Encyclopedia of Politics, the Media, and Popular Culture

Encyclopedia of Politics, the Media, and Popular Culture

BRIAN COGAN AND TONY KELSO

GREENWOOD PRESS
An Imprint of ABC-CLIO, LLC

A B C  C L I O

Santa Barbara, California • Denver, Colorado • Oxford, England

Library of Congress Cataloging-in-Publication Data

Cogan, Brian, 1967–
    Encyclopedia of politics, the media, and popular culture / Brian Cogan and Tony Kelso.
        p. cm.
    Includes bibliographical references and index.
    ISBN 978–0–313-34379–7 (hard copy : alk. paper) — ISBN 978–0–313-34380–3 (ebook)
1. Mass media—Political aspects—United States. 2. Communication in politics—United States. 3. Popular culture—Political aspects—United States. I. Kelso, Tony. II. Title.
P95.82.U6C62   2009
302.230973—dc22   2009026719

13 12 11 10 9   1 2 3 4 5

This book is also available on the World Wide Web as an eBook.
Visit www.abc-clio.com for details.

ABC-CLIO, LLC
130 Cremona Drive, P.O. Box 1911
Santa Barbara, California 93116-1911

This book is printed on acid-free paper ∞

Manufactured in the United States of America

Contents

List of Entries for Part II

Introduction

This work systematically describes and analyzes the intersection between popular culture, politics, and media in the United States. Accordingly, it seeks to examine the most important interactions between these three areas over the past 200 years. Because we wish the book to have a greater air of recency than many other works that have examined American political history, however, the encyclopedia concentrates more on developments since the dawn of the twentieth century, when movies were already in circulation and what would become the first broadcast medium, namely radio, was coming into being.

ARRANGEMENT

The encyclopedia is divided into two parts. The first section contains longer chapters, each of which explores connections between popular culture and politics in relationship to a particular medium or major format, including movies, documentaries, radio, television, news, music, advertising, and online and other "new" media.

The second part of the book is devoted to an extensive series of A–Z entries. These shorter accounts cover everything from political cartoons and media representations of presidents to political scandals and campaign rituals such as kissing babies. To facilitate navigation between the two parts, A–Z topics that are mentioned in the longer chapters are set in bold to alert the reader that additional discussion of these issues can be found in the corresponding entries in Part II. With the *Encyclopedia of Politics, the Media, and Popular Culture*, we have endeavored to (1) highlight the connections between politics, media, and popular culture that have not received sufficient treatment and (2) reexamine previously researched topics through the lens of popular culture and media to reveal fresh meanings and interpretations of political events. We realize that despite its considerable length, the book is still incomplete—unfortunately, no work can exhaustively capture the fascinating ways in which Americans have used media and popular culture to generate meaning and engage in politics and, conversely, fully spell out the array of tactics that politicians have employed to exploit media and popular culture as a means of appealing to potential voters. Instead, our goal is limited: We simply hope that the work sparks in readers a renewed interest in politics. In this manner, we regard the encyclopedia as an engagement device to help students, scholars, and other concerned citizens start their own conversations about the proper role of the media and popular culture in U.S. politics. To this end, the book highlights the perhaps frightening yet always intriguing links between media, popular culture, and politics, and how their interplay offers new opportunities for Americans to engage in that most mysterious of all human activities, the political process.

ACKNOWLEDGMENTS

Along the way, many people assisted in the creation of this encyclopedia and helped inform its writing. Some directly served as consultants or research assistants. Others, including a number of colleagues and former professors, played an important role through their general influence on our work and our approach to the political system in the United States. Although many people richly deserve our appreciation, we would especially like to thank the following: Lila Bauman, Marco Calavita, Sue Collins, Robert Conway, Sal Fallica, Todd Gitlin, Mike Grabowski, Josh Klein, Ted Magder, William McCarthy (no descendant of Eugene or Joseph!), Terrence Moran, Gwenn Morreale, Bill Phillips, MJ Robinson, Laura Tropp, and Jonathan Zimmerman. We would also like to express our warm thanks to our families—without the enormous emotional support and understanding we received from Tony's wife, Tricia, his son, Emil, and Brian's wife, Lisa, we could never have put in the commitment it required to finish such an extensive project. Finally, no work is complete without the substantial effort of a patient editor. We are happy to say that our editor, the redoubtable Kristi Ward, provided invaluable advice and wisdom during the production of this work—we thank her for her grace throughout the process.

Part I

Chapter 1

Political Movies

Since the creation of motion pictures at the end of the nineteenth century, when the power of the moving image captivated the American imagination, movies have been used for political purposes. Although movies made purely for propaganda purposes and sponsored or made by governments for the purposes of propaganda are inherently political by nature, such as the *Why We Fight* documentaries during World War II, for the most part in the second half of the twentieth century there were fewer overt attempts by the American government to influence the political message of nondocumentary films. However, with the cultural and social changes from the Civil Rights Movement to the student protests of the late 1950s and 1960s, many films made from the 1960s to the present have also been far more critical of American institutions and foreign policy than in previous decades. Films such as *Easy Rider*, *The Parallax View*, and *All the President's Men* in the 1960s and 1970s, and later on films such as *Bullworth*, **Bob Roberts**, *Wag the Dog*, and **Dave** in the 1980s and 1990s demonstrated that political films could still be critical of American values and policies, even in a time period that many critics considered to be more socially conservative. But no matter what the ultimate political orientation of the filmmaker, films that have dealt with political issues have fascinated the American public, and some of the most highly controversial political films of the past century have helped to spark and maintain debates on important issues.

Throughout the twentieth century and into the twenty-first, films have been a key method for analyzing the relationship of Americans to popular culture, and representations of politics or political figures in American films have been key areas for determining how Americans regard the dominant political institutions of America. Films, while not causal and not overt representations of the will or vision of the American people, still sometimes are reflections of undercurrents in society that only film can articulate in terms of popular culture. Also, many films have openly challenged the dominant ideology of America. While analyzing films cannot simply find a causal relationship to how Americans feel about politics, they do give us valuable insights into the ways in which the American film industry has had a contentious relationship with government almost since its inception. Much in the way that the American people feel a dualistic sense of reverence and ambivalence around authority, the relationship between Hollywood and politics has also been a long and contentious relationship.

Some of the best and most resonant political movies have also mirrored the American fascination with a sense of cynicism and dissatisfaction with the political arena. As writer Mark Aucoin noted in an article in the *Boston Globe*, "the trajectory of a political career, as seen in the movies, leads almost inevitably from idealism to compromise to cynicism" (Aucoin 1997, B.6), and Aucoin is correct in noting that in many political films (particularly biographical ones) the ascent of the major character is only matched by his or her rapid descent, as demonstrated in such films as *All the King's Men* (1949), *The Candidate* (1972), and *The Seduction of Joe Tynan* (1979). But, many political films as diverse as *Mr. Smith Goes to Washington* (1939) and *Bullworth* (1998) and even Oliver Stone's *W.* (2008) show some optimism in a political world that, although corrupt, still has glimmers of hope. The film industry has long attempted to follow trends in American politics in popular culture, and the trajectory of American films about politics may help to express both American ambivalence and American optimism in the political system.

EARLY FILMS AND POLITICS

While many of the earliest films were simple experiments in an attempt to decipher the language of the new medium, early on some of the greater directors of the silent era in America were able to use film to express certain ideological aims. The common view of early films seen by most contemporary Americans is of crudely made and poorly told stories. Numerous early filmmakers were attempting to create great works of socially conscious art, including blatant "message" films about crime, poverty, social ills, and immigration. Early giants such as D. W. Griffith, one of the pioneers of cinema grammar and language, was concerned with making films that the audiences would want to watch as well as be sources of instruction and enlightenment. Griffith, who made hundreds of films early in the twentieth century long before his most fertile period, often made films that championed the underdog from wealthy interests that threatened the poor. An early film, *A Corner of Wheat* (1909), is a typical example of Griffith's populist nature. In the film, a wealthy wheat baron corners the market on wheat, leading to a bread shortage. According to film historian Tom Gunning, the populist movement of the late nineteenth century had been a major influence on Griffith and "Griffith, having come to maturity during the heyday of muckraking journalism, was strongly impressed by their revelations of the gritty realities of life and the new social consciousness that inspired them" (Gunning 1991, 242). Film scholar Kay Sloan noted in the chapter "The Loud Silents: Origins of the Social Problem film" that "small film companies often turned to the literary and political milieu of the muckrakers and the progressives for storylines" (Sloan 2002, 44). From an early age, film had already realized that the new medium was not merely an efficient and entertaining way to tell stories, but it could tackle social issues and be instructive as well as entertaining.

Many other early filmmakers were heavily influenced by the social movements at the turn of the twentieth century, as evidenced by films such as Bannister Merwin's *The Usurer's Grip* (1912), which showed the plight of a desperate couple, who get increasingly into debt until they were rescued by the financially prudent Russell Sage

Foundation. The film was made as a partnership between the Edison Company and the Russell Sage Foundation and was an early precursor of modern television message films laced with advertising. According to Kay Sloan, this demonstrated how "through melodrama, the Edison Company and the Russell Sage Foundation advertised direct social reform and suggested that direct philanthropic measures might remedy urban poverty" (2002, 49). Numerous film plots at the turn of the century often involved the politics of poverty and the plight of the working class in a depressed economy. Griffith was particularly attracted to films of this nature, and his early films, such as the proto-gangster film, *The Musketeers of Pig Alley*, a silent film from 1914 that involves the unwitting involvement of a musician and his wife in a large-scale gang war, also illustrate the squalid working conditions that many Americans were working in at that time. Griffith, of course, is best known for his most brilliant and problematic work, ***The Birth of a Nation*** (1915), a sprawling and technically innovative epic film about the Civil War. The problematic nature of the film is in its treatment of African Americans, where marauding slaves (played mostly by white men in blackface) are represented as bestial savages in league with unscrupulous northern carpetbaggers, only contained at the end by the virtuous Ku Klux Klan, a clearly racist and repugnant position by today's standards, but to many surviving southern veterans of the Civil War it was a vindication of sorts and the film was extremely popular. Although it is now mostly dismissed as an urban legend with little factual basis, many film scholars have cited then President Woodrow Wilson as proclaiming that the film was "history writ by lightning." This movie also led to the rise of film criticism. Some critics at the time were impressed by the film's technical majesty and epic length, but disgusted by its distortion of history. While the first half of the film is more or less about the tragedy of war and how it sets family against family, the second half, with its depictions of freed slaves during the Reconstruction Era haphazardly running the statehouse, and with their feet up on desks and smoking big cigars, is clearly problematic. The evil Senator Stoneman and his mulatto protégé Silas are portrayed as opportunistic invaders, with Silas in particular lusting after the white women who surround him just out of his reach. The film was a spectacular success at the box office, but was also protested by the the National Association for the Advancement of Colored People (NAACP) who organized a successful boycott in Boston and caused the film to be banned in several states. Griffith, incidentally, was not the only filmmaker to tackle the subject of the Civil War. The great silent comedian Buster Keaton also addressed the war in his 1927 comedic masterpiece, *The General*, which sidestepped the question of slavery altogether. Needless to say, from a political standpoint, depictions of African Americans in early Hollywood films are unacceptable by today's standards.

While *The Birth of a Nation* is seen by many as the epitome of Griffith's career, his next film, the epic *Intolerance* (1916), was also an attempt at a political statement where the suffering of innocents is contrasted with the forces of good (including some politicians) working to alleviate the misery of the poor. Other silent films were just as political, if less progressive, Fred Niblo's *Dangerous Hours* (1920) involved a Bolshevik plot to infiltrate American industry and foment strikes. Still other directors, such as Erich von Stroheim, with his massive truly epic film *Greed* (1923) (originally ten hours long, later cut down to a more manageable three hours) involved the persecution of immigrants by capitalists in California. It is interesting to note that early on, Hollywood had not yet become as politically conservative in terms of subject matter as it would be in years to come after the advent of the Hays code, which provided explicit instructions as to what was permitted in a film and what was considered lewd or obscene.

World War I also had a lasting effect on Hollywood, and while many popular actors such as **Charlie Chaplin**, Douglas Fairbanks Sr., and Mary Pickford had worked on **War bond drives**, many were disillusioned with the war in its aftermath. In a rare early antiwar film, King Vidor examined the horror of the first great global conflict in his film *The Big Parade* (1925). Vidor followed that up with a parable on, according to film scholars Terry Christensen and Peter Hass, "urban alienation and isolation" (71) in *The Crowd* (1928). In terms of comedy, films by directors such as Chaplin and Mack Sennett also frequently targeted rich landlords and crooked businessmen, icons of repression in an age of reformist impulses. Chaplin's everyman tramp character often fought against bureaucracy, most notably in his later films such as *Modern Times* (1936) and *The Great Dictator* (1940), which attacked mechanization and fascism, respectively. Chaplin was growing increasingly political as the decades wore on, and his socialist views would later cause him to become a controversial figure in the United States until he was forced out of the country in the 1950s.

The end of the silent era in the late 1920s led to changes in not only how films were made (by then the studio system had been solidified) but also in what subjects films were allowed to broach. While certain political films were becoming increasingly successful, and antiwar epics, such as the film version of the book *All Quiet on the Western Front* (1930) directed by Lewis Milestone, demonstrated that politically risky films were possible, many films took the social concerns of the 1920s silent films and updated them with sensationalistic themes. Crime films and films involving the plight of "fallen woman" soon became extremely popular. In the early 1930s some of this populist message lived on in films where interests, presumably landlords and large corporations, were assailed. One of the key messages of the films of the 1930s was the lone man, often a senator or reformer, working to fight the sinister anonymous enemies of freedom who were seeking to impose fascist rule in America. Films such as *Washington Masquerade* (1932) and *Washington Merry-Go-Round* (1932) both dealt with ordinary men attempting to make a difference in a world increasingly controlled by large corporate interests.

At the same time, movie studios themselves were facing a new form of censorship. The Hayes code, which curtailed taboo subjects in films such as partial nudity or use of drugs, demonstrated that no evil could win at the end of the film or crimes could go unpunished. By 1927 the Hayes code was effectively working as a form of censorship that was based not only on moral concerns but also on political concerns, as evidenced by the fact that Hayes also produced an index of books and plays deemed unsuitable for filming for moral or political reasons. The Hayes code, which would be followed by most of Hollywood for the next several decades, was a key example of how the industry sought some control over the increasingly maverick directors who challenged the studio system's natural reflexive action of churning out films with little controversial or political content.

Some films produced during the 1930s were decidedly right wing in tone, such as the controversial *Gabriel Over the White House* (1933), which featured Walter Huston as a politically corrupt president who is possessed by the angel Gabriel, sends the army to shoot criminals, and disbands Congress for the good of the nation. The film, which was influenced by William Randolph Hearst (and partially written by him), suggested that a strong leader was the best solution to the problems of the depression besetting the nation. However, other films such as *The President Vanishes* (1934) continued in the populist vein of the little man fighting against the interests of large corporations and shadowy fascists.

The influence of **Frank Capra** on political films and pop culture is incalculable, and his contribution to the debate about how much influence the ordinary people should have on government seemingly gone amuck was evident in films he made in the 1930s: *Forbidden* (1932), *Mr. Deeds Goes to Town* (1936), and *Mr. Smith Goes to Washington* (1939), all of which deal with outsiders taking on political corruption. In *Forbidden* and *Mr. Deeds* the forces of evil are represented by corrupt politicians and goodness is represented by lone individuals who choose to take on corruption and face down the men who really run the show. In *Mr. Smith*, perhaps his most famous and most evocative film, Capra again deals with an ordinary man, Jefferson Smith, who idealistically fills a Senate appointment and tries to fulfill his goal of starting a boys' ranch for his pet project, the Boy Rangers. When Smith finds out that not only is most of Washington corrupt but so is his idol, senior senator Joseph Paine (Claude Rains), who is also on the take, Smith leads a famous filibuster in order to stop passage of a bill that would develop a corrupt water project instead of the ranch that Smith envisioned. Smith as a representative of the people ultimately wins, as Capra heroes inevitably do, when supported by the common man. While many critics dismiss Capra's work as sentimental, his movies in the 1930s and his work for the government in the 1940s marked Capra as a concerned American, yearning for small-town values in a world dominated increasingly by depression and looming war. Although his work was primarily in the western, iconic director John Ford also made his mark as a classic envisioner of lost America in a series of films starting with *Young Mr. Lincoln* (1939) and continuing with his masterful exploration of the West as a sort of a representation of how American values were contested and finely honed.

FILMS DURING WORLD WAR II AND THE 1940s

The advent of World War II drastically changed the nature of the film industry as many actors, directors, and writers wanted to do their part for the war effort, with even huge stars such as Jimmy Stewart and Clark Gable enlisting and facing combat and others working on instructional films for the army or other branches of the armed services. Also, in terms of content, most films were no longer addressing controversial or domestic issues, except as background for larger issues—most were dealing with the war effort or patriotism. While anti-Nazi films had been made previously to the war, such as *Confessions of a Nazi Spy* (1939) or *The Great Dictator* (1940), they had been met with skepticism, particularly from those in the German American community (*Confessions* in particular led to some animosity, including a theater being burnt down in Milwaukee). But Warner Brothers in particular was keen for U.S. involvement in the upcoming war, and when war was declared in 1941, Warner Brothers was ready to rush films into production. One of the first major films to address the war was the classic *Casablanca* (1942), which portrayed the fight against the Nazis as a noble cause for even the most disinterested of the isolationist crowd. Buoyed by *Casablanca*'s success, the studios began to produce more and more war movies, most of them blatant propaganda, but many of them successful; however, many of them were too simplistic (such as *The Hitler Gang* [1944] and

Hitler's Madmen [1943]). Other films were specifically designed purely as propaganda, such as the pro-Russian *Mission to Moscow* (1943) and *The North Star* (1943).

At the same time the U.S. government was using some of the best American talent to produce instructional films in an effort to educate American soldiers on the reasons they were fighting. As many Americans had been isolationists before the war, the government knew that it needed to produce films that were both educational and entertaining. The result was the *Why We Fight* series of educational films directed by Frank Capra with animation from Walt Disney. Although the films were highly entertaining, equating the Nazis with American gangsters by sometimes using outright fabrications or half-truths in order to try and convince the troops of the necessity of fighting the Axis powers, the films were ultimately not that convincing according to later studies. However, the idea that training films were effective led to a whole subsection of American training films that were used in schools and for civics groups over the next two decades.

After the war was over, Hollywood began to address other issues as well, such as the plight of returning veterans to America in the award-winning film *The Best Years of Our Lives* (1946). The late 1940s, however, mostly saw Hollywood shy away from films considered too controversial, as the Justice Department's antitrust lawsuit against the studios and the House Committee on Un-American Activities (HUAC) investigations of the late 1940s and early 1950s saw Hollywood return to escapist fare or treat politics as the 1930s films had, as sometimes corrupt as in *State of the Union* (1948), another Capra film about the corrupting power of politics, and *All the King's Men* (1949), a grim look at the potential for fascism in the United States based on Robert Earl Warren's book on populist demagogue **Huey Long**. Change was again in the air during the late 1940s, and certain studios found it easier to work in arenas that were not necessarily as transparent as the social problem or simple political corruption film. In the 1950s the enemy was no longer the political machine, and in many cases it was not even of this earth.

FILMS OF THE 1950s: COLD WAR SCARES AND ALIEN INVASIONS

Not all early 1950s films were overtly political, but many films did try to address the growing Cold War with the Soviet Union and the threat of a new global war. Anti-communist films soon grew in frequency, with 33 films about anti-communism being made between 1947 and 1954, some of these more apparent than others. Some films skirted political issues for social issues, such as juvenile delinquency in epics such as *The Wild One* (1953) and *Rebel Without a Cause* (1955), which can be analyzed in hindsight as films that criticized the conformity of middle-class existence, but were also made as much for an excuse to appeal to a teen market as they were cautionary tales. As the studio system began to fail, many films were now being made by independent companies, leading to a rash of films in previously avoided genres such as teen exploitation films and, especially, science fiction.

Science fiction films are the perfect vehicles for cultural and political critiques, as they take place in futuristic societies or feature protagonists not of this world, but the viewer has to make a leap of recognition to see the allegory present. Sometimes that led to 1950s films that analyzed both the threat of communist military might, as well as the dangers of the atomic age, and even corporate conformity. The original *Invasion of the Body Snatchers* (1956) film can be seen as an allegory not only of alien invasion but alien ideology as well, as the alien takeover literally removes all emotions from the transformed humans, leading to a world of conformity and unity that resembles a society of communists, or as the bland conformity of American corporate and social life during the 1950s. The film is open to interpretation depending on which side of the political aisle one is on. Likewise, films such as *The Thing from Another World* (1951) and *Them* (1954) can be seen as allegories of nuclear power causing untold havoc with nature (creating giant ants, mutants, and in Japanese films, Godzilla) and of the soulless nature of others, and perhaps ourselves. The alien in *The Thing* could be read as the mind-numbing effects of ideology; whether it was communism or consumer culture, the result was the same—a loss of humanity.

For all of the backward-looking historical critiques that analyzed the 1950s as an era of craven conformity, the decade was filled with as many controversial and socially mature films as it was of cheaply made propaganda. For every movie such as *I Married a Communist* (1949) and *My Son John* (1952), which simply attacked communism as a menace, there were also more nuanced films that worried about McCarthyism, such as was shown with the allegorical sellout of the townspeople of *High Noon* (1952), or such films as *On the Waterfront* (1954), which allowed that both naming names and fighting against oppressive authority might be possible at the same time.

Hollywood also came to regard the new medium of television as potentially problematic. The potential for television to be used as a source of propaganda was evident, and one of the key critiques of mass media from the 1950s, *A Face in the Crowd* (1957), combined the political with a critique of television, where small-town grifter Larry "Lonesome" Rhodes rises to power by using television to become a political force, backing an isolationist senator in his attempt to become president. He is exposed as a hypocrite on live television and in the end retreats to his luxury apartment alone, shouting grandiose speeches into the night accompanied by the uproarious laughter provided by his laugh track machine. Politics were also viewed through the lens of nostalgia, of yearning for a time when things were simpler and political machinery more benevolent, as in John Ford's *The Last Hurrah* (1958) in which the political boss Frank Skeffington (Spencer Tracy) knows that the new mediated age of politics via television is destroying the old localized system, with Skeffington's opponent defeating him in an homage to Nixon's "**Checkers Speech**." The 1950s were a time when the old studio system had decayed to the point where new independent films, as well as more experimental films from the studio system, could continue to question the way Americans related to political issues. The next two decades would see this trend continue as the retirement or death of longtime directors such as Ford and Capra paved the way for a new generation of filmmakers who wished to address important political and social issues of the time.

THE 1960s AND 1970s: VIETNAM, *EASY RIDER*, AND WATERGATE

The 1960s and 1970s saw the further demise of the studio system and the continuing financial success of independent films, sometimes ones that challenged the dominant political ideology of the time. While television was slow to deal with the political and social issues of the 1960s, Hollywood was not shy in approaching complex social problems; albeit many of the films that tackled issues such as free love, the hippie movement, and drug usage were exploitative cheap films, such as Russ Meyer's camp classic *Beyond the Valley of the Dolls* (1970) or the LSD-themed

The Trip (1967). Other films were more explicitly political and well made. The early 1960s saw films such as the antinuclear war *On the Beach* (1963) that saw the last survivors of a nuclear war glumly awaiting their inevitable death from radiation poisoning. A more humorous exploration of a serious topic was Billy Wilder's classic Cold War comedy **One, Two Three** (1961), which featured James Cagney as a beleaguered Coca-Cola executive trying to strike a deal with the East Germans, while simultaneously turning his boss's daughter's communist new husband into a capitalist by the time the boss arrives. Otto Preminger's *Advise and Consent* (1962) about a beleaguered nominee for secretary of state (Henry Fonda) also gleefully skewered the left and right as blocking consensus on important issues, while holding out hopes that compromise is still the hallmark of democracy.

As the 1960s progressed, many films began to tackle the issue of the Cold War in more detail, leading to the rise of the political thriller. One of the most successful film franchises of all time, the **James Bond** series, starting with *Dr. No* (1962) demonstrated that the Cold War was best fought by a daring and resourceful agent, battling enemy agents with a Walter PPK, his wits, and a vodka martini, shaken, not stirred. Other films were more serious in tone. In films such as the **Manchurian Candidate** (1962) the threat of possible brainwashing and an inexplicable alliance of right-wing ideologues and communist agents almost doom America. Still more radical and more subversive than almost any political film to this day was Stanley Kubrick's masterpiece *Dr. Strangelove, or How I Learned to Stop Worrying and Love the Bomb* (1964), which presented a world where everyone was essentially crazy, paranoid, or both, with various characters gleefully plotting how many women it would take to repopulate the world, and others worrying about how communists wanted to steal our "precious bodily fluids." If *Strangelove* was a black comedy about the end of the world, other films that addressed the issue, such as *Failsafe* (1964) in a plot similar to *Dr. Strangelove* where the president is forced to make a hard decision when a plane attacking Russia cannot be recalled, took a more conciliatory tone, as did the thriller *Seven Days in May* (1964) where the threat was not from the Russians, but ambitious and ruthless American generals. A classic Cold War paranoia film was the James Coburn political comedy *The President's Analyst* (1967), which starred Coburn as a psychiatrist treating the president and becoming increasingly unstable and paranoid himself, all the while pursued by Russian, American, and British secret agents.

Despite the fact that the controversy over the war in Vietnam was causing upheavals across the nation, Hollywood largely avoided the war during its heyday, with only John Wayne managing to get funding for his film, *The Green Berets* (1968), which shows the righteous American forces fighting the good fight against the cowardly and despicable North Vietnamese. Despite the fact that public opinion was turning against the war, the Wayne vehicle was the last major film to be made about Vietnam until the 1970s.

Race was also a particularly divisive issue in America during the 1960s, and soon films that dealt with America's Civil Rights Movement were becoming more ubiquitous. Films such as *In the Heat of the Night* (1967) and *Guess Who's Coming to Dinner* (1967), both starring Sidney Poitier, addressed the issue of how Americans in both the South and the North, respectively, dealt with racial assimilation and animosity. Later, films that dealt with race evolved into the "blaxploitation" craze of the early 1970s with films such as *Shaft* (1971) and *Foxy Brown* (1974) that did not exactly advance the Civil Rights Movement, but did, however, provide more roles for black actors and allow a more visible on-screen presence for African Americans.

Some of the more prominent political films were released in the late 1960s. A film that explored the political implications of the counterculture (albeit in a sometimes incoherent fashion) was *Easy Rider* (1969), which followed two societal dropouts (Peter Fonda and Dennis Hopper) on a motorcycle trip across an imaginary land called America, where in the end they realize there may be no hope for a dying giant. Other films share the cynicism of the late 1960s, including Haskell Wexler's visually stunning but often-numbing *Medium Cool* (1969), which also attacks the media for its callousness and cynicism. As the decade closed, more explicitly political comedies, while not overtly mentioning Vietnam, could not be read outside of the time period, such as *M.A.S.H.* (1970) and the film adaptation of the classic antiwar novel *Catch-22* (1970), both of which highlighted the absurdity of war and its often surrealistic consequences. Although these films were not always the most popular films, they did demonstrate that in the 1960s, the studio system and independent filmmakers were trying to make films that resonated more with audiences who increasingly wanted more realistic fare rather than just entertainment.

The early to mid-1970s also saw the trend toward antiestablishment films continue with thrillers such as Robert Redford's cynical look at tarnished idealism in *The Candidate* (1972) and more paranoid political thrillers that hinted at shadowy conspiracies that no one could stand against in films such as *The Parallax View* (1974) and *Three Days of the Condor* (1975), again with Redford, where the cynicism that rooted in American filmmaking from the Kennedy assassination onwards manifested itself in conspiracy theories and overt contempt for established authority.

By the mid-1970s, the very real specter of the **Watergate scandal** gave new ammunition to those who questioned the American system, and also led to impressive cinematic feats in *All the President's Men*, which starred Robert Redford as Bob Woodward and Dustin Hoffman as Carl Bernstein, the real-life reporters from the *Washington Post*, whose investigative journalism had led to the exposure of the Watergate scandal and the first ever resignation of a sitting president of the United States. The film, which exposed the methodical nature of the reporters' investigation, was released in 1976, and some critics have suggested that it might have been a factor in Jimmy Carter's victory over Gerald Ford in the presidential election that year, thanks to a growing backlash against the Republican Party. More realistically, however, Ford's pardon of Nixon was surely more important than the film *All the President's Men*—for more information about the Ford presidential campaign, see Chapter 7. Other films once again began to challenge the power of television, and a key film that exposed the vapid nature of the news industry was the classic news parody *Network* (1976), where the "mad prophet of the airwaves" Howard Beale is slowly seduced from his truth telling to become a corporate hack and eventually the victim of an on-air assassination. *Network* demonstrated the deep ambivalence that many Americans were feeling about the political situation and the influence of mass media. Although made in 1976, the script by noted television writer Paddy Chayefsky seems as timely today as it did over 30 years ago.

By the end of the 1970s the film industry had changed drastically and the Young Turk directors of the early 1970s, such as Francis Ford Coppola, Martin Scorsese, George Lucas, and Steven Spielberg, had come to dominate an industry that was increasingly becoming reliant on blockbusters. Although nuanced political films such as *The Seduction of Joe Tynan* (1979) were still being made, the shift in the industry's focus toward blockbusters and the end of the 1970s led to a new administration and a new political trend toward the conservative end of the political spectrum. (As demonstrated in Peter Biskind's book *Easy Riders, Raging Bulls*, the rise of the new directors was also tied into a new concern for box office and opening weeks, leading to less financing for more provocative films.)

THE 1980s: "THIS TIME DO WE GET TO WIN?"

The conventional wisdom about the 1980s in general and the film world in particular is that the 1980s was a decade of entrenchment and a conservative trend both in culture and in Hollywood films. While there are certainly some grains of truth in this, the opposite may be just as true, as nothing energizes a political base and social causes more than a socially conservative president. However, while there were many films that tackled political causes, many films made in the action adventure genre were certainly right of center. The Rambo trilogy in particular has been singled out as a prime example of the latent conservatism in Hollywood at this time period, and a cursory glance at the character of John Rambo (developed and played to perfection by Sylvester Stallone) certainly has right-wing overtones, especially in the third film. However, the first Rambo film in the trilogy, *Rambo: First Blood* (1982), is less a feel good "let's kill them all" movie than an indictment of the consequences of Vietnam and the neglect of deeply traumatized Vietnam veterans. When Rambo is first introduced, he is not a glorious warrior but instead is a paranoid drifter, scared, traumatized from experiences he initially will not reveal, who simply wants to be left alone to drift wherever the road takes him. When a small-town sheriff first bullies him and then arrests him, Rambo's natural instincts kick in with disastrous consequences for local law enforcement officials who clearly do not know how to handle a threat of the magnitude of Rambo and his superior survival skills.

The second film, *First Blood II*, takes a turn toward wish fulfillment as Rambo is allowed to go back to Vietnam to find and rescue POWs, who were abandoned by an uncaring government. Although the film is similar to the first movie in its treatment of the scarred psyche of John Rambo, it also walks an uneasy line between action and political commentary, made plain early on in the film when Rambo, after being assigned his mission, asks his handler, Colonel Troutman (Richard Crenna), "this time, do we get to win?" By the time the third film, *Rambo III* (1988), was made, Rambo had gone to fight against the Russians with the mujahideen, and the silliness implicit in the material had caused the once nuanced character to be turned into caricature, albeit with sufficiently violent carnage to satisfy its younger audience. In retrospect, the popularity of the movies may have been due to the spectacular special effects of the series and the action quota more than the overt political messages of the time.

Of course, action films did dominate the screen in the 1980s, and the militaristic themes that ran through many action films were probably inspired by what Hollywood perceived as the prevailing political current of the times. Future California governor **Arnold Schwarzenegger** starred in a series of action films as a strong wisecracking killer, always ready to take action when no one else would take on the enemy. Other action heroes such as Chuck Norris also fought against the enemy, in this case the invading Soviets. In the film *Invasion U.S.A.* (1985) Norris takes on the invading hordes of Soviets and Cubans, who have inexplicably decided to invade Florida. While the film seems over the top and absurd in retrospect, it is nowhere near as absurd as the classic of the anti-Soviet genre, *Red Dawn* (1984), where the Soviets invade Colorado and only a small band of high school teammates, the Wolverines, stand up to them in partisan attacks. Although the teens are eventually all wiped out, it is indicated at the end that their sacrifice, much like the French partisans of World War II whom they are supposed to resemble, inspired a widespread resistance movement that eventually defeated the Soviet invasion. Other films, such as the Tom Cruise vehicle *Top Gun* (1986), showed American navy flyers in combat with unspecified (but presumably communist) fighters, who are easily defeated by the American airmen.

While the predominant critical view of the 1980s was that the overall emphasis was on simplistic right-wing films, from the start of the 1980s the opposite was also true, with overtly left-wing films such as Warren Beatty's *Reds* (1981) getting a special screening at the White House by Beatty's old friend from his acting days, President Ronald Reagan. Newer directors, who had grown up in the 1960s, were also starting to make films that captured some of the resistance that epitomized some aspects of politics in the 1960s. **Oliver Stone** in particular took overt aim at capitalism in films such as *Scarface* (1983) and *Wall Street* (1987), both of which, not unlike DeMille's biblical epics, manage to both criticize and glorify their subjects. In *Scarface* the "hero," Tony Montana, rises to the top of the drug trade and enjoys the fruits of his labors for much of the film, before he is gunned down in a hail of bullets. (This later inspired a cult-like devotion to the film in the hip-hop world where the authenticity of the gangster was sometimes praised to ridiculous extremes.) *Wall Street* (1987), based on the insider trading scandals of the 1980s, was also a grittily realistic portrayal of an Ivan Boesky-type corporate raider (Stone even includes a paraphrase of Boesky's real-life declaration that "Greed is good"), who seduces a young trader to the dark side of capitalism. The film is almost Capra-esque in its contrast of the saintly father and longtime workingman who guides his son back to the right path. Like *Scarface*, the film almost revels in the trappings of capitalism before eventually getting back to the main character's redemption. Stone's other political films such as the Vietnam epic *Platoon* (1986) and *Born on the Fourth of July* (1989) also take critical looks at American foreign policy during the height of when the country was supposed to have gone resolutely to the right. The 1980s and the early 1990s also saw the rise of new independent films and the rise of distribution that allowed filmmakers such as John Sayles, Spike Lee, Richard Linklater, and later Kevin Smith and others to succeed. However, the blockbuster had been established as the backbone of Hollywood, and political films could be financed in the 1990s by mainstream studios, as long as they were likely to turn a profit.

THE 1990s AND BEYOND

It is unclear whether the 1990s and beyond reflected a new sense of cynicism in political films or a new sense of optimism. Many directors, intrigued by the Clinton presidency, were inspired to make movies where the protagonist showed that an ordinary American was still capable of changing the course of the country, as in the Kevin Kline vehicle *Dave* (1993), or that politicians, although deeply flawed in many ways, were still capable of greatness, as in the Clinton presidential campaign satire *Primary Colors* (1998). There were some extremely cynical voices still out there, notably Tim Robbins whose overt critiques from the left were some of the angriest and most abrasive political films made in the 1990s, starting with the classic *Bob Roberts* (1992), a satire about a right-wing folksinger running for president while deliberately obfuscating his message, or later films such as the antideath penalty *Dead Man Walking* (1995) or the nostalgic but unrealistic look at socialist theater in *Cradle Will Rock* (1999) also demonstrated an ambivalence about American culture and politics that Robbins would pursue to the present day.

Some directors started looking to past presidents for inspiration, as Oliver Stone did in his many political films, most notably his sympathetic, but still scathing **Nixon** film, *Nixon* (1995), and his examination of the various conspiracy theories around the assassination of **John F. Kennedy** in *JFK* (1991). Despite the fact that many had argued that the country was tilted to the right, the fact that a major studio would finance the production of a film suggesting government involvement in the murder of a recent president was still a powerful indication that potential box office was a more powerful rationale for green-lighting a film than the politics of the film. As the Clinton era began in 1993, a plethora of political films were green-lighted, leading to some of the more overt nonwar related films of the past several decades. The concept of the beneficent liberal president, wise and all knowing, became a reality (at least in film) in *Dave* (1993) and *The American President* (1995) where the presidents (or as in *Dave*, the ordinary man who becomes president) are shown as decent people, surrounded, as in a Capra film, by schemers and political hacks who do not have the best interests of the people at heart. As the 1990s progressed, some films became more overt at attacking what they saw as the corruption of large industries, such as the Warren Beatty vehicle *Bullworth* (1998) where the presidential candidate is killed by the consortium due to his attacks on the health care industry.

The optimism engendered by the Clinton years seemed to lead to new optimism among the major studios, buoyed by the prosperity and relative security during this period. Even the damaging revelations of the Clinton sex scandals of the late 1990s (see **Political Scandals**) could not damage the left's fascination with Clinton and perhaps the most interesting film (which was originally a book by journalist Joe Klein) about the Clinton years, *Primary Colors* (1998). It revealed the duality of Clinton (portrayed as Governor Jack Stanton in the film) and his attempts to rein in his dark side and womanizing, along with a genuine effort to help America. Hollywood seemingly could forgive Clinton his sins, based on his enormous popularity with the American electorate. However, the hypercritical *Wag the Dog* (1997), which suggested that an American president might resort to simulating a war in order to divert public attention from a sex scandal, indicated that by the late 1990s the cynicism of the 1970s had not been totally dissipated. A key film that demonstrated this, and one of the few films to this day to examine the Gulf War of the early 1990s, was David O. Russell's *Three Kings* (1999) where a group of bored soldiers try to steal a cache of gold bullion, leading them to conformations with members of the Iraqi military and some unpleasant realizations about the collateral damage caused by American foreign policy. While not considered an overtly political film by some, one of the most overt critiques of capitalism may have come from fantasy or science fiction films. The first *Matrix* (1999), directed by the Wachowski brothers, can be read in many different ways, Christian allegory, science fiction escapist film, cyberpunk adventure; but to many Marxist critics, it was not difficult to decode the film as one that attacked the capitalist system, as one that pulled the wool over the eyes of most in consumer culture, or as one that showed we live in a world where humans are enslaved and blinded to the reality of their enslavement (much like the John Carpenter film *They Live* [1988]). Another film, *The Truman Show* (1998), both satirizes the public's fascination with reality shows and critiques a world where product placement is the norm as a human is kept captive in an imaginary world where his every movement is used as entertainment and the construction of personal meaning in a world of mindless idiots, who spend all of their time glued to the television set. It would seem that the end to the 1990s may have seen the resurgence of well-made films that critiqued and questioned the nature of politics, but by the start of the next century, it was clear that after September 11, producers and directors would have to rethink that nature of the film industry.

Political Movies after 9/11

After September 11 some pundits claimed that the political landscape had changed and that there would be fewer films that questioned the role of the United States in world affairs. Although many films made after 9/11 were patriotic in nature, it appears as though a new sensibility, one that intentionally avoided politics, was present, or at least one that did not allow for overtly critical major motion pictures to be made for several years. Even when Oliver Stone finally made a film about 9/11, it was the apolitical *World Trade Center* (2006) that analyzed the heroism of the rescue workers rather then presented Stone's usual critique of American foreign policy. The only other World Trade Center films to be made so far are the realistic (and tragic) *United 93* (2006), which examined the heroism of the passengers of that doomed plane, and the Adam Sandler vehicle *Reign Over Me* (2007) that examined the aftermath of 9/11 from the perspective of a man who lost family in the tragedy. (Also see **9/11 Films.**) While other films have been made that examined social issues, most notably *Hotel Rwanda* (2004), it seems as though many filmmakers are waiting to see what kinds of films the American public wants. It could be that as of this writing the industry is in a holding pattern, still relying on blockbusters and remakes (such as the update of the *Manchurian Candidate* [2004]), while waiting to see what the next trend in successful political filmmaking will be. There have been some films that were extremely critical of U.S. foreign policy, such as *Syriana* (2005), and those that were, in retrospect, fairly right wing or libertarian, such as *Team America: World Police* (2004); but these films seem to be anomalies as opposed to the norm.

Oliver Stone finally got around to making his planned biopic of George W. Bush in *W.* (2008), which was surprisingly not as biting or vicious as many critics had predicted. Other films, although set in the past, also seemed to evoke either directly or indirectly the ongoing war on terror. The Tom Hanks vehicle *Charlie Wilson's War* (2007) was a broad comedy drama that looked at how a rogue congressman helped to originally finance the Afghanistan mujahideen warriors during the Reagan years and directed the viewer to the fact that the United States had funded fighters such as Osama Bin Laden years before they turned against the United States. Another film that addressed the concerns over civil liberties in light of the Patriot Act was the George Clooney film *Good Night and Good Luck* (2005), which was ostensibly a dramatization of the epic slugfest between pioneering journalist Edward R. Murrow and Joseph McCarthy, but could also be seen as a critique of the Bush administration. Other films that looked at contemporary politics included the Saudi Arabia–based *The Kingdom* (2007) and the more overtly political *Rendition* (2007).

Additional recent political films included the biting political satirization of the tobacco industry in *Thank You for Smoking*, the true life story of a longtime Soviet spy in the FBI in *Breach* (2007), and even director Ron Howard's film version of the play *Frost/Nixon* (2008) about the epic televised duel/interview between an unrepentant Richard Nixon and British journalist David Frost.

FURTHER READING

Aucoin, Don. "Hollywood Votes the Rascals Out." *Boston Globe*, November 4, 1990, B.6.

Christensen, Terry, and Peter Hass. *Projecting Politics: Political Messages in American Films*. Armonk, NY: M. E. Sharpe Press, 2005.

DeBauche, Leslie Midkiff. *Reel Patriotism: The Movies and World War I*. Madison, WI: University of Wisconsin Press, 1997.

Dickenson, Ben. *Hollywood's New Radicalism: War, Globalisation and the Movies from Reagan to George W. Bush*. London: I. B. Tauris, 2006.

Franklin, Daniel. *Politics and Film: The Political Culture of Film in the United States*. Lanham, MD: Rowman & Littlefield, 2006.

Giglio, Ernest. *Here's Looking at You: Hollywood, Film & Politics*. New York: Peter Lang Publishing, 2007.

Gunning, Tom. *D. W. Griffith and the Origins of American Narrative Film: The Early Years at Biograph*. Urband and Chicago: University of Illinois Press, 1991.

Richards, Jeffrey. "Frank Capra and the Cinema of Populism." In *Movies and Methods: An Anthology*, ed. Bill Nichols. Berkeley: University of California Press, 1976, 65–77.

Sloan, Kay. Excerpt from "The Loud Silents: Origins of the Social Protest Movie." In *Movies and American Society*, ed. Steven Ross. Malden, MA: Blackwell Publishing, 2002.

Chapter 2

Political Documentaries

Documentary films have typically not sparked as much interest as their fictional, usually Hollywood, counterparts. Yet even if they only rarely attract the large audiences that highly publicized fictional movies regularly draw, many documentaries still reside in the realm of popular culture. Moreover, because they commonly take on political themes, documentary films especially deserve attention in any examination of the intersection of politics, media, and popular culture.

DEFINING THE DOCUMENTARY FORM

Defining what constitutes a documentary is not a completely simple task. Over the years, scholars and creators of documentary films have debated exactly what distinguishes them from fictional movies—their conclusions have changed over time. The British documentary filmmaker and theorist John Grierson, who is widely considered one of the main founders of the form, is generally credited with actually coining the term. To him, the documentary involves, "the creative treatment of actuality" (Grierson 1966). Similarly, current scholar Michael Renov states it entails "the more or less artful reshaping of the historical world" (1993, 11). Often a documentary film is interchangeably referred to as a nonfiction film. Yet the line between fiction and nonfiction is inevitably a blurry one. Like Hollywood directors, documentary filmmakers sometimes stage reenactments, rehearse actions, add lighting to scenes, and score their movies with music that was obviously not playing at the moment of filming. Furthermore, creators of nonfiction films must choose what to include in—and consequently exclude from—the frame, decide on camera angles and lenses, and edit shots just as any maker of fictional movies does. Thus the form cannot possibly mirror real life in an unadulterated fashion. Another area that is debated is the extent to which the people in documentaries go about their business as they would if they were not being filmed. In other words, do they consciously (or even unconsciously) modify their behavior and "perform" for the camera? The persons who appear in documentaries are expected to "be themselves" and serve as *social actors* rather than professional actors. But knowing they are being watched likely has an influence on how these "real people" conduct their affairs.

Despite these overlapping tendencies, there are still key differences between nonfiction and fiction films. Bill Nichols, an authority on documentaries, for instance, contends that documentaries "address *the* world in which we live rather than *a* world imagined by the filmmaker" (2001, xi). In addition, generally much more so than the creators of fiction movies, documentarians seek to give the impression of authenticity. Rather than entirely fabricate a world for their audiences, makers of nonfiction films select portions of actual lived experience from their original context and arrange them in ways to make an argument. The documentary, therefore, "is not a reproduction of reality. It is a *representation* of the world we already occupy. It stands for a particular view of the world, one we may never have encountered before even if the aspects of the world that is represented are familiar to us" (Nichols 2001, 20). Although documentaries are sometimes perceived by the public as "objective," in effect, subjectivity inevitably enters the picture. The very process of making choices—subject, shot selection, and the like—guarantees that the outlook presented will reflect the stance of the film's creator. Nichols explains that fiction films ask their audiences to suspend disbelief, while documentaries hope to inspire belief, to convince their audiences to accept their filmmakers' interpretations of events as true. Accordingly, the author claims that documentaries correspond with the rhetorical tradition. In both cases, the filmmaker or orator uses certain tools of persuasion to structure a communicative act as a means of advancing a position and influencing an audience. Thus metaphorically, a documentary is a type of visual essay. It sometimes entertains its viewers but it is designed to do more than that. Not surprisingly, then, documentaries frequently carry political implications.

Documentary Genres

Nonfiction films can be assigned to various subgenres. For instance, many documentaries emphasize clear-cut scientific, nature, and educational issues. What is commonly called the *social documentary* is the nonfiction form most often associated with political themes. This type of documentary, too, can be divided into subgenres. In his definitive history of the documentary, Erik Barnouw (1993) divides documentaries up into the functions its practitioners fulfill, including the *prophet*, the *explorer*, the *advocate*, the *poet*, the *chronicler*, the *observer*, the *catalyst*, and so on. Other scholars have devised somewhat different genre categories for nonfiction films. Direct cinema, cinéma vérité, experimental, and further designations have been used to classify documentaries in an attempt to facilitate a better understanding of their purposes and how they communicate meaning. Regardless of how they are defined, each subgenre has included films that are loaded with political import.

Yet trying to discern exactly what constitutes a political documentary is itself problematic. Some theorists would maintain that every product of the mass media has political connotations. Yet such a conclusion yields an analysis of the intersection of politics and documentaries essentially meaningless. The field can be narrowed by focusing on forms that are directly political, such as nonfiction films that either function as government propaganda or deliver alternative perspectives on the status quo. Documentaries that revolve around "identity politics"—issues involving gender, race, sexual orientation, and other defining characteristics—are generally overtly political as well.

THE ORIGINS OF THE DOCUMENTARY

Many scholars trace the documentary's roots to the early films, or *actualités*, of the Frenchman Louis Lumière in the late nineteenth century. For example, the film *Workers Leaving the Lumière Factory* displays, as the title indicates, people simply exiting their place of employment. Such films seem to faithfully document everyday events as they happened (although, even here, it appears as though scenes were sometimes rehearsed). Yet a documentary tradition that went beyond merely recording either mundane activities (such as a train arriving at a station) or sensational events (such as a circus performance) to acquire a "voice," or a manner of expressing a point of view or argument, did not transpire until the 1920s. During that decade, more sophisticated documentaries emerged in the Soviet Union, France, Germany, Holland, England, and North America. The leading Soviet documentarians of the period, such as Esfir Shub, Dziga Vertov, and Sergei Eisenstein, were particularly influential on their counterparts in the United States, as well as government officials interested in using documentaries to further political policies. But the nonfiction feature that film historians generally point to as the one that gave birth to a full-fledged documentary form in the United States is *Nanook of the North* (1922). Produced by Robert Flaherty, who is universally regarded as one of the documentary's "founding fathers," it depicts an Inuit family's struggle to survive in the bitter conditions of the Arctic.

A BRIEF HISTORY OF THE POLITICAL DOCUMENTARY IN THE UNITED STATES

In 1896, the film *William McKinley at Home* showed the candidate for president in the midst of his political campaign. Soon after, *President McKinley's Inaugural Address* presented the newly elected president giving his speech—yet his actual words were not heard because the arrival of sync sound was still decades away. Similar to the primitive *actualités*, these short pieces merely recorded McKinley engaged in political activity without providing a clear stance on the events.

The U.S. government produced several rudimentary propaganda films as early as 1911. In one, farmers in the East were encouraged to move to the newly developed territories in the West. Once the country joined forces with its World War I allies in 1917, propaganda films promoting support for American involvement and hatred of the enemy were released, including *Pershing's Crusaders*, *America's Answer*, and *From Forest to France* (also see **World War Propaganda**).

Although *Nanook of the North* is widely heralded as the first great American documentary film, it does not explicitly forward a political argument. Vaguely anthropological, still, the feature has political implications, even if they were not broadly recognized by its large and receptive audience when it was first screened. Despite Flaherty's sympathetic portrayal of Nanook and his family, the filmmaker's work presents their daily life—at least subtly—through a colonialist lens. *Nanook of the North* is also significant in that it established right from the start the blurry boundaries between fiction and nonfiction film. Flaherty requested that his social actors reenact routines—sometimes even activities they had long abandoned for newer practices.

The 1930s: Documentaries Become Institutionalized

As the nation entered the Great Depression, a number of filmmakers from the left end of the political spectrum began producing numerous documentaries that delivered sharp critiques of the capitalist enterprise and other aspects of U.S. society. In 1930, the Workers' Film and Photo League (later the word "Workers" was dropped from its title) was formed to train photographers and documentarians, with the goal of producing films from a Marxist perspective. Part of the group's mission was to expose images and issues that were generally not covered by the standard news services. Although audiences for these films were usually smaller than those enjoyed by Hollywood, figures from the realm of popular culture, including such luminaries as the actor and eventual screen director Elia Kazan, as well as actors Burgess Meredith and James Cagney, sometimes participated in their creation. In 1934, three key figures of the Film and Photo League (FPL) left the organization to establish Nykino. Its first well-promoted film poked fun at turning to religion for feelings of hope regarding an afterlife rather than considering the hunger that already exists in life on earth.

In contrast to the FPL and Nykino was the more politically centrist or possibly right-leaning series *The March of Time* (MOT). Sponsored by Time-Life-Fortune, Inc., and backed by the corporation's head, Henry Luce, the MOT released a new film each month. These short movies covered current affairs in a journalistic fashion and played before the feature selections at popular movie theaters.

Meanwhile, various government agencies were producing and disseminating documentaries as well. Rexford Guy Tugwell, who had been appointed by Franklin Delano Roosevelt to head up the Resettlement Administration (RA), turned to the documentary as a tactic for championing FDR's New Deal initiatives. Tugwell hired **Pare Lorentz**, who would become the force behind several notable government-supported documentaries. Eventually, though, partly because of resistance from Republicans and corporate leaders who were hostile to the New Deal, filmmaking efforts such as Lorentz's would come to a halt as financial support dwindled.

Other private and corporate concerns also released documentaries that provided commentary on the matters perplexing the nation during the 1930s. For instance, *The Spanish Earth*, an antifascist perspective on the Spanish civil war, was produced by the Contemporary Film Historians, Inc., whose members included the playwright Lillian Hellman and the novelist Ernest Hemingway, who wrote and narrated the film. The conflict was revisited years later in the film *The Good Fight* (1984), directed by Mary Dore, Noel Buckner, and Sam Sills, and narrated by Studs Terkel. Frontier Films, which succeeded Nykino, created a variety of documentaries, several of which dealt with labor unrest from a left-wing point of view. Elia Kazan directed *People of the Cumberland*, a film that featured the trials of coal miners in Appalachia and their efforts at organized resistance to exploitative practices. The actor Paul Robeson narrated *Native Land*, which examined workers' rights and unions. *The City* dealt with urban planning and received much attention at the New York World's Fair of 1939. Although well-known personalities contributed to these and other like-minded films, most of the time these documentaries suffered from poor funding and distribution and, consequently, were not screened by the kind of sizable crowds associated with popular culture. Often, they were screened in art house theaters by especially politically engaged audiences. Probably, then, these left of center, nongovernmental, nonfiction films had minimal impact on the general population. After the Japanese attacked Pearl Harbor, support for critical documentaries diminished; in their place arose ones that promoted national unity in the cause of defeating the Axis powers.

The 1940s: Entering World War II

Both British and Canadian documentaries were distributed in the United States before the Japanese invasion of Pearl Harbor, which might have contributed to boosting sympathy for the Allied cause even before direct U.S. involvement. Once President Roosevelt had committed troops, documentarians from all three English-speaking nations exchanged footage, and audiences in all three countries were able to see one another's films centered on the war. Not only did documentary filmmakers in the United States work on behalf of the military effort, but fiction movie producers joined the cause as well. Together, they served the function of gaining popular support for U.S. involvement. Along the way, documentaries received far more screenings than they had during the 1930s.

Some of the nonfiction war materials produced simply consisted of training films. These straightforward explanations of various military techniques were not documentaries per se, in the sense defined above, because they did not advance arguments. Yet they were an important part of the war filmmaking venture nonetheless.

Other films created throughout the war period would qualify as full-fledged documentaries. Propaganda films in particular were backed by the government to influence citizen attitudes and heighten troop morale. Probably the most notable propaganda movies made in this vein are the seven that comprise the *Why We Fight* series, which were designed to turn over 9 million American citizens into soldiers and other military workers. The famous Hollywood director **Frank Capra**, a lieutenant in the war, was in charge of production.

A number of Hollywood veterans besides Capra also played a major role in producing propaganda films and other types of war documentaries, including John Ford and John Huston. Some of these movies featured actual or reenacted battle scenes. Ford, for example, personally filmed action for *The Battle of Midway* (1942) and was seriously wounded in the process. Yet his bravery led to special recognition when his film won an Academy Award. Ford also used miniatures and special effects to recreate the attack on Pearl Harbor in his film *December 7th* (1943).

Huston's *The Battle of San Pietro* (1945) is considered by many to be the best American wartime documentary ever crafted. The director also wrote and narrated the film. In the movie, American and German forces in Italy fight ferociously for control of the Liri Valley. Yet by picturing the excruciating costs of war, including shots of civilian casualties, it did not operate as sheer propaganda.

Shortly after the United States entered the war, the Roosevelt administration established the **Office of War Information** (OWI), which was given the task of coordinating all of the government information provided to the media, as well as charged with producing its own materials to educate and persuade the public. (Also see **World War Propaganda**.)

Postwar Documentaries before Television

While scores of nonfiction films were disseminated and more people than ever before had viewed this form of motion picture during the war, documentaries did not build on that momentum and gain widespread popularity immediately afterward. Following World War II, less funding was available for documentaries, fewer film-makers participated in the genre, and, accordingly, fewer of these films were created and distributed. The Hollywood professionals who had made documentaries on behalf of the nation returned to business as usual, once more supplying fictional enter-tainment for moviegoers. Nonfiction education and training films flourished while documentaries with a strong voice and artistic vision found far fewer outlets. Com-mercial theaters typically shunned them, relegating them to classrooms, corporate boardrooms, and similar venues.

Moreover, resistance to the New Deal had pressured the government to pull back on releasing documentaries that endorsed domestic policies. And with the war behind them, Franklin D. Roosevelt (FDR) and other officials had little need to sponsor the kind of output they had financially backed when the conflict was still in motion. The OWI was totally abolished; meanwhile, the Department of Agricul-ture still engaged in production, albeit on a smaller scale, and the International Motion Picture Division of the Department of State continued to ship propaganda films abroad. Private industries sometimes provided funding, but generally with the intention of enhancing company profits rather than showing concern for the common good. Nonprofit associations, other interest groups, and independent social documentarians (especially on the left), in contrast, were often hesitant to boldly take a critical stance toward issues, in part, because McCarthyism was on the rise. Makers of controversial films risked being accused of Communist sympa-thy, which could result in the loss of their careers. The late 1940s, in general, reflected neither the hardships of the Great Depression nor the turmoil and threat of fascism of World War II. It appeared that the motivation to express strong politi-cal statements through film had diminished. In the midst of the Cold War climate, documentaries, by and large, were usually tamer than many of their antecedents had been. Nonfiction films as a whole, then, lost their edge and sense of creativity. Still, one contentious area that did make its way into documentary production involved race relations. For example, Frank Sinatra sang in *The House I Live In* (1945), a theatrical short that spoke out against anti-Semitism. Yet the overall impact of films of this nature before the Civil Rights Movement took hold was likely dubious.

Television: A New Channel for Documentaries

If the immediate postwar years were a time of lull for documentaries, the rise of television in the 1950s became a period in which nonfiction films proliferated like never before. (For a discussion of politics and nondocumentary forms of television entertainment, see Chapter 4.) Although the technology for television had existed well in advance of the war, the medium was not heavily marketed until after its con-clusion, which coincided with a renewed emphasis on the consumer economy. By 1950, there were roughly 4 million sets in U.S. homes. The next year, TV was avail-able from coast to coast. Also in 1951, as *The March of Time* came to a close, a new CBS series was beamed through the airwaves. ***See It Now***, a spin-off of the radio show *Hear It Now*, helped newsman **Edward R. Murrow** gain even greater fame. The other major networks also broadcast informational shows, mostly as a means of satisfying their licensing requirements to serve the public interest. In 1953, National Educational Television (which would later become the Public Broadcasting Service [**PBS**]) was born. As a noncommercial network partly funded by the government, it offered many opportunities for documentarians to put their work on the air.

See It Now is generally considered to be television's first regular television documentary series. Yet as it took up more and more controversial issues, advertisers increasingly withdrew support. Eventually the weekly show was reduced to an occasional special, and then supplanted by *CBS Reports*. Murrow's role was decreased, although he still anchored *Harvest of Shame*, a critically acclaimed installment of the program.

In 1960, NBC launched *White Paper*, a documentary series that applied many of the same conventions of CBS's public affairs programming. While covering a variety of pressing stories of the day, such as the Bay of Pigs invasion and the death of Soviet dictator Joseph Stalin, it generally stayed clear of inciting the kind of heated reactions its CBS rival sparked. For its part, ABC introduced a number of one-hour documentaries under the title, *Close-Up!* One of them, "Yanki No" (1960), dealt with anti-Americanism in Latin America. Another noteworthy film in the series, "The Children Were Watching" (1960), portrayed white segregationists and a family whose daughter hoped to be the first to attend a formerly all-white school. Racial themes were also evident in "Walk in My Shoes" (1961), which depicted life in Jim Crow America from an African American point of view.

Later, CBS inaugurated *60 Minutes*, one of the news magazine format's—if not television's in general—most successful ventures. Started in 1968, the investigative journalism vehicle achieved such success that spin-offs, such as ABC's *20/20* and *Dateline NBC*, eventually followed. These types of public affairs shows have almost completely replaced long-form documentaries on commercial broadcast television. At the same time, however, the broadcast medium has brought nonfiction works to more people than movie theaters ever did.

Direct Cinema and Cinéma Vérité

By the late 1950s, film technologies were becoming lighter, more mobile, and more flexible, thus offering filmmakers opportunities to establish new techniques. Out of these developments emerged two related documentary methods. Cinéma vérité (film truth) was mostly of French invention, thanks largely to the work of Jean Rouch. In the United States, an approach to recording situations in everyday life became known as "direct cinema." Perhaps the main difference between them has to do with the extent to which the documentarians intervene in what they are filming. The artist engaged in cinéma vérité directly participates in the action, sometimes even functioning as a provocateur, hoping to trigger reactions that reveal a deeper truth about the situation captured for the screen. On the other hand, the direct cinema director attempts to remove himself or herself from the scene and act as an objective observer, an uninvolved bystander. Direct cinema, then, often requires very long takes, as the documentarian waits for something to unfold that can hold an audience's attention. Cinéma vérité deliberately tries to present moments that would have never happened without the presence of a camera. Direct cinema, conversely, intends to show behavior that supposedly would have occurred even if the film crew were absent. One of the early major documentaries to become associated with the practices of direct cinema is *Primary* (1960), produced by Drew Associates. The film was also the first of its kind to comprehensively cover a political campaign while providing a behind-the-scenes perspective.

Today, the two labels (cinéma vérité and direct cinema) are often used interchangeably although this undercuts their original point of difference. Debate has centered on whether a filmmaker can ever achieve pure objectivity or if a camera (unless it is hidden) can actually serve as a "fly on the wall." Rouch and his fellow practitioners of cinéma vérité dismissed the notion of objectivity and instead sought to take a strong point of view toward the subjects they filmed. Both styles, however, usually gain political import by focusing more on individuals that relate to larger social issues than on broad concerns in the abstract. Generally, too, they take the shape of a narrative more than a film essay composed of shots from diverse sources that are edited in a way to advance a particular argument.

The 1960s and 1970s: Documenting a Time of Political Unrest

In the late 1960s and the 1970s, funding came from many supporters and thus a considerable amount of notable documentaries were produced. Emile de Antonio resurrected the left-wing tradition, creating scathing critiques of elements of American life. (He sometimes referred to his work as "the theater of fact.") His first successful film, *Point of Order* (1963), received a considerable run in movie theaters. It revisited the 1954 Army–**Senator Joseph McCarthy** hearings and debunked the politician's tactics. In 1971, the director released *Millhouse: A White Comedy*, which levied attacks against the character and activities of Richard Nixon the year before he was reelected as president. He also produced a documentary in 1975 about the radical group the **Weather Underground**.

Reflecting the controversies surrounding the U.S. military endeavors in Southeast Asia, a number of documentaries about Vietnam were also created during this period, most of them challenging the government's line on the intervention. De Antonio delivered one himself, in a highly critical history of U.S. involvement in Vietnam. *In the Year of the Pig* (1968) portrays a number of haunting images, including scenes of American soldiers burning villages and terrifying women and children. On the other hand, *Why Vietnam?* (1965), produced by the Department of Defense and distributed to schools, presented a pro-war point of view.

As the disconnection between the government's official version of the war and the media's firsthand view of it became more pronounced, dissenting voices increasingly surfaced. *Letters from Vietnam* (1965), created by Drew Associates and aired on ABC TV, however, does not take a hostile stance per se yet poses questions about U.S. involvement. The film's scenes are scored with excerpts from audiotape letters that a helicopter pilot had sent to his daughter back home. Through them, the soldier reveals the harsh realities of war, including the conditions faced by child victims. A few years afterward, Joseph Strick won an Academy Award for best short documentary for his film, *Interviews with My Lai Veterans* (1970). In the piece, former soldiers, seemingly still numb from their participation in the war, disclose stories about the massacre that U.S. troops committed in the Vietnam village identified in the film's title.

One of the most famous Vietnam films of the period, an Oscar winner for Best Documentary, is Peter Davis's *Hearts and Minds* (1974), which paints a history of the conflict and explores the damage done on all sides. The film was rereleased in 2004, probably because distributors felt it contained parallels between U.S. involvement in Vietnam and the twenty-first-century occupation of Iraq.

Ultimately, many government officials at least partially blamed the media for the nation's Vietnam defeat because of the critical standpoint some television and documentaries presented. A number of patriotic thinkers have continued this line of argument until the present day. Others counter that the media should not be used as a scapegoat and that America's failure in Vietnam was a result of an array of complicated factors.

Meanwhile, the Newsreel Collective, later named Third World Newsreel, produced and disseminated, often to college campuses, dozens of short pieces of agit-prop on additional matters. Founded in 1967 in New York, the organization moved to other cities across the country. It took on a number of contentious topics, including student protests at Columbia University, the plight of working-class women, and a variety of issues faced by people of color. Over time, Third World Newsreel has expanded its operations and continues to distribute films today about many marginalized peoples.

Frederick Wiseman was a foremost contributor to the direct cinema tradition. Many of his films, such as *The Titicut Follies* (1967), which examines a hospital for the criminally insane, and *Law and Order* (1969), about the work of the Kansas City Police Department, following the conventions of the form, do not convey a bold viewpoint yet are certainly capable of triggering political thoughts in viewers, depending on the predispositions they bring to the documentaries.

Other Documentaries with Political Implications.   As the women's movement gained steam in the 1970s, not surprisingly, documentaries with feminist themes or implications also surfaced. Before the decade, relatively few women had directed documentaries. By the close of the 1970s, many women had produced films on a range of personal and political topics. Barbara Kopple gained considerable recognition throughout the decade, especially for her Academy Award–winning documentary, *Harlan County, USA* (1976), which offers a sympathetic view of Kentucky coal miners who were locked in a bitter strike. Later, Elizabeth Barrett also turned her lens on coal mining, but her film, *Coal Mining Women* (1982), specifically emphasizes women who were working in a predominantly male world. Connie Field looked at women in the labor pool as well, yet within a different context. *The Life and Times of Rosie the Riveter* (1980) is an historical examination of the women who toiled in the factories when there was a shortage of male workers during World War II. In 1972, the distribution company Women Make Movies was launched, designed to "address the underrepresentation and misrepresentation of women in the media industry" (quoted from the Women Make Movies Web site, http://www.wmm.com/about/general_info.shtml). Most of the feminist films of the decade, however, never achieved popular status and had to settle for play outside the theatrical market. Still, Women Make Movies remains active today, funding films produced by women and helping to ensure they gain exhibition.

Other documentaries also highlighted the cause of labor in general. In *The Wobblies* (1978), for example, Deborah Shaffer and Stewart Bird show the organizing activities of the Industrial Workers of the World (nicknamed the Wobblies) throughout the first half of the twentieth century. Additional themes that grew out of the 1960s social movements, including racial equality, gay rights, and environmentalism, received treatment as well.

In addition, the 1972 political party conventions were covered by a group of alternative filmmakers known as "Top Value Television," or TVTV. Taking a guerrilla approach to events, they offered a very different perspective of the rallies than that communicated through conventional media.

Yet no documentary achieved more success in the decade than *Woodstock* (1970), which presents an elaborate collage of the rock concert by the same name. Not overtly political, the film is yet significant for its depiction of hippie culture, which indeed signified, at least in part, collective resistance to certain events and dominant ideas in the U.S. society at large. In 1973, another concert documentary was created for a primarily African American audience. Mel Stuart's *Wattstax* captures the spirit of a performance that symbolized, in a sense, the Black version of Woodstock.

The 1980s: Video Makes Its Entrance

For years, documentary filmmakers had relied on 16mm film, a lighter and easier format to use than the wider 35mm version preferred by Hollywood. Entering the 1980s, videotape production was becoming more popular. Cheaper and simpler to employ than any kind of film, it enabled many more people to participate in documentary production at a variety of levels, from crudely amateur to highly professional. Still, hoping to secure profits in a satiated environment proved difficult. Yet the growth of cable and satellite television supplied additional venues for reaching audiences. HBO, in particular, telecast a number of significant documentaries and continues to do so until this day. A&E, The History Channel, The Learning Channel, The Discovery Channel, and others have relied extensively on nonfiction films to fulfill their programming requirements. Yet only rarely have any of these commercial cable offerings (as opposed to a premium venue such as HBO) provoked considerable political debate or controversy, which has usually been the case with the advertising-driven medium of television at large. Many of the documentaries on these channels consist of titillating or human interest material, or straightforward accounts of scientific developments, activities in nature, and similar fare. Films such as *Justiceville* (1987), about a group of homeless activists in Los Angeles, were broadcast on The Discovery Channel only in its early days and are in no way typical of programming trends in general. Many of the nonfiction films on these cable stations follow predictable formulas and serve to satisfy the needs of corporate sponsors.

Not that every documentary film made in the period was devoid of impact or political reference. For instance, **Errol Morris**'s *The Thin Blue Line* (1988), which challenges the conviction of a man serving a life sentence for the murder of a police officer, was screened in many theaters and actually contributed to the release of the wrongfully incarcerated man.

A serious film about the nuclear age, *If You Love This Planet* received an Academy Award for Best Documentary Short. Although it was produced by a Canadian organization, it received attention in the United States. The U.S. Department of Labor, under the Ronald Reagan administration, classified the film as "political propaganda" and required copies exhibited in the United States to carry a warning label that identified it as such.

Charles Guggenheim, a renowned documentarian, created several films of political consequence. *Note from Little Rock*, an Academy Award winner, recounts the events of the Arkansas school integration crisis. Guggenheim had earlier acquired an Academy Award for *Robert Kennedy Remembered*, a biography he completed just weeks after the presidential candidate's assassination. Later, he received two more Academy Awards, including one in 1995 for *A Time for Justice*, a documentary that explores the Civil Rights Movement.

Several additional important political nonfiction films were released during the 1980s. Some of them explored the dubious involvement of the United States in Central American insurgencies and counterinsurgencies. Pamela Yates and David Goodman won an Academy Award for their documentary, *Witness to War: Dr. Charlie Clements* (1985), about a Vietnam veteran working in El Salvador to heal wounded rebel soldiers. Barbara Trent, the head of the Empowerment Project, produced *Destination* (1986) and *Coverup: Behind the Iran Contra Affair* (1988), and later received an Academy Award for *The Panama Deception* (1992), which delivers a scathing critique of U.S. policies in that nation. Today, Trent continues to create documentaries, some of which express an antiglobalization perspective. Robert Richter, in the 1990s, carried on the motif of unsavory U.S. intervention in Latin American conditions. Both *School of Assassins* (1994) and *Father Roy: Inside the School of Assassins* (1997) expose the training of eventual Latin American human rights abusers by U.S. personnel at the Army's School of the Americas in Georgia. The actress Susan Sarandon narrated each film. Meanwhile, Yates turned her attention to poverty in the United States in the 1990s with a trilogy of films.

Some Vietnam documentaries continued to emerge, perhaps reflecting the war's lingering influence on the national consciousness (a tendency that still seems active, given that, even in the twenty-first century, a few nonfiction films on the Vietnam era have been produced—see below). For example, calling to mind the film *Letters from Vietnam*, Bill Couturiè created *Dear America: Letters Home from Vietnam* (1988). This time, the correspondence of several soldiers is heard, their words read by a group of well-known actors. Produced for HBO, the feature resulted in an Emmy Award for Couturiè. Several films returned to even earlier wars. For instance, *The Day after Trinity* (1980) profiles J. Robert Oppenheimer, one of the major forces behind the creation of the atomic bomb that was used to decimate Hiroshima and Nagasaki, Japan, during World War II. *The Atomic Café* (1982), made by Kevin Rafferty, Pierce Rafferty, and Jayne Loader, is a satirical commentary on U.S. propaganda films that had sought to incite fear in the population about the threat of a Soviet-led nuclear holocaust; the documentary enjoyed a successful run in numerous theaters. Another documentary on the birth of the atomic era, Robert Stone's *Radio Bikini* (1987), shows U.S. authorities permanently evacuating the residents of Bikini Atoll to conduct bombing tests, as well as the nation's own soldiers, who were provided neither protection nor information on the harm that nuclear fallout would cause, innocently watching the explosions in the distance.

Documentaries tackling racial and ethnic controversies emerged as well. In 1979, eight black producers formed the National Black Programming Consortium in response to the lack of African American shows on PBS. Henry Hampton, who in 1968 had established Blackside, Inc., the largest African American–owned film outfit at the time, served as executive producer of the PBS series *Eyes on the Prize*. The episodes comprehensively cover the history of race relations in the United States; some of them, after receiving funding to clear up copyright problems with archival footage, have been recently rebroadcast on PBS. Marlon Riggs also made several films on African American themes and sometimes sparked controversy when his work aired on PBS. *Ethnic Notions: Black People in White Minds* (1987) uncovers media stereotypes of African Americans, a subject he revisited in 1989 with *Color Adjustment*. Asian Americans produced documentaries that treated identity politics as well. One of the most highly regarded Asian American nonfiction films of the period is Christine Choy and Renee Tajima's *Who Killed Vincent Chin?* (1988). The feature investigates the murder of Chin, who was beaten to death outside a fast-food restaurant after his bachelor party in the suburbs of Detroit, Michigan, a city where many residents were feeling resentment over the Japanese encroachment on Detroit's automotive manufacturing dominance. It appears his attackers assumed that Chin, a Chinese American, was Japanese. Over the years, the PBS Minority Consortium has supported works by Native Americans and Latinos as well.

Following the 1969 Stonewall Riots in New York City, which marked a turning point in the gay rights movement, more homosexual filmmakers used documentary to make their voices heard. Nearing the 1980s, the Mariposa Film Group released the pioneering film, *Word Is Out: Some Stories of Our Lives* (1978). In 1984, Robert Rosenberg, John Scagliotti, and Greta Schiller chronicled the history of gay culture, persecution, and resistance in the United States in *Before Stonewall*. Also in 1984, *The Times of Harvey Milk*, by Rob Epstein and Richard Schmiechen, received significant attention. The documentary centers on the career of Harvey Milk, the first openly gay person to win an election for public office in California. Roughly a year after his term had begun, he and the mayor of San Francisco were murdered by another council member. Later, Rob Epstein joined Bill Couturiè and Jeffrey Friedman to make *Common Threads: Stories from the Quilt* (1989), a documentary that attempted to raise consciousness about the AIDS epidemic, which had hit the gay population especially hard. Made for HBO and narrated by Dustin Hoffman, the program drew a sizable audience. Documentaries and experimental cinematic pieces on lesbian-feminist issues also came to the fore through the efforts of Barbara Hammer, a pioneer in the area who has produced dozens of films since the 1970s.

Meanwhile, Marlon Riggs did not produce documentaries only about the black experience per se. A gay man, he generated controversy with his frank and sexually charged portrayals of urban, African American gay men in *Tongues Untied* (1988). In response to the film's scheduled appearance on PBS, some politicians debated the merits of the government funding work they perceived as obscene. Amidst the verbal storm, a few public stations backed out of running the show, although most PBS outlets broadcast it as planned. Yet the contentiousness surrounding the documentary might have had an influence on the eventual National Endowment for the Arts decision to no longer provide financial support for individual artists, including filmmakers.

The nature of the relationship between documentaries and television in general reached a turning point when, in 1984, the Federal Communication Commission (FCC) relaxed its guidelines regarding broadcasters' requirement to serve the public interest. TV executives, forever nervous about risky programming, therefore, had less motivation to devote significant airtime to nonfiction films on controversial matters. Just four years earlier, CBS had suffered attack for its telecasting of *The Uncounted Enemy: A Vietnam Deception*, which alleged that General

William C. Westmoreland had deliberately misled the government, the public, and the military itself about the size and strength of the Vietnamese forces. The outcry culminated in Westmoreland filing a suit against CBS (he later dropped it). But the legal proceedings revealed that CBS had indeed engaged in some dubious practices in making the documentary. With commercial networks pulling back on hard-edged investigative reports, PBS became of even greater importance to documentarians wishing to exhibit their work on the small screen.

Documentaries in the 1990s and into the Twenty-First Century

As the number of potential outlets for exhibiting documentaries has increasingly multiplied, the line between fiction and nonfiction, many film scholars contend, has grown even blurrier. Furthermore, with more time to fill on ever more cable and satellite stations that include nonfiction formats, the quality of many documentaries has arguably declined. Networks eager to promote themselves, satisfy their advertisers, decrease costs, and meet tight deadlines are sometimes compelled to make compromises, even to the point of occasionally misrepresenting facts. At the same time, documentarians working for television (premium channels like HBO perhaps being an exception) do not usually enjoy the same degree of autonomy or film rights as their independent counterparts, resulting in formulaic products that meet the needs of network executives. Broadcast television networks, anxious about losing audiences to cable, are typically still more risk averse than they were in the past; consequently, challenging documentaries almost never receive the play they did during the medium's early days. On the flip side, however, because of the expansion of available high-quality, lightweight, low-cost, digital video equipment, documentary filmmaking, like other media production, has become noticeably democratized. More aspiring artists than ever can participate in creating nonfiction films—or any other kind of visual material that interests them.

Yet public television, with far fewer pressures from advertisers, has remained a fruitful venue for documentaries. In 1988, Congress committed funds toward an independent PBS operation. Some of that money found its way to the establishment of the Independent Television and Video Service (ITVS), whose very mission involves tackling matters that commercial stations generally will not touch, and ensuring that more voices are heard and underserved audiences are addressed. Much of ITVS's production has consisted of documentaries, which often appear in one of two series—*P.O.V.* or *Independent Lens*. Another PBS feature, *Frontline*, has won many awards and, for years, has represented the nation's only TV public affairs documentary series to be regularly broadcast. Launched in 1983, the program has televised over 500 episodes, covering many political and social justice issues along the way. The criminal justice system, in particular, has received considerable attention, often at the hands of producer Ofra Bikel, who has been with the show since its first season. Moreover, beginning in 1988, every four years *Frontline* has produced a special feature entitled *The Choice*, which profiles the Democratic and Republican nominees for president.

Still, since its inception, PBS has faced rebuke from primarily conservative politicians who have taken issue with its sometimes critical perspective. On occasion, government officials have reduced funding or threatened to pull it all together. Thus even public television has had to strike a balance between airing provocative programming and avoiding heated government response. In her book, *Public*

Television: Politics and the Battle Over Documentary Film, B. J. Bullert (1997) explains the struggles that documentarians have encountered in trying to get PBS to broadcast their films on contentious subjects. Barbara Trent, for instance, secured an Academy Award for her documentary *The Panama Deception* (1992), despite the fact that PBS had earlier refused to telecast her film, just as it had rejected her 1988 nonfiction feature, *Cover-Up: Behind the Iran-Contra Affair*. While some observers perceive a documentary series like *Frontline* as bold exposé, others acknowledge it covers divisive topics, but say it does so through self-censored, diluted executions.

Probably the documentarian who has received the most fame through PBS is **Ken Burns**. Though many of his works are not especially political, his 1990 set of films, *The Civil War*, is politically significant because it covers a major moment in U.S. history.

Elsewhere, independent nonfiction filmmakers have continued to find ways of obtaining funding to produce and distribute their work. Often, drawing from diverse approaches, they render documentaries intended to expose transgressions, challenge attitudes, or activate change. Barbara Kopple, for example, turned to labor strife again in *American Dream* (1991), a look into a meat-packers' strike in Minnesota. For the second time, Kopple took home an Oscar for her work. Meanwhile, Jonathan Stack teamed with Liz Garbus to create *The Farm: Angola USA* (1998), then joined with Simon Soffer on *The Wildest Show in the South: The Angola Prison Rodeo* (1999). Both films explore Angola Prison in Louisiana and provide social commentary on the country's prison system in general. Mixing the personal with the political, a common combination since the rise of identity politics, Judith Helfand and Daniel B. Gold treat the issues of the modern toxic environment by, among other things, showing scenes of Hefland's parents' vinyl-sided home in *Blue Vinyl* (2002). An especially political film that generated considerable attention is D. A. Pennebaker and Chris Hegedus's **The War Room** (1993), which provides an inside look at Bill Clinton's 1992 presidential campaign. Released in 2004, *The Road to the Presidency* also follows the 1992 campaign trail but did not spark as much interest. R. J. Cutler and David Van Taylor covered another campaign—the U.S. Senate race in Virginia between Charles Robb and Oliver North, who had once been heavily implicated in the controversial Iran-Contra Affair—in the documentary, *A Perfect Candidate* (1996).

Recent Theatrical Releases.   In general, throughout their history, documentaries not produced for television have gained much less notice and drawn far smaller audiences than the fictional features of Hollywood. Those presenting dissenting points of view, in particular, have usually been marginalized by commercial television and corporate theater chains. In a sense, then, documentaries have rarely achieved the status of "popular culture," at least if that term is associated with mass fame. Yet the meaning of "popular" is a relative one. At what point does a work cross the line from comparatively unknown to popular? How big must the audience be? Certainly a home movie seen only by friends and family would not qualify as a product of popular culture insofar as reaching many viewers (although there are other ways of defining popular culture—for instance, products made by everyday people for everyday people—that would lead to the conclusion that even this amateur practice could be included within the category). Yet many documentaries have been seen by enough people to be construed as popular on some level—or at least on the margins of popular culture and, therefore, by reflecting some of its defining characteristics, intertwined with it. A number of film festivals, for instance, devote some, or sometimes all, of their screenings to documentaries. Although nonfiction films have been included in festivals since this form of exhibition first emerged, the number of festivals in general and those committed to documentaries in particular has dramatically increased in recent years. One chain of festivals that especially emphasizes films with a political bent is the series of Human Rights Film Festivals that is staged around the world, including the United States. These events feature a broad selection of both fiction and nonfiction films. Some U.S. festivals completely dedicated to documentaries are the Hot Springs Documentary Film Festival in Arkansas and Full Frame in New York. Yet probably no film festival has done more to popularize and legitimize the documentary than the Sundance Film Festival, held every year in Utah. Its founder, actor Robert Redford, is a documentary enthusiast and has pushed for a strong nonfiction presence at the competition. With its own cable network, Sundance also telecasts some of the documentaries that received praise during the festival. Furthermore, Sundance and other festivals have provided a forum that has generated enough interest in certain documentaries to bring them to popular movie theaters.

Then again, from time to time, since the birth of the form, particular documentaries have enjoyed notable runs in the same movie theaters that project the products of Hollywood. Flaherty's *Nanook of the North* was a big hit in theaters in the 1920s. The following decade, Pare Lorentz's *The River* and *The Plow That Broke the Plains* reached big audiences in neighborhood movie theaters. Many World War II documentaries also received substantial theatrical screening. With the advent of television, however, documentaries in the 1950s and 1960s, with a few exceptions, left the big screen for the smaller confines of the TV set. They made somewhat of a comeback in theaters in the late 1960s and 1970s, when independent filmmakers, influenced by the social and political conflicts of the Vietnam era, took special pains to obtain exhibition.

Yet the twenty-first century has represented a renaissance of sorts for the theatrically distributed documentary. In fact, 8 of the 10 top-grossing documentaries of all time have been produced since 2002. Why the renewed interest in the documentary form has occurred is a subject for conjecture. Some critics contend that the ongoing corporatization and supposed "dumbing down" of the news has left people yearning for more investigative coverage and diverse points of view that challenge the government's and the business world's version of events.

The movie that perhaps signified a turning point is *Hoop Dreams* (1994). Tracking the lives of two inner-city basketball players who aspire to become stars, the documentary examines the pressures they face. Yet it is more than a biographical depiction—along the way, *Hoop Dreams* explores the social conditions of low-income, urban culture and how many young people, especially African American males, perceive their only path of escape to success is via the basketball court. The film won the Audience Award for Best Documentary at the Sundance Film Festival, garnered wide critical acclaim, grossed over $7 million dollars at the theaters, and was eventually broadcast on public television. Accordingly, it demonstrated that a thoughtful documentary could indeed translate into financial reward.

In 2004, Harry Thompson and Nickolas Perry gained a limited theatrical run for their film *The Hunting of the President*, based on a book by Joe Conason and Gene Lyons, about the alleged decade-long effort by some Republicans to politically destroy President Bill Clinton. Ten years earlier, the film *The Clinton Chronicles* indeed attacked Clinton for a variety of supposed transgressions. Video sales of the video were promoted by the Reverend Jerry Falwell on both television and radio.

The documentarian who has lately attracted the most attention—both positive and negative—is **Michael Moore**. His rise to fame began with his release of *Roger & Me* (1988), which enjoyed considerable success at film festivals. Subsequent releases include *Bowling for Columbine* (2002), which draws from the late 1990s student massacre at Columbine High School to explore the nation's relationship with guns and violence; and *Fahrenheit 9/11* (2004), a brutal indictment of the George W. Bush administration that was intended to help sway the presidential election of 2004 in Senator John Kerry's direction.

Through his films, Moore has established a personal style that mixes considerable on-camera involvement with humor, irony, and satire. Along the way, he has achieved an unprecedented degree of celebrity for a documentarian, extending his film work into other venues, including popular books, television programs, and live events. Moore won an Oscar for Best Documentary for *Bowling for Columbine* and a Palme d'Or at the Cannes Film Festival for *Fahrenheit 9/11*, which became the highest grossing documentary of all time by far (supplanting *Bowling for Columbine* for that distinction). In 2007, Moore generated additional controversy with the release of *Sicko*, which takes a highly critical look at the health care system in the United States. Through comparison with health care programs in Canada, Cuba, France, and the United Kingdom, Moore argues that the nation should socialize its health services and institute universal coverage.

Another film that received far more attention than is typically the case with documentaries is ***An Inconvenient Truth*** (2006). Centering on a presentation delivered around the world by former vice president and 2000 presidential candidate Al Gore, the movie provides considerable evidence in support of the general view held by most scientists on climate change and examines the potentially devastating consequences of global warming. Becoming the fourth largest grossing documentary film in U.S. history, *An Inconvenient Truth* also received numerous honors, including Academy Awards for best documentary and best original song.

The Rise of "Reality" Television.   Beginning in the 1990s, a new television genre gained popularity and has now become a staple feature in programming line-ups. "Reality TV," at the same time, has rendered the demarcation between fiction and nonfiction more difficult to discern than ever. Put into its historical context, Reality TV is not only of recent vintage. Arguably, it began in the 1950s with the show *Candid Camera*, which revolved around pulling pranks on unknowing, every-day people. In 1973, the 12-part series *An American Family* tracked the daily lives of a seven-person family residing in Santa Barbara, California. It generated debate about some of the defining characteristics of documentary and ethical concerns already associated with the form. During the course of the show, tensions between family members were evident, including the announcement of Pat Loud to her husband that she wanted a divorce. Observers speculated whether the program was portraying the "truth"; that is, would the participants have behaved in the same way if the camera had not been present? Or in their awareness of being filmed, were they somewhat performing for an audience? More generally, to what extent does editing distort the picture? Is the result "real" or fiction? Furthermore, questions emerged as to the responsibility of the documentarian toward his or her subjects.

Is the filmmaker instrumental in evoking conflict among the social actors, and if so, is this appropriate? Have the cast members been violated?

All of these discussions and tendencies were only exacerbated with the introduction of MTV's *Real World* in 1992 and, later, of shows such as *Survivor* and *Big Brother. COPS* also stands as a progenitor of the phenomenon. Since the arrival of these programs, reality shows have dramatically multiplied in the twenty-first century. Yet most of these offerings highlight sensational, interpersonal encounters and clashes—it would be a stretch to say they carry any direct political import.

Still, a reality show that conveys the spirit of social documentary sometimes seeps through the cracks. **Morgan Spurlock**, for example, created a program entitled *30 Days*, in which each episode places a participant (often Spurlock himself but sometimes other everyday people) into an unfamiliar situation for 30 days as a means of challenging thought on an issue.

Recent War Documentaries.   Military conflict has often provided fertile ground for documentary exploration. Though it terminated decades ago, the war in Vietnam, for example, has continued to be probed through nonfiction film. For instance, in an effort to come to terms with her husband's death, Barbara Sonneborn produced a personal account of her visit to Vietnam and conversations with both Vietnamese and other U.S. widows. *Regret to Inform* (1998) won several film festival awards, was nominated for an Academy Award, and aired on PBS's *P.O.V.* in 2000. Another American woman returns to Vietnam in *Daughter from Danang* (2002). Yet her quest is not to reconcile the loss of her husband but to try to locate her birth mother. She is disturbed to learn that her mother had slept with her birth father, a U.S. solider, while struggling as a prostitute during the war. In *The Trials of Henry Kissinger* (2002), based on a book by Christopher Hitchens, filmmakers Eugene Jarecki and Alex Gibney indict the once powerful government official as a war criminal, not only for his role in Vietnam, but also because of his alleged support of genocide in East Timor and his influence on the coup of the democratically elected socialist Salvador Allende in Chile. Errol Morris won the 2003 Oscar for Best Documentary for *Fog of War: Eleven Lessons from the Life of Robert S. McNamara* (2002), a treatment of the man who had served as secretary of defense during much of the Vietnam War.

More recent or current military activities have inspired documentary activity as well. The Iraq war following the September 11 terrorist attacks in particular has been the impetus behind the production of a number of nonfiction films. Shortly after the nation first attacked Iraq in an effort to depose of its dictator, Saddam Hussein, in 2003, various nonfiction filmmakers set their lenses on the conflict.

Yet not only independent filmmakers, but officials in government also took an interest in producing documentaries about the country's involvement. As is commonly the case during times of war (see, for example, **World War Propaganda**), the nation's leaders mounted a comprehensive propaganda campaign, which included films, to stir up citizen support for the cause. For instance, in the lead-up to the incursion into Iraq, the government propaganda film *Operation Enduring Freedom: America Fights Back* (2002) was released. Hosted by then Secretary of Defense Donald Rumsfeld and featuring Lee Greenwood singing "God Bless the USA," the piece attempts to gain public backing for a protracted military response to the brutal 9/11 attacks on the World Trade Center and Pentagon. Two years later, in *Buried in the Sand: The Deception of America* (2004), filmmaker Mark Taylor, although not contracted with the government, symbolically buttressed the mission by taking a pro-war stance and reinforcing the reasons why he thought the nation was justified in driving a maniacal Saddam Hussein from power.

On the other hand, the U.S. invasion and subsequent occupation of Iraq motivated many documentarians to either offer counterinterpretations to the Bush administration's views on the war or examine the conflict in other ways. Barbara Kopple, for example, released the film *Bearing Witness* (2004), which tracks the activities of five female journalists reporting from dangerous regions in Iraq. The same year, Kopple served as executive producer of the documentary *WMD: Weapons of Mass Deception* (2004). Directed by Danny Schechter, the film exposes the dubious government justifications for the war and argues that the media were complicit in the run up to it. From Schechter's vantage point, the media system in the United States functions as a tool of state propaganda because it merely restates the official positions of the country's leaders without seriously challenging them. In *Voices of Iraq* (2004), Eric Manes, Martin Kunert, and Archie Drury took a populist approach to the altercation. The filmmakers distributed over 150 video cameras to everyday Iraqis, requesting that they use them and then pass them on to other people. Edited from over 400 hours of footage, the documentary conveys, as the title suggests, a diversity of voices from the population that has actually had to endure the bloodshed in its midst. Elsewhere, within the context of American involvement in Iraq, U.S. Marine Lieutenant Josh Rushing compares the FOX news network to the Arab news service, al Jazeera, in Jehane Noujaim's nonfiction film *Control Room* (2004), a look inside the operations of this Middle Eastern newcomer to journalism. The documentary garnered considerable attention and, interestingly enough, Rushing eventually joined the al Jazeera news staff.

Meanwhile, **Robert Greenwald**, a longtime maker of fictional entertainment films, turned to the political arena to either direct or assist in producing a series of documentaries that are highly critical of President George W. Bush. He also created two films that look at the circumstances in Iraq. *Uncovered: The War on Iraq* (2004) follows the Bush administration's efforts to build support for the attack on Iraq and spells out the consequences of the invasion as explained by former diplomats, politicians, previous ambassadors, ex-members of the CIA, and a former secretary of the army. Greenwald constructs an impressive case against the wisdom of the Iraq assault through relentless deconstruction of the various claims of the Bush administration in its rationale for the mission. In 2006, Greenwald released another documentary that offers a scathing critique, this time in relationship to companies that benefit from the destruction overseas. *Iraq for Sale: The War Profiteers* argues that private contractors hired by the government have been irresponsible in their workmanship and are actually subjecting American soldiers and Iraqi citizens to greater danger, putting profits above safety.

A number of nonfiction films approach the struggle from the perspective of the U.S. troops in the field. *I Am an American Soldier* (2007), produced and directed by John Laurence, presents a year in the life of the members of the 101st Airborne Division of the U.S. Army. Though it emphasizes the soldiers' bravery, it also sheds light on the hardships they endure. The considerable adversity faced by the troops is the subject of several other notable documentaries. For example, Patricia Foulkrod's *The Ground Truth* focuses on the problems, including post-traumatic stress

President Bush, speaking during a news conference in the Rose Garden of the White House, 2006, was the frequent subject of film documentaries from 2004 on. (AP Photo/Ron Edmonds)

disorder, many soldiers suffer upon their return from the battlefield. In a series of interviews, military personnel and their families and friends discuss their experiences before, during, and after the soldiers' participation in the war. Ellen Spiro and former longtime talk show host Phil Donahue produced and directed *Body of War* (2007), which tracks the life of Thomas Young, a U.S. Iraq war veteran, after he was paralyzed from a bullet to the spine. The documentary traces Young's heroic attempts to cope with his immobility and exposes how he is now questioning the government's decision to launch the conflict with Iraq. The Emmy Award–winning documentary *Baghdad ER* (2006), which was distributed and televised by HBO, also unveils some of the trauma that was unleashed by the military operation. The film centers on a military hospital in Baghdad and features the doctors', nurses', and other health workers' valiant efforts to save the lives or heal the wounds of injured soldiers. Its brutal depictions reveal the gruesome nature of war—an account rarely seen on commercial television or in movie theaters. *Last Letters Home: Voices of American Troops from the Battlefields of Iraq*, by Bill Couturiè, was also presented by HBO. The documentary explores the ultimate cost of war—death itself. Using a similar technique to one he employed in *Dear America: Letters Home from Vietnam* (1988) (see above), in this case, rather than have actors deliver the soldiers' accounts, the director has family members read on camera the final letters they received from their deceased loved ones while they were still alive.

Some Iraq documentaries actually gained attention at the annual Academy Awards shows. *Operation Homecoming: Writing the Wartime Experience* (2007) was nominated for Best Documentary Feature for the 2008 event. Directed by Richard E. Robbins, the film, like some of those just mentioned, examines—through the writings of American soldiers—the troublesome experiences they had in either Iraq or Afghanistan, the site of a related U.S. conflict. The documentary also later aired on PBS. Another film that received a nomination the same year is *No End in Sight* (2008), directed by Charles Ferguson. The documentary illustrates the serious mistakes that were made by the Bush administration in executing the war and proposes, as the title indicates, that given the current circumstances, the battle will go on indefinitely. Yet the winner of the Oscar for Best Documentary Feature at the 2008 ceremony dwells on neither American soldiers nor government officials, and locates its action not in Iraq but in Afghanistan. Alex Gibney's *Taxi to the Dark Side* (2007) follows the case of Dilawar, an Afghan taxi driver who, though seemingly innocent of any wrongdoing, was captured, questioned, and finally beaten to death by American soldiers. The film serves as a vehement indictment of the Bush administration's policies on interrogation and torture.

Another Academy Award nominated film (honored in 2007) that shows the horrors, as well as some of the positive consequences, that have resulted from the invasion of Iraq is *Iraq in Fragments* (2006), directed by James Longley. The movie offers portraits of Iraqi citizens from the perspectives of three major demographic groups in the country—Shiites, Sunnis, and Kurds. *My Country, My Country* (2006), too, was nominated for Best Documentary Feature in 2007. Like *Iraq in Fragments*, it explores the daily lives of everyday Iraqis under occupation.

Prominent documentarian Errol Morris added to the mix of nonfiction films that investigate the situation in Iraq with his production of *Standard Operating Procedure* (2008). Morris challenges viewers to reflect on the Abu Ghraib scandal, which had sprung to worldwide attention when disturbing photos depicting American soldiers torturing Iraqi prisoners were brought to light in 2004. The film probes the topic through interviews with some of the participants and by revealing additional shocking pictures that had barely been seen before in the media.

Yet no documentary that draws from the Iraq war had more impact than Michael Moore's *Fahrenheit 9/11*. Although the film serves as a fervent denunciation of President George W. Bush in general, it nonetheless also includes a critique of the invasion of Iraq to make its case.

Dozens of other documentaries on the Iraq conflict have been produced and distributed since the first bombs were dropped. Yet most of them have not played to large audiences. Still, together they demonstrate the extent to which bloodshed on the battlefield can stir nonfiction filmmakers into generating works that ask viewers to consider difficult truths about the nature of war. While some documentarians—especially those working for commercial television—offer stories of bravery that mostly endorse the cause, probably many more nonfiction film artists hope to incite resistance to the violent confrontations waged by political leaders yet fought by everyday people.

Another documentary that explores the war activities of the United States in general is Eugene Jarecki's *Why We Fight* (2005). The film opens with President Dwight D. Eisenhower's warning that the creation of the "military-industrial complex" could spell trouble for the nation. Jarecki implies that the country has fallen into the trap, and suggests that the military industry not only financially benefits from war but is accordingly compelled to promote it.

The 2004 Presidential Campaign. The renewed interest in documentaries coincided with the heated 2004 presidential campaign between incumbent George W. Bush and Democratic challenger, Senator John Kerry. Nonfiction filmmakers on both the left and the right entered the fray in their both indirect and direct attempts to persuade voters to endorse one candidate or the other. President Bush had proven to be a controversial figure, and many political pundits noted the nation had become polarized between adamant Bush supporters and those who just as vehemently opposed his policies and activities in office.

Michael Paradies Shoob and Joseph Mealey co-directed *Bush's Brain*, an investigation of Karl Rove, a key Bush strategist commonly held to be a central influence on the president's outlook and approach to politics. The film portrays Rove as a conniving, malicious, Machiavellian scoundrel, retracing some of the unsavory tactics, including the dishonest smearing of rivals, he had allegedly used in previous campaigns.

Neither the Bush nor the Kerry side produced officially authorized, full-length, promotional films. Yet others stepped up to fill the gap. In *Brothers in Arms*, Paul Alexander recaps Kerry's service in Vietnam, depicting him as a war hero who had looked out for the lives of the soldiers he commanded. The documentary also shows Kerry's transformation into a critic of the war, including his testimony before Congress of atrocities committed by U.S. soldiers, and the backlash that resulted. George Butler also explores Kerry's Vietnam years and offers a similar sympathetic interpretation of the candidate in *Going Upriver: The Long War of John Kerry*. To counter these positive portrayals, a group calling itself **Swift Boat Veterans for Truth** produced a series of commercials (as well as a complementary book that became a best seller) that presented Kerry as a traitor who had lied about receiving war medals. It appears its work had more impact than Alexander's and Butler's—many political analysts concluded after Bush held onto his office that the Swift Boat campaign had helped swing the election. Yet the group's major claims were eventually uncovered as misleading.

The Swift Boat's perspective was echoed by others. *Stolen Honor: Wounds That Never Heal*, for instance, contends that the soldiers' confessions before Congress of brutal conduct were fraudulent. The Sinclair Broadcasting Group had planned to air the film on all of its over 60 stations. Yet once the documentary sparked controversy, Sinclair pulled back and broadcast only an edited version on fewer stations.

Some pro-Bush documentarians took a different course of action. Created to appeal to evangelical Christians, *George W. Bush: Faith in the White House* pictures the president as a devoutly religious man and, consequently, more suitable for office than a supposed unbeliever. The film was available to churches and other interested individuals and groups on DVD.

The documentarian Errol Morris did not produce any full-length films for the campaign, but he nonetheless contributed to the battle by directing a series of political commercials portraying "Republican switchers," that is, people who had voted for George W. Bush in 2000 but were now prepared to cast their ballots for John Kerry. Morris received financial backing from the liberal political interest group **MoveOn.org**. The organization posted over 15 of Morris's spots on its Web site as well as distributed several of them to TV stations in several swing states.

Michael Moore's *Fahrenheit 9/11*, however, gained more attention than any other partisan documentary during the 2004 campaign season. Accordingly, it evoked considerable retorts through pundit appearances on newscasts, Web sites, books, and documentaries offering brutal rebuttals.

THE FUTURE

Any analysis of future events inevitably entails speculation—it is no different with pondering the fate of documentaries. Yet some trends seem clear. The boundaries between fiction and nonfiction will likely continue to blur. When documentaries are presented in the form of narratives—or stories—which is becoming increasingly common, the line between them and fiction movies tends to become less distinct. Reality TV represents a recent dramatic case in point. Over the years, documentarians have incorporated the techniques of fiction filmmakers and vice versa. Yet the categorical designation "documentary" is so well established and resonant that it is doubtful it will be abandoned altogether. Concurrently, the borders involving the creation of nonfiction films are converging as well. Often, financing and producing documentaries is now an international endeavor, as the world, at least in some aspects, takes on characteristics of what the late media theorist Marshall McLuhan called the "Global Village." A third pattern appears to be the collapsing line between the producer and the consumer of documentaries. As media technologies become ever more affordable and accessible, an unprecedented number of people have the opportunity to present their point of view through the nonfiction moving image. Through the Internet and its populist Web sites such as **YouTube,** anyone able to log on to a computer has the potential to post a piece online and, if enough viewers discover it and tell others, attract a sizable audience. Documentary production, then, like other forms of media, has become more democratized, offering everyday citizens a means of empowerment.

The Documentary and Activism

As more people—both professionals and amateurs (another pair of distinctions that is growing hazier)—enter the ranks of the documentarian, the capacity to use diverse forms of nonfiction material in hope of activating social change is greater than ever. Some recent films point toward the possibilities. In *The Yes Men* (2004), Chris Smith, Sarah Price, and Dan Ollman track the activities of "Andy and Mike," the self-labeled "yes men," who provide a satirical critique of global capitalism by staging hoaxes at prominent affairs and conferences, posing as, for instance, World Trade Organization officials. Globalization is also a topic of concern of the Guerrilla News Network, an activist group that, with the help of everyday individuals, attempts to make and distribute nonfiction pieces to inform audiences, especially young people, on a range of issues and critical developments and stir political involvement. Another grassroots organization, Big Noise, similarly strives to persuade primarily young audiences about the excesses of capitalist exploitation. When the World Trade Organization met in Seattle, Washington, in 1999 amidst unexpectedly large protests, Big Noise, as well as the Seattle Independent Media Center and others, documented the uprising, offering an alternative perspective to the one transmitted by traditional news channels.

As documentaries and other types of persuasive media continue to proliferate and advance divergent points of view from the full political spectrum, audiences will be increasingly challenged to resolve conflicting messages in forming interpretations of important issues and societal events.

FURTHER READING

Barnouw, Erik. *Documentary: A History of the Non-Fiction Film*. 2nd rev. ed. New York: Oxford University Press, 1993.

Barsam, Richard Meran. *Nonfiction Film: A Critical History*. Bloomington: Indiana University Press, 1992.

Bullert, B. J. *Public Television: Politics and the Battle Over Documentary Film*. New Brunswick, NJ: Rutgers University Press, 1997.

Curtin, Michael. *Redeeming the Wasteland: Television Documentary and Cold War Politics*. New Brunswick, NJ: Rutgers University Press, 1995.

Devine, Jeremy. *Vietnam at 24 Frames Per Second*. Austin: University of Texas Press, 1995.

Ellis, Jack C., and Betsy A. McLane. *A New History of Documentary Film*. New York: Continuum, 2005.

Grierson, John. *Grierson on Documentary*, ed. Forsyth Hardy. London: Faber and Faber, 1966.

McEnteer, James. *Shooting the Truth: The Rise of American Political Documentaries*. Westport, CT: Praeger, 2006.

Nichols, Bill. *Introduction to Documentary*. Bloomington: Indiana University Press, 2001.

Renov, Michael. "Introduction: The Truth about Non-Fiction." *Theorizing Documentary*, ed. Michael Renov. New York: Routledge, 1993.

Zimmermann, Patricia Rodden. *States of Emergency: Documentaries, Wars, and Democracies*. Minneapolis: University of Minnesota Press, 2000.

Chapter 3

Politics and Radio

Until recently, radio has not received the academic attention it deserves. Instead, scholars have immersed themselves in television, the nation's most dominant and sophisticated form of mass media throughout the latter half of the twentieth century. Yet understanding the impact of radio is crucial to comprehending the role of mass media in U.S. society because it represents the country's first broadcast medium and greatly established the basic political economic structure that television would later adopt. A close examination of the medium reveals that political implications enter into the very origins of radio because of the controversy associated with who actually "invented" it. Similar to other new developments, radio did not emerge through the efforts of one person but resulted from the work of many innovators, including Nikola Tesla, Alexander Popov, and Jagdish Bose. Still, the person most often cited as the "founder" of radio is Guglielmo Marconi, who secured the initial patent for the technology, awarded by England in 1896, and later received numerous U.S. patents. Yet in 1943 the U.S. Supreme Court essentially undermined the case for Marconi as the inventor of radio and attributed its creation to Tesla. What distinguishes Marconi from the other developers, however, is that, financially backed by influential figures in the United States, he was the first person to significantly commercialize a practical system. Clearly, then, he was interested in profiting from the new form of communication. But Marconi—or any of the other inventors—could have never envisioned the path that radio would eventually take.

Indeed, in a sense, for Marconi, radio was simply an extension of the telegraph, an improved method for instant point-to-point communication across distances. Unlike its predecessor, the "wireless" required no cables and would ultimately replace the reliance on Morse Code with the transmission of the human voice. After Marconi helped establish the British Marconi Company at the turn of the century, the radio was primarily used to link communication between stations on land and ships at sea. Yet, for years, radio remained a largely unregulated industry, which triggered a chaotic environment in the ether and finally led to the Radio Act of

1912 as a way to minimize the confusion. Thus began a long battle between power-ful institutions and common citizens over who owns the airwaves and should have control over them.

THE FUNCTION OF RADIO: SERVING COMMERCIALISM OR DEMOCRACY?

From Ham Operators to Commercial Radio

In the early days of radio, the greatest number of operators consisted not of naval or commercial personnel, but of amateurs who would come to be known as "hams." Immeasurable hobbyists, mostly male, took pleasure in building homemade sets, often in sheds and attics, with whatever materials were available. Given the limited radio frequency spectrum, though, as more and more enthusiasts entered the arena, the airwaves became congested and interference among competing users threatened to turn radio into an unruly realm. To bring the situation under control, the U.S. Congress stepped in and passed the Radio Act of 1912, which stipulated that the airwaves were public property yet could be temporarily licensed to individual or corporate applicants by the Department of Commerce and Labor. In addition, while government and commercial operators were assigned large portions of the spec-trum, amateurs were granted only undesirable short wavelengths of 200 meters and less and limited to just one kilowatt of power.

Yet once the United States changed its stance from neutrality to dynamic partici-pation in World War I, the government banned amateur activity altogether and closed down ham stations to prevent any interference with naval transmissions. But despite this brief respite during the country's engagement in the Great War, amateur operators proliferated in the early 1920s, far outnumbering their corporate and government counterparts.

So for more than 20 years after its invention, radio served primarily as a point-to-point means of communication. Broadcasting in the United States did not actually begin in earnest until 1920, when KDKA in Pittsburgh transmitted updates of the Harding-Cox presidential election results, foreshadowing a link between politics and popular culture right from the start. Although other stations have staked their claim to being the first professional radio broadcaster, KDKA is generally credited with the achievement. Yet in its infancy, broadcasting was not primarily commer-cially sponsored. Much of the motivation behind broadcasting to a mass audience was to simply expand radio sales by offering content that people would want to tune in to, thereby creating a profitable consumer market. Indeed, for years, the idea of transmitting selling messages into the homes of everyday citizens was a controversial issue, which some critics viewed as especially crass and as a practice that listeners would thoroughly reject.

The breakthrough for commercial broadcasting came in 1922, when AT&T, which, along with RCA (a company that had been formed, in part, by buying out American Marconi's stations and patents) and other corporations, represented one of radio's major corporate participants, set up a small studio and extended the opportunity for any interested party to broadcast self-selected material for a fee. Following the pattern it had established with the pay telephone, AT&T thus put in motion a form of transmission that was dubbed "toll broadcasting." Once compa-nies discovered that people in their homes not only tolerated sales pitches but sometimes even responded to them and became customers, the commercial model of radio was quickly established, a paradigm that has been perpetuated ever since.

Eventually radio shows—such as dramas, comedies, "soap operas," and variety formats—flourished. Yet unlike the current practice typically followed by both radio and television, wherein brief commercials are inserted into the programming established by the networks or stations, advertisers generally purchased full blocks of time and sponsored entire shows. Moreover, they were actually responsible for producing them. Thus a company was empowered not only to deliver direct sales messages at the beginning of a program or in-between segments but also to include its brand in the very name of the show (for example, the *Eveready Hour*) and even create content conducive to promoting its products, sometimes prefiguring the convention today known as product placement.

Commercial Radio and the Threat to Democracy

As radio evolved into a medium mainly financially supported by selling audiences to advertisers, intellectuals, critics, and business practitioners debated the merits of such a system and its possible impact on democracy itself. Some critics mounted a vigorous critique, one that continues to circulate today and challenges the distribution of power within the modern media and the ideology they allegedly disseminate. Early commentators, such as the journalist and poet James Rorty, who, early in his career, had held positions in advertising, contended that the centralization of radio stations into the hands of very few companies and the role of advertising enabled corporations to exercise too much control over the population through their mostly covert diffusion of programming that bolstered the standing of big business, subverting democratic ideals along the way. In essence, these critics, usually identified with the political left, were questioning the very nature of America's capitalist economy. Once the roaring 1920s were supplanted by the Great Depression, their account gained even greater energy. Yet rather than confront an economic apparatus that yielded hardship for many, radio encouraged its audience to maintain its confidence in the status quo. Rorty and his cohorts argued that business was defining the public interest and indirectly—or sometimes even directly—censoring what citizens could hear. Promoting their own interests, corporations, these opponents believed, reinforced a media structure that narrowed the range of voices allowed on the air, especially those radical ones that were numerous during the country's economic plunge. In this sense, commercial radio spread a type of propaganda. The corporate monopoly of radio signified the capacity to unduly shape the audience's ethical standards and worldviews. Content was limited to what was acceptable to advertisers and their need to sell goods and services within a suitable symbolic climate. Feeling threatened by a type of commercial fascism, critics worried that radio would only intensify the undemocratic impulses capitalism had already unleashed on the nation for decades, diminishing the vigorous flow of free speech and thought. They were not against the medium of radio per se. Instead, for them, radio had the potential to educate and enlighten if placed in the right hands, yet it had been reduced to a sales device for big business. Moreover, because access to radio required large financial resources, the "voice of the people" could not compete.

The commercial critique of radio was sounded by many critics and was typified by a consumer movement in the 1930s that preceded the one that would become well known in the 1960s. The activists involved in this pressure group wished to transform the nature of radio. By 1935, however, their strivings had largely failed and commercialism in radio had mostly won the day.

Commercial Radio as a Vehicle for Democracy

On the other side of the debate were those who asserted that commercially funded radio *was* democratic. Unlike a media system owned by the state and in the service of government, American radio, thanks to private control, let the people decide for themselves what they wanted to hear by listening to the shows they liked best. Only a *laissez-faire*, free-market economy could provide common citizens with their right to receive the programming they demanded. Radio producers merely acted on behalf of the people who "voted" with their tuning dials. Consequently, business did not mold public opinion; rather, quite the opposite was in effect: popular opinion determined which shows would survive and which ones would fail. The privatization of radio, accordingly, guaranteed protection against state tyranny and ensured a democratic approach to the airwaves. The disputation that these two sides generated would not go away. In truth, it would carry on through the advent and maturation of television and proceed until the present day.

Commercial Radio Reigns Supreme

But the perspectives represented by the two camps have not only manifested themselves through verbal debate. For in one way, the history of radio can be seen as a never-ending contestation between top-down, corporate interests and bottom-up, individualistic rebels, between the forces of conformity and the renegades who desired to flout convention. During the 1920s, as more and more stations were licensed, just as it had before the Radio Act of 1912, the ether became mired due to constant interference. In response, Congress passed the Radio Act of 1927, which gave birth to the Federal Radio Commission (FRC), the forebear to the Federal Communications Commission (FCC), which came into being in 1934. The year after the Act was established, the FRC developed a spectrum reallocation plan that privileged "general public service" stations over ones with narrower interests. The ruling, in practice, translated into a regulatory framework that was more sympathetic to networks than smaller stations, including community, educational, and nonprofit outlets. Starting in the late 1920s, then, the networks dominated the airwaves. NBC, CBS, and later, ABC reigned into the 1950s, until television exploded onto the cultural landscape. Moreover, local programming was generally superseded by network feeds, especially during prime time hours. Still, though the commercial environment of radio has generally biased the needs of business, countercurrents have always found ways of slipping through the cracks. Even today, for instance, independent ham operators (those without licenses are now commonly referred to as "pirate" broadcasters—see "Pirate Radio" below) continue to express themselves through the airwaves (although the Internet has quickly established an alternate mode for such individualistic transmission).

The 1950s and Musical Rebellion

In the 1950s, many observers felt that the birth of television would sound the death knell of radio. Instead, radio adapted to the new medium and changed its emphasis. Far less attention was devoted to dramas, comedies, and variety shows, all of which translated well on television and took up residence there. Music, which had always filled a considerable portion of the radio schedule, now became the mainstay. At the same time, in adjusting to television's challenge, radio began to segment its markets, yielding more individualistic, fragmented patterns of listenership. In essence, radio traveled on the path toward decentralization. Listening in the 1950s was, in general, less communal and more personal than it had been throughout the 1930s and 1940s. The networks, in turn, channeled the bulk of their energy toward television, which, from its infancy, largely followed the model that radio had already established. National advertisers funneled most of their dollars to television as well. In this sense, radio shifted from what could be called a network era to a format era; accordingly, local rather than national advertising provided much of the funding.

Into this atmosphere emerged disk jockeys (DJs) who especially appealed to young people by promoting a unique generational identity and thereby offering them the opportunity to rebel against their elders, which incited a kind of moral panic. Their prominence had been foreshadowed by DJs who had focused on airing recorded music on some of the relatively small number of independent stations that were still in existence even after radio became largely commercial. In the 1950s, orchestra and other traditional forms of music were feeling the threat of popular music, particularly rock and roll. Teenagers embraced the new sounds, while their parents railed against them and worried that popular music was somehow leading their kids astray. By the end of the decade, wishing to acquire the music they heard on the radio, teenagers were purchasing more records than their parents. Although many advertisers were at first loathe to sponsor "pop" music because they did not want to associate their goods with its supposed decadent values, they had difficulty resisting for long because they recognized its profitability. Yet while station managers endeavored to enforce the standardized playlists of the "Top 40," a format that advertisers favored because it smoothed the edges of what they perceived as somewhat dangerous fare, numerous DJs fought back and won the battle to choose their own records for air. Simultaneously appropriating and adding to their young audience's language, some of these DJs, including such notables as Wolfman Jack, Dewey Phillips, and Alan Freed, achieved huge popularity. As rock and roll gained a greater hold on the airwaves, adults feared that it was somehow contributing to juvenile delinquency and antisocial behavior. Conversely, the fresh songs peppering the radio dial resonated with young people hoping to both stand out and fit in with their peers. In 1959, a trauma struck the radio industry, one that dramatically reduced rock and roll DJs' autonomy and even ruined many of their careers. Known as the *payola scandal*, the practice of record companies supplying incentives to DJs in return for playing certain releases came to public attention, producing a general outcry and a congressional probe. Various scholars contend, however, that the attack on payola was nothing more than a war on rock and roll itself. After all, quid pro quo arrangements were hardly unique to the music industry. To a significant degree, some researchers argue, the backlash against rock and roll conveyed substantial racial overtones. (See "The Threat of Rock and Roll" below.) Moreover, the conflict had serious political implications because the music provided the potential for its audience to oppose the current state of race relations. Ultimately, commercial forces regrouped and, through the help of marketing research, the Top 40 format became a fixture, which minimized DJ autonomy, reduced programming uncertainty, and, once more, promoted standardization. Radio was again mostly under corporate control.

Revolting Against the Status Quo in the 1970s

As much impact as the payola scandal had on the radio industry, however, it by no means brought cultural politics or resistance to commercial dominance in the ether to an end. In the late 1960s and early 1970s, a new brand of renegade surfaced. Renouncing the AM band for the relatively undiscovered terrain of the FM spectrum, countercultural entrepreneurs and DJs produced highly original programming far removed from the repetitive style of Top 40 radio.

The FM spectrum was nothing new. Howard Armstrong was the key figure behind its development and introduction in the late 1920s and early 1930s. Yet its potential lay dormant for decades. Finally, though, in the early 1960s, the FCC recognized that the AM band was, once more, becoming too crowded. Consequently, the regulatory agency promoted the use of the FM spectrum. Eventually, a 1967 ruling opened the door for FM radio to acquire greater prominence.

FM's friendlier regulatory environment coincided with the rise of the youth counterculture movement of the 1960s. In reaction to AM radio's homogeneity and incessant, crass commercialism, many young people turned to FM broadcasts for programming that revolted against the status quo. And for a brief window of time, they were not disappointed. On the one hand, there arose numerous community radio stations (see **Pacifica and Community Radio**), which were commercial-free and relied on listeners for financial support. These broadcasters targeted an audience that cut across age categories. But more importantly for the younger crowd, "**free form**" radio reawakened the rebellious attitude that had held sway in the 1950s. Its audience consisted of many people aligned with the counterculture that grew out of the social upheaval of the 1960s. Free form DJs played an eccentric array of music, as well as aired conversations that challenged the political status quo, sometimes inviting voices that were rarely heard in media. But as FM gained greater popularity, station executives again stepped in to promote a rock format that appealed to young audiences, without the left-wing political leanings that might alienate advertisers.

Pirate Radio

Throughout the decades, though, ham operators continued to broadcast, albeit to far smaller and specialized audiences. Many of them, in an expression of rebellion, deliberately defied the law by transmitting their programming without licenses, a form of broadcasting that has come to be known as pirate radio (sometimes referred to by its proponents as "micro-radio"). An offshoot of this practice actually started soon after radio began to be regulated by government agencies in 1912. To get around legal requirements, some independent operators would set up their stations south of the U.S. border yet aim their material to the states above. Although the U.S. government did not approve of these stations and sometimes worked to prohibit them, it did not seriously hinder their operation until well into the 1980s. Yet like the amateur hobbyists who experimented in the airwaves at the very dawn of radio, while far fewer in number, ham operators challenged authority from rooftops, garages, or surreptitious locations by tapping into frequencies within the United States. Some of these renegades carried on the hobbyist tradition, while others aimed to further larger goals and establish community support and participation. For example, beginning in 1969, Allan Weiner and several of his friends launched a handful of stations throughout the New York City area and maintained their broadcasts until federal government agencies finally discovered them and closed them down two years later. Weiner and one of his colleagues were arrested and sentenced to one year's probation. Hundreds of other pirate stations, some barely noticed and others that actually attracted loyal audiences, came and went throughout the years. Then, in the mid-1980s, probably at least partially in reaction to community radio's dwindling impact (see **Pacifica and Community Radio**), commercial radio's increasing corporate consolidation, and the now prohibitive costs of starting up an independent, licensed station, an especially low-powered type of local broadcasting, a spin-off of its predecessors, made its entrance. Known as microbroadcasting (or low-power FM radio), it would lead to a controversy that involved the commercial radio industry, citizen groups, and government, over the very nature of the airwaves and who should have access.

Two of the early leading proponents of microbroadcasting were Walter Dunn and DeWayne Readus (who later named himself M'banna Kantako). Both black men, they recognized its potential to reach underserved audiences of color (for a full discussion of the tendency to marginalize African Americans in particular, see "African Americans and Radio" below). Kantako used his outlet, launched in 1987, to expose what he perceived as abusive police practices within his local community. Despite efforts by the government to silence him, Kantako has continued to operate, in one way or another, into the twenty-first century. Moreover, largely due to Kantako's and other similar-minded people's influence, by the late 1990s, hundreds of additional microfacilities had sprouted up all over the country, sometimes moving from place to place to avoid detection by the FCC. One station in particular that gained considerable attention was Free Radio Berkeley, the creation of Stephen Dunifer, another person who became an important advocate of low-power FM.

Thus the battle began between opponents, usually from the realm of business, who insisted that micro-radio posed a threat to established radio because it would create interference, and proponents who countered that with improved technologies that had greatly enhanced a more efficient use of the spectrum (as evidenced by the intense expansion of cell phone usage, for instance), micro-radio's low-powered signals could easily coexist with its commercial neighbors. Some legally run low-power FM stations had actually existed from 1948, when an FCC ruling helped give rise to them, until the late 1970s, after the FCC, notably influenced by public radio broadcasters, issued another order that essentially banned them. Over 20 years later, the push was on to resurrect low-power FM. Advocates of micro-radio believe that it better serves the interests of local communities and groups, including ethnic and racial minorities and working-class populations such as farmers, that are often marginalized by its corporate-controlled counterparts (for related discussion, see "Race, Class, and Gender in Radio" below). Many of the pirate, microstations that proliferated during the 1980s and 1990s had a decidedly, often radical, political bent, with identifying labels such as Black Liberation Radio and Mutiny Radio. Proponents of micro-radio argue that they are more "public" than the public radio stations (especially **National Public Radio** [NPR]) that actually go by that name because low-power FM outlets, unlike current public radio, encourage everyday people to fully participate in generating the content of the programming.

After a prolonged series of conflicts both within the micro-radio movement and between it and outside adversaries, during which time many stations were forced to either temporarily or permanently close shop, the situation finally came to a head. Microbroadcasters ultimately lobbied representatives in Washington to pass legislation that legalized low-power, independent stations. Their activism was vehemently opposed by the National Association of Broadcasters (NAB). The FCC actually gave serious consideration to granting microbroadcasters the right to operate. It was probably motivated, in part, by the wish to bring illegal pirate radio under control. In 1999, it issued a ruling that showed a considerable degree of sympathy toward the micro-radio community's cause. But the commercial radio industry, led by the NAB, quickly responded and was able to hold up implementation of the new proposal. Yet in 2000, the FCC announced a plan that was even more favorable to noncommercial microbroadcasters. The NAB followed with a lawsuit. Throughout the process, NPR also fought to prevent the licensing of low-power FM stations. In the end, Congress stepped in and approved legislation that mostly catered to the interests of the NAB. The FCC, however, still approved licenses for a limited number of stations, but under the significantly restrictive guidelines that had been imposed by Congress. Most of the stations could start up only in sparsely populated territories, away from many of the urban areas that, micro-radio supporters contend, also need them. About half of the originally granted licenses went to religious groups. Although micro-radio was not entirely killed, it was dealt a serious blow, while commercial owners secured a nearly complete victory.

The Future of Radio and Its Relationship to Democracy

Since the dust dissipated in the clash between microbroadcasters and commercial stations (although, even now, it has not totally settled), the established radio industry has witnessed ever increasing consolidation. But instead of operating within the network dominance of yesteryear, today's radio is profoundly managed by chain ownership. Not long after the Telecommunications Act of 1996 allowed companies to own as many as eight stations in some markets and an unlimited number of them nationwide, only three companies dominated much of the radio landscape. Critics have charged that the concentration of radio has produced increasing homogeneity and nearly eliminated local control. Through the use of ever-refined marketing techniques and new technologies, large radio conglomerates are able to centralize their operations and offer standardized fare for their dozens of stations without the need for local DJs. The radio industry answers that it has simply perfected the system of giving listeners, fragmented into various audiences, exactly what they want.

Although it appears that the forces of commercialism now reign, the political tension between them and those who resist them is likely to continue. And as other vehicles enter the mix, scholars can only speculate as to how the nature of audio transmission will develop. Recently, satellite radio leapt into the arena and became a threat to the broadcasting industry. Rather than financing its services by selling audiences to advertisers, this direct form of radio drew on the model of raising revenue through listener subscriptions. But in just a few years since its full 2001 launch, more and more advertising is creeping into its programming. Meanwhile, the Internet represents yet another stiff challenge. Although the Internet offers the potential for every participant to serve as both a producer and a consumer of media, including exclusively aural content, conflicting powers and institutions are busy working to advance their own interests and help shape the Internet's structure. What form the Internet eventually takes, scholars reason, will have large implications for democracy. If the Internet retains open access and treats all content providers equally, then, it appears, it will foster a democratic spirit. But if advertisers and established media companies can push for a system that best meets their needs, then the Internet, it seems, will simply replicate the mostly top-down structure that most forms of media in the United States have exhibited since their origins.

RACE, CLASS, AND GENDER IN RADIO

The political friction between commercial and noncorporate influences has not been radio's only notable instance of power struggle during its over 100 year history. Another major issue involves decades of the medium's expression of gender, racial, and class biases. In other words, radio privileged certain groups, while marginalizing others. Because, for a sizable window of time before the advent of television, radio was the nation's most prominent medium for cultural dissemination, its impact on individual and group identity indirectly yielded political consequences. For example, broadcasting only rarely offered specialized programming to recent immigrants in their own languages. On the other hand, they were not entirely dismissed. Radio content usually conveyed assimilationist values to immigrants, functioning to affirm Anglo-American ideas and principles. Radio's approach to the working-class population had political implications as well. While everyday workers were welcomed as consumers, any labor activists within their midst were almost completely disregarded. Unlike programming that supported a friendly business climate, voices in the workforce did not play well with advertisers. Though corporate spokespersons frequently received airtime, union leaders, for instance, were perceived as too "controversial."

African Americans and Radio

An understanding of the nation's racial politics can be more fully grasped through an examination of the history of the relationship between African Americans and radio. From the birth of radio broadcasting in the 1920s until the Civil Rights Movement of the 1950s and 1960s, African Americans were significantly barred from and often belittled through radio. During the 1920s through the 1940s, blacks represented a relatively small percentage of the population in the northern states, where most of radio's institutions of power resided. Moreover, nationwide, not only were blacks disproportionately poor and isolated, but their rates of radio ownership were low as well. Consequently, advertisers, radio's primary financial supporters, did not view them as important consumers and felt no need to appeal to their interests. At the same time, given the degree of racism that existed in the United States, especially in the South, the industry feared alienating its core white audience by featuring programming that might appeal to African Americans. Although some radio targeted toward blacks did slip through the cracks, for the most part they were marginalized in a number of ways. For instance, very few radio stations were owned by African Americans in the 1920s or 1930s. In fact, in 1939, none of the country's 778 radio stations were owned and operated by black Americans. Yet blacks did find work as performers. Many of the African Americans who played in the bands and orchestras whose music was broadcast actually participated anonymously. Moreover, when they did receive recognition, it was often in vehicles labeled as "coon acts." Black roles in radio comedies and dramas were often filled by white actors. The most notorious example of this incongruity was heard on *Amos and Andy*, which, for years, was by far the most popular show on radio. On other programs, African American characters usually reflected the prevalent stereotypes of the day.

Mammies, butlers, petty thieves, and various buffoons composed much of the standard list of black representations. Words that were offensive to African American ears, such as "nigger" and "darkie," often crept into broadcasts as well.

Of course, as is generally true with all forms of media, some chinks in the armor did appear, permitting voices of black resistance to sometimes prick the consciences of those who were uneasy with the prevailing racist social structures. For instance, in the 1930s and 1940s, before McCarthyism would sweep aside most liberal political critique, radio writers associated with the Cultural Front (a group interested in inserting a politically radical perspective into the radio environment) conveyed left-wing perspectives that included the portrayal of African Americans and the children of immigrants as quintessential U.S. citizens, and espoused racial justice. In addition, prior to what would become another surge of consumer culture after World War II, to fulfill one of its mandates before the FCC, networks would often produce shows with public interest themes, although they would often broadcast them during the periods in their schedules that received low ratings, a practice that led to these offerings being known as "sustaining programs." One 1939 drama, *The Pursuit of Happiness*, sometimes put multiethnic exchange and interracial relationships in the workplace in a positive light. Another, *New World A-Coming*, produced in the mid-1940s, depicted African American experiences and politics in Harlem, and protested race-based discrimination. ***America's Town Meeting of the Air***, which was designed to bring the spirit of the traditional town-hall political meeting to radio, sometimes directly addressed racial themes for a general audience.

With an emphasis on public affairs, sustaining programs that focused on race actually served a government function during World War II. Political officials wished to promote national unity in support of the conflict. In this environment, it would not be efficacious to symbolically exclude the people of color who comprised a small yet significant portion of the population and supplied a disproportionate number of troops. Still, the programs that celebrated its black citizens generally emphasized their "positive achievements" and nondivisive black heroes such as George Washington Carver. On the other hand, they seldom covered contentious matters on the order of Jim Crow or segregation in the military. *America's Town Meeting of the Air*, though, stood out in this respect. Once African American soldiers returned from the war only to face the same segregation that they had experienced before the conflict, the push for equal status would only intensify.

The Threat of Jazz.   Yet the overall historical hesitancy to allow black Americans entrance into mainstream radio transmission was exemplified through the rise of popular music in the twentieth century and how some forms were more readily embraced by industry executives than others. When jazz music, for instance, gained popularity in the 1920s, it sparked considerable debate. Presaging similar arguments about certain types of music today, opponents contended that jazz represented a kind of "low" culture that would only debase traditional values. Yet some scholars maintain that resistance to jazz, which was mostly the product of African American artists, revealed racial undertones. Many people feared a certain cultural miscegenation, perceiving that Anglo conventions could be infiltrated and degraded by black expression. Critics of jazz felt the music contained lewd lyrics and promoted dancing that smacked of indecency. They associated it with "the jungle" and "savage" impulses. That more and more white audiences were finding enjoyment through the music only heightened their antagonism. Largely because of the controversy surrounding jazz, many talented black singers and musicians were initially kept off of the airwaves, and scores of songs were blacklisted (this word itself, some would say, carries racial implications). Eventually, though, jazz secured a degree of legitimacy when white artists began to incorporate its rhythms into their compositions, thus transforming what some referred to as "race music" into a more acceptable offshoot often labeled as "sweet jazz." As jazz continued to build a following, then, radio could no longer deny the potential its popularity signified and more African Americans were invited to the microphone. By the late 1920s, artists such as Duke Ellington and Cab Calloway were building their legacies with the help of radio. The floodgates were not opened, however. Radio networks refused to hire black studio musicians until the late 1930s, and they continued to monitor and censor black jazz music, influencing blacks, at the risk of diminishing a sense of authenticity, to often accommodate network gatekeepers by softening any edges that could be interpreted as rough. The net result, according to some researchers, is that black jazz music was significantly restrained by radio.

The Threat of Rock and Roll.   Similar tendencies were on display during the dawn and growth of rock and roll in the 1940s and 1950s. Once again, black artists were the chief creators and innovators of the new genre. The teen audience was becoming an important target segment, and was increasingly turning to rock and roll as a badge of identity and means of rebellion. Recognizing the trend, in an atmosphere that still mostly excluded black announcers, a number of white DJs attempted to sound "black." The backlash against rock and roll, many academics assert, was, at least in part, yet another reaction to the threat of cultural miscegenation. The music indirectly challenged the unofficial segregation in the North and its Jim Crow counterpart in the South. While television, at first, mainly perpetuated the proclivity to exclude and trivialize African Americans, the multiplying number of small, independent radio stations offered a parcel of space for black culture to tenuously occupy, especially since television was not serving the needs of people of color. Through market segmentation, not only did some black performers have the opportunity to connect with primarily white audiences but more radio stations were dedicated to African American listeners as well. By 1955, for example, more than 600 stations were programming either part or all of their schedules for black audiences, although few were actually owned by nonwhites. WDIA in Memphis, Tennessee, which went on the air in 1947, was the first station devoted exclusively to black programming. Concurrently, curious white listeners were turning their dials and discovering more black music and points of view. At least one scholar has even argued that the cultural hybridity that radio inadvertently fostered provided some small measure of symbolic inspiration for the incipient Civil Rights Movement. Although advertisers were originally tentative about supporting rock and roll (sometimes seen as another form of "race music"), just as they did with jazz, they eventually recognized a threshold of popularity had been reached and could no longer ignore coming on board. Once advertisers funneled their dollars toward broadcasters of rock and roll, however, the forces of commercialism inevitably worked to mutate the music into a form that was safer and more palatable to radio executives as well as to the older generation that feared its influence. In this sense, critics argue, "Top 40" represents one of the industry's efforts to commercialize and pacify the music, and rein in the DJs' autonomy. Following this line of thinking, 1960s Motown could also be viewed as a less threatening version of black music. Along the way, reproducing the acts of incorporation by the white jazz musicians of the past, white artists such as Elvis Presley and Jerry Lee Lewis integrated the rock and roll style into their performances, which likely helped trigger the eventual toleration of the music by a larger portion of the population. Entering the 1960s, radio had become the most integrated mass medium in the nation.

Recently, many writings have pointed out that the pattern has been repeated with rap music and radio's initial reluctance to give it airtime. A number of critics have—sometimes derisively, sometimes as a mere observation—called attention to the penchant for many young white people to present themselves as "wiggers," i.e., white "niggers," a word that has been repositioned by the hip-hop community to denote not a racist designation but a term of endearment. But the history of radio demonstrates that the appropriation of black culture into white identity is nothing new. In the 1920s, jazz music enabled white listeners, like the minstrel show participants before them, to symbolically assume "blackface" and thus experiment with an emotional release that existed outside the constraints of traditional white codes. Rock and roll afforded the same possibilities. Many a white teenage fan of black performers eagerly poached "black" slang and played out a renegade role in opposition to the perceived social conformity of the 1950s, an inclination captured by Norman Mailer in his 1957 piece "The White Negro." A significant agent of cross-cultural flow, radio allowed black performers to enter white homes even as it enabled white fans to try out black jargon and customs as a way of implementing what they viewed as freer expression. Some scholars argue that the medium thus functioned to promote racial integration. Others counter that by granting esteem to the African American as an entertainer, one of the few roles that, throughout U.S. history, has given blacks an opening to economic success, radio unwittingly perpetuated stereotypes and unknowingly advanced a subtle form of the minstrel show tradition. In recent years, blacks have achieved standing as an important market segment, albeit within the context of commercialized radio. Yet the number of stations owned or run by black Americans remains small. At the same time, however, radio renegades such as M'banna Kantako and his Black Liberation Radio have (often illegally) provided a space of resistance for black voices that do not cohere to the standards of discourse advertisers find acceptable.

Women and Radio

Women, too, although not as severely as African Americans, have been marginalized in comparison to (white) men through radio for much of its history. Early ham operators were almost exclusively male. Furthermore, the ideology that relegated women to subordinate status in the culture at large was, unsurprisingly, rarely challenged by radio broadcasts.

It was not as though women were not valued. But their worth was assessed within the context of their power as consumers. During radio's first decades, the dominant cultural ethos strongly suggested that women should be consigned to the home. Accordingly, married women, far more than their husbands, were recognized as the primary purchasers of domestic goods. As the advertising model of radio took hold, broadcasters wished to transfer the instrument from the garages of amateurs to the living rooms of families. Moreover, the industry marketed radio as a means of reducing the drudgery of women's day-to-day chores, providing them with a comforting companion. Daytime radio, then, especially catered to women, although in ways that did not empower them as much as reinforce their stereotypical roles as mothers and wives. Shows often focused on issues such as home decoration, making clothes, and raising children. Among these programs appeared the quintessential domestic genre aimed at women—the radio "soap opera." Its very name indicates the fusion of drama and commercial sponsorship (soap companies often funded the shows and even frequently participated in their production). Soap operas, which proliferated during the 1930s and 1940s, generally buttressed traditionally feminine and domestic values and helped to make certain brands household names.

Nor did women make up much of the ranks within the radio industry itself. They commonly worked as receptionists and secretaries, but rarely as executives. On the other hand, dramas and comedies required female actors if programming were not to reflect an all-male world. Yet women seldom gained positions as announcers, a bias that, while not as pronounced, continues to this very day. The decision makers in radio held the notion (also supported by some audience surveys of the time) that a woman's voice did not sound as authoritative as a man's. Consequently, women were also greatly underrepresented as anchors and reporters, even as news eventually took up an increasing part of the radio schedule.

Today, in spite of the increasing fragmentation of the audience, there is very little in the way of "women's programming" on radio in the order of that which is found on television cable stations such as Lifetime, We, and Oxygen. Although more female voices and performers are on the air than in previous decades, male performers still represent far more than their share of roles based on the composition of the U.S. population at large.

Other Marginalized Groups

One more example can clarify the tendency that radio had to bestow higher social standing to some groups over others. During the medium's commercial development, people living in rural areas—especially farmers—were underserved. Only a small amount of programming was specifically targeted at this demographic. Most of the broadcasts that reached people outside the cities, some scholars argue, did not generally emphasize the issues that mattered most to this audience, such as agricultural reports or announcements of local community events. Instead, radio addressed rural citizens in a manner that encouraged them to give up the "backward" ideas of the country and embrace the urban cultural values reflected by the networks centered in New York. Programming tended to endorse integration into a city sensibility rather than acknowledge the distinct needs of rural dwellers, an approach that helped to define people in the country as consumers and thus better served radio's corporate sponsors. When rural characters were presented on shows, more often than not, they took on the roles of "hillbillies" and "hicks."

RADIO AS A GOVERNMENT TOOL OF PROPAGANDA

Most scholars would affirm that propaganda is a fact of modern life. And as various academics have noted, during times of war, managing the messages the public receives is especially crucial—democracies, in particular, require the consent of the people. Since the dawn of the twentieth century, government and military officials have gained access to an increasing array of media to convey the ideas and positions they wish the citizenry to embrace. Radio has been one of the tools in the propaganda arsenal.

During World War I, the United States launched what was arguably the most comprehensive propaganda campaign the world had ever known (see **World War Propaganda**). The prevailing attitude among the populace before American involvement was isolationist. Once the decision was made to send U.S. troops to the front, the government needed to shape public opinion to support its military mission. George Creel was appointed to head up the Committee on Public Information (CPI), which became known as the "Creel Commission." Creel drew from all of the forms of communication at his disposal to transform resistance to U.S. entry into the war into fervid backing of American intervention. At the time, though, radio had not evolved into a mass medium and thus did not play a key role in the CPI's tactics.

Propaganda and Franklin Delano Roosevelt

By World War II (WWII), though, radio was central to the lives of Americans. Consequently, the government has employed radio—sometimes directly, sometimes indirectly—throughout every major conflict to encourage patriotism and propagate messages in line with military goals. Yet since the rise of television, it has merely served as a supplementary medium. During WWII, however, radio stood as the nation's most popular mass medium. Thus the use of radio for the objective of disseminating propaganda in support of World War II provides an exemplary case study (also see **World War Propaganda**). The government broadcast propaganda to people abroad to help advance the American point of view on the existing state of affairs. At the same time, some expatriates, in acts of betrayal, were employed by the Nazis to convey anti-Ally messages to populations outside Germany, including U.S. soldiers. But the Franklin Delano Roosevelt (FDR) government's creation of propaganda for domestic consumption perhaps sheds the most light on how the interplay of politics and popular culture came together for the purpose of buttressing internal support for American involvement in the war.

Even outside the realm of direct government intercession, however, radio in the 1930s and 1940s subtly but fundamentally accomplished a tendency that national leaders could use to their advantage: allowing for tensions on the margins, it helped create a national community, at least an imagined one. Given that only three national networks supplied the lion's share of programming throughout the country, at any moment in time, listeners from coast to coast were brought together to simultaneously share the same event. The feeling of unity that radio could sometimes foster not only benefited the government but also worked to meet the interests of the corporate world; as radio became increasingly privatized into the hands of big business, it consistently offered content that depicted consumerism as part and parcel of the "American Way of Life."

More overt government efforts during the run up and execution of the war were commonly channeled through radio news. Although slow to occupy much space on the radio dial in the 1920s, news content enjoyed a greater and greater foothold—and secured the backing of sponsors—over the course of the next two decades. Partly because it tended to use more accessible language than its print-based counterpart, by the early 1940s, radio had become citizens' primary and most trusted source for news. FDR had already used radio to convey propaganda well before the United States joined forces with the Allies. Assaying to lead the population in a dramatically new economic direction during the Great Depression, the president vigorously employed the medium—as well as other communication vehicles—to explain and promote his New Deal policies. His work was cut out for him, however, because the public was apprehensive about anything that had the scent of propaganda. Many people came to realize that they had been misled in the buildup to World War I through false atrocity stories and other misrepresentations, and did not wish to be fooled again. Academics and other intellectuals, too, had been warning for years that radio was a powerful mass medium with the capacity to be especially exploited for propagandistic purposes. Moreover, people were becoming increasingly aware of how the Nazis were utilizing radio to instill their perverse doctrines. Still, with the establishment of the National Recovery Administration (NRA), Roosevelt launched his campaign. The radio networks, knowing that they were dependent on the government for their very right to exist and for the rules they must follow, donated considerable noncommercial time to the NRA to make its case, despite the resulting loss of advertising revenue. One of the largest NRA productions was hosted by the popular singer Kate Smith and featured other notable entertainers. With the assistance of commercial writers and actors, a number of federal agencies produced and broadcast hundreds of advertising-free programs in support of the president's domestic agenda. Other shows pulled from the domain of entertainment as well, merging politics and elements of popular culture along the way. In addition, FDR initiated his series of "Fireside Chats." In these discussions, creating the impression that he was an invited guest into living rooms across the country, Roosevelt presented himself in a conversational and avuncular manner that was appealing to many citizens; a sizable portion of the population tuned in to the chats.

Resistance to FDR

The FDR administration's messages did not go unopposed, however. Big business developed its own counterpropaganda campaign in opposition to Roosevelt's New Deal plans, which were hugely unpopular with the corporate world. The Great Depression planted a seed of doubt about the very nature of capitalism in people's minds because so many of them were experiencing hardship. The New Deal, to the business set, signified socialist reforms and a threat to capitalism itself. Most newspapers at the time were also not sympathetic to the policies, which is another reason why Roosevelt relied so strongly on radio. Scores of corporate-backed, entertainment programs included voices of resistance to the New Deal. For example, both General Motors and Ford sponsored symphony music shows that featured "intermission talks" on the benefits of the free enterprise system. The National Association of Manufacturers produced *The American Family Robinson*, a serial that portrayed the businessman as a societal hero. Besides corporations battling FDR on the airwaves, popular radio personalities such as **Huey Long** and **Father Charles Coughlin** also fueled the fire. In the end, it is debatable as to whom achieved the upper hand. Perhaps the safest view would suggest that FDR reached a compromise with his detractors. Recognizing he could never deeply undermine capitalism (it is doubtful that he ever intended this to begin with), he softened his New Deal measures over time and, based on the ways in which the unfolding war propaganda campaign eventually grew more privatized, seemed to partner with business in affirming the U.S. system of free enterprise.

Franklin Delano Roosevelt, circa 1936. (Photofest)

Propaganda and World War II

But the outbreak of World War II represented a turning point for government-run propaganda. The focus shifted from acceptance or rejection of the New Deal to the role of the United States in the conflict. Business, though skeptical of FDR's political intentions, worrying that he might utilize war messages to distract the public from his underlying domestic goals, was willing to cut a wartime president more latitude. While the radio networks advocated impartiality in their news coverage, journalists, although with some exceptions, were mostly favorable toward Roosevelt's stance on intervention even before the Japanese invasion of Pearl Harbor; once the United States was attacked, the posture was still more pronounced. Based in Britain for CBS news, the legendary **Edward R. Murrow**, for instance, implicitly sounded the theme that England needed the help of the United States. Straightforward reporters spawned news commentators, some of whom became very popular. Two such notables, H. V. Kaltenborn and Raymond Gram Swing, both appeared to endorse the cause of U.S. involvement. At the same time, many powerful spokesmen of FDR's foreign policy were granted access to the airwaves. It appears that radio news, overall, facilitated in building a climate suitable to the nation's entry into World War II. Furthermore, once the United States went to battle, government and military officials attempted to manage the flow of news through various techniques designed to discreetly censor news reports.

Direct government-produced propaganda programming related to the war, however, probably did not achieve the same level of success as less overt forms. Unlike news, which the public generally perceives as information emanating from a third-party, government-created shows of the time risked coming across as blatantly biased. Moreover, citizens were more liable to have their guard up after enduring not only the propaganda campaign of World War I but also the bold persuasive tactics behind FDR's New Deal communication. In addition, the government shows were often slated in poor time slots or had to compete head-to-head with more amusing commercial fare. Meanwhile, though, FDR's Fireside Chats continued and received thousands of letters from everyday people commending the president on his talks and approach to the war.

One of the early examples of government-produced, noncommercial war propaganda occurred before direct U.S. participation. Drawing upon the services of well-known writers and actors, including Bette Davis and Robert Montgomery, *The Treasury Star Parade* brought politics and popular culture together to promote the purchase of defense bonds and stamps. Soon, the government founded the Office of Facts and Figures, which was charged with overseeing all information and propaganda initiatives on behalf of defense. Later, the agency was renamed the **Office of War Information** (OWI). A chief goal of the OWI was to simply explain to the populace the reasons for the nation's intervention in the war. People were well aware that the United States had been attacked at Pearl Harbor, yet, given the messy complexity of the multicountry confrontation, they were not exactly sure who the United States was (and was not) fighting and why.

A number of both news- and entertainment-based, noncommercial dramas and documentaries were devoted to the mission. Just eight days after the bombing of Pearl Harbor, James Stewart, Orson Welles, and other celebrities starred in the show, *We Hold These Truths*, which celebrated the Bill of Rights and made it clear that its survival was worth fighting for. President Roosevelt supplemented the broadcast with a brief public address. For 13 weeks, another propaganda vehicle, *This Is War!*, was carried on all the major networks and garnered high ratings. The show and other similar offerings sought to personalize the conflict by depicting everyday life for the soldiers and bringing the sounds and imagined images of war directly into people's living rooms, sometimes even symbolically placing listeners in the middle of the action.

The government also created programming targeted toward ethnic and immigrant groups whose first language was not English. A central objective of this subpropaganda campaign was to encourage a sense of national unity among the country's diverse audiences, especially the Italian- and German-speaking populations who might be torn by whether they should be loyal to their land of residence or ancestral home. Shows aimed at these segments of the population included *Uncle Sam Speaks*, which tried to recruit foreign-language volunteers and drum up feelings of American patriotism, and *We Fight Back*, which used vignettes from German culture in an attempt to resonate with German-speaking people. Sometimes the government sidestepped the use of propaganda altogether and simply closed down non-English speaking radio stations.

Several shows intended to stir up pro-war passion in the audience by demonizing U.S. enemies. Because the Roosevelt administration had decided it would be wise to fight in Europe before Asia, one major challenge involved convincing Americans that Germany should be the primary target and not Japan. After Pearl Harbor, citizens were already predisposed to feelings of hatred toward the Japanese; the Germans, on the other hand, although dangerous abroad, had not directly harmed the nation. (Some scholars argue that racism also entered the picture—while Japan signified the yellow-skinned "other," Germany affirmed the white skin, European ancestry of the U.S. majority.) The drama *You Can't Do Business with Hitler*, which portrayed the German people as suffering under Nazi rule, scored well in the ratings. *This Is Your Enemy* followed some of the same conventions and also evoked positive responses from many listeners. At the other end of the spectrum, the OWI developed programming meant to trigger sentiment toward American allies, which was often a harder sell, in part because the population did not necessarily trust its partners. For instance, Russia's system of government was already held in suspicion; at the same time, many people felt that Great Britain was not doing enough on its own to protect itself. *An American in England*, for example, consequently appeared to fall flat. Though it was produced for a U.S. audience, it actually had more British listeners.

Once the U.S. war effort had been established for a while, business and conservative politicians were less willing to let government propaganda go unchecked. In 1943, Congress cut the domestic division of the OWI's budget by two-thirds, fearing that it was functioning as FDR's personal vehicle for advancing other elements of his political agenda (after the war, it was eliminated altogether). The move seriously undercut Roosevelt's ability to run an effective noncommercial, government radio propaganda campaign, which came to a crawl.

Corporate Propaganda During World War II.   Advertising and corporate-sponsored programming, on the other hand, also served propagandistic functions and thrived throughout the war years. Just after the United States had entered the storm, the advertising industry changed the name of its Advertising Council to the War Advertising Council (WAC). The government turned to advertising agencies to develop campaigns on government positions. Many businesses, conversely, shifted their attention from direct sales pitches for their products and services, which had the potential to come off as overly crass in a time of war, to advancing patriotic, "public service" messages of support for the cause (sometimes claiming that their companies were in some way actually enhancing the nation's ability to fight) and themes regarding the need for all citizens to do their part to ensure victory (sometimes explaining techniques for rationing and ways in which company products could help by, for example, making it easier to conserve) and, in a more directly self-serving manner, announcing that the system of free enterprise would once again flourish once the conflict was settled. Advertisers also occasionally used the more subtle tactic of inserting pro-war messages into their sponsored entertainment shows to evoke advantageous associations for their brands in the minds of consumers. These implicit intersections between advertising and propaganda somewhat worked to turn the antagonism between the corporate world and the FDR administration into a collaborative enterprise.

Radio Entertainment Propaganda During World War II.   Concurrently, in a practice that explicitly brought together politics and popular culture, the government both circuitously and overtly inserted propagandistic motifs into commercial radio shows themselves. Through the OWI's Network Allocation Plan (NAP), the radio industry was instructed to regularly integrate war messages into its programming. In practice, the Radio Advisory Committee (RAC) asked government agencies to provide every major advertiser with a schedule of war messages they wished to address. These points were in turn passed along to writers and producers to effectively insert (generally seamlessly) into the entertainment shows. Despite the lack of legal enforcement, radio executives were generally willing to comply, given that, among other circumstances, their licenses were granted by a government agency and were based, in part, on serving the public interest. Consequently, radio during the war years still centered on advertising-sponsored, crowd-pleasing entertainment even as it disseminated government propaganda. Popular comedy programs such as *The Jack Benny Show*, *Bob Hope*, and *Fibber McGee and Molly*, at one time or another, covered various issues that were of importance to the government, including why the public should accept gas and sugar rationing, an understanding of various war organizations, and the sacrifices everyday people were being asked to make. Whether it was an endorsement of the scrap metal drive or a call for everyone to unite behind the country's military mission, various radio comedy shows did their part to serve the nation at a critical juncture. In 1942, **Bob Hope** began the tradition of broadcasting his shows from army and naval bases, a practice he would later bring with him to television. By going right to the field, Hope went beyond OWI expectations by representing the voices of the actual soldiers called for battle.

Radio soap operas, which were endemic when the United States crossed the threshold into war, were also implicated in the OWI master propaganda plan. Appealing to a largely female audience, these shows were in a position to assist in furthering goals related to gender, including enticing women to seek wartime employment and ideologically shifting the role of women from domestic worker to wage-earning laborer. Even before the NAP was announced, soap opera writers, who generally tap into current events and were perhaps feeling the pull of patriotism as well, were already incorporating war-based themes into their serials. The trend was further solidified once the NAP went into effect. *Pepper Young's Family*, for instance, featured the main character's sister joining him in the factory. The association between the male-dominated OWI, which sometimes engaged in preapproving scripts, and soap opera producers was not always a harmonious one, however. Although they did slot war plots into their scenarios, soap opera creators sometimes resisted going too far for fear of alienating their stay-at-home, female base of fans. Many listeners, in fact, despite the tenor of the times, did not look kindly on women who left behind their child-rearing and wifely duties for gainful employment in the marketplace. Overcoming years of domestic socialization was no easy accomplishment. Thus writers often balanced meeting the wishes of the OWI with satisfying the demands of their audiences, showing, for example, that housewives were also central to the war effort. Moreover, not every woman who entered the workforce was portrayed in a positive manner. For example, her absence might be presented as the chief reason for her children falling into delinquency, or she could be shown as unhappy and lonely because of her choice to work. In other genres as well, the wage-earning female was sometimes depicted as less than feminine, even perhaps mannish and crude. This ideological tension was eventually resolved when, after the war, women were again mainly expected to return to their homes and hand their jobs back over to the soldiers returning from battle. Some soap opera plots featured women once more assuming traditional roles, not only reclaiming their household chores but also nurturing physically or emotionally damaged men who had suffered in the war. The backlash against stereotypical representations of womanhood was still at least a decade away.

The Impact of World War II Radio Propaganda.   Overall, though, these less obvious propaganda techniques involving the placement of propagandistic messages into regularly scheduled shows were probably more successful than the direct federal, noncommercial programming because much of the audience likely interpreted the comedies, soap operas, and related fare as mere entertainment and was not fully aware of the embedded messages on behalf of government. For example, the OWI once requested that the producers of *Fibber McGee and Molly* plant a recruitment message for merchant seamen into one of its episodes; on the day after its airing, the number of people who signed up was twice as high as usual. To a significant extent, as U.S. involvement in WWII continued, the OWI's NAP supplanted government produced shows in disseminating propaganda. Through the mutual and coordinated efforts of the OWI, the radio industry (via the NAB's Victory Council and the networks' Network Relations Committee), and radio advertisers (via the WAC and its RAC), therefore, the propaganda mission was essentially privatized, which benefited both the Roosevelt administration and the corporate world. Although there is not sufficient data to know how they responded to the material, millions of citizens were unwittingly exposed to government propaganda every day.

THE USE OF RADIO IN POLITICAL ELECTION CAMPAIGNS

A more easily recognized form of political propaganda is that associated with messages aimed to promote candidates during election seasons. Moreover, this type of persuasion is generally significantly more contradictory because the two major parties, as well as other minor parties and special interest groups, disseminate widely divergent claims and arguments. Since the birth of the United States, political candidates and their supporters have drawn upon every available media resource in their attempts to sway the vote their way. Yet before the twentieth century, the only influential mass medium in existence was print, through newspapers, books, flyers, posters, and similar materials. As the nation's first broadcast medium, radio came to represent, at least in its capacity to efficiently reach thousands or even millions of voters simultaneously, a sea change in how political campaigns would be waged.

Instituting Guidelines for Political Coverage

As radio gained prominence in the 1920s, many politicians and social critics hoped that it would help engender a more informed electorate, build a sense of national unity, and counteract the hostile partisanship that had been typical of newspapers. Yet at first, broadcasters had little guidance as to how they should participate in the political arena. The Radio Act of 1927 began to lay out their responsibilities in relationship to politicians. In an effort to cultivate fairness, the Act specified that if a station agreed to air paid advertising from a candidate, it was then required to accept advertising from all of his or her rivals. The Communications Act of 1934, however, made it clear that licensees were not obliged to accept any political advertising to begin with, although they were encouraged to do so. At the same time, stations were not mandated to provide free air time. Thus, in practice, better funded candidates had an advantage in accessing the airwaves with their advertising in comparison to opponents with smaller financial bases, making it more difficult for the latter to compete.

Most stations were willing to broadcast political advertising and other political programming as one means of demonstrating they were not reluctant to devote at least some of their schedules to the public interest. Furthermore, even before the federal government issued its 1927 and 1934 regulatory framework, the major networks had already informally established their own common policies. They agreed to mostly work with only national candidates from the two major parties and limit political programming to just one hour per day. Consequently, parties besides the Democratic and Republican, including the Socialist and Communist Parties, received far less access to broadcast facilities, partly because, perceiving them as too far removed from the mainstream, networks did not wish to risk alienating listeners, and partially due to these parties not having the financial resources to buy substantial chunks of time.

Yet special occasions called for more than 60 minutes of political broadcasting per day. For example, in 1924, over 300 stations broadcast the federal election results on election night, many of them dedicating the entire evening to the event or interspersing coverage with their regular programming. Just four years earlier, only a single station had done the same, as KDKA in Pittsburgh inaugurated its service—and broadcasting in general—on the night of the federal election. Overall, though, stations usually enjoyed greater profits when allocating time to commercial clients and so preferred to minimize the portion of its schedule assigned to political broadcasts. As radio evolved, broadcasters needed to weigh their desire to secure as much revenue as possible with their obligation to serve the public interest. This balancing act was especially difficult during campaign seasons. In 1928, both NBC and CBS agreed to broadcast, free of charge, the Republican and Democratic conventions. The coverage helped the networks gain favor from the parties that had the authority to influence regulations and radio licensing, but at considerable financial sacrifice. Networks also donated airtime for speeches, inaugurations, and other noteworthy political events to demonstrate devotion to public affairs and ward off unfriendly regulations. Election night reporting became increasingly sophisticated; building on the inherent drama of the evening, the networks tried to outdo one another in demonstrations of technical wizardry, which probably made the broadcasts more entertaining for a substantial slice of the audience.

Incumbency had its advantages. Networks often allowed the president and members of Congress the microphone without charge during nonelection periods. A Roosevelt Fireside Chat, positioned as a presidential address to the people, for instance, could nonetheless function as a reelection campaign tool. At the same time, though, networks at least tried to remain nonpartisan.

Campaigning through Entertainment

Initially, networks were also averse to granting time to politicians who wished to campaign through forms generally linked with entertainment, such as drama, rather than through straightforward speeches or announcements. Yet some staged scenarios, indeed, slipped through the cracks, especially on stations not owned and operated by the major networks. In many cases, programming was presented as mere entertainment but was actually designed to politically proselytize. Over time,

U.S. Secretary of Commerce Herbert Hoover, in cabinet of Calvin Coolidge, listens to the radio broadcast on March 11, 1922, of "Air News." (AP Photo)

candidates became more adept at getting around network restrictions and exploiting the medium for their political purposes. Networks, for their part, were inconsistent in enforcing their ban on dramatized political campaign content. For instance, in 1944, celebrities, including Lucille Ball and Irving Berlin, endorsed their favorite presidential candidate during the radio broadcast, the "Roosevelt Special." Four years later, a series of comedic shows targeting women in the home was produced for the Democrats and their choice for president, Harry Truman. The programs featured songs, pointed jokes, and contests aimed at involving the listener.

Early Political Radio Campaigns

Although radio, in its early years, tended to focus on national politicians, the first candidate to use the medium to campaign was then incumbent New York City mayor John F. Hylan in 1921. His opponent, Henry F. Curran, quickly followed suit. Still, such incipient political programming was relatively primitive—the technology was not always dependable, scheduling had not yet become standardized, and, as mentioned above, guidelines had not been established—and politicians themselves did not at first fully understand how to best use radio to meet their goals. It did not take long, however, for politicians to realize that they could save much energy by replacing some of the grind of day-to-day campaigning with the efficiency of reaching a mass audience through radio. Some early advocates of radio argued that the medium could reduce political stress in general because politicians would no longer have to engage in lengthy speaking tours. Furthermore, radio was able to deliver a feeling of intimacy seldom achieved on the campaign trail.

Before radio, few voters ever got to see a candidate live, and even fewer actually got to shake hands with a politician. Yet, for many people, radio gave the impression that a candidate was speaking to an audience member one-on-one in his or her own home. Politicians soon discovered that they needed to add radio to their arsenal. Conversely, for reasons already noted, the radio industry also realized that it needed the support of politicians. This quid pro quo arrangement, in part, helped radio rapidly develop into an effective campaign instrument. And the medium could also be put to use to advance an agenda by politicians already in office.

Although he was not the first one to deliver a speech via radio, Calvin Coolidge is usually identified as the earliest president to significantly exploit radio's potential. In 1923, he delivered the first State of the Union address ever transmitted through the airwaves. Before then, just a proportionately small number of people had ever had access to the words of a president as the utterances were actually unfolding—they could only hear them within earshot at a live event. People enthusiastically gathered around radio sets in homes and offices; stores selling radios even projected the speech to passersby. Although it was not designed as entertainment, the speech generated the kind of stir that could be associated with popular culture. Yet Coolidge did not so much speak from a studio directly to an audience as orate before a live audience, which was then simultaneously carried on radio. Later, Herbert Hoover turned to radio often but he, too, situated his broadcasts within an impersonal context. Franklin Delano Roosevelt would be the president to perfect the utilization of radio in a way that realized much of its potential for conveying a feeling of audience intimacy. By the time he approached the end of his initial year in office, he had given 24 speeches over the radio networks, with four of them billed as Fireside Chats.

At the same time as broadcast presidential speeches were becoming more common, radio usage for political campaigning continued to rise as well. The 1924 season probably marks the first one in which radio played a consistent role in both parties' efforts. The broadcast of the Democratic convention proved to be a media sensation. Unfortunately for the party, however, much of the stir was evoked by the highly contentious and protracted proceedings, which likely contributed to its 1924 presidential defeat. In general, probably neither party, still accustomed to the traditional campaigning methods they had employed for years and inexperienced with the new medium, realized radio's potential. By 1928, though, politicians were growing increasingly savvy in their application of broadcasting. For both parties, radio costs represented the largest line item of their total campaign expenditures. The Democrats provided an early instance of fusing campaign politics with popular culture, producing 30-minute shows that allocated 10 minutes to speeches and the remaining time to musicians and actors from stage and screen. Radio plays and five-minute advertising spots also emerged during the 1928 campaign season. Voter turnout exceeded the previous election's by over 5 percent. To what extent radio was responsible for the bump, however, is a topic for debate.

The Impact of Radio on Politics

Radio outlays for presidential campaigns continued to increase throughout the 1930s. Yet the fact that the losing party in four straight elections (1928, 1932, 1936, and 1940) invested more money in radio than its opponent attests to the dubious impact the medium had on results—it was an important campaign tool but could not single-handedly determine outcomes when so many other factors were

Calvin Coolidge, seen here in 1929, was the first U.S. president to make considerable use of the radio. (Photofest)

at work. Still, radio had altered the campaign landscape. For example, candidates could sometimes be held more accountable for contradictory positions: taking a particular stance in a stump speech in one U.S. region, then offering a conflicting perspective in another area could appear foolish if a nationally broadcast speech belied the messages spoken at one of the face-to-face encounters. What is more, even if determining what effect radio had on voter turnout is problematic, some scholars contend that radio at least in some measure helped popularize politics and make it more interesting and accessible to everyday people. Before the medium, it would have taken a politician hundreds of speeches over the course of weeks to reach the number of people that he or she could now accomplish with just one radio speech. In a sense, radio created a massive town square, bringing together individuals and small groups of people gathered in living rooms or even cars. FDR, an obvious advocate of radio, contended that the medium actually raised the level of campaign communication because it removed citizens from noisy crowds and the heightened emotions they inspired, and, instead, allowed them to arrive at opinions in a rational manner in the quiet of their own homes. Some observers claimed at the time that, unlike the days of the partisan press when constituents would gravitate toward their favorite biased newspapers, radio enabled people to hear a range of speeches and, consequently, attain a more neutral state of mind.

In one of the most legendary research projects conducted on media campaigns and voting behavior, entitled in its printed form as *The People's Choice*, Paul Lazarsfeld concluded that the media—and radio in particular—had little impact on how people actually voted. In the great majority of cases, he reported, the media either activated internalized positions or reinforced already existing views—only infrequently did media campaigns yield conversion, that is, sway voters to change their minds regarding which candidate would receive their votes.

The Impact on Presentation Style.   At the same time, politicians had to adjust their styles to accommodate the new medium. Many of the conventions followed in speeches before large crowds did not translate well on radio. Screaming into a microphone could overwhelm listeners, while dramatic gestures could not be seen. Moreover, the traditional stump speech was generally attended by many partisans; the mass radio audience was more diverse and required different skills to reach. Listeners could simply turn the dial if they did not like the sound of a politician—or not tune in at all. Thus, speakers needed to consider making their speeches more entertaining to hold an audience, especially given that they were competing with comedies, dramas, sports, and variety shows for the listeners' attention. Newspapers even began to critique performances and comment not only on the content of a speech but the style of the candidate uttering the words as well. Some politicians were more adept than others in modifying their communication approaches, which, consequently, in some cases, probably had an influence on who was elected. Because they could not assess crowd response as they could at live encounters, candidates began to increasingly rely on audience measurement and polls to better gauge how effective their speeches had been. All of these factors suggest, as many observers did at the time and as some researchers maintain today, that radio actually revolutionized the political campaign process. Yet others counter that radio did not simply replace earlier electioneering techniques as much as supplement and amplify them. Pamphleteering, mailed materials, and personal appearances, for example, continued unabated and still constituted major parts of the campaign war chest. Yet radio—through speeches and other political programming—and mass advertising probably intensified the merging of information and entertainment, and blended a personal approach with mass dissemination. In addition, there is evidence that demonstrates some citizens were directly touched by politicians' personal appeals. Herbert Hoover, for example, received thousands of letters after each radio address. Later, FDR received even more feedback (see **Fireside Chats**).

Radio's Diminishing Impact.   After World War II, when the age of networks and national audiences gave way to the dawn of more local broadcasting and fragmented listenership, radio took on less and less importance as a crucial campaign instrument. By adding visuals to the aural dimension, television, in the 1950s, supplanted radio's dominance as a means of persuasion during election seasons. While the medium is still a part of the campaign media mix, it has mostly been consigned to use as a supplementary tool.

TALK RADIO: PARTICIPATORY POLITICAL CONVERSATION

Another way in which radio has functioned as a political medium, beyond its role in the dissemination of messages by political candidates, governments, corporations, and other interest groups hoping to achieve particular goals, is through its use as a forum for political dialogue and debate, a phenomenon that has come to be known as political *talk radio*. Since the 1980s, the genre has gained the kind of high ratings that observers would say signifies it has established a place within the rubric of popular culture. Even more so than the early broadcasts of political speeches, conventions, and related political material, political talk radio, some scholars argue, represents a type of town square, or perhaps better still, the coffeehouses and similar outlets of the past, which were places where the citizenry could engage in lively political conversation on what it perceived as the most pressing topics of the day. Whereas the political programming during radio's initial decades mostly involved one-way transmission from the source of the broadcast to people symbolically congregated into an imaginary, unified populace, political talk radio allows listeners to actually participate—in real time—in the discussion of timely issues and thus contribute to the creation of the shows' very content. It enables people who feel there are few vehicles through which everyday citizens can make their voices heard an opportunity to call in and express their perspectives on current affairs. Moreover, numerous adherents claim, political talk radio has the potential to present a more diverse set of viewpoints than is typically offered in the contemporary, hard-to-access, consolidated media environment. Others would add, however, that the format is not as egalitarian as the town meetings of the past: program producers screen callers and decide who will have the chance to talk with the shows' hosts, and the on-air personalities themselves directly control the flow of conversation.

Today's political talk radio was foreshadowed by several figures who gained notoriety by animatedly and heatedly advancing (often controversial) political viewpoints on the shows they hosted. Father Charles E. Coughlin and Senator Huey Long, who both achieved large followings in the 1930s, are two notable examples. Yet these men's programs and others like them did not (partly due to limited technological capacity) make the airwaves available for listeners to join in the live discussion. Later, in the 1960s, shows such as *Rambling with Gambling* featured more talk than music, yet they, too, did not generally accept live phone calls from the audience, nor take on controversial matters. The contemporary version of talk radio surfaced in the late 1970s; from the early part of the 1980s to the mid-1990s, the number of stations with an all-talk or combined news and talk format had increased fourfold, becoming one of the most popular genres on the air. The growing cell phone market facilitated talk radio's expansion—people could now call in while driving in their motor vehicles. At the same time, media deregulation and satellite technology gave the radio industry the capability to syndicate shows and build a national audience, somewhat reversing the trend toward fragmentation that had been going on for decades. Talk radio provided a major boost to AM in particular. Over the years, more and more people had abandoned its frequencies for the better clarity of the FM signals. Talk radio supplied one significant solution to reenergizing AM's cultural relevance. Part of what distinguished talk radio was that, unlike most commercial programming of the past, it actually encouraged controversy. The style of vocal delivery is, by design, often decidedly impassioned. Despite its contentious tone, many advertisers were quick to support the format because they perceived that the talk radio audience consisted of a greater percentage of active listeners than those who tuned into music stations as a form of background atmosphere. Because of its political bent and argumentative character, notwithstanding its populist aura, it has sparked several critiques by scholars, journalists, and other commentators. One point of attack by critics of talk radio centers on its supposed uncivil nature. Show hosts often shout, insult public figures or even listeners, and convey sentiments that opponents regard as hostile toward women, people of color, and other minority groups.

Talk Radio's Present Personalities

"Dr. Laura" (**Laura Schlessinger**) is one of the prominent radio talk show personalities who has generated controversy. Yet most of the other notable stars in the field are male. Widely regarded as a host who embodies the abrasive conventions associated with the genre, **Howard Stern** was among the first personalities to achieve considerable attention for his work in talk radio and is considered one of the preeminent "shock jocks," a label commonly used in connection with this inflammatory form.

Don Imus, who first went on the air in 1968, is also generally included in the pantheon of famous shock jocks, although his work has been qualitatively different from Stern's. Although Stern's comments have often had indirect political implications, he has not devoted most of his attention to major political issues and government officials. Imus, on the other hand, though held as generally crude as well, became much more explicitly political beginning in the late 1980s.

Another allegation persistently raised by adversaries of political talk radio is that it is overly right wing in its ideological slant. The most notorious personality in this regard is **Rush Limbaugh**, whose manner and popularity have inspired numerous spin-offs. Limbaugh's relentless political tirades were a chief factor in bringing political talk radio into the national consciousness. By 1992, he commanded the format's largest audience.

The Impact of Talk Radio

Political talk show celebrities have commonly maintained that they have a major influence on public opinion. There is some evidence to support their position, although to what extent they have shaped outcomes is a contestable point. To shed light on the issue of right-wing bias in political talk radio and what impact it had actually had on events, the Times Mirror Center for People in the Press conducted an investigation in 1993. Based on a survey of 1,500 listeners and 112 talk show personalities, it concluded that most listeners were male and twice as likely to be politically conservative than liberal. Two years later, the audience consisted of nearly three times as many conservatives as liberals, and a follow-up study revealed that regular listeners paid more attention to news in general and were more politically active than the public at large. The fans who were interviewed divulged several reasons why they regularly tuned into political talk radio, including that it furnished views that were typically regarded as especially risky and therefore excluded from other media venues. A 2007 study co-conducted by the Center for American Progress and Free Press indicated that an imbalance had grown over time. The institutions' report stated that out of 257 news/talk stations owned by the top five commercial companies, 91 percent of the discussion was conservative. Ninety-two percent of the stations did not air any liberal talk, as defined by the researchers, at all.

Talk Radio as a Backlash against Women and Other Marginalized Groups. Another major criticism of political talk radio, although not articulated as often, relates to the manner in which it has ostensibly operated as a backlash against the Women's Movement and attempted to define what the nature of masculinity should be. Some historians contend that, following the second-wave feminism of the 1960s and 1970s, general anxiety about manhood started to become prominent. Within this cultural environment, talk radio, these critics say, provided a safe haven for mostly white men who longed to reassert themselves and forego expressions of "political correctness" toward women and people of color. Talk radio's brand of masculinity, however, rebelled against the rules of decorum supposedly typified by the corporate executive and, instead, emphasized the verbal aggression and course qualities that are purportedly emblematic of the working-class male, thus subtly perpetuating a breed of class politics as well. According to this critique, talk radio has offered men a feeling of empowerment and endeavored to reinforce a kind of patriarchal structure that positions a more primal man at the top of society's hierarchy. During a period that has witnessed considerable business deregulation and, consequently, greater corporate consolidation and centralization of power, the format has tended to be populist in its attitude, critical of both government and big business, and hostile toward any version of social justice programs that might smack of a feminine touch. Howard Stern, Don Imus, and Rush Limbaugh have all been accused of perpetuating sexist and racist perspectives. For example, in 2007, Imus evoked a storm of criticism by labeling the players on the Rutgers University women's basketball team, the runner-up in the 2007 NCAA basketball tournament, as "nappy-headed hoes" (Steinberg 2007). Soon afterward, he was fired from CBS radio and **MSNBC**, which had also carried his show on television (for further discussion, see **Don Imus**). As a woman, Dr. Laura (Laura Schlessinger), on the other hand, would seem to offer a contradiction to the backlash perspective. Yet as a conservative radio host with traditional views on gender and an oppositional stance toward homosexuality, perhaps she is not as far removed from her male cohorts as it might appear at first glance.

Noncommercial Alternatives

There are two other notable versions of programming that fall under the umbrella of talk radio, both of which are mostly noncommercial. Community radio, best exemplified by the chain of Pacifica stations (see **Pacifica and Community Radio**), features extensive news coverage and political discussion, generally from a left-wing or radical point of view. These offerings often invite listeners to call in and join in the dialogue. But the much more popular noncommercial talk programs are broadcast on public radio stations around the country. A large part of their content is supplied courtesy of NPR, founded in 1970. Few would argue that NPR mirrors the coarseness, male orientation, or far-right-wing leanings for which some of the most popular commercial political talk radio programs are frequently attacked. Yet for many listeners, NPR, like these shows, also provides an alternative to the kind of interpretations they usually associate with other forms of media, particularly TV network news.

Unlike commercial radio, public radio receives little financial support from advertisers, instead relying on government funding and donations from listeners. At the same time, as a nonprofit institution, its mission goes beyond maximizing ratings—more than its corporate-owned competition, public radio has traditionally placed an accent on serving the public interest. Consequently, through music and other formats, it has usually reached out to frequently marginalized groups to a much greater extent than commercial stations catering to general audiences.

It is clear that radio in the United States did not have to evolve into a commercial form of communication—similar to the medium's development in other countries, it could have followed a public model. In the 1920s, many critics, especially those aligned with the Progressive Movement, which was a movement dedicated to further instituting a flourishing democracy, proclaimed that profit-driven media were incompatible with the maintenance of a dynamic marketplace of ideas and the health of democracy itself. Some noncommercial radio stations, many operated by universities, did indeed exist in the 1920s and 1930s. But commercial broadcasting eventually dominated the airwaves, as public service stations were not able to compete with the tantalizing fare and the corporate resources of their advertising-supported rivals. Proponents of commercial radio, moreover, argued that public radio was innately paternalistic, implying that broadcasters knew what was best for listeners rather than the audience itself. Throughout the initial decades of broadcast radio's existence, most historians would agree, public service outlets, with their limited backing, never lived up to their promise. Offered frequencies on the virtually unknown FM dial and transmitting content throughout the 1940s and 1950s, public radio, with its elite, "high culture" programming principles, was not widely accessible and did not resonate with a sizable portion of the populace. The creation of the Corporation of Public Broadcasting (CPB), a result of the Public Broadcasting Act of 1967, was designed to revive the form. Although the Act was established primarily in relationship to television, as an almost afterthought, it was applied to radio as well and NPR was born. The intention of the legislators was that NPR should cater to underserved communities, yet also reach larger audiences than public radio had in the past. In 1971, NPR's first major program was launched, entitled *All Things Considered* (*ATC*). The show's original philosophy emphasized that *ATC* should not merely mimic the conventions of standard journalism, with its focus on simply reporting political events and government affairs. Instead, it should provide a much fuller discussion of the issues, as well as incorporate the perspectives of everyday people into its coverage. Yet it did not, at first, achieve the popularity for which its creators had wished. Over the years, therefore, according to some scholars, while still retaining its distinctiveness, to attract a larger audience, *ATC* somewhat modified its approach by no longer stressing multicultural egalitarianism as much as its authoritative voice.

In due course, similar to the predominantly AM political radio programs, *ATC* rose in prominence during the 1980s and became NPR's most famous news and talk show. In 1979, *Morning Edition* (*ME*), a comparable offering for morning listeners, was added to the lineup and also achieved successful ratings. Yet unlike their commercial talk radio counterparts, *ATC* and *ME* are widely regarded as utterly civil in tone. Their announcers and commentators are generally held to be highly articulate, with smooth, evenhanded vocal deliveries. NPR's group of listeners is customarily perceived as being more educated, financially sound, and politically liberal than the average audience, although studies have yielded contradictory findings about the degree to which this depiction is accurate (Douglas 2004, 320). Another point of departure from commercial talk radio is that, while both *ATC* and *ME* often converse with everyday people during their live discussions and in their taped reports, they do not regularly encourage audience members to call in and become part of the broadcasts.

By the mid-1970s, *All Things Considered* enjoyed the largest audience of any noncommercial radio program in U.S. history (Douglas 2004, 320–21). Both *ATC* and *ME* became recognized for their reporting that, like some of the dramatic World War II broadcasts of the 1940s, symbolically brought the audience into the scene through the use of natural sounds and conversations on location. In its early days, NPR demonstrated a willingness to take on or even dwell on events that other venues would not touch or fully address. For example, in 1978, it became the first network to air a Senate debate live. Soon afterward, instead of furnishing quick daily wrap-ups of the Iran-Contra Scandal (see **Political Scandals**), NPR supplied hours of live coverage of the hearings. Although this comprehensive approach continues to characterize NPR, some critics claim that its investigative reporting and proclivity for treating controversial issues has weakened over the years, largely due to decreased government funding and the subsequent growth of corporate sponsorship. (Although NPR does not allow full-length, traditional commercials, it has increasingly permitted advertisers to receive on-air mentions.) They state that NPR is no longer eager to take risks for fear of losing a major source of financial support or alienating conservative politicians who can squeeze its share of the federal budget. They also question whether the network's broadly viewed left-of-center reputation still rings true and if it, in fact, represents a choice that is fundamentally different from commercial media. Others counter that, despite its limitations, NPR features a wider range of voices than those heard on privately owned radio stations.

THE FUTURE OF RADIO

Despite dramatic changes in the media environment since its inception, radio has adapted every time it was threatened and maintained its vitality. But the current array of emerging new media pose perhaps the greatest challenge traditional radio has ever faced. As digital broadcast radio, direct satellite radio, and the Internet continue to evolve, people will have hundreds or even a seemingly limitless number of channels and other options from which to choose. The capacity already exists—with MP3 files, on-demand programming, and other developing technologies—for audience members to listen to whatever they want, when they want. Media convergence through digitalization allows operations that have not been in the audio business, such as newspaper Web sites, to add to the fray. This also means, conversely, that standard radio broadcasters will have the ability to transmit text, pictures, and video to their listeners.

What impact the new media will have on public radio, which has customarily taken its responsibility to serve the public interest more seriously than its commercial competitors, is of special concern to academics. Some observers say that because public radio has built a significantly strong niche audience, it might hold onto its loyal base by simply doing more of what it does best through additional modes of delivery. They caution, though, that public radio must retain its commitment to public service and not parrot commercial stations if it hopes to survive. More broadly, scholars wonder what influence new media will have on the notion of the public interest in general. Optimistic critics contend that, however the aural landscape plays out, there will be more program diversity than ever before, which will be greatly beneficial to the nation's state of democracy. In this proliferating media marketplace, people will be addressed not only as consumers but as citizens, thereby yielding a type of electronic public sphere. Perhaps the type of programming that advocates of micro-radio have called for will be realized on the Internet. More pessimistic scholars counter that, given radio's history and the country's deeply entrenched commercial media model, it is more likely that corporations will find methods for ensuring that the new forms of media remain friendly to the interests of advertisers and simply amplify the trends that have been in place for decades. In March 2007, for instance, a panel of judges raised the royalty charges that Internet stations playing music would have to pay. Immediately, hundreds of stations, many of which targeted small niche audiences interested in hearing material rarely heard on commercial outlets and were run by private citizens with their own money, closed down. In addition, the cost of satellite and Internet services, based on this school of thought, could prevent many people from fully enjoying the expanding selection of vehicles. The issue of "net neutrality" could become a factor as well. Presently, the Internet is democratic in its nature, regarding every source—whether individual or corporate—more or less equally. If net neutrality were to be undermined, however, some content providers would be treated more favorably than others through a fee arrangement. Those able to pay higher premiums would gain quicker and easier access to Internet users than those incapable of handling the costs. This development, skeptical critics contend, would render an Internet that to a large extent merely reflects the commercial arrangement that has prevailed throughout the country's media history, contributing little to a revitalized democracy. Moreover, satellite radio and the Internet are regulated differently than broadcast media and, at least for now, are under no obligation to satisfy the public interest. Consequently, so this argument goes, transmissions that reach out to marginalized groups and promote social justice causes will likely see little time of day. Many advocates of the current broadcasting system, on the other hand, declare that a reformed approach to new media is unnecessary because the traditional media structure has more than adequately addressed public interest concerns through free market forces. Ultimately, they say, the audience votes for what it wants by listening to material that meets its needs and disregarding the rest. In a democracy, the majority should rule and the industry should not be required to appeal to unprofitable segments of the population.

One development that almost all analysts would agree on, however, is that digitization will ensure radio will be more interactive and conform less to the one-way transmission model that has characterized broadcast radio since its infancy. This in itself, some would state, is good for democracy. Today, there are already Internet radio operators supplying content meant to cultivate civic participation. What forms radio takes in the future and to what degree they democratically serve the citizenry remain questions for vigorous speculation.

FURTHER READING

Barnouw, Erik. *Tube of Plenty: The Evolution of American Television*. 2nd rev. ed. New York: Oxford University Press, 1990. (The first two chapters provide an excellent history of radio.)

Craig, Douglas B. *Fireside Politics: Radio and Political Culture in the United States, 1920–1940*. Baltimore: John Hopkins University Press, 2000.

Douglas, Susan J. *Listening In: Radio and the American Imagination*. Minneapolis: University Press of Minnesota, 2004.

Hilmes, Michele. *Radio Voices: American Broadcasting, 1922–1952*. Minneapolis: University of Minnesota Press, 1997.

Hilmes, Michele, and Jason Loviglio (eds.). *Radio Reader: Essays in the Cultural History of Radio*. New York: Routledge, 2002. (See, especially, Chapters 1–3, 8, 10, 11, 13, 16–19, 21, 23, and 24.)

Horten, Gerd. *Radio Goes to War: The Cultural Politics of Propaganda during World War II*. Berkeley: University Press of California, 2002.

McChesney, Robert W. *Telecommunications, Mass Media, and Democracy: The Battle for Control of U.S. Broadcasting, 1928–1935*. New York: Oxford University Press, 1993.

Steinberg, Jaques. "Talking Politics, Drawing Viewers." *New York Times*, December 23, 2007, 34.

Walker, Jesse. *Rebels on the Air: An Alternative History of Radio in America*. New York: New York University Press, 2001.

Chapter 4

Politics and Television Entertainment

If radio, throughout its history, has involved a protracted political battle between profit-seeking corporations and the democratic forces of everyday people for control over the airwaves (see Chapter 3), then television has not followed suit. Although it took dozens of years after its birth for business interests to prevail in dominating the radio environment, television in the United States was a commercial enterprise right from the start. Indeed, as television made its way into the living rooms of American homes, it immediately adopted the economic model, based on the financial support of advertisers, that radio had already established through trial and error.

The development of television had begun well before it became a fixture in the lives of U.S. citizens, however. Because so many people were involved, both explicitly and indirectly, in bringing television to fruition, it is difficult to point to one inventor of the medium. Technological innovations that were necessary for the creation of television were already occurring in the nineteenth century. Yet it would take decades for television to come to realization.

Perhaps the first significant event to widely demonstrate TV's potential was NBC's broadcast of the opening of the World's Fair in New York on April 30, 1939. Franklin Delano Roosevelt gave the welcoming address, making him the first incumbent president to ever appear on television. (Before he became president, Secretary of Commerce Herbert Hoover had presented a speech on an experimental telecast in 1927.) Two years later, though, the screens went almost entirely dark. With the outbreak of World War II, the television industry deemed it futile to roll out a major innovation for a distracted population.

Once the war had concluded, television enjoyed a rebirth and quickly picked up steam. Probably the first major attempt to broadcast a regularly scheduled series can be traced to 1946, when NBC introduced a variety show called *Hour Glass*, which ran for 10 months. Yet overall, the network shows and reception signals paled in comparison to today's expectations. Still, a threshold had been reached. In 1947, the opening of Congress was telecast for the first time. By the end of 1951, a coast-to-coast infrastructure was in place. In 1948, less than 1 percent of the homes in the United States had owned a television. Five years later, in 1953, the percentage had bounded toward 50 percent. By 1960, nearly 90 percent of households had purchased a television.

THE COMMERCIAL MODEL: DEMOCRATICALLY SERVING "THE PEOPLE" OR BENDING TO CORPORATE AMERICA?

Although news often obviously taps into political content, programming that is commonly regarded as sheer entertainment can carry political implications as well. (For a full discussion of television news, see Chapter 5.) As television usurped the dominant role that radio had played in the culture, it also appropriated the advertising supported economic system that its forbearer had crystallized. Consequently, from a political perspective, since the very origins of television as a mass phenomenon, the influence of advertising has had a considerable impact on the type of content the medium has generally broadcast, often reflecting the interests of big business more than offering a marketplace of ideas that, according to the spirit of the First Amendment, is fundamental to the needs of a democracy. Advertisers demand not only high ratings, but also a symbolic climate that is suitable for the promotion of goods and services. Accordingly, advertisers usually frown upon any kind of content that generates controversy, challenges fundamental assumptions about U.S. culture, or triggers deep contemplation. For the advertising industry, risk is, to a large extent, a four-letter word.

The Roots of Advertising's Influence on Programming

The prominent media historian Erik Barnouw once explained how advertising began to shape the nature of programming during the early days of television, a pattern that has mostly been followed ever since. A variety of early dramas, including a number of those carried by such notable anthology series as *Kraft Television Theater* (1947–1958), *Philco Television Playhouse* (1948–1955), *Goodyear Television Playhouse* (1951–1960), *Omnibus* (1953–1957), and *Playhouse 90* (1956–1961), addressed, in a profound manner, some of the troubling issues that ordinary people confronted in everyday life. These shows, telecast live, resonated with audiences and achieved high ratings. "But one group hated them" (1990, 163), Barnouw stated: the advertising industry. As he put it:

> Most advertisers were selling magic. Their commercials posed the same problems that Chayefsky [one of the renowned television writers who worked within the genre] drama dealt with: people who feared failure in love and in business. But in the commercials there was always a solution as clear-cut as the snap of a finger: the problem could be solved by a new pill, deodorant, toothpaste … or floor wax….
> … [T]he "marvelous world of the ordinary" seemed to challenge everything that advertising stood for. (1990, 163)

Eventually, faced with criticism from its sponsors, television executives learned an important lesson that still guides industry leaders today. Decision makers must balance the wishes of the audience with the demands of the advertisers that fund the programming. Television fare that highlights economic problems or has other political implications is almost always anathema. Beginning in the 1950s, then, to ensure lines were not crossed, interference from advertisers, such as involvement with script changes, became commonplace. Then again, partly because broadcasters have been charged by the Federal Communications Commission (FCC) to serve the public interest, some challenging programming inevitably slips through the cracks.

On the other hand, there are certain entertainment formats that advertisers are very willing to back. "Law and order" dramas, for example, especially those that reinforce the U.S. legal system, have been acceptable ever since television first began broadcasting in earnest. Westerns that mythologized the American frontier, including *Cheyenne* (1955–1963), *Gunsmoke* (1955–1975), and *Maverick* (1957–1962), proliferated during the 1950s and remained popular in the first half of the 1960s. This genre, too, had no difficulty finding support from advertisers.

From Sponsorship to "Spot" Advertising.   Yet early on, just as had been the case with radio, advertisers not only sponsored shows, but oversaw production as well. Because of this arrangement, advertisers could directly mold programming to their benefit. The event that led to the demise of advertising-produced programming was the "Quiz Show Scandal." Shows with high payouts, such as *The $64,000 Question* (1955–1958), drew sensational ratings and captivated millions of viewers. Yet in 1959, a black cloud was cast over the television industry when it came out that some of these shows were being rigged in the service of advertisers. Designated contestants, chosen for their audience appeal in hope of maximizing ratings, were being fed answers—and even coached on how to credibly deliver their replies—in advance of the contests. As the scandal came to a head, congressional hearings into the situation were launched. The public, which, in general, trusted in television with a type of naiveté, given the medium's rapid growth and almost magical quality, was disillusioned. One result was that television executives mostly replaced the quiz shows with other programming. But the larger outcome—one that had a major impact on television's very structure—was that the networks soon disallowed advertisers to be considerably in charge of program production and scheduling. Instead, to ensure a higher degree of integrity, they indicated that they would themselves oversee the creation and scheduling of all the shows in the TV lineup. But to continue to receive the financial support of advertisers, the networks fully implemented an economic model that was already in motion: they would welcome advertisers to insert short commercials into the breaks between shows or during the programs themselves. Known as "spot advertising," it satisfied both the networks' need for funding as well as the advertisers' desire to market their products through the airwaves. This quid pro quo arrangement between the advertisers and the networks and stations has been in place ever since.

Political Critiques of Commercial Television

In general, a television station or network seeks to balance its drive to maximize profit with the need to satisfy the government's FCC's requirement that it must serve the public interest if it hopes to hold onto its license. The former goal is usually pursued through the broadcasting of entertainment programming while the latter is most often met with news and other public affairs offerings. Most observers would contend that the "serious" formats receive short shrift in comparison to shows and programs that focus on various types of amusement. Because of this perception, ever since the first mass telecasts, television has garnered more than its share of rebuke. Critics argue that by putting the accent on "mindless" fare, television is not giving people enough worthwhile information and is therefore shortchanging democracy. They feel that the FCC has rarely done more than pay lip service to ensuring that broadcasters promote the public interest. Such a harsh evaluation was exemplified in 1961 by then FCC chairman Newton N. Minow, who proclaimed that television was a "vast wasteland." His words have been echoed through the years in one way or another by scores of detractors. Yet others counter that this stance is elitist—the television industry is simply providing the populace with what it wants. They reason that high ratings indicate a vote of confidence in a show. On the other hand, if people are tuning out, then a program is cancelled. Accordingly, they say, the television business is especially honoring the spirit of democracy.

Cable TV: Expanding Commercial Communication

Until the 1970s, the television industry was dominated by just three national networks: CBS, NBC, and ABC. Most people received "free" (besides the cost of a television set and electricity there were no other direct charges) programming through the airwaves via the antennas that were already installed on their TVs. Cable television initially emerged mainly to bring station feeds to rural homes that were out of range of broadcast signals.

But eventually cable sought to extend its reach. Thus began the gradual loosening of the traditional broadcast networks' lock on power, as more and more viewers subscribed to cable services. Broadcast network ratings started to decline, a tendency that has continued until the present. Today, audiences have dozens, sometimes even hundreds, of channels from which to pick. Nor is cable the only option— direct satellite television, videotape or DVD rentals, and even programming available on the Internet and cell phone have further weakened the relatively long reign of CBS, NBC, and ABC.

When cable first burst onto the scene, many advocates declared that, in breaking apart the broadcast network oligarchy, it would function as a force for democracy by providing viewers with far more choices. Moreover, the possibility existed that cable fees could reduce the need for funding from advertisers, therefore enabling "the people" to have more influence over industry programming decisions than sponsors. Yet commercialization crept into cable right from the start. Currently, besides the "premium" channels, such as HBO and Showtime, cable channels are laden with advertisements. Critics pronounce that the spread of advertising and other recent pro-business policies have undermined any democratic potential cable represented. Instead, they claim, the proliferation of channels has merely reinforced the advertising supported economic model that had already been implemented and has generated only more of the same kind of programming that had become standard fare. In short, the debate about whether television either extends or emasculates the democratic impulse continues.

Educational and Noncommercial Television

Of course, public television offers viewers an alternative to the standard formats that commercial television typically delivers. From television's birth, numerous parties were interested in the possibility of using the medium as a vehicle for education. Yet television was so dominated by commercial interests that educational goals were largely shoved to the side. In the 1950s, most attempts to promote noncommercial, educational television were largely futile.

Interestingly, when television was first introduced into other Western nations, it was regarded as a public resource—commercialism came later. Yet in the United States, the tables were flipped: it would be years before public television finally took its place beside its commercial counterparts. In November 1967, backed by President **Lyndon Johnson**, the Corporation for Public Broadcasting was legally established. In the beginning, public television was funded mostly through government subsidies and viewer donations. A major part of its mission involved devoting far more attention to serving the public interest than the advertising-supported networks appeared to be doing. To this end, emphasis was placed on program diversity and reaching particular groups, including traditionally marginalized populations, whose needs were not being satisfied by commercial offerings designed to appeal to massive audiences.

In its early years, public television indeed featured more controversial fare than that typically seen through commercial channels. Makers of documentaries, in particular, turned to public television as a fertile venue for nonfiction films that challenged conventional views. Moreover, freed from the tyranny of maximizing ratings, it could set aside considerable time for public affairs coverage. During the **Watergate** crisis, for example, public television was able to air the congressional hearings live during the daytime and repeat the presentations at night—something that commercial television could in no way duplicate. Because many citizens were highly engaged in learning about the scandal (in a sense, making Watergate a popular culture event), the extended, live broadcasts breathed new life into public television. Stirring up the waters continued into the following decade. In 1988–1989, for instance, the four-part PBS (Public Broadcasting Service) series *Secret Intelligence* bravely revealed the covert and unsavory practices of the CIA since its founding in 1947.

Entertainment shows on public television also sometimes pushed the envelope by tackling risky themes. For example, launched in 1971, *The Great American Dream Machine* (1971–1972), which consisted of a string of short comedic scenarios, was iconoclastic in lampooning government activities. The political satire was so biting that it evoked angry cries in Washington.

Such heated rebuke was not unusual—in fact, public television has never been immune from political pressures. Like commercial television, which relies on the FCC for licensing, public television is dependent on the government—but to a much greater extent because Washington furnishes it with much of the money it needs for its very survival. Thus, public television must generally avoid broadcasting programs that might trigger too much hostility from political authorities and jeopardize its funding. From time to time, government officials, especially on the conservative end of the spectrum, have threatened to reduce financial backing or eliminate public television entirely. In 1995, for example, Republican Speaker of the House Newt Gingrich announced his intention to tighten up the purse strings in retaliation for PBS's perceived liberal bias.

Today, PBS documentary series such as *Frontline* (1983–present) and *P.O.V.* (1988–present) still treat topics that commercial stations usually will not touch. Yet critics charge that even these high-minded programs tend to play it safe.

They argue that not only the fear of political backlash but also the increased influence of corporate benefactors has compelled PBS to become more inhibited over the years. When public television was initially established, it strove to maintain a commercial-free environment. But facing constant economic difficulties, public television eventually invited, with growing regularity, corporations to sponsor shows. Along the way, PBS allowed advertising to creep into its programming. At first, corporate promotions consisted of brief oral announcements with minimal visual support (nor could companies directly pitch specific products). Currently, what could only be identified as full-fledged commercials commonly appear in between programs. PBS is by no means as commercially driven as its competitors; yet, like its advertising-based competition, it cannot altogether avoid the temptation to "soften" its lineup to appease its sponsors. Some observers bemoan this state of affairs, contending that PBS has started to resemble the commercial networks. Others counter that perhaps public television has run its course, given that its ratings continue to decline and that cable networks, such as the Discovery Channel and Bravo, now occasionally provide the same kind of information and formats that formerly could be found only on PBS. More than ever, public television is struggling to retain its distinctiveness and demonstrate that it is worth saving.

Alternative Media, Noncommercial Television, and Voices of Dissent.   At the same time, though, given that television is not monolithic but a complex institution, perspectives that challenge dominant points of view occasionally surface. During the Vietnam era, for instance, some forms of noncommercial television (and even commercial television for that matter), including National Education Television (NET), a forerunner of PBS, offered words and images of dissent. In 1967, the Ford Foundation funded the creation of the Public Broadcast Laboratory (PBL), which launched a series of shows that were made available to dozens of educational television stations across the country. PBL programming gave voice to the nation's subculture, accenting themes that commercial networks typically disregarded. Today, vehicles such as the current affairs program *Democracy Now* (the show started on radio in 1996, then eventually joined television as well), owned by the Downtown Community Television Center (DCTV), are distributed to generally low-rated educational or otherwise noncommercial cable stations for small audiences that wish to view controversial material they usually cannot find elsewhere.

MCCARTHYISM

The meddling of advertisers was not the only factor that, early on, encouraged the television industry to drain its programming of controversial political inferences. Although the end of World War II brought peace to the nation, a new, "softer" conflict emerged, one that would be waged more through symbolism and propaganda than with arms. The "Cold War" between the United States and the Soviet Union would guide foreign policy decisions and be embedded in the American conscience for decades, finally coming to a close with the fall of the Berlin Wall in Germany in 1989. The atmosphere surrounding the perceived Soviet communist threat had a profound impact on the entertainment industries, including television. In October 1947, a new government formation, the House Committee on Un-American Activities, opened proceedings in regard to the purported influence of communism in

Hollywood. Months later, a group of writers was charged with contempt of Congress for refusing to answer questions posed by the committee. All of them served time in prison. Soon, a blacklist was developed to identify anybody suspected of harboring communist sympathies. Any person included in this secret list generally found it impossible to find work in the entertainment industries.

Hollywood was the first media field to face investigations into possible links to communism. Soon, however, the world of broadcasting was confronted as well. The "witch-hunt" gained momentum entering the 1950s. A publisher created by three former FBI agents followed up an earlier document with the release of *Red Channels: The Report of Communist Influence in Radio and Television*, which, often based on exceedingly indirect or flimsy evidence, identified 151 communist sympathizers who were infiltrating the broadcast industry. Many of the people on the list were noted celebrities, including Lucille Ball (fortunately for her, she was one of the lucky ones to ultimately be "cleared" of posing a threat). Being implicated in any number of politically "liberal" actions, including such seemingly minor incidents as formerly opposing one of the fascist leaders in World War II or currently resisting race discrimination, could land a person on the roll.

Into the fray stormed a U.S. Senator from Wisconsin, **Joseph R. McCarthy**, after whom the movement to purge communist leanings from the nation would eventually be named. McCarthy became the symbolic leader of the mission, bringing his zeal to a cause that already smacked of paranoia.

Throughout the era of McCarthyism, the blacklists were carefully shielded from view and the procedures used to flush out "controversial" figures were especially furtive. Faced with ruin, some artists even took their own lives, including Philip Loeb, star of *The Goldbergs* (1949–1954), who, after the cancellation of the show due to his name's appearance in the pages of *Red Channels*, overdosed on sleeping pills. The chilling effect of McCarthyism was pervasive. Writers and their superiors were averse to taking on any risky subject matter.

One of the developments that possibly contributed to McCarthy's downfall was **Edward R. Murrow**'s investigative coverage of the senator and his tactics on the CBS news show *See It Now* (1952–1955). Soon after a series of episodes on the theme, hearings involving a dispute between the army and McCarthy were also televised. In his testimony, McCarthy conveyed a repugnant image. Following the proceedings, the Senate voted to condemn McCarthy, 67 to 22.

Yet McCarthyism did not vanish right away, even after the senator's death in 1957. Television professionals continued to suffer the loss of viable careers if they became even loosely linked with communism through often dubious evidence. The McCarthyism era finally came to a close shortly after John Henry Faulk, who had worked for CBS radio as a disk jockey and had made frequent appearances on CBS television, won a lawsuit against an organization (and affiliated individuals) that was yet committed to rooting out the communist threat it felt still existed. After the June 1962 ruling, numerous artists who had been blacklisted began to resurface, and issues that earlier would have been seen as too risky were now more apt to receive attention.

THE INFLUENCE OF THE GOVERNMENT ON PROGRAMMING

McCarthyism represents an example of government officials putting acute pressure on the media industries to tame their programming. Yet the government in general has a certain degree of influence over content decisions. Although it rarely directly censors television shows (some wartime news coverage being one exception), the government can apply its authority in more subtle ways. For instance, because television stations must obtain and renew their licenses through the FCC and abide by its regulations, television executives are leery of broadcasting anything that might deeply offend the government.

The government has seldom overtly meddled into entertainment programming in particular. On occasion, however, especially during the early days of television, certain shows that received airtime were in fact created by government agencies or at least had officials involved as advisors or in helping out in other capacities. For example, produced by the Department of Defense, *The Armed Forces Hour* (1951) featured short films and musical performances by members of the military that served to promote the armed forces. Retired Rear Admiral Ellis M. Zacharias served as technical consultant for *Behind Closed Doors* (1956–1959), a spy drama based on actual episodes of Zacharias's experience in naval intelligence. Conceived by Lieutenant Carl Bruton, *The Big Picture* (1953–1959) was a U.S. Army documentary series that enjoyed a particularly long run and was well received by many viewers. *I Led Three Lives* (1953–1956), based on the book of the same name by former FBI spy Herbert A. Philbrick, functioned as anti-Communist propaganda. Philbrick himself worked on the show as a technical consultant. Moreover, FBI Director J. Edgar Hoover added his implicit endorsement—each script was sent to his agency for approval before production.

Again, though, such direct government intervention into television entertainment is rare. Symbolic support for government policies and activities is generally indirect, emerging from what some scholars argue is the medium's ideological tendencies (see "Television and Ideology" below). On the other hand, U.S. officials have probably been more influential in shaping the role that television has played in other countries.

Television and Foreign Propaganda

Sometimes the U.S. government has directly promoted the distribution of media products abroad. For example, in the 1950s, the U.S. Information Agency (USIA) began supplying emerging television stations in over 15 countries with American films. In this manner, the United States was subtly fostering the spread of the nation's worldview, thus implementing a type of propaganda program. In particular, within a Cold War climate, the films were meant to counteract the extension of communism. The secretary of state at this time, John Foster Dulles, was instrumental in exploiting the media, both domestically and internationally, to position the U.S. capitalist and democratic approach to life as superior to anything communism had to offer. The secretary of state became a recognizable television personality, even inspiring the comedian and actress Carol Burnett to sing a humorous tribute to him, which was called "I Made a Fool of Myself over John Foster Dulles," on an episode of *The Jack Paar Show* (1957–1962).

Cultural Imperialism.   Yet the influence of U.S. media on other parts of the world has not always been a result of direct government intervention. More often, it has been a by-product of companies involved in the U.S. media industry simply seeking greater profits by moving into foreign territory. As European nations and other countries began developing their own television systems, they were frequently willing to buy

U.S. shows instead of broadcasting their own because they could save money. The American interests that owned the programming had already reaped handsome returns domestically—consequently, they were prepared to market their already completed high-quality shows for a price that the studios in the foreign nations, faced with the prospect of creating programs from scratch, could not match. Along the way, although it was not intentional, U.S. television fare functioned as propaganda by transmitting the "American Way of Life" into the homes of people throughout the world.

With American television came American advertising agencies, which increasingly set up branches abroad. Their clients, corporations based in the United States, were only too eager to gain tremendous access to foreign markets, enabling them to pitch their goods and services across the ocean. The U.S. government might not have been the key player in this expansion, but it was certainly sympathetic to it, seeing it as a means of further halting communism in its tracks. Accordingly, the government initiated aid programs that facilitated the process.

As this scenario unfolded, cries of American cultural imperialism, the tendency to undermine a country's symbolic environment by imposing one's own, were sounded by artists, teachers, and other critics outside the United States, an accusation that continues to this day. In an attempt to stem the flow of U.S. media products, foreign governments applied various measures, yet could not prevent American television from gaining a significant foothold. Many opponents feared that, with its wealth, media dominance, and military might, the United States would remake the world in its own image.

Not everyone was opposed to the cultural "invasion," however. Entrepreneurs, advertising agencies, and numerous other proponents have argued that international audiences are well served by the media vehicles that the United States, with its abundance of talent and resources, can produce. Moreover, they caution, just because citizens in foreign nations are viewing American shows does not mean that they are turning into "Americans"—different people evoke different meanings based on the cultural lenses through which they screen them. Worldwide distribution of television programs does not inevitably lead to worldwide homogenization. Furthermore, those who dismiss protests of cultural imperialism say, cultural currents travel in both directions. The recent integration of Latin and African sounds into some of the popular music produced in the United States is a case in point. Cultures have been intermixing and affecting one another throughout the millennia.

TELEVISION AND IDEOLOGY

Numerous media scholars argue that nearly every product of the mass media—especially television—has political implications. According to this line of reasoning, by emphasizing certain depictions while leaving out others, television and other forms of media tend to convey messages that sustain the status quo. In this manner, they claim, television indirectly fulfills an ideological role. The concept of ideology, as used by academics in media studies and cultural studies, is concerned with the deep-rooted, shared beliefs and values that define a culture, endorse a particular worldview, and cultivate an approach to living that maintains the current distribution of power in society. The "dominant" ideology is that to which most people subscribe, even though it benefits those in positions of cultural authority (i.e., government leaders and corporate leaders) more than everyday citizens. In other words, the circulation of dominant ideology helps to prevent ordinary men and women from resisting the current state of affairs. The primary way in which television inadvertently facilitates this ideological feat is by rarely challenging viewers to bring to mind fundamental questions about the very structure of society. Instead, taken for granted assumptions (for example, capitalism is the best economic system on earth or the United States has established a model of democracy that all other nations should follow) are continuously reinforced. The undesirable consequences of the nation's executed policies (for instance, families struggling with poverty or covert military operations in foreign countries) receive far less attention. From this vantage point, even the most "mindless" situation comedy or "escapist" drama contributes to preserving the American Way of Life by perpetuating a sense of cultural equilibrium and not giving a platform for voices of dissent. In most cases, a show's part in this scenario is hardly obvious.

Reflecting the Political Climate of the Times

Yet some programs have more plainly served an ideological function. Seldom do television producers intentionally seek to convey propagandistic messages. Rather, the process is more subtle. By simply reflecting the political climate of the time and operating within the economic structure of the television industry, they inadvertently create programming that tends to reinforce status quo perspectives.

The spy genre is a case in point. In the mid-1960s, stories centered on espionage burst onto the American airwaves. At this time, citizens were starting to learn about covert CIA involvement in clandestine affairs abroad, including its role in a coup in Iran that established the Shah as its leader (ultimately leading to negative consequences when the Shah was finally overthrown at the beginning of the **Iran Hostage Crisis** in 1979) and the Bay of Pigs invasion in Cuba. These disclosures were upsetting to a portion of the populace because they flew in the face of the image of the United States as only an agent of benevolence in the world. Through sheer repetition and by conveying the theme that some threats were so fierce that they demanded underhanded response, spy stories, in a sense, presented the opportunity for viewers to come to terms with the idea that government organizations were engaged in secret—and possibly morally dubious—behavior.

In general, the spy programs emphasized that there were demonic, conspiratorial forces that had to be eradicated, even by ignoble means if necessary. In short, good (the United States) must ultimately triumph over evil (the nation's enemies). Along the way, the spy series justified the use of deception. A somewhat similar type of programming resurfaced in the 1980s during the presidency of Ronald Reagan, who frequently engaged in intense Cold War rhetoric and endorsed a number of military interventions in Latin American nations to stop the supposed spread of communism.

The Vietnam War supplied another context in which shows could indirectly affirm foreign intervention to halt the communist menace. Although few programs specifically turned to Vietnam as a setting, a number of shows in fact highlighted military ventures, usually drawing from World War II, a less controversial conflict, to provide a dramatic or comedic backdrop. Most likely, television insiders were not furtively and deliberately endorsing government policies, merely reflecting them.

Throughout the 1960s, though, there was an almost surreal juxtaposition between the real world events on the ground and the images presented by television entertainment. The Civil Rights Movement, the Vietnam War and its accompanying protests, and the Women's Liberation Movement contrasted sharply with TV programs such as *My Mother the Car* (1965–1966) and *F Troop* (1965–1967). Broadcast news could not avoid coverage of the various forms of strife that were manifesting themselves across the country. But when it came to prime time television, the cultural disruptions were almost entirely absent from the screen. Some critics would charge that television was, again, inadvertently performing an ideological function by celebrating the American Way of Life and diverting attention from issues of political import, thus enabling those in the positions of power to go about their business without worrying about encountering overwhelming resistance from the public. Many television advocates, on the other hand, would say that, after a day of work and other stresses, the typical person does not seek to be reminded of unpleasant, real life affairs; instead, he or she turns to the television for escape and relaxation. In this sense, once more, television is merely giving viewers what they want.

Going against the Grain.   Interestingly, some popular television entertainment in the 1970s actually challenged fundamental American assumptions that had held sway for so long. Perhaps, if they hoped to stay pertinent, broadcasters could no longer avoid reflecting the turmoil that had made its imprint on the culture. One program, ***All in the Family*** (1971–1983), especially stood out, as it took on issues of bigotry, sexism, and other controversies. Yet instead of driving viewers away with its frank portrayals, as those who contend that audiences desire only simplistic fare might predict, it received very high ratings, even climbing to number one on the charts and generating various spin-offs, including ***Maude*** (1972–1978). Other shows hesitantly followed suit, allowing greater inclusion for people of color, homosexuals, and other marginalized groups. Over the years, "relevant" programming—from the socially conscious *Welcome Back, Kotter* (1975–1979) and *Barney Miller* (1975–1982) in the 1970s and early 1980s, to today's multifaceted *Law & Order* (1990–present)—has offered not only engaging entertainment but opportunities for reflection as well.

Recent Ideological Trends

Still, throughout television history, this type of programming has hardly been the norm. Most of the time, television entertainment has tended to shy away from formats that ask people to consider difficult truths. For instance, just as spy stories in the 1960s gave indirect justification for covert government activity, today, according to various critics, certain entertainment programs inadvertently make disturbing behavior seem more palatable. Since President George W. Bush declared a "War on Terror" after the September 11, 2001, terrorist attacks on New York City and the Pentagon, a number of revelations have surfaced that many people find troubling. For example, investigative reporters have exposed the use of torture by U.S. soldiers and the CIA's role in "extraordinary rendition," a process that involves captives suspected of illicit and dangerous transgressions being piloted to nations known for their abusive treatment of prisoners. Well before these and other alarming leaks had emerged, the U.S. government had already upset many people around the world by creating and supporting the operation of a makeshift detainee center in Guantá-namo Bay, Cuba. Hundreds of alleged enemy combatants had been rounded up and deposited there and, running counter to traditional U.S. justice procedures, were neither officially charged with a crime nor given the hope of a trial.

Within this political atmosphere arose movies and television programs that featured torture as a perhaps unfortunate, yet necessary means toward a worthy end. The TV show that probably best exemplifies the trend is *24*, which first aired in November 2001, only two months after the brutal 9/11 terrorist attacks. Having achieved notable popularity, it is still running today as this book goes to press. Clearly reflecting the "War on Terror," *24*'s hero, Jack Bauer (played by Kiefer Sutherland), a "Counter-Terrorism Unit" expert, routinely strives to prevent an array of especially catastrophic terrorist threats to the nation. Furthermore, acts of torture, committed by U.S. agents against monstrous enemies, frequently enter into the scenario. Seen through the lens of ideology, these representations, according to many scholarly observers, indirectly justify the use of otherwise objectionable (and probably illegal) violence when the situation demands it. At the same time, then, they circuitously sanction the questionable policies and activities of the government. Other post-9/11 series, such as *The Shield* (2003–2008) and *Lost* (2004–present), have also incorporated into their narratives portrayals of torture to ensure that "good" triumphs over "evil."

The Ideology of Consumerism

Another common ideological message that television continuously conveys, critics point out, is the attractiveness of consumerism, that is, the continuous buying and using up of products. Because of the economic structure of television, which is rooted in the monetary support of advertisers, the industry is compelled to offer programming that provides a climate suitable to the promotion of goods and services. Media content analyses have consistently demonstrated that the world of television is disproportionately populated by characters who are financially well off (see "Television and Socioeconomic Class" below). Rarely do themes center on, for example, the real life issues of living paycheck to paycheck, losing a job, or coping with poverty. From this perspective, not only do the commercials endorse the accumulation of merchandise—the shows themselves also reinforce the pursuit. On the other hand, the negative consequences of rampant consumerism—environmental damage, the exploitation of low wage workers, and so on—receive little play. Politically, the concerns of big business are symbolically served more than those of the millions of everyday citizens who do not reap their share of the benefits of capitalist enterprise.

The Impact of Ideology

Other critiques have focused on the notion that television, as a constant source of amusement, distracts people from engaging in the sort of political activity that could help improve their lives. Rather than regularly drawing attention to government and corporate abuses that might challenge people to get involved in political affairs, television supplies endless entertainment that typically generates a passive state of mind.

Not every media scholar agrees with this assessment of television's ideological impact and political implications. Rather than assume television—or any form of mass media for that matter—is somehow manipulating or "brainwashing" citizens into adopting attitudes and behaving in ways that work against their best interests, many thinkers contend that viewers are in fact active and use the media on their own terms. To suggest that television is inducing a kind of hypnotic spell over people, one that undermines their ability to take full control of their lives, is, to these media researchers, to take an elitist and paternalistic stance. Expressing a more populist approach, they maintain that audiences are not hoodwinked by broadcasters but engage with television simply because they obtain, to one extent or another, satisfaction in it.

TELEVISION AND IDENTITY POLITICS

Similar to radio (see Chapter 3), in its early days and for years afterward (and, according to some critics, even today to some extent), television tended to marginalize certain groups in relationship to gender, race, and other distinctions. Many media scholars contend that this is an important point to consider when assessing television's political impact. Because of the medium's major presence, it plays a role in expressing cultural expectations about what people are (or should be) like. In this manner, television contributes to ways in which different types of people are perceived and form their own identities, a process that indeed has political implications.

Television and African Americans

When television first took root in people's homes, African Americans were dramatically underrepresented. Still, black performers were frequent guests on variety shows right from the start. Ed Sullivan, for instance, featured African Americans as early as 1948 in his show, *Toast of the Town* (later renamed *The Ed Sullivan Show* [1948–1971]). *Broadway Minstrels* (1948), originally described as an "all colored revue," was designed to be network television's first all-black show. After two weeks, however, white artists also came on the program, which was renamed *Broadway Jamboree*, and then cancelled in less than two months.

Usually, though, when they appeared on the screen, African Americans were portrayed in a stereotypical fashion. This pattern was exemplified by the situation comedy *Amos and Andy* (1951–1953). The show had already enjoyed a hugely popular run on radio. A pair of white men, Freeman Gosden and Charles Correll, had played the roles of the two lead African American characters, complete with "black accents." Yet putting black makeup on white men had become socially unacceptable after World War II. Thus, African Americans were cast for the show. But the demeaning depictions that Gosden and Correll had established were simply adopted by the black actors, Alvin Childress and Spencer Williams, Jr.

Yet the situation improved over time, particularly after the Civil Rights Movement of the 1960s. The television industry began to show more cultural sensitivity toward nonwhite people. Throughout the coming decades, African Americans were included in a number of TV series. Still, a lot of the characters they played were viewed by critics as "token" roles. Moreover, from the original release of *Amos and Andy* to 1984, only four other shows that aired on broadcast television for more than one season featured predominantly black casts—all of them were situation comedies.

Bill Cosby, though, made headway in *I Spy* (1965–1968), becoming the first black performer to star in a regularly scheduled dramatic series. African American Greg Morris soon followed suit, playing a lead character in another and especially popular spy series, *Mission Impossible* (1966–73). Another significant program was *Julia* (1968–1971), which represented the first time that a black female performer (Diahann Carroll) starred in her own series in a "respectable" role (she was a nurse instead of, for example, a domestic servant). Yet a number of critical viewers argued that the main character was merely a "white woman in dark skin." The show rarely alluded to the nation's racial problems. Nor did Julia interact with many black characters—she was fully integrated into the almost entirely white environment the show depicted.

In 1977, the miniseries *Roots*, about a man who was captured and sent to America to serve as a slave and the struggles of his descendants for emancipation, took the country by storm, with its final episode commanding the largest audience of any sponsored telecast up until that time. It compelled many of its approximately 100 million viewers to confront the history of the country's horrific practice of slavery. On the other hand, not everybody was enthusiastic about the drama. These people maintained that, with its ultimately uplifting ending, *Roots* only functioned to help whites purge their feelings of guilt without evoking any significant change.

The following decade, *The Cosby Show* (1984–1992) portrayed an upper-middle class, successful black family. The attractive and likeable clan was headed up by Cliff Huxtable (played by the renowned Bill Cosby), an obstetrician, and his wife, Clair (performed by Phylicia Rashad), an attorney. The situation comedy became a major hit, occupying the top spot in the ratings for years. Scores of fans celebrated the show because it went against the grain of traditional stereotypes and demonstrated that a largely white audience could identify with a black family. Others were less enamored with the program, saying that it misrepresented African Americans by not calling attention to the structural racism that prevented most black people from achieving high status in the country. They objected to the show's suggestion that if African Americans would only work hard enough, they too could be like the Huxtables, when, from these critics' point of view, such aspirations were an illusion for many.

Perhaps part of the problem was that, because there were still relatively few representations of African Americans on television, the image of the Huxtables came to symbolize the entire black population. From this perspective, what was desired was a range of depictions that recognized the diversity that existed among blacks. Put simply, there needed to be more shows centered on African Americans that collectively captured the full socioeconomic spectrum.

In fact, *The Cosby Show* did pave the way for the numerous primarily African American programs that followed, although these shows tended to entail only a limited range of African American representations. Today, the percentage of African American characters on television nearly parallels the proportion of the actual U.S. population composed of blacks. Yet they are still underrepresented in some formats, especially public affairs and advertising. Moreover, one of the main critiques waged by media scholars today is that, while overtly offensive depictions seldom occur, stereotypes are perpetuated in subtle ways. For example, African Americans are far more likely to appear in athletic or comedic roles than in "serious" ones. While black situation comedies pepper the programming lineup, an African American drama almost never emerges. Consequently, a black basketball player reinforces the distorted perception that African Americans are more physical than intellectual. And the focus on humor vaguely keeps alive the minstrel show tradition of the nineteenth and early twentieth centuries—in these variety acts, African Americans further darkened their faces—or sometimes, to appear as African Americans, whites darkened their faces—with makeup and performed grossly racist sketches for white onlookers. For some academics in media studies, the endless scenes of hip-hop "thugs," with their long chains, oversized clothes, and gold-plated teeth, also resurrect the minstrel show mentality.

Many observers point out that one major reason why African Americans and other people of color have been underrepresented and overly stereotyped is that television's labor force has traditionally been disproportionately white. Consequently, images of diverse groups have tended to be produced and viewed, so to speak, through a white lens. Over the course of television history, people of color have had less access to employment in the industry than their white competitors—especially in relationship to decision-making positions of power—although the situation for nonwhites continues to improve. Some scholars also believe a path toward more equitable portrayals of all races and ethnicities would involve a commitment to developing a wide range of multicultural programming aimed at children. The hope is that by exposing people to the full demographic spectrum of U.S. society, television could inspire greater acceptance of diversity at large.

Television and Native Americans

The treatment of people of color in general has followed a similar pattern as that for African Americans. Before the Civil Rights Movement and pressure from various political interest groups, nonwhites gained little inclusion on the screen and were usually stereotyped. With a few exceptions, for example, Native American men have been vastly underrepresented on television and often depicted as "noble savages" or mystical, "wise sages." The Western genre, a staple in the 1950s and 1960s, pictured white cowboys battling hostile and animalistic "Indians" who needed to be shoved aside in the name of progress. In these shows and others like them, Native American women were often presented either as self-sacrificing, princess-like Pocahontas figures or as sexually promiscuous "squaws."

Television and Latinos

Latino men have frequently been portrayed as lazy and clownish, or as "Latin lovers." The Western *The Cisco Kid* (1950–1956), a carryover from Hollywood films, for example, featured the lead character as a type of "bandito," while his sidekick, Poncho, expressed himself through a gross caricature of broken English. In *The Adventures of Kit Carson* (1951–1955), the hero's subordinate Mexican partner was actually played by a white actor. Another Western, *Zorro* (1957–1959), included a number of Mexicans, yet they generally served as villains or buffoons, or in minor roles. Another white actor fulfilled the part of a simpleminded Mexican on *The Bill Dana Show* (1963–1965). Dana's character, Jimenez, worked as a lovable but inept bellhop for a hotel.

The most prominent Latino actor in television's early days, though, was Desi Arnaz, who was Lucille Ball's husband, both in real life and in the hugely popular show *I Love Lucy* (1951–1961). To a large extent, Arnaz, who was Cuban, was actually presented in a positive way, albeit with a touch of the Latin lover quality. Still, when he lost his composure over Lucy's mishaps, he frequently descended into Spanish-speaking outbursts that conformed to stereotypical imagery.

For their part, Latinas were often relegated to disguising their cultural origins. What is more, when they were allowed to express their ethnic identities, it was frequently as the classic "luscious Latina" seductress.

Yet as the industry began to recognize the potential of the Latino market, circumstances slowly took a turn for the better. A greater number of programs in the 1970s and 1980s featured Latino roles—although they contained traces of earlier stereotypes, they did not perpetuate the crass caricatures of previous decades. Finally, in 2000, *The Brothers Garcia* was promoted as the first English-speaking situation comedy with an all-Latino cast and creative team. A show that garnered even more attention, however, was *The George Lopez Show* (2002–2007), starring the comedian by the same name. The series focused on the amusing adventures of Lopez, the manager of an airplane factory in California, and the rest of his Latino family. In 2006, America Ferrera was cast in the lead role in *Ugly Betty*, a spin-off of the Columbian telenovela, *Yo Soy Betty, la Fea* (I am Betty, the ugly one). The comedy centers on the less-than-glamorous Betty, who works in the pretentious world of fashion and struggles to fit in. Regarded as distinctive because of its offbeat quality, the show, which is still running, has received critical acclaim, including three Emmy awards in 2007.

Despite the gains Latinos have made on television, today they are still very underrepresented, especially given that their population now exceeds that of African Americans and is expected only to grow larger, partly due to the increasing flow of immigration from Mexico, Central America, and South America to the United States.

Television and Asian Americans

One of the common stereotypes of Asian Americans before television—and subsequently reinforced by the medium in its infancy—related to "the yellow peril," the idea that Asians are somehow a threat to the nation's culture. The portrayal, as is commonly the case, grew out of the political climate of certain periods, such as the resentment toward the large migration of Chinese into the country in the nineteenth century and the war with Japan in World War II. These depictions entailed shifty, diabolical Asian men whose heinous intentions must be stopped. On the other hand, Asian men have also often been pictured as asexual—rarely has an Asian male been cast in a romantic lead. Instead, they are seen as brainy and without physical attractiveness. Women, conversely, have been frequently represented as hypersexual, either as passive "China dolls" or as aggressive "Dragon ladies." Critics have also complained that Asians are too regularly associated with martial arts.

The initial Asian depictions on television occurred in 1949, on *Mysteries of Chinatown*. In this show, staring a white actor as Dr. Yat Fu, the "mysterious Asian" stereotype was prevalent. *The Adventures of Fu Manchu*, a rehash of earlier Hollywood films, came to the air in 1956 and lasted only one season. The nefarious Dr. Fu was clearly yet another manifestation of the dreaded yellow peril. The following year, the sexless Charlie Chan, also a character previously established in movies, came to the small screen in *The New Adventures of Charlie Chan*. Its main role played by a white actor, the show, too, lasted just one season.

The following decade, the adventure series *Hong Kong* (1960–1961) underlined the generalized perception of Asian men as devious and Asian women as sexy. In addition, the eventual legend Bruce Lee was cast in *The Green Hornet* (1966–1967). In this crime drama, Lee used his martial arts prowess to help bring criminals to justice. Interestingly, Lee was under the impression that he would play the lead role in another series focusing on an Asian environment, *Kung Fu* (1972–1975).

Yet the white actor David Carradine was hired for the role because, according to the show's producers, they felt a Chinese man could not be accepted as a hero by an American audience. Carradine's portrayal arguably perpetuated the caricature of the mysterious Asian male. Perhaps the program that offered the most complex representations of Asians was the police drama *Hawaii Five-O* (1968–1980). This long-running series probably conveyed hints of Asian stereotypes, yet included at least three Asian regulars who were not limited to the narrow symbolic confines once exhibited by Fu Manchu and Charlie Chan.

Still, even into the 1970s, the humble servant figure made its appearance from time to time. *Bachelor Father* (1957–1962) relied on an Asian "houseboy," *Bonanza* (1959–1973) included the Chinese cook, Hop Sing, and *The Courtship of Eddie's Father* (1969–1972) presented audiences with a docile Asian housekeeper in service to Eddie and his single father.

Asian Americans secured a larger number of supporting roles in the 1980s. Then, in 1987, Japanese American actor Pat Morita was cast in the lead role in the police detective series *Ohara* (1987–1988). The program was not free from stereotypes, however, as Ohara drew on mystical patience in pursuit of criminals and resorted to martial arts when the situation demanded it.

Another breakthrough was achieved in 1994, when the comedienne Margaret Cho acquired the principal part in *All-American Girl*. The situation comedy involved a culture clash between the assimilated Korean American girl Margaret Kim (Cho's role) and her mother who adamantly held to her traditional ways. This show offered sympathetic portrayals of Asian Americans yet lasted but one season.

One of the most well-known Asian American movie and television performers today is Lucy Liu, who starred in *Ally McBeal* (1997–2002) and episodes of *Ugly Betty*. Yet some media scholars illustrate that, even in the twenty-first century, Liu has a tendency to reinforce the dragon lady image. It appears that some stereotypes die hard. Moreover, Asian Americans continue to be underrepresented on U.S. television.

Television and Women

In 1978, Gaye Tuchman wrote an article, "The Symbolic Annihilation of Women by the Mass Media," that is still widely circulated today. In the piece, she argued that women were omitted, trivialized, and condemned in the media, including television. In short, women were represented less often than men and were too frequently portrayed as subordinate or in other inferior ways. For example, in early family situation comedies such as *I Married Joan* (1952–1954), *The Adventures of Ozzie & Harriet* (1952–1966), *Father Knows Best* (1954–1963), and *Leave It to Beaver* (1957–1963), women were inevitably positioned as housewives and mothers. Tuchman explained that, furthermore, when women were shown working, they usually labored in lower status jobs than their male counterparts and repeatedly displayed incompetence. A lot of evidence seems to support her position. In the 1950s through the 1970s, only 20–35 percent of speaking characters were female.

Yet even by the mid-1980s, more than twice as many men as women could be viewed on the small screen. Women were especially underutilized in dramas, while appearing more regularly on comedies. Still, similar to other marginalized groups, women made gains over time and improvement continues today. Just as the Civil Rights Movement challenged the media in terms of race, the Women's Liberation

Movement of the late 1960s and 1970s called into question the traditional expecta-tions associated with women. One program that seemed to lead the way was *The Mary Tyler Moore Show* (1970–1977). The actress after whom the situation com-edy was named played Mary Richards, a single career woman who worked as an associate producer for a local news broadcast. In a sense, she symbolized the image of the independent woman that had a degree of cultural resonance in the 1970s. On the other hand, she had to meet the demands of her male superiors, especially the gruff head producer, Lou Grant. Several years later, the police drama *Cagney & Lacey* (1982–1988) was significant in that it demonstrated a "buddy" series starring two women in typically male roles could attain popularity.

In the 1990s, *Ally McBeal* (1997–2002) generated considerable attention from media scholars for its gender portrayals. The show was lauded for revolving around the life of a successful female lawyer. Yet critics also countered that the main char-acter was still stereotypically desperate for a man. Moreover, the actress in the lead role, Calista Flockhart, paid no service to women wishing to escape from the cul-ture's dominant standard of beauty—she was utterly thin, even, some suspected, anorexic. Another series that sparked a wide and passionate following was *Sex in the City* (1998–2004). Too racy for commercial television, the situation comedy was carried by the premium cable network HBO (although a sanitized version of the series continues to circulate via syndication). The show was notably provocative for its strong, professionally employed female characters who engaged with explic-itly sexual themes and undermined traditional gender stereotypes. The program was not immune from criticism, however—a number of observers claimed it promoted the idea that women could achieve full equality with men only through the savvy use of their bodies, thus buttressing the perception of women as sex objects. Compared to their predecessors from the situation comedies of the 1950s, however, these women had truly come a long way.

But most academics of television would state that, overall, programming only rarely fundamentally challenges the gender roles that are broadly accepted in the culture. No doubt, women are more likely to be as intelligent and talented as men than they were in decades past. But typical conventions of masculinity and feminin-ity remain. Moreover, even today, men occupy a greater number of starring roles than women. At the same time, the television workforce is still dominated by men, particularly in key decision-making positions.

Television and Socioeconomic Class

The media researcher Richard Butsch has repeatedly illustrated that the working-class population is underrepresented on television (as well as in other media), while people in the professional or managerial ranks are overrepresented. Much of his emphasis has been on situation comedies in particular, which, he claims, frequently flip typical gender role expectations. Butsch asserts that when working-class men appear, they are almost always depicted as buffoons—conversely, their wives are seen as competent (2003). Over the years, Ralph Kramden of *The Honeymooners* (1955–1956), Fred Flintstone of *The Flintstones* (1960–1966), Archie Bunker of *All in the Family* (1971–1983), and Homer Simpson of *The Simpsons* (1989–present) have all fit the bill. On the other hand, he claims, when a family is middle class or of still higher economic standing, the male in the household is usually not pictured as clownish. Ideologically, then, these situation comedies seem to be making an indirect statement about socioeconomic class and the unacceptability of not making a lot of money. Many other scholars have also demonstrated that people from the lower economic classes are consistently underrepresented in the media, including television, in general. Moreover, when they are displayed, it is more likely that they will be shown in less glamorous ways than their financially well-off counterparts. Part of the reason for this imbalance, some critics contend, is that because television is largely funded by advertisers, TV executives are more apt to feature a symbolic world that is far richer than real life. In this manner, television tends to continuously reinforce the ideology of consumerism.

Of course, because television is so complex, there are always exceptions to every tendency. For instance, a long-running show that to a large extent sympathetically portrayed a working class family (the Conners) was *Roseanne* (1988–1997). True to form, the father was not a strong leader—the mother was the most dominant force. Yet the Conners, despite their eccentricities and financial difficulties, were a loving family.

One genre that has more prominently featured people of lesser socioeconomic standing is the daytime tabloid talk show (often scornfully referred to as "trash TV talk shows"), such as *The Jenny Jones Show* (1991–2003), *The Montel Williams Show* (1991–2008), and *The Jerry Springer Show* (1991–present). On these programs, the guests often come from the fringes of society and display qualities that are perceived as decidedly outside the norm (cross-dressers, extreme racists, highly promiscuous men and women, and so on). The emphasis is usually on creating heated debate and, sometimes, even physical conflict (*The Jerry Springer Show* is notorious for its staged altercations). In a sense, the abrasive tone is similar to that of many radio talk shows, except that they tend to be more socially liberal and at least indirectly address a type of identity politics. Those who dismiss this format as vulgar and as a negative cultural influence usually contend that many of the guests convey demeaning representations of lower-class people. The shows, however, are not without their academic supporters. Some proponents argue that, regardless of their excesses, the programs have helped the public gain a greater awareness of marginalized people and have promoted tolerance toward them. Furthermore, the talk shows have brought previously hidden subjects to light, including transgenderism, incest, and domestic abuse, which has provided therapeutic benefit to many viewers.

Television and Sexual Orientation

For most of television history in the United States, gays and lesbians were considerably excluded from programming; when they were shown, they were usually depicted in grossly stereotypical ways. Even in the 1990s, the sight of two men in bed together—but not touching—on *Thirtysomething* (1987–1991), and an unprecedented kiss between two women on *Ellen* (1994–1998), generated considerable controversy and withdrawal of advertising support. Not until 2000 did the first romantic male-to-male kiss take place on commercial television, in an episode of *Dawson's Creek* (1998–2003).

From the dawn of television through the 1970s, homosexuals were largely absent. In the 1980s, a regular gay character, who struggled to gain acceptance from his family, was included on *Dynasty* (1981–1989). Yet elsewhere, gays and lesbians still received little play.

Representations of nonheterosexuals increased in the 1990s. But not until near the turn of the twenty-first century did true breakthroughs occur. At one point, *Will & Grace* (1998–2006) was the fourth highest rated program in the country, even though Will, one of the two main characters, was gay (yet played by a heterosexual male). But various critics complained that Will was essentially nonsexual—he did not engage in affectionate activity with any men. Some went on to point out that, if anything, the show sometimes indicated that Will might cross over and actually become romantically involved with Grace, a woman. Overall, the image of Will was made palatable to a heterosexual audience uncomfortable with blatant homosexual display.

In 2003, perhaps more than any television show had ever done, *Queer Eye for the Straight Guy* (2003–2007) brought mainstream visibility to homosexuality. The hit "reality" show, about five homosexual men who in each episode gave a heterosexual man a "makeover," started on the cable network Bravo, then came to NBC once it had demonstrated that it did not pose a serious risk to advertisers. Although the program did not emphasize sexuality, its five stars were openly gay and highly likeable.

But no show was as bold in presenting an at least somewhat authentically gay world as *Queer as Folk* (2000–2005), which started in Great Britain, then traveled to the United States in 2000. Homosexual romance was a central element of the drama. Yet it appears that advertisers were not willing to back such a frank depiction of homosexuality, given that the show was telecast by the premium cable channel Showtime. (After its original run, *Queer as Folk* was picked up and edited for commercial television by Logo, a cable station targeted toward gays and lesbians —see "Targeted Channels for Marginalized Groups" below.) Several years later, lesbians finally had their turn, as Showtime originated *The L Word* (2004–2009), a drama centered on the lives of homosexual and bisexual women.

Two genres that have also lately helped nonheterosexuals emerge from television's closet are the daytime, tabloid talk show and the "reality" show. MTV's reality show *The Real World* (1992–present), for instance, has consistently included gay characters, many of whom are appealing to general audiences. *Survivor* (2000–present), a reality show that pits contestants against one another in surmounting various mental and physical challenges, presents another case in point. In its very first season, a gay man, Richard Hatch, won the contest. Although most viewers found him to be unpleasant, they did not necessarily arrive at this opinion due to his sexuality, but because he was simply an objectionable character per se. Some scholars argue that Hatch's not being exclusively defined by his sexual orientation represented a significant stride toward securing widespread acceptance for nonheterosexual people. Many other reality shows have also included homosexuals and portrayed them in a nonjudgmental manner.

In general, though, even today, lesbians and bisexuals appear far less often on television than gay men. And representations of transgendered people are even rarer. Most media researchers agree that the "queer" community has made considerable gains on television but that there is still a long way to go.

Targeted Channels for Marginalized Groups

One development that has enabled television to better serve marginalized people is the recent dramatic increase of channels—especially through cable or satellite systems

—that are available to all sorts of niche audiences. For example, Black Entertainment Television (BET) is aimed at African Americans. Latinos can turn to Univision, Telemundo, or other Spanish-speaking stations. Asian Americans do not have as many options (one probable reason is that they still make up a small portion of the U.S. population and are therefore not seen as having much market potential) but there are stations that target them, especially in large, multicultural cities. "Women's television" includes Lifetime, We, and Oxygen. In 2005, Logo was introduced—since then, the GLBT (gay-lesbian-bisexual-transgender) community has finally had a station it could call its own. A search through any cable or satellite channel lineup will often reveal many stations that cater to other demographic groups as well.

How television evolves in its relationship to an increasingly diverse U.S. population will continue to have important consequences in terms of identity politics. Through its representations of various groups, television will play a role in defining social expectations and either encouraging or subverting the movement toward full equality for all of the nation's citizens.

POLITICIANS AND CELEBRITY

Because many politicians, especially at the national level, are highly visible, they sometimes, in a sense, assume the status of celebrity. More than any other medium, television provides the opportunity for politicians to become household names and public personalities. During any presidential campaign, for example, competing candidates for high office are continuously seen in news and public affairs shows, commercials, and, from time to time, even entertainment programs. (For a comprehensive treatment of political campaigns, advertising, and other types of promotion, see Chapter 7.)

Probably the earliest president to attain the level of television celebrity was **John F. Kennedy**. Widely regarded as the nation's first "TV President," he demonstrated

John F. Kennedy's good looks and ease on camera were thought to have contributed to his 1960 election as president. (AP Photo)

a mastery of the medium like no other politician before him. Handsome, witty, and charming, Kennedy vividly displayed his command of the airwaves during the televised **Kennedy-Nixon Debates** in 1960, an event that likely played a significant role in his election victory. When the president was assassinated on November 22, 1963, a tragedy caught on film, it triggered the largest television media event that had ever occurred up until that time; symbolically bringing people together in a collective ceremony of mourning, television, to many observers, helped unite the nation as the population tried to recover and understand the meaning of such an unexpected and deeply felt loss.

Lyndon B. Johnson, who inherited the presidency after Kennedy's assassination, dramatically lacked his predecessor's charisma. Despite his less than magnetic persona, however, Johnson was nearly obsessed with managing television coverage while he was in office. According to the media historian Erik Barnouw (1990), the president kept three televisions lined up side-by-side in the White House, each tuned to one of the major networks. Nor was he above taking matters into his own hands when he witnessed a newscast that offended him—he was known to have personally phoned anchors and other television journalism professionals to subject them to a heated tirade when he believed the situation called for it. Today, every major politician strives to shape media coverage to his or her liking, a complex propagandistic enterprise that inevitably comes with the territory. Lyndon Johnson, though, perhaps represents the first particularly intense attempt by a president to control his public image and perceptions of his administration's practices (especially its involvement in the Vietnam War) in the age of television.

Richard Nixon, too, sought to direct television in a manner that cast him in a positive light. Generally perceived as awkward on camera (an interpretation that might have even benefited him at times, since he could avoid accusations of being a slick, "Hollywood type"), he often conducted ignoble affairs in secrecy and orchestrated events that made him seem presidential. For example, his travels to the Soviet Union

Former President Lyndon B. Johnson in December 1969, in a CBS special with Walter Cronkite, *Why I Chose Not to Run* (for second term, in the 1968 election). (CBS/Photofest)

and China enabled him to come across as open-minded, boldly diplomatic, and even heroic. On occasion, Nixon worked to soften his curmudgeon image by tapping into elements of popular culture as well.

Yet the next president after Kennedy to gain a kind of celebrity standing was Ronald Reagan. Not only was he adept at managing news coverage, but, drawing on his career as an actor, he was a great performer who skillfully presented himself as a highly likeable and engaging leader. (For more discussion on Reagan as a celebrity, see "Former Entertainers as Politicians" below.) Bill Clinton, too, at least until the Monica Lewinsky scandal, was commonly recognized as possessing a charming on-camera presence and as being effective at handling media coverage

Another politician who appears to have joined the ranks of celebrity is the current president, **Barack Obama**. Now and again described by journalists during his election campaign as having obtained "rock star status" or, rather more ominously, having evoked a "cult of personality," Obama frequently drew huge audiences to his rallies, which were sometimes staged in a sports stadium or other large venue. Recognized as a dynamic speaker (even, partly because his father was black, bringing to mind for some people shades of Martin Luther King Jr.), the then 47-year-old candidate attracted young voters in particular, sparked comparisons to John F. Kennedy, and inspired expression that relates to the realm of popular culture, including a music video that made the rounds on the Internet and a series of **Obama Girl** and other **YouTube** episodes.

Because of their high profile, U.S. presidents have often been represented in entertaining ways in the media. For an examination of some of these depictions, see the names of various presidents and their media portrayals in Part II.

Former Entertainers as Politicians

A number of politicians did not rise to the level of celebrity via their visible political activity per se. Instead, they had already achieved star status through their work in entertainment before they decided to transition into the political sphere. Several of the most well-known performers to later obtain office came from the world of film—some of their movies also eventually appeared on television. These stars include **Clint Eastwood** (mayor of Carmel, California, from 1986 to 1988) and **Arnold Schwarzenegger** (current Republican governor of California).

Other election winners first found fame in professional sports, a television staple. Some notable performers in this category include the following:

- *Bill Bradley*. A Rhodes Scholar and Oxford graduate who played for the New York Knicks for 10 years, Bradley won two championships with the team, in 1970 and 1973. After his illustrious career ended in 1977, he was inducted into the NBA Hall of Fame in 1983. In 1978, Bradley ran for the U.S. Senate in New Jersey and won, going on to serve three terms. Following his departure from the Senate in 1996, he sought the Democratic presidential nomination in 2000 but lost to Al Gore, despite the support he received from basketball greats Michael Jordan and Bill Russell.

- *Jim Bunning*. A star pitcher for the Philadelphia Phillies who retired from major league baseball in 1971, Jim Bunning went on to serve in the Kentucky Senate and the U.S. House of Representatives. Then, in 1998, he was elected to represent Kentucky as a Republican U.S. Senator, a position he currently holds as this book goes to press. Bunning is also the only U.S. Senator to be in the baseball Hall of Fame.

- *Jack Kemp*. After a 13-year career as an American Football League (AFL) quarterback (earning most of his success with the Buffalo Bills), Jack Kemp won—in Buffalo, New York—a Republican seat in the U.S. House of Representatives in 1971, and retained the position until 1989. In 1988 he ran for president but was defeated in the primaries by George H. W. Bush, who eventually appointed him as Secretary of the U.S. Department of Housing and Urban Development (HUD), an office he held until 1991. During his tenure, he advocated innovative "Urban Enterprise Zones" to boost inner-city economic growth. Then, in 1996, he was the vice-presidential candidate on the ticket of **Bob Dole**, who was soundly defeated by incumbent Bill Clinton. In May 2009, Kemp died of cancer.

- *Steve Largent*. Largent retired from the Seattle Seahawks in 1989 after enjoying a reputable career as a wide receiver that earned him induction into the NFL Hall of Fame in 1995. Just one year before his football recognition, he was elected to the U.S. House of Representatives, where he served until 2002.

- *J. C. Watts*. Watts was elected in Oklahoma to the U.S. House of Representatives in 1990. An African American, he became a rising star in the Republican Party until he left politics for the private sector in 2001. Before entering the realm of politics, he had gained sports fame as the quarterback for the University of Oklahoma, leading the football team to two Big Eight championships, in 1980 and 1981.

Numerous television shows have also functioned as launching grounds for political ambition. For example, George Takei, who had played Mr. Sulu on *Star Trek*, ran unsuccessfully for Los Angeles City Council in 1973. Sheila Kuehl, known for her role as Zelda on *The Many Loves of Dobie Gillis*, later became a California state senator and recently filed a "Statement of Intention" to run for California Secretary of State in 2010. Nancy Culp, who had achieved fame as Miss Jane Hathaway on the *Beverly Hillbillies*, made an unsuccessful run for Congress in Pennsylvania in 1984—she lost a close race, perhaps partly because her one-time co-star Buddy Ebsen had taped radio ads for her opponent claiming that Culp was "too liberal." Also liberal was Ben Jones, who had portrayed the character Cooter Davenport on *The Dukes of Hazzard*, and was afterward elected to represent Georgia in Congress, serving two terms from 1988 to 1992. Ten years later, he ran again, this time in Virginia, but failed in his attempt to win a congressional seat. Fred Grandy, a Harvard graduate who became the popular character "Gopher" on *The Love Boat*, was subsequently elected in Iowa to serve as a Republican congressman from 1986 to 1995, and eventually went on to host radio talk shows. Alan Autry, i.e., Bubba Skinner from the television show *In the Heat of the Night*, became mayor of Fresno, California, in 2000 and served until 2008.

Originally gaining fame as a pop music singer with his wife, Cher (together they simply billed themselves as "Sonny and Cher"), in the 1960s, Sonny Bono soon also starred with her in the very popular *The Sonny and Cher Comedy Hour*, a variety show that aired from 1971 to 1977. Once his entertainment career had ended and he and Cher had divorced, he went into politics. In 1994, after serving as mayor of Palm Springs, California, he was elected as a Republican to the U.S. House of Representatives by California's 44th District. In Congress, Bono became best known for the Sonny Bono Copyright Extension Act, which aided the music industry but was also controversial. The Act granted an additional 20 years to a copyright before a product entered the public domain. Tragically, Bono died in a skiing accident in 1998 and was succeeded by his wife Mary Bono for the rest of his term and in subsequent elections. Although his public persona as an entertainer was one of a lovable goofball, he was a respected congressman at the time of his death.

Throughout the 1970s and 1980s, **Jesse Ventura** garnered attention from his days on the mock-sport, heavily televised pro wrestling circuit. In 1998 he was elected as governor of Minnesota, a position he decided to relinquish after one term.

The large number of former television stars who became politicians demonstrates that name recognition and acting skills can be valuable assets for future politicians. It appears that the nature of celebrity somehow adds a layer of legitimacy to the political pursuits of many candidates, even though, due to rules regarding fairness that the television industry follows, their programs are not shown while they campaign.

Finally, no former entertainer ever attained higher political standing than President Ronald Reagan, who, as an actor, had mixed both film and television appearances. He embarked on his performance career as a radio sportscaster in the 1930s. From there, he turned to acting and appeared in dozens of motion pictures, most of which, however, are regarded as "B" movies. His first major venture into politics occurred when he became president of the Screen Actors Guild. At that time, he was perceived as a liberal. His gradual transformation to conservative icon started once he was hired to host a TV series sponsored by General Electric (GE). While under the employ of GE, he also traveled the country as a spokesman for the company, espousing the marvels of free enterprise and limited government. He began to gain notice when he gave a stirring televised speech on behalf of Republican presidential nominee Barry Goldwater in 1964. Coming across as a natural politician, Reagan ran for governor of California in 1966 and won the election. He finished two terms, and then competed against incumbent Gerald Ford for the Republican presidential nomination in 1976. He lost only narrowly. The following presidential election season, however, Reagan secured the Republican nomination and handily defeated incumbent Jimmy Carter. Four years later, his reelection was almost a foregone conclusion.

As president, drawing from both his acting and political experiences, Ronald Reagan was masterful on camera. Apparently exuding warmth, sincerity, and patriotic sentiment—yet with a stern, fatherly hand when the situation warranted it—the ever-avuncular Reagan played a role in helping many citizens, after the disillusionment of the Vietnam era and the poor economic performance under Jimmy Carter, feel better about their country again. Although he was often accused of being an intellectual lightweight who merely functioned as a rhetorical showman for the Republican Party, the criticism rarely stuck, earning him the nickname of "the Teflon president." His public appearances were generally heavily stage managed out of fear that any inadvertent bumbling or unfortunate ad-libbing might undermine the inspiring persona he radiated whenever he read from a script. Somehow Reagan was so adept at making a positive impression that he was even able to survive the Iran-Contra crisis relatively unscathed (see **Political Scandals**).

Today, for many Republicans, Ronald Reagan's legacy has taken on almost mythic proportions. He is seen by many as the person who reinvigorated the conservative movement and championed some of its most fundamental tenets. During the 2008 Republican primary season, for instance, each of several candidates indicated that, rather than carry on the mantle of the increasingly unpopular incumbent George W. Bush, he would lead his administration according to the model Reagan had established. Just four years earlier, following the president's death after a lengthy bout with Alzheimer's disease, Reagan's six-day funeral ceremony had turned into a genuine mass media event.

Appearances on Television Entertainment by Politicians

Since the dawn of television, politicians have increasingly appeared on entertaining television shows, frequently as a means of promoting a run for office or as a way of simply enhancing their public image. Serving as a guest on a talk show has been especially common.

Sometimes the situation is reversed and a one-time politician leaves the field to fully enter the world of entertainment. Former Cincinnati council member and mayor Jerry Springer, for example, went on to host the daytime tabloid TV talk show, *The Jerry Springer Show*, which debuted in 1991 and is still in circulation today. Springer has made a number of other television appearances but is best known for the show named after him. In fact, Springer generated so much attention from the program that eventually a Hollywood movie was made about him, entitled *Ringmaster* (1998). For his part, **Fred Thompson** has bounced back and forth. Originally an attorney who served in the government realm for years, he later became a character actor in 1985. Then, in 1994, he was elected as a Republican U.S. Senator and continued in office until 2003. At the end of his second term, he joined the cast of *Law & Order* (1990–present), playing the role of New York City District Attorney Arthur Branch. Next, he left the show in 2007 to seek the 2008 Republican nomination for president. His campaign failed miserably, however, and he soon left the race without winning a single primary delegate.

Other people involved in politics make a name for themselves by serving as political pundits, or sometimes even as hosts, for televised news or public affairs shows. Several highly visible examples include former White House appointee and Republican presidential candidate Pat Buchanan; current Democratic strategist **James Carville** (who gained initial fame through his appearance in the political documentary, *The War Room*); previous Democratic presidential candidate and longtime social activist Jesse Jackson Sr., who once hosted his own syndicated TV talk show; and Democratic strategist George Stephanopoulos (who "co-starred" with Carville in *The War Room*), the current host of ABC's *This Week with George Stephanopoulos* (2002–present).

Celebrity Activism

Many entertainers never run for office yet vigorously engage with politics through activism. Whether campaigning on behalf of political candidates or advocating in support of various causes, these performers work to affect social change. A by-no-means-comprehensive list of notable celebrities who have channeled considerable energy in this direction includes the following actors, athletes, and musical performers:

- *Actors*—Ed Asner, Warren Beatty, Harry Belafonte (also a singer), Marlon Brando, George Clooney, Matt Damon, **Jane Fonda**, Charlton Heston, Angelina Jolie, Paul Newman, Chuck Norris, Sean Penn, Robert Redford, Tim Robbins, Susan Sarandon, Martin Sheen, Oprah Winfrey (also a TV talk show host who is involved in many other media enterprises), Joanne Woodward

- *Sports Figures*—Kareem Abdul-Jabbar, **Muhammad Ali**, Earvin (Magic) Johnson, Bill Russell, Bill Walton

- *Musical Performers*—Joan Baez, **Bono**, Jackson Browne, Tracy Chapman, the **Dixie Chicks**, **Bob Dylan**, Arlo Guthrie, **Woody Guthrie**, George Harrison, **John Lennon**,

John Mellencamp, Willie Nelson, Pete Seeger, Bruce Springsteen, Barbara Streisand (also an actress), Stevie Wonder, Neil Young

Critique of the Intersection of Politics, Celebrity, and Entertainment

The merging of politics, celebrity, and popular culture—especially television—has evoked substantial debate among scholars in terms of its impact on American democracy. One school of thought can perhaps be captured by Neil Postman (1985), who declared that television, by its very nature, has been a major factor in trivializing the political process. According to him, the print media, on the other hand, have a tendency to promote analytical deliberation. Thus, in the nineteenth century, before the onslaught of movies and television, when citizens relied on newspapers and other printed materials for their information, they might have been inclined to take a highly rational approach to politics. Conversely, from Postman's perspective, television downplays words in favor of visual images, which generally incite emotional reactions. At the same time, television presents an entertaining framework for nearly everything it depicts—including political events and campaigns. Extensive argumentation and debate are supplanted by sound bites and talk show appearances by politicians. Sustained media coverage of the issues is replaced by gossip and innuendo. The result is that citizen involvement in politics, a purportedly serious endeavor, is akin to following sports or celebrity performers, a supposedly frivolous activity. Along the way, the media do not empower the citizenry but undermine democratic potential.

Other academics adopt a far more optimistic stance toward the blending of politics, celebrity, and entertainment. They say that television and other elements of popular culture do not necessarily contaminate the realm of politics—in fact, they can even generate more interest in the political issues that affect everyday lives. Liesbet van Zoonen (2005), for example, suggests that politics in the United States have always incorporated aspects of entertainment based on the communication tools available at the time. From this point of view, there is nothing wrong with political engagement being pleasurable or fun. Popular culture can actually evoke greater political passion and expand awareness. Ultimately, the media are instrumental to the practice of democracy and, despite their current limitations, have the potential to stir citizen participation.

Many critics have drawn attention to declining voter turnout, political apathy, and cynicism as signs of television and popular culture's corrosive influence. Why, they ask, are many people more willing to vote for a contestant on *American Idol* than a candidate for the presidency? Still, perhaps the intersection of politics and entertainment is inevitable, given that both institutions involve performance. Scores of observers have pointed out that there is a greater emphasis on style, appearance, and personality than there was in the distant past. The question is whether this drives people away or pulls them in.

Looking at the 2008 presidential election season, a case could be made that the contemporary media environment is in no way alienating voters. The turnout in Democratic primary polls and caucuses, for instance, was unprecedented. Part of the excitement could be attributable to the fact that both of the leading candidates, one a woman (**Hillary Clinton**), the other a mixed-race man who identifies as black (Barack Obama), pointed to the possibility that, for the first time in U.S. history, a female or person of color could attain the nation's highest office. Moreover, Obama epitomizes the idea of the politician as celebrity. Handsome, charismatic, inspiring, as well as a master orator, Obama sometimes delivered a stump speech in an indoor stadium filled to capacity. From time to time, a person in attendance even fainted, a reaction that is reminiscent of the grip The Beatles once had on an audience. Will.i.am of the music group, The Black Eyed Peas, produced a pro-Obama video for YouTube that received millions of hits. Journalists occasionally referred to the candidate as having "rock star" status; at first, some even worried that he was triggering a "cult of personality" that foregrounded style over substance. Yet whatever pundits make of it, there can be no doubt that thousands of people were drawn into the political process who probably would not have been otherwise; indeed, Obama clearly stated that one of his central goals was to get everyday citizens excited about and involved in politics. His presidential victory over John McCain in the general election produced the greatest voter turnout in decades. Based on the phenomenon he generated, it would be hard to argue that the blurring of politics, celebrity, and entertainment automatically yields apathy and cynicism. Here, the result appears to be quite the opposite. Perhaps, therefore, the impact of politics combining with popular culture depends on the inherent drama associated with a particular political event or campaign—it varies from context to context.

Celebrity activism, too, has received heavy criticism. Politicians seeking endorsements from entertainers, opponents say, cheapens the democratic process. Actors, musicians, and other entertainment performers do not always possess substantial political knowledge and should not have a disproportionate influence on the system. In contrast, some scholars state, celebrity activists can produce widespread interest in important causes, such as hunger, AIDS, and economic injustices, which can lead to positive change. Furthermore, if it is true that citizens are feeling more detached from traditional political parties and their major politicians, then celebrities can fill a gap by forming opinions from the same resources available to everyday people, thus offering perspectives that audiences can relate to.

POLITICAL TELEVISION SHOWS AND GENRES

Since the birth of broadcast television, many commercial programs, instead of conveying political implications through ideology, have had explicitly political themes or narrative contexts. Premium cable channels, especially HBO, have also offered entertaining shows with political backdrops. Indeed, freed from commercial influence, these shows have sometimes challenged dominant cultural perspectives far more than is usually true with commercial fare. Nonetheless, because advertising-supported television reaches much larger audiences than subscription-based services, it has had much greater impact. What is widely regarded as primarily informative programming, such as news, public affairs, and documentary vehicles, has, of course, often directly related to politics (for more exploration of these formats in relationship to politics, see Chapters 2 and 5). Indeed, a number of political news stories in the television age have had such social significance and have attracted so much interest that they could arguably be viewed as instances of real life merging with popular culture, although with an especially serious tone. Major political episodes that became highly rated, protracted, televised media events might include, for example, the Watergate crisis (1972–1974) and the September 11, 2001, terrorist attacks on the World Trade Center and the Pentagon (also see **Political Scandals**). Yet a variety of shows and genres that are generally assigned to the broad category of entertainment per se have also overtly drawn from the realm of politics.

Spy and Foreign Intrigue Shows

A number of programs that foreground espionage mirror the current political environment in which they air. Accordingly, the content of the shows is either expressly or implicitly political. In these shows, talented spies who are often members of federal agencies or at least loosely in line with government objectives engage in secretive and sometimes ethically ambiguous activity as a means of undermining threats to the nation, especially from foreign adversaries. Along the way, they tend to reinforce the idea that the United States is a force for "good" that must do whatever it takes to root out "evil." Shows of this ilk that have appeared through the years (along with brief descriptions) include:

- *Dangerous Assignment* (1951–1952). U.S. undercover agent Steve Mitchell was sent to locations around the world to battle various international problems.
- *Doorway to Danger* (1951–1953). The chief of a top-secret government agency, John Randolph supervised a group of agents involved in tracking down U.S. enemies.
- *Foreign Intrigue* (1951–1955). In the beginning, American foreign press correspondent Robert Cannon encountered war criminals and other seedy characters. The cast and locations changed over time but the general themes remained the same.
- *The Hunter* (1952–1954). Master of disguise Bart Adams worked to thwart sinister plans, often conceived by communists. Frequently, he had to rescue a person from the Red menace.
- *I Spy* (1965–1968). Tennis player Kelly Robinson and his trainer, Alexander Scott, served as secret agents for the U.S. government, working to undermine the Soviet threat abroad.
- *Mission Impossible* (1966–1973, 1988–1990). In each episode of this highly popular series, the leader of the Impossible Missions Force received a tape-recorded message instructing him about that week's assignment, which frequently involved a threat from a foreign power that needed to be subverted.
- *The Exile* (1991–1995). A former U.S. agency spy who was framed for murder, John Phillips (aka John Stone) engaged in furtive secret assignments while trying to clear his name.
- *Air America* (1998–1999). Rio Arnett, whose code name was Air America, worked undercover for the Office of Strategic Implementation.
- *The Agency* (2001–2003). The activities of the CIA were the focus of this series.
- *Alias* (2001–2006). After spying for an agency she mistakenly believes is aligned with U.S. interests, Sydney Bristow joined the CIA to fight her former secret employer and keep the nation safe from terrorism.
- *24* (2001–present). Every season agent Jack Bauer is faced with only 24 hours to save the United States from a major terrorist scheme. Each "real time" episode in the season features one hour in his excruciatingly stressful day.
- *The Unit* (2006–present). A top-secret team of soldiers engages in undercover missions—often involving counterterrorism—throughout the world, while the operatives' families cope with their absence and attempt to protect their cover.
- *Burn Notice* (2007–present). In a twist on the traditional format and infused with a comedic edge, this series finds Michael Westen, a spy once in good standing with

U.S. intelligence, privately freelancing his covert services in an effort to finance his personal quest to determine why he has been "burned," that is, blacklisted from official duty.

- *Chuck* (2007–present). In another surprising and comedic deviation from the standard formula, this show centers on the socially awkward Chuck Bartowski, who, after opening an e-mail that suddenly embedded an entire database of secret government information into his brain, now must work to foil would-be terrorists and other evildoers, even as U.S. agents attempt to regain the lost intelligence.

Science Fiction

Political science scholar Rex Brynen (2000) argues that certain science fiction programs, similar to particular spy series, have reflected—and simultaneously contributed to—political trends of the time. The legendary *Star Trek* (1966–1969), for example, drew upon the idealism that was in the air in the 1960s, often presenting motifs of multicultural tolerance and metaphorically projecting a romanticized version of American society. Decades later, scoring very high in the ratings, *The X-Files* (1993–2002), with its accent on conspiracies, captured the feelings of political paranoia that had emerged after a population subjected to events such as Watergate and the Iran-Contra scandal (see **Political Scandals**) had grown increasingly cynical about the government and its affairs.

Preceding both programs, *Voyage to the Bottom of the Sea* (1964–1968), one of television's most successful science fiction series, followed the crew of the *Seaview*, a futuristic atomic submarine, as it traveled the seas seeking to dispose of both human and alien villains. In a sense, the show functioned as a counterperspective to *Star Trek*: whereas the latter conveyed the 1960s sentiment of liberal optimism, *Voyage to the Bottom of the Sea* reminded viewers that threats of all kinds (especially from various bastions of communism) remained ever present.

Military Situation Comedies

War, of course, has overt political implications. A number of shows have taken a comedic approach to military conflict. Sometimes, it seems as if such a framework has lampooned conflict. On the other hand, various critics would contend that situation comedies with a military backdrop, despite their emphasis on amusement, actually normalize, and thus inadvertently justify, the need to execute bloody battles. Some of the programs in this category that have aired over the past several decades include *The Phil Silvers Show* (1955–1959), *McKeever & The Colonel* (1962–1963), *Ensign O'Toole* (1962–1964), *McHale's Navy* (1962–1966), *Gomer Pyle, U.S.M.C.* (1964–1970), *The Wackiest Ship in the Army* (1965–1966), *Hogan's Heroes* (1965–1971), *Operation Petticoat* (1977–1978), *Private Benjamin* (1981–1983), and *Major Dad* (1989–1993). One show that especially stands out is *M*A*S*H* (1972–1983), which, most observers would agree, provided a critical outlook on the hardship of war.

Military Dramas

Most television military dramas have not seriously challenged U.S. interventions, but have, instead, portrayed war as an exciting adventure. Some of the programs within this genre include *O.S.S.* (the acronym for the U.S. World War II agency, the

Office of Strategic Services—1957–1958), *The Gallant Men* (1962–1963), *Combat* (1962–1967), *Twelve O'Clock High* (1964–1967), *The Rat Patrol* (1966–1968), *Garrison's Gorillas* (1967–1968), *S.W.A.T.* (technically a police drama, but one involving army-style warfare in major U.S. cities—1975–1976), *From Here to Eternity* (1979–1980 miniseries), *Tour of Duty* (1987–1990), *China Beach* (1988–1991), *Soldier of Fortune* (a drama that contained elements of espionage as well—1997–1999), *Pensacola: Wings of Gold* (1997–2000), and *NCIS* (mostly a criminal investigation show that also includes doses of comedy, it nonetheless features a special team of naval and marine personnel within the context of conflicts abroad—2003–present).

Yet a potentially critical outlook has sometimes entered the picture. For instance, *Over There* (2005) dealt with the Iraq War even as it was occurring, examining the effects of the conflict on a group of soldiers and their families. The drama, which lasted only one season, did not appear to strongly advance an agenda, thus allowing viewers to form their own points of view on the intervention.

Another military-related program, this time from a different genre, was the "reality" show *Boot Camp* (2001). In this series, which lasted just one season, 16 "recruits" were subjected to raw physical tests in a military environment to see who had the mental discipline and stamina to avoid elimination and rise to victory. Adding to the aura of authenticity, *Boot Camp* featured real-life marine drill instructors putting the contestants through the drills.

Political Situation Comedies

Many situation comedies have, on occasion, included material of a political nature. *All in the Family* (1971–1983) and *The Simpsons* (1989–present) are two cases in point. *Murphy Brown* (1988–1998) also provides a notable example. The show caused a stir when the lead character rejected two suitors and, instead, opted to raise as a single mother the baby she had recently given birth to. Then Vice President Dan Quayle condemned the fictional Brown's decision, citing it as an instance of the way in which family values in the nation had supposedly declined.

A variety of other situation comedies have incorporated the realm of politics into their very fabric, featuring fictional government officials or other political participants as main characters. These shows (along with brief descriptions) include:

- *The People's Choice* (1955–1958). City council member Socrates ("Sock") Miller encountered various amusing difficulties, including his relationship with the mayor's daughter, as he tried his best to help the community.
- *The Governor & J.J.* (1969–1972). Governor William Drinkwater, a widower, relied on his daughter to serve as "first lady."
- *All's Fair* (1976–1977). Set in Washington, D.C., arch-conservative political columnist Richard Barrington and his ultraliberal girlfriend, Charley Drake, somehow managed to maintain their love for each other.
- *Benson* (1979–1986). African American Benson served as Governor Eugene Gatling's butler. Yet Benson also proved so adept at assisting Gatling with political decisions that he was eventually appointed state budget director. Later, Benson became lieutenant governor and even ran against his former employer for the governorship (the election result was never revealed, however).
- *Hail to the Chief* (1985). Centered on the zany life in the White House of Julia Mansfield, the first woman to be elected as U.S. president, the series lasted only several months.

- *Mr. President* (1987–1988). Another show about the U.S. president, this time played by the renowned actor George C. Scott and centered on the home life of the nation's top official.

- *Hearts Afire* (1992–1995). Set in Washington, D.C., revolving around the romantic relationship between legislative assistant John Hartman and senator press secretary Georgie Anne Lahti (who later added Hartman to her name after their eventual marriage), the show alluded to various political topics.

Several political situation comedies have had a more explicitly satirical bent. Included among them are the following:

- *D.C. Follies* (1987–1989). The show's title stood for the name of the D.C. bar at which the main characters met for social interaction. Most of the principles, though, were not live human beings but puppets—many of them depicted high government officials, including then President Ronald Reagan and first lady Nancy, and former presidents Richard Nixon, Gerald Ford, and Jimmy Carter.

- *The Powers That Be* (1992–1993). Prominent executive producer Norman Lear was behind this spoof of Washington insiders that followed the life of a dim-witted senator and his dysfunctional family.

- *Spin City* (1996–2002). Prone to frequent gaffes and unable to competently govern, New York Mayor Randall Winston was compelled to rely on his staff, especially Deputy Mayor Mike Flaherty, who was adept at handling the media.

- *That's My Bush* (2001). This short-lived program mercilessly parodied President George W. Bush shortly after he had won the nation's highest office.

- *Lil' Bush* (2007). Echoing the tone of *South Park*, this highly irreverent cartoon show featured President George W. Bush and some of his top officials (including Vice President Dick Cheney, Secretary of State Condoleezza Rice, and Donald Rumsfeld, Bush's first Secretary of Defense) as mean-spirited childhood friends engaged in devilish pranks during the George H. W. Bush administration.

Political Drama

Similar to certain situation comedies, numerous dramas have sometimes integrated political content into their episodes. Whether it was the exploration of Soviet dictator Joseph Stalin or the Nuremberg Nazi trials in *Playhouse 90* (1956–1961); the social issues raised by *Lou Grant* (1977–1982); the horrific rendering of the quest to survive a nuclear holocaust in the made-for-TV movie *The Day After* (1983); the portrayal of GIs acclimating to everyday life after returning home from their assignments during World War II in *Homefront* (1991–1993); or the spotlight on an Irish family reacting to events in the turbulent 1960s in *American Dreams* (2002–2005); televised drama has occasionally offered the opportunity for viewers to contemplate matters of consequence.

Then again, several dramas have had a more explicitly political focus. Perhaps surprisingly, however, throughout U.S. television history, there have been few shows that have been identified with the genre known as political drama. Some of the most noteworthy ones (along with brief descriptions) include:

- *Treasury Men in Action* (1950–1955). Based on actual cases from the files of the U.S. Treasury Department and broadcast live, the series depicted government agents triumphing over various scoundrels. Somewhat functioning as propaganda (the government recognized it for its public service), it also occasionally featured real-life government officials.

- *Cavalcade of America* (1952–1957). An offspring of its radio counterpart, this dramatic anthology presented stories of American heroes, including many political figures.
- *Slattery's People* (1964–1965). Amidst professional and personal troubles, state representative James Slattery promoted causes and advocated for reforms.
- *The Senator* (1970–1971). Idealistic in the face of opposition from entrenched interests, Junior Senator Hayes Stowe sought to better society by doing what he felt was right.
- *Backstairs at the White House* (1979). This miniseries provided a view into the private lives of eight U.S. presidents through the eyes of White House staff.
- *Top of the Hill* (1988–1989). The youngest and newest member of the U.S. Congress, idealistic Representative Thomas Bell strove to satisfy his conscience by taking on corruption, pollution, and other political concerns.
- *First Monday* (2002). While heroically attempting to make the right decisions, recently appointed U.S. Supreme Court Justice Joe Novelli often represented the swing vote in an evenly politically divided court.
- *Commander in Chief* (2005). Although the show was short-lived, it was notable for fictionally featuring the first woman to become the president of the United States.

Most of these series had only brief runs. Yet the political drama that stands out from all the others, not only in terms of its years on the air but also because of its popularity, critical acclaim, and attention from academics, is *The West Wing* (1999–2006). For a full discussion of this show involving the activity of a fictional U.S. president, see *The West Wing*.

Talk Shows

Many entertaining talk shows have tapped into the political world. During television's infancy, for example, Edward R. Murrow frequently conversed through a screen with political notables in their homes on *Person to Person* (1953–1961). More recently, **Barbara Walters**, from time to time, has also used the straight interview format with politicians on the sporadically broadcast *Barbara Walters Special*. Other programs, designed to advance a decidedly partisan agenda, have somewhat blended the traditional public affairs interview genre with the standard talk show style, a method perhaps best exemplified by *Rush Limbaugh* (1992–1996), a spin-off of the radio program also hosted by **Rush Limbaugh**. Then again, there have been numerous straightforward interview shows that have conveyed considerably more balance. Some of the most notable ones have included public television's long-running *The Charlie Rose Show* (1991–present), whose host has often conversed with political players of all stripes, as well as cable television's many offerings, especially *Larry King Live* (1985–present), which has enjoyed over two decades of telecasts. Although the venerable, ever-suspenders-wearing King has invited far more figures from the realm of popular entertainment into his studio, he has also interviewed scores of politicians, sometimes even particularly powerful ones. To date, for example, a total of eight either former or then current U.S. presidents have appeared on his show.

Yet late night talk shows have especially drawn attention in connection to politics. The genre is associated with those programs that generally air after the last edition of the local news on weeknights and feature a host who opens with a comedic monologue or other amusing material, and then interviews one or more invited guests, most of whom have already attained some kind of celebrity status. A few of the best-known current late night talk shows include *The Tonight Show* (presently hosted by Conan O'Brien) and *Late Night with Jimmy Fallon* on NBC, *Late Show with David Letterman* and *The Late Late Show with Craig Ferguson* on CBS, and *Jimmy Kimmel Live!* on ABC.

The popular form intersects with politics in a number of ways. To begin, the comedic hosts regularly draw from current affairs, particularly the realm of politics, for topics they can turn into satire during their introductory monologues. Over the years, these stars have delivered literally thousands of jokes with a political bent. Political scandals, such as the affair between former President Bill Clinton and Monica Lewinsky (see **Political Scandals**), especially provide fodder for ridicule. *Politically Incorrect*, also a late night talk show of sorts, takes a different approach. It actually invites celebrities and political guests to engage in a round-table (and generally humorous) discussion and debate on the issues of the day. On one episode, host **Bill Maher** generated considerable political controversy (resulting in the cancellation of his show, which was originally telecast on Comedy Central from 1993 to 1996, by ABC—only to be quickly picked up by pay channel HBO) when, shortly after September 11, 2001, he contended that the suicide mission of the terrorist attackers was not an act of cowardice.

Yet the blending of amusement and politics comes through in another manner on the traditional late night talk show. Although the majority of guests hail from the world of pure entertainment per se, on occasion, a politician will also appear. That a politician was not averse to visiting such a venue was in evidence even during the early days of television. Richard Nixon, for example, a then former vice president and eventual president, once turned up on an episode of *The Jack Paar Program* in 1963. Mixing his political persona with a touch of musicianship, Nixon actually performed one of his own compositions on the piano. **Jack Paar** had taken over *The Tonight Show* in 1957 after it had gone through several mutations (including name changes) and then left the program in 1962 to host a similar show named after him. Given his influence in the industry, Paar is recognized as a pioneer of the late night talk show form. Moreover, not every political interview he conducted blended with entertaining performance. For example, Paar had earlier engaged Nixon in a serious conversation on *The Tonight Show* during the politician's run for the presidency in 1960. His opponent and soon-to-be winner of the top office, John F. Kennedy, was also interviewed by Paar on another installment of the show.

The kind of lighthearted moment Nixon provided in his 1962 talk show appearance, however, was not typical for years. A common perception was that a politician playing loose on television would somehow cheapen his (or, rarely, her) image. Although there was never a clear and solid dividing line, nonetheless, politics and entertainment were seen as two separate fields. Even Nixon's stint on the piano occurred only after he had retired from politics (although he would eventually emerge again in the 1968 presidential season).

One political moment in talk show history that is frequently cited involved Bill Clinton during his first run for president in 1992. Hoping to reach youth voters, he made numerous appearances on entertaining television venues, including *The Arsenio Hall Show* (a late night talk show that ran from 1989 to 1994 and that for a time was very popular, especially with younger audiences). Donning dark sunglasses, Clinton whipped out his saxophone and used his musical skills in an attempt to connect with young viewers, who are often perceived as being more amenable to entertainment than serious political discussions. Through this gesture, Clinton hoped to render the older, relatively staid Republican candidate, President George H. W. Bush, old-fashioned in contrast. A major difference between Nixon's piano performance in 1962 and Clinton's musical presentation 30 years later, though, is that Clinton was actually in the midst of running for president. The first "baby boomer" candidate to seek the position, Clinton was instrumental in making more ordinary the tactic of fusing politics and popular culture as a means of reaching youth voters.

Since Clinton's somewhat raucous performance, talk show appearances by politicians have become increasingly common. Indeed, one of the notable features of the 2000 presidential campaign was the more extensive use of talk shows in general as a way of reaching the public in a setting that usually does not involve challenging questions. One of the central reasons a politician will become a guest on a late night talk show is to try to carve out an affable public persona and connect with voters on a more personal level. As candidates and office holders have turned to entertainment vehicles with greater regularity, the practice has gained a higher degree of acceptability and the distinction between politics and entertainment has become hazier

Arkansas Democratic presidential hopeful Governor Bill Clinton appears on *The Arsenio Hall Show* during a taping at Paramount Studios in Hollywood, California, June 4, 1992. Clinton played the saxophone during the show's musical opening. (AP PHOTO)

than ever. Some observers view the tendency as problematic, feeling that it debases the political arena. Other onlookers counter that it can actually rejuvenate political participation by meeting people in the symbolic environments that considerably resonate with them and through which they find consistent pleasure.

Some recent late night talk show visits by politicians, however, have truly stood out from their previous manifestations. When Arnold Schwarzenegger came on *The Tonight Show* (then hosted by Jay Leno) in October 2003, he did not simply exploit the appearance to boost his run for the governorship of California—he actually announced his candidacy itself. Throughout history, the declaration of an intention to pursue a high office was viewed as a serious affair, one expected to be staged in a formal or traditional setting. Yet Schwarzenegger virtually eradicated the wall between politics and entertainment with his break from convention. Some critics would argue, however, that his bold move should not be seen as totally unexpected. After all, Schwarzenegger had achieved fame as a professional body builder and, later, as an actor, well before shifting to the realm of politics. Still, other former entertainers had transferred to the political field, but none of them had ever commenced a run for governor on late night, broadcast, television.

Then again, something similar had happened just one month before, albeit on cable television, which usually draws a significantly smaller audience than its broadcast competitor. John Edwards announced his candidacy for the nation's most prestigious political office—the presidency of the United States—on a different yet related venue. The Democrat declared his intention to run for the top spot on the ticket for the White House on the satirical, news parody program *The Daily Show with Jon Stewart*. Here was an instance of forgoing a "real" talk show for a "fake" news program.

Four years later, Fred Thompson, a sometimes actor, other times politician, whose starring acting performances on the popular television series *Law & Order* were currently in circulation, combined Schwarzenegger's choice of popular culture vehicle with Edwards's high aims by, in fact, announcing his plan to seek the presidency on *The Tonight Show*. Interestingly, Thompson, a Republican, made this proclamation on the very same day as a Republican candidate debate that he declined to participate in had been televised on the FOX network.

Late night television talk shows have collectively functioned as one of the primary products of popular culture to blend politics and entertainment in a way that seems mostly palatable to the public. Today, there is no sign that the political exploitation of the format will lessen in the future—if anything, given the growing propensity to merge politics and popular culture, the practice will likely increase.

Morning News Shows

Ostensibly a vehicle for news coverage, television morning news shows also blend in elements of entertainment. The genre began in the United States in 1952, when NBC introduced *The Today Show* (also known simply as *Today*), which still airs nationally for four hours (over the years its length has increased) each weekday morning, making it one of the longest running television programs of all time. *Today* inspired a number of spin-offs, whose producers hoped to emulate the format and achieve similar success. In 1975, another very popular morning news show, *Good Morning America*, debuted on ABC. Since then, these two programs have battled one another for the top spot in the morning ratings. CBS, for its part, has not been able to develop a show that consistently competes with NBC's and ABC's offerings for ratings supremacy. Currently, *The Early Show* occupies the morning slot in CBS's schedule. Launched in 1999, it replaced *CBS This Morning* (later abbreviated to *This Morning*), which was a descendant of other comparable CBS morning ventures. One cable station, **FOX News**, also produces a morning news show that attracts a sizable audience. *FOX & Friends* made its entrance in 1998 and, like other programs on the network, is generally recognized as framing issues from a conservative or right-wing perspective.

Although morning news shows devote some time to traditional "hard" news, they are usually regarded as "softer" than their evening counterparts, featuring far more "lifestyle" stories, such as human interest coverage and interviews with celebrities, thus blurring the line between news and entertainment. Many scholars and critics have complained that this "dumbing down" of the news has increasingly leaked into all forms of television journalism. Perhaps the plainest recent example of the cross-pollination between AM and PM formats occurred when Katie Couric, who had gained wide fame on *Today*, was assigned to replace Dan Rather on *The CBS Evening News* in 2006.

Because of the view that morning news shows provide a friendly television environment, politicians sometimes prefer to appear on them rather than other news programs. Those who are facing an election, in particular, reason that they will encounter a less intense line of questioning than they would on the evening news broadcasts. Ross Perot, a former independent candidate for the presidency, who ran against Republican George H. W. Bush and Democrat Bill Clinton in 1992, was one of the first politicians to markedly exploit this tactic on the campaign trail. His morning television program stops included *Good Morning America*, as well as daytime talk shows.

Since then, morning news show appearances by politicians have become commonplace. For instance, the top two candidates for the 2008 Democratic nomination for the presidency—Hillary Clinton and Barack Obama—as well as the Republican nominee—**John McCain**—all hit the morning show circuit during their campaigns. On a single day in December 2007, for example, in preparation for the first contest of the primary season, the Iowa Caucuses, Clinton was interviewed on *Good Morning America*, *Today*, *The Early Show*, *FOX & Friends*, and *Morning Joe* (a morning news show on cable station **MSNBC**). Obama made several visits during his campaign as well, including an appearance with his wife, Michelle, on *Today*. Their joint effort was meant to display a united front in diffusing a controversy that had emerged. Earlier, it had been exposed that the family's church pastor, Jeremiah Wright, had delivered remarks that were especially inflammatory and vehemently critical of U.S. policies. Quickly, speculation arose as to whether Barack shared Wright's views, which were widely depicted as un-American. Michelle, too, had been accused of expressing a lack of love for her country. By coming together on *Today*, they hoped to dispel such rumors and portray themselves as a warm, level-headed, and patriotic couple. John McCain also turned to *Today*, *Good Morning America*, and other morning news shows to discuss his positions and present a likeable image.

It seems almost certain that morning news shows will continue to be one of the tools in the complete campaign arsenal, as well as a forum for any major politician who wishes to get a point across without the threat of a serious challenge from an interviewer. On occasion, then, these programs serve as a keen illustration of news and entertainment merging with political discourse.

Political Satire

An array of variety or sketch comedy shows have placed considerable emphasis on satirizing political officials and events. A few of the most important entries in this category include *Rowan & Martin's Laugh-In* (1968–1973); *The Smothers Brothers Comedy Hour* (1967–1975 and 1988–1989), a show that also featured the presidential "candidacy" of **Pat Paulsen**; *Saturday Night Live* (1975–present); and *Mad TV* (1995–present). Several news parody programs have also presented scathing political satire.

Political Cameos

Politicians have not only traveled the talk show circuit in an act of self-promotion, but have, on occasion, played minor roles in televised series. Richard Nixon, for instance, once came on *Rowan & Martin's Laugh-In* and uttered "Sock it to me," an oft-heard phrase on the show. Over the years, a number of politicians have either served as a guest host on *Saturday Night Live* (1975–present), including former New York mayors Edward Koch and Rudolph Giuliani and former Vice President **Al Gore**, or at least made an appearance, such as 2008 presidential candidates Michael Huckabee, Barack Obama, and Hillary Clinton. Other television genres have also featured cameos by famous politicians. Gerald Ford and his wife, Betty, as well as Henry Kissinger, for instance, showed up in the drama *Dynasty* (1981–1989). In another case in point, Boston resident and then Speaker of the House Thomas "Tip" O'Neill appeared on a 1983 episode of the long-running, Boston-based sitcom *Cheers*. During his brief stint, O'Neill played a bar patron, which, in some roundabout fashion, probably reinforced his long-held contention that "all politics is local."

Politicians and Consumer Advertising. While political advertising is an important component of any major campaign (see Chapter 7), from time to time, in a noteworthy instance of mixing politics and popular culture, a politician makes a cameo-like appearance in a commercial that is not promoting a candidate but an everyday consumer product or service. Some of the most famous spots in this vein include the following:

- **Anne Richards and Mario Cuomo Doritos Commercial.** Former governors Anne Richards (Texas) and Mario Cuomo (New York) came together in an amusing commercial for Doritos corn chips that was broadcast during the Super Bowl on January 29, 1995. In the spot, Cuomo and Richards (who is apparently packing up her office now that her reign as governor has come to a close) talk about changing times, with the initial implication being that they are referring to a shifting political climate. As it turns out, however, they are merely commenting on the new design of the Doritos bag. At a New England presidential dinner later that month, then President Bill Clinton joked that he had been so impressed by the commercial that he had eaten "three bags of Doritos since then." While the advertisement was meant to generate humor by having politicians poke fun at their own images, it also signified a trend toward accepting consumer commercials that feature politicians as nothing out of the ordinary. Though the Doritos spot did not represent the first time a former politician had been involved in pitching a product, previously, popular sentiment held, any ex-high-ranking, government official who engaged in such a practice generally ran the risk of compromising the dignity of the office he or she had once occupied. Arguably, the Doritos commercial opened the door for the famous Bob Dole Viagra and Pepsi spots that were to come.

- **Bob Dole Viagra Campaign and Pepsi Commercials.** After serving as a U.S. senator from 1969 to 1996 and losing a run for the presidency, Bob Dole, who had successfully overcome prostate cancer in 1991, began performing in television commercials for the erectile dysfunction drug, Viagra, in 1999. Though his role as spokesman for the pill provided fodder for late night comedians, it also brought attention to the sexual complications that can develop for prostate cancer survivors and also perhaps helped to reduce the stigma associated with male impotence. The commercials, as well as appearances on other popular culture venues, such as talk shows, seemed to indicate that Dole was comfortable with making light of himself, which flew in the face of the image he had earlier cultivated as a politician—dull, stilted, and serious.

    Later, during the 2001 Academy Awards, Bob Dole made a splash in a commercial for Pepsi. The spot features a singing and gyrating Britney Spears intercut with various onlookers apparently riveted by her dancing prowess. The final admiring spectator is Bob Dole, seated in an easy chair, with a dog by his side. As the commercial comes to a close, he utters "Easy boy," a double entendre that could be interpreted in relationship to the dog or Dole's possible erection. Roughly two months earlier, Dole had starred in another commercial for Pepsi during the 2001 Super Bowl. A parody of his Viagra campaign, the spot leads the viewer to believe it is a promotion for the drug, with the same tone and language (Dole speaks about, for example, "a product that put real joy back in my life") the audience would associate with commercials for the tablet. Soon, however, once the setup is complete, the "little blue friend" turns out to be not a dosage of Viagra but a can of Pepsi.

    Besides acting in these much discussed commercials, Dole has appeared in a variety of spots for other goods and services, including the Visa credit card, Dunkin' Donuts, and Target retail stores.

- **James Carville and Bill Frist Coca-Cola Commercial.** Democratic strategist and political pundit James Carville and former Republican Senator (from 1995 to 2007) Bill Frist also starred in a Super Bowl commercial, which was broadcast during the game in 2008. The spot for Coca-Cola opens with political opponents Carville and Frist arguing on a pseudo-panel discussion news show. Soon, Carville treats Frist to a bottle of Coke. This shared moment ostensibly, in the blink of an eye, transforms their relationship: in successive scenes, they ride a Washington tour bus together, attend a museum together, sit for the painting of a dual caricature portrait together, and cheer at a basketball game together. The final shot displays them clinking their bottles together while viewing the Washington Monument, which is centered between them in the distance. The humorous montage reinforces the theme that is captured in the lyrics of the song sung in the background—"Why don't we go outside and change our view?"

Consumer advertising offers the potential to earn a substantial sum of money after a political career has subsided—with the exception of Carville, who has never run for office, all of the figures in the commercials described above have left the realm of politics behind. At the same time, similar to cameos on other popular culture formats, performances in commercials can help humanize a politician and make him or her seem more likeable. Yet in the case of a retired official, rather than serving as a campaign tool, they could represent part of a strategy to enhance a legacy by changing the public perception of a former elected leader from "just another politician" into "an everyday person."

It is clear that throughout television's history, politics, popular culture, and televised entertainment have intersected in a variety of ways. What this means for democracy in the United States continues to be a topic of much debate.

THE FUTURE

Television will almost certainly persist as a force in how democracy is practiced in the United States. It is likely that the blurring of politics and entertainment will only continue as well. Yet the nature of television itself is changing. Gone are the days in which viewers would turn to mostly CBS, NBC, and ABC for programming. With remote controls and digital recording, audiences now have the opportunity to watch what they want, when they want. Moreover, the consequences of television's further convergence with the Internet are grounds for considerable speculation. Today, people can bypass television altogether by accessing the medium's fare on the Internet, whether on computers, iPhones, or BlackBerry devices. In addition, through YouTube and other similar sites, every person has the potential to post his or her own content for anybody else to screen. Many scholars are hopeful about these developments, arguing that the transformations are serving to democratize the media—and by extension, politics. They claim that slowly but surely, power is shifting from the few to the many, from a relatively small number of corporations and political institutions to millions of consumers. Less optimistic observers caution that the economic and political entities that have been responsible for much of the structure of the mass media will simply adapt and maintain their grip on the new media environment. (For a full discussion of the unfolding role of new media in politics, see Chapter 8.) How the intersection between politics, media, and popular culture continues to unfold remains to be seen.

FURTHER READING

Barnouw, Erik. *Tube of Plenty: The Evolution of American Television*. 2nd rev. ed. New York: Oxford University Press, 1990.

Brynen, Rex. "Mirror, Mirror? The Politics of Television Science Fiction." *It's Show Time! Media, Politics, and Popular Culture*, ed. David A. Schultz. New York: Peter Lang, 2000.

Butsch, Richard. "Ralph, Fred, Archie, and Homer: Why Television Keeps Re-creating the White Male Working-Class Buffoon." *Gender, Race, and Class in Media: A Text-Reader*, ed. Gail Dines and Jean M. Humez. 2nd ed. Thousand Oaks, CA: Sage, 2003.

Corner, John, and Dick Pels (eds.). *Media and the Restyling of Politics: Consumerism, Celebrity and Cynicism*. London: Sage, 2003.

Doherty, Thomas. *Cold War, Cool Medium: Television, McCarthyism, and American Culture*. New York: Columbia University Press, 2003.

O'Connor, John E., and Peter C. Rollins (eds.). *The West Wing: The American Presidency as Television Drama*. Syracuse, NY: Syracuse University Press, 2003.

Postman, Neil. *Amusing Ourselves to Death: Public Discourse in an Age of Show Business*. New York: Penguin, 1985.

Riegert, Kristina (ed.). *Politicotainment: Television's Take on the Real*. New York: Peter Lang, 2007.

Street, John. *Politics & Popular Culture*. Philadelphia: Temple University Press, 1997.

Van Zoonen, Liesbet. *Entertaining the Citizen: When Politics and Popular Culture Converge*. Lanham, MD: Rowman & Littlefield, 2005.

West, Darrell M., and John Orman. *Celebrity Politics: Real Politics in America*. Upper Saddle River, NJ: Prentice-Hall, 2003.

Wilson, Clint C., II, Félix Gutiérrez, and Lena M. Chao. *Racism, Sexism, and the Media: The Rise of Class Communication in Multicultural America*. 3rd ed. Thousand Oaks, CA: Sage, 2003.

Chapter 5

Entertaining News and Political News Satire

Media critics and scholars have debated the influence of the news in informing, and sometimes entertaining, the public. Numerous scholars of journalism and the history of news, such as Mitchell Stevens, James Carey, Jay Rosen, and Michael Schudson, have argued in various ways that the nature of news in America has never been the serious and purely informative enterprise that many journalists (and journalism schools) seem to think it is. Many believe that the very nature of what is news goes through a selective and interpretive process that involves not only what is to be covered but what can be considered newsworthy, and what is ultimately covered out of the myriad of stories that could possibly be presented as news. By nature there is only so much room for so many stories to be reported on the nightly news or in the daily paper (or today, online), and it is through a process of selection and framing that news broadcasts and newspapers are organized. As news organizations (at least mainstream ones) are almost universally dependent upon advertising, certain unofficial rules are also considered part of the average news package. (There are many programs on public television that provide more in-depth sources of news, but they are also usually funded by some form of sponsorship by large corporations.) Because advertising is not as effective when viewers or readers are depressed, the news must also report on subjects that, while not vital to the average Americans life, nonetheless are entertaining and amusing.

AMUSING OURSELVES TILL THE NEXT COMMERCIAL

In his book *Amusing Ourselves to Death: Public Discourse in the Age of Show Business*, the late media critic Neil Postman argued that the American news broadcast does not provide a coherent presentation and analysis of the day's events of note, but instead presents a disconnected and disjointed world of random events, tied together in packages of events where the anchor men and women alternately look sad, serious, and happy as the news dictates. To Postman, the news as presented on television "has no order or meaning and is not to be taken seriously" (Postman 1985, 99). As Postman along with longtime television news insider Steve Powers pointed out in another book (*How to Watch Television News*), because of the nature of advertising and sponsorship, that news "in its worst form, can also be mainly a 'filler' a 'come-on' to keep the viewers attention until the commercials come" (Postman and Powers 1992, 25). The main point of the nightly news is then not to inform, but to keep viewers in their seats and give them information that will not overly depress them so that they cannot accept the transition to advertisements for increasingly larger careers, even brighter teeth, or some new form of "totally extreme" potato chips. Another example of this could also be programs such as *Today*, which also mixes small doses of news with lifestyle and entertainment reports in order to get the presumed viewer up and out of bed, and perhaps even amused on the way to work.

Postman and Powers point out that because news, especially television news, is structured as it is, with an imperative to constantly boost ratings caused by advertising, it is worth considering in detail why news is structured with stories being presented quickly and then segued into other stories, wildly fluctuating in mood and message, until commercials come, in which case the lead-out story is also slightly cheery and upbeat in order to avoid associating a negative story with the product being advertised. As Postman pointed out in *Amusing Ourselves to Death*, news anchors (used to) use a connective phrase "and now ... this" to indicate that the next story had no real connection to the last one, or at least nonlinear or logical connection. This means that the viewer "has thought long enough on the previous matter (approximately 45 seconds) and that you must not be morbidly preoccupied with it (let us say, for ninety seconds) and that you must now give your attention to another fragment of news or a commercial" (Postman 1985, 100). The switch to a commercial must be seamless in a way that does not distract the viewer or make him or her worry too much to enjoy a commercial for McDonald's or a large sports utility vehicle that he or she will never drive off-road. While ideally the nature of news is the presentation of important information to the general public in a way that allows the organization of events to be made in a logical and coherent manner, in reality news is often packaged into entertaining sound bites, easy to swallow and consider for a limited amount of time before one turns one's attention to the commercial messages that are the real point of a news program.

This has also led to a presentational style that, outside of coverage of war or natural disaster, has led to a form of news delivery where the news itself is presented in a lighthearted way, one that emphasizes that although we have just shown you images of fire, burglary, murder, and recession, nonetheless, the news team, or news family, is still there to find coherence for you, show you a human interest story in order to make you chuckle or smile to yourself, and then provide the sympathetic ear of the weatherman and sportscaster. By sympathetic ear, we are implying that the function of sports and weather, particularly prominent in local news (where a majority of Americans get their information) serves as a distracting or reassuring voice at the end of the program. Sports reporting often features a gruff but lovable reporter who shakes his head sadly at the foibles of the local teams and demonstrates acts of heroism and bravery in order to provide a more satisfying conclusion to the end of the day, or provide hope for the future, in that sports teams (a stand-in for the hopes and dreams of the presumed viewer) will always have next year. The weather presenter (sometimes a meteorologist) is often the focus of slightly derivative laughter on the part of the news team, as it is indicated that rain or other inclement weather is somehow the fault of the weather reporter and that the news teams' entreaties for the weather reporter to provide good weather have simply gone in vain. While this level of camaraderie and joking discussion on television has become a sort of a cliché, and does not occur as much on network news broadcasts (outside of the unique approach of the much-maligned Katie Couric on CBS, who was originally vilified by many critics, but who was praised during the election campaign of 2008 for her no-holds-barred interview with vice-presidential candidate Sarah Palin), it has been so accepted that the faux camaraderie exhibited in the news spoof *Anchorman* (2004) was perhaps the least hilarious part of the movie, because viewers were simply so used to joviality being part of the news package. Perhaps Postman has a point in his assertion that modern news presents more entertainment than pure factual news, but it also could be that the presentation of news is inherently structured in a way that entertainment is a necessary part of the packages and that viewers would be "depressed" by nothing but hard news. Or, another theoretical perspective is that the structure of most American television news is an attempt to do something quite different, to legitimatize a system that could otherwise be questioned.

News as a State Apparatus

Many argue that to analyze the American news media system without analyzing the imperatives of capitalism is to miss the underlying assumptions and worldview that inform the presentation of information in television and print news. Because America is a capitalist society, the news, unlike the BBC and other news organizations across the world, is nominally free of government supervision and censorship. But, as American television lacks a government-generated source of revenue such as the television license fee that users in Great Britain must pay, alternate means of sponsorship must be used. The earliest form of commercial advertising in early television was the sponsorship system, where large American companies, such as General Electric or Texaco, would sponsor a program by paying for many of the costs involved in the program in return for favorable mentions on the program. In his book *The Sponsor: Notes on a Modern Potentate*, the classic look at the relationship between sponsorship and content, the late television historian Erik Barnouw argued that the control by sponsors and advertisers on television programming had become so prevalent that those who critiqued this role tended to be marginalized. Arguments that the system itself was the problem could be dismissed as radical or fringe attacks on an entrenched system, one that had worked well since the age of radio. But as Barnouw also argues, despite the fact that "sponsorship is basic to American television," it is also something that "demands analysis and appraisal" (Barnouw 1978, 4). And the power of the sponsor, whether wielded outright or not, is that the sponsor has "reached the ultimate status; most decision making swirls at levels below him, requiring only his occasional benediction at this or that selected point. He is the potentate of our time" (4). What Barnouw refers to as the sponsor is no longer the individual sponsor that would have been named in programs such as General Electric Theater (hosted by future president Ronald Reagan from 1954 to 1962), but is now a group of large corporations that can afford to advertise on network television and premium cable. But analyzing the role of the sponsor as a group of large corporations that influence television through purchases of advertising also fits into the argument that the sponsor is merely reflective of a system that effectively controls network and print news through indirect control. To Douglas Kellner, author of *Television and the Crisis of Democracy*, while television can be used as a source of social change, it also "reproduces the status quo in a highly conservative manner . . . " (Kellner 1990, 6). Kellner, borrowing from the theoretical framework of Marxist philosopher Louis Althusser and the neo-Marxist standpoint in general, notes that television serves as an ideological state apparatus, one that constantly reinforces the dominant ideology though hegemony. To Kellner and others who analyze from a neo-Marxist point of view, television tends to silence those who critique capitalism (Kellner 1990, 9). Television advertising is a system of control, where news that might challenge the dominant worldview is excluded, not always openly in terms of editorial selection, but where dissenting voices are simply not recognized as legitimate, and therefore not included in debates. News functions according to the neo-Marxist critique, as an apparatus that aids in providing social control and maintaining the dominant system. While polls consistently indicate that many news anchors are left of center in their political views, the large corporations that they work for would not allow them to truly question the dominant system, even while minor critiques of individual power brokers may be permissible from time to time.

In his groundbreaking work on media, *The Whole World Is Watching: Mass Media and the Making and Unmaking of the New Left*, media scholar Todd Gitlin applied Erving Goffman's work on frames to the ideological analysis of media pioneered by Stuart Hall and other writers. Gitlin argued that because we as individuals cannot directly experience most of the world ourselves, we must rely on the mass media to create "frames" or "persistent patterns of cognition, interpretation, and presentation of selection, emphasis, and exclusion, by which symbol handlers routinely organize discourse whether verbal or visual" (1980, 7). All mass media must by necessity select which events to emphasize and which to exclude based on considerations of time and efficiency, "thus, for organizational reasons, frames are unavoidable" (Gitlin 1980, 7). But Gitlin and others argue that television does not simply report the world "as it is" but frames reality "as it should be." While much of Gitlin's work relies on Marxist assumptions about the hegemonic nature of the press, one need not be a Marxist to argue that there is a dominant American ideology that the mass media supports both in principal and in practice. As most Americans rely upon the mass media for much of their information about the outside world, it seems reasonable that mass media, such as newspapers and television, function as "a significant social force in the framing and delimiting of public assumptions, attitudes and moods" (Gitlin 1980, 9). Kathleen Hall Jamieson in her book, *Dirty Politics: Deception, Distraction and Democracy*, argues that because of the nature of news, politics contains numerous complex and no easily explainable ideas; therefore a function of news is to necessarily "frame" news by providing "schemas" that "simplify, organize and enable us to process the world with out confronting each situation anew. Once triggered a schema helps us to fill in consistent information that has not actually been provided by an observable event" (Jameison 1992, 166). In watching the news, events are compared in the mind to previous events and easily filed away in categories that have been preestablished. Thus political issues are framed in certain ways that can be easily understood. When the news broadcasters and papers present an issue in a certain way, it is easier for the mind to try and categorize the new events not as discreet and unique but as familiar and routine.

Many scholars have suggested that news media help to determine the public "perception of what is news in pervasive ways" (Iyengar and Kinder 1987). While Barnouw, Postman, and Kellner would agree that the dominant ideology of television is one of consumption rather than one that airs serious coverage of legitimate issues, they would disagree on ideological grounds. However, all these critiques acknowledge that, at least since the time of television, the idea of news in America has become degraded and that for various reasons entertainment is often privileged over legitimate news. In an age where Britney Spears, Lindsay Lohan, and others are more recognizable than numerous public officials, it seems as though something has happened to news to make it, if not more entertainment oriented, at least less serious.

But is this really the case? Certainly many argue that the idea of news has always been contested, and that even early American newspapers were also filled with salacious gossip. Most American papers before the twentieth century were partisan by nature and often featured attacks on political opponents that today would have been considered libelous. Even, as Mitchell Stevens points out, the first newspaper published in America in 1690, *Publick Occurrences, Both Foreign and Domestic*, had more than its share of reporting on scandals rather than what today would be called "hard" news. In his analysis of the history of news in America, *Discovering the News: A Social History of American Newspapers*, sociologist Michael Schudson points out that the concept of objectivity in news is a creation of the nineteenth century, based upon the rise of the Associated Press in 1848, whereupon the new organization, in order to be considered useful by the newspapers that would take stories from the new service, realized that "it could only succeed by making its reporting 'objective' enough to be acceptable to all its members and clients" (Schudson 1978, 4). According to Schudson, when this belief in objectivity was in and of itself a fallacy, as there was no operative mechanism used by journalists to define or explain what objectivity meant, how could it vary so much from (then) newspaper to newspaper depending on the language and metaphors used by that particular paper? As Schudson asks: why in journalism, where none of the features that guarantee objectivity in law or medicine exist or are likely to exist, should objectivity still be a serious issue? (9). If news itself is a construction that serves to report information based on concerns other than objectivity, then news (from a slightly cynical point of view) can be seen as a delivery device for advertising, one that is malleable to outside interests, such as advertisers, and ripe for exploitation and abuse from the networks and larger corporations who own the networks that depend on advertising revenue in order to stay in business. If network news shows (and the Fox News Network, MSNBC, and CNN, all of whom are owned by the same corporations that own the major networks) need to appeal to an audience who still watches news broadcasts and therefore must compete for an audience that is increasingly shrinking thanks to the Internet and alternative sources of news, then they must also try to make their news more compelling, more up-to-date, and more entertaining. It is a vicious cycle: while pundits decry the paucity of real serious political coverage on news networks, the viewers consistently tune into broadcasts that are more concerned with soft news, health reports, and style than with in-depth political examinations or debate.

There has always been a compromise between hard news and soft news, whereupon journalists are allowed to do certain "difficult" hard news stories in return for doing softball pieces designed to boost rating, as in the *Person to Person* series done by **Edward R. Murrow** from 1953 to 1959 (the show continued with host Charles Collingwood till 1961). Originally Murrow had wanted the series *Person to Person* "to, in spite of television, revive the art of conversation." But as Murrow did not have control of the program, ultimately, "what was demonstrated that the image was as significant as the conversation" (Battone). Even though Murrow tried originally to broadcast series interviews with politicians and celebrities such as Marlon Brando, Fidel Castro, and Robert F. Kennedy, he still had to also smile and sit through interviews with Liberace and others out to plug their new movies or show off their fine art collections. Murrow's experience demonstrates the compromise that is part of the engine of the news industry: unless people watch the programs, advertisers will not sponsor the news, in which case viewers will go elsewhere for their information. Morning news shows such as *Good Morning America*, *Today*, and *CBS This Morning* (formerly the *CBS Morning News*) further blurred the line between news and gossip and celebrity information. This was apparent early on as *Today* originally featured a chimpanzee named J. Fred Muggs as co-host with David Garroway, from 1953 to 1957. While the morning shows usually provide solid information in the first half hour, later on they essentially report celebrity news, entertainment, and other forms of soft news. By the time most people are awake and watching the programs, they have essentially left any hard news reporting behind.

Other major news networks have also become increasingly preoccupied with "softening news" in an effort to obtain more viewers. When in 1976 Barbara Walters resigned from the *Today* show to become co-anchor of the *ABC Evening News* with Harry Reasoner, experts bemoaned the way in which news was becoming increasingly oriented toward both celebrity news and the increasing rise of news anchors as celebrities themselves. Even Walter Cronkite, the dean of modern news reporting, was appalled at the hiring of Walters and remarked at the time, at hearing the news that Walters had been hired for $1 million a year for five years, that "at first there was a wave of nausea, a sickening sensation that we were going under, that all our efforts to hold network television aloof from show business had failed" (Barkin 2003, 126). Then CBS news president Richard Salant pulled no punches when he remarked at the time that "this isn't journalism—this is a minstrel show" and mockingly compared the hiring of Walters to CBS hiring a celebrity such as "Cher," adding that "if this circus attitude continues and I have to join in, I'll quit first" (126). While it is questionable if similar comments would have been made if an entertainment-oriented male journalist had been hired as a co-anchor, similar problems arose when Dan Rather was replaced in 2006 (Bob Schieffer was the interim anchor for most of 2005–2006) by former *Today* show host Katie Couric. Numerous critics, perhaps some also motivated by chauvinism, also attacked CBS for going for style over substance. After keeping quiet for some time after his forced retirement, Rather eventually attacked both CBS and Couric in a remarkably candid interview. Leo Standora in the *New York Daily News* noted Rather's comments during an interview on **MSNBC**, "Speculating on the program's declining ratings, Rather said, 'The mistake was to try to bring the "Today" show ethos to the "Evening News" and to dumb it down—tart it up in hopes of attracting a younger audience.' Then in a kinder vein, he said Couric 'tried to change networks, which is always difficult, and change the programs at the same time.' Then he opened fire again. He said the program 'trend line' continues to lean toward excessive and overdone celebrity coverage" (Standora 2007).

Rather's opinion was naturally colored by personal experience, but other critics also noted that Couric had approached the news in a "softer fashion," and for once, the ratings may have indicated that Rather had a point, after an initial ratings boost to over 13 million views, by 2007, the viewership had been cut more than half to just above 6 million viewers. On September 19, 2007, Rather filed a $70 million dollar lawsuit against CBS and parent company Viacom, claiming that he had been cheated out of promised stories of *60 Minutes II* and had been forced out of his anchor position unfairly. At the time of this writing, CBS had defended itself against the suit and is promising to fight it vigorously in court.

Other celebrity journalists include Geraldo Rivera, who famously discovered the empty vault of Al Capone, and were more of the rule than the exception in the 1980s and 1990s as journalists increasingly were promoted by their networks. (Although Rivera had been a serious journalist in the 1970s, uncovering the abuses at the Willowbrook facility on Staten Island, by the 1980s and 1990s he had become a celebrity journalist best known for his personality rather than the quality of stories he covered.) The new CNN and Fox networks made celebrities out of war correspondents such as "Scud Stud" Arthur Kent and Geraldo Rivera who went into combat during the second Gulf War as an embedded journalist. The rise of celebrity programs such as *Entertainment Tonight* (1981–present), *Access Hollywood* (1996–present), and the *E* channel have made news about celebrities as easily accessible as regular news broadcasts. Even though these programs make no claims to be "hard news," the graphics, opening music, and presentational style are intentionally highly reminiscent of regular news broadcasts and suggest that the line between news and entertainment may have irrevocably blurred. As Steve Barkin argued in his book *American Television News: The Media Marketplace and the Public Interest*, the line between what information the public deems necessary and what the news media deems necessary may be blurred as a function of the way modern news is not constructed. As Barkin noted, "large audiences are not surprisingly attracted to celebrities and stories about entertainment. But the celebrity news nexus implies something more: that journalism invests entertainment with greater weight in the culture than it might otherwise receive and that journalism accordingly shapes the values of a culture where celebrity is exalted" (Barkin 2003, 133). As Neil Postman had previously argued, perhaps the way in which news values entertainment over hard news, not the exclusion of all hard news but the loss of valuable news time to soft stories, shows that the only way to find real news is to look to news programs that are intentionally meant to entertain. Perhaps the best sources of news on contemporary American television may be those that were created primarily to amuse, rather than to inform, and paradoxically, unlike the major cable or broadcast networks, actually succeed at both entertaining and informing.

Political News Satire

In an age where many argue that serious analysis of political and social events in American life has been replaced by "info-tainment," it has also been suggested that satirical programs such as **The Daily Show with Jon Stewart**, **The Colbert Report**, **Saturday Night Live**'s "Weekend Update," the various programs of Dennis Miller and **Bill Maher**, and the satirical news weekly **The Onion** provide not only a source of entertaining satire but also both a real source of information and a new kind of space that provides a real form of political participation, albeit an entertaining kind (also see **News Parodies**). In his book *Entertaining Politics: New Political Television and Civic Culture*, Jeffrey Jones argues that "television has begun to [use] multiple avenues for presenting politics in imaginative ways, treatments that can offer voices, positions and perspectives not found in traditional television presentations of politics" (2005, 9), and that "entertaining politics offers a *cultural* site where new issues, languages, approaches, audience relationships to politics are occurring" (2005, 14).

Satire of the news is as old as the news itself, and when network news became more organized in the 1950s, parodies of the stylistic presentation of the news as seen on television soon began. Movies, always quick to try and disassociate themselves from the presumed lowbrow approach of television, have presented numerous critiques of network news. Early films such as *A Face in the Crowd* (1957) showed the news media as being easily manipulated by media-savvy politicians and entertainers. Later films such as *Network* (1976) skewered network news so accurately and presciently that it seemed more of a prophecy than a contemporary satire. Other films such as *Broadcast News* (1987), *Anchorman* (2004), *Bruce Almighty* (2003), and even two science fiction films that envisioned a particularly info-tainment-esque world, Paul Verhoeven's *RoboCop* (1987) and *Starship Troopers* (1997), showed the news media providing either mindless entertainment or political propaganda for the dominant political powers.

There were also several television shows that analyzed television news from a satirical point of view, including the Emmy Award–winning television show *The Mary Tyler Moore Show*, which documented the day-to-day life of a television station. A later shorter-lived program was the highly acclaimed *Sports Night*, which bore more than a passable resemblance to the brilliant Canadian parody *Newsroom*. A more recent example is the news satire *Back to You* (2007), which starred Kelsey Grammer and Patricia Heaton as feuding anchors on a television network. The program was one in a long line that looked at the absurdity of the news-gathering and broadcasting industry.

Cartoons have also been a fertile place for news parodies, and *The Simpsons* have the clueless and self-important local TV news anchor Kent Brockman who once, mistaking a space shuttle full of science project ants floating free, proclaimed his allegiance to "our ant masters." *Futurama*, also created by Matt Groening, continues this parody, where in the future the news is anchored by an alien, Morbo, co-anchor of A2 news, who is waiting for his fleet to arrive and destroy earth, and Linda, a blond giggling co-anchor who laughs frequently at Morbo's "jokes" but never seems to get Morbo's references to Earth's coming destruction. *Family Guy* also parodies the news on a regular basis, with clueless and sometimes sadistic anchors Tom Tucker, Dianne Simmons and, as she is referred to on the program, "Asian correspondent Tricia Takanawa." *American Dad*'s Greg Corbin and Terry Bates, the bickering gay partners who anchor the local news, provide another example. Most of the programs that examine the news agree on one thing, that television news is easily parodied because of its vacuous nature where entertainment and the trivial are much more likely to be aired than actual news. A Canadian program that was broadcast on PBS in the United States was Canada's much more subtle *Newsroom*, which skewered Canadian news in a way that was applicable to any struggling news station where entertainment came before news.

The Daily Show with Jon Stewart

One of the most discussed and debated and certainly one of the most influential sources of satirical looks at news programming, or what Jones calls "entertaining politics," is *The Daily Show* with host Jon Stewart. *The Daily Show* was created in 1996 with then host Craig Kilborn as the master of ceremonies on a program that analyzed popular culture, celebrity, and current events. The show was created by writer and correspondent Liz Winsted as a spoof of network news with a roving group of correspondents (who later included such now-famous alumni as Steve Colbert, later of *The Colbert Report*, and Steve Carell, of *The Office* television show as well as movie fame). Stewart took over the show after the acrimonious departures of both Winsted and Kilborn in 1999. Following Stewart's becoming the host, the show changed over the course of several years into a witty, sometimes caustic, and daring examination of politics and political foibles rather than becoming another "Weekend Update" type satire of current pop culture icons such as Paris Hilton and Lindsay Lohan. (Although from time to time pop culture figures would be satirized, depending on what was going on the political stage that week.) *The Daily Show* became popular, particularly with the younger demographic advertisers find attractive, by 2004.

The Daily Show has attracted a rabid and consistent fan base of close to 2 million regular viewers during weeknights on cable's Comedy Central channel, and presumably more who watch it on repeats and on the various international syndications that air across the world. Questions arise though, as to exactly how informed this fan base is, or whether fans of a particular program have the ability to engage in genuine political participation, or whether *The Daily Show* is a substitution for real political involvement. In her book *Entertaining the Citizen: When Politics and*

Jon Stewart, hosting the 43rd annual Grammy Awards, 2001, in Los Angeles. (AP Photo/Kevork Djansezian)

Popular Culture Converge, noted media and political analyst Liesbet van Zoonen argues that the mechanisms of fandom are much akin to genuine political participation. As van Zoonen wrote, we can accept "fandom as a basis for rethinking engagement with politics" (2005, 17). In this view the idea that being a "fan" of a sports star or celebrity is akin to the same process that is involved in participating in the political process.

Daily Show viewers may be both entertained and amused while watching the program, but are sometimes also involved in a complicated process where entertainment serves to stimulate in-depth thought and discourse, rather than simply distract or serve as a distraction.

While surveys have shown that viewers of *The Daily Show* are not the "stoners" that Fox News pundit **Bill O'Reilly** has called them, they may or may not be more motivated than voters who are concerned with civic issues or voters who listen to conservative talk show radio. Regardless of how effective it is in motivating civic participation, *The Daily Show* is a needed corrective when other satires of news programs such as "Weekend Update" on *Saturday Night Live* concentrate mainly on celebrity parody, it is refreshing that *The Daily Show*, unlike most of the mainstream press, takes one thing seriously, its position as a comedic watchdog, keeping government on its toes. Other programs that could be analyzed in a similar way, but that look at the news from a humorous fashion, would include Keith Olbermann's program, *Countdown with Keith Olbermann*, and to a lesser extent even Bill O'Reilly's program, *The O'Reilly Factor*, which also use humor as a tool to disseminate information.

The Colbert Report

The Colbert Report (the correct pronunciation is the French pronunciation, with the "t's" silent in both "Colbert" and "Report") is a news parody program spun off from the popular *The Daily Show with Jon Stewart*. It features anchor Stephen

Stephen Colbert, host of TV's *The Colbert Report* on the Comedy Central network, does one of his customary salutes during a show on January 18, 2007, in New York. (AP Photo/Adam Rountree)

Colbert as a pseudo-right-wing pundit based loosely on Fox News's Bill O'Reilly. Colbert, who began his career as the token "conservative" reporter/commentator who rarely made any sense on *The Daily Show*, soon showed his flair for comedy and keen improvisational skills, and in 2005 it was suggested that his show be spun off into a parody of *The O'Reilly Factor* program, complete with guests designed to be skewered and numerous instances to increase the character's already formidable ego. Colbert relies on a series of running gags on the show, including hawking his own "formula 401 Sperm"; as he told *New York Times* columnist Maureen Dowd, "the more Stephen Colberts' in the world the better" (Dowd 2006, 54). Colbert also has a running list of people and institutions that are "dead to me" and has asked that Congress build a wall, complete with "moat with flames, fireproof crocodiles, predator drones and machine gun nests to keep out immigrants" (Dowd 2006, 54). In April 2006 Colbert famously lambasted President George W. Bush at the White House Correspondents' Dinner where he advised Bush to ignore his lousy approval ratings because they were based on reality "and reality has a well-known liberal bias." Colbert also made no friends in the crowd when he advised them to remember the rules of covering the White House: "The president makes decisions . . . the press secretary announces those decisions, and you people of the press type those decisions" (Moraes 2007). As the president sat in stony silence, barely cracking a smile, Colbert went on to mock not only the war in Iraq but also Bush's fabled anti-intellectualism and propensity for photo ops, noting that "I stand by this man. I stand by this man because he stands for things. Not only for things, he stands on things. Things like aircraft carriers and rubble and recently flooded city squares" (Patterson 2007). Colbert noted that *The Colbert Report* was an instant success, with Colbert immediately becoming almost as popular in the ratings as *The Daily Show*, and within months *The Colbert Report* was averaging over 1.5 million viewers on a daily basis, more than most shows on basic cable. Like its predecessor, *The Daily Show* (which engages in a mock feud, instigated by Colbert with Jon Stewart) is respected for the serious authors that it brings onto the air and has had appearances by authors such as Frank Rich, Carl Bernstein, Tina Brown, George Will, Andrew Keen, Tom Hayden, and Andrew Shrum, as well as celebrities and politicians such as Al Sharpton, **Jane Fonda**, and Bill O'Reilly himself.

The 1/2 Hour News Hour

The 1/2 Hour News Hour was a satirical fake news program created by Joel Surnow, creator of the popular program *24*, which attempted to recreate the success of *The Daily Show with Jon Stewart* in a similar vein, including fake commercials by vapid celebrities and segments including conservative commentator **Rush Limbaugh** as president with conservative pundit Ann Coulter as vice president. The program drew respectable ratings at first, but lousy reviews, and an erratic production schedule caused a downturn in ratings. The program was canceled in August 2007. While the time may have been ripe for a conservative response to *The Daily Show with Jon Stewart*, *The Colbert Report*, or *Weekend Update*, perhaps as the critics suggested, the fault was not in the programs politics, but in the quality of the writing and acting. Fox announced plans to retool the program and relaunch it at an unspecified date in the future.

FURTHER READING

Barkin, Steve. *American Television News: The Media Marketplace and the Public Interest.* Armonk, NY: M. E. Sharpe, 2003.

Barnouw, Erik. *The Sponsor: Notes on a Modern Potentate.* Oxford: Oxford University Press, 1978.

Battone, Richard. "Person to Person." http://www.museum.tv/archives/etv/P/htmlP/persontoper/persontoper.htm (accessed May 12, 2007).

Dowd, Maureen. "America's Anchors: Jon Stewart and Stephen Colbert Faked It until They Made It, Now They Are the Most Trusted Names in News." *Rolling Stone*, issue 1013, November 16, 2006.

Gitlin, Todd. *The Whole World Is Watching: Mass Media and the Making and Unmaking of the New Left.* Berkeley: University of California Press, 1980.

Hill, Doug, and Jeff Weingard. *Saturday Night: A Backstage History of Saturday Night Live.* New York: Vintage Books, 1986.

Iyengar, Shanto, and Donald Kinder. *News That Matters: Television and American Opinion.* Chicago: University of Chicago Press, 1987.

Jamieson, Kathleen Hall. *Dirty Politics: Deception, Distraction and Democracy.* Oxford, U.K.: Oxford University Press, 1992.

Jones, Jeffrey P. *Entertaining Politics: New Political Television and Civic Culture.* Lanham, MD: Rowman & Littlefield, 2005.

Kellner, Douglas. *Television and the Crisis of Democracy.* Boulder, CO: Westview, 1990.

Moraes, Lisa. "Colbert Still Digesting His Correspondents' Dinner Reception." http://www.washingtonpost.com/wp-dyn/content/article/2006/05/01/AR2006050101558.html (accessed September 1, 2007).

Patterson, Troy. "Dinner Theater: Why Stephen Colbert Didn't Bomb in D.C." http://www.slate.com/id/2140921/nav/tap2 (accessed September 1, 2007).

Postman, Neil. *Amusing Ourselves to Death: Public Discourse in an Age of Show Business.* New York: Penguin, 1985.

Postman, Neil, and Steve Powers. *How to Watch TV News.* New York: Penguin Books, 1992.

Schudson, Michael. *Discovering the News: A Social History of American Newspapers.* New York: Basic Books, 1978.

Schudson, Michael. *Advertising, the Uneasy Persuasion: Its Dubious Impact on American Society.* New York: Basic, 1986.

Standora, Leo. "Dan Would Rather Not See Katie's Changes." *New York Daily News*, June 12, 2007, 66.

Van Zoonen, Liesbet. *Entertaining the Citizen: When Politics and Popular Culture Converge.* Lanham, MD: Rowman & Littlefield, 2005.

Chapter 6

Politics and Popular Music

Politics and popular music have been tied together for thousands of years and American music has often been resolutely political. From the time of the American Revolution, songs, slogans, and musical chants have been used to ridicule and parody opposition candidates. While we assume that the most virulent songs in opposition to politicians come from recent times, actually the tradition of vicious attacks and of lionizing one's own candidate in song and chants goes back to almost the start of American politics. A classic example occurred during the election campaign of Grover Cleveland—when it was alleged that he had fathered an illegitimate child, his opponents were all ready for his campaign stops with chants/sing-alongs of "Ma Ma, Where's my Pa, gone to the Whitehouse, Haw Haw Haw!" Not the most subtle of attacks, but very memorable. Chants, songs, and music were always a staple of American politics and appear to be valuable parts of the political process for the foreseeable future.

Most campaigns since the earliest years of the presidency used music as a way of highlighting issues and gaining attention for their candidates. While many of the songs used by candidates and about political movements were fairly uninspired, many were quite astute and were used to great effect in campaigns where many Americans, especially in the nineteenth century, were only functionally literate and had to rely on slogans, songs, chants, and alliteration to remember important details in a vestige of an earlier oral culture. Political songs helped make campaign themes memorable, and therefore were highly effective ways of rallying the troops.

Although there were numerous songs about George Washington, some treating him with almost fatherly reverence, others merely deifying him, the first true campaign song was most likely from the election of 1800 where the song "Jefferson and Liberty" written by Robert Treat Pain Jr. served as a rallying cry of Jefferson's supporters versus his opponent John Adams (strangely enough, Pain had also previously written songs in support of Adams, but switched allegiances by the 1800 election). Andrew Jackson used the song "Hunters of Kentucky" to great success, but it was not until the election of 1840 that a song truly caught the popular imagination. According to Stuart Schimmler, the song "Tip and Ty," which was based on the slogan "Tippecanoe and Tyler Too" became a nationally popular song. It was written by Alexander Coffman Ross and put to the tune of "Little Pigs," a popular song of the day. According to Irwin Silber, the *American Review* called it, "in the political canvas of 1840 what the 'Marseillaise' was to the French Revolution. It sang Harrison into the presidency" (Schimmler 2002). The election of 1860 and the bitterly fought contest between Lincoln and Douglas led to a plethora of songs attacking or praising both politicians. Lincoln used the haunting "Lincoln and Liberty," written by Jesse Hutchison, based on the old Irish standard "Rosin the Beau." Douglas relied on the explicitly political "Dandy Jim of Caroline," which boldly said:

> We'll raise our glorious banner high, "Douglas and Johnson," live or die;
> We'll vindicate our glorious cause, the constitution, and its laws:
> Aristocrats we do despise, for they the poor would disfranchise.
> The constitution is our plan, that gives to all the rights of man.

Later presidential candidates did not always rely upon songs adapted from popular songs, but used popular music of the time that they felt applied to their campaigns. Theodore Roosevelt used the ragtime classic "A Hot Time in the Old Town Tonight" as his theme song, demonstrating that popular tunes of the day could be adapted for campaign use. Even popular singers could be used to further the campaign theme, as demonstrated when Warren Harding employed Al Jolson to sing "Harding You're the Man for Us" (Schimmler 2002). Franklin Roosevelt used a variety of theme songs, such as "On the Right Road with Roosevelt" by Robert Sterling and "We Want a Man like Roosevelt" by Kenneth Wardell, both of which optimistically claimed that Roosevelt would fix America's crushing unemployment. However, Roosevelt took up the challenge explicitly with his main campaign song, the uber-optimistic "Happy Days Are Here Again."

Naturally politicians found that songs that identified with the candidates, not necessarily with their themes, were also powerful tools for invigorating the voter base, as Harry Truman found out when he naturally chose "I'm Just Wild About Harry" as the theme song to his 1948 election campaign. Dwight Eisenhower employed veteran Broadway songwriter Irving Berlin for his "I Like Ike" song, which was also later the title of a popular calypso song from Trinidad celebrating the president's accomplishments. **John F. Kennedy** also took a song by Broadway pros, "High Hopes" by James Van Heusen, with a rewrite by Sammy Cahn to update the lyrics. After the 1960s, as politicians started to choose rock songs for their campaign theme songs, the quality went down noticeably. Although songs like "Go Go Goldwater," "Nixon's the One," and even Fleetwood Mac's "Don't Stop Thinking 'bout Tomorrow" were adequate songs, most candidates from the 1970s onwards did not stick to one song for that long. In the 2008 race for president, **Hillary Clinton** held an online vote to see which campaign song would best fit her campaign. The winner was a treacley ballad from Canadian singer Celine Dion, "You and I," first used in a commercial, which demonstrated why it might be wise to have several good songs on tap in case a real clinker is chosen by the electorate. One reason for the change was that many songwriters objected to specific politicians using their material (as in Bruce Springsteen objecting to Ronald Reagan using his song "Born in the USA" as a campaign song) as well as the fact that many songwriters, especially rock musicians, were writing songs for other purposes, not to support candidates and politics but to oppose them. This does not mean that candidates will stop using theme songs, only that in a televisual age, the purpose of the campaign song may be less useful in an age of **YouTube** mash-ups than in previous decades. (For more information about political campaigning in general, see Chapter 8.)

MUSICIANS AND PROTEST SONGS

By the time of the twentieth century, advances in the production of sheet music, as well as the advent of the phonograph, had increased the ubiquity of protest music or music made for political aims. As long as there have been politics, there have been protest songs against the dominant ruling class. From English political songs and Irish protest songs, the American version grew from songs that satirized first America's colonial British masters, and later American political figures as well. While protest songs and campaign songs and chants were always effective tools, the use of music to protest political problems grew, evolved, and saw a renaissance in the 1960s with the rise of the modern protest movement.

In the 1960s folk music and rock and roll reestablished the importance of the folk song. Some early examples of political musicians include the contributions of **Joe Hill**, **Woody Guthrie**, Pete Seeger, **The Weavers**, Leadbelly, and others in the embryonic folk scene, especially Joan Baez, **Bob Dylan**, and **Phil Ochs**. Numerous other folk and rock groups in the 1960s became politicized, and protest songs performed by rock musicians became ubiquitous in the 1960s, including songs by artists such as Neil Young, The Doors, Country Joe and the Fish, Jefferson Airplane, and numerous others. From the 1970s to the present punk rock has also served as a source of protest, particularly in the subgenre known as hardcore where bands such as Minor Threat, Dead Kennedys, Bad Religion, Reagan Youth, Youth of Today, NOFX, Green Day, Anti-Flag, Against Me, Nation of Ulysses, and many others have railed against the political status quo. The D.C. punk scene in the 1980s was particularly politically oriented, with Jeff Nelson from the D.C. punk band Minor Threat organizing a series of protest posters that proclaimed "Meese is a pig," in reference to Attorney General Ed Meese in the Reagan administration, and others in what was called "Revolution Summer" in 1985 also organizing protests and demonstrations and trying to arouse the youth of America (or at least the punk contingent in the D.C. and Arlington, Virginia, areas) to take on the system and advocate noisily for social change.

While the heavy metal scene was traditionally not as politicized in America until recently, some players in the heavy metal scene were politically active, such as singer Dee Snider from the band Twisted Sister, who, although he wrote protest anthems that were unclear about what they were protesting ("We're not gonna take it"), nonetheless turned out to be an eloquent and well-prepared opponent of music censorship when he appeared before the senate committee investigating obscenity and violence in rock lyrics (at the behest of the Parents Resource Music Center). Nonetheless, most of the metal bands of the 1970s and 1980s were not politically active (although one could argue that many heavy metal songs were antimainstream religion and were therefore political in their own way). Many modern bands were more politically active, in particular **Rage Against the Machine**, who were prominent as a political band in the 1990s, noisily assailing the American political machine during their prime and after their reunion in 2007.

Numerous rap groups were also politically active, including Public Enemy, Paris, Ice Cube, and N.W.A., who also attacked mainstream culture. Some, such as Paris, were extremely specific in their political satire. On his 1992 record *Sleeping with the Enemy*, Paris rallied against then President George H. Bush and had a cover illustrated of the rapper taking aim in a rifle site at the president, eventually leading Paris to be dropped from his label, Tommy Boy. (Paris returned to the headlines when his 2003 record, *Sonic Jihad*, depicted a plane flying toward the White House in a deliberate echo of 9/11.) While other rappers were more political, an actual agenda other than noting the problems of the world was hard to make out. Public Enemy put out several amazing protest records, but their lack of political focus and comments in interviews bordering on the anti-Semitic (leading to the eventual ouster of Professor Griff, who astoundingly asked in an interview, "why do you think they call it Jewelry?"). Flavor Flav's later buffoonish antics on several VH1 reality programs further undermined the group's message. Some politicians also tried to pick fights with rappers, which includes President Bill Clinton's public fight with Sister Souljah in 1992, or the repudiation of rapper Ice-T for his punk project Body Count, which featured the song "Cop Killer" (before the record label removed the song on subsequent versions of the album), and the list goes on to this day.

Other musicians were also active in politics from a right-wing perspective, although this was rare outside of **country music**. Aside from the **Dixie Chicks** there were not that many mainstream country acts who were outspoken politically from a left-wing perspective. Numerous patriotic country songs were released, especially in the aftermath of 9/11, including songs by The Charlie Daniels Band, such as his answer to 9/11, "The Last Fallen Hero," and Clint Black performed pro-war songs. Toby Keith recorded the pro-war "Angry American." Political country songs are nothing new, but country music has always had its provocateurs. Johnny Cash did a few anti-Vietnam songs. Merle Haggard did the antihippie classics "Okie from Muskogee" and "Fightin' Side of Me," but he also performed a pro-union song around the same time, angering many. More recently, Steve Earle, Emmylou Harris, and Kris Kristofferson all did anti–Iraq War and George W. Bush songs.

Some notable politically right-wing rock stars include the always outspoken Ted Nugent, the late Johnny Ramone, Michael Graves from the second version of the Misfits, and Dave Smalley from Down by Law. Some musicians were more active in politics than others, such as Jello Biafra from the Dead Kennedys, who ran for mayor of San Francisco in 1979 and finished with a respectable 3.5 percent of the vote, and Fat Mike from NOFX, who organized the grassroots activist movement, punkvoter.com, in an attempt to aid voter registration efforts at punk concerts, particularly in the punk package Warped Tour. Recently John Hall from the band Orleans (known for their hit song "Still the One") was elected to a term as a congressman from upstate New York in 2006.

POLITICAL THEMES IN ROCK MUSIC

There had been much written about the politicization of rock music during the 1960s, but it should be remarked from the start that music had been involved in politics for centuries beforehand. Folk songs, madrigals, satirical lyrics, and campaign songs were well known in Europe and across American well before the twentieth century. However, with the advent of rock and roll in the late 1940s to early 1950s, it can be argued that music was inherently politicized as rock and roll music was itself an inherently political act. (Although many dispute when the first real rock and roll song was written or when the genre came into being, many scholars locate the origins as a developing merger of blues, rhythm and blues, and other forms of music that coalesced in the late 1940s and early 1950s.) This is not to say that all rock and roll songs or indeed most early rock songs were political in nature. Some genres by themselves were more suited to political topics, such as folk music and punk rock, but if rock and roll is looked upon as an expression of transgressive impulses, it can be seen in and of itself as a form of rebellion against the dominant social mores of the time. Rock and roll's relationship to race, as most early rock and roll was made by African Americans and was in many cases appropriated by white teens (and record companies) for their own needs, is also complex and can be looked at as a political act. In an era when segregation was the norm in America, for white teens to listen and dance to African American music can be seen as a political act. While we are not arguing that rock and roll was responsible for the end of segregation in America, it was a major political force in the 1960s, and therefore the focus of this chapter will primarily be the examination of the role of rock music from the 1960s to the present in terms of how it influenced and was influenced by American politics.

During the 1960s many musicians were politicized by their opposition to the growing conflict in Vietnam, and groups, such as Jefferson Airplane, Crosby, Stills, Nash and Young, Country Joe Macdonald and the Fish, sang eloquent protest songs. Some groups in the 1960s were outright radical in their demands for social change. Detroit's angriest proto-punk band, the MC5, angrily denounced mainstream culture. With their spiritual guru John Sinclair demanding a new era of "dope, guns and fucking in the streets" and the MC5 telling the kids that it was time to "Kick out the Jams, Motherfuckers!" it was no wonder that people looked for an artist with a cohesive political agenda; one man to whom many looked with optimism was legendary chameleon Bob Dylan.

Although Bob Dylan was always seen as one of the most eloquent political writers of the 1960s, much of his work does not denounce particular events or people, but comments more obliquely on world problems or involves looking at the persona in a political sense. In a way, many of Dylan's lyrics (outside of songs such as "Masters of War" are so oblique as to invite the listener to try and interpret them in any way they can, with multiple interpretations being the norm as much as Dylan playing radically different versions of the same song on subsequent tours. Noted media expert and Bob Dylan scholar Sal Fallica summed up Dylan's attitude toward politics by noting that

> The best analysis of Dylan's politics comes from Dave von Ronk who describes Dylan generally as being on the left, but with little interest in the rudiments of politics; he's obviously sympathetic to the downtrodden, hence his use of Woody Guthrie as a role model but von Ronk describes Dylan as having the sensitivities of a left leaning troubadour but certainly not in any way ideological; there is a very famous incident where Dylan in 1963 was being given an award by this leftist group, and in his acceptance speech Dylan sort of said that he saw a little of himself in Lee Harvey Oswald—and this was anathema to the left and caused a great uproar. (Fallica 2007)

Throughout the 1960s, Dylan loved playing the provocateur, needling critics who dared to question the meaning behind his obtuse lyrics, and deliberately trying to obscure the meaning of his music in a political context. Dylan's political stance then may have simply an impulsive antiauthoritarian streak.

If the 1960s folk and rock movements were key elements in the American counterculture and protest movements, in the 1970s the punk movement was the center of protest, although many of the bands that are best remembered for their political commentary are the British punk bands such as the Sex Pistols, The Clash, Crass, Subhumans, Conflict, and others fighting the good fight for anarchy (even if some of them had no idea what it meant) and protesting the Thatcher administration. One of the most political punk bands from North America, D.O.A. (who released the classic track "Fucked up Ronnie" about President Ronald Reagan), were Canadian, but were equally involved in punk's tradition of protest. Although many early American punk bands such as the Ramones (who only released a politically partisan song in the 1980s when they recorded the anti-Reagan "Bonzo Goes to Bitburg") were not political, they and early bands such as Television, Richard Hell and the Voidoids, The New York Dolls, and Suicide were all anticonformist and antiestablishment. While most punks were saddened by what they saw as the sad but benign Jimmy Carter as president, most punks did not become as politically active until after the Reagan election. Even the Dead Kennedys, one of the most politically astute of the Californian punk movement, initially wrote a protest song against Governor Jerry Brown, an old school leftist, and later had to update the song to refer to what they saw as the real danger.

In the 1980s many musicians began working to actively change social and political conditions, and projects such as USA for Africa, **Live Aid**, **Band Aid**, and 20 years later Live Eight. While many of these concerts and compilations had the best intentions, such as feeding the starving in Ethiopia and freeing South African leader Nelson Mandela, the records themselves were almost always allowed to stand as statements on their own; with the exception of notables such as Bob Geldof and later **Bono**, few rock stars actually followed up to see if the situations had improved. This can be seen as the epitome of the 1980s "protest" movement. Some of the most pivotal moments in the intersection of politics pop culture and music were tied to specific moments in time. For instance, the late 1960s saw a plethora of anti-Vietnam songs such as the Jefferson Airplanes' "Volunteers," Country Joe and the Fish's "Feel like I'm Fixing' to Die Rag," and even Jimi Hendrix's version of "The Star-Spangled Banner" played on an electric guitar at Woodstock. However, during the 1980s, little that could be classified as mainstream rock and roll from a commercial viewpoint could also be called protest music. When rocker Bruce Springsteen put out his album *Born in the USA*, many took it for a patriotic anthem, as opposed to the sad song it really was beneath all the bombast. The 1990s saw the resurgence of punk rock (which had never truly died, but was just ignored by mainstream media for most of the past several decades) and many newer punk bands began to become as politicized as the punk bands of the early 1980s who had a vested interest in protesting the administration at the time.

During the presidency of George W. Bush, many musicians became politically active, especially during the ongoing war in Iraq. Bands such as NOFX organized sites such as punkvoter.com to mobilize the supposedly apolitical youth voter, and they organized tours and records to combat the Bush administration's policies.

POLITICAL THEMES IN PUNK

While it has been argued that almost any kind of music can be considered political under the right theoretical lenses, some genres of music are more political by their nature. Punk rock since the mid-1970s has had some of the most politically volatile music and messages, from all ends of the political spectrum.

While many of the punk bands mentioned above are anarchist or left wing, many members of the punk community were right wing politically as well. Most skinheads, whether racist skins or antiracist skins, were usually very pro-American and often sported American flag patches sewn into their jackets. Dave Smalley (DYS, Dag Nasty, All, Down By Law) is well known for his centrist views and is an eloquent spokesman for moderate political positions in punk rock. Most famously of all, Ramones guitarist Johnny Ramone (John Cummings) was well known for his right-wing ties and used his induction into the Rock and Roll Hall of Fame to praise President Bush onstage. Still today, many punks are divided on issues such as the war in Iraq, although certainly there are more punks on the left side of the spectrum than the right.

However, punk by its nature had several left-leaning tendencies, and the lip service paid to the political philosophy of anarchism (mostly inspired by British anarchists such as Crass and even the Sex Pistols) led to an ideological aspect of the early British revolution that America did not initially have. The most famous and influential in terms of punk look and spreading the appeal of anarchy (albeit, not on a serious ideological manner) were Britain's the Sex Pistols.

While the Sex Pistols were an English band, they were one of the most influential bands in not only spreading punk music to the United States in the late 1970s but also, although sometimes unintentionally, spreading the inherent antiestablishment message of punk rock. While it is debatable as to how much the Sex Pistols believed in some of the messages they were encoding in their songs (parts of their image were created by manager Malcolm McLaren and artist Jamie Reid, both influenced by Guy Debord and the Situationist International), the Sex Pistols arrived in America

Musician Henry Rollins, front man of the punk group Black Flag until 1986, discusses music and politics during the S X SW Film Festival and Conference in Austin, Texas, 2006. (AP Photo/Jack Plunkett)

in January 1978 and avoided playing the major venues in large cities such as New York City, Chicago, and Los Angeles, relying instead on playing in small concert halls across the South before ending the tour at the Winterland Ballroom in San Francisco on January 14, 1978. Lead singer Johnny Rotten ended the chaotic show by taunting the audience with the now classic line "Ever get the feeling you've been cheated?" Although numerous other British and American bands were both more explicitly political and more articulate, much of the interest from the American media at the time of the Sex Pistols was not about American punk (despite the vibrant scenes in New York City, Los Angeles, and San Francisco during that time period, which had actually greatly influenced the Sex Pistols, as opposed to the other way around), but concentrated on the antics and presumed debauchery of the British punks. As the punk movement spread, many American punks introduction was the Sex Pistols album *Never Mind the Bollocks, Here's the Sex Pistols*, which, through songs such as "Anarchy in the UK" and "God Save the Queen," inspired many American punk bands, as well as the growing punk audience in the United States, to question authority and, much more importantly, to form their own bands and question the structures of American music. While many British bands such as Crass (true anarchists who lived in a collective and shared their royalties among other bands on their DIY record label) were more politically organized and dedicated to political change, the Sex Pistols, albeit somewhat by accident, were among the most influential bands in spreading the ideology of the punk movement across America.

The initial punk bands from England and America influenced the second wave of American punk rock called hardcore, which was a more politicized and working-class version of punk rock. In the late 1970s and early 1980s, bands assailed consumer culture, capitalism, and the presumed wasteful American way of life, and political targets were chosen from both the left and the right. A prime example of this is the legendary San Francisco–based punk band the Dead Kennedys (the name itself, a darkly humorous joke at the expense of the American political dynasty), who attacked both the hypocrisy of the religious right, as well as the left-wing governor of California Jerry Brown as a proto-hippy/fascist in their song "California Uber Alles." As mentioned previously, punk took some of the best potshots against authority, as by its nature punk was supposed to be antiauthoritarian. The Reagan administration was a particular target, and numerous punk bands united in various compilations for wider dissemination of their protest. Biafra, through his label Alternative Tentacles, also released the classic anti-Reagan compilation *Let Them Eat Jellybeans*, which featured tracks from the Circle Jerks, Black Flag, and others who were also militant in their opposition to authority and freedom of expression. Other early bands that attacked the Reagan administration included Reagan Youth, The Misfits, and especially MDC (Millions of Dead Cops) who railed against huge corporations and what they considered to be the police state in songs such as "Born to Die," which started with the furiously chanted "No War, No KKK, No Fascist USA."

The band Toxic Reasons notoriously wrote in their song "White Noise," "standing in the streets of El Salvador/the last son of freedom won't fight no more/ the Vietnam era and Khrushchev have died/but the war goes on and I'm asking why." While some assailed U.S. foreign policy, others simply assailed the United States. Black Flag wrote in their classic "Police Story" that regarding the police, "they hate us, we hate them/we can't win, no way!" while other bands such as

Suicidal Tendencies simply sang about shooting Reagan in their song "I Shot Reagan." While some of the aforementioned songs were done tongue in cheek, other punks were more serious in their political opposition.

Particularly active were the D.C. punks in the mid-1980s who organized massive protests, campaigns of active graffiti writing, health clinics, and funding for enterprises that feed the hungry such as Food Not Bombs. During the "Revolution Summer" of 1985, the D.C. punks became more daring, starting to mix the political back with the personal, realizing that to save the world they would have to save themselves, leading away from explicit protest songs and more toward a politics that embraced individual freedom and self-expression.

As the punk scene fragmented (not for the first or last time) during the mid to late 1980s, some bands remained active and spread the message. One of the most intelligent and most compelling was the band Bad Religion, originally based in California, who started out with broader pronouncements such as "Fuck Armageddon, this is Hell!" but soon began to become more diligent in crafting their lyrics, writing lengthy polysyllabic songs that expressed disappointment with the way the world worked and the way in which the forces of authority drained the creative potential and real authority of the people as in "You Are the Government." While few punk bands with a political message toured as relentlessly in the late 1980s to early 1990s, other punk bands soon became embraced, such as Green Day, who were only to become political later in their career. Still others such as the relentlessly entertaining Canadian band Propaghandi frequently crossed the border to agitate for a variety of causes. New American bands, such as Anti-Flag, Rise Against, and Against Me!, provided a positive punk message for a new generation of punks who desired to know what all the fuss was about. While the modern punk bands may not be as well known as some of the bigger names in protest music today, some bands such as NOFX, whose lead singer Fat Mike organized a serious of compilations against the Bush administration, as well as founding punkvoter.com, proved that punk music will continue to take an antiauthoritarian stance into the next decade at the very least.

Many have complained recently that the political climate post-9/11 has led to fewer overt signs of protest in mainstream music, as it would be considered unpatriotic in a time of war. Pearl Jam has always been a politicized band, but has been more vocal recently about their opposition to President Bush and his policies. At the Lollapalooza festival in August 2007, a live broadcast of Pearl Jam was censored during an Internet simulcast by AT&T's blue room Web site when lead singer Eddie Vedder began chanting "George Bush, leave this world alone!" For 16 seconds, the Web site mysteriously went silent. AT&T later had to publicly apologize for the censorship and blamed it on a subcontractor, Davie Brown Entertainment. The band responded angrily, with guitarist Mike McCready writing in a statement that "When one person or company decides what others can hear, that is totalitarian thinking" (Scagg 2007, 30). Although the censorship may have been inadvertent, many critics of the Bush administration such as the Dixie Chicks found themselves the subjects of boycotts and harsh criticism when lead singer Natalie Maines denounced President Bush at a concert in 2004

FURTHER READING

Cohen, Norman. *Folk Music: A Regional Exploration.* Westport, CT: Greenwood Press, 2005.

Crew, Danny. *American Political Music: Volume 1: Introduction, Alabama–New York*. Jefferson, NC: McFarland and Company, 2006.

Dylan, Bob. *Chronicles Volume One*. New York: Simon and Schuster, 2004.

Eyerman, Ron, and Andrew Jamison. *Music and Social Movements: Mobilizing Traditions in the Twentieth Century*. Cambridge, U.K.: Cambridge University Press, 1998.

Fallica, Sal. Author's interview with on March 4, 2007.

Lankford, Ronald. *Folk Music USA: The Changing Voice of Protest*. New York: Schirmer Trade Books, 2005.

Scagg, Austin. "Pearl Jam: Censored." *Rolling Stone* issue 1034, September 6, 2007, 30.

Schimmler, Stuart. "Singing to the Oval Office: A Written History of the Political Campaign Song." February 13, 2002. http://www.presidentelect.org/art_schimler_singing.html (accessed June 1, 2007).

Chapter 7

Political Campaign Advertising

The fusion of political campaigns and popular culture is not a phenomenon that has emerged in the United States only recently. Even by the turn of the twentieth century, this convergence was already becoming established. Building throughout the nineteenth century, during any presidential campaign season, in towns and cities across the country, swarms of citizens would line walkways and cheer as they viewed the spectacle of bands, dignitaries, flags, colorful banners, badges, and smiling faces streaming by. Modern advertising, which emerged and began to assume its pervasive presence in the cultural landscape during the second half of the nineteenth century, had its political forms as well.

The idea that advertising functions as an element of popular culture, however, is a contestable issue. Many critics would argue that advertising actually interrupts the modes of entertainment (television shows, for instance) that people seek out. Yet other scholars would answer that, in the United States, because advertising represents such a dominant part of the symbolic landscape and not only operates as the chief means of support for most forms of mass media but also has a profound influence on the very content the media deliver, it is impossible to separate advertising from the rest of popular culture: the two communication systems are intertwined. This tendency is in effect with political advertising just as it is with general consumer advertising; despite the myriad protests heard during any campaign season in relationship to the plethora of campaign ads and commercials that pepper the mass media, numerous people still discuss them in their day-to-day conversations. Today, various Internet enthusiasts who are especially politically engaged even create their own independent political commercials and post them on video Web sites such as **YouTube**; some of these low-budget creations achieve popular status and circulate widely as other Internet users forward them to acquaintances, friends, and family members.

THE ROLE OF ADVERTISING IN THE POLITICAL CAMPAIGN

Political advertising refers to placing political messages in purchased media space for the purpose of persuading a mass audience on behalf of a candidate, issue, or cause. Yet advertising is but one component of a comprehensive political campaign. During a typical presidential election season, for example, the candidates, their campaign staffs, and scores of volunteers will participate in planning and executing innumerable duties, including the following activities:

- **Speeches.** The politician running for office will implement an elaborate schedule of speeches, delivered at campaign rallies and other organized events in towns and cities throughout the country. Although it will frequently be reviewed by the candidate before it is presented, a speech will generally have been written by one or more persons belonging to his or her team of speechwriters. Given the sheer number of talks that will be performed during any campaign, the candidate will often rely on a "stock speech" or "stump speech," which is a standardized speech suitable for many occasions. At each stop, if necessary, minor adjustments can be made to the stump speech to tailor it to each audience. At the same time, a large pool of well-trained "surrogates" will also travel and make speeches on behalf of the candidate. These stand-ins could include other politicians, family members, respectable friends, or celebrities. Frequently, campaign speeches, depending on the location and setting, receive local or national news coverage, which provides additional promotion for the candidate. Such exposure is generally the result of coordinated efforts between journalists and some of the candidate's campaign operatives.

- **Public relations activities.** Developing, carrying out, and monitoring a public relations (PR) plan is an enormous part of a political campaign and encompasses so many practices that it is difficult to spell them all out. Some of the most important and common PR responsibilities fall under the categories of *media management*, the attempt to control, manipulate, or influence media coverage so that it advances rather than undermines the goals of the campaign; *image management*, the process of crafting and maintaining a consistent and electable persona for the candidate by attending to details of appearance, presentation, and style; and *political marketing*, which comprises the dozens of promotional activities that do not belong to the category of advertising per se. Examples of media management include sending out press releases with newsworthy information that is favorable to a candidate, orchestrating **press conferences** when a politician has something important to announce and desires the attendance of journalists and other key observers, and arranging appearances on various media venues, such as Web sites, news shows, talk shows, or even more overt entertainment productions. Choosing the right clothes and hair style for a television encounter, coaching a candidate on diction and speech patterns, and helping a politician eliminate awkward gestures are all instances of image management. Political marketing could entail anything from a publicity stunt at a state fair to a town hall meeting conducted by a candidate's avatar in the virtual computer world of "Second Life."

  Perhaps the main characteristic that defines PR apart from advertising is that it is often "free" publicity earned through third-party mediation. For example, campaigns do not have to pay news organizations for any coverage they receive. On the other hand, print space in newspapers and air time on television for advertising is always bought. Consequently, PR messages are frequently perceived as more "credible." Whereas advertising is easily recognized as a form of purchased propaganda, reporting through the press or newscasts is usually perceived as originating from the work of journalists rather than a politician's campaign staff.

- **Party conventions.** Although conventions are the sites at which candidates are officially nominated, over the years they have evolved from contentious affairs to major PR events. In the past, conventions were filled with argumentation and dissention as politicians hashed out who would eventually gain the parties' nominations. Today, choosing who will run for the presidency at a convention is usually a mere formality; the gatherings are heavily orchestrated in such a manner as to convey party unity and themes that are conducive to winning the election. More often than not, the central messages that emerge from a convention become the platforms that are emphasized throughout the rest of the campaign. Many of these themes are revisited and reinforced in the political advertising that follows, so the conventions still play a vital role in the election process and serve as a springboard for forming and implementing an advertising strategy (also see **Political Conventions**).

- **Political debates.** Televised presidential debates were not always staged in previous decades, but now they have evolved into a standard element of any election season. Not only do the major party nominees debate, but intraparty debates also normally occur during the primary periods. Each occasion stands as an important opportunity to make positive impressions on the electorate, while avoiding any mishaps. Because a widely watched debate, which inevitably receives substantial news discussion afterward, can sometimes become a key contributing factor in winning or losing an election, a candidate's campaign team is thoroughly involved in prepping the politician for the event, generally coaching him or her in advance on what questions to expect and how they should be answered.

In spite of the daunting array of practices that are put in motion for a political campaign, advertising yet represents one of the most important aspects of the total initiative. Indeed, political advertising has evolved into such a force that, currently, its cost is typically the largest line item in a campaign budget during any major party run for president. Buying many units of time on television, in particular, is exceptionally expensive. Political advertising is commonly regarded as the main means through which presidential candidates directly convey their messages to the populace. What is more, the sophisticated development of political advertising unfolded mainly in the United States and more money is spent on it in the United States than in any other country. Furthermore, because it is associated with propaganda, advertising is probably the most controversial component of a political campaign. For these and other reasons, political scholars and critics have taken an increasingly keen interest in the role of political advertising in the democratic process.

The Producers behind Political Advertising

There are many organizations (and even individuals) that contribute to the creation of advertising during any national campaign season. For a presidential election, for example, each candidate will hire or form his or her own agency or team to plan and execute an advertising campaign. In addition, the parties (the Republican and Democratic ones being the biggest) to which the candidates belong will generally create their own advertising in support of their nominees. Beyond these obvious sources, however, are many independent groups that also mount campaigns to either indirectly advocate on behalf of a candidate or work toward his or her defeat (by law, they cannot directly mention the candidate). Political pressure groups have existed throughout the history of the United States. But their formal function in election politics has intensified over the past few decades, to the extent that they sometimes have more influence over audience perceptions on certain topics than the political parties themselves. A ruling in 1976 facilitated the sharp rise of the political action committee (PAC), which is a group devoted to a single issue, encompassing anything from the environment to abortion. After that, for years, although donations to specific candidates were restricted, PACs were allowed to contribute unlimited funds (termed "soft money") to the national parties, which could then funnel the resources into advertising or other activities. Moreover, many PACs constructed their own political advertising campaigns. Yet in 2002, Congress passed legislation that barred the parties from raising or spending soft money ("hard money" donations, i.e., those going straight to the candidates themselves, remained legal, with their limits even being increased). A largely unintended result of the ban on soft money was the dramatic proliferation of so-called 527 groups, named after the federal tax code that grants them tax-free status if their work is devoted to political causes that are not coordinated with the parties or their candidates. In essence, during the 2004 presidential election, the first one to transpire under the new financing law, much of the soft money that would have been directed to the parties was simply channeled into 527s.

Thus, during any federal campaign season, there are many sources behind the political advertising in support of each candidate. Yet to members of the audience, the ads and commercials are likely to appear as if they are coming from one point of origin for each major candidate. Although it is a legal requirement that the organization funding each advertisement be identified, usually such reference is underplayed and, consequently, viewers are not always able to distinguish the group behind what they see or hear.

THE EVOLUTION OF POLITICAL CAMPAIGN ADVERTISING IN THE UNITED STATES

A comprehensive history of political advertising would encompass national, state, and local campaigns, as well as survey the myriad forms of advertising that have appeared over the years and the various media through which they have been delivered. Yet national, presidential general elections typically generate the most interest among the electorate and, with their vast financial resources, exploit the domain of popular culture more than any other political campaigns. In addition, television has received the greatest amount of attention from observers because it was with this medium that political advertising became a principal component of campaigning and topic of controversy. Discussions and debates about political advertising generally center on its televisual forms (although, as the use of the Internet continues to expand, this is changing) far more than its radio, print, and other media manifestations.

Early Forms of Presidential Campaign Advertising

Throughout the nineteenth century and early twentieth century, political advertising per se was not one of the core tools in the campaign war chest. The only form of mass media in existence was print, which included books, magazines, and newspapers. Politicians and their backers indeed used the press to reach audiences, but much more through partisan news coverage and opinion pieces than directly produced and placed ads. During any election season, people were exposed to posters, parade banners, and pamphlets. Yet these were usually not distributed nationally, nor were mass audiences exposed to them simultaneously. Thus citizens' engagement with these local advertising vehicles was more interpersonal in nature than it would be with the media to come.

Still, campaign advertising, including partisan handbills, broadsides, and posters designed to appeal to the emotions and imagination, was a staple publicity tactic by the dawn of the twentieth century. Precursors to other modern advertising formats had surfaced in the nineteenth century as well. For example, popular songs that foreshadowed the advertising jingle were starting to be perceived as particularly effective ways of mobilizing public opinion. During Grover Cleveland's second presidential race, for instance, supporters of his opponent charged that Cleveland had fathered an illegitimate child and serenaded campaign appearances with shouts of, "Ma, ma, where's my pa? Gone to the White House, haw, haw, haw!" Sloganeering, an advertising device commonly employed to reduce an idea to its barebones essence in a way that drums up sentiment among large numbers of people, was also coming into play. As a case in point, throughout the campaign of 1840, William Harrison was enshrined in the alliterative phrase, "Tippecanoe and Tyler Too." The expression was intended to remind citizens of Harrison's role in a battle against the Shawnee Indians at Tippecanoe in 1811, an event of questionable merit that resulted in the massacre of Indians yet weakened their strength. The reference, cleaned up for the purpose of mythologizing the candidate, was even encoded in song. Supplemented with parades and symbols that signified Harrison was a man of the people (though he was solidly a member of the well-to-do), such as the display of log cabins, the distribution of hard cider, and the donning of coonskin caps, the cheer of "Hurrah for Tippecanoe" could be heard loud and clear at campaign gatherings. Yet advertising's potential as a central instrument of promotion during election seasons awaited the rise of the nation's first broadcast medium.

Radio Campaigns and the Mass Audience

Although radio was introduced at the turn of the twentieth century, it originally operated as a point-to-point form of communication. It was not until the 1920s that it developed into a mass medium. Much of the impetus behind the creation of a radio broadcasting system was the desire of corporations connected to the industry to simply sell radios. Advertising as a primary revenue stream did not occur until after 1922, when AT&T experimented with a type of transmission that was dubbed "toll broadcasting." Like the management of its pay telephone service, the company offered any person who or business that wished to convey a message via the airwaves to enter its studio for a fee. A real estate agency in Long Island, New York, is generally identified as the first company to demonstrate the potential of advertising to fruitfully reach people listening to radio within the comfort of their own homes. After hearing the Queensboro Corporation's sales pitches for its apartments away from the congestion of Manhattan, many people responded and became potential or actual customers. Stimulated by this success story, scores of businesses took to the ether with their own selling messages. Once the business world recognized radio's considerable capacity as a promotional vehicle, it was only a matter of time before commercial sponsorship would become the dominant model of broadcasting in the United States.

Politicians, too, took to the airwaves in the 1920s. In terms of direct campaign tactics, radio eventually supplanted parades and brass bands in importance. Moreover, it offered an expanding array of opportunities for reaching the populace at the level of popular culture. Yet candidates at first relied far more on broadcast speeches and coverage of political conventions than explicit advertising itself. In 1928, a rudimentary kind of political advertising finally found a place on the radio dial. The Republican Party hired thousands of "Minute Men" to present brief radio talks in support of its candidates. Operatives wrote scripts, which were sent in advance to readers across the country so that the same message could be heard nationwide on the same day. Meanwhile, New York Governor Al Smith's failed run for the presidency featured a radio play portraying his life story, as well as five-minute radio speeches, which, due to their brief length and paid placement, could be considered an early sort of political broadcast advertising. In addition, the Democrats created 30-minute shows that fused political speeches with entertainment, such as music and celebrity appearances.

Indeed, as political candidates' understanding of radio matured, as a means of indirect promotion, they continued to learn ways of inserting campaign messages into programming that had the appearance of mere entertainment. In 1944, for instance, on the *Roosevelt Special*, a number of big-name celebrities, including Tallulah Bankhead, Irving Berlin, and Lucille Ball, provided brief endorsements for the candidate whose name supplied the show with its title. As most radio historians agree, Roosevelt became the president who best demonstrated the efficacy of radio for establishing a bond with the public. Four years later, during Harry Truman's run for president, the Democratic Party placed campaign themes into a series of humorous programs it produced and targeted toward women at home during the day.

Political Advertising through Newsreels

At about the same time as radio was evolving as a popular mass medium, the interplay of politics and popular culture in the service of campaigns found another new expression through newsreels. These short films were screened by movie patrons before the featured selections. Mostly a forerunner to the contemporary television news show (in fact, the introduction of television quickly led to the newsreel's extinction), the newsreel was also exploited by political candidates for self-promotion, somewhat prefiguring political television advertising. For example, Hollywood was called into service to help defeat Upton Sinclair, a socialist running for governor of California in 1934. Actors were hired to play the roles of everyday citizens who conveyed anxiety regarding the prospect of a newly elected Sinclair. The following year, **Huey Long**, the senator of Louisiana, unwittingly undermined his own campaign by participating in a newsreel produced by *The March of Time*. Little did he realize that the makers of the short film were partial to Long's competitor; presaging television attack commercials, the newsreel was edited in such a manner as to make him appear ridiculous.

The Role and Advantages of Radio in the Political Advertising Mix

Yet once television took the U.S. population by storm following World War II, it replaced both newsreels and radio as the most potent mode of political advertising. Radio advertising for candidates and political issues, though, did not simply vanish and, in fact, is still in use today. The medium offers several advantages. First, radio advertising is much cheaper to produce and air than its television counterpart, which is especially important for candidates with small budgets such as city and state office seekers. Second, it can reach potential supporters during their drive-time commutes. Third, although television increasingly supplies opportunities for targeting niche audiences, radio can sometimes be even more efficient in appealing to particular groups of voters due to its specialized formats. In general, radio continues to be a part of a comprehensive political campaign.

Television and the Rising Importance of Political Advertising

Observers often point to the advent of television as a pivotal period for political advertising. Election campaigns themselves, encompassing many promotional activities—some of which could even be entertaining to a certain extent—and exploiting every available communication medium, had been waged since the forming of the nation. Yet historically, advertising per se was but one supplementary element within a comprehensive run for office, and broadcast commercials in particular had only been in existence since radio's mass introduction in the 1920s. Once U.S. audiences eagerly embraced the new medium of television, advertising evolved into one of the most central features of a campaign, especially those for federal elections. Candidates continued to incorporate other forms of advertising, including radio commercials and print ads, into their campaigns. But television advertising has garnered the most attention for at least the past 50 years. Some critics argue that political advertising, with its dependence on innovative technologies and large coffers, has turned campaigns into a type of entertaining spectator sport that contributes to audience passivity and leads to less participation at the voting booth. Others would contend that not only is political advertising a reality of today's sophisticated campaigns and not going away, but that it also represents an important form of free speech and an efficient vehicle for communicating with the populace.

Early Resistance to Political Advertising on Television.   Although television technology had been on hand decades earlier, the new visual medium was not fully marketed to the public until after World War II; the industry and its key patrons held that the disheartening conflict and its surrounding tensions did not provide a suitable climate for the launch of a major media invention. The first presidential campaign to include television advertising, then, did not occur until after the troops had returned and the nation was ready to settle into a more routine way of life, albeit, one that enjoyed an expanding emphasis on a consumer economy. In 1948, Rosser Reeves, a top executive of the Ted Bates advertising agency and an influential figure in the field at large, turned to Thomas E. Dewey, the governor of New York and the Republican candidate for president, and discussed with him the possibility of running spots as part of Dewey's campaign. Reeves had seen that television commercials could persuasively sell everyday products and services and assumed that they could also be employed to promote politicians. Dewey declined, however, feeling that such a display would be perceived as improper. Bruce Barton, of Batten, Barton, Durstine & Osborn (BBDO), was also interested in assisting Dewey. But the politician only followed Barton's lead following his presidential defeat and during his run for reelection as governor. Instead of producing and placing commercials, though, the campaign staged an 18-hour television event in which voters around the state asked questions on camera and Dewey offered replies from a studio. With the help of this effort, Dewey retained his governorship. Yet the extent to which his victory was a result of the broadcast is uncertain, as many other factors are at work in any political campaign.

The Advent of the Political Media Consultant

Initially, even as advertising became a greater force during election seasons, media consultants played relatively minor roles and did not function as topmost campaign planners. Not until 1964 did the ad team begin to assume fairly equal status with other major tacticians in a campaign. Sometimes completely separate agencies have been temporarily formed in support of a presidential candidate. Today, a media advisor for a national campaign is generally a powerful figure in charge of the advertising strategy and often, for its overall communication strategy as well. Political media consulting has grown into a full-fledged profession.

Presidential Campaign Advertising in the Age of Television

The earliest significant use of television advertising for a presidential election was for the campaign of 1952 between Democrat Adlai Stevenson, the governor of Illinois, and Republican General Dwight D. Eisenhower. Since then, television has represented the most dominant medium in a presidential advertising campaign, although its supremacy could eventually be undermined as politicians increasingly turn to the Internet and other interactive forms of communication to promote their candidacies. Regardless of how the contemporary media landscape develops, however, political advertising will continue to be a crucial component in any run for the presidency.

1952 U.S. Presidential Advertising Campaign

During the 1952 presidential campaign, it appears that the Democrats, led by candidate Adlai Stevenson, were uneasy about soliciting the help of Madison Avenue, just as the major candidates had been in the previous election season. Although it invested in spot advertising, the Democratic Party spent far less than the GOP on it and, instead, threw more of its weight behind the airing of 30-minute programs that featured speeches by Stevenson and other political endorsers. Some of the themes in his advertising included his purported courage; the political inexperience of his Republican opponent, General Dwight D. Eisenhower; Eisenhower's association with the anti-Communist crusader **Senator Joseph McCarthy**; the purported threat of Republican leadership sinking the citizenry into another depression echoing the Great Depression; and the notion that Stevenson was someone, as the spots put it, who would "talk sense to the American people."

Soon-to-be-President Eisenhower, on the other hand, was probably the first national candidate to demonstrate the efficacy of televised political advertising. The Republican National Committee awarded its advertising account to BBDO, with Ben Duffy heading up the agency's initiative. The Citizens for Eisenhower Committee also retained an agency, which eventually produced TV programs, commercials, and, in conjunction with the Disney studio, a cartoon that featured an "I Like Ike" jingle. Eisenhower backers believed he possessed a likeable personality that would play well on the new medium. Some suspected that his charm could be better delivered through short, casual-feeling appearances than formal speeches. Later, several independent Republican operatives called on the services of the highly regarded advertising man, Rosser Reeves, who enthusiastically championed the use of spot advertising, which would be placed between two regularly broadcast network shows. Working with Michael Levin, an employee of Erwin, Wasey & Co., they devised an advertising strategy that emphasized simplicity and, unlike Stevenson, who rarely appeared in his campaign commercials, Eisenhower himself as the chief on-camera presenter. The General indicated some discomfort in selling himself like a product, yet was ultimately willing to go along with the plan, resulting in the **"Eisenhower Answers America"** series of commercials. Some of the common advertising themes in the Eisenhower campaign included the candidate's leadership potential and Stevenson's connection with the incumbent Democratic president, Harry Truman, who had become very unpopular. While the Stevenson side advanced the campaign slogan, "You Never Had It So Good!" the Eisenhower team countered with "It's Time for a Change." Given Truman's standing with the public, the Republican slogan probably had more resonance.

The Republicans also employed additional television tools, such as broadcast speeches, a drama, and other political shows. On the whole, their TV campaign was in all probability viewed as more entertaining than the Democrats' fare. Yet it was the Republicans' advertising that represented the biggest innovation of the election season and signified how future campaigns would be waged. Reeves and many others concluded, however, that Eisenhower would have won even if they had not developed the commercials. Indeed, the General had gained a reputation during World War II as a hero and, afterward, was a hugely popular public figure. In 1952, a poll conducted by Roper found that Eisenhower was the most admired living American. The GOP's 1952 advertising legacy is that it triggered concerns about the appropriate role of political advertising that are still lively debated today (see "Controversies Surrounding Political Advertising" below). Moreover, the 1952 campaign conducted by both parties signaled the beginning of the end for the long-form televised speech in favor of shorter formats, especially TV spots.

1956 U.S. Presidential Advertising Campaign

The 1956 presidential election pitted the same two men who had run against each other in the previous campaign—Democrat Adlai Stevenson and now incumbent Republican President Dwight D. Eisenhower. This time around, the Democratic Party was not as resistant to the services of Madison Avenue, recognizing that to successfully compete with an exceedingly popular man in the White House, it had to exploit the same tools as its competitor. The party also launched a type of advertising that generated controversy and continues to be disputed to this day, namely, the negative, attack TV commercial. While the form had been foreshadowed in 1952, the accusations in that year's spots were mostly mild and indirect in comparison to their 1956 descendants. The Democrats forcefully took on Eisenhower in a series of commercials entitled "How's That Again General?" Each spot first lifted footage from the 1952 campaign that showed the soon-to-be president making a promise, then offered a response by Stevenson's running mate, who explained how the pledge had not been fulfilled.

The Democratic candidate's team pointed the finger at the vice president as well, suggesting that **Richard Nixon**, who was not held in high regard by the populace, could wind up as president should Eisenhower, who had recently suffered several ailments, including a heart attack, pass away. A number of scholars indicate that the set of produced commercials based on this theme actually ran. Yet the political campaign scholar Kathleen Hall Jamieson (1996), who interviewed Stevenson's director of PR, states that the anti-Nixon spots never aired, partly because the candidate was opposed to particularly overt negative advertising. But despite the actual broadcast advertising challenge to Eisenhower, in the end the election result was the same as it had been four years before; this time, though, the greatly admired Eisenhower won in a landslide in retaining his office.

1960 U.S. Presidential Advertising Campaign

In 1960, many social critics were of the opinion that, given its continuous advancement as a persuasive form, advertising could be a central factor in deciding the next president. Yet the most well-known television event to emerge from the election season was the **Kennedy-Nixon debates**. One of the most significant strategies the 42-year-old **John F. Kennedy** used in his advertising, against the counsel of some of his advisors, was to discuss his Catholicism head-on, in hope of disarming those who worried that a first-time Catholic president would take his orders from the pope in Rome. Spots on this issue were aired in West Virginia during the Democratic primary season to help fend off Kennedy's top opponent, Hubert H. Humphrey. Kennedy continued to address the issue during the general election season, with commercials that pulled footage from a question and answer session he had held with a group of Houston Protestant ministers; his performance during the event is widely acknowledged to have been a masterful one.

For his part, Republican Richard Nixon wished to distance himself from the dubious reputation of Madison Avenue and so formed Campaign Associates, an in-house advertising agency staffed by practitioners who had taken temporary leave from their various agencies to join the Nixon campaign. The candidate was not particularly amenable to his consultants' advice, nor, it appears, accessible for filming. Thus Gene Wyckoff, a filmmaker who had been hired by the in-house agency, produced a number of five-minute spots, each of which focused on an edited series of still photographs; Wyckoff preserved a sense of motion by panning and zooming the camera over the photos. Despite its reliance on frozen stills, the technique, according to Wyckoff, proved to be effective and gave Nixon a heroic appearance. In addition, Nixon was on hand enough to participate in a string of short spots in which he spoke straight to the camera. Some of these commercials contained echoes of the "Eisenhower Answers America" campaign—Nixon heard a question asked by an off-screen announcer, and then he delivered his reply.

Some Kennedy spots featured the candidate talking directly to the camera; others relied more heavily on either a hired voice-over announcer or a third-party, famous political endorser, such as the candidate's wife, Jacqueline Kennedy. The Kennedy team also included a jingle in several of its commercials—the phrase, "Kennedy, Kennedy, Kennedy for me," was its most memorable line.

Given how close the actual voting results were, it could be that the advertising made a difference in tilting the election toward Kennedy. Still, because advertising is but one variable among many others in the voter decision-making process, it is impossible to know what impact the advertising had.

1964 U.S. Presidential Advertising Campaign

As the 1960s continued, the hard-sell advertising approach advocated by major advertising practitioner Rosser Reeves and many others was being challenged by more soft-sell techniques, exemplified by the work of the legendary advertising figure

Bill Bernbach, which emphasized emotional appeals, even humorous ones, over straightforward sales claims. Bernbach, a founder of the full-service consumer advertising firm Doyle Dane Bernbach (DDB), is often cited as the leading figure behind "The Creative Revolution" in advertising. The Reeves method of advertising, Bernbach felt, was too intrusive and did not treat the consumer with the proper measure of respect. Bernbach believed that a campaign did not have to force-feed consumers to be successful. The best advertising, he maintained, could both sell a product or service, as well as entertain or amuse. Often viewed with almost reverence by creative practitioners ever since, Bernbach was hugely influential in the advertising industry and the impact of his philosophy toward creativity in the business is still in evidence today. Although his ideas were developed primarily in relationship to consumer accounts, they carried over into the political arena as well. At the same time, the advertising agencies, which had been mostly linked with a pro-business, Republican sensibility, were becoming more diverse, with a greater percentage of self-identified Democrats and politically liberal-minded professionals joining the ranks. This evolving advertising environment would play a part in the presidential election of 1964.

After the traumatic assassination of John F. Kennedy, Vice President **Lyndon Johnson** assumed office and ran for reelection. He was opposed by the Republican candidate, Barry Goldwater, who had gained a reputation for making particularly incendiary comments, which the Johnson campaign would take advantage of.

The most talked about television episode to emerge from the 1964 election season, indeed, a piece often credited as the most famous (and controversial) political commercial of all time, was the Johnson "**Daisy**" spot, which strongly suggested that a vote for Goldwater risked the possibility of the Republican starting a nuclear war. The histrionic spot, which was pulled after only one airing yet continued to reverberate because of the hubbub and news coverage it generated, probably reinforced the perception that Goldwater was too explosive to competently handle presidential duties. The commercial was followed up by other spots that, while perhaps not as unrestrained as Daisy, were yet harsh and (sometimes misleadingly) depicted the Republican candidate as a far too risky choice for president—not only was he pictured as a threat to peace but as someone who would destroy the nation's popular Social Security program as well.

In one attack commercial, the leader of the Alabama chapter of the Ku Klux Klan offered an implicit endorsement of Goldwater (although, it appears, the spot was never broadcast because the Johnson staff itself felt it stretched the bounds of fairness too far). Another spot that did air (again only once) presented a young girl who was licking an ice cream cone while being invisibly poisoned by Strontium 90, a likelihood brought about, the commercial alleged, by a Goldwater presidency. The advertisement is also notable because it was perhaps the first political spot to ever employ a female voice-over. Meanwhile, the Republican Party went on its own attack with a commercial that rendered a vision of moral decay under Johnson. Overall, however, the Goldwater spots lacked creativity by mostly focusing on the candidate talking straight to the camera. In the end, Johnson won the election in a landslide, outpacing his opponent 486 to 52 in the Electoral College.

1968 U.S. Presidential Advertising Campaign

As the 1968 presidential campaign approached, the party primary system was expanding. In 1964, there were only three primary contests; by 1992, the number had expanded to 35. Consequently, to efficiently cover broadening territory, targeted advertising campaigns became increasingly necessary. Concomitantly, research technologies, including demographic data systems and opinion polls, were achieving greater sophistication, enabling politicians to better pinpoint constituents they especially wished to reach with customized messages.

Meanwhile, by the time of the 1968 election, the Civil Rights Movement and the Vietnam War had made a deep imprint on the nation. President Lyndon B. Johnson, dismayed by his role in the unpopular conflict, announced he would not run for reelection. Subsequently, Hubert Humphrey won the Democratic primary and headed up the party's ticket. On the Republican side, after an eight-year respite, Richard Nixon decided to once again vie for the presidency.

One of Nixon's key media consultants was Roger Ailes, who was the executive producer of the daytime TV talk show, *The Mike Douglas Show*. Blending politics and popular culture, Nixon had actually appeared on the program, where he met Ailes and was so impressed with him that he later invited him to apply his expertise to the Nixon campaign. Frank Shakespeare, an executive with CBS, also joined the team. The candidate's heavily managed race exemplified the growing complexity of using media, especially television, to seek office, so much so that it inspired the author Joe McGinniss to fully describe and analyze it in what would become a classic text on political campaigns, *The Selling of the President* (1969).

Probably the most controversial commercial produced by the Nixon team took advantage of the discord that had occurred at the Democratic convention, when protesters, consisting of mostly students, were beaten by the police, while inside the hall the ruckus went largely ignored. The spot presented scenes of the mayhem, as well as shots from Vietnam, and then cut to a smiling Hubert Humphrey, giving the impression that he relished these disturbing images. The ensuring backlash prompted the Nixon campaign to pull the commercial from the airwaves, although, in a less coarse manner, it created others with a similar theme, linking domestic and foreign disruption to the incumbent vice president.

On the competing side, Humphrey went in what had become the more traditional route by hiring a full-fledged advertising agency, the renowned DDB. Even though it provided an innovative and strategically advanced plan, DDB later lost the account partly due to its large proposed budget and the Humphrey operatives' rejection of the spots it pitched. Ultimately, Joe Napolitan, a veteran of past campaigns, supervised the Democratic candidate's media efforts and headed up his advertising. One notable production was a half-hour telecast that featured a biographical account of Humphrey and the singing of Jimmy Durante. "What Manner of Man" was broadcast seven times on network television and shown on many more occasions by other stations. An example of a spot that generated controversy was a frequently run commercial attacking the Republican vice-presidential candidate, Spiro Agnew, who was lowly esteemed by much of the population. Hired for his creative ability, Tony Schwartz, who had become a political advertising guru of sorts, produced the advertisement. While the line "Spiro Agnew for Vice President" was displayed on screen, the sound of a man laughing uproariously provided an ironic commentary.

On the eve of the election, Nixon and Humphrey each staged a two-hour telethon with celebrity appearances, including Jackie Gleason on the Republican broadcast, and Paul Newman and Frank Sinatra on the Democratic program. In the end, both parties had spent far more money on TV advertising than any other vehicle.

The election result was a razor-thin victory for Nixon, who won by less than 1 percent of the total vote.

1972 U.S. Presidential Advertising Campaign

Feeling the need for a more coherent structure than the one that was in place in 1968, incumbent Richard Nixon formed an in-house team dubbed the November Group, which was paid by the also internally organized Committee to Re-Elect the President (often casually referred to by its less than noble sounding acronym, CREEP). Headed up by adman Peter H. Dailey, the November Group was designed to temporarily hire practitioners from various agencies and then be disbanded after the election.

Opposing Nixon was George McGovern, who ran on the platform that he could get the country out of the unpopular Vietnam War and shift priorities from national defense to domestic issues. Political campaign veteran and masterful documentary filmmaker Charles Guggenheim tried to bolster McGovern's chances with several long-form broadcasts, as well as a series of five-minute and shorter commercials. Some of the spots used a straight cinéma-vérité approach (footage crafted to look unstaged, a technique Guggenheim was known for) or combined it with shots of McGovern speaking directly to the camera.

The November Group put its emphasis on short spots displaying the incumbent in action. One notable commercial advanced the themes of Nixon as a man of peace and, based on his diplomatic visit to Russia while in office, Nixon as a statesman. Yet, in a tactic meant to put the candidate in a warm light, it supported the messages by featuring the president discussing the ordeal of a 12-year-old girl named Tanya, who had borne the hardships of World War II in Russia. Other spots also attempted to humanize Nixon, who was generally observed as cold and distant. For example, his daughter Tricia told the story in one commercial of how her father had slipped a personal and endearing note under her door on the night before her wedding. The Republican's media managers, in general, wished to exploit the advantages of incumbency by presenting Nixon as president rather than as a mere candidate. Still, the November Group went on the attack as well. One of the most famous spots (channeled through a subgroup, "Democrats for Nixon," to distance the president from any appearance of personally mudslinging) to emerge from the campaign was an assault on McGovern's purported weakness on defense. Using toy soldiers, the commercial showed a hand removing several of them at a time while an announcer stated McGovern's plan to cut back on military expenses.

Because McGovern was so far behind in the polls as November's vote drew near, his staff felt the need to create a negative campaign, a common strategy for a candidate who is significantly trailing his or her opponent in the last days of an election season. One commercial even focused on the notorious **Watergate** break-in; since the illegal activity had not yet escalated into a full-blown public scandal, though, the advertisement had little effect. As the Democratic side became even more desperate, Guggenheim stepped aside and was replaced by the highly regarded Tony Schwartz. But all of the last-minute toil was to no avail, as Nixon won reelection in a rout.

1976 U.S. Presidential Advertising Campaign

Nixon's 1972 election triumph was short lived. The Watergate scandal came crashing down on him about a year later, soon resulting in his resignation from office in 1974 (see **Nixon Farewell Speech**). **Gerald Ford**, who had become vice president after Spiro Agnew's earlier resignation, assumed the presidency and ran for election (his first, giving him the distinction as the only person in U.S. history to become both vice president and president without a vote) in 1976 to maintain office. Following the hiring and firing of two media teams in several months, he turned to the political consulting firm Bailey, Deardourff and Associates for help. The business in turn hired copywriter Malcolm MacDougall, who had gained prominence through his work with clients such as Oldsmobile and Titleist. The Democratic candidate, **Jimmy Carter**, a relative unknown at that point, secured the services of Gerald Rafshoon, a former publicity and advertising director for Twentieth Century Fox, who had worked on Carter's campaigns for governor of Georgia in 1966 (which he lost) and 1970 (which he won). Because of amendments that had been added to the Federal Election Campaign Act in 1974, the 1976 contest became the nation's first heavily federally funded presidential campaign and each side operated with the same amount—about $22 million. Ultimately, roughly 50 percent of the budget went to advertising, with about 60 percent of this ad expenditure going toward television. These percentages, which have held relatively steady throughout the years, attest to the ever-progressive significance of advertising during presidential campaigns. Equal spending limits in general, however, favor the incumbent, since he or she typically receives much additional media coverage, free of charge, by simply carrying out the duties of the office.

To familiarize the population with Carter during the primary elections, Rafshoon produced a five-minute film that depicted the candidate as a "real" man, wearing blue jeans and boots, and walking through a peanut farm. On the other side, despite his image as a "nice guy," Ford had, whether fairly or unfairly, acquired the reputation of being a "bumbler" (thanks in no small part to Chevy Chase's parody of him, complete with stumbling and pratfalls, on the comedic variety show *Saturday Night Live*; also see **Ford, Gerald [Media Portrayals]**). Thus the Ford team set out to depict him as a strong leader. The staff produced a campaign theme, "I'm Feelin' Good about America," and a jingle to deliver it over visuals of happy people. Ford advertising also presented biographical material designed to help the public better know the candidate and inspire it to regard him as warm and upright. Carter's staff also took a high road of sorts, showing him as a family man with traditional American values. Against the backdrop of Watergate, both candidates wished to demonstrate that they were men of strong moral character. Consequently, their commercials tended to be less polished than those that had aired during the three previous election seasons. Instead, the spots often employed more straightforward techniques, such as the candidates directly addressing viewers and everyday people giving personal testimonies.

In the final days leading up to the election, Carter brought in Tony Schwartz, who had acquired a reputation as a seasoned, political advertising expert, to produce a series of radio and television spots, several of which, just in case, took an attack approach, and some of which were targeted toward particular constituencies. Ford's campaigners also segmented their market; in one memorable series of programs aimed at key states, the baseball celebrity Joe Garagiola leant his endorsement. Attack spots rounded out the advertising arsenal. On the evening before the vote, both candidates broadcast long-form shows. The next day, Carter won the presidency in a close contest.

1980 U.S. Presidential Advertising Campaign

By the end of Jimmy Carter's term in the White House, a common perception was that, although he appeared to be a decent human being, the president was "weak" and his administration was inept. **Ronald Reagan**, the Republican candidate in 1980, meanwhile, quickly earned the distinction of being a master of television. Given his earlier career as an actor and a commercial spokesperson, especially for General Electric, he was comfortable with the medium. Accordingly, Reagan spoke directly to the camera in his commercials, much more than candidates had done in recent presidential election seasons. Peter H. Dailey, the media specialist who had assisted Richard Nixon in 1972, was hired to head up an in-house agency, named Campaign '80. John Anderson, running as an independent, rounded out the field, but eventually dropped out.

Despite Carter's low standing, he still had the advantages of incumbency, and his campaign team, again led by Gerald Rafshoon, attempted to depict him as a world leader. In some spots, for example, he was shown in action during the Camp David accords, which were regarded as one of his top success stories. On the other hand, some commercials went negative, with messages that included the projection that Reagan's economic policies (originally termed by **George H. W. Bush** during the Republican primaries as "voodoo economics") would hurt the nation and the insinuation that Reagan, at 69, was too old and mentally feeble for the presidency. Carter's team also strove to reinforce the fear that Reagan might be too predisposed to starting a war.

On the Republican side, the commercials for Reagan mostly sounded a positive tone. Reagan's strategy played to his strengths: whether accurately reflecting the real man or not, his media image was nearly untarnished (except for the belief held by many that he was overly hawkish). A five-minute advertisement that aimed to paint an inspirational summary of Reagan's life and political record was heavily broadcast. At the same time, the candidate was not entirely averse to waging attacks, although they were often indirect or at least kept Reagan out of the picture. For example, the GOP lifted and broadcast footage from speeches Edward Kennedy had given during the Democratic primaries, in which he had blasted Carter on his performance as president. Such a tactic has often been implemented, especially when one side's candidate has all but been assured while the other party's nominee has had to survive a hotly contested primary season. Primary campaigns, indeed, often provide fodder for later attack advertising—one party can resurrect criticism once directed at the eventual winning candidate from the other party by an intraparty challenger who ultimately failed to gain the nomination. Using a "surrogate," rather than the candidate himself or herself, in attack advertising is also very common. Political consultants frequently believe that personally engaging in mudslinging can weaken the perception of a candidate, making him or her appear too vindictive and unsuitable for office. Letting others carry out the attacks, they reason, will help the candidate stay above the fray and seem more honorable.

It appears that Carter's advertising was never able to counter his reputation as a weak leader. What is more, unlike the Democratic National Committee (DNC), the Republican National Committee ran a considerable amount of advertising of its own, some of which instructed the audience to "Vote Republican for a Change." Finally, in response to a 1976 Supreme Court Ruling that allowed independent organizations to spend money on political campaigns, a number of PACs produced advertising as well—these PACs channeled far more expenditures toward the support of Reagan than Carter.

On the night before the election, both candidates aired long-format shows. Carter's 20-minute program was narrated by the actor Henry Fonda. Meanwhile, Reagan's 30-minute vehicle did not physically include any celebrities. Yet during his talk, Reagan referred to John Wayne, the famous actor who had recently died, as an emotionally moving symbol of the country. On Election Day, Reagan easily won the presidency, besting Carter by nearly 10 percent in the popular vote and 489 to 49 in the Electoral College. To a considerable extent, Ronald Reagan represented how far political campaigns had come in embracing the services of television. In 1948, Harry S. Truman had flat-out refused to run television advertising. Just over three decades later, Reagan obtained the nation's highest office, in part, because of his ability to deliver inspiring performances on the small screen in commercials and other formats.

1984 U.S. Presidential Advertising Campaign

In 1984, President Ronald Reagan's reelection was all but certain. He was a very popular president and was in a position to realize the advantages of incumbency. Following the example Nixon had established in 1972, the Republicans formed an in-house election team. Capitalizing on the good feelings Reagan evoked in many citizens, this group of professionals developed a soft-sell series of flag-filled commercials entitled, "**Morning in America**," which became one of the most memorable and broadcast campaigns of the 1984 run for top office. In other advertisements, the Reagan effort further tapped into patriotic sentiments with the help of a song by country musician Lee Greenwood entitled, "God Bless the USA."

Democrat Walter Mondale's team attacked Reagan on his vulnerabilities, yet its attempts ultimately failed to achieve its objectives. The Republican side proved adept at blunting accusations and sustaining its own case. In probably the most discussed political commercial of 1984, the GOP showed a bear that came face-to-face with a young man holding a gun. At the close of the commercial, however, the bear took a step back, suggesting that the man had stood down the threat. The accompanying voice-over announcer made it clear that the bear symbolized the Soviet Union and that President Reagan was the man who could keep a potentially dangerous USSR at bay.

Throughout the months leading to Election Day, Mondale never represented a serious challenge to the incumbent and suffered the worst defeat in the Electoral College since 1936.

1988 U.S. Presidential Advertising Campaign

The advertising campaign for Vice President George H. W. Bush, the Republican candidate for president, unlike his predecessor's, Ronald Reagan, was anything but sweet. The Bush staff vehemently attacked the Democratic challenger, Michael Dukakis, portraying him as too liberal to successfully lead the nation. Subsequent to airing a series of commercials designed to convey a positive image of the Republican candidate, the Bush campaign turned aggressive and went for the jugular. For instance, one spot, using deceptive tactics, blamed Dukakis for the horribly polluted conditions in Boston Harbor. Yet the commercial that stood out from all the others—and some scholars argue, had a large impact on the election results themselves—was the one known as the "**Furlough**" spot or as "Revolving Door," which, combined with spin-offs produced by other interest groups, in misleading fashion, cast Dukakis as weak on crime.

Another attack spot that generated a strong reaction used actual footage from a Dukakis campaign stop. In the commercial, Dukakis was shown riding in an army tank. His manner and expression, however, made him look terribly out of place and silly. Once again, this commercial implied, the candidate was too soft for office. The point was underscored by an announcer who presented greatly distorted claims about the governor's record on defense. The Dukakis team tried numerous ways to dampen the Republican offensive, including the use of several spots that presented what some observers would contend were clumsy (and belated) rebuttals. A number of Democrats also charged that the GOP was staging a dirty campaign in general and "Revolving Door" in particular was racist because it resorted to stereotypes and played into typical Caucasian fears. Earlier, an independently produced spot had established the theme that, under a furlough program in Dukakis's home state of Massachusetts, some criminals were allowed weekend passes and committed crimes while on leave. As a case in point, the commercial specifically called attention to Willie Horton, a black criminal, and his victims, who were white. Although the "Revolving Door" advertisement created by the Bush team never explicitly mentioned his name, by centering on the same furlough message, the commercial triggered associations of Horton and his violent misdeeds. (Even today, political scholars debate whether the allegation of racism holds merit.) At the same time, Dukakis and his staff employed the services of David D'Alessandro, an agency professional who had made a name for himself by creating a highly esteemed advertising campaign for John Hancock Mutual Life Insurance, known as "Real Life, Real Answers," which featured slice-of-life vignettes that appeared very realistic. When the technique was applied to election politics, however, it seemed to come off as fake and the spots were quickly retired. The Dukakis campaign also aired a set of commercials that questioned Bush's choice of Dan Quayle, commonly regarded as inexperienced and inept, as his candidate for vice president.

In the end, all of the Democratic efforts were to no avail. After the votes were tallied, having garnered about 54 percent of the popular vote, Bush was again headed to the Oval Office, this time not as the number two man, but as the top person in office.

Various members of the academic community and other critics often point to the 1988 election as an especially poignant example of the problematic role of television commercials—it has even been cited as the most malicious presidential campaign in the history of televised politics (although some claim the 2004 run rivals it). Moreover, a number of scholars even identify the Bush advertising campaign as one of the most important factors, if not *the* most important one, in Dukakis's fall. There is probably enough evidence to indicate it indeed influenced voters' assessments of the candidates. Polls revealed, for instance, that as "Revolving Door" continued to run, more and more people viewed the Democrat as soft on crime. Dukakis's standing in relationship to the environment also deteriorated once the Benton Harbor spot had made an impression through the airwaves. Such negative representations, some critics say, produce a more cynical electorate. Others note that the attacks were grossly deceiving, a characteristic that TV commercials, through editing and contrived juxtapositions, can readily nurture. Yet defenders of political television advertising counter that maligning opponents, engaging in deception, and image making have always been a part of the election process. In addition, they answer, voters have plenty of sources from which to get information and advertising is but one influence among many others. (Also see "Controversies Surrounding Political Advertising" below.)

1992 U.S. Presidential Advertising Campaign

By the election season of 1992, incumbent George H. W. Bush's popularity had precipitously decreased. It appears that attention had shifted from the victorious battle abroad during the 1991 Gulf War to the less than stellar performance of the economy at home. The team of **Bill Clinton**, the governor of Arkansas and Democratic contender, seized on the issue, using it to define one of its central themes. Meanwhile, a third candidate, Ross Perot, unlike so many other independents before him, mounted a serious challenge to the Democratic and Republican nominees.

Bill Clinton's staff included communications director George Stephanopoulos and chief strategist **James Carville**, both of whom achieved a type of fame through their performances in the documentary *The War Room*, a film that presented a behind-the-scenes look at the Clinton campaign and received an Academy Award nomination for best documentary. Meanwhile, the GOP pulled from Madison Avenue in forming the November Group. The in-house agency featured a number of people who had worked on Bush's previous campaign. Only after abruptly dropping out of the race in July, and then reentering it in October, did Perot hire the services of the Temerlin-McClain agency, which renamed itself the 270 Group, signifying the number of electoral votes needed to win the election.

Democratic political strategist James Carville, in a 1991 photo. (AP Photo/George Widman)

Besides featuring longer format biographical films on various occasions, the Clinton side produced a number of radio and television commercials that attempted to depict an empathetic candidate as well as attack Bush's record. One of its TV techniques was to contrast actual statements pulled from the Republican's speeches with revelations by an announcer and textual documentation that undermined Bush's claims and sought to reinforce him as deceitful. As is frequently the case with political advertising, sometimes these spots presented facts in misleading ways.

Just as they had done in 1988, Bush's strategists opted to run another negative campaign; indeed, they broadcast proportionately more oppositional ads than any prior presidential campaign during the television era had ever implemented. One commercial that stood out displayed two people, whose faces were blocked out, side-by-side. The announcer noted a position that the "candidate on the left" stood for, and then called attention to an opposite stance held by the "candidate on the right." At the end of the commercial, the faces were revealed and the viewer learned that both people were Bill Clinton. Another spot, one that sparked controversy due to its deceptive use of statistics, featured several workers from various backgrounds; underneath each person, the amount of the additional taxes he or she would supposedly pay under Clinton was displayed. In a third notable commercial, a *Time* magazine cover with the headline "Why Voters Don't Trust Clinton" was reproduced on screen. Yet in many cases, when mounting attacks, the Republicans saw Clinton's tacticians working to defuse each one through commercials of their own. Not all of the Bush spots were negative, however. Because Bush held an advantage in the polls on international affairs, his positive spots often endeavored to deflect attention from domestic policies and indicate the president's prominence as a world leader. One commercial, for example, contained shots of the Gulf War and Russian President Boris Yeltsin.

Ross Perot manifested a novel, if somewhat eccentric, approach to running for the presidency. His most significant innovation consisted of giving rebirth to the half-hour political commercial. During a five-week period, Perot aired 11 such programs. In several of them, the candidate talked frankly, challenged the status quo, and employed a broad array of homemade looking charts, using a pointer to present his arguments. The shows attracted a large audience and demonstrated that the long-term format could still be effective.

On Election Day, George H. W. Bush received about 38 percent of the vote, while Perot garnered roughly 19 percent. Bill Clinton, who despite capturing just 43 percent of the ballots, the fourth lowest total for any winning presidential candidate in U.S. history, earned victory. Political pundits often contend that Perot perhaps cost Bush the election because he siphoned off more Republican than Democratic votes.

1996 U.S. Presidential Advertising Campaign

The 1996 presidential election season was, for the most part, uneventful. President Bill Clinton, backed by a relatively strong economy and no serious foreign threats to the nation, was able to almost completely realize the advantages of incumbency. Republican candidate Senator **Robert (Bob) Dole** of Kansas had little ammunition with which to defeat him. As he had done in the previous election, Ross Perot again entered the race, this time as the Reform Party candidate, but never generated the kind of formidable challenge he had posed four years earlier.

Clinton mounted an advertising blitz over the summer, before Dole, still focused on warding off Republican opponents during the party's primary season, could direct his attention to the general election. One central message the Clinton campaign team attempted to convey was to portray Bob Dole as an aging and frail conservative who was out of touch with the common citizen. In the end, the presidential election result was decisive. Although Clinton, once more, did not receive over 50 percent of the popular vote, he beat Dole by over eight percentage points. In the Electoral College, the tally was 379 to 159. Perot's totals were less than half of what they had been in the previous election.

2000 U.S. Presidential Advertising Campaign

The 2000 presidential vote was one of the closest and most controversial elections in U.S. history. On the evening of the balloting, it was becoming clear that whoever won the state of Florida would claim victory in the Electoral College. After the polls were closed, the broadcast news shows originally projected that current Democratic Vice President **Al Gore** would carry the state. Later, however, the networks retracted their declaration, and then eventually announced that Republican candidate and current governor of Texas **George W. Bush** had prevailed. Yet the number of votes separating the two in Florida was so small that Gore asked for a recount. Thus set in motion about a month of contentious recounts, court trials, and public relations maneuvering on both sides, a process that was incessantly covered by the news media and followed by millions of anxious viewers. Finally, the issue went before the Supreme Court, which, in a contentious move that continues to be disputed even today, demanded the recount be stopped, essentially awarding Bush the presidency. The election controversy was further exacerbated by the campaign of Green Party candidate Ralph Nader. Some angry Gore backers felt that Nader was responsible for the vice president's defeat because he had supposedly siphoned off more Florida votes that would have otherwise gone to Gore than the mere 537 that ultimately determined the contest.

When the 2000 election season had begun, the incumbency of Al Gore was a mixed blessing. On the one hand, the U.S. economy had prospered under President Bill Clinton's and Gore's leadership. On the other hand, Gore was linked to Clinton, who had recently endured impeachment for lying to—or at least seriously misleading—the populace about his extramarital affair with his one-time intern, Monica Lewinsky (see **Political Scandals**). Meanwhile, Republican George W. Bush was relatively inexperienced in politics and had gained the reputation, whether fairly or unfairly, of lacking intelligence.

One of the distinctive aspects of the 2000 election season was the wider use of talk shows for political promotion. Indeed, the tendency to exploit a variety of popular culture vehicles had become increasingly common over the years (see "Political Promotion, Popular Culture, and Youth Voters" below). In targeted "battleground" states—those the campaigns felt would decide the election—advertising played a central role. Although Gore was an incumbent, he and his Democratic supporters actually produced more negative attack commercials than the Bush campaign, perhaps because opinion polls usually showed that the Republican had a slight lead. The issue the Democrats seemed to focus on in their spots more than any other was health care, contending that Bush would attempt to privatize the system and, consequently, in their view, dramatically weaken its

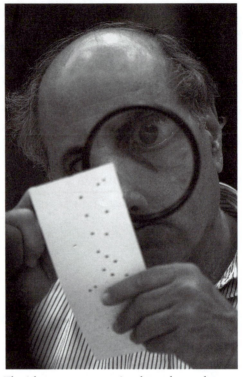

A Broward County, Florida, vote canvassing board member uses a magnifying glass to examine a disputed presidential ballot November 2000, in Fort Lauderdale, Florida. (AP Photo/Alan Diaz)

protections. They also heartily challenged Bush's tax cut plan. On the Republican side, one of the top issues appeared to be education. The Bush campaign regularly rebuked the Clinton-Gore performance on schooling, even though education had traditionally been a subject discussed more often by Democrats. In one spot, the announcer asked, "Is the status quo in America's schools good enough? Under Al Gore and Bill Clinton, national reading scores stagnated. America's high school students place almost dead last in international math tests." Further, mirroring tactics that had been utilized in past presidential campaigns, Bush staff members also produced advertising that presented statements by Gore, followed by evidence that contradicted those assertions. In this way, they hoped to reinforce the idea that Gore often offered false accounts. Finally, Bush's advertising repeatedly endeavored to connect Gore with Clinton as a means of questioning the vice president's sense of morality.

After the Supreme Court's decision, despite Gore gathering more popular votes than the Republican contender, George W. Bush won the Electoral College, 271 to 266, and took up residence in the White House.

2004 U.S. Presidential Advertising Campaign

If the 2004 presidential campaign season was not as controversial as its predecessor of four years earlier, it was still a polarizing event resulting in a very close election. The incumbent, George W. Bush, had become a highly contentious figure during his first term in office. Particularly after the calamity of September 11, 2001, when terrorists had crashed planes into the World Trade Center in New York City and the Pentagon in Washington, Bush took measures and conveyed attitudes that some people found deeply troubling while others roundly applauded. Critics of Bush contended that a number of actions represented a draconian response to the crisis of September 11; defenders often acknowledged that these tactics were extraordinary but held that the times demanded such an approach—the president was simply doing what was necessary to protect the citizenry. Keeping the country safe from terrorism and other threats became one of the defining issues of the 2004 campaign.

The advertising campaigns for Bush and his Democratic challenger, Senator John Kerry, reflected the mood of the dueling camps inspired by the president's first term in office. The run for president in 2004 was the most expensive one in history, and a large percentage of each side's budget was devoted to advertising. At the beginning of the general election, the Bush team produced commercials that emphasized the candidate's positive attributes. Yet a spot entitled "Safer, Stronger" set off debate early on because it featured a shot of firefighters handling a flag-draped body at the site of the World Trade Center attacks, a scene that angered some viewers, who thought its use was cynical and exploitative. Soon the Bush side also employed negative techniques. In a spot dubbed "100 Days," its producers claimed that if Kerry were elected, he would raise taxes by $900 billion by his hundredth day in office. Another commercial pronounced that Kerry would impose a gasoline tax that would harm American families. Besides the prospect of Kerry raising taxes, a central theme conveyed by the Bush campaigners was the idea that the Senator was a "waffler"; that is, he was prone to making initial declarations, then contradicting those statements later on. A notable spot that vividly reinforced this accusation portrayed a windsurfing John Kerry. As an announcer cited conflicting Kerry positions (for example, "Kerry voted for the Iraq war, opposed it, supported it and now opposes it again"), the Democrat was shown moving in one direction until the scene flipped to depict him surfing in the opposite direction. At the end of the spot, the announcer concluded, "John Kerry. Whichever way the wind blows."

Many political pundits agreed that Kerry often did not help his own cause in diffusing such attacks: numerous critics labeled him as dull, a problematic characteristic in an age of television. In his advertising, Kerry would, on occasion, directly rebut Bush charges (in one commercial, the announcer contended, "John Kerry has never called for a $900 billion tax increase"). His staff also created positive biographical spots that pictured him as a leader or even a hero. For instance, some TV advertisements included testimonials from Vietnam veterans who had served under Kerry that recalled his bravery in battle (these endorsements would later be contested by the group "**Swift Boat Veterans for Truth**"). Kerry sometimes turned negative as well—his advertising confronted Bush on health care, the economy, the Iraq war, and other topics. For both sides, however, a sizable portion of the most brutal presentations was left to 527 organizations, such as **MoveOn.org**, the Media Fund, and the Progress for America Voter Fund, possibly because, by allowing surrogates to execute the dirtiest advertising, the candidates themselves would be distanced from allegations of mudslinging.

Yet the 527 group that gained the most notoriety—and whose advertising perhaps had the most impact on the election—in 2004 was called "Swift Boat Veterans for Truth." Its television campaign called Kerry's reported Vietnam heroism into question, even though many of its claims would later be discredited. Some postelection analyses even supported the possibility that the Swift Boat assault was a major determining element in Bush's reelection. Then again, deceptive advertising was also produced by the Kerry campaign team and is commonly used in election seasons in general. Once more, as with just about any voting contest, to what degree the 2004 campaign commercials actually swayed citizen's behavior at the polls is an open subject. Attempting to isolate the influence of advertising from the other factors at work, including election news coverage, convention speeches, and presidential debates, is a difficult, if not impossible proposition.

Although, as he had in 2000, Ralph Nader entered the race, his impact seemed negligible. After the ballots were cast, George W. Bush retained office, receiving about 51 percent of the vote, while Kerry settled for just over 48 percent. In the Electoral College, the tally was 286 to 251 (one vote went to John Edwards, Kerry's vice-presidential choice, since one elector pledged to Kerry defied convention and voted for Edwards instead).

2008 U.S. Presidential Advertising Campaign

Preceding the 2008 U.S. presidential general election, the Democratic primary season—a process used to determine the Democratic nominee for president—was unlike any other in the nation's history. First, it involved a very close, highly contested, protracted battle that lasted well over a year before producing a clear nominee. What especially made the primary distinctive, however, was that each of the top two Democratic candidates offered the potential to disrupt the unbroken reign that white men had held on the presidency. **Hillary Clinton** was a woman. And **Barack Obama**, a man, was a person of color. Far more people than ever before participated in the primary elections and caucuses, which helped to generate an unprecedented level of excitement and a blitz of media coverage for a process that for many if not most citizens generally goes largely unnoticed. As is commonly the case, particularly since new forms of media had recently begun proliferating, each candidate had to endure various controversies.

For her part, Hillary Clinton attempted to portray Barack Obama, relatively unproven on the national stage, as not ready to lead the nation, especially in regard to potential violent threats from abroad. In one of her most notable commercials, while the sound of a phone was heard, a voice-over announcer informed the audience that it was "3 AM" and "there's a phone in the White House and it's ringing. Something is happening in the world." As the scene cut between images of children sleeping safely and soundly in their comfortable beds, the announcer asked the audience who it would rather have answering the phone. Although some political pundits contended the spot artfully conveyed a powerful message, a number of critics countered that it was tainted with faintly racist tones. Their argument was that, by showing only white children in a suburban setting and inciting fear of Obama, the advertisement subtly exploited the traditional concern of a "black threat" to orderly society held by a portion of the white population. The Obama team, which sought to position Clinton as a symbol of the status quo, quickly responded (something it became known for throughout the campaign) with a counterattack. The spot appropriated the beginning of the Clinton commercial, portraying the same sleeping children and depicting the identical 3 AM scenario. Once more, the advertisement implicitly asked the viewers who they would prefer to pick up the phone. This time, though, the action shifted to images of Obama while the voice-over continued,

"When that call gets answered, shouldn't the president be the one—the only one—who had judgment and courage to oppose the Iraq war from the start?"

The 2008 Democratic Primary and Popular Culture. Although the 2008 Democratic primary season did not generate nearly as much output from the realm of popular culture as the 2004 general election had stirred, nevertheless, a few moments stand out, which include:

- An online promotional video for Hillary Clinton that parodied *The Sopranos* (see **Hillary Clinton**).
- A video posted on **YouTube** by a backer of Obama that mocked Clinton by combining footage of the candidate with scenes from the famous **Macintosh "1984" Commercial**, followed by a similar production from a Clinton supporter in rebuttal (see **Hillary Clinton**).
- Obama's supposedly preferential media treatment was parodied on two episodes of *Saturday Night Live* (see **Hillary Clinton**). Yet Obama's luster was soon tarnished as the contentious primary calendar continued.
- A series of YouTube videos featuring "**Obama Girl**," a woman who declared she had a crush on the senator.
- A widely circulated online music video produced by Will.I.Am of the popular music group The Black Eyed Peas, which celebrated the message contained in Obama's campaign slogan, "Yes We Can."

Yet perhaps the most significant connection between the Democratic primary campaign and popular culture involved Barack Obama's "rock star" status itself. To begin, the candidate was especially popular with youth voters. Moreover, demonstrating a capacity to connect with the younger crowd on its own turf, his team masterfully executed an ongoing online initiative that garnered small donations from more people than any primary campaign in U.S. history and maintained enthusiasm by continuously sending out e-mail messages that invited other forms of participation. Touring the country, with his good looks and dynamic oratory skills, the candidate frequently delivered speeches before tens of thousands of cheering supporters, sometimes filling indoor stadiums. News stories reported that, on occasion, a person in attendance would even faint, supposedly overwhelmed from seeing Obama in person. His impact on an audience eventually evoked a kind of backlash, with some journalists decrying the "cult of personality" Obama had incited—one pundit on **FOX news** even compared him to Hitler because of the way in which both figures could move a crowd.

The 2008 Republican Primary Season. The 2008 Republican primary campaign was to a large extent upstaged by the Democratic contest, which received more media attention and spawned a greater sense of public interest, probably because, among other reasons, the Republican incumbent president had become so unpopular that he had tarnished his party's reputation and the prospect of either a woman or a man of color occupying the White House seemed to offer a change of direction. Moreover, the Republican primary season contained far less drama than its Democratic counterpart.

Initially, a crowded field of candidates began to take shape, including **Fred Thompson**, a former U.S. Senator and then current cast member of the television show, *Law & Order*. Mixing politics and popular culture, Thompson officially declared his intention on an episode of *The Tonight Show*. Meanwhile, former

Governor of Arkansas Mike Huckabee, commonly perceived as a dark horse candidate, received the endorsement of "tough guy" actor Chuck Norris. In the end, however, **John McCain,** who had competed against eventual winner George W. Bush for the Republican nomination in 2000, rose to the top and secured the nomination.

The 2008 General Election.   Largely due to improvements in organization and media technologies, the advertising war between Senator Barack Obama and Senator John McCain was unparalleled in the sheer volume of commercials both sides released and the rapidity with which they produced them. During the primary season, Barack Obama had made foreign affairs—particularly the wars in Iraq and Afghanistan—a major issue. Initially, he continued to foreground concerns abroad in the general campaign as well. Again and again in his advertising, when on the attack, Obama attempted to link McCain to the policies of the incumbent president, George W. Bush, whose approval ratings had become abysmal. In support of this message, his advertising reiterated that McCain had voted in agreement with Bush 90 percent of the time. Meanwhile, Obama's central campaign slogan—"Change We Can Believe In"—offered an alternative to the widely unpopular positions of the Bush administration. Still, much of Obama's advertising refrained from direct challenges to his opponent and was positive in tone, emphasizing values he purportedly stood for such as "hope," "values," and "hard work."

Interestingly, John McCain promised change as well, an unusual approach for a candidate belonging to the party currently in power. Yet because any association with President Bush had become so toxic, McCain hoped to distance himself from the incumbent. Through his advertising and other tactics, McCain continuously reinforced his image as an independent "maverick" who would even defy the Republican Party when needed to advance the cause of, in the words of his campaign slogan, putting "Country First." But much, if not most, of McCain's advertising actually focused on Obama. Wishing to undermine his opponent's pledge to move the nation in a fresh direction and adopt the agent of change mantle himself, McCain strove to define his opponent as overly liberal, a proponent of tax increases, and a "celebrity" who was not fit to lead. If change was the defining theme of the general election, then McCain sought to convince the populace that his version was backed by years of experience his adversary could not match.

Later in the campaign, in response to shifting conditions at home and afar, Obama altered the stress of his advertising. For weeks, the media had consistently depicted the "surge" (a term used to indicate the added troops President Bush had sent earlier in the year to help reduce the level of violence in Iraq) as "working," which diluted the force of Obama's assertion that he was against the war from its inception. Meanwhile, starting in September, the United States was hit with a credit and mortgage crisis that threatened to send the economy into a tailspin not seen since the Great Depression. Thus Obama's advertising devoted greater attention to McCain's ties to Bush on domestic, rather than foreign policies. In one notable commercial, the Obama team represented McCain as fundamentally out of touch with the common person by referring to a remark McCain had made about being unsure of how many houses he owned (it was revealed to be seven).

Before the economic meltdown, however, McCain introduced his vice-presidential pick, Sarah Palin, a onetime mayor of Wasilla, Alaska, and the current governor of the state. Yet by choosing Palin, not only did he undercut his experience argument, but McCain chipped away at his ability to mock his opponent as a mere star figure as well.

Indeed, Palin, recognized for her physical attractiveness and plainspoken expression, immediately took on celebrity status, often drawing more people to her rallies than McCain himself. Yet her lack of national experience was soon clearly conveyed in two news interviews, one with Charlie Gibson of ABC and the other with Katie Couric of CBS. Palin stumbled badly in both appearances, so much so that she was ridiculed in several parodies on *Saturday Night Live*. The sketches involving Tina Fey, who played Palin, became one of the biggest popular culture phenomena of the season. Posted on YouTube, the satires were viewed by millions of people following their original broadcasts. Along the way, McCain's advertising turned from attacking Obama on his inexperience to contending that the Democrat was a dangerous choice because the public allegedly did not know enough about him.

But one aspect of the 2008 presidential campaign that truly distinguished it from its predecessors was the degree to which the Internet was used for advertising and other purposes—especially, as alluded to above, by Obama and his staff. If the 2004 campaign was seen as the first "Internet Election" (see "The Future" below), then Obama seized the trend that was led by former presidential hopeful Howard Dean four years earlier and advanced it exponentially. Obama wholeheartedly embraced the Internet as a powerful tool for fundraising, delivering his message, and recruiting and mobilizing thousands of volunteers.

Obama's new-media team was led by Joe Respars, who had cut his teeth on the 2004 Dean campaign. Added to the group was Chris Hughes, a co-founder of the hugely popular social networking site **Facebook**, Kate Albright-Hanna, an award-winning producer with **CNN**, and Scott Goodstein, an expert on text messaging. The new-media strategy assisted the campaign in securing an unprecedented number of small donations and organizing hundreds of thousands of supporters.

Thanks in large part to Albright-Hanna, Obama emerged as the star of his own channel on YouTube. Over 1,000 videos were uploaded on the Web site and viewed by millions of people. Moreover, in a measure designed to involve everyday citizens, the YouTube channel also featured many unknown Obama backers. For example, one 13-minute video portrayed students in a high school in the Bronx, New York, discussing their reaction to Obama's landmark speech on race, spurred by controversy over the comments of his former pastor, Jeremiah Wright, who had criticized whites and suggested that the events of 9/11 might have been just retribution for white racism. Many of Obama's advertisements were also included on the channel. Consequently, the candidate's total advertising campaign had far more impact than it would have had if it had centered on television alone.

At the same time, Goodstein launched an integrated mobile phone program that incorporated text messaging and Obama-themed "wallpaper" and ring tones. By receiving text messages, potential voters were able to keep up with the day-to-day activities of the Obama campaign and receive information about upcoming television appearances and events. Furthermore, the system promoted reciprocity—a staff was in place to answer any questions sent via text from Obama supporters. Perhaps the peak moment of the mobile plan occurred (not without glitches, though) when the campaign declared it would announce its vice presidential pick by text. Unfortunately for the McCain side, it never mounted a serious cell phone challenge of its own.

In addition, unlike McCain, Obama and his team drafted candidate profiles for a variety of social networking sites, including not only Facebook and its chief competitor MySpace.com but also lesser known venues such as AsianAve.com and BlackPlanet.com. At the heart of the Internet initiative, however, was the campaign's home Web site, My.BarackObama.com, overseen by Hughes. New-media specialists generated incalculable e-mails and placed advertisements throughout the Web as a means of attracting people to the site, which contained many of the videos that were also available on Obama's YouTube channel. Furthermore, in a departure from what had come before, My.BarackObama.com (nicknamed MyBO) encouraged interactivity. By signing up, visitors could **blog**, join groups, plan their own events, engage in fundraising efforts, and volunteer in many other ways. Also, because guests were given the opportunity to communicate with one another, some of the work was carried over to the offline world through thousands of "house parties," phone solicitations, door-to-door calls, and other activities. Not only that, MyBO actually allowed participants to express dissent. For instance, users formed the group, "President Obama, Please Get FISA Right," which was devoted to criticizing Obama's backing of a controversial bill. For a while, it was the largest sublocation on the MyBO network. Here again, although McCain had his own Web page and other online tactics, according to most political observers, they paled in comparison to the level of sophistication and wizardry displayed by the Obama Internet program. Many pundits declared that the new-media strategy implemented by the candidate's talented staff revolutionized the use of the Web as a political tool and changed the face of how future political campaigns would be run, providing a case study that would be analyzed for years. (For additional discussion on the role of new media in campaign advertising, see Chapter 8.)

After the highest voter turnout in decades, Barack Obama claimed victory in the election, winning the Electoral College 365 to 173. As the son of a father from Kenya and a white woman from Kansas, he became the first African American, biracial president in U.S. history. His support among youth voters (aged 18–29) was especially strong, probably due in no small part to his capacity to synthesize politics with popular culture. Not long afterward, *Time* named him its "Person of the Year."

TRENDS IN POLITICAL TELEVISION ADVERTISING IN THE UNITED STATES

Looking at the big picture—especially since the dawn of the television age in the 1950s—several trends in the history of presidential campaign advertising can be identified. Although a list is seldom exhaustive, it can point to several of the most evident developments:

- **The rising prominence of the media consultant.** In 1952, during the first presidential campaign season to feature political television advertising, Democratic candidate Adlai Stevenson was strongly resistant to accepting the assistance of TV professionals in his drive for the presidency. The Republican and eventual winner, Dwight D. Eisenhower, too, although willing to participate in the making of commercials, displayed discomfort with the activity. Moreover, in the early years after television's introduction, political media practitioners typically operated as technicians who simply carried out the tasks that needed to be accomplished to produce and run advertising. By 1964, this approach was in notable transition. Currently, media consultants are viewed as key and indispensable members of the campaign team—they no longer serve as mere functionaries but are instrumental in planning a campaign, including crafting the themes that the advertising is intended to convey. In developing message strategies, they even play a role in carving out a candidate's policy positions. Whereas the media team of the 1950s consisted of a somewhat haphazard collection of practitioners who were not particularly well versed in politics, today political media consulting is a full-fledged industry. Any serious attempt to reach the White House now requires the backing of a large staff of professionals engaged in a complex process involving intense research, collection and interpretation of statistical data, planning, strategizing, implementation, evaluation, and adaptation to conditions that can change dramatically from day to day.

- **Advertising agencies are eager to back both major parties.** Before 1964, advertising agencies and their personnel were often hesitant to work on behalf of Democratic candidates out of fear that it would alienate their existing clients. Given that agencies handled the accounts of large corporations, they were more sympathetic to offering their talents to the GOP, which was widely regarded as the party of big business. Agency decision makers themselves often leaned to the right. Over time, however, people entering the ranks of the agency world were more politically diverse. In addition, corporations have increasingly come to realize that it is in their best interest to express goodwill toward both parties (even if, overall, Republicans usually secure greater financial contributions from big business than Democrats). For years, some Democratic hopefuls struggled to obtain media consultants willing to join their campaigns. Yet in 1964 DDB signaled a breakthrough for Democrats when it openly confessed that it wished to create advertising for President Lyndon Johnson as a means of trying to keep Republican Barry Goldwater from office. Today, there are scores of firms ready to take on political clients regardless of their party affiliations—some of them primarily specialize in Republican causes, while others are mostly loyal to the Democratic side.

- **Shorter TV commercials.** When politicians began to use television in earnest during the 1950s in support of their presidential campaigns, they frequently devoted much, if not most, of their emphasis to longer formats. Thirty-minute shows were common, as were five-minute spots. Recently, although extended programs have still appeared, especially on the evening of an election, far more weight is placed on short, generally 30- or 60-second commercials. In 1992, independent candidate Ross Perot revived the long form, but his work represents more the exception than the rule.

- **Increasingly expensive campaigns.** The cost of campaigning has risen exponentially over the years, and television advertising represents a major element behind escalating expenses. Although various measures have been taken by legislators to regulate the ways in which money is raised and spent, the financial resources it requires to mount a campaign have only increased and this trend is likely to continue.

- **Dominance of television.** After exhibiting an initial tentativeness toward embracing television as a campaign tool, candidates quickly recognized its irresistible potential and it became central to the process. Before 1950, television was not a factor in elections. Yet by 1960, more money was channeled toward television advertising than any other type, a pattern that has been in place ever since. Still, it is unclear whether television will continue to dominate media expenditures in the future. With its rising significance and popularity, the Internet could challenge TV as the politician's medium of choice.

- **More sophisticated techniques and higher production values.** In 1952, soon-to-be President Eisenhower made an impact with primitive commercials, each of which merely depicted a person asking a question, and then Eisenhower offering a brief response (see "Eisenhower Answers America"). It is improbable that such an execution would be efficacious today. As technologies and experience have expanded, political advertisers have become more adept at applying the latest techniques to campaigns. Moreover, research methods have steadily advanced. Campaign teams commonly gather feedback about commercials from audiences before deciding if they will release the spots for broadcast. Pretesting advertising is not foolproof, but it can often help prevent crucial mistakes. Through research and an understanding of consumer psychology and motivation, media professionals are better able to infuse advertising with symbolism that plays on their audiences' emotions. Just as the creators of general consumer advertising tend to appeal more to feelings than intellect, so too do campaign teams often endeavor to pack their advertising with sentiment rather than a significant amount of information about their candidates' policies. In seeking office, politicians throughout history have tapped into the hopes and dreams, as well as the fears and anxieties, of the populace. But the degree to which media consultants can currently survey voter values and attitudes and then reflect them in the advertising they develop for their candidates is unprecedented.

Other tendencies in political advertising are more debatable. Some scholars claim that with the rise of television, advertising puts much greater focus on image than policy positions. Yet others counter that the cultivation of an image has always been a part of politics, even if it was not termed as such. There is probably more consensus, however, regarding the idea that image management is indeed a crucial factor in modern campaigns and that there are more resources available than ever before for any campaign team attempting to construct a favorable persona for its candidate. Many critics also argue that negative or "attack" advertising has intensified over time. But here again, other observers contend that heaping scorn on political opponents has occurred throughout the nation's past. The proportion of advertising devoted to attacks cannot be indicated with a linear, upward sloping line—it varies from campaign to campaign. Still, despite the controversy it generates, negative advertising is a consistent component of election seasons and will in all probability only persist.

TYPES AND FUNCTIONS OF POLITICAL ADVERTISING

A number of scholars and practitioners have attempted to sort political television advertising into categories based on its common features, a nomenclature that can be summarized. For instance, drawing from the work of Kathleen Hall Jamieson and L. Patrick Devlin, Brian McNair (2007) outlines eight variations. The *primitive* commercial refers to a spot created during television's infancy, when producers had not yet accumulated a storehouse of tools they could use to construct high quality advertising. The 1952 "Eisenhower Answers America" campaign provides a prime example for this designation. A *talking head* commercial is a straightforward execution that displays a candidate highlighting an issue by speaking directly into the camera. Only a politician who has the skill to adapt his or her delivery to the requirements of television, such as former two-term (1980–88) President Ronald Reagan, is likely to succeed with this kind of spot. Reagan is commonly identified as someone who could speak to a mass audience yet appear as though he were personally talking to each viewer one-on-one.

The *negative* spot comes in many forms but is characterized by its attack on an opponent. To avoid making the candidates appear too harsh and less than honorable, the scornful messages in these commercials are often delivered by surrogates. For example, during Richard Nixon's 1972 run for reelection, the president's handlers established a group called "Democrats for Nixon" and allowed this subsidiary to produce and air anti–George McGovern spots. In this way, Nixon could steer clear of any association with "dirty politics." Eight years later, in some of his advertising, President Carter himself attacked his Republican opponent, Ronald Reagan, a decision that probably harmed his reputation as a decent and principled man.

Sometimes, primary seasons supply ammunition for potential negative advertising. Intraparty accusations can be picked up by the opposing party and used in its advertising throughout the general election period.

In a *concept* commercial, the candidate usually does not appear; rather, an idea is advanced through a variety of visual, aural, and narrative practices. For instance, in the 1964 campaign for Democratic President Lyndon Johnson, the highly touted DDB agency produced an array of concept spots designed to make dramatic points. In one, taking advantage of a volatile statement that Johnson's opponent, Republican Barry Goldwater, had made—"Sometimes I think this country would be better off if we could just saw the Eastern Seaboard and let if float out to sea"—DDB shot a dimensional map of the United States, with a saw carving through the Eastern states. As the scene proceeded, an accompanying announcer reiterated the controversial Goldwater remark.

Cinéma-vérité commercials are those that portray a candidate in ostensibly "real life" settings, although the action is generally rehearsed. A spot of the 2004 Democratic candidate, Senator John Kerry, shaking hands with people at a rally embodies this technique. *Testimonial* advertising entails on-camera endorsements by well-known figures or, in its *man [or woman]-in-the-street* version, everyday people. For instance, in 1980, actress Mary Tyler Moore provided support for Jimmy Carter, while, during the primaries, actor Carroll O'Connor revealed his loyalty toward Democratic challenger Edward Kennedy. Four years earlier, in a commercial for incumbent Gerald Ford, several "average" citizens explained why they backed the Republican, with comments that included, "I think he offers solidarity" and "I think he's a strong person." Finally, in the *neutral reporter* format, the audience is offered, usually via an announcer and suitable visual footage, a series of statements, and then asked to draw its own judgment. Whereas the advertising claims are devised to appear objective, they are actually arranged in such a way as to render the conclusion inevitable and favor the advertised candidate. In 1968, for instance, a spot for Democrat Hubert Humphrey depicted a weather vane in the form of Republican opponent Richard Nixon, with each of his index fingers pointing in opposite directions. As the announcer alternated between drawing attention to one statement once uttered by Nixon and a contradictory position also articulated by the candidate, the weather vane shifted back and forth and eventually spun rapidly. Along the way, the viewer was led to deduce that Nixon was inconsistent in his stands on issues. (Nixon operatives later repeated the weather vane approach in a similar commercial used to attack McGovern in 1972.)

Although these eight categories are by no means exhaustive and can often overlap, they begin to identify patterns that are useful for understanding the rhetorical tactics at work in political commercials. Edwin Diamond and Stephen Bates (1992) supply another insightful classification scheme by focusing on what they call the four phases of a political advertising campaign. The first phase consists of *ID spots* that introduce and establish the basic identity of a candidate. As a case in point, in 1980, during the Republican primaries and before he settled for a spot on the ticket as the vice-presidential candidate, George H. W. Bush was relatively unknown. Consequently, his campaign staff developed a set of commercials, entitled "Magnitude," that attempted to make the candidate seem enormously popular. Frequently, ID spots are biographical, such as a 1988 Michael Dukakis commercial that employed scenes from a family album to picture the Democrat as a rousing example of the American Dream.

In the second phase of a campaign, media operatives typically produce *argument spots*, which are intended to sketch out a candidate's fundamental policy positions. The 2000 advertising for George W. Bush that declared his "compassionate conservative" approach to politics exemplifies this stage. The politician in the third phase goes on the attack, drawing on the spectrum of strategies available for creating commercials that discredit the opposition. Last, in phase four, which Diamond and Bates label "I see an America ...," a candidate engages in a sort of retreat and, instead, accents positive themes and inspirational messages. On the evening before the 1992 vote, for instance, Bill Clinton's team aired a short biographical program that borrowed the tone of *A Man from Hope*, an emotionally stirring film that had been shown at the Democratic convention.

Often, a campaign does not proceed cleanly from one phase to another—but the model supplies a helpful framework for thinking about the advertising during an election season. Yet even before the first phase of a general campaign launches, the *meta-campaign* is played out. During this stage of the process, promotion is aimed not at the general public but at the political elite—i.e., large financial contributors, party workers, and other potentially influential backers—in an endeavor to secure the support it will take for any candidate to have a chance of becoming the party nominee. Another major target of the meta-campaign is the press, since candidates hope that initial positive news coverage can help jump-start a successful run.

An additional constructive approach to analyzing political advertising involves dividing it into its functions. William L. Benoit et al. (2003) discuss three central groupings for political communication in general. Politicians can *acclaim*, that is, emphasize their positive characteristics and accomplishments; *attack*, by criticizing their opponents' positions, qualities, or record; or *defend*, which demands refuting any attacks delivered by their challengers. All of these methods of classifying political advertising can assist critics and researchers as they evaluate campaigns.

CONTROVERSIES SURROUNDING POLITICAL ADVERTISING

Throughout its history, especially since the advent of television, political advertising has generated considerable controversy. The most common complaints about political advertising, as well as the familiar rebuttals to these objections, can be loosely categorized.

- **Escalating campaign costs.** Television advertising is one of the main elements that has dramatically driven up campaign expenditures over time. Critics charge that the high costs involved in election seasons prevent less than affluent citizens from running for office. From this perspective, candidates are not occupying a level playing field—the one who is able to raise the most money holds a significant advantage. In this sense, elections can be "bought." For example, Michael Bloomberg, one of the richest people in the world, who had switched from the Democratic Party to the Republican Party so he could run for mayor of New York City in 2001, was able to personally fund his winning campaign and significantly outspend his opponent on advertising, which included the distribution of video tapes to individual households. In addition, because so much money is needed to mount a campaign, incumbents are forced to devote considerable time to raising funds for their reelection rather than concentrate on fulfilling the responsibilities of their offices. Yet defenders of political advertising answer that no amount of money can salvage a poor campaign; many instances in which a candidate with meager resources beat a well-heeled opponent can be cited.

Moreover, some proponents assert that advertising performs an educative function for voters and, accordingly, is well worth the cost. For instance, many citizens have little knowledge of what goes on in Congress from day to day. Yet if a representative or senator casts a vote that, were it exposed, could be unpopular, a challenger in the next election can highlight this decision in an advertisement. Some scholars claim that, since many people are dissatisfied with news coverage and pay less attention to it than political advertising, commercials and ads have the capacity to provide more information to an audience than journalism. Other observers note that advertising expenditures could be lessened if television stations were required to provide free airtime to politicians (which is the case in many other countries). The counterargument to this position is that such government intrusion into private enterprise would violate the free-market system.

- **Too much negativity**. Critics contend that attack advertising has a damaging impact on the democratic process. They say that the vehement accusations lobbed back and forth are so disturbing that many citizens turn away from political discourse and even shun the polls. These observers draw attention to decreased voter turnouts and indicate that negative advertising is at least partly to blame—it evokes cynicism and disengagement. On the other hand, advocates of political advertising state, it is difficult to determine to what degree negative advertising has contributed to depressed turnout because there are many other factors at work. News coverage of corruption, for example, could incite greater feelings of alienation than a 30-second commercial. Furthermore, these defenders maintain, there was never a utopian age in which the voting rate was exceptionally high—throughout history, there has been a substantial portion of the eligible electorate that has declined to cast ballots during elections. At the same time, evidence goes both ways: it appears that in some cases, a negative advertising campaign influenced numerous people to refrain from voting, while in other instances, it actually drove citizens to the polls to vote against the candidate behind what they perceived as an unfair attack. Especially heated battles might even provoke greater interest. The 2004 campaign between incumbent George W. Bush and Senator John Kerry, for instance, was filled with brutal remarks on each side. Yet the percentage of voters who ultimately went to the polls was higher than it had been in years. In the end, attack and defense are as central to politics as inspiring declarations and self-acclamations.

- **Degrading of political discourse**. Many political and media scholars believe that political advertising debases political discussion. First, because they generally appear in 30-second versions or other abbreviated formats, advertisements present reductive arguments. Policies that require elaboration and substantial supporting evidence in order to be fully understood and accepted are instead simplistically condensed into visual gimmicks and short sound bites. Second, because of its visual bias, television advertising in particular tends to frame issues in entertaining ways, thus trivializing the nation's very system of democracy. Dominating the political advertising landscape, TV promotes image over substance, and targets emotions over intellect. Candidates are marketed in the same manner as chewing gum and shampoo. Third, mass advertising has lessened the need to stage rallies and live appearances; as a result, people no longer feel an interpersonal connection to candidates. Consequently, politics has become a spectator sport—citizens are indirectly encouraged to watch the show rather than actively participate in the democratic process.

Conversely, there are various lines of thought offered in rebuttal. First, a considerable amount of information can be delivered in 30-second spots or other short-format vehicles. Perhaps a politician cannot spell out all the reasons for a particular stance in an advertisement, but he or she has enough time or space, in many instances, to clearly articulate a position on a specific issue, which is valuable information in itself. Not only that, although it might be true that an advertisement expresses only a brief message, taken together, the many spots and ads that comprise a complete campaign can be viewed as a protracted argument. Often, each advertisement is simply a compressed version of a point made in a campaign speech. Indeed, a candidate's acceptance speech at a convention and subsequent stump orations frequently supply the themes that are simply reinforced by the advertising. Furthermore, the practice of abridging complex subjects into pithy slogans was transpiring well before the advent of television. The phrase, "Tippecanoe and Tyler too," for example, was coined in 1840 in support of candidate and eventual president William Harrison. Alternately, a long presentation does not necessarily better serve the populace—it too can still smack of shallowness, or it might be so awkwardly constructed that audiences are left feeling confused.

Second, political discourse that is also entertaining should not inevitably be dismissed. It could be that amusing political advertising actually engages more people than dry, stilted discussion. Nor has the political arena ever been devoid of entertaining elements and attempts to shape candidate images at the expense of weighty exposition. Also, if a campaign attempts to manufacture an image that is severely incongruous with a politician's real personality, the disparity will likely be exposed by opponents, the press, or other sources, which would render the advertising ineffective. At the same time, voters have never decided their choices on the basis of logic alone; feelings have always been a central influence on voting behavior. Furthermore, there is evidence that indicates emotions not only do not automatically detract from rational contemplation but are actually necessary for its operation—feelings and thought are intertwined. Also, communication imbued with emotion is more capable of engaging the citizenry than entirely logical discourse devoid of passion. In any event, today's audiences, immersed in media their entire lives, are media savvy and therefore likely to see through any manipulative tactics in advertising.

Third, though politicians often do not schedule as many personal appearances as their forbearers, they yet attend many live events. Furthermore, in the days when candidates or their supporters engaged in more face-to-face encounters, only a small percentage of the population was ever willing or able to be on hand. Political advertising on television or carried by other media enables an unparalleled percentage of the populace to have at least symbolic connection with a politician. Finally, the forces of modernization preclude any move away from mediated politics and toward a largely in person type of campaigning, so to lament the role of television and other media is a waste of energy.

- **Sleaziness reigns**. Opponents of political advertising often cite how often it degenerates into misleading claims, nasty mudslinging, and unfair attacks. Sometimes advertisements outright lie—or at least seriously distort the truth. Independent PAC and 527 advertising is especially brought up in this regard because it is frequently not held to the standards of accountability to which the candidates and their teams are expected to conform. These groups from time to time take much greater risks and deliver far more controversial statements than most candidate campaigns would feel comfortable expressing. By law, they are required to operate independently from the candidates they support, which perhaps partly explains why they are sometimes willing to be particularly daring. In reality, though, these organizations often coordinate—albeit indirectly and technically lawfully—their efforts with the major parties.

Yet other observers counter that, here again, "dirty" tactics are as old as politics itself. Thomas Jefferson was derided as a heinous atheist, Martin Van Buren was branded a morally suspect transvestite (although different terminology was used at the time), and Grover Cleveland was portrayed as an abusive husband. It could even be argued that modern political advertising is actually a cleaner type of expression than that used by campaigns in the past because it is unavoidably sanitized for home consumption. Perhaps a middle-ground perspective could be honored if political advertising was more heavily regulated. Unlike its general consumer counterpart, political advertising containing even blatant falsehoods will generally not result in government intervention or reprisal. This lax framework is rooted in free speech philosophy and the belief that in the open marketplace of ideas, the best ones will rise to the top while the worst thoughts will be relegated to oblivion. Over the years, rather than the government, the media have increasingly facilitated the weeding out of disreputable declarations in political advertising. Functioning as an advertising watchdog, various media segments, usually housed in news divisions, perform fact-checking responsibilities and seek to debunk deceptive assertions and practices for their audiences. No comparable service in the distant past was ever instituted to offer corrections to the underhanded smears delivered by ruthless politicians.

- **The importance of media consultants over politicians.** According to some observers, the prominence of political advertising has rendered a situation in which politics is conducted by advertising agents rather than politicians. These media professionals care only about winning the election, the number one criterion for remaining in high demand. Given that after the ballots are cast they will move on to other campaigns, they are not especially interested in how well their candidates will govern if they obtain office. To secure victory at all costs, media consultants will actually influence their candidates' policy positions, which could prove damaging should the politicians implement (or renounce) these stands after their postelection celebrations. From the reverse point of view, however, media practitioners are no more liable to be ethically compromised than politicians and other "insiders" themselves. As third-party intermediaries, they have greater potential than emotionally close campaign associates to furnish objective advice. Nor can media consultants shove an attitude or an issue down a candidate's throat—the person running for office can always veto any recommendation.

In summary, critics highlight a number of problems with political advertising. Yet this form of promotion is just one component of a comprehensive political system that, in a complex world, will always be flawed. There has never been a golden age when political campaigns were exempt from the scornful commentary of interested onlookers. Similarly, today's advertising can be regarded as a continuation of the process that began with the short messages of the banners and broadsides of the nineteenth century. Still, further debate about the merits and disadvantages of political advertising can lead to modifications that will benefit the electorate. Yet eliminating any already entrenched form of political advertising is probably untenable and would likely be renounced by many politically engaged people as a severe infringement on free speech.

THE DUBIOUS IMPACT OF POLITICAL ADVERTISING

A key issue to politicians, their media consultants, scholars, and other observers is assessing to what extent political advertising has an impact on events. Despite abundant research and speculation, discerning its influence is problematic and evidence about the effects of political advertising is, by and large, inconclusive. It might seem that, given how much money is spent on it, advertising must work. But its efficacy is unclear. In a classic text on general consumer advertising, *Advertising, the Uneasy Persuasion* (1986), Michael Schudson argues that advertising's power to affect purchasing behavior is limited or even possibly negligible because there are so many other aspects behind why someone chooses one brand over another, including the pull of family members, peers, societal expectations, and other mitigating factors. Furthermore, measuring the effect of advertising by isolating it from all of the other shaping variables involved in a purchase is generally difficult, if not impossible to achieve. Political communication researchers, too, usually point to the complexity of the voting decision-making process and concede that apprehending exactly what role advertising plays in any given scenario is a complicated and often unattainable endeavor. Knowledgeable observers will often claim that even excellent advertising cannot sell an otherwise unpopular candidate. Moreover, other real events or media stories that occur outside the carefully crafted campaign can belie preplanned themes. Other factors being equal, a political incumbent generally has a strong advantage over a challenger because the former has far more access to free of charge media as he or she simply goes about fulfilling the duties of the job—consistent news coverage for a president, for instance, is ensured. Still, research into political advertising's effects continues and, regardless of its flaws, can indicate some probable conclusions. It appears likely, however, that debate about political advertising's part in persuading voters will persist.

Research on Mass Media Effects

Investigation into mass media effects began in the 1920s, partly out of concern that they represented a potentially harmful force. In particular, the war time propaganda of World War I and, later, World War II (see **World War Propaganda**) seemed to demonstrate media's capacity to manipulate attitudes. For decades, many researchers subscribed to what was later termed the "hypodermic needle" model of media, which is to say that the impact of the media is direct, uniform, and very powerful. Yet in the 1940s, in a highly acclaimed study eventually labeled *The People's Choice*, head researcher Paul Lazarsfeld presented findings supporting the idea that the media had very little influence on voting behavior in terms of single-handedly motivating people to change their minds about for whom they would mark their ballots. For years, then, this "limited effects" perspective held sway for the media in general. In recent times, scholars have endorsed various views between these two poles. Generally, researchers convey an understanding that the media are just one of many elements involved in the formation and maintenance of attitudes and behaviors. Different people will interpret messages in diverse ways depending on external cues as well as their own predispositions.

Research into specific media effects on political beliefs and voting performance runs into several problems. Surveys, such as public opinion polls, can yield divergent findings based on how the questions are worded. Some critics argue that these polls can sometimes affect outcomes in their own right: For example, if a voter learns that the candidate he or she favors trails an opponent in the polls by a wide margin, he or she might be less inclined to make a trip to the voting booth, feeling such an effort is futile. Even if actual voting results are interpreted, the relationship between an advertising initiative and the consequent balloting tallies is hard to distinguish. A winning candidate might have run a campaign that was widely regarded as weak; conversely a losing candidate might have executed advertising that reviewers considered especially robust. Experimental research, moreover, suffers from the fact that any investigation is conducted in conditions that do not reflect real world settings. Again, though, in spite of these limitations, some research has produced significant implications. For instance, one study (Rosenberg and McCafferty 1987) provided evidence that a candidate's appearance—his or her dress, facial expressions, etc.—can shape the way the politician is perceived. It seems to be the case that, since the dawn of television, politicians have had to modify their approach to delivery if they hoped to inspire the electorate. A direct and intimate mode of address reads better on the medium than a cold and formal presentation. For example, political historians contend that the ease with which John F. Kennedy, the first "TV president," handled TV was a key factor in his victory over Richard Nixon, who looked less than comfortable on the small screen. If this is true, then the physical style that is portrayed in a candidate's advertising is an important production area to keep in mind.

Contemporary research on the effects of political advertising per se, given its qualifications, has nevertheless rendered a number of insights. Some of it indeed suggests that advertising's influence is greatly moderated by the existing political attitudes of its audience members. If certain people like a candidate, for instance, they will look with favor on advertising that puts this politician in a positive light and tend to dismiss negative information about the candidate from the opponent's campaign. In this sense, Lazarsfeld's study from the 1940s still has relevance. Other research indicates that political advertising's effects are in inverse proportion to the amount of knowledge an audience has of the candidates or issues—the more information it has digested, the less it will be susceptible to advertising. It also appears that aesthetic qualities do not necessarily make a difference: even a well-done commercial might have no impact on its intended recipients. Ultimately, what can be stated about the influence of political advertising is that producers have control over the construction of the campaign, but not the manner in which the audience will interpret it. Strategically sound messages that are packaged in artistically compelling ways are more likely to benefit a politician or cause than poorly conceived themes and shoddy executions. Political operatives, relinquishing extraordinary sums of money, presume that advertising must have some effect. Accordingly, they do their best to achieve their objectives, sometimes succeeding and other times failing. Put simply, some advertising works, while some does not. Many political historians point to the furlough commercials (e.g., "Revolving Door") aired during George H. W. Bush's 1988 campaign as having made a difference in the election (see **Furlough Commercial**). Conversely, various scholars would assert that even if Adlai Stevenson had run highly captivating advertising in 1956 he still would not have been able to drive the ever-popular Dwight Eisenhower from office.

To what degree advertising affects voting behavior is just one of the questions of interest about its overall impact. Some academics and other critics contemplate its influence on the democratic process itself. One school of thought postulates that advertising manipulates rather than informs voters, and cheapens or trivializes the election atmosphere by commercializing a serious activity. The counterargument is centered on the assumption that politics has never been a fully rational procedure, and that manipulation, image making, and truncated arguments have always been a part of it. Nor are political trends always consistent. Richard Nixon's image was not commonly placed in high regard, yet, before the Watergate scandal, he won two straight presidential elections. At the same time, voters are not foolish dupes and are able to see through deceptions and arrive at conclusions on their own terms. Finally, advertising does provide useful information and can trigger further exploration to learn about candidates and issues by consulting the plethora of other sources available. Through mass advertising, these proponents state, more people than ever are invited to participate in the democratic system.

Another critique of political advertising, as noted earlier, emphasizes the high cost of running a modern media campaign. Critics point to the disproportionate number of elected federal officials who are economically affluent or even highly rich. Political power, based on this perspective, becomes something that can be bought. Yet, others would answer, money does not guarantee victory—a candidate who squanders funds on a deficient campaign can be defeated by a politician with far fewer dollars.

Finally, many political scholars argue that televised political advertising in particular has contributed to the decline—but by no means the end—of the influence of the two major parties. For years, major presidential candidates have conducted campaigns that are usually parallel to, yet independent of the promotional activities of the party with which they are affiliated. Through TV, and now the Internet, politicians can more easily speak directly to the population rather than work within the traditional party structure. Television, therefore, has the capacity to mobilize attention far more quickly and comprehensively than political parties can accomplish through grassroots efforts. Accordingly, the backing of party leaders has been partially supplanted by the expertise of media consultants. Perhaps this is one reason why the political primaries, during which, in former times, closed door meetings often produced nominees, have over the past 50 years become more democratic—today, popular primary elections and caucuses help decide who will run for office, usually making the nomination process at the party political conventions a mere formality. Some observers decry this diminution of the role of the Democratic and Republican parties. Others counter that the straighter link between politicians and citizens is a healthy development for democracy. They also sometimes add that when the party machinery was in full operation, corruption and cronyism were frequently rampant. Often, an everyday citizen made a ballot decision not on the basis of which candidate he or she judged as the best choice, but because a favor—for example, a job, a pledge to push through a piece of legislation, or even a covert monetary bribe— would be granted in exchange for the person's vote.

POLITICAL PROMOTION, POPULAR CULTURE, AND YOUTH VOTERS

The intersection of political campaigns and popular culture is especially apparent in regard to reaching potential youth voters, typically classified as those eligible citizens between the ages of 18 and 29. Although the realm of popular culture is so vast that, at least on some level of interest, it appeals to nearly everyone, it is particularly associated with the young. Over the years, politicians have increasingly recognized the potential of popular culture for targeting this demographic.

Throughout most of the nation's history, while national campaigns often focused more attention on some regions of the country than others based on the strategic importance of certain states for winning enough electoral votes to carry elections, they did not have the sophisticated arsenal of research and marketing tools to segment their audiences according to narrower demographic categories, such as gender, age, and race. But in the 1950s, as television was rapidly becoming a cultural phenomenon and radio was adjusting to TV's challenge by breaking up its national programming model into more specialized formats, advertising and marketing professionals in general were gaining a greater understanding of the benefits of segmentation and learning to better tailor campaigns toward different markets. Today, as media technologies and choices continue to proliferate, marketers essentially take for granted that the national audience is exceedingly fragmented and, consequently, channel considerable energy into devising ever more refined tactics for reaching smaller and smaller niches (even sometimes customizing messages for each individual).

Youth voters are usually branded as more politically apathetic and unmotivated than the population at large. A large body of statistics supports the case that the proportion of young people who vote is generally smaller than the portion of older citizens who cast their ballots at the polls. Yet because they represent a sizable constituency, youth voters are still identified as an important market, especially when an election is expected to be close. Lately, to activate this hard-to-stimulate segment, campaigns and interest groups have experimented with a number of novel approaches.

Early Youth Targeted Campaigns

One of the first notable examples of attempting to mobilize young people occurred in the 1968 election season, when Senator Eugene McCarthy entered the Democratic primaries. The McCarthy team recruited scores of energetic and politically engaged young volunteers to support its leader's candidacy, in an effort that was nicknamed a "Children's crusade." Youth voters took on even higher significance in the next election. In 1971, the Twenty-sixth Amendment to the U.S. Constitution had lowered the legal voting age from 21 to 18, largely due to a voting rights movement that grew out of the nation's involvement in the Vietnam War. Thousands of people of college age protested that most of the men drafted to serve were not allowed to vote for the very leaders who were responsible for sending them abroad. The slogan, "Old enough to fight, old enough to vote," captured their feelings of injustice. George McGovern, the Democratic candidate in 1972, strongly opposed the war and pledged to bring American troops home if he were elected. Given that people in their late teens and early 20s were the ones most directly affected by the war, many young adults were drawn to his campaign. Youth from around the country formed a grassroots movement backing McGovern—many of them volunteered on behalf of his run for the presidency. At the same time, the DNC produced advertising that simply encouraged young people to register, believing that they would likely vote for Democrats. Incumbent Richard Nixon's team countered with a youth advertising campaign of its own. Wrapped around the theme of "Young Voters for the President," the ads and spots perhaps had an impact. The DNC's assumption that youth registrations equaled Democratic votes seemed ill founded when nearly half of the new voters chose Nixon on their ballots.

"Rock the Vote" and Other Youth-Centered, Political Interest Groups

Over the past two decades, one of the most visible initiatives that has brought popular culture and politics together for the goal of evoking more civic participation among young people is **Rock the Vote** (RTV). On its Web site, the organization's mission reads, "Rock the Vote is dedicated to protecting freedom of expression and empowering young people to change their world."

Since the founding of RTV, a number of similar independent organizations that fuse politics and popular culture as a means of targeting youth audiences have emerged, some of which are either spin-offs from RTV or at least seem to have been inspired by the group. The 2004 presidential election season pitting incumbent George W. Bush against Senator John Kerry provides an exemplary case study on how various youth-centered initiatives have employed elements of popular culture to achieve their aims. RTV itself was again active in its attempts to mobilize youth voters. But RTV was not alone. Several groups turned to the domain of hip-hop in hope of appealing to black youth in particular. The Web site initiative, MoveOn.org, for instance, produced a commercial that mimicked the conventions of a rap music video. Elsewhere, the highly successful rap performer Sean "P. Diddy" Combs launched what he termed the **"Citizen Change"** campaign. Rap the Vote, an offshoot of RTV that originated in 2000, added its energy to the mix. The **Hip-Hop Summit Action Network** (HSAN), introduced by the hip-hop mogul Richard Simmons in 2001, also fanned the political flames. In the words of its mission statement, HSAN "is dedicated to harnessing the cultural relevance of Hip-Hop music to serve as a catalyst for education advocacy and other societal concerns fundamental to the empowerment of youth." Based on "the belief that Hip-Hop is an enormously influential agent for social change," among its many endeavors during the run-up to the 2004 election, HSAN sponsored a 2003 summit at which over 10,000 attendees registered to vote and partnered with World Wrestling Entertainment's "Smackdown Your Vote" to try and influence still more young adults to register. Meanwhile, the first ever National Hip Hop Political Convention brought together 3,000 participants to explore the issues that they deemed important through panel discussions, speeches, and performances.

Still other organizations, such as America Comes Together, New Voters Project, and Declare Yourself, sought to target youth in general with comparable tactics, honed by the products of popular culture. The music channel MTV, a vehicle that is commonly identified as a key component of youth culture, again sponsored its "Choose or Lose" campaign. In a related yet distinctive venture, the documentary filmmaker and activist **Michael Moore** delivered humorous yet politically charged speeches on campuses around the country in his "Slackers Uprising Tour."

Sean "P. Diddy" Combs arrives in Milwaukee in 2004, representing "Citizen Change," a nonprofit, nonpartisan group, where he kicked off his "Vote or Die" tour to emphasize the importance of voting. (AP Photo/Stephan Savoia)

To maintain their tax exempt status, these and other similar political interest groups were usually presented as nonpartisan. Generally, their main stated goal was to simply help generate a high youth voter turnout. Still, many observers complained that most of these organizations displayed a pro-Kerry bias. The public sentiment during the 2004 presidential campaign was highly polarized, with one camp widely dubbed as the "anybody but Bush" contingent. Given the perception that young people vote more often for Democrats than Republicans, these critics were sensitive to the possibility that an initiative legally bound to not support a specific candidate could yet do so in an indirect manner. Their critique had some merit, as a number of the celebrities, including P. Diddy, were on record as being opposed to President Bush's reelection. Despite the political leanings of their backers, though, these groups had to at least operate under the guise of neutrality. At the same time, based on the sheer quantity of parties associated with the organizations, the people working or volunteering for them represented positions along the political spectrum.

In the end, over 4 million more 18–29-year-olds voted in 2004 than in the previous presidential election—an almost 10 percent increase. Yet many pundits gave mixed reviews about young people's level of participation. Although they had, in fact, cast more ballots for John Kerry, youth voters did not have an appreciable impact on the election because turnout had increased across demographic categories. On the other hand, the number of young adults who voted exceeded the goal of MTV's Choose or Lose campaign.

Afterward, RTV encountered difficulties and tensions, and today is nearly defunct. Momentum appeared to have diminished for several of the other youth-oriented organizations as well. Yet it seems probable that the objectives and approaches toward new media and popular culture these groups established will continue to be a factor in coming elections, especially if the youth vote is viewed as an important market segment.

Candidate Promotions and Popular Culture

Over the years, various campaigns for political candidates themselves have shown a growing tendency to exploit popular culture for the purpose of reaching a younger crowd. When Richard Nixon appeared on the irreverent comedy sketch show *Rowan and Martin's Laugh-In* in the 1960s, his action was broadly regarded as novel and even risky. Yet such behavior eventually became more predictable and is common today. In 1992, for instance, Bill Clinton played his saxophone while wearing dark sunglasses on *The Arsenio Hall Show* and, in front of a studio audience on a program for MTV, disclosed his preference of underwear. Four years later, Republican challenger **Bob Dole** came on the *Live with Regis and Kathie Lee* show to publicize an autobiographical book he had just completed. In 2000, major presidential candidates were guests on various entertainment talk shows, including *The Tonight Show, Late Night with David Letterman,* and *The Oprah Winfrey Show.* Elsewhere, Al Gore discussed the merits of rap music in a televised "town hall" meeting on MTV. Democrat John Edwards officially announced his candidacy on *The Daily Show with Jon Stewart* the following presidential election season. Presently, this cable program in particular regularly includes political guests, who generally utilize their visits as a platform for enhancing their images with young audiences. It appears that a carefully orchestrated plan that incorporates ingredients of popular culture will remain a consistent component of any future presidential campaign.

Importance of Pop Culture in Political Advertising

The political science scholar Glen W. Richardson Jr. (2003) argues that many political advertisements, particularly those that appear to have achieved some measure of success, clearly draw from the realm of popular culture, even if their creators might be unaware of this connection. The expressions of popular culture follow certain conventions that trigger specific audience expectations, a process that relates to the concept of *genre*, or a type of media narrative characterized by a distinctive style, such as a soap opera. Richardson identifies several popular culture genres according to which various political advertisements over the years could be classified, including horror, satire, pornography, dystopia, testimonial, tabloid TV scandal, family melodrama, altered states, and action hero. For example, with its grainy, black and white photography and ominous music, a 1988 George H. W. Bush commercial that portrayed rival George Dukakis as soft on crime displayed the typical qualities of the horror film (see **Furlough Commercial**). In 1996, the Clinton campaign used a melancholy solo piano track and soft focus photography to produce a mini-family melodrama that asserted Clinton's opponent, Robert Dole, was a threat to the American family. From this genre-centered perspective, political advertising and popular culture often directly intertwine. Moreover, a fruitful evaluation of an advertisement requires more than simply breaking down its logical claims or exploring its substantive content in terms of whether it takes a "positive" or "negative" approach, or focuses on "issues" or "image." A political spot is more than a straightforward argument—similar to movie directors or TV show producers, in their commercials candidates present stories that pull from common cultural associations and understandings to appeal to audiences through both reason and emotion.

Other recent campaign commercials provide further examples. In the 1998 Minnesota race for governor, former pro-wrestling entertainer Jesse Ventura's media team devised a spot that mimicked the production techniques of a toy commercial for an action figure. In the advertisement, which embodied the action hero genre, two boys played with a **Jesse Ventura** doll battling another toy man who represented "special interest groups." Two years earlier, a commercial for presidential candidate Pat Buchanan had captured the look and feel of a "reality" police show. Sometimes campaigns borrow a popular song to convey a symbolic message. An independent organization in support of Ronald Reagan, for instance, purchased rights to Lee Greenwood's country song "God Bless the USA" to furnish its commercial with an inspiring tone.

Occasionally, especially when it is intended to target potential youth voters, a political advertisement is markedly overt in linking to a product of popular culture. During the 1998 run for governor in California, for instance, Libertarian candidate Steve Kubby mocked the two major parties and their nominees with a commercial that featured the characters and crude animation style of *South Park*. In another example, prior to the 2008 primaries, in her bid for the presidency, Hillary Clinton appeared with her husband and former president, Bill Clinton, in a direct parody of the final episode of the highly popular HBO series *The Sopranos*. Posted on Clinton's campaign Web site, the spot received additional recognition through blogs, news coverage, and other venues. If future candidates maintain their interest in targeting young voters in the coming elections, the production of commercials that blatantly reference elements of popular culture will likely only increase.

THE FUTURE

Currently, the state of political advertising is in considerable flux. Although television is liable to continue to dominate campaign expenditures, the Internet and other forms of new media could challenge its reign. Scholars point out that the 2004 run for the nation's highest office was the first "Internet Election." Roughly 75 million Americans turned to the Internet for political information, to engage in political e-mail discussion, to make campaign donations or volunteer time, or to participate in more than one of these activities. Web logs, known as "blogs," also entered into the fray. Since then, these online practices have only escalated.

Internet Advertising Tactics

There are several types of Internet advertising available to resourceful politicians. Candidate Web sites themselves serve as a kind of advertisement. On occasion, spots that receive initial exposure on television are then placed on the Internet for added attention, sometimes in enhanced versions that are not suitable for broadcast. At other times, original commercials are designed specifically for the Internet and e-mailed to millions of recipients. Frequently, these advertisements are infused with humor or interactive features that stir some people to forward them to friends and family members, which further benefits the originators of the messages. In addition, campaigns can place advertisements on blog sites or generate blogs themselves.

The Internet has created the possibility for an unprecedented number of groups— or even individuals—to produce and distribute political advertising. For example, in 2004, the online advocacy organization MoveOn.org sponsored a contest that invited people to submit commercials depicting their impressions of George W. Bush in 30 seconds. JibJab, a two-person operation, crafted a spoof that satirized both Bush and his opponent John Kerry. The cartoon, through "viral" distribution, became so popular that it even received play on network television. Although it was not a commercial per se, it demonstrated the sort of impact a well-conceptualized political advertisement could have as well. During the 2008 election season, an initially undisclosed creator posted a commercial on YouTube that mixed footage from "1984," a famous Apple Computer commercial (also see Macintosh "1984" Commercial), with the face of Hillary Clinton to mock the 2008 presidential candidate. Soon afterward, another spot, drawing from the same Apple source, took shots at Democratic opponent Barack Obama. There is considerable conjecture regarding how campaigns will manage their political advertising as long-established media combine with the Internet, podcasts (audio files that can be downloaded), distribution on cell phones, and the other new media developments that will surely unfold. For now, politicians will continue to grapple with the best methods of using the fresh tools on hand to gain their objectives. (For a full discussion on the role of new media in politics, see Chapter 8.)

FURTHER READING

Benoit, William L., et al. *Campaign 2000: A Functional Analysis of Presidential Campaign Discourse.* Lanham, MD: Rowman & Littlefield, 2003.

Diamond, Edwin, and Stephen Bates. *The Spot: The Rise of Political Advertising on Television.* 3rd ed. Cambridge: MIT University Press, 1992.

Jamieson, Kathleen Hall. *Dirty Politics: Deception, Distraction, and Democracy*. Oxford, U.K.: Oxford University Press, 1992.

Jamieson, Kathleen Hall. *Packaging the Presidency: A History and Criticism of Presidential Campaign Advertising*. 3rd ed. New York: Oxford University Press, 1996.

Mark, David. *Going Dirty: The Art of Negative Campaigning*. Lanham, MD: Rowman & Littlefield, 2007.

McGinniss, Joe. *The Selling of the President*. New York: Penguin, 1968.

McNair, Brian. *An Introduction to Political Communication*. 4th ed. London: Routledge, 2007.

Richardson, Glenn W., Jr. *Pulp Politics: How Political Advertising Tells the Stories of American Politics*. Lanham, MD: Rowman & Littlefield, 2003.

Schwartz, Tony. *The Responsive Chord*. Garden City, NY: Anchor, 1973.

Trent, Judith S., and Robert V. Friedenberg. *Political Campaign Communication: Principles & Practices*. 5th ed. Lanham, MD: Rowman & Littlefield, 2004.

Williams, Andrew Paul, and John C. Tedesco (ed.). *The Internet Election: Perspectives on the Web in Campaign 2004*. Lanham, MD: Rowman & Littlefield, 2006.

Chapter 8

Politics Online

Although rudimentary forms of computer technology had been in service for decades, it was not until the 1960s that a concerted effort was made toward the development of a system that would eventually result in what is today known as the Internet. Backed by the U.S. Department of Defense, innovators perceived that a network of interconnected computer terminals could greatly benefit government projects by facilitating the flow of information. Before the decade had come to a close, a precursor to the Internet, namely ARPANET, was born. A fully functioning Internet came into operation in the 1980s. Yet for years, these communication tools were used primarily by researchers, scientists, and other academics. Consequently, they functioned in relative obscurity. As the Internet began its move into the commercial realm in the late 1980s, however, its public recognition quickly intensified. Still, at first, navigating the network was not easy for the everyday person without technical skill. But soon after the introduction of the World Wide Web (WWW) in the early 1990s, the number of people engaging in online activity grew exponentially. Though the terms "Internet" and "WWW" are often spoken interchangeably, they are not one and the same—the Internet provides the infrastructure to potentially connect citizens around the world, while the WWW is a format of interlinked documents that enables users to easily browse the system. Some scholars suggest that the expansion of the Internet into the fabric of day-to-day life represents nothing less than a full-scale communication revolution. While many others are less bold in their assertions, almost no observer of media would deny that the Internet has had a dramatic impact on modern culture, including politics.

THE POTENTIALLY DEMOCRATIC CHARACTERISTICS OF THE INTERNET

The very structure of the Internet distinguishes it from other forms of mass media. Indeed, it is not clear whether the Internet can be considered a mass medium in the traditional sense at all, although it sometimes functions as such. The Internet departs from its media predecessors—including television, radio, and print vehicles—in several ways that carry political significance. These defining characteristics include:

- **Users can be both senders and receivers of messages.** Unlike a mass medium (television or radio, for example), which typically involves relatively few large institutional communication sources transmitting messages to thousands or even millions of audience members, the Internet allows every participant to both send and receive information. Because the mass media require sizable financial and technological resources for their operation, few people—mostly only those professionally employed in the media industries—are able to contribute to the production of television shows, radio broadcasts, newspapers, magazines, and other media products. On the other hand, any able-minded person with an Internet connection can send e-mail, build a personal Web site, post pictures to **MySpace** or **Facebook** (see "Social Networking and the Democratization of Media" below), start a blog (see "Political Blogs" below), or share a video on **YouTube** (see "Online Video Sharing Sites" below). The number of people reached through these online expressions is often quite small. Yet sometimes, especially when a transmission goes "viral," even a single user can garner a worldwide audience.

- **Interactivity.** A person viewing a television show or reading a magazine has limited opportunity to offer feedback to the source of the communication. Phone calls to TV stations or letters to the editor are hardly immediate or efficient responses. Nor do they usually generate much, if any, reply in return. Conversely, the Internet provides the potential for continuous feedback. For instance, people can interact in real time through instant messaging (IM) services. Or a reader can quickly post a comment in reaction to an article on an online news site (see "Online Political Journalism" below). Put simply, the audience has scant short-term control over what happens in the mass media yet can be a co-participant in online communication. Accordingly, one-way transmission can become two-way (or multiway) exchange.

- **Lack of hierarchal structure.** Unlike the channels of mass media, which are dominated by several huge media conglomerates, such as Viacom and The Walt Disney Company, the Internet, at least in its current formation, is not subject to the overarching rule of any government or private enterprise. Instead, disintermediation, or the reduction in the ability of big media insiders to manage the flow of information, is the order of the day. In other words, people no longer have to rely on "professional" journalists for their news or turn to movie studios, record labels, or broadcast networks for their entertainment. Through the Internet, people can bypass traditional gatekeepers and, for example, learn about events from seemingly countless "citizen" journalists, or gain amusement by calling up any one of the millions of amateur-produced videos posted on YouTube.

The political implications of these characteristics associated with the Internet center on the manner in which online activity democratizes the media environment. No longer must audiences act as passive consumers of the products of mass media. Now nearly every citizen can add to the marketplace of ideas. Today's Internet users have an unprecedented degree of control of their experience in comparison to their forebears who could only settle for the top-down model of traditional mass media. Moreover, individuals can symbolically join with multitudes of other like-minded people more rapidly than ever before to promote a cause or movement.

Still, not every observer is as optimistic about the democratic potential of the Internet. Some critics fear that the present crop of media conglomerates will discover ways of adapting so they can retain their overpowering grip on the media landscape. Those who present a less sanguine assessment point to the rising influence of advertisers, which are vigorously working to transform the Internet into just another instrument for selling goods and services. Currently, however, advertisers have not developed the techniques to gain consistent success in their appeals to consumers on the Internet. To be sure, the spread of online media has incited panic within the advertising industry. With the plethora of available choices, not only through the Internet but through all the other forms of media as well, the mass audience has become fragmented into much smaller groups. Furthermore, because they have the increasing capacity to use the media on their own terms—to get what they want, when they want it, and wherever they want it—people can readily dismiss the advertising messages that come their way.

The concept of "net neutrality" also relates to the issue of the Internet's democratic possibilities. Currently, the Internet generally treats every user equally. Yet there is a push among some companies behind the present online infrastructure to institute a fee configuration that would privilege content providers with the means to pay (such as corporations) over those who cannot (such as everyday people). If this development were to prevail, critics argue, then the Internet would simply perpetuate the commercial model that has reigned with other media and do little to bolster a reinvigorated democracy. Thus whether the Internet, still in its infancy, eventually falls under the spell of the corporate world like its mass media ancestors or evolves into a force for democracy—or somehow integrates both possibilities—is very much an open question.

Another factor is not only a defining element of the Internet but has had a major impact on the very nature of other forms of media as well. The Internet is a product of computer digitization, a process that has eventually penetrated all of the electronic media. By gradually replacing their analog systems with digital technology, television, radio, and other communication vehicles have facilitated the movement toward media convergence. What this means is that once a media product has been digitized—a television show, a movie, a printed document, and so on—it can be accessed in any number of ways. For instance, a television program can be watched on the Internet, on a cell phone, and, of course, on a television. Or a Web site can be screened on the same three formats. Or to take yet another example, a song can be heard on the radio, on the computer, through the television, or on an mp3 player. Here again, convergence provides the flexibility that enables the audience to take greater control of its media experience. Accordingly, power has shifted from the mega-media corporation to the everyday viewer, listener, or reader. Thus digitization, a central component of the Internet that has stretched well beyond the computer, has further democratized the total media environment.

SOCIAL NETWORKING AND THE DEMOCRATIZATION OF MEDIA

One of the ways in which the democratization of media space has been evidenced is through the emergence of social networking sites such as MySpace, Facebook, and LinkedIn. These Internet destinations allow a member to easily construct a personal Web site and build a network of "friends" with whom the user can communicate online. MySpace was launched in 2003 and quickly became the nation's most popular social networking site. Older minors and young adults, in particular, embraced the site and were largely responsible for its explosive success.

The following year, Facebook was introduced. But unlike MySpace, Facebook was initially designed to service only college students. Later, it was opened up to high school students and, eventually, to the general population. Over time, Facebook surpassed MySpace in worldwide popularity. LinkedIn was put online before the other two networks yet, with its emphasis on business rather than social interaction, has never attracted nearly as many visitors as its two rivals. Since the birth of these Web sites, a number of similar venues have surfaced as well, although some of them are targeted toward more specific audiences, often centering on a particular area of interest. Still, MySpace, Facebook, and LinkedIn remain three of the most recognized sites of their kind.

Overall, however, these established social networking sites are not major hotbeds of political activity. Most participants mainly use them to casually interact with friends and family, share pictures, promote themselves, and engage in other generally fun interpersonal activities. On the other hand, a user of a site such as Facebook can join a group of other like-minded people under the banner of, for instance, "Christian Democrats" or "Lipstick Republicans." During the 2008 U.S. presidential campaign season, thousands of visitors clicked in to scores of groups in alignment with one of the two central tickets. The names of online organizations associated with the election included anything from "Sarah Palin is NOT Hillary Clinton" to "Obama, the ANTICHRIST." Yet rarely do such groups lead to serious mobilization that translates into a concerted push for political influence. Instead, members are far more likely to simply toss comments back and forth about the subject that defines the affiliation. Moreover, for every group that at least loosely connects to some political issue there are dozens more that focus on celebrities, forms of entertainment, hobbies, and other kinds of amusement.

Then again, during the 2008 run for the presidency, Barack Obama was the first candidate for the nation's highest office to make significant use of social networking sites to drum up support. The soon-to-be president drew up personal profiles for both well-known vehicles and venues aimed toward relatively niche audiences.

ONLINE POLITICAL SPECIAL INTEREST GROUPS

Although most social networking sites carry only marginal political import, many other online locations, especially those managed by certain special interest groups, are directly involved in political affairs. One of the most renowned Web organizations of this ilk is MoveOn.org. Launched in 1998 during the impeachment of President Bill Clinton to gather signatures for an online petition that asked Congress to censure President Clinton for lying under oath about his sexual affair with an intern (see **Political Scandals**) and then "move on" to more significant concerns, MoveOn.org has evolved into an influential liberal political advocacy group, with membership in the millions. Loyal to the Democratic Party, since its founding MoveOn.org has backed many political candidates at both state and national levels. Besides requesting donations on behalf of politicians it endorses and in order to keep itself running, the site attempts to involve its members in several additional ways. For example, during the 2004 presidential campaign season, MoveOn.org challenged visitors to create and submit a 30-second commercial that attacked George W. Bush. Entries were judged and the winning advertisement was placed on television. Distributing online polls to glean its members' opinions on various issues is another common tactic. Furthermore, through constant e-mail contact with its registered users, the group organizes protests and a variety of other grassroots political events, including door-to-door canvassing, phone bank solicitations, and "house parties," in which individuals volunteer to host small gatherings of people united by a common theme or cause.

While MoveOn.org has received both considerable acclaim and scathing criticism, it is by no means the only one of its kind. Representing both sides of the political spectrum, innumerable other special interest groups use the Internet in a similar fashion. Although some of them began online, most of these organizations were created in a traditional manner and then incorporated the WWW into their structures. Several of the most notable include America Coming Together and EMILY's List on the left, and Progress for America and Club for Growth on the right.

ONLINE MEDIA AND POLITICAL CAMPAIGNS

Probably the first significant use of the Internet by political candidates running for the nation's highest office occurred during the 1996 campaign season. Throughout the Republican primaries, most of the main contenders created and posted campaign Web sites. After the nomination had been determined, both Republican Bob Dole and Democrat Bill Clinton, who did not face any primary opposition because of his incumbency, included Web sites as part of the media mix in their general election campaigns.

Yet these Internet efforts were rudimentary at best. Before entering the twenty-first century, simply establishing any presence at all on the Web was enough for candidates to indicate they were on the cutting edge of the latest media trends. Indeed, the Internet was still a novelty to much of the population. Furthermore, candidate Web sites tended to be no more than online translations of printed materials, providing information about the politicians but offering visitors little, if any, opportunity for interactive engagement. By no means were these Web sites central components of the campaign arsenal.

It was not until the 2004 battle for the presidency that online campaigning began to come of age. During the primary period, Democrat Howard Dean unexpectedly catapulted into the limelight thanks in large measure to his team's ability to exploit the Internet to solicit a vast number of donations and cultivate a force of loyal supporters. After Dean dropped out following an infamous gaffe that destroyed his candidacy, John Kerry, the eventual Democratic nominee, also utilized the Internet more aggressively to raise funds, recruit volunteers, and motivate citizens to cast their vote for him. Republicans, including the incumbent candidate George W. Bush, who would win reelection, and special interest groups such as **Swift Boat Veterans for Truth**, also instituted savvy online tactics. No longer on the margins of political activity, the Internet became a major campaign tool, so much so that many observers identify the 2004 contest as the nation's first "Internet Election."

As President Bush's term in office was coming to a close, his eventual successor, Barack Obama, embraced the Internet like no candidate before and demonstrated just how powerful a resource it could be. Although any single influence is difficult to measure, it appears as though the Obama campaign's sophisticated Internet initiative played an instrumental role in his victory. Many pundits and observers pointed to Obama's system of online tactics as the exemplar that not only politicians but consumer marketers as well should emulate. (For a more comprehensive discussion of Obama's use of the Internet, see Chapter 7.) It is probably safe to assume that, from now on, the Internet will be a vital element of any major political campaign. In comparison to other modes, political Internet advertising features several advantages, which include: (1) it is cheaper to produce and distribute than television commercials; (2) in response to changing conditions, ads and commercials can be revised almost immediately; (3) it raises the potential to target audiences to new levels, even to the extent that an advertisement can be individually customized to reach a particular viewer; (4) it allows the opportunity for audiences to interact with the commercials and ads they see; and (5) at least for now, it is not subject to the same regulatory restrictions as its print and broadcast counterparts. On the other hand, the loose environment makes it more difficult for candidates to maintain control over their promotion and ensure that consistent messages are sent.

Whether or not the Internet usurps the authority that television has enjoyed over the past half century is not at all clear. What is certain, however, is that the online medium has come a long way in campaign politics since it made its appearance in 1996 and was perceived almost as a gimmick.

ONLINE POLITICAL JOURNALISM

Newspapers, a staple throughout the nation's history, have been experiencing a growing threat since the rise of the Internet. People wishing to gather in-depth information and commentary about current events are not nearly as reliant on printed pages of news as they once were. Sales are down. Circulations have decreased. At home delivery, for an increasing number of people—especially the younger crowd—seems outmoded or almost quaint. The Web offers an apparently infinite number of journalistic sources—many, if not most of them available free of charge. Meanwhile, as more and more citizens turn away from the newspaper for the possibilities they find online, scores of advertisers are eliminating or reducing the expenditures devoted to buying newspaper space for their paid publicity—or at least rethinking their positions. Moreover, given the manner in which the Internet has made it easier for people to be not only consumers but producers of media, a whole cottage industry of "citizen journalists" has surfaced, to some extent diminishing the importance and redefining the role of the professional press. The newspaper business, consequently, is facing difficult times, some leaders even showing signs of panic.

One response by major newspapers has been to create online versions of their traditional printed materials. Yet they are grappling with how to make this transition suitably profitable. By conceding the need to embrace the Internet if they hope to appear up-to-date, they further weaken the standing of the newspaper. At the same time, readers who formerly paid for the daily paper have shown resistance to parting with even a nominal fee for news online.

Further complicating the picture has been the emergence of commercial news entities that forswore the printed format right from the start, instead opting to publish directly online. Today, many of these online newspapers or news magazines exist. But two of the most popular ones, which also happen to place considerable interest in political stories and opinion, are *Slate* and *Salon*.

Michael Kinsley, a former editor of the print magazine *New Republic*, founded *Slate* in 1996 with the corporate backing of Microsoft. One of his goals was to perform a service for his audience by wading through what he perceived was an ocean of online news information, pulling out the most significant issues, and bringing succinct and synthesized reporting of them together under one source. As part of its mission, *Slate* provides a daily summary of what major newspapers are currently covering. Overall, its emphasis is not so much on uncovering fresh information—digging after "scoops" that it can use to beat the competition—as much as offering cohesive overviews, relatively short features, blogs, and commentaries on the most pressing news of the day. Yet early on, *Slate* did include one distinctive format—a section of real-time dialogue between staff and guest writers. It also hosts the Web site for the political cartoon **Doonesbury**, supplying a link to each day's edition.

Slate is generally regarded as having a mildly liberal political slant. In the 2004 presidential election, the majority of its regular writers expressed a preference for Democrat John Kerry over incumbent Republican George W. Bush, which appears to add support to this interpretation of the magazine's political inclinations. Interestingly, *Slate* is not shy about revealing its staff's biases—it actually publishes the voting choices of its writers and other personnel.

In 2002, Kinsley left the online publication (eventually, though, he began to make writing contributions, a practice he still performs on occasion today). Two years later, the *Washington Post* acquired *Slate* from Microsoft. Since June 2008, David Plotz has served as chief editor. A decade before, *Slate* had experimented with charging a subscription fee, one of the first news Web sites to do so. The plan backfired, however, and the online current-affairs magazine returned to presenting its content for no charge. Consequently, it relies on revenue from advertisers to maintain its presence. Like its traditional newspaper counterparts that had made the move online, it found that too many people, used to not having to pay for most material on the Web, were unwilling to relinquish money for online news.

Viewed as a "progressive" online publication, *Salon* leans further to the left of *Slate*. *Salon* was founded in 1995 by David Talbot, a former arts and features editor with the *San Francisco Examiner*, with some financial support from Apple Computer. He relinquished his role as chief editor in 2005 and was replaced by Joan Walsh, who still holds the position today.

Initially, *Salon* operated as a biweekly source of cultural and political commentary. But to build traffic, Talbot decided to produce an issue each weekday and include new and breaking coverage of current affairs, as well as investigative journalism. In 1998, the online magazine gained attention with original exposés, including a story that disclosed then House Judiciary Committee Chair Henry Hyde had had an affair with a married mother of three children. Today, *Salon* is continuously updated throughout the week. Like its competitor, *Salon* devotes space to the arts, culture, and other "softer" news and reviews, while placing considerable emphasis on political coverage and analysis. Yet in contrast to *Slate*, it features a greater number of longer articles. Furthermore, *Salon* has achieved a degree of success with charging fees. In 2001, *Salon* launched "Salon Premium," which allowed only subscribers full access to the magazine. Soon, though, the news source backpedaled somewhat by extending another means of entering the site to those unwilling to pay. To view content, readers were asked to first look at an advertisement placed by a sponsor. For the most part, this economic model has held steady ever since. Everyone can gain the privilege of perusing most of *Salon*'s material, yet subscribers enjoy several extra benefits. At the same time, the publication supplements user fees with advertising revenue.

At the moment, there is much speculation by scholars, cultural critics, and other observers as to how journalism and the nature of news will evolve as digital media in general gain an ever-greater grip on the populace. Yet because the future is ultimately unpredictable, there is no consensus among them—only time will tell how news coverage and its reception by the audience will unfold in the age of the Internet.

POLITICAL BLOGS

The term "blog" comes from the word "weblog," which was introduced into the cultural lexicon in the late 1990s and was designated to refer to a type of diary or journal produced online. What exactly constitutes a blog is sometimes a slippery subject. (For example, are only the people who initiate original postings bloggers, or are the readers who post responses bloggers as well? Does it include only opinion or also straightforward reporting? Is it only an individual enterprise or can it be the product of a group?) Yet in an authoritative book on the topic, *Blogwars*, David D. Perlmutter defines a blog as follows:

> (a) written in the style of a personal essay, journal entry, diary, or memoir, (b) interactive, (c) containing posts of varying lengths in reverse chronological order, (d) embedded with hyperlinks within text, (e) providing permalinks and allowing trackbacks [discussions that are taken up on other blogs], and (f) listing other blogs. (2008, 61)

Not every Web site that is commonly regarded as a blog, however, fulfills all six criteria. Based on its looser, popular conception, a blog can consist of any kind of subject matter—from one person's regular postings about a trip abroad to a commercial site that focuses on recurrent contributions from multiple participants who analyze and provide information on financial affairs. A political blog, as the expression indicates, is an online journal of political thought and commentary. The most popular blogs extend the opportunity for exchanges between authors and readers. Because blogs can deal with any topic, most of them are not political. Yet for those that are, with their diverse array of individual voices and varying levels of interactivity, certain blogs can give the impression of personalizing political communication. Previously, only the "mass media" (television, radio, books, and so on) were capable of reaching huge audiences. Now a single person, if he or she strikes the right cord, can build a readership of comparable size. Blogging is playing a part in partially supplanting the "top down" model of media, wherein a small number of mighty corporations transmit messages to the citizenry, with a "bottom up" approach in which ordinary people are capable of having a disproportionate impact on the national conversation. In general, bloggers reject the standard "objective" mode of the mainstream media in favor of strong and openly partisan biases.

The Debate about Blogging: Is It Good for Democracy?

Today, there are literally thousands of either amateur or professional writers who are involved in producing material for political blogs—and their numbers continue to climb. Some blogs are published by individuals, while others are the product of a staff of people. Although there are likenesses among them, given that there are so many variations of the form, it is nearly impossible to neatly categorize political blogs. As their presence has grown, scholars and other observers have increasingly joined in a vigorous debate as to their significance, especially in relationship to democracy.

Some observers fear that political blogs—and the Internet in general—will function not to unite the nation, but to divide it into myriad factions and, thus, partisanship will rule the day. For example, left-leaning blogs are more likely to link to other blogs with similar political outlooks and, likewise, conservative blogs tend to offer connections to other right-leaning pages. Moreover, critics complain, the dialogue on political blogs can often lack civility, instead descending into name calling, blatant distortions, and foul language—particularly when someone from one "camp" visits the opposing side. A portion of potential participants, averse to the heat, might opt to drop out of the discussion altogether, striking a blow to democratic engagement. Even instances of identity theft have occurred via blogs, including imposters who pretend to be their political rivals in an effort to discredit or defame their adversaries. In addition, the blogs that receive the heaviest traffic become prime real estate opportunities for advertisers. Once a blog accepts sponsorship, it is open to the same commercial pressures to water down its content as any other advertising-funded medium (for the example of radio, see Chapter 3; for the example of television, see Chapter 4). Another line of critique centers on the supposed confusion that arises when just about anybody with access to a computer can post material online. Unlike paid journalists, everyday people do not have a set of standards to conform to nor are they prone to vigorous fact checking. Consequently, so the thinking goes, readers hoping to navigate the Internet waters for useful political information and interpretation will be deluged by unreliable and erroneous opinions.

Proponents of political blogging present several counterarguments. First, they point out that resistance to a new form of media technology is nothing new. For instance, before becoming fully integrated into society, radio and television, too, had endured more than their share of rebuke. Like it or not, it appears as though the Internet is here to stay and the importance of online communication to both political campaigns and those simply seeking political information will only expand. Similarly, partisanship has been around for generations. Most of the newspapers from the founding of the country and throughout the nineteenth century, for example, were strongly biased in their political perspectives. Second, though fierce partisanship can split people into opposite sides, it can also inspire those of common mind to come together and possibly mobilize in an attempt to evoke change—blogs, without question, facilitate the process of finding comrades who hold a similar worldview and subscribe to equivalent political positions. From this vantage point, blogging invigorates the marketplace of ideas that, ideally, stands as a central characteristic of democracy. As a range of "interest groups" face off in a verbal war, their transaction can lead to social progress. Third, even if partisanship were to be accepted as problematic, there is no conclusive evidence that audiences of blogs are completely shielding themselves from conflicting opinions. Plenty of political blogs indeed link to some sites on the opposite end of the spectrum—or at least reference them in making their own points. Many citizens, exposed to multiple interpretations, will inevitably modify stances over time. In the end, supporters contend, blogging actually democratizes the flow of ideas by circumventing the professional gatekeepers of the past, thereby allowing more people than ever to become active in the political process. In other words, citizens have the power to sidestep the "professionals" and access information directly on their own terms. They need no longer be content with merely consuming the banter of the paid pundits. They can contribute to the fray as producers as well. Depending on talent and marketing ability, however, some bloggers will reach far larger audiences than others. But to worry about too many people having the ability to disperse their ideas, according to those with a positive regard for blogging, is to take an elitist, rather than a populist, attitude.

Big Moments in Blogging's (Short) History

Regardless of its pros and cons, blogging, it seems, has become a fact of life. The computer itself (through the use of e-mail, Web sites, and other online materials) became a prominent, though underdeveloped, tool in the campaign chest in 1996. Yet blogging as a major campaign component awaited discovery. Beginning with the presidential contest of 2004 between Republican incumbent George W. Bush and his challenger, Democratic Senator John Kerry, the majority of major political campaign strategies have included a blogging component.

Blogging started coming to light in the late 1990s but did not explode into a cultural phenomenon until several years later. Matt Drudge (see *The Drudge Report*) presaged the rise of the "blogthrough" (a news item first revealed on a blog that quickly becomes so huge that it gains wide coverage on traditional mainstream media) when he disclosed in 1998 that *Newsweek* magazine had killed a story involving then President Bill Clinton's extramarital affair with a White House intern, a scandal that eventually threatened to drive Clinton from office (see **Political Scandals**).

The blogthrough as a true political force fully arrived in 2002, when former Senate Majority Leader Trent Lott made what were arguably racist comments during a celebration of then Senator Strom Thurmond's 100th birthday. The big media outlets paid little attention to his remarks. Yet the "blogosphere" rapidly circulated discussion of Lott's effusive endorsement of Thurmond, who had acquired the reputation of a hardcore segregationist during his run for the presidency in 1948. Finally, the floodgates were opened and mainstream journalism had to respond. The incident likely played a part (although to what extent is by no means clear) in the later resignation of Lott, whose image had been severely tarnished by the coverage of his birthday party speech.

In the early days of blogging, established news agencies tended to be dismissive of them (some still are). Yet once it was apparent that bloggers could have an impact on actual events, journalists were forced to come to terms with them. Soon, mainstream outlets were filing reports about them and citing them as sources, realizing that when a story reached a certain threshold of attention online it could no longer be ignored. A number of major episodes precipitated a storm of blogging that probably had an influence on the way in which they were treated in the traditional news media, including the September 11 terrorist attacks in 2001, the U.S. invasion of Iraq in 2003, the London terrorist bombings in 2005, and the Hurricane Katrina disaster that leveled large sections of New Orleans less than two months later. Yet three blogthroughs especially stand out in bringing blogging wholesale recognition.

The 2004 Howard Dean Campaign.   The 2004 presidential race is often pointed to as the first "Internet election." The person who is generally credited as the initial presidential candidate to comprehensively demonstrate the power of the Web is former governor of Vermont and former chair of the Democratic National Committee Howard Dean. In 2003, the Dean team pioneered the use of blogging as part of its online initiative, creating its own blog site along the way. Individual supporters were also encouraged to start their own blog sites and link them to

Dean's. The campaign was instrumental in influencing the mainstream media to acknowledge the growing importance of blogging.

Dean, who in the early stages of the campaign was not identified by the media as a leading contender, presented himself as a "Washington outsider," a man of the people. The perception caught on and the candidate surprised the pundits by gathering a devoted following of citizens, especially among the young. The Dean staff, headed by strategist Joe Trippi, strove to bypass the established channels of media and reach the population directly through the Internet. Momentum escalated as more and more people spread the word online and organized themselves into a reputable force. Accordingly, an association of Dean bloggers was born. The campaign obtained the sought-after aura of a populist crusade. Dean rapidly catapulted from relative obscurity to celebrity status.

Still, the online endeavor was not immune to substantial flaws and, consequently, its impact should not be overstated. For one thing, it was not as interactive as it could have been in theory. Despite the will to energize the citizenry, a politician also understands the need to control the central messages of a campaign. To allow an Internet strategy to become a bona fide free-for-all could backfire. Not to mention that there are not enough hours in the day for every participant who posts an entry to be addressed by someone at campaign headquarters. The Dean team, then, struggled to walk a fine line between mobilizing its backers and not letting the presidential run take on a life of its own. In short, the campaign was not utterly populist, a discovery that eventually alienated some Dean enthusiasts. Many people offered suggestions to Dean's Web site but received no feedback—or merely a rote response—in return.

In the end, however, Dean's online effort was indeed a novel, if not revolutionary, political development. Moreover, the candidate's swift fall from grace cannot be attributed to blogging. One of the most talked about events of the 2004 presidential race in general was Dean's infamous "scream" speech in Iowa. Just after he had lost that state's primary caucus battles, Dean mounted the stage in hope of rallying his troops. Although it came across as merely an enthusiastic address by those present at the live meeting, when shown on television, because of the faulty way in which it had been recorded, Dean came across as maniacal, as someone far too volatile to be trusted with the presidency. For days, the television news media played clips from the speech and discussed its damaging effect (and, by endlessly playing snippets and casting them in a negative light, probably helped to make the oration's destructive blow a self-fulfilling prophecy). Following the Iowa contest, the first of the primary season, Dean immediately fell in popularity and never recovered.

Swift Boat Veterans for Truth.   A group known as Swift Boat Veterans for Truth, created for the goal of discrediting Democratic Senator John Kerry's heroic service in Vietnam, initially circulated its rumors on the Internet. Soon, its distorted accounts migrated from there to a series of televised commercials that received extensive news coverage. The Swift Boat smear campaign is often identified as being one of the significant factors that contributed to the defeat of Kerry by incumbent George W. Bush in the 2004 presidential election. (For a full account of Swift Boat Veterans for Truth and the role it played in Kerry's downfall, see **Swift Boat Veterans for Truth.**)

Dan Rather and "Memogate."   In September 2004, on an episode of CBS's *60 Minutes II*, longtime news anchor veteran Dan Rather delivered a story that questioned incumbent President George W. Bush's 1970s service in the Alabama National Guard, alleging that he had improperly abandoned his military duties to work on a political campaign. To support this position, Rather presented supposed copies of evaluations written by one of Bush's former Guard supervisors. The revelation, if true, could have proven particularly controversial, given that Bush was currently running for reelection.

Immediately after the telecast, bloggers, especially on the conservative Web site Free Republic, started challenging the legitimacy of the memos Rather had shown on the program. The accusation arose that the documents were, in fact, fake. Writing on powerlineblog, Scott W. Johnson and John H. Hinderaker contended that such was the case—their post, "The Sixty-first Minute," was eventually widely cited by the mainstream media and helped powerlineblog garner the "Blog of the Year" award from *Time* magazine.

Once the charge that the Rather memos were forgeries spilled into conventional media coverage, the storm escalated. CBS finally admitted that it could not fully verify the documents' authenticity. Dan Rather, who had been a journalist for over 50 years and had worked for CBS for over 40 of them—with nearly a quarter of a century spent as the network's lead anchor—was fired soon afterward. Although the reasons for Rather's termination are likely multifaceted, it appears as though the blogosphere, indeed, was a major factor in destroying the venerable newsman's career. Interestingly, the allegation that President Bush had cheated on his military responsibilities was never demonstrated to be false (or true for that matter)—only the credibility of the memos used as the main evidence to back the claim were called into dispute.

The three historical episodes spelled out above strongly indicate that the 2004 presidential campaign season represented a watershed moment for blogging. By the end of the election, it seemed that the format had definitely arrived as a player in the political landscape and could no longer be brushed away or ignored. From there, the blogworld continued along the path of professionalization, functioning as another force to be reckoned with in the realm of journalism at large. Most bloggers remain amateurs. Yet a significant number of them—especially those who receive heavy reader traffic—are paid and taken seriously by both common citizens and the mainstream media.

Categories of Bloggers

Although candidates running for office have increasingly employed blogging as a tactic, the vast majority of political blogs are not directly associated with parties or politicians. A good many of them are produced by everyday people with a passion for politics. (Still, it must be mentioned that, at least currently, not every person has equal access to the Internet because of differences in socioeconomic status. In this sense, then, blogging is not utterly populist, nor does it unequivocally represent the voice of "the people.") The bulk of these bloggers, however, reach just small audiences. Only the rare talent rises to the level of attracting a mass following. Some of the most notable blogs, in this regard, include RealClearPolitics, Taegan Goddard's Political Wire, and Wonkette; the conservative sites, Red State, Town-Hall, and Little Green Footballs; and the liberal site, MyDD. Yet three names that have especially made their mark are Matt Drudge of *The Drudge Report*, Arianna Huffington of the *Huffington Post*, and "Kos" (real name, Markos Moulitsas Zúniga), writer of the *Daily Kos*. See Part II for entries on these sites.

Blogging by Traditional Journalists.   In a sort of "if you can't beat 'em, join 'em" mentality, scores of mainstream news agencies now include blogs by some of their staff journalists as part of their output. For example, all three of the major network television news divisions—CBS, NBC, and ABC—feature blogs that are written by their correspondents for their Web sites. Newspapers, too, have incorporated blogging into their online sites. The *New York Times*, for instance, carries many blogs, including several written by their regular columnists, such as Paul Krugman and Nicholas D. Kristof. Readers are also invited to "blog" about the op-ed pieces they read. In addition, a number of conventional news outlets have even co-opted former independent bloggers, further blurring the distinction between the traditional field of journalism and the blogosphere. All of these blogs are designed to come across as more timely and spontaneous than the media organizations' traditional reports and columns. Extended current events can provide excellent occasions for blogging. For example, on the night of an important primary election during the 2008 presidential campaign, the *New York Times* assigned a writer to post updates on a blog throughout the evening.

One of the major consequences of established journalism outlets joining their independent competitors in the blogosphere is that the news cycle is continuously shrinking. The accent is increasingly on immediacy over other considerations. One of the drawbacks to this approach, however, is that the news—especially as presented through blogs—is more prone to inaccuracies. Even minor blemishes—such as spelling errors—that readers would generally not expect from a professional resource have grown in number. Still, the focus on speed appeals to the person hungry for the most current information that is available on a news story.

The Functions and Influence of Blogs

The role and influence of blogs has been a matter of much dispute. Yet as blogs keep expanding in number and commanding ever-greater attention, even detractors are being forced to come to grips with the idea that this new form of journalism is here to stay. Accordingly, media scholars have been attempting to evaluate the impact of blogs. Because the blogosphere is such a fresh development, however, reaching hard conclusions is no easy task. How blogging will continue to evolve and affect journalism is anybody's guess. On the other hand, a number of ways in which blogging is functioning can be at least tentatively described.

In relationship to political campaigns, a blog can enable a candidate's team to bypass traditional media channels and relatively inexpensively appeal directly to possible voters, providing a means of, for instance, raising money or energizing a base of followers. One of the main uses of the Web, particularly blogs, in this regard, entails bringing people together for a common purpose. Political campaigns can exploit online resources in an attempt to organize people in support of their goal, while everyday individuals can employ them to organize themselves. Political power often enlarges as numbers increase. Some observers contend that online "communities" are the modern equivalent of the coffeehouses and other public settings of yesteryear, where common citizens would gather to discuss and debate the issues of the day. Yet others counter that a "virtual" community lacks the richness and reasonable manners of a face-to-face collective.

Bloggers in general, according to David D. Perlmutter, an authority on the phenomenon, "can serve the public as informants, investigators, collators, and compilers, and revisers and extenders of political information" (2008, 110). Because the sheer quantity of information on the Web can be overwhelming to the average reader, the blogger who surveys and synthesizes material into a digestible overview of some of the most important current political affairs is conducting a beneficial activity.

When they are present at a live event, bloggers, with their quickly derived postings, can bring audiences into the scene, supplementing the information that flows from traditional channels. Sometimes, faced with fewer pressures from corporate executives and advertisers, they can even cover topics and details that large news agencies are loathe to touch. Likewise, bloggers occasionally give voice to certain people or groups that are often marginalized in mainstream media.

Some bloggers engage in investigative reporting, that is, deeply follow a usually controversial story over time in an effort to bring truth to light. The standard media organizations, with their focus on objective "balance," have reduced the amount of coverage they devote to this style of reporting. It is also time-consuming and costly, two factors profit-driven, corporate news agencies would rather avoid. Although most bloggers do not have the financial resources to properly perform investigative journalism, nonetheless, by carefully and responsibly scrutinizing a large amount of secondary (existing) reports and other materials, especially talented practitioners are capable of exposing troublesome issues and activities that many readers wish to learn about.

One of the most fundamental ways in which bloggers have changed the nature of journalism is by undermining the clout of the so-called "experts." No wonder they have been attacked, in particular, by the mainstream media, although major news agencies are increasingly coming to terms with blogs, as evidenced by them rolling out their own versions. At the same time, though, "everyday" intelligent and well-informed people can work as analysts and critics, thus opening political debate to a far wider range of points of view. Mainstream news companies have often been accused of allowing only pundits who hover near the center of the political spectrum to express their opinions. Bloggers fall on the extreme ends of the left-right political divide—and everywhere in between. Consequently, they considerably add to the "marketplace of ideas" that is a central tenet of the U.S. political system. Yet not all observers celebrate this development. Proponents claim that bloggers help democratize the political process and stir greater citizen involvement, while critics complain that the cacophony of online commentary only degrades the nation's political discourse and spreads confusion.

Related to the bloggers' challenge to the traditional media's authority is the part that some of them play as political watchdogs. Here again, the "old" media organizations have often been blamed of late for allegedly not taking enough of an adversarial stance toward political figures. For generations, one of the most expected functions of the journalism profession has been to hold the powerful to account. Many critics contend that, due to a number of pressures, including the need to gain access to the corridors of government, the mainstream media have turned into political bedfellows, operating as mere stenographers for officeholders rather than as questioners of their policies and practices. Likewise, owned by corporations and funded by advertisers, traditional news media are generally unwilling to passionately confront any of the ignoble activities of big business. On the other hand, a lot of bloggers truly relish this responsibility. Episodes such as highlighting Trent Lott's divisive comments and putting Dan Rather's evidence of President Bush's alleged abandonment of military duty to the test are instances of bloggers fulfilling a watchdog role.

To a growing degree, they have demonstrated the capacity of pushing news stories that might not have been covered otherwise into the mainstream media—or at least bringing them to surface more quickly than would probably be the case if the conventional news agencies were left to their own devices. Bloggers have from time to time beat the established media to an important "scoop." Thus, the political blogosphere not only adopts a skeptical attitude toward government and the corporate world, but also toward the very field of journalism. The blogging realm, unsurprisingly, is not without its serious flaws and irresponsible practitioners. Yet an optimistic outlook of the impact of blogging would suggest that, despite its problems, it is carrying out a crucial service for the public—and maybe even journalism itself. It could be that as they become more and more intertwined, political bloggers and mainstream news agencies will realize they both need each other.

But it bears repeating that blogs are in their infancy and how they unfold is grounds for speculation. It is highly unlikely that the blogosphere will completely supplant the traditional news profession. What does seem clear at this point, however, is that blogging has indeed changed the rules of the game. Various observers even posit that the most influential posters—such as Kos, who, like others, is actually courted by politicians and is sometimes hired as a consultant (see *Daily Kos*)—are joining the ranks of the media elite and mutating into part of the very establishment they had originally intended to defy, becoming a new wave of gatekeepers in the process. Belying their grassroots reputation, some blogs have been charged with planting "sock puppets," i.e., professional advocates posing as ordinary citizens. Certain groups, in particular, have been accused of enforcing group unity to the extent that it closes down lively debate.

Yet the blogosphere is a highly complex and contradictory domain. Hence, its influence will almost surely be variegated and felt at different levels. As blogging takes its place beside the already deeply assimilated forms of media that came before it, the interaction between them will touch politics and popular culture in ways that remain to be seen.

ONLINE VIDEO SHARING SITES

Another recent online development to further contribute to the democratization of the media environment is the rise of online video sharing sites. At these venues, any user can upload a video for visitors to see and share with others. Thus participants can operate as both producers and consumers of media content. The most popular site of this type by far is YouTube.

Launched in 2005, YouTube quickly exploded in popularity. Soon after it came on the scene, literally millions of videos were being posted and screened online. By 2006, YouTube had been purchased by Google. The quality of the material ranges from amateurish home videos to professional-grade productions that have been appropriated from third-party sources (generating a number of copyright controversies along the way). Accordingly, most of the pieces, usually relatively short in length, receive rather limited attention. Yet some videos, particularly those that are rapidly passed on from viewer to viewer via e-mail and other online channels, a process known as "going viral," can gain an audience over time that easily matches those achieved by the big broadcast television networks.

The great majority of the uploaded offerings are not political in nature. Then again, YouTube is sometimes used for political purposes. For example, during his

2008 run for the presidency, Barack Obama started his own channel on YouTube. At the same time, many everyday people also added fuel to the fire. One of the most notable videos, anonymously posted by a supporter of Obama, transformed the legendary **Macintosh "1984" Commercial** into a spot that poked fun of his Democratic rival Hillary Clinton. Meanwhile, the "**Obama Girl**" became an overnight sensation with a music video uploaded on YouTube that featured a scantily clothed woman revealing why she had a "crush" on Obama.

RELATED NEW MEDIA AND POLITICS

Coinciding with the evolution of the Internet, other related forms of new media that owe their very existence to digital technology have also grown into cultural phenomena. In the United States, the cell phone, which has been available for decades, is not only used to make telephone calls but to access the Internet, screen videos, and send text messages as well. Marketers have discovered that text messaging, in particular, can be an advantageous tool for reaching customers. By extension, politicians, who during campaigns must take on the role of marketer in addition to their many other responsibilities, have also begun to put text messaging to work. As a case in point, just as it had with the Internet, Barack Obama's campaign team demonstrated political skill during Obama's run for the presidency with a well-developed mobile phone program that involved supporters through text messaging and other tactics, an approach his Republican rival, John McCain, never matched. Furthermore, text messaging can be utilized to mobilize people in grassroots movements. Although this potentiality has not firmly caught on in the United States, it has occurred elsewhere. In 2001 in the Philippines, for instance, thousands of citizens used text messaging to coordinate large-scale protests that led to the peaceful overthrow of the then current president, Joseph Estrada, with his vice president, Gloria Macapagal-Arroyo, replacing him, an event commonly known as the Second People Power Revolution (the first had occurred before cell phone technology had become established).

One of the latest media applications to have sparked a stir in the realm of popular culture makes combined use of Internet and cell phone technologies. Twitter, a type of social networking application and "micro-blogging" tool, enables registered members to keep in continuous contact with a list of "followers" by sending a stream of "tweets," or short text-based messages no more than 140 characters in length. In turn, members are able to receive tweets from the subscribers they follow. Participants can access Twitter through either the Web on any computer or a properly equipped mobile phone. Logging on to Twitter via cell phone is especially popular with users because its portability is compatible with the nature of the service. Based on the company's original concept, each tweet is designed to answer the simple question, "What are you doing?" Subscribers can post replies to the question—and read their fellow members' updates—as many times a day as they wish. Moreover, they can stay in touch not only with friends and family but also with celebrities, corporate marketers, and other well-known figures who make themselves available through Twitter as a public relations tactic.

Again, as with nearly all of the social networking systems, most tweets do not convey anything of particular political importance. Yet like its digital relatives, Twitter offers people the possibility of using it for political purposes. For example, citizens can receive tweets from participating politicians. Not surprisingly, given all of the new media devices it fruitfully employed, the Barack Obama team also sent out tweets from the campaign trail to interested Twitter members during the candidate's 2008 run for the presidency.

What other forms of new media or online vehicles emerge in the days ahead is anybody's guess. Since the dawn of the Internet, the communication environment has been going through rapid change, with innovations breaking out in quick succession. Most of these inventive developments swiftly come and go. But every once in a while one catches hold of the public imagination and moves beyond being merely a fad of popular culture to become a media fixture. Two scenarios do seem likely to continue indefinitely, however. The digital technology that supports the Internet will persist in creating the conditions in which people can interact with media and one another wherever they want and whenever they want. And all of the new media products that stick will find their way into the world of politics, involving both politicians and everyday citizens alike.

FURTHER READING

Armstrong, Jerome, and Markos Moulitsas. *Crashing the Gate: Netroots, Grassroots, and the Rise of People-Powered Politics*. White River Junction, VT: Chelsea Green, 2006.

Gillmore, Dan. *We the Media: Grassroots Journalism By the People, For the People*. Sebastopol, CA: O'Reilly Media, 2006.

Keren, Michael. *Blogosphere: The New Political Arena*. Lanham, MD: Lexington Books, 2006.

Perlmutter, David D. *Blogwars*. New York: Oxford University Press, 2008.

Rigby, Ben. *Mobilizing Generation 2.0: A Practical Guide to Using Web 2.0 Technologies to Recruit, Organize and Engage Youth*. Indianapolis, IN: Jossey-Bass, 2008.

Trippi, Joe. *The Revolution Will Not Be Televised: Democracy, the Internet, and the Overthrow of Everything*. Rev. ed. New York: Harper, 2008.

Williams, Andrew Paul, and John C. Tedesco (ed.). *The Internet Election: Perspectives on the Web in Campaign 2004*. Lanham, MD: Rowman & Littlefield, 2006.

Part II

A

AFRICAN AMERICAN STAND-UP COMEDIANS. There is a long tradition of political activism in the African American stand-up material, from the political comedy of Richard Pryor, to Dick Gregory, to Redd Foxx, to the present; there has been a long tradition of saying things in the form of comedy that cannot be said in a serious discussion without causing offense. Two of the most notable modern comedians to use heavily political material in their acts are **Chris Rock** and **Dave Chappelle**. Although the two comedians are widely disparate in their approach, they come from a unique perspective related to the tradition of African American comedy and are allowed more leeway than many traditional comedians to address serious issues regarding race and politics. Others who have recently made a difference in terms of political comedy are D. H. Hughley, most recently as a commentator on **CNN**, Larry Wilmore and Wyatt Cenac from *The Daily Show*, and David Alan Grier on the Comedy Central faux news program, *Chocolate News*, which ran briefly in late 2008.

AIR AMERICA. Air America is a liberal radio network founded by Sheldon and Anita Drobny in 2004 to challenge the presumed right-wing dominance of the airwaves. After funding the initial idea, the network was bought by Evan Cohen and Mark Walsh, who ran it for several years before ownership changes and shake-ups hurt the financial stability of the network. Regular hosts included on Air America were Randi Rhodes, Janeane Garofalo, Chuck D. from the rap group Public Enemy, and **Al Franken**. The station went through various versions of restructuring due to money problems during the first few years of its existence, before being bought following a 2006 bankruptcy by left-wing tycoon Stephen Green who appointed his brother, perennial political candidate and former New York City public advocate, Mark Green as president of Air America. While the network is an interesting idea politically, it never seemed to have jelled as a concept or as a real alternative to right-wing talk radio. A reason for this may be that the celebrity hosts were not as used to the format of radio, or that the network's chronic underfunding and constant talent turnover never helped create a distinct identity for Air America. The network continues to this day, including a program hosted by Rachel Maddow, who now also has a successful television show started in 2008 on **MSNBC**, *The Rachel Maddow Show*. Air America programs may yet eventually evolve into a legitimate challenge to conservative radio giants such as **Rush Limbaugh** and **Sean Hannity**.

ALI, MUHAMMAD. Muhammad Ali (1942–) is the iconic American boxer formerly known as Cassius Clay who was a heavyweight champion of the world on three separate occasions. In the early 1960s Clay became politicized and associated with the Black Muslim movement and changed his name to Muhammad Ali after converting to Islam, announcing this dramatically after his stunning defeat of heavyweight champ Sonny Liston in 1964. Always outspoken in the ring and outside, Ali soon made a name for himself as a political agitator and provocateur par excellence. When Ali was drafted in 1967, he refused to serve and was taken to court by the U.S. government. He was eventually sentenced to five years in prison, fined $10,000, and also barred from fighting. Although Ali stayed free on appeal, he was able to fight only once (in Georgia where there was no boxing commission) before his conviction was finally overturned on appeal in 1971. Today Ali is still a legendary American fighter, but unfortunately Parkinson's disease has led to his departure from the American stage. Ali represents the kind of outlandish sports figure, who, during his heyday in the 1960s and 1970s, was a keen and humorous commentator on American social and political life. In the film *Ali* (2001) he was portrayed by Will Smith.

ALIAS. *Alias* was a politically charged spy television program created by J. J. Abrams and starring Jennifer Garner that ran from 2001 to 2006. The show detailed the exploits of undercover spy Sydney Bristow as she traveled the world working for SD-6, an agency she believes is part of the CIA, but which is actually a branch of the international spy organization The Alliance of 12. When Sydney discovers this after the death of her boyfriend, she works with the real CIA to fight the international espionage organization and save America from terrorism and attack. The show was incredibly convoluted, but demonstrated that the political thriller, assumed dead in the latter half of the twentieth century, was alive and well and that the spy genre could be resurrected again and again.

ALL IN THE FAMILY. *All in the Family* was a politically charged sitcom created by Norman Lear (based on a British sitcom, *Till Death Us Do Part*), running from 1971 to 1979, which dealt with the loudmouthed, bigoted Archie Bunker, his meek and ready-to-please wife, Edith, and his liberal daughter and son-in-law, Gloria and Mike. While Archie is presented as a somewhat sympathetic character, he is also a retrograde bigot and defender of blue collar white America. The program was a huge, if very controversial, success with some members of the audience watching to root along with Archie. The program was an effort by Lear to push the envelope on American television and try to make a program that represented the realities of life in America after the Civil Rights and antiwar movements. Archie's clear discomfort with other races, women's lib advocates, and gay rights made for entertaining, if somewhat didactic, explorations of American social and political problems. Even though Archie serves as the proto-typical bigot of the program, the show later introduced a black family, the Jeffer-sons (characters later were spun off into their own sitcom), that included a black patriarch, George Jefferson, just as bigoted against Caucasians as Archie was about everyone. After its end in 1979, the show briefly continued, after the depar-ture of the rest of the cast, as the reformatted sitcom *Archie Bunker's Place* from 1979 to 1983. *All in the Family* is regarded today as one of the most important television shows in American history, and certainly the most groundbreaking in terms of social and political taboos. Norman Lear went on to more advocacy as the founder of People for the American Way (1980), a group that fought against religious influence in America during the 1980s and 1990s.

AMERICAN FLAG, WEARING. Abbie Hoffman (1936–1989), the 1960s radical and fugitive from justice, created a stir when he was arrested in October 1968 for wearing a shirt patterned after the American flag. This was considered radical at the time and Hoffman was held in a maximum-security prison when arrested, sent to trial, and convicted of desecrating the American flag. Undeterred, Hoffman later appeared on *The Merv Griffin Show* in 1970 wearing another American flag shirt that was blacked out by censors afraid of offending some Americans. It is ironic that at the time period the move was incredibly controversial, but as of this writing rock stars such as Kid Rock wear garments patterned after the American flag and flag-patterned clothing is readily available at many major clothing outlets. In 2005 Air Force General Richard Myers, Chairman of the Joint Chiefs of Staff, was photo-graphed wearing an American flag shirt while leaving a wreath at the Vietnam War Memorial, demonstrating that times had changed in terms of what clothing was con-sidered patriotic and what was not.

AMERICA'S TOWN MEETING OF THE AIR. A radio show that began in 1935 and was intended to promote a sense of democracy by transporting the atmos-phere of a traditional town-hall political meeting to the airwaves, *America's Town Meeting of the Air* holds significance for identity politics because it occasionally dedicated segments to racial themes for a general, mixed-race audience. In a sense, it was instrumental in broaching and moving to the forefront of societal con-sciousness a topic that had usually been regarded as beyond the acceptable boun-daries of public discourse. *Town Meeting* broadcast racially themed segments with titles such as, "Let's Face the Race Question," "Should Government Guarantee Job Equality for All Races?" and "Are We Solving America's Race Problem?" During these airings, prominent black intellectuals were sometimes invited to join the show's panels. On occasion, they even articulated especially controversial (to a white audience) views or radical positions. The programs sparked lively reaction, with many listeners sending letters—some positive, many others highly critical—to *Town Meeting*'s staff. Despite black participation in the discussions, however, most programs addressing contentious issues usually featured more white pundits; black women were almost if not entirely absent. Moreover, the black voices that did achieve access and question the status quo frequently evoked white resistance and hostility.

The show continued for roughly two decades, finally going off the air in 1956 (it was simultaneously carried on television in 1948, 1949, and 1952 as well).

AMOS AND ANDY. Begun as a radio show in 1928, *Amos and Andy* was deeply controversial in terms of identity politics because of its stereotypical portrayals of African Americans. The two main characters were played by white actors, Freeman Gosden and Charles Correll. For years, however, it was the most popular program on the air. It was such a hit, in fact, that it was also translated (although, out of visual necessity, with the use of black actors) into a highly rated television show in the 1950s. Exceedingly degrading to African Americans, the program to a large degree signified the continuation of the U.S. blackface minstrelsy tradition. Yet, at least to a substantial sector of the population, the radio show had such cultural resonance that many businesses adjusted their hours and work schedules to accommodate listening.

When the show moved from radio to television in 1951, the lead roles were played by the African American actors Alvin Childress and Spencer Williams Jr. Yet the situation comedy was still produced by Gosden and Correll, who merely passed the stereotypes they had developed to Childress and Williams (some observers point out, however, that some characters were pictured in reputable positions, such as attorneys and business owners). Although it did not achieve the same impact as the radio version, the television show, the first to feature an all-black cast, was nevertheless a hit. It ran on national television for two years, and then appeared on local stations for about the next decade. Eventually, though, pressure from interest groups, especially the NAACP (National Association for the Advancement of Colored People), led to the show's demise in 1966.

Amos and Andy (NBC Radio), 1936. Shown from left: Freeman Gosden (as Amos) and Charles Correll (as Andy). (Photofest)

APPLE PIE (AS SYMBOL). For decades the apple pie has been one of the enduring symbols of American culture and politics, and the images of freshly baked pies in paintings by illustrator Norman Rockwell are evocative of the myth of small town America where common values are celebrated by family dinners ending with a delicious slice of pie. It has been suggested that the apple pie is a metaphor for American assimilation and is a distinctively American food. However, apple pies were popular in Europe and particularly in England before they became the epitome of American food. Today apple pies, although there are various varieties and recipes, are usually made the same way as they were in England at the end of the sixteenth century, and the first recorded apple seeds brought over were by the pilgrims in 1620. While today apple pies are regarded as desserts, in colonial times apple pies were primarily served as a part of a regular meal. Some credit the Pennsylvania Dutch for this innovation, although the history of how it gradually became a dessert food is unclear. Politically speaking, most modern candidates who run on a platform of American values are well advised to be shown eating an apple pie at some point during their campaign. Mark Twain, writing about the foods he missed while over in Europe in 1878 prominently listed pies, particularly apple, as uniquely American dishes that he had trouble finding while in Europe. It is unclear exactly how many politicians have used the apple pie as a political prop, but it is clear that its use as an American symbol dates back to the first president. Martha Washington's "Book of Cookery" listed a recipe for an apple pie that advised "If you would gave yr apples looke green, coddle them in fair water, then pill thenm & put them in ye water again, & cover them very close" (Olver, Lynne. "American Apple Pie." http://www.foodtimeline.org/foodpies.html#applepie [accessed September 6, 2007]). Ultimately, William Grimes, a *New York Times* food critic, may have put it best when, after considering whether the temperance movement caused the loss of hard cider as a popular drink, and how the hungry union and confederate soldiers scavenged for apples to make pies for extra nutrition, he concluded his examination of the pie by noting that "it may be as simple as this: apples grow in profusion all over the United States and the colonists, who brought the English pie making habit with them, simply put one and one together" (Grimes, William. "The Endlessly Unimproved American Pie." *New York Times*, October 20, 2004, F4).

ASHCROFT, JOHN. Former U.S. Senator from Missouri and U.S. Attorney General under **George W. Bush** during his first term from 2001 to 2005, John Ashcroft (1942–) is also known for yet another talent: his several albums of inspirational Christian music released on an unknown label. Ashcroft's albums included songs such as the famous "Let the Eagle Soar," which included the line, "Only God, no other kings."

A clip of Ashcroft singing the song was featured on a **CNN** program, was used by **Michael Moore** in his film *Fahrenheit 9/11* (2004), and was also parodied by *The Daily Show*. It can now be found on **YouTube** where presumably numerous younger listeners watch it for its kitsch value. Ashcroft had also sung with a Senate group called the "Singing Senators" including Trent Lott, James Jeffords, and Larry Craig for some time in the 1990s, although mp3s of their music are not readily available to the public.

B

BAND AID. Band Aid is a British charity music group from 1984 that inspired the Live Aid and "**We Are the World**" movements in the United States in 1985. The first single was organized as a Christmas single in England by singer Bob Geldof (of the Boomtown Rats) and Midge Ure (from Ultravox), with an all-star cast that included **Bono**, Paul Weller, Sting, George Michael, Boy George, and many others. The single was designed to raise money and awareness for the famine in Ethiopia as well as to raise U.S. awareness of starvation and deprivation across all of Africa. While the results are debatable, it did demonstrate a growing political awareness by rock stars, one that would increase into the 1990s.

BECK, GLENN. Glenn Beck is a popular political analyst, comedian, and radio DJ, best known for his early-evening *Glenn Beck* program televised Monday through Friday on the **Fox** cable television channel. Beck is also the host of a popular syndicated radio program, broadcast in 300 cities in America. Before working at Fox, Beck hosted a program on **CNN**'s Headline News station from 2006 to 2008. He was also a top 40 radio DJ for several years, starting in Florida in 1983. Beck's books include *The Real America: Messages from the Heart and the Heartland*; *An Inconvenient Book*; and *The Christmas Sweater*. While Beck is particularly beloved by many conservatives for his evangelical fervor and libertarian stance, some critics have accused him of grandstanding, with his trademark of being on the verge of tears as he reports on stories, making him the subject of much pop culture analysis. Beck, a practicing Mormon, is also a vocal proponent of gun ownership rights. In addition, he is the host of several lecture tours that are combinations of stand-up comedy as well as political analysis. Along with **Sean Hannity** and **Bill O'Reilly**, Beck has emerged as a popular voice for conservative values on the Fox cable channel. According to an article in the *New York Times*, "With a mix of moral lessons, outrage, and an apocalyptic view of the future, Mr. Beck . . . is capturing the feelings of an alienated class of Americans" (Stelter,

Brian, and Bill Carter. "Fox News' Mad, Apocalyptic, Tearful Rising Star," *The New York Times*, March 30, 2009, p. A1).

BEETLE BAILEY. *Beetle Bailey* is a long-running syndicated newspaper comic strip about a private in the army and his regular run-ins with his abusive sergeant, Sgt. Snorkel. *Beetle Bailey* was started in 1950 by cartoonist Mort Walker, who still works on the strip to this day aided by his son Greg Walker. The strip started with Bailey as a college student, but with the start of U.S. involvement in Korea, the character enlisted in the army where he has remained to this day through numerous wars and conflicts. The strip frequently highlights the everyday contradictions and inefficacy of the American military, but at various occasions is also extremely patriotic and supportive of American soldiers. The strip also caused controversy in 1970 with the introduction of Lieutenant Flap, a black character that led the military paper *Stars and Stripes* and several southern papers to drop the strip, although numerous others picked up the strip in response. Recurring characters include the inefficient General Halftrack and his vivacious and frequently sexually harassed secretary Miss Buxley, as well as Corporal Yo, an Asian character. In contrast to the prevailing mood about the military, Walker, a World War II veteran, has always attempted to keep the strip largely out of larger issues about war and more about bureaucracy and human foibles. (For discussion on political cartoons in general, see **Political Cartoons**.)

BERNAYS, EDWARD. Edward Bernays (1891–1995) is considered by numerous authors, such as Stewart Ewen and Mark Crispin Miller, as the father of modern public relations and American propaganda. Bernays, who was the nephew of the founder of psychology, Sigmund Freud, was a progressive who believed that propaganda was useful in maintaining a dynamic and ordered "mass society" where an "invisible government" influenced the average citizen for his/her own good. In an increasingly complex and industrialized society during the 1920s and 1930s, it was seen by many progressives (including Walter Lippmann, the author of *Public Opinion* [1922], one of the key media theorists of the early part of the twentieth century) that it had become difficult for average citizens to choose between a dizzying array of possible choices, and therefore they needed guidance from benign organizations and educated individuals who could help make the correct choice clearer. During World War I, Bernays (along with Lippmann and others) was part of the U.S. Committee on Public Information, which helped market World War I and "sell" it to the average American. The techniques developed by the committee were essential in both World War I and all subsequent wars.

Bernays was also responsible for campaigns for tobacco, including a memorable march of "flappers" walking down Fifth Avenue on Easter Sunday in 1929, in a publicity stunt for the American tobacco industry. Bernays also worked domestically for clients as diverse as General Electric, propagandizing against public ownership of utilities, as well as the United Fruit Company, with whom he worked with the U.S. government, and the CIA to create the climate for a CIA-led coup in 1953. Bernays lived his long life as an apologist for propaganda, but did in later years campaign against one of his earliest clients, the tobacco industry. Modern political propagandas (Joseph Goebbels was influenced by Bernays) and the public relations industry are part of the legacy that Bernays leaves behind. (For related discussion, see **World War Propaganda**.)

BILLY BEER. Billy Beer is a novelty beer endorsed by former President **Jimmy Carter**'s brother, Billy Carter (1937–1988), in 1977. In promoting/endorsing the beer, the colorful plainspoken brother of the president became a semi-celebrity and an ubiquitous presence on television shows such as *Match Game* and various talk shows. Today the beer is no longer manufactured and cans or six packs of it are available for sale on Web sites such as eBay for high prices, although many collectors have long since concluded that the only value of the beer is as a kitschy historical artifact. Billy Beer is part of a long tradition of memorabilia associated with presidents that are often manufactured quickly and with little thought of how if would affect the image of the sitting president. Billy Carter is also an example of how family can embarrass their presidential relatives, as in the case of **Roger Clinton**, the half brother of former president **Bill Clinton** who was arrested for possession of cocaine in 1984 and for drunk driving in 2001.

THE BIRTH OF A NATION. *The Birth of a Nation* is an incendiary, brilliant, and extraordinarily controversial 1915 film by pioneering American director D. W. Griffith. The film, although innovative and groundbreaking, is also universally regarded today as racist and patronizing, but must also be analyzed in the context of its time period and in the context of cinema history. Griffith was one of the first great directors and storytellers in American history, and he was responsible for numerous innovations in editing, camera placement, use of close-ups, and other early developments in the grammar of cinema. The film itself is a retelling of the days of the Civil War and Reconstruction in the South, primarily as it affects one southern family, the Camerons, and a family of northern abolitionists, the Stonemans, their communities, and (to a lesser extent) the slaves that live in the southern community as well. While the old South is glamorized as a place of dignity and grace, where slaves are allowed to live in relative harmony with their white owners, Austin Stoneman, the northern abolitionist, is shown as intolerant and power hungry. After the end of the war and the assassination of Lincoln, Stoneman, along with his evil mulatto aid, Silas Lynch, disastrously empowers southern blacks, almost all of whom are depicted as buffoons or brutes. Finally, Ben Cameron, the remaining Cameron son, is forced to form the Ku Klux Klan to save the day from power-hungry freed slaves and restore order and grace to the South, where the newly freed slaves are promptly disenfranchised again from voting.

While the movie is obviously and patronizingly racist, it was also a brilliant piece of filmmaking that used innovative techniques such as split screens, montage editing, iris shots, fade-ins, and fade-outs that marked it as technically miles ahead of any other film yet made at that time.

The film was an enormous success in its time period, and then President Woodrow Wilson was alleged to have said that watching the film was like watching "history writ with lightning," although many modern film scholars have disputed this. The film also was the source of numerous demonstrations at the time of its release, especially by the NAACP who condemned the film as racist. Griffith, who denied that he was racist, nonetheless did set out to make an openly political film. According to Christensen and Hass, Griffith "saw film as an educational tool, and he set out to use it as such—an intention that was itself political. *The Birth of a Nation* was the first important American political film, not only because it reshaped the image of the South, but also because of the way it influenced American thought toward politics—in addition to its encouragement of racism and the revival of the Ku Klux Klan" (Christensen, Terry, and Peter Hass. *Projecting Politics: Political Messages in American Films*. Armonk, NY: M. E. Sharpe Press, 2005, p. 68). Griffith set out to make an epic film that would make people consider political issues seriously, and unfortunately, he succeeded. Today, the film is a milestone in American filmmaking and an example of how controversial and divisive a political film could be back in its time period as well as today.

BLACK PANTHERS. Black Panthers is a radical African American political organization that was started in 1966 to promote rights for black Americans, which often used violence to achieve its ends. The Panthers, who also did community outreach, opening kitchens to feed the poor in order to both empower lower-class neighborhoods and also to recruit new members and foment revolutionary consciousness as well as provide weapons training, were primarily active during the "black power" era of the 1960s and are largely defunct as of this writing. During their prime, the fiery speeches and publicity stunts of Panther leaders, such as founders Huey P. Newton and Bobby Seale, soon courted controversy with their militant agenda. Although the group gained headlines for their protests and confrontations with the police, the Black Panthers also garnered many white supporters, including numerous celebrities, leading social critic Tom Wolfe to write a book, *Radical Chic and Mau-Mauing the Flak Catchers* about a fund-raiser that conductor Leonard Bernstein had held for the Black Panthers in 1970. Wolfe's coining of the term "radical chic" was originally in a shorter *New Yorker* article describing the party, but in the book version Wolfe developed the term and, according to a *Time* magazine article at the time, "thus described the tendency among bright blooded, moneyed or otherwise distinguished New Yorkers lately grown weary of plodding, via media middle-class institutions like the Heart Ball, the U.J.A. and the N.A.A.C.P. to take up extreme, exotic, earthy and more titillating causes" (Foote, Timothy. "Fish in the Brandy Snifter." 1970. Available at http://www.time.com/time/magazine/article/0,9171,904627,00.html [accessed August 1, 2007]).

BLOGS. A political blog is usually an online political journal of political thought and commentary that allows for exchanges between authors and readers. Each original posting is generally in the form of an "essay," which may be as formally written as a piece published in an authoritative newspaper or as loosely composed as a string informal musings. The writer of the original piece then allows for responsive comments by readers of the original posting. Previously, only the "mass media" (television, radio, books, and so on) were capable of reaching huge audiences. Blogging is helping to partly replace the "top down" model of media, where a small number of powerful corporations transmit messages to the citizenry, with a "bottom up" approach in which ordinary people are capable of having a substantial impact on the national conversation. In general, bloggers reject the standard "objective" mode of the mainstream media in favor of strong and openly partisan biases. Many mainstream political writers for newspapers, magazines, radio, and television have also begun to blog on Web sites for their employers or for themselves. For examples of political blogs, see *Daily Kos*, *The Drudge Report*, and *Huffington Post*.

BOB ROBERTS. *Bob Roberts* is a political satire from 1992, written and directed by Tim Robbins. The film involved a folk-singing political candidate who runs for a senate seat in Pennsylvania against the incumbent (played by writer Gore Vidal). The charismatic Roberts comes across initially as a charming self-made million-aire, but his pseudo-populist message later is shown to hide a darker agenda. Acceding to the *New York Times* review by Vincent Canby, Roberts is charis-matic because "he appropriates gestures and language associated with 1960's pro-test movements and uses them in the cause of his own brand of 1990's right-wing rabble-rousing. He calls himself a 'rebel conservative'" (Canby, Vincent. "Bob Roberts." 1992. Available at http://movies2.nytimes.com/movie/review?_r=1&res=9E0-CE7D91E31F937A3575AC0A964958260&oref=slogin&page-wanted=print). Robbins's "mockumentery" style captures both the minutiae of the long campaign (as the film *The Candidate* did previously) but also updates it to analyze how populist messages can easily be twisted with the right amount of audiovisual persuasion. While clearly partisan, the film also takes several well-warranted slaps at network anchors and vacuous political operatives.

BOND DRIVES. During World Wars I and II, bond drives were essential in order to raise money for the wars, and they also served a secondary role as a source of information and a call to patriotism during the wars. Numerous celebrities were enlisted to aid in bond drives during both wars, such as **Charlie Chaplin** and Douglas Fairbanks. Even fictional characters on radio, such as Batman and Superman, did their part in raising money in bond drives, as did numerous radio comedians and dra-matic actors. This demonstrated how popular culture could be used in wartime propaganda. (Also see **World War Propaganda**.)

BOND, JAMES. While James Bond was a British secret service agent in literature and film, he also was representative of certain attitudes both toward the Cold War and toward sexual liberation and personal freedom that appealed to many Americans in the 1960s. Bond was created by former British secret agent and writer Ian Fleming (1908–1964), also the writer of the children's favorite *Chitty Chitty Bang Bang* (1964), who decided to base a character loosely on some of his own experiences, albeit quite exaggerated, as a secret agent. The first Bond novel, *Casino Royale*, was released in 1952, becoming much more popular with the release of the first James Bond film, *Dr. No*. In 1962, Bond quickly became a hugely popular character and the lynchpin of a lucrative franchise. Between 1962 and the present, there have been 22 "official" Bond films released, one parody (the first *Casino Royale* in 1967), and one film made as an attempt to wrest control of the franchise, the Sean Connery vehicle *Never Say Never Again* (1983). The films' immense popularity as well as Bond's enduring stature as an iconic pop culture figure, with numerous licensed products and tie-ins, has led to Bond becoming the ultimate representation of the secret agent. Bond, the quintes-sential suave and dangerous secret agent, is not just a popular book and movie character but has also been used as a form of social commentary on American (and British) politics, as well as a useful metaphor for pundits to use as an exam-ple of some foreign espionage enterprise gone wrong. Like his eventual predeces-sor Jack Bauer of popular television show *24*, Bond does not play within the rules, he literally has a license to kill as an "00" agent and does not hesitate to

Sean Connery as James Bond, 007. (From the *Ultimate Super Heroes*, a Bravo television special, 2005. Bravo Television/Photofest)

resort to brute force or torture in order to find out specific information relevant to the plot of one world threatening conspiracy with another. Bond is an amoral ladies' man, not afraid to use a femme fatale as a shield if she betrays him, but also a quintessential gentleman, one who opens the door for the lady before he takes her to bed. Many commentators have criticized the Bond series for its apparent sexism and old-fashioned image of the world as a black/white or east/west political dichotomy, but the truth is actually far more complex. The Bond character does not impose a pro-Western ideology of the viewer, but instead, as Bond experts Bennet and Wollacott have noted, "moves the viewer to a new set of ideological coordinates" (Bennett, Tony, and Janet Wollacott. *Bond and Beyond: The Political Career of a Popular Hero*. New York: Methuen Books, 1987, p. 5). In other words, one does not have to agree with Bond in order to identify with the character or to find the movies entertaining.

Other critics argue that Bond was a sort of Cold War relic, fighting ideological battles long settled, but from early on the villains were rarely Russians, and the ones who were (as in *From Russia with Love* [1963]) saw renegade Russians acting against their country's orders. In many films (such as *The Spy Who Loved Me*) Bond actually found himself working with the Russians to stop a genocidal madman. In reality, despite the limitations of the action/adventure genre that he was inextricably tied into, Bond was actually an ecumenical pop culture figure, still sexist but a self-acknowledged dinosaur, one that fought with a wink and a witty line, ready to garrote a foe and seduce whatever comely absurdly named woman (Pussy Galore anyone?) who he met along the way. With the dawning of a new century, a problem was recognized by the producers, that in appealing to the public as a pop culture figure, Bond's success had become a problem, and that his campiness had subverted an important aspect of the character, his cold rationality. With the twenty-first official Bond film, the character was brought back to his origins, and now played by the icy Daniel Craig in the remake of *Casino Royale* (2006), and in its sequel *Quantum of Solace* (2008), Bond is once again a taciturn killer, one who apparently still fits the public imagination (and in a post-9/11/24 world, Bond may well need to be more calculating and less hedonistic to retain his place in the public's imagination) and will for some time to come.

BONO (PAUL HEWSON). The lead singer of popular and long-running Irish band U2, Bono (Paul Hewson; 1960–) is one of the best-known singers and celebrities in the world; his band has sold millions of copies of its albums since 1980. While the other members of U2 have been sporadically involved in political events such as **Live Aid**, Bono is well known for his longtime political activism for a variety of issues. While some of Bono's early issues, such as famine relief in Africa and oblique comments on the Northern Irish political system, were less focused, in the late 1990s and for the past several decades, Bono has spent extensive time working for African debt relief and aids activism. In the course of his work, Bono famously met with Treasury Secretary Paul O'Neill and lobbied him and, through him, the Bush administration for African debt relief. Bono remains to this day one of the most outspoken rock stars, one who actually uses his leverage with politicians and fans to agitate for real political change.

BOONDOCKS. *Boondocks* was an extremely political comic strip from 1996 to 2006 (and later a cartoon on Cartoon Network) by Aaron McGruder that satirized the political dimensions of race in America. (McGruder put the comic on indefinite hiatus in March 2006.) The comic strip, and later cartoon, featured the adventures of the Freeman clan: Huey, the politically conscious older brother; Riley, the wannabe gangster; and their cantankerous older grandfather who takes care of them and is constantly exasperated by Huey's proselytizing. The *Boondocks* television series was on Cartoon Network for several seasons, but is currently available only on their Web site. During its prime, the cartoon strip was one of the most ardently political strips in America, and several of the more confrontational episodes were pulled by various newspapers or placed on the editorial page. McGruder also collaborated on a graphic novel with artist Kyle Baker and writer Reginald Hudlin in 2004 called *Birth of a Nation: A Comic Novel*, which imagined the town of East St. Louis seceding from the Union to form a town called "Blackland" when black voters are disenfranchised. McGruder's incendiary strips featured during its heyday some of the most vicious attacks on presumed American hypocrisy and delusions about racial equality. While many would (and did) disagree with the central thesis of the *Boondocks*, it at least brought to light a subject not often discussed in comic strips. (For discussion on political cartoons in general, see **Political Cartoons**.)

BORIS AND NATASHA. Boris and Natasha are cartoon Soviet-style spies from the mythic Pottsylvania who appeared regularly as villains on the Rocky and Bullwinkle programs *Rocky and his Friends* (ABC 1959) and *The Bullwinkle*

Show (NBC from 1961 to 1964). (To make things even more confusing, Rocky and Bullwinkle originally appeared in *The Frostbite Falls Review* in the late 1950s, and after the cancellation of *The Bullwinkle Show* in 1964, the program was repackaged and syndicated as *The Adventures of Rocky and Bullwinkle*.) Boris Badenov and Natasha Fatale were constant foes of Rocky and Bullwinkle, who always had a secret plan that reflected in some way American concerns about the presence of Soviet agents during the Cold War. Their leader, known as Fearless Leader, was obviously a Soviet autocrat. In later movies Boris was played by Dave Thomas and later Jason Alexander, and Natasha was played by Sally Kellerman and then Renee Russo; in a bizarre bit of casting, Robert De Niro played Fearless Leader in the film version of *The Adventures of Rocky and Bullwinkle* (2000). Boris and Natasha are examples of the humorous way in which the realities of the Cold War trickled down into the lives of average Americans and the way in which entertainment served to put a human and comedic face on the unknown. (For discussion on political cartoons in general, see **Political Cartoons**.)

"BORN IN THE USA." The iconic and seemingly patriotic song by Bruce Springsteen, "Born in the USA" is from the album (1984) of the same title. Many who viewed the song as a patriotic anthem misinterpreted it, but in reality it was a gritty and uncompromising look at inequality and the plight of Vietnam veterans. "Born in the USA" was one of the more popular songs of Springsteen's career, and its iconic title made it adaptable for multiple interpretations. The song was briefly used by the Reagan reelection campaign in 1984, before complaints by Springsteen forced the campaign to stop using it. Like "Fortunate Son" (Creedance Clearwater Revival, 1969), another song often mistaken for a patriotic song, "Born in the USA" is an example of how the overall anathematic feel of a song can obscure the lyrics of it, leading to misinterpretation.

BRILL'S CONTENT. *Brill's Content* was a magazine that covered the intersection of media and politics, founded by millionaire mogul and founder of *Court TV*, Steve Brill, in 1998. The magazine regularly featured stories on media ownership, consolidation, and journalism in an age of increasing chumminess between politicians and journalists. Although the magazine was more or less geared toward insiders, it regularly lost money and after several tries at restructuring, eventually folded in October 2001. *Brill's Content* was an unusual magazine in that it covered the media's role in politics with a critical eye and was a frequent critic of the coziness between journalists and government, as well as media consolidation.

BRUCE, LENNY. Lenny Bruce (1926–1966) was a famous and tragic stand-up comedian (real name Leonard Schneider) who was hounded by authorities for his freewheeling, often obscene rants against the government and authority. Bruce started out playing nightclubs in Brooklyn and his comedic act, as much free-form jazz-like improvisation as actual comedy, soon enraptured audiences who had never seen anything quite like Bruce. Bruce was also the author of a biography co-written with Paul Krassner and first serialized in *Playboy* magazine

(Hugh Hefner was a longtime supporter of Bruce), *How to Talk Dirty and Influence People*, released in 1967 after Bruce's death.

Broke (facing jail time for public obscenity), almost unable to get a gig thanks to his notoriety and the nervousness of club owners fearing arrest, and in debt, Bruce died of a drug overdose in 1966. Bruce received a posthumous pardon from then New York Governor George Pataki in 2003, the first case of a posthumous pardon in New York history. Bruce's life was also dramatized in the play *Lenny* (1971), later made into a movie with Dustin Hoffman. The legacy of Bruce and similar comics, such as Mort Sahl, who relentlessly attacked the system was to expose the hypocrisy surrounding the ongoing debate about obscenity and free speech. While some of Bruce's later material verged on the paranoid (reading aloud from his court transcripts and explaining the techniques the police used to arrest him), Bruce's earlier material still holds up on some of the many recordings done during his life and several released posthumously. Lenny Bruce's name has now become synonymous with resistance to authority and standing up for free speech despite regulations. Lenny Bruce was also one of the celebrities mentioned in the REM song "It's the End of the World as We Know it, and I Feel Fine" in 1987. (Also see **Stand-Up Comedy and Politics**.)

BUCKLEY, WILLIAM F., JR. Author, editor, journalist, harpsichord player, and television host, William F. Buckley Jr. (1925–2008) also founded the influential conservative magazine *National Review* in 1955. Buckley had also been the leading voice of intellectual conservatism ever since the appearance of his first book, *God and Man at Yale*, in 1951. Since the 1950s and the founding of his influential magazine, Buckley had also served as the host of the long-running debate show

William F. Buckley Jr., the conservative pioneer and television *Firing Line* host, smiles during an interview at his home in New York on July 20, 2004. (Frank Franklin II) (AP Photo)

Firing Line (1966–1999), which despite several well-known skirmishes, featured rational debate, a stark contrast to the raucous debates and shout-downs of current television debate programs such as *The O'Reilly Factor* on **Fox News**. Buckley was also a frequent guest on numerous talk shows and even appeared as himself on an episode of the popular show *Rowan and Martin's Laugh-In*. Buckley won an Emmy, was awarded the Presidential Medal of Freedom, received the American book award for best mystery in 1980, and is well known for his series of novels featuring CIA agent Blackford Oakes. Buckley's diverse talents made him an ubiquitous figure in American politics (he ran unsuccessfully for mayor of New York in 1965, claiming that if he won, the first thing that he would do is demand a recount, and his brother James served as a senator from New York) as well as popular culture, where his urbane wit and political consistency and grace served to spread the conservative gospel on talk shows for over 50 years. Buckley was the father of Christopher Buckley, author of *Thank You for Smoking* and other popular books. Buckley's legacy is that in his long career he has been the face of the conservative movement to the general public, especially before the presidency of **Ronald Reagan**. Buckley represented a dying breed of public intellectuals who could argue their opinions forcefully but without malice on American television. Buckley had also been parodied for his mannerisms by comics such as Robin Williams and Joe Flaherty on *Second City Television* and even by a talkative Gremlin in the film *Gremlins 2* (1990). Buckley died at his home on February 27, 2008.

BUGS BUNNY. Comedic long-running cartoon rabbit with a fetish for carrots and dressing up in women's clothing, Bugs Bunny (usually voiced by Mel Blanc [1908–1989]) has become a lasting part of American popular culture. Bugs was also active during World War II, where he found himself fighting against the Nazis and Japanese in various cartoons. Mel Blanc was also part of the war effort, voicing the character of Pvt. Snafu in training films for the soldiers written by Theodore S. Geisel, aka Dr. Seuss. Bugs Bunny has not only been used for propaganda but is probably one of the best-known cartoon characters in the world and is a representative of American ingenuity and resourcefulness. Long after the years of the classic cartoons, Bugs and his friends live on in the popular imagination. (For discussion on political cartoons in general, see **Political Cartoons**.)

BURNS, KEN. Ken Burns (1953–) is a documentarian, best known for his work produced for **PBS**. Although his films are not generally highly political, some of them carry political import because of their focus on major conflicts in U.S. history. The 1990 series *The Civil War*, for example, is socially significant for its comprehensive historical presentation of a bloody, yet seminal event in the country's domestic development. The set of films received wide critical attention and drew a particularly large audience for PBS (indeed, PBS stations still air it from time to time, especially during pledge drives). In *The Civil War* and other documentaries, Burns has cultivated a recognizable style, one that has influenced a number of film artists ever since. In 2007, he turned his lens on another wide-scale confrontation—aired on PBS, *The War* offers a distinctive perspective on World War II through the personal accounts of several Americans involved in the hostilities.

BUSH, GEORGE H. (MEDIA PORTRAYALS). George H. Bush (1924–) was the forty-first president of the United States and served for one term beginning in 1988 before being defeated by President Bill Clinton in 1991. While Bush was in office, his patrician mannerisms and "wimp factor" caused him to be the source of some comedic imitation, most notably by *Saturday Night Live* cast member Dana Carvey who parodied the president's catchphrases such as "A thousand points of light" and "Not gonna do it" as well as the president's pronunciation of the name "Saddam Hussein" to great comedic effect. Carvey's good-natured ribbing of the first Bush president stands in contrast to the venom heaped upon the second President Bush by many pundits. Carvey continued the Bush impression after the president's retirement. Bush also appeared as a character on *The Simpsons*, when he caused a furor when he moved in across from the Simpsons, leading to a fight with Homer that ends only when Bush moves out, only to be replaced by former President Gerald Ford.

BUSH, GEORGE W. (MEDIA PORTRAYALS). The forty-third president of the United States and one of the most controversial mainly due to his handling of the Iraq War and other foreign policy ventures, President George W. Bush (1946–), son of President **George H. Bush** (from 1988 to 1992), found himself the source of continuous satire, starting with *Saturday Night Live*'s portrayal of him as a bumbling frat boy during his debates with **Al Gore** during the 2000 election, continuing through such television shows as *The Daily Show*, *The Colbert Report*, *The Tonight Show with Jay Leno*, *Late Night with David Letterman*, *The Conan O'Brien Show*, and many others.

Bush was also the subject of a short-lived television show on Comedy Central, *That's My Bush*, created by *South Park* moguls Trey Parker and Matt Stone. The program essentially mocked Bush in the same way that *Saturday Night Live* had, as a bumbler a la Gerald Ford. The show was cancelled because of low ratings, although Parker and Stone, noted conservatives, felt it might also have been based on subtle government pressure.

In 2007, Comedy Central launched a new program entitled *Lil' Bush* featuring Bush and members of the Bush administration as Little Rascals–type versions of themselves. Bush was also the subject of several parodies on Cartoon Network's *Robot Chicken*, where among other things, Bush discovered that he was really a Jedi and used his powers to compel Laura Bush into a threesome with Condoleezza Rice, as well as tried to convince an aid that the war in Iraq was going well with the use of Jedi mind tricks.

C

THE CANDIDATE. Directed by Michael Ritchie, the political satire *The Candidate* starred Robert Redford as Bill McKay, an idealistic liberal candidate for the U.S. Senate from California who has a rude awakening when he is forced to compromise his principles in order to have a chance in a tough campaign. His political manager, Lucas (Peter Boyle), pressures him into compromising his principles on numerous issues, until by the time the campaign is over, McKay is unsure of where he stands or what principles he has left. The film was directed by Michael Ritchie and written by Jeremy Larner who won an Oscar for best screenplay. One of the late 1960s and early 1970s wave of politically cynical films that questioned the effectiveness of the American political system, *The Candidate* was also one of the more realistic films about the finances and institutional workings of a political campaign. According to Mick La Salle of the *San Francisco Chronicle*, "over time 'The Candidate' has come to be regarded as a remarkably prescient and authentic portrayal of the vagaries of modern politics, showing the inside deals that lead to votes and the wearing away of idealism by the quest for power" (La Salle, Mick. "Sundance Kid Looks Back: 'Bagger' Director Redford Reflects on 40-year Career." *San Francisco Chronicle*, October 29, 2000, p. 51). According to a *New York Times* article, the film was also an inspiration to former Vice President Dan Quayle, which inspired him to go into politics. Life later imitated reality, when candidate **Jimmy Carter**, also inspired by Redford's role in *The Candidate*, used Redford as a debating coach while running for president.

CAPRA, FRANK. Frank Capra (1897–1991) was an Italian-born naturalized American director best known for populist films featuring ordinary people fighting corruption and impersonal authority figures. In films such as **Mr. Smith Goes to Washington**, *Mr. Deeds Goes to Town*, **Meet John Doe**, and even *It's a Wonderful Life*, Capra portrayed the resilience of small-town America against assorted corrupt politicians, bureaucrats, and land barons. Although some of Capra's films could be seen as a critique of American politics, they can also be seen as representative of how the best aspects of small-town political structures, local organizations, savings and loans, the Boy Scouts, were actually symbolically more powerful then even the U.S. Senate. During World War II Capra was responsible for the famous *Why We Fight* series of films that attempted to justify for U.S. soldiers the reasons we were involved in World War II. Capra, along with Walt Disney and others, brought Hollywood techniques to the propaganda documentaries and made them as entertaining as they were informative, with dissolves, quick cuts, mistranslations, and other cinematic techniques that equated the Nazis to American gangsters. After the end of the war, Capra returned to making Hollywood films (including one of his enduring classics, *It's a Wonderful Life*), but his output suffered and he finally retired from filmmaking in the early 1960s. Although Capra's Hollywood films were never political in a partisan sense, they did demonstrate both a critique of large-scale capitalism and, at the same time, a reverence for the vanishing American dream. Capra was nominated for an Oscar 11 times for best picture and best director and won three times for best director.

Capra was also an inspiration to numerous politicians who imagined themselves as outsiders, from **Bill Clinton** to **Jimmy Carter** and perhaps even **John F. Kennedy**. But to film scholar Allen Roston, the candidate who styled himself the most after a Capra hero such as Mr. Smith was former President Carter. To Roston, the small-town, deeply religious, and self-reflective Carter was a natural successor to the mantle of the Capra hero, usually a single individual from a small town trying to uphold its virtues in a cynical and complex world. According to Roston:

> Most important, Carter presented himself as an outsider untouched by Washington's political machinations and sordid past. His campaign implicitly sounded the populist themes of Capra's cinema—metropolitan corruption, suspicion of sophistication, the virtue of the rural, distrust of politics, and fear of government. He was, like Mr. Smith, a modern imitation of Christ driving the moneychangers out of the temple of government. As Carter's campaign speech-writer Patrick Anderson put it, Carter viewed himself as something "out of Horatio Alger, with a touch of Frank Capra thrown in, a Sunday-school hero writ large"—a "spunky little fellow" who gets the best of "the big bullies, uppity women, and city slickers of the world" because he is "canny and honest and pure." (Roston, Allen. "Carter and Capra." *Journal of Popular Film & Television* 25, no. 2 [Summer 1997]: 59.)

Although Carter's success was limited and his eventual naiveté proved his undoing, it proves the resonance of Capra's vision of political America that the character that Carter presented himself as was based upon the vision to the most prominent visionary of American small-town values presented on film in history.

CARTER, JIMMY (MEDIA PORTRAYALS). Former President Jimmy Carter (1924–) was not parodied as much on television as some of his successors would be, but he was the source of some comedic satires portrayed by Dan Aykroyd on *Saturday Night Live* during the late 1970s. Carter, because of his former career as a peanut farmer, was sometimes also portrayed as an anthropomorphic Mr. Peanut, while some of the attacks focused on Carter's quirks, such as Aykroyd's portrayal of Carter as oversexed due to his interview with *Playboy* magazine where he admitted to "lusting after other women in his heart."

Other portrayals, such as *Doonesbury*'s images of the Carter administration as benign new agers, also gently satirized the president, but not as savagely as Nixon before him or Bush afterwards.

CARVILLE, JAMES. James Carville (1944–) is one of the preeminent political advisors, campaign managers, and writers of the latter half of the twentieth century. He first came to prominence as a campaign manager in the mid-1980s running campaigns for Governor Robert Casey in Pennsylvania and Senator Frank Lautenberg in New Jersey. His most important accomplishment was, along with George Stephanopoulos, running the 1992 **Bill Clinton** presidential campaign. This media savvy strategy was captured in the 1993 documentary *The War Room*. Since the Clinton years, Carville has found success as a consultant, pundit, and campaign manager for other candidates. In a strange twist, Carville married former Bush aide Mary Matalin in 1993. He currently hosts a weekly satellite radio sports show and is on the faculty of Tulane University.

CAVETT, DICK. Dick Cavett (1936–) is an erudite talk show host and prolific writer who interviewed some of the most important American public figures of the late twentieth century. Cavett, who started as a writer, performer, and stand-up comedian, found his true calling as a low-rated but always erudite and witty talk show host, first on *The Dick Cavett Show* (ABC 1969–1974, ABC 1975, **PBS** 1977–1982, later CNBC 1989–1996). Cavett's career proved that intensive political discussions could be held without devolving into a series of shouting matches, and along with **William F. Buckley**'s *Firing Line*, Cavett proved that, if presented correctly, audiences could be attracted to serious issues. During his run on television, Cavett tackled politics, sports, science, literature, and art in a way that is almost unimaginable in terms of today's later night television talk shows. Today only the satirical news program *The Daily Show with Jon Stewart* (see **News Parodies**) even comes close to addressing the wide breadth of issues that Cavett did.

CBS REPORTS. In 1958, largely because of the controversies it inspired, *See It Now*, hosted by news giant **Edward R. Murrow**, was replaced by the semiregular series *CBS Reports*. Murrow had been active in challenging taken-for-granted views and the assertions of **Senator Joseph McCarthy** on *See It Now* and, thus, CBS eventually found it hard to maintain advertising on the public affairs show. Murrow was still allowed to participate in the new program, albeit to a lesser extent. Still, in 1960, he anchored its critically acclaimed segment entitled, *Harvest of Shame*. Soon afterward, Murrow entered the realm of government as the director of the U.S. Information Agency. *CBS Reports* continued, however, and from time to time still addressed series social issues. "Hunger in America" (1968) and "The Selling of the Pentagon" (1971) stand out in this regard. The latter show highlighted the military's substantial public relations apparatus, disclosing that the Pentagon spent millions each year producing and distributing propaganda films, sometimes hosted by celebrities such as Jack Webb or John Wayne. The broadcast triggered stern rebukes of CBS President Frank Stanton and a congressional investigation into its fairness. Shortly afterward, Stanton reduced *CBS Reports*, like *See It Now* before it, from a regular series to a sporadic "special."

CHAPLIN, CHARLIE. One of the all-time great actors of the silent era and beyond, Charlie Chaplin's (1889–1977) career started in England and he quickly became extremely popular in America in large part because of his engagingly physical appeal. He wrote, directed, produced, and composed most of the music for his own films during his lengthy career. His political involvement dates back to World War I when he appeared in a series of short films designed to make Americans buy War Bonds. (One memorable short has him knocking out the German Kaiser with a large hammer labeled "War Bonds" [for related discussion, see **Bond Drives**].) He also made one of the first films to directly parody and attack Adolf Hitler in *The Great Dictator* in 1940 where he played Adenoid Hynkel (the Dictator of Tomania) as well as a Jewish barber who is mistaken for Hynkel and impersonates him later in the film. At that time many opposed Chaplin's political message as it was seen as premature when most Americans were still pro-isolationist. Despite the later widespread support for the war amongst Americans, many people, unaware of the seriousness of the Nazi threat, did not want to get engaged in what many saw was just another "European conflict." Later, this film gained greater critical appreciation as America entered the war. After World War II Chaplin caused more controversy with his outspoken left-wing and socialist views and helped to financially support the Russian struggle against the Nazis during World War II. During the late 1940s, the HUAC committee subpoenaed him to appear. When Chaplin responded by telegraph that he was not a member of the Communist party, HUAC declined to take his testimony. Five years later, when Charlie Chaplin went to London for the premier of *Limelight* (1952), the government denied him an entrance visa (Chaplin never formally became a U.S. citizen). After leaving America he went to live in Switzerland in 1952 (he also kept a home in Ireland) full time. He returned to the United States in 1972 to receive an honorary Oscar for his contributions to film, not long before his death in 1977. Chaplin was one of the first outspoken movie stars who used his position to campaign for causes he believed in and demonstrated that movie stars could command political clout, paving the way for later politically active movie stars such as Tim Robbins and Susan Sarandon on the left and Ronald Reagan, **Arnold Schwarzenegger**, and Bruce Willis on the right.

CHAPPELLE, DAVE. Dave Chappelle (1973–) is a stand-up comedian originally best known for his routines about smoking pot, who became a star on the edgy and unpredictable *Chappelle's Show*, which included sketches about a blind (and black) white supremacist, scenarios about what would have happened if President Bush had been black, as well as less political but equally hilarious send-ups of Rick James and Prince. Although the primary focus of the show was on pop culture and racial relations, Chappelle also frequently satirized the average American's ideas about power, as in the black Bush sketch, and indirectly challenged America's comfort ratio in talking about race. Chappelle famously walked away from the show during production for a third season and has kept a low profile since then, appearing occasionally to do stand-up unannounced at various clubs. Chappelle, a practicing Muslim, was an expert at skewing the American idea that racial divisions are a thing of the past, and his astute sense of humor also probably contributed to his decision to leave the constraints of the television sketch comedy format. (Also see **African American Stand-Up Comedians** and **Stand-Up Comedy and Politics**.)

Dave Chappelle poses for photographs before the start of Directors Guild of America Honors ceremonies 2004. (AP Photo/Julie Jacobson)

"CHECKERS SPEECH." One of the most legendary televised political speeches ever presented was **Richard Nixon**'s "Checkers" address, delivered in 1952. The talk represents an early use of television to reduce the political fallout from a scandal. The impetus for the speech was the allegation that Nixon, the Republican candidate for vice president, had been siphoning money from a secret fund put together for him by California campaign supporters.

After a poll by Republican Thomas Dewey found that Nixon was increasingly becoming a liability to the ticket, the party decided to act before he dragged the ticket down. On September 23, 1952, the Republican National Committee bought 30 minutes of time on 64 television stations, as well as several hundred radio stations, to broadcast a rebuttal to the charges against Nixon. Following a brief close-up of his calling card, the camera pulled back to reveal Nixon sitting at an official-looking desk with his wife Patricia Nixon sitting silently off to one side watching her husband. Throughout the speech, Nixon absolved himself from any misconduct. Subsequent to telling the American public that the $18,000 and "other money" (Nixon never mentioned on the broadcast what the "other money" actually was) in question had been spent on legitimate political purposes, Nixon then shifted focus away from the economic issues in a brilliant bit of rhetorical flourish (possibly inspired by a dog story that then President Franklin Roosevelt had previously used to great effect). Nixon explained:

A group of images shows vice-presidential candidate Richard Nixon explaining his $18,000 expense fund on television in 1952, during an appearance nicknamed the "Checkers" speech, in reference to his family's dog, which, he said, was the only contribution he received for his personal use. (AP Photo)

One other thing I should probably tell you, because if I don't they'll probably be saying this about me too, we did get something—a gift—after the election. A man down in Texas heard Pat on the radio mention the fact that our two daughters would like to have a dog. And, believe it or not, the day before we left on the campaign trip we got a message from Union Station in Baltimore saying they had a package for us. We went down to get it. You know what it was? It was a little cocker spaniel dog in a crate that he sent all the way from Texas. Black and white spotted. And our little girl—Tricia, the six-year-old—named it Checkers. And you know the kids love that dog and I just want to say this right now, that regardless of what they say about it, we're going to keep it!

(Barnouw, Erik. *Tube of Plenty: The Evolution of American Television.* 2nd rev. ed. New York: Oxford University Press, 1990, p. 138.)

Nixon's reference to the dog was designed to drum up sympathy and to show that if he had accepted any "bribes," it was only in the form of an adorable animal. After presenting Checkers as a distraction, Nixon then asked viewers to write the Republican National Committee to let it know if he should stay on the ticket, pledging that even if he were dropped, he would still vigorously campaign for the Republican Party. Presidential candidate Dwight D. Eisenhower, who was watching the speech in Cleveland, remarked to Republican chairman Arthur Summerfield, "I think you got your $75,000 worth" (Barnouw, Erik. *Tube of Plenty: The Evolution of American Television.* 2nd rev. ed. New York: Oxford University Press, 1990, p. 139). Viewed live by almost half of the television-owning families in the country, Nixon's performance is widely credited with saving his candidacy and preventing him from withdrawing from the race. Through his masterful diversion from a controversial matter and his skillful use of television, he helped deflect a potential crisis. Although Nixon would continuously demonstrate awkwardness with television over the next several decades (see **Richard Nixon [Media Portrayals]**), the Checkers speech is a key example of how early television was exploited by politicians to shift attention from serious issues and to directly and powerfully appeal to the emotions of the potential voter. Despite not employing a video image of the dog or bringing him on stage, Nixon painted a mental picture that was sufficient to mollify many voters. Later, he happily posed with the dog in many photos. Unfortunately for Nixon, Checkers died in 1964, long before **Watergate**.

CHRISTIAN COALITION. The Christian Coalition is a Christian political activist group founded by Pat Robertson, the famous and often controversial televangelist, perhaps one of the best-known television ministers of the past 40 years (because of his 1988 presidential bid). The group was reorganized by Ralph Reed, one of the new groups of younger evangelists in the 1980s, although Reed did not officially run the organization after the initial first years.

The Christian Coalition is dedicated to lobbying for political and social change based on Christian values, and at its peak in the 1980s and early 1990s many pundits credited the Christian coalition for helping to elect conservative candidates on the local and national levels. As the mission statement on its Web site states, the

Christian Coalition of America is a political organization, made up of pro-family Americans who care deeply about becoming active citizens for the purpose of guaranteeing that government acts in ways that strengthen, rather than threaten, families. As such, we work together with Christians of all denominations, as well as with other Americans who agree with our mission and with our ideals. (Christian Coalition. "About Us." Available at http://www.cc.org/.)

The Christian Coalition was most active during the early 1990s, and although they still maintain a robust presence in some elections, they have mostly lost their influence (with the departure of Reed, who went on to unsuccessfully run for lieutenant governor of Georgia in 2006). Reed has also been linked by some reports to the Jack Abramoff lobbying scandal (a scandal that involved the undue influence of lobbyists in the **George W. Bush** administration and probably helped Reed to lose the election). Like the Moral Majority before it, the Christian Coalition demonstrates the growing power of evangelical voters (along with mainstream Protestant and Catholic allies) and their social and political concerns. The Christian Coalition, with its glossy ads and ubiquitous presence in politics, for many years was an example of grassroots Christian political organizing that targeted younger hipper evangelicals as well as the traditional base.

CHRISTIAN ENVIRONMENTALIST MOVEMENT. While during much of the twentieth century many fundamentalist Christians (and many others of various faiths or no faith) were not concerned with the environment, from the late 1970s to the present there has been a new movement, called the Christian Environmentalist Movement, of Christians who have devoted themselves to environmental causes. During the 1980s many fundamentalists, such as James Watt, Secretary of the Interior during the early Reagan administration, were not concerned with the environment, looking at earth as a place God had given in abundance to be used as man saw fit. Recently though, Christian groups began to look at the environment as a sacred trust left by God for Christians to tend. New groups and Web sites such as the "What would Jesus drive?" Web site, www.whatwouldjesusdrive.org/, launched originally in 2002, have made the movement increasingly public, and groups such as the Evangelical Environmental Network have been involved in lobbying attempts to spread the twin messages of Christian redemption and environmental awareness. While the popular image of evangelical Christians in politics (especially as represented on television and in movies) has been of intolerant holy rollers, the Christian environmental movement demonstrates that some evangelicals are becoming more concerned with practical issues as opposed to just being interested in matters of faith. This is another example not only of evangelical political engagement but also of how evangelical culture is becoming increasingly aware that new technologies and social networking sites online are providing new inroads for faith-based initiatives in popular culture, as well as demonstrating the diversity of opinion in the evangelical community.

CITIZEN CHANGE. Launched by the famous rap performer Sean "P. Diddy" Combs, "Citizen Change" was an organization and movement aimed at youth voters during the 2004 presidential campaign and at least indirectly designed to help swing the vote in Senator John Kerry's direction. Yet its mission was more objectively stated. According to its Web site, Citizen Change was meant "to make voting hot, sexy and relevant to a generation that hasn't reached full participation in the political process" (www.behaviordesign.com/work/case_studies/images/ctz/canned_site/home.html [accessed December 16, 2006]). During the 2004 election season, the organization implemented an assortment of publicity activities, including events held at various venues such as college campuses. Citizen Change's slogan, "**Vote or Die,**" was featured on a fashion line of T-shirts marketed to young people. It is questionable as to how effective the organization was in the long run, or whether the now dormant Citizen Change organization will be revived in the future. (Also see **Rock the Vote**.)

CLINTON, BILL (MEDIA PORTRAYALS). Bill Clinton (1946–) was the forty-second president of the United States and one of the most frequently caricatured presidents because of his penchant for food and women, as well as his affable personality and considerable charm. Clinton, who had what his aides called frequent "bimbo eruptions" (where yet another woman accused the president either of improper advances or of having an affair with her in the past) was first caricatured as a glutton, as on early *Saturday Night Live* episodes, or later as a skirt chaser (a notorious sketch had Clinton as played by Darrell Hammond settling down after his presidential terms were over with his new wife, Monica Lewinsky, who played herself in the sketch), or, in one instance, as holding a "low key" victory party to celebrate his victory in the impeachment hearings against him, drinking beer instead of champagne in a sign of remorse and national reconciliation (for related discussion, see **Political Scandals**).

During the campaign of 1992, Clinton also proved a master of allowing himself to become a part of pop culture. While campaigning for president, Clinton made numerous successful attempts to connect with youth voters during the 1992 presidential election, including appearing on numerous television programs including *The Arsenio Hall Show* and MTV where he talked to average Americans and

Bill Clinton and Everett Harp play their saxophones during the Arkansas Ball at the Washington Convention Center in D.C., Wednesday night, January 20, 1993, the day that Clinton was inaugurated as president of the United States. (AP Photo/Greg Gibson)

played his saxophone. Clinton, a fair saxophone player, used his musical skills to connect with a younger audience more used to entertainment than serious political discussions and made the older, more staid, Republican candidate, President **George W. Bush**, seem old-fashioned in contrast. Clinton was the first of the "baby boomer" generation to hold public office, as a result of that he was more suited for a media environment that gave pop culture more time and reportage than rational notions of discourse.

Clinton was also the subject of a thinly disguised portrayal of him as a domineering, junk food addict and womanizing southern governor with an overbearing control-freak wife in the book and movie versions of *Primary Colors*. The book by *Newsweek*'s Joe Klein was a runaway best seller and the source of much speculation as to the author. The 1998 movie version of *Primary Colors* starring John Travolta as Jack Stanton, the Clinton stand-in, was a slightly more sympathetic version of a flawed but idealistic man who did more good than harm despite his womanizing. A more positive fantasy approach to the Clinton presidency was the television series *The West Wing*, which starred Martin Sheen as the optimistic and dynamic president Josiah Bartlett who, despite much soul searching, always managed to do the right thing.

Not all Clinton parodies have been that sympathetic though, and recently Bill Clinton was parodied on the show *Family Guy* where a drunken pot-smoking and partying Clinton becomes best friends with the lead character, Peter Griffin, and eventually sleeps with both Peter's wife, Lois, and later Peter himself, much to Peter's surprise. Clinton was especially in the news in the 2008 primary season, where he campaigned for his wife, while trying not to upstage her scripted performances with his own personal charisma. While Clinton was much hated by many on the right, his ease with television and other forms of media made him one of the most telegenic presidents in history, perhaps second only to Ronald Reagan.

CLINTON, HILLARY. Hillary Clinton (1947–) is an American politician, former first lady, two-term senator from New York, was a candidate for the Democratic presidential nod in 2008, and is currently Secretary of State. She has long polarized opponents on the right who objected to her influence within the **Bill Clinton** White House, and who have long used her as a bogeyman in terms of fund-raising, as her name mentioned on a letter often galvanizes the Republican Party base. Clinton has always been a pop culture figure and has been parodied on numerous television shows such as *Family Guy* and *The Simpsons*, as well as on *Saturday Night Live*.

During the buildup to the 2008 presidential primaries, Democratic candidate Hillary Clinton and her political team engineered a Web-based parody of the finale of the long-running HBO series *The Sopranos*. In the final episode of *The Sopranos*, the anti-hero Tony Soprano and his family sit in a diner and eat onion rings as "Don't Stop Believing," a song by lite rockers Journey, plays in the background. After various suspicious possible hit men pass by the table, the screen goes dark and soundless, leading to countless fan protests and speculation. In the Hillary Clinton parody of *The Sopranos* finale, Hillary sits in a diner in Mount Kisco, New York, playing the Tony Soprano role and looking for songs on the jukebox. After putting on the same Journey song, her husband, Bill Clinton, arrives and is disheartened that Senator Clinton has ordered a bowl of carrots for the table, as opposed to the onion rings (that Bill Clinton had clearly wanted) that were featured in the Sopranos finale. As the two Clintons speculate as to what Internet voters had picked as her new campaign song (the choices appear on the jukebox, but the eventual winner as found on the Clinton campaign Web site later was the song "You and I" as sung by Canadian singer Celine Dion), Bill Clinton asks how the campaign is going. She responds, "Well, like you always say, 'Focus on the good times.'" He then asks her what the winning song is, adding, "My money's on Smash Mouth. Everybody in America wants to know how it's going to end." Then, mirroring the Sopranos again, where menacing people walked by the Sopranos' table, a grim-faced man walks by scowling at Hillary Clinton, played in a cameo by actor Vincent Curatola (Johnny Sack on *The Sopranos*). When the menacing man is gone, Hillary asks "Ready?" as she puts a coin in the jukebox and the screen goes blank as in the Sopranos. Then a screen advises viewers to go to the Hillary Clinton Web site for more information on what song was chosen as the campaign song. The untitled video created by Mandy Gunwald, Jimmy Siegel, and Danny Levinson became extremely popular and was accessed on the Web site **YouTube** and her Web site hundreds of thousands of times within a week of its release.

The video not only demonstrated an attempt by her staff to humanize the often cold and calculating public image of Senator Clinton, it also demonstrated how savvy she and her staff had become about using technology. It countered a previous use of the Internet by an (unauthorized) member of the **Barack Obama** campaign team, who had mashed a Clinton stump speech to the **Macintosh famous "1984" commercial** (released on March 5, 2007). This clip also demonstrated the increasing use of viral videos to spread information and campaign information quickly, without having to spend large amounts on network or cable advertising. With audiences increasingly segmented and more and more political dollars going toward specific issue advertisements, it seems likely that Senator Clinton's strategy will be repeated by other campaigns during the 2010 election, as well as afterwards. During the campaign there was also talk that the media was focusing too much on her negatives to the benefit of her primary opponent, Barack Obama. This was parodied on *Saturday Night Live* on two occasions (February 23 and March 1, 2008) where the press was portrayed as fawning over Obama to Clinton's detriment. Clinton also guest starred on March 1, 2008, when she appeared alongside Amy Poehler (appearing as Hillary Clinton) to mock both the supposed softball treatment given to Barack Obama during the debates, as well as her notorious laugh. Clinton later graciously accepted the post of Secretary of State, without an accompanying YouTube video.

CLINTON, ROGER. Half-brother of former president **Bill Clinton**, Roger Clinton (1956–) was often an embarrassment to the presidency (a particularly embarrassing revelation had been that Roger Clinton had served time in prison for dealing cocaine during the 1980s) and was involved in several public scandals while Clinton was president (from 1992 to 2000) and immediately afterwards. The most prominent scandals involving Roger Clinton were the embarrassing revelations that several people had paid Clinton tens of thousands of dollars to be considered for parole, including Rosario Gambino, a reputed soldier in the Gambino crime family, as well as former executive J. T. Lundy, who had offered Roger Clinton an interest in a

Venezuelan coal mine. Roger Clinton was also pardoned by his brother as one of his last acts as president in 2001. Presidential relatives have often been in the public eye, and stand-up comedians and satirical shows such as *Saturday Night Live* often use them as fodder for their routines and demonstrate that the foibles of presidential relatives are often a way for the general public to gain insight into the character, and often humanity, of politicians.

CNN. CNN was the first cable all news channel and one of the most influential sources of information for the American public for over the past three decades. Originally founded by Maverick businessman Ted Turner in 1980, the network soon grew from its small Atlanta home base to now reach over 90 million households.

For most Americans, the first Gulf War (1990–1991) was the first war in which television brought live eyewitness accounts of the war directly into their living rooms. In particular, cable all-news channel CNN was watched frequently by many for its in-depth coverage of the war. Unlike previous wars, where newsreel footage and radio were the only options for information, and unlike the Vietnam war, where footage shot on film had to be developed before it could be shown, causing delays before the public could see the footage, during the first Gulf War, audiences were seeing live satellite transmitted footage, commented on by anchors and correspondents who were often as confused as to what was going on as the audience. Some of the more ardent correspondents strived to get closer to the war zone, and hence to a better opportunity to get a good story, and one reporter, Arthur Kent, was nicknamed the "scud stud" for his good looks and propensity to be near the places where missiles hit. This change to an expectation of "real time" war coverage has changed for Americans, making it more immediate and also more compelling. (Also see **Televised Wars**.)

THE COLBERT REPORT. *The Colbert Report*, which started on Comedy Central in 2005, is a spin-off of *The Daily Show with Jon Stewart*, but the two shows frequently "cross over" and the two hosts talk to each other at the end of *The Daily Show*. While *The Daily Show* started as a parody of the traditional news program and worked itself into a hybrid of a news program and a satirical examination of the political conventions, *The Colbert Report* started out as a parody of the popular *The O'Reilly Factor* of **Fox News**, featuring conservative commentator **Bill O'Reilly**. Eventually O'Reilly and Stephen Colbert came face to face in a series of comedic summit meetings on both programs.

The encounter was somewhat strained and awkward, and sometimes hilarious. While Bill O'Reilly seemed sometimes flattered and sometimes bemused by Colbert's straight-faced parody of O'Reilly's politics and Colbert's respectful, sometimes humbled attitude, Colbert remained resolutely in character, looking up graciously at the man he called "papa bear" and had cited numerous times with a poker face as the inspiration for both *The Colbert Report* and his persona. O'Reilly, who at times did not seem to be sure whether an elaborate gag was being played on him or whether he was in on the joke, could only really query with his usual antagonism whether Colbert's name was pronounced "Col-bear" or "Coalbeart." O'Reilly, who has previously called the viewers of *The Daily Show* "Stoned Slackers," tried to find out from Colbert what *The Daily Show* experience had been like for him:

O'Reilly: It's all me. It's all me. Now who watches you? What's your audience? Do you do research? Do you know who . . .

Colbert: Well, Bill, that's one of the reasons I want to do my show. OK? I emulate you.

O'Reilly: Yes.

Colbert: I want to bring the message of love and peace to a younger audience. People in their 60s, people in their 50s, people who don't watch your show.

O'Reilly: OK, so people in the 50s and 60s, too young for "The Factor" are watching your show.

Colbert: . . . Bill. What are you on? What gives you the strength? Jesus Christ or Pat Robertson's protein shakes?

O'Reilly: I'm motivated by the fact that you need material, that the more I'm on, the more successful you will be . . .

O'Reilly: But every left-wing critic loves you. Why? Is it because you're French? Is that why?

Colbert: That must be it, Bill. I'm using that to pull the wool over their eyes. So they—see, that's the sugar that puts my medicine into the system.

O'Reilly: You must be doing something. You must be doing something.

Colbert: I'm doing you, Bill.

In 2007 Colbert announced his candidacy for the president and tried to get on the Democratic primary ballot in South Carolina. However, the Democratic party of South Carolina denied Colbert a spot (despite his willingness to pay the filing fee), so Colbert's presidential ambitions are on hold for the moment.

COMIC BOOKS. Comic books have long been indicators of popular culture. Since their inception, comic books have reacted to events in American history and have often been keen observers and social commentators. In the 1940s, comic books "went to war" during World War II with characters such as the iconic Captain America and his sidekick Bucky, the Human Torch and the Sub-Mariner, as well as Superman, banding together to fight against the axis powers. Captain America, in his first issue *Captain America #1* was already seen punching a particularly evil-looking Adolf Hitler in March 1941, anticipating the American involvement in the war, likely thanks to the justified anxiety held by Jewish comic creators such as Joe Simon and Jack Kirby, the creators of Captain America, about the growing Nazi menace. As Bradford Wright mentions in his book *Comic Book Nation: The Transformation of Youth Culture in America*, "comic books launched their propaganda efforts long before the American government. Many of the young Artists creating comic books were Jewish and liberal. Morally repelled by the Nazis, they expressed their politics in their work" (Wright, Bradford. *Comic Book Nation: The Transformation of Youth Culture in America*. Baltimore & London: The John Hopkins University Press, 2001, p. 35). Kirby, along with comic giants such as Will Eisner and Jerry Siegel (co-creators of Superman), also later enlisted during the war. During World War II the nature of comic books also changed, as the new naturally patriotic characters became hyperpatriotic, abandoning their pursuit of bank robbers and other criminals to sometimes literally fight on the front lines. At a time when the United States needed to intensify propaganda efforts to get the war machine going at home (see **World War Propaganda**), comic books were no exception in the propaganda offensive.

As Wright also noted "Comic books urged all Americans, including children to participate in the war effort. Those who remained aloof or pursued selfish interests appeared as misguided fools at best, traitors at worst. The comic books war effort, much like the real one, left no room for ambiguity or debate on most issues" (Wright, Bradford. *Comic Book Nation: The Transformation of Youth Culture in America*. Baltimore & London: The John Hopkins University Press, 2001, p. 44). Although the comic books world was united in their support of America during the good war, later wars proved more ambiguous. Later heroes such as Iron Man, first introduced in 1963, started out by fighting the Vietnamese before turning their attention to regular supervillains when the war began to cause dissention among comic book fans. By the late 1960s, younger comic book writers began to turn away from the jingoistic cheerleading of the past to concentrate more on social commentary although there were several notable exceptions, such as the laudatory comic book appearances of President John F. Kennedy.

Numerous politicians have also made cameo appearances in comic books, but few were initially as popular as the young and vibrant Kennedy who appeared in both Marvel Comics' the Fantastic Four, and as a friend of D.C. Comics' Superman. Kennedy and Superman were apparently so close (and Kennedy so full of free time) that Kennedy could disguise himself as Clark Kent to fool the extremely gullible Lois Lane, as he knows Superman's secret identity. A Superman comic (scheduled for November 1963 release) featuring the president had to be quickly rescheduled after Kennedy's assassination and was rescheduled as a tribute several months later.

Later politicians were not treated as reverently. President Richard Nixon and Vice President Spiro Agnew appeared in numerous underground comic books, mostly unflattering and some potentially libelous. During the 1960s countless underground comics mocked politicians of all stripes, so while Nixon may have been amongst the most reviled, he was certainly not alone.

Some superheroes seemed to have more overt political connections than others. Superman in particular met numerous presidents as well as Kennedy. Although Superman was around during the Franklin Roosevelt (FDR) to Dwight Eisenhower years, none of those presidents appeared in any of the Superman comic books, although in several issues decades later on, Superman is shown meeting FDR after the fact. In 1986 Superman also met then President Ronald Reagan in the miniseries *Legends* where Reagan temporarily forbade superheroes from using their powers. (In that series Reagan also met the Martian Manhunter, who saved Reagan from an assassination attempt by disguising himself as the president.) When Superman briefly "died" (no major character is ever killed off forever in a comic book) in 1993, Bill and Hillary Clinton were seen delivering a eulogy for Superman in *Man of Steel #20*. The Clintons also appeared in a dream sequence in the indie comic book *Strangers in Paradise*. George W. Bush has made appearances in numerous contemporary comic books and comic strips, including an appearance where he made a congratulatory call to Dagwood and Blondie on their 75th anniversary (although Dagwood refused to believe it was the president). During Marvel's *Civil War* crossover, President Bush is seen sponsoring legislation for the registration of superheroes and eventually meets with heroes Yellow Jacket, Iron Man, Mr. Fantastic of the Fantastic Four, and vigilante from the future Deadpool. Bush also met several members of the Rising Stars, a group of superheroes created by J. Michael Straczynski. Needless to say, Captain America also had encounters with numerous presidents of the United States during his long career (as well as being given a secret mission in 1976 by then Secretary of State Henry Kissinger), and in one speculative issue of *What If?* Captain America ran for president as an independent against both Carter and Reagan in 1980 and was elected. During the height of their popularity in the 1940s through 1980s comic books were a way for readers to imagine alternative worlds much like this one, but in a more spectacular way, where superheroes could fly over buildings and defeat any dangers, and where politicians did the right thing and were effective. (For discussion of other ways in which U.S. presidents have been depicted in the media, see entries on presidents beginning with **John F. Kennedy**.)

COMMANDER IN CHIEF. *Commander in Chief* (2005–2006) was a short-lived dramatic program with a story line involving the first female president of the United States, MacKenzie Allen, played by Geena Davis, and her problems in dealing with a hostile Congress and her own administration. The program lasted only one season, although this is most likely a response the overall quality of the program, as opposed to any deep-set American opposition to having a woman president.

COUGHLIN, FATHER CHARLES. Father Charles Coughlin (1891–1979), known as the radio priest, was a noted political commentator who was one the most popular fixtures on radio during the early part of the twentieth century. Fr. Coughlin started his career on children's station WJR in Detroit in 1926 and with his Radio League of the Little Flower quickly grew in popularity during the early 1930s. Like Roosevelt, Coughlin knew and appreciated the power of radio to make connections with unseen speakers, and he was able to use the medium to his advantage. After being dropped by CBS in 1931 for being too controversial in his attacks on communists and bankers, Coughlin formed his own version of a network by buying time on a series of local stations. While Coughlin initially supported Roosevelt when the president was working towards the interests of the poor over large corporations, Coughlin turned against Roosevelt as the president began to examine international issues. Coughlin upped his political rhetoric into vitriol and anti-Semitism (including calling the New Deal, the "Jew Deal"), and he increasingly became a pariah to the hierarchy of the Roman Catholic Church and the National Association of Broadcasters, which established the fairness doctrine partially as a countermeasure against Coughlin. After the early 1940s, Coughlin was forced off the air, although he continued to be active as a parish priest and agitator until his retirement in 1966.

Coughlin's legacy is tied in with the legacy of Roosevelt and others who sought to use radio as a populist medium. Early broadcasters found that radio audiences were deeply involved with speakers who touched them on a personal level and those like Coughlin who could use the warmth of the medium to agitate for political change demonstrated that politicians and political activists of all stripes would need to learn the nuances of radio (and later television and the Internet) if they wished to appeal to the majority of Americans.

COULTER, ANN. Ann Coulter (1961–) is a right-wing radio and television commentator who has caused much controversy over the years, particularly with her attacks on the "9/11 widows." Coulter began her career as a Cornell law school graduate who eventually worked her way up to the U.S. Senate Judiciary committee in 1994. In 1996 she began appearing on **MSNBC** as a legal correspondent, and her glib way with a word and her ability to craft a witty sound bite on demand soon made her a viewer favorite. She began to appear as a pundit on **Fox News** as well as **CNN** and many other cable outlets. Coulter is also the author of seven books currently, all of which went on to become best sellers, the most controversial being the book *Godless: The Church of Liberalism*, where she attacked the widows of 9/11 victims who had gone into politics as "harpies," which displeased as many of her fans on the right as her foes on the left. Her latest book, *Guilty Liberal "Victims" and Their Assault on America*, was released in January 2009. In 2007 Coulter also courted controversy when she jokingly referred to then presidential candidate John Edwards as a "faggot." Despite frequent controversies, Coulter has long refused to apologize for her actions, and many, even on the left, such as **Bill Maher**, find her refreshing for her outspoken behavior.

COUNTRY MUSIC. While many could argue that American Country Music (also called Country Western music) contained right-wing and sometimes reactionary points of view, critics have noted that in the past few decades, in contrast to folk music, rock, or punk, country music often leans in a more conservative direction than other genres of music. (This may also be a classic misinterpretation of the genre.) Classic country artists such as Johnny Cash, Merle Haggard, and even Hank Williams all wrote pious songs in praise of small-town American values and religion in the 1940s, 1950s, and even 1960s (yet they also wrote and sang many apolitical songs, as well as songs that celebrated drunkenness, drugs, and living a debauched life). An example of this might be Haggard's "Okie from Muskogee," a song about the small-town values of the people in Muskogee, which Haggard later backtracked and claimed was his attempt to write a song from the perspective of his father's generation. (Nonetheless, many country fans read the song as a conservative answer to the hippie movement.) Johnny Cash in particular wrote numerous political country songs, such as the "Ballad of Ira Hayes" in 1970, about the tragic death of the native American soldier who helped raise the flag at Iwo Jima.

The outlaw genre of music in the 1960s and 1970s also led to new material that dealt with issues such as divorce, the breakup of the traditional American nuclear family, and the fear that political unrest was wreaking havoc with America. Artists such as Willie Nelson, David Allan Coe, and Waylon Jennings chronicled the contradictions of country politics in their recordings of the 1970s.

After 9/11, numerous country stars rushed to write and record songs in praise of America and patriotic values. **The Dixie Chicks**, in an unusual move for a country group, openly criticized President **George W. Bush** on stage in Texas and as a result found themselves the focus of several boycotts, threats, and eventually a documentary by Barbara Kopple and a subsequent triumphant return in 2006. Country music remains one of the most conservative of American music genres, still keeping faith (mostly) with God and country. (For a comprehensive discussion of politics and music in general, see Part I, Chapter 6.)

CRONKITE, WALTER. Walter Cronkite (1916–2009) was the longtime anchor for *CBS Evening News* from 1962 to 1981. Cronkite was extremely popular and

Former *CBS News* anchor Walter Cronkite speaking during a forum at the John F. Kennedy Library in Boston, October 2005. (AP Photo/Steven Senne)

was often called "the most trusted man in America." It also turned out that he was politically powerful as well; many attribute the lack of confidence of many Americans in the war in Vietnam to Cronkite declaring the war a failure in January 1968. As a biographer noted about Cronkite and Vietnam, after:

> returning from Vietnam after the Tet offensive Cronkite addressed his massive audience with a different perspective. "It seems now more certain than ever," he said, "that the bloody experience of Vietnam is a stalemate." He then urged the government to open negotiations with the North Vietnamese. Many observers, including presidential aid Bill Moyers speculated that this was a major factor contributing to President Lyndon B. Johnson's decision to offer to negotiate with the enemy and not to run for President in 1968.
>
> (Museum.tv 2006. Available at http://www.museum.tv/
> archives/etv/C/htmlC/cronkitewal/cronkitewal.htm)

Cronkite was an iconic presence for many during political events in the 1960s and 1970s, and his calm, reassuring voice helped Americans contextualize tragedies such as the 1963 Kennedy assassination in which Cronkite openly wept on air. Cronkite, still alive and an elder statesman of American news at this writing, has had a formidable career, and many believe he was perhaps the last of the truly dignified news presenters who stepped down in his prime.

D

DAILY KOS. The founder of *Daily Kos*, Kos (birth name Markos Moulitsas Zúniga; 1971–) has grown into a political force in his own right. Not only has he served as a consultant to political campaigns (including his work as a technical consultant for the 2004 Howard Dean run for the presidency), but his annual convention for bloggers, the "YearlyKos" (renamed "Netroots Nation" in 2008), now draws hundreds of attendees. Even high profile politicians make an appearance. For instance, both major candidates for the 2008 Democratic presidential nomination, **Hillary Clinton** and **Barack Obama**, felt compelled to show their faces at the convention. Along with fellow prominent blogger Jerome Armstrong, Kos is the co-author of the oft-cited book about blogging, *Crashing the Gates: Netroots, Grassroots, and the Rise of People-Powered Politics*.

Kos unveiled his left-leaning political blog in 2002. For years, it has been one of the nation's most popular collaborative **blogs**. *Daily Kos* allows other bloggers to embed their own online diaries within its site, thus encouraging a high level of participation. Like the *Huffington Post*, it features a large collection of regular contributors and promotes interactive discussion between its writers and its readers. Yet in contrast to Huffington's creation, *Daily Kos* has a much more activist mission, which chiefly entails influencing and building up the Democratic Party. The site regularly seeks donations from readers for candidates Kos supports. Indeed, Kos was a major factor behind the rise of what has come to be known as the "netroots," a loosely organized online, politically progressive community devoted to changing the state of politics through the vehicle of the Democratic Party. Some political observers—as well as members of the group themselves—liken the netroots to a full-fledged mass movement.

As he has grown in stature, Kos has generated his fair share of controversy. His strongly worded opinions sometimes draw the ire of people from both ends of the political spectrum. One notable episode, which developed during the 2008 Democratic primary season, involved an intraparty squabble between pro-Clinton bloggers and other posters, including Kos himself, who offered stern criticism of the candidate. One unpaid blogger, "Alegre," with the backing of a number of like-minded colleagues, called for a "writers strike." Given the provocative tone of some of *Daily Kos*'s rhetoric, it seems almost certain that the political blog will continue to stir up discord in the future (an outcome that Kos might even desire). (See Part I, Chapter 8, "Politics Online.")

THE DAILY SHOW WITH JON STEWART. *The Daily Show with Jon Stewart*, which airs on Comedy Central, has been the most successful venture in turning news into outright entertainment in modern political history. *The Daily Show* regularly brings in an audience of over 1.2 million viewers (Dowd, Maureen. "America's Anchors: Jon Stewart and Stephen Colbert Faked It until They Made It, Now They Are the Most Trusted Names in News." *Rolling Stone*, issue 1013, November 16, 2006), many from highly coveted younger demographics, and many whom, it seems, turn to programs such as *The Daily Show* for actual news as opposed to simply entertainment. (*The Daily Show*'s coverage of elections and other special events were collected on DVD sets as *Indecision 2004*, other DVD sets have been best sellers, and *The Daily Show* has received extensive coverage in numerous major newspapers, national magazines, and news programs.) Jon Stewart has been given the coveted Peabody award for excellence in journalism several times, and his comments on a notorious episode of **CNN**'s *Crossfire* about the vacuity of most news debate programs apparently struck a chord with those fed up with the American news media.

The *Indecision* segment led to ratings improving to an all-time high. *The Daily Show* has garnered a series of major awards, such as six Emmy awards and a prestigious Peabody award. In 2004 the program was also nominated "as one of television's best broadcasts by the TV critics association" (Dowd, Maureen. "America's Anchors: Jon Stewart and Stephen Colbert Faked It until They Made It. Now They Are the Most Trusted Names in News." *Rolling Stone*, issue 1013, November 16, 2006), and Jon Stewart was named by *Newsday* as the most important newscaster among anchors of the major cable, network, and public broadcasting stations (Dowd 2006). This is all from a program that was not designed to deliver news to the general public, but to point out the inherent absurdity not only of the major networks and cable stations that delivered news on a nightly basis, but also to point out the absurdity of the way in which modern reporters did not question information that was given to them, but (according to *The Daily Show*) merely parroted back the official point of view presented by those in authority. When Stewart famously went on CNN's *Crossfire* just before the 2004 presidential election, he quietly but firmly made a case that programs like the (since cancelled) *Crossfire* did not spark real debate, but instead served to confuse and mislead audiences. To Stewart, who delivered the message that, regarding programs such as Crossfire, "I felt it wasn't fair and I should come here and tell you it's not so much that it's bad as it's hurting America." When hosts Tucker Carlson (on the right) and Paul Begala (on the left) challenged him and tried to dismiss Stewart's attack as another joke, Stewart still maintained his calm and responded, "I'm here to confront you because we need help from the media and they're hurting us." Begala then asked Stewart, "So, the indictment is that *Crossfire* reduces everything to left, right, black, white?"

"Yes," said Stewart. At this, Begala looked pained and then responded, as if explaining something painfully obvious to a small child, "It's because we are a debate show." In between Tucker and Begala's frequent interjections, Stewart finally was able to respond, "No, that would be great, to do a debate would be great, but that's like saying that pro wrestling is a show about athletic competition." While Stewart was not able to convince the hosts of *Crossfire* that they were not engaging in substantive political debates, he did make a valuable comparison between the idea of television news as a source of serious political discourse and the talking/shouting head format that had begun to dominate many news-based programs toward the end of the twentieth century.

DAISY COMMERCIAL. Aired in 1964 on behalf of President **Lyndon B. Johnson's** run for reelection, "Daisy" is widely held as the most famous (and controversial) political commercial in U.S. history. The Democrats had secured the services of Doyle Dane Bernbach (DDB), which was headed up by the celebrated creative advertising figure Bill Bernbach. DDB's strategy partly centered on attacking Republican opponent Barry Goldwater for his purported instability, hawkishness, and overall conservative extremism. The agency hired the consultant Tony Schwartz, who came to be regarded as a giant of political advertising, even though he had never worked for an agency himself and was, instead, self-employed and largely self-taught (he later became an insightful writer on media and a professor at Fordham University). In the midst of Cold War fears about nuclear destruction, Schwartz created the Daisy political advertisement.

The commercial features a little girl picking off petals from a flower and counting them from one to ten. Then, the girl looks up with a startled expression as the shot freezes and the camera zooms into her eye until the screen is completely black. At the same time, her voice is replaced with the voice of a male announcer who counts backward from 10. The commercial next cuts to the explosion of an atomic bomb, presumably killing the girl and possibly everyone else on the planet. A statement pulled from a Johnson speech plays under this dramatic and frightening image: "These are the stakes—to make a world in which all of God's children can live, or to go into the dark. We must either love each other, or we must die." The commercial ends with an announcer, who says: "Vote for President Johnson on November 3. The stakes are too high for you to stay home." The message of the ad was clear: under a Goldwater administration, the presumably hot-tempered Republican would lead the country into a nuclear confrontation with Russia.

The commercial aired only once (on *Monday Night at the Movies*), which was enough to receive an immediate and vigorous reaction. Johnson was reportedly happy with it. But it sparked a large storm as many people accused the commercial's producers of portraying Goldwater unfairly by branding him as a warmonger. Some in the audience, especially those on the Goldwater campaign staff, were simply outraged. Even countless numbers of those who had not originally viewed the spot later heard about it or saw it replayed on television newscasts. The chair of the Republican National Committee filed a formal complaint, contending that the Daisy commercial had violated ethical codes and was libelous. Though the Johnson campaign ultimately distanced itself from the spot, the damage (to Goldwater) had already been done. The genius of the advertisement, according to Schwartz, was that it did *not* mention Goldwater at all. As Schwartz noted in his book, *The Responsive Chord*, he made this choice because most people do not need to be told explicitly about something they might already believe.

To Schwartz, "commercials that attempt to *tell* the listener something are inherently not as effective as those that attach to something that is already in him [*sic*]" (Schwartz, Tony. *The Responsive Chord*. Garden City, NY: Anchor Books, 1973, p. 96).

The Daisy commercial is now seen as one of the most effective and evocative pieces of campaign propaganda in U.S. political history. It demonstrated that a message does not always have to be conveyed repeatedly to be effective—the right theme and execution can work even if it is only momentarily televised and then quickly withdrawn, stirring up news coverage along the way. With the current ubiquity of **YouTube**, political campaigns can use similar strategies without having to rely on network news to broadcast and discuss the clips.

Although likely overstated, Daisy cemented in incalculable minds the image of Goldwater as someone who was too volatile to be trusted. For example, in the October before the election, a poll revealed that, by a factor of five to one, people thought Goldwater was more liable to start a nuclear war than Johnson, who went on to win the election in a landslide.

DAVE. *Dave* is a 1993 political movie satire that stars Kevin Kline as an ordinary man who happens to be a virtual double (although for some reason he has never noticed this before) for the corrupt president of the United States. Initially drafted by the president's political cronies to step in for the president during public appearances, Kline's character is later used to replace the president full time when the incumbent has a stroke. Of course, Kline's character proves to be a better president, fulfilling the populist suspicion of many Americans that they could also do a better job as president. The film featured a variety of celebrities for the political and entertainment worlds such as Tip O'Neill, **Arnold Schwarzenegger**, Tom Harkin, **Chris Matthews**, Larry King, Jay Leno, and even a suspicious **Oliver Stone** who pokes fun at his own penchant for conspiracy theories. *Dave* is yet another pre-911 populist fantasy where an everyman is allowed to use the most powerful office on earth for good. *Rolling Stone* magazine referred to *Dave* as the "first political fable of the Clinton era" (Travers, Peter. "Dave." Available at http://www.rollingstone.com/reviews/dvd/5948265/review/5948266/dave [accessed July 13, 2007]), which reflected the general optimism on the left for the Clinton presidency.

DEATH OF A PRESIDENT. *Death of a President* is a British film from 2007 directed by Gabriel Range that used archival footage of the real president **George W. Bush** mixed in with doctored footage to create a scenario where the president is assassinated and to show what the aftermath would have been in such a scenario. The film was attacked by many critics as being either an attack on the president or simply a show of bad taste. The film was strangely enough only mildly controversial, perhaps because it did not receive much publicity; otherwise it may have had more of an impact on popular culture.

DIXIE CHICKS. The Dixie Chicks (Natalie Maines, Emily Robison, Martie Maguire) are an all female country group who got into some trouble with its fan base, country radio stations, and conservative commentators when on March 10,

The Dixie Chicks, from left, Martie Maguire, Natalie Maines, and Emily Robison, shown in Santa Monica, California, during the launch of MTV's Rock the Vote, 2003, a campaign to get young voters to register. (AP Photo/Nick Ut)

2003, at a concert in London, Natalie Maines, a singer in the group, informed the audience that "just so you know we're ashamed the president of the United States is from Texas" (Easton, Jake. "Dixie Chicks and Alex Baldwin: Fighting for 'Centre Square' on *The Hollywood Squares*?" *Radok News; Tabloid Column*, April 23, 2003 [accessed March 12, 2007]). The uproar that followed was both unexpected and, at least since the tumult of the 1960s, unprecedented. The fan base was outraged with thousands of fans calling country stations to complain and many country stations dropping the Dixie Chicks from their playlists, with one station WDAF-AM (610), 61 Country, in Kansas City even organizing a "trashing" of Dixie Chicks records to be returned to the record company. At first the band initially issued apologies for Maines's statement, but on March 14, Maines issued a statement saying:

> As a concerned American citizen, I apologize to President Bush because my remark was disrespectful. I feel that whoever holds that office should be treated with the utmost respect. We are currently in Europe and witnessing a huge anti-American sentiment as a result of the perceived rush to war. While war may remain a viable option, as a mother, I just want to see every possible alternative exhausted before children and

American soldiers' lives are lost. I love my country. I am a proud American. (Easton. "Dixie Chicks" [accessed on August 10, 2007])

The band found touring more difficult in the South than in the North, and after a while began to regret their initial apology. In 2004 they joined the politically charged Vote for Change tour with Bruce Springsteen, Pearl Jam, and REM among others, which tried to get youth voters interested in participating in the 2004 presidential election. Documentary filmmaker Barbara Kopple followed the Dixie Chicks with a camera for the next three years to document audience reactions and how the women dealt with death threats and audience negativity. The film was released in 2006 as *Dixie Chicks: Shut Up and Sing* (supposedly named after an angry fan letter the Dixie Chicks had received). A follow-up record, *Taking the Long Way*, was released in 2006 and went on to win five Grammys, but was most notable for the defiant song "Not Ready to Make Nice," which pointedly addressed the controversy and the free speech issues involved. Ironically, it left the Dixie Chicks more popular than when the controversy had begun three years earlier.

While the Dixie Chicks were not the first musicians to ever criticize American foreign policy, they were one of the rare country groups to take a nuanced stand against a polarizing but still popular (at the time) president. The ensuing issues and issues of free speech versus respect for the office of the president and whether a standing president should be criticized during wartime date back to the start of the American presidency, but in terms of the music industry it may have never previously come from a band as mainstream and unthreatening as the Dixie Chicks. While most country music has a history of being politically conservative and patriotic (see **Country Music**), the Dixie Chicks incident allowed most Americans to see that country music was not monolithically on one end of the political spectrum, and that issues of free speech are especially important during wartime.

DOLE, BOB. Bob Dole (1923–) is one of America's best-known Republican politicians who spent 27 years in the Senate from 1969 to 1996 and several terms as Senate majority and minority leader. Dole was also a decorated World War II veteran who lost most of the use of his right arm due to a war injury. In 1996 Dole led an unsuccessful bid for the presidency against incumbent **Bill Clinton**, and subsequently retired from political life. Dole, who successfully fought prostate cancer in 1991, started appearing in television commercials for the erectile dysfunction drug Viagra. While this naturally was fodder for late-night comedians, it also helped to raise public awareness of the problems faced by prostate cancer survivors. Dole seemed much more comfortable poking fun at his image after his retirement from politics and was a frequent guest on talk shows where he proved to be an amiable and bipartisan guest. Dole also appeared as himself in an episode of *Futurama* in the late 1990s. He appeared in a Pepsi ad featuring pop star Britney Spears, in 2001, where he parodied his own appearances as a Viagra spokesmen, telling a dog who barks happily at an image of Spears, "Down boy." Presumably, Dole was referring to the dog.

DOONESBURY. *Doonesbury* is one of the most popular and controversial political comic strips in American history. It has been running more or less continuously since September 30, 1968 (with a hiatus from 1982 to 1984, returning after an off-Broadway musical recounted events that took place during the hiatus), when it first appeared in a student newspaper as *Bull Tales*. In October 1970, it started appearing in 28 papers across the country retitled *Doonesbury* (and soon became extremely successful), and has been written and drawn by creator Garry Trudeau since its inception. While the strip ostensibly has followed a group of students from the fictional Walden College from campus protests in the 1960s to their lives in the present day, the strip has often been to many the most intelligent and biting comic strip available (although in some newspapers it is on the editorial page). The main characters of the strip are the titular Michael Doonesbury and his college classmates, B. D., Boopsie, Zonker Harris, Mark Slackmeyer, Kim, Zipper, and others. Over the past four decades the comic strip has tackled **Watergate**, Koreagate, Oil Companies, the tobacco industry (including the popular recurring character, the life-size talking cigarette Mr. Butts, who has also appeared in ads for the American Cancer Society, among other organizations), Dan Quayle, **George H. Bush, George W. Bush, Ronald Reagan, Jimmy Carter**, Jerry Brown, **Richard Nixon**, the Internet, gay marriage, oil companies, among many others. The series recently received acclaim for its sensitive portrayal of Gulf War (I and II) veterans having problems readjusting to society. The series is one of the most important (and long-running) politically oriented comic strips in American history, and it is unclear whether it has had more awards or condemnations by political figures. (For related discussion, see **Political Cartoons.**)

DRUDGE, MATT. See Part I, Chapter 8, "Politics Online," and *The Drudge Report.*

THE DRUDGE REPORT. It is unclear whether the politically conservative Matt Drudge (1966–), founder of *The Drudge Report* Web site, is even a blogger in the purest sense of the term. Yet he is often lumped into the classification and appears to occasionally fulfill some of the functions associated with **blogs**. In any case, Drudge is an influential Internet reporter and Web site editor. He is most famous for breaking the **Bill Clinton**–Monica Lewinsky scandal in 1998 (see **Political Scandals**). On January 18, Drudge first disclosed on his Web site, *The Drudge Report*, that *Newsweek* magazine had killed a potential report on a White House intern's involvement with then President Bill Clinton. A day later, Drudge was the first to reveal the name Monica Lewinsky to the general public. Not long afterward, the controversy snowballed.

Drudge launched *The Drudge Report* in 1994 through an e-mail to friends, but it soon grew to 300,000 subscribers, which led to his hiring by Wired.com and then aol.com for the purpose of providing news and celebrity gossip. Soon his Web site was breaking important stories, thanks to a developed network of informants. Drudge detailed his adventures in his 2000 biography, *The Drudge Manifesto*, which was co-written by the late Julia Phillips, author of the Hollywood memoir *You'll Never Eat Lunch in This Town Again*. Drudge demonstrated that, instead of always relying on traditional news operations, information could increasingly be derived from the Internet, via e-mail newsletters and blogs produced by everyday people. He also showed that salacious gossip could still serve as fodder for news stories in the late twentieth century. Owners of less popular Web sites were often beneficiaries of Drudge. A link on his Web site could result in a copious amount of traffic for those fortunate enough to be in his favor.

For others, however, Drudge could be notoriously fickle, sometimes cutting off their links without a word.

Although Drudge is not as relevant as he was in the 1990s, he is still a prominent voice in the online world (a 2008 report by quantcast.com, for example, ranked *The Drudge Report* as the seventh most visited news Web site). Yet *The Drudge Report* serves mostly as a clearinghouse for various news items and, due to greater competition, rarely breaks major stories. Some of Drudge's most notable revelations over the past decade have come at the expense of Democrats, such as coverage of presidential candidate **Al Gore**'s dubious visit to a Buddhist monastery for a fund-raiser in 2000, and reports about John Edward's $400 haircut when he was running for the nation's highest office in 2007. Drudge also hosts a weekly syndicated radio program that is carried by over 200 stations. Though Drudge is not (and has never claimed to be) a traditional journalist, he has significantly contributed to changing the nature of news in the age of new media. His emphasis on immediacy has sometimes forced the hand of mainstream media outlets that are slow to respond to breaking stories that have not yet been thoroughly fact checked. (See Part I, Chapter 8, "Politics Online.")

DUKE, DAVID. David Duke (1950–) is a white supremacist politician who ran several close campaigns for governor and senator from Louisiana in 1990 and 1991. Although Duke, an ex-member of the Ku Klux Klan, claimed that he was no longer a racist while running, it was clear that a great many residents of the state of Louisiana were sympathetic to his aims. He first ran for office in 1989, narrowly winning a seat in the Louisiana House of Representatives, beating a fellow Republican who had been publicly backed by then President **George H. Bush**. Duke's candidacy and openly racist views (although he challenged the use of the term) gained him national notoriety, and in 1990 he ran a campaign in an open primary for the U.S. senate in Louisiana where he gained 44 percent of the vote against Democratic incumbent Bennett Johnson. Duke's next major race was for the governorship of Louisiana in 1991 against former Governor Edwin Edwards. The campaign was the focus of media outcry and public appeals by the Republican Party for voters not to vote for Duke, which in some districts also probably helped his appeal to disenchanted and poor white voters, who thought of him as the second coming of the segregationist **George Wallace**. Wallace later repudiated his earlier views, something Duke has failed to do. Duke lost the election, even though he garnered over 50 percent of the white vote. He went on to run in several more elections, less successfully every time, and later turned his attention to anti-Semitic pursuits. In 2002 Duke published a book entitled *Jewish Supremacist: My Awakening on the Jewish Question*, an anti-Semitic attack supported by European and Ukrainian white supremacists. In December 2006, Duke made an appearance at the "Review of the Holocaust: Global Outlook" conference organized in Tehran, Iran, by Iranian president Mahmoud Ahmadinejad. To many critics, Duke symbolizes the fact that not only are there still racist, anti-Semitic, and other despicable views held by average Americans, but the art of using notoriety for self-promotion is still very much alive. Just as George Wallace had previously used segregationist views to achieve national stature, David Duke also was able to use his notoriety to extend his 15 minutes of fame well beyond its usual shelf life. Duke also maintains a Web site and blog where he discusses his views and opinions quite candidly. It is questionable in terms of media presence whether stories reported about Duke caused him to gain more followers or to continue to lose the respect of those who misguidedly supported him in the past.

DYLAN, BOB. The artist known as Bob Dylan (1941–; born Robert Zimmerman, but took the surname Dylan from the Welsh poet Dylan Thomas) is widely regarded as one of the most respected and renowned American songwriters of the twentieth century and beyond. Although not gifted with a particularly beautiful voice, Dylan has for years been the poet laureate of American music, and he has inspired several different generations into joining political and social movements. Always a mysterious figure, Dylan, an ardent fan of **Woody Guthrie**, arrived in New York City in 1961 from Minneapolis and quickly established himself on the burgeoning New York City folk scene. He was aided by other artists, such as The Clancy Brothers and Tommy Makem, and developed a persona as an artist equally concerned with the compelling images he conjured with his words as with melody. Moving away from traditional folk ballads, Dylan's songs increasingly began to deal with social and political issues as the 1960s wore on, such as "Masters of War" and "Blowing in the Wind" as well as many others that addressed such issues as war and the empowerment of teenagers. Although Dylan largely stopped recording and performing overt protest music as the years went on, his lyrics have always tended to be either vague by nature or very socially aware. Dylan is so revered by his many fans that his persona has taken on the aura of a counterculture jester/philosopher, whose every pronouncement is regarded as having come from another realm, which is probably at least half true. Ironically, as Dylan himself has mentioned, for all of his cultural capital with the protest movement of the 1960s and early 1970s, his politics were not always to the left. In his autobiography, *Chronicles*, Dylan mentions that in the early 1960s, "I have a primitive way of looking at things and I liked county fair politics. My favorite politician was Arizona senator Barry Goldwater" (Dylan, Bob. *Chronicles Volume One*. New York: Simon and Schuster, 2004, p. 283). Dylan is a towering figure in American popular music and popular culture and has influenced countless musical artists, an entire generation of new lyricists, and is most often cited by critics as the poet laureate of the popular music set. He is often inscrutable and hard to pin down and define, as the recent 2007 movie *I'm Not There* demonstrated by having Dylan played by multiple actors to express the many symbolic "Dylans" that existed in different stages of his work. (For further discussion of Bob Dylan, as well as politics and music in general, see Part I, Chapter 6.)

E

EASTWOOD, CLINT. Clint Eastwood (1930–), the iconic American actor, is known not only for playing politically resonant characters, such as the right-wing Dirty Harry, and directing such World War II films as *Flags of Our Fathers* (2006) and *Letters from Iwo Jima* (2006), but also for his brief role in American politics. In 1986 he was elected mayor of Carmel-by-the-Sea, California, and served one term. As mayor, he was known for his efforts to "clean up the town," albeit in a war on litter as opposed to a war on crime. Eastwood did shift his position slightly to the left as mayor of Carmel; he opposed off-shore oil drilling and spent $5 million of his own money to keep developers out of town and to preserve the wetlands near the town. Eastwood has been known for making politicized films, especially in his early years (in the 1960s and early 1970s) when the Dirty Harry series of films were considered right wing by many film critics. Although Eastwood denied a right-wing agenda in his work, he did attend Republican fund-raisers, voted Republican in the 1960s, 1970s, and 1980s, and was associated with other right of center actors such as John Wayne and Glenn Ford. In later years, Eastwood took a more libertarian stance and was on record as both opposing the second war in Iraq but also threatening (jokingly) to kill **Michael Moore** if he showed up on his doorstep (as Moore had done famously to Charlton Heston in the film *Bowling for Columbine*). Eastwood is primarily known as a director today, and while many try and find overt patriotic or anti-American images in his later films, Eastwood demanded that they be judged simply on an artistic level. Whether as director or as iconic actor, Eastwood is one of the more politicized actors of his generation and his films can be seen as an example of how movies can be politicized and how the line between public figures and actors has been increasingly blurred over the past 50 years.

"EISENHOWER ANSWERS AMERICA." The first presidential candidate to make extensive use of television as a tool for advertising in an election season was General Dwight D. Eisenhower in 1952. The most notable campaign consisted of a series of commercials dubbed "Eisenhower Answers America." In each usually 20-second commercial, an everyday citizen asked a question about one issue and Eisenhower gave a generalized response on how he would handle the problem. Today's advertising practitioners would probably agree that the spots lacked creativity. Still, given the context in which they ran, the commercials surely made an impression on many people. In the end, Eisenhower handily won the election over Democratic challenger Adlai Stevenson. Yet the impact the advertising campaign had on Eisenhower's victory is uncertain. Most scholars concur that given the General's popularity, he probably would have won even if he had not executed a comprehensive advertising campaign. Still, Eisenhower's advertising effort likely stood as the most novel development of the 1952 election season and strongly indicated the manner in which future political promotional campaigns would be conducted, a process that has received considerable criticism.

EISNER, WILL. Will Eisner (1917–2005), one of the most influential artists and storytellers in comics' history, was also responsible during World War II for creating instructional comic book characters designed to teach American soldiers safety and proper etiquette as a soldier. Along with army training films, comic books were often effective tools for teaching basic safety, rules, and mechanical lessons such as how to drive a Jeep and how to clean a rifle. Eisner, who had an award named after him in the comic world, continued to work on Army training manuals and instructional books following the war, while at the same time writing some of the more groundbreaking work in comics such as his work on the Spirit comic series, leading to the rise of the graphic novel and a new sense of comics as a legitimate form of popular culture, if not high art. Eisner was also an early proponent, if not one of the originators, of the large-scale book-length comic books known as graphic novels. (See also **Comic Books.**)

F

FACE THE NATION. See Sunday Morning Political Shows.

FACEBOOK. See Part I, Chapter 8, "Social Networking and the Democratization of Media."

FAHRENHEIT 9/11. *Fahrenheit 9/11* is a 2004 documentary by **Michael Moore** about the perceived failures of the Bush administration's policies after the terrorist attacks on the United States on September 11, 2001. Because of its strongly critical stance, it generated considerable controversy. Hoping to actually influence the results of the 2004 presidential election between **George W. Bush** and his Democratic opponent, Senator John Kerry, Moore released the movie (after his original backer, Disney, had earlier refused to distribute the film, which only added to the publicity surrounding it) just months before November's vote. *Fahrenheit 9/11* argues, among other claims, that President Bush stole the 2000 election from **Al Gore**; had oil connections with family members of Osama bin Laden, the mastermind behind the catastrophic terrorist attacks of September 11, 2001; misled the nation into its war with Iraq; and was undermining the rights of U.S. citizens through surveillance operations sanctioned by the Bush-endorsed U.S. Patriot Act. One of the highlights of Moore's decidedly partisan documentary is footage of President Bush reading to an elementary school class the book *My Pet Goat* for seven minutes even after being informed that planes had hit New York's twin towers. Interestingly, although, as in his other works, he narrates the film, Moore appears on camera far less than in most of his documentaries. After winning the Palme d'Or award for best picture at the Cannes Film Festival, it stirred more anticipation than probably any documentary in history. Once it came to the theaters, it at least shared center stage in the country's realm of popular culture. News outlets covered and debated the film. It evoked both laudatory and hostile responses—from both the right and left ends of the political spectrum.

On the oppositional end of the spectrum, political pundits assailed him, anti-Moore Web sites sprouted up, and David T. Hardy and Jason Clarke co-authored the book *Michael Moore Is a Big Fat Stupid White Man*, whose title was a parody of Moore's own text, *Stupid White Men*. At the same time, at least four full-length documentaries were produced as counterattacks. *FahrenHype 9/11: Unraveling the Truth about Fahrenheit 9/11*, *Celsius 41.11: The Temperature at which the Brain Begins to Die*, *Michael Moore Hates America*, and *Shooting Michael Moore* all, in one way or another, rebuke Moore's political positions and argue that Moore's filmmaking techniques render gross distortions of events. Still, none of these documentaries had the financial backing or the production quality of Moore's film; the size of their audiences paled in comparison as well. Various observers have reasoned that both Moore and his adversaries probably reinforced the thoughts and attitudes of their respective like-minded viewers far more than influenced any people to change their minds about the candidates running for the White House.

In the end, whether *Fahrenheit 9/11* had any impact on voting decisions in the 2004 presidential election is difficult to ascertain—with Bush's reelection, certainly Moore's goal was not obtained. Its commercial significance, though, is clear. *Fahrenheit 9/11* broke the box office record for a documentary film (securing over 15 millions viewers in its first month of release and a total gross of nearly $120 million), far surpassing the previous leader, none other than Moore's *Bowling for Columbine* (whose total gross was about $21.5 million [imbd.com]).

FIRESIDE CHATS. Franklin Delano Roosevelt (FDR) is generally regarded as the first president to master the use of radio to further a political agenda. In particular, he turned to the medium as an instrument of propaganda to promote his domestic policies as well as to secure support for U.S. involvement in World War II. His talks scored well in the ratings—from January 1940 through February 1942, a period of national crisis, for example, his speeches reached an average of 53.8 percent of American homes. Some of his addresses were labeled as "fireside chats," designed to promote a feeling of intimacy between the politician and the listener. FDR especially liked radio because it enabled him to bring his messages directly to the citizenry and circumvent the press, a vehicle he greatly distrusted, given that most newspaper leaders were hostile toward his New Deal policies. That he was able to, so to speak, enter the homes of everyday people while masking his physical disability from polio, moreover, was no small factor as well. Radio addresses allowed him to bypass personal appearances during which he could not easily conceal his confinement to a wheelchair.

Apparently, Roosevelt's personal approach indeed moved many listeners. After a fireside chat, for instance, he generally received considerable feedback through the mail. Often, a letter indicated that Roosevelt had come across in a "human" manner, or that he even seemed like a member of the family. Still, such fan mail decreased over time, as radio lost its novel quality and began to work its way into the fabric of everyday life.

Roosevelt was instrumental in establishing the need for politicians to modify their communication styles if they hoped to successfully appeal to the populace through radio. A more conversational tone played far better, for example, than the loud mode of address that had always been suitable for speeches at live political events.

Recently, President **Barack Obama** has been encouraged by political commentators to use the fireside chat model to speak to the American public about the ongoing serious economic crisis of 2009, although on television, rather than radio, and, more often, online via a video appearance on **YouTube**.

FIRING LINE. *Firing Line* was a long-running political talk show hosted by brilliant conservative gadfly **William F. Buckley** (1925–2008) and guest commentators from all points of the political spectrum. The show began in 1966 inspired by a previous talk show hosted by David Susskind in the 1950s, *Open Mind*, in which civil conversations could sometimes go for two or three hours on complex topics if the debate was still lively and dignified. Buckley started the program (first an hour long, and toward the end of the show one-half hour) hosting notable guests who included Hugh Hefner, Groucho Marx, Mother Teresa, **Muhammad Ali**, Jack Kerouac, Allen Ginsberg, frequent sparring partner Norman Mailer, and numerous presidents. Whatever political spectrum the guest was from, the dialogue was always interesting, unhurried, and often deeply philosophical and introspective. In comparison to modern programs such as *Hardball with Chris Matthews* and *The O'Reilly Factor*, *Firing Line* was the height of grace and civil conversation. It is difficult to imagine a program of this level of depth and discourse not only because the nature of television is biased against serious discourse but also because such a program would find it difficult to find sponsors who could pitch products to an audience who could sit still for up to an hour without commercial interruption.

THE FIRST FAMILY AND THE FIRST FAMILY RIDES AGAIN (TWO VOLUMES). Satirical recordings that made fun of the early days of the John F. Kennedy presidency, the record *The First Family* was recorded by Vaughn Meader in 1962 and included dead-on parodies of the Kennedy clan and, in particular, Kennedy's thick Boston accent. The records were considered very popular in their time period, but that period was not to last. After Kennedy's assassination in 1963 the records were removed from record stores and Meader's career went into a tailspin from which he never recovered. An apocryphal tale has **Lenny Bruce** doing a stand-up routine on the night of the Kennedy assassination and telling the crowd, "Boy, is Vaughn Meader screwed." *The First Family* records were as much affectionate send-ups of the Kennedy family quirks and less a truly vicious attack, as done by other political comedians.

The second record, the *First Family Rides Again* (1981), was a send-up of the Reagan family by noted caricaturist Rich Little, who brought back Vaughn Meader for some of the updated material. Because of its time period, the second record did not receive nearly as much attention as the first.

FLYNT, LARRY. Larry Flynt (1942–) is best known as the publisher of the popular pornographic magazine *Hustler* (as well as several others including *Barely Legal*) who challenged free speech restrictions in several famous trials in 1976. Flynt was also a crusader against political hypocrisy and, starting in 1998, offered a reward for any information on politicians having secrets. A film was made in 1996 about his various lawsuits, called *The People vs. Larry Flynt* (directed by

Milos Forman) starring Woody Harrelson as Larry Flynt and Courtney Love as his doomed wife Althea Leasure. Flynt still publishes *Hustler* at this writing, and continues on his Web site to offer rewards for politicians caught in embarrassing sexual circumstances. Most recently Flynt took credit on his Web site for the revelations about Louisiana Senator David Vitter's name appearing in the "black book" of Washington, D.C., madam Deborah Jeane Palfrey in July 2007. Flynt remains to this day a successful pornographer and an advocate for free speech as well as an opponent of the sexual hypocrisy of politicians.

FOCUS ON THE FAMILY. Focus on the Family is a religious advocacy group dedicated to monitoring the media to see if television is making family-oriented programs or programs that were not appropriate for family viewing. The group was founded in 1977 by Rev. James Dobson as a way to engage Christian voters, as well as to alert them to media depictions considered antifamily. According to liberal activist and free speech organization People for the American Way,

> Dr. Dobson is heard daily on more than 3,400 radio facilities in North America, in 15 languages, on approximately 6,300 facilities in 164 countries. Dobson's estimated listening audience is over 220 million people every day, including a program translation carried on all state-owned radio stations in the Republic of China. In the United States, Dobson appears on 80 television stations daily. (pfaw.org)

In essence, the group both encourages political participation, much in the sense that **Rock the Vote** does, only with a distinct focus on how an evangelical Christian can cope with a secular society where most pop culture is oriented away from a Christian mind-set. The group's Web site has regular updates on media, including movie, television, and music reviews and suggestions about family-friendly programming. Increasingly, politically activist groups engaged with popular culture in the last half of the twentieth century, and right wing or not, Focus on the Family provides a source of critiques that evangelicals can use to analyze current trends in media. In terms of political engagement, it is unclear how much influence Focus on the Family has on voters, but for the past several decades evangelical voters have helped in close presidential campaigns and swing states.

FONDA, JANE. Jane Fonda (1937–) is a controversial actress better known to some for her left-wing politics than her lengthy acting career. Although Fonda had been a star for some time in the 1960s, it was a provocative series of antiwar statements that she made and an ill-advised two-week tour of North Vietnam in July 1972, where she was used for propaganda purposes by the Vietnamese government, even being photographed at one point wearing a helmet and posing with applauding soldiers on an anti-aircraft gun, as well as meeting with captured POWs and accepting their assurance (under torture) that they had been treated with dignity and respect, that led to her being given the derogatory nickname "Hanoi Jane" by conservative pundits. Fonda's actions were sharply criticized by many who found it difficult to defend Fonda's actions (except under the right to free speech), but it also illustrates the great American tradition of being able to say whatever one wants to say, no matter how ill-informed.

FORD, GERALD (MEDIA PORTRAYALS). While former President Gerald Ford (1913–2006), the thirty-eighth President of the United States, may have been one of the most affable and (aside from his one huge controversial move, pardoning former president Richard Nixon) least controversial American presidents, his occasional bumbling and pratfalls led to a fertile source of parody for *Saturday Night Live*'s Chevy Chase, who played the president as unable to stand on his own for more than a few seconds without hitting his head or taking a spill. While Chase's parody was more good-natured than some presidential parodies, the real President Ford had been an athlete most of his life and even swam frequently up until his death. A comic image of Ford also appeared on the animated show *The Simpsons*, where Ford replaces former President **George H. Bush** as Homer's neighbor and finds that he and Homer have a lot in common, including their propensity for accidents and falling down.

FOX NEWS. Fox News is a cable news network started by Rupert Murdoch's News Corp on October 7, 1996, to counter what he perceived as a liberal bias in the news world. According to Murdoch and news president Roger Ailes, the new network would stand in contrast to what they perceived as the liberal bias of **CNN** and other stations, but would make sure that the news sections were deliberately nonpartisan. When the network was founded, **National Public Radio** reporter Philip Boroff interviewed news chief Roger Ailes who talked about the new station's slogan, "we report: you decide," and why it would be different from other news networks:

> Chief Roger Ailes, the former Republican political consultant, says its news will be fairer than other news outfits, which he claims usually lean to the left. Fox News features sports, show biz, politics, psychology, a family program and two hours a week on pets. But Ailes says it will have a hard news edge, a harder edge than the new **MSNBC**, from NBC and software giant Microsoft. (Ackerman, Seth. "The Most Biased Name in News." 2007. Available at http://www.fair.org/index.php?page=1067 [accessed March 18, 2008])

The new network quickly came under fire by analysts such as Fairness and Accuracy in Reporting who, since the inception of the Fox News Network, have attacked what they consider the right-wing slant of the network. According to Seth Ackerman in an article posted on the FAIR Web site:

> Since its 1996 launch, Fox has become a central hub of the conservative movement's well-oiled media machine. Together with the GOP organization and its satellite think tanks and advocacy groups, this network of fiercely partisan outlets—such as the *Washington Times*, the *Wall Street Journal* editorial page and conservative talk-radio shows like Rush Limbaugh's—forms a highly effective right-wing echo chamber where GOP-friendly news stories can be promoted, repeated and amplified. Fox knows how to play this game better than anyone. (Ackerman 2007)

While Fox may or may not have a natural conservative bias, their main commentators, such as **Sean Hannity, Bill O'Reilly,** and other guest hosts such as Dennis Miller and **Oliver North,** certainly are more right wing than other commentators on cable. The late former Fox News reporter Tony Snow had previously worked for the **George H. Bush** administration, and later went on to become press secretary for **George W. Bush**. Whether there is an overtly conservative bias to Fox News, or even a liberal bias to other news stations, has been hotly debated over the past several decades; however, media critics contend that Fox News is an overt attempt to reinforce a particular brand of ideology on a consistent basis on a televised news channel. Ailes, the mastermind behind the much criticized "Willie Horton" ads of the 1988 George H. Bush campaign (see **Furlough Commercial**) and former Nixon aide, makes no pretense of claiming a strong nonpartisan journalistic ethic. Ultimately, with ratings that consistently trounce CNN and MSNBC, Fox News has proven itself to be a success in a volatile news marketplace. This does not address the most important issue, though, of how a partisan news network should operate. While many media analysts, such as Jay Rosen and the late James Carey, have questioned the idea of journalistic objectivity and suggested that news should reposition itself to become public advocates rather than supposedly objective sources of information, it seems as though Fox is an advocate, albeit a partisan one. (For more information see Part I, Chapter 6.)

FRANKEN, AL. Al Franken (1951–) is one of the foremost comedic political commentators working from a leftist perspective, originally a comedy writer and performer who went on to run for the U.S. Senate from Minnesota in 2008. He has worked on political comedy/analysis since the early 1970s and is best known for his stints writing and performing on *Saturday Night Live*, his long-running radio show on the **Air America** network, and his books on politics. Franken originally started as a writer and performer along with collaborator Tom Davis on the first season of *Saturday Night Live* where he helped the show shape much of its cutting-edge political commentary. Franken also worked as a reporter and commentator on the show from 1985 to 1995. After his tenure on *SNL* was over, Franken became more vocal in his support of left of center political causes, and he became a prolific author. His first book, an attack on inaccuracies by **Rush Limbaugh**, titled *Rush Limbaugh Is a Big Fat Liar*, was released in 1996, the first of a series of hilarious but pointedly political polemics Franken

Comedian Al Franken on his 2007 radio show on Air America, in Minneapolis, announcing he will run for the U.S. Senate in 2008. Franken eventually won the Minnesota senate seat in July 2009 over incumbent Republican Senator Norm Coleman in a hard-fought election that went through a recount and had to be decided by the state supreme court. (AP Photo/Ann Heisenfelt, POOL)

would continue to produce for the next decade. In 2004 Franken accepted a position as a host on the newly minted leftist radio network Air America, where he quickly became one of its more popular hosts, until leaving in 2007 to run for the Senate seat of the late Paul Wellstone currently held by Republican Norm Coleman of Minnesota. Franken's astute political commentary and urge to mock the pompous makes him one of America's most fascinating satirists. After a much contested election, a recount, and lawsuits, Franken was eventually elected to the U.S. Senate. (Also see **Stand-Up Comedy and Politics.**)

FREE FORM RADIO. In the late 1960s and the 1970s, "free form" radio (also known as underground, alternative, or progressive radio) grew in popularity, largely due to recent government regulations that encouraged greater use of the FM spectrum. It appealed mainly to younger audiences, particularly those associated with the counterculture that had emerged during the social strife of the 1960s. Brought to the forefront by Tom "Big Daddy" Donahue and Larry Miller (who had started in Detroit) in San Francisco, and other pioneers, free form represents a notable moment in radio's cultural and political history. The emphasis was on long-form music, including rock songs that were mostly excluded on AM and other genres, as well as conversation, such as antiwar discourse, that opposed the dominant political views of powerful institutions. Sometimes people who were highly unlikely to have their voices heard on other venues, such as members of the **Black Panthers,** were invited to express their views. Although a variety of stations in previous decades had presaged underground radio, two of the ones most often cited as ushering in the loose format are KMPX in San Francisco (where Donahue worked) and WOR in New York. By 1968, there were over 60 such operations scattered throughout the United States. On these stations, DJs had far more independence than their AM counterparts and often experimented with programming that flowed in an eclectic or especially eccentric manner. For instance, a raucous rock song could be followed by a folk tune, and then a jazz offering. In addition, much less time was devoted to commercials. Some of the DJs, as a means of identifying with their perceived counterculture audience, subversively projected the image that they were under the influence of illegal drugs during their broadcasts. At first, national advertisers did not trust this unconventional approach to radio. So local advertisers, particularly record stores, stereo outlets, and other emblems of youth culture, picked up the slack. Still, as FM grew in popularity, in yet another manifestation of the tug-of-war between commercial and anticommercial forces, the former eventually came out on top. The free form style peaked in the mid-1970s. By then, station executives were working to diminish the format's left-wing leanings and musical heterogeneity, while retaining a rock sound that could continue to attract a youth audience with money to spend. Moving into the 1980s and 1990s, stations increasingly relied on consultants and market researchers to craft content that maximized advertising revenue. Along the way, however, FM, which had mostly sat on the shelf for years, nearly crushed its AM competition, which was ultimately forced to reassess itself.

FURLOUGH COMMERCIAL. "Furlough Commercial," also known as "Revolving Door," was the title of a commercial produced by the **George H. Bush** presidential campaign team in 1988 that attacked Bush's opponent, Michael

Dukakis, indicating his stance was too liberal toward criminals. During Dukakis's term as governor of Massachusetts, furloughs had been granted to some murderers serving life sentences, including Willie Horton, a name that would become notorious throughout the last part of the presidential election season. In April 1987, Horton had received a weekend furlough and proceeded to flee his home state, break into a home in Maryland, and then stab the man and rape the woman inside the house. The Republicans leaped at the chance to link this brutal crime with Dukakis. The commercial their party produced depicted a revolving door at a prison, with lines of frightening-looking prisoners entering and leaving the facility. As ominous music sounded in the background, an announcer stated: "His revolving door prison policy gave weekend furloughs to first-degree murderers not eligible for parole. While out, many committed other crimes like kidnapping and rape, and many are still at large." Other independent Republican groups, including Americans for Bush and the Committee for the Presidency, also produced commercials with the furlough theme, one of which highlighted the case of Willie Horton. These messages were also heavy-handedly reinforced through print and radio venues. Together, the advertisements were intended to make Dukakis seem "soft" on crime and cast doubt on his sense of values. The "Revolving Door" commercial took on a life of its own, receiving much free play on newscasts, which thus offered it greater potential to persuade. The accusation contained in the furlough spots, however, was misleading—Dukakis had not instituted the crime program himself but had inherited it from his Republican predecessor. Many political observers believe the furlough commercials played a key role in catapulting Bush to the presidency. Some scholars also contend that the spots contained racist undertones, reinforcing the stereotype of the black male threat to white safety.

G

GEORGE. *George* was a magazine founded by **John F. Kennedy Jr.** that examined political and social issues, as well as entertainment and popular culture. The magazine debuted with a picture of model Cindy Crawford dressed as George Washington in 1995 and, after some missteps, became regarded as a magazine that looked at the role of politics in everyday life in a serious, but lighthearted manner. The magazine's most prominent coup was its exclusive interview with Fidel Castro. After Kennedy's death in 1999, Frank Lalli took over, but the loss of the iconic Kennedy and the softening advertising market eventually caused the magazine to fold. *George* ceased publication in January 2001.

GET SMART. *Get Smart* was a classic 1960s secret agent parody created by Mel Brooks and Buck Henry in 1965 and starred Don Adams as bumbling secret agent Maxwell Smart. The series was a parody of the other secret agents currently in vogue during the Cold War (such as the Man from U.N.C.L.E. and **James Bond**). Smart fights against various surrealistic villains based on Bond villains and other television and movie villain stereotypes. Smart was accompanied in his quest by the beautiful (and never named) Agent 99, his exasperated boss "The Chief," and occasional helpers such as the robot Hymie (who when questioned about his name simply repeats his creators' refrain that "My Father's name was Hymie"). The show featured liberal use of gadgets such as Max's famous shoe phone (a precursor to the cell phone perhaps?) and the inexplicably useless cone of silence (which was supposed to mask any conversations but in reality made it impossible to hear anything the other person was saying). *Get Smart* was cancelled in 1970 but led to several sequels during the 1970s and 1980s, and today is regarded as not only one of the cleverest spy spoofs ever to appear on American television but also an example of how to parody the prevailing social and political climate without seeming heavy-handed. A movie version starring Steve Carell that bore little resemblance to the original show came and went quickly when it was released in 2008.

THE GOLDWATERS. One of the stranger instances of political folk music was a 1964 pro–Barry Goldwater group, named for the then Republican candidate for president. The Goldwaters, who wore matching AuH2O T-shirts (Au is the elemental symbol for gold, and H2O for water), released a record called *The Goldwaters Sing Folk Songs to Bug the Liberals* (1964). The Goldwaters were created by two brothers, Mark and Buford Bates, and consisted of Fred Quan on banjo, Bob Green on guitar and vocals, Jim Vantrease on bass, and Ken Crook on lead vocals. The group played folks songs in favor of Goldwater's candidacy for president, a rare example of a right-wing folk group when most folk music espoused liberal causes. The band (minus Vantrease, the bass player) went on tour with Barry Goldwater on many campaign stops and played numerous rallies, including several with the "Goldwater girls" (Goldwater cheerleaders who dressed as cowgirls) and other motivational speakers, including at one rally **Ronald Reagan**. The band dissolved after Goldwater lost in a landslide in the 1964 presidential election, and as recently reported on the CONELRAD Web site have no plans to re-form. The back of the record humorously informs the listener:

> CONSERVATIVES UNITE! Bug the liberals . . . Give this beautiful, multi color long play album to one of your liberal "friends." Pokes fun at the foibles of the Left Wingers. Cuba, Bobby, the Other Bobby, Stereos, The Doll House, Gold Reserve, Welfare State, Foreign Aid, National Debt, Managed News, Pinkos, A.D.A., Harvard, C.I.A. . . . ad infinitum. It's all in the groove designed to keep you chuckling for hours.
>
> An Ideal Gift. Order several . . . Help spread the Conservative message . . . No doubt, you will convert a liberal! (Conelrad. "The Goldwater Who Came in from the Cold: The Exclusive Conelrad Interview." Conelrad.com: Cold War Music from the Golden Age of Homeland Security. Available at http://www.conelrad.com/media/atomicmusic/sh_boom.php?platter=25 [accessed July 25, 2007].)

GORE, AL. Former vice president of the United States (1993–2001) and presidential contender (2000), Al Gore (1948–) is also known as one of the most visible political figures in the United States and a strong proponent of environmental change and global warming awareness. Although Gore was often derided as being stiff and wooden while campaigning (he was notoriously mocked on *Saturday Night Live* as a wooden debater, constantly referring to how he would put the economy in a "lock box"), he was later able to mock his image with appearances on *Saturday Night Live*, as well as in the cartoon science fiction show *Futurama* (his daughter was a writer for the program at the time). Gore is perhaps best known today for his 2006 documentary *An Inconvenient Truth* warning about the perils of global warming. The movie went on to make respectable money at the box office, won an Academy Award in 2006, and transformed Gore into a pop culture icon and certainly one of the best-known former vice presidents in history. Gore has also had much success in his postgovernment career and has been able to mock his formerly stiff image, including a recent appearance on *Saturday Night Live* where he refused to leave the set of *The West Wing*.

GRAHAM, BILLY. Billy Graham (1918–) has been one of the most influential clergymen in America from his start in the 1940s to the present day. Graham, a Southern Baptist Evangelical, has acted as a spiritual adviser and mentor to presidents since Dwight Eisenhower, and his massive crusades—including stadium-filling ones beginning in the 1950s—have made him a major political force in American political and civic life. His reputation has been mostly for fairness and a concern with spirituality and taking control of one's life (he counseled **George W. Bush** when the future president was struggling with alcoholism, and was also an advisor to Johnny Cash for most of the singer's life). Graham was also one of the first television ministers who used the budding medium to circulate his sermons amongst a larger audience. Although Graham has presented himself as a centrist and populist preacher who made fundamentalist Christianity less harsh and more open to other denominations, Graham was enveloped in some controversy over the years. He was an early supporter of **Senator Joseph McCarthy**'s crusade against communists both real and imaginary, and he was also known for some ill-advised comments over the years, especially when tapes were leaked of Graham and Nixon talking where Graham made several critical comments that bordered on the anti-Semitic. Graham has also been criticized by many who feel that his (presumed) influence at the White House is a threat to the separation of church and state.

Overall Graham has been a powerful conduit between the presidency and spirituality, and his influence in the White House as well as through his revival meetings, public ministry, and television specials has been immense. He has demonstrated the force and influence of religion in American political life and also showed that many presidents, even if less than pious in real life, often consider it to be politically advisable to be seen with Billy Graham as a sign that they support not his political views, but the power of religion in American political and social life. His influence will be felt years after his death, because, as Harold Bloom wrote in his profile of the influential reverend in a *Time* magazine article, "He is an icon essential to a country in which, for two centuries now, religion has been not the opiate but the poetry of the people" (Bloom, Harold. "Heroes and Icons: Billy Graham." http://www.time.com/time/time100/heroes/profile/graham01 [accessed July 25, 2007]).

GREENWALD, ROBERT. Known for most of his career for his work on fictional, entertainment films, director Robert Greenwald (1945–) has shifted his attention to creating documentaries with a highly political slant. In 2003, he directed *Uncovered: The Whole Truth about the Iraq War*. Greenwald's funding and distribution tactics represent a fresh development in political activism through film. For instance, Greenwald has received financial support from the left-leaning Internet advocacy group, **MoveOn.org**. Not only has it facilitated production, but MoveOn has also sponsored "house parties" as a means of putting Greenwald's documentaries before the public. Through its Internet operation, the organization invites members to host or attend gatherings devoted to screening a film, and helps coordinate the events. Rather than rely on initial showings in theaters, then, Greenwald has generated a following through these informal encounters and online DVD sales, which, in turn, have led to actual theatrical exhibition. His production methods seem to emphasize pragmatic concern with making an argument over stylistic flair. Accordingly, the accent is on getting a message out quickly instead of striving for artistic appeal.

Apparently, the election of **George W. Bush** had triggered an impulse in Greenwald to quickly make and release political films. Just a year before *Uncovered*, the filmmaker had teamed with Earl Katz to produce Joan Sekler and Richard Ray Perez's

Unprecedented: The 2000 Presidential Election, which argues that the Bush campaign employed unscrupulous measures to achieve victory in an election that Bush's challenger, then Vice President **Al Gore**, had actually won.

Uncovered is a venomous rebuke of President Bush and a dismantling of his reasons for going to war in Iraq. It features numerous on-camera appearances by government insiders who debunk the claim that the war on Iraq was initiated because it supposedly possessed weapons of mass destruction. Shortly after releasing *Uncovered*, Greenwald went to work on *Outfoxed*, a documentary that asserts the **Fox News** Network is a shrill for the Republican Party. Soon, Greenwald produced another film in what appears to be an anti-Bush series. *Unconstitutional: The War on Our Civil Liberties* takes the president to account for impinging upon the freedom of U.S. citizens in his administration's execution of the "war on terror." The documentary points out how Islamic immigrants were rounded up and imprisoned without charge, and explores the abuses committed by U.S. soldiers at the Abu Ghraib prison in Iraq.

GUTHRIE, WOODY. Woody (Woodrow Wilson) Guthrie (1912–1967) was perhaps the most influential and important American folk and protest song singer of the twentieth century. His songs (especially the highly politicized "This Land Is Your Land") have become staples at left-wing protests and his music directly influenced the protest movement of the 1960s, as well as the career of his most famous disciple **Bob Dylan** (Robert Zimmerman), who was inspired by Guthrie to become a folk and protest song singer.

Guthrie, after traveling around the country and performing with various other musicians including Matt Jennings and Cluster Baker in the Corncob Trio (Guthrie also married Jennings's sister Mary Esta Jennings in 1934), first started writing his own music circa 1932, and by 1935 he had become a prolific songwriter. In 1935 Guthrie was particularly inspired by a natural disaster of epic proportions, a vicious dust storm in Pampa, Texas, that inspired one of his most famous songs, "So Long, It's Been Good to Know Yuh" (aka "Dusty Old Dust"), which demonstrated Guthrie's increasing comfort with writing topical songs about the poor and downtrodden. Guthrie increasingly became influenced by communism and in 1939 began to write a column for the *People's World*, "Woody Sez" in 1939. By 1940, Guthrie, inspired by hearing "God Bless America" one time too often, wrote his most famous song, originally titled "God Blessed America," which later became known as "This Land Is Your Land," as a populist/socialist response to what he saw as the jingoism of American patriotic songs. Although Guthrie wrote it early in his career, it was not recorded until several years later thanks to World War II. The lyrics, which call for an America without borders or "no trespass" signs, are among the best known of all American folks songs, despite their relative and beautiful simplicity.

Guthrie's career was further boosted by the help of musicologist and field recorder Alan Lomax, who recorded archival material by Guthrie including songs and stories, provided airtime on his radio program *Columbia School of the Air*, and later arranged for further recording sessions to disseminate Guthrie's music on a wider basis.

Guthrie is best known for two collections of songs recorded in 1940 called *Dust Bowl Ballads Vols. 1 and 2*, released originally on several 78 rpm records. The dust bowl ballads are some of the most evocative American folk songs ever written about the plight of poor farmers trying to make ends meet when nature itself has conspired against them. After the relative failure of the *Dust Bowl Ballads* records, Guthrie moved around the country several times, eventually dropping his communist party column over issues of orthodoxy, and moved in with Pete Seeger and the Almanac Singers communal house, where he played with the embryonic **Weavers** lineup and recorded several albums with the Almanac Singers. After Germany declared war on Russia, Seeger, Guthrie, and the others somewhat hypocritically shifted from an antiwar to a pro-war stance and Guthrie, after being divorced by his wife, Mary, had to join the Merchant Marines where he served for several years, before briefly serving in the army toward the end of the war.

After the war Guthrie recorded prolifically with other singers such as Leadbelly until a hereditary degenerative disease, Huntington's disease, curtailed his performances and recordings in the early 1950s. Guthrie lingered on till 1967 when he died in Creedmoor State Hospital in Queens, New York. Ironically, Guthrie's career took off after his incapacity, with numerous of his songs becoming popular standards in the folk revival of the mid-1950s and with both the Weavers and the Kingston Trio having major hits with Guthrie compositions. Guthrie was also a major influence on Bob Dylan, who journeyed to meet Guthrie in the hospital in December 1960 and on numerous occasions afterwards.

Guthrie's music remains some of the more successful and populist protest songs of the twentieth century, and his influence on the folk revivals and politicization of that genre in the 1950s and 1960s is immeasurable. Today grade schools across America include Guthrie songs as part of the curriculum, and his best-known song, "This Land Is Your Land," is sung (albeit with several of the verses omitted for their attacks on capitalism) by numerous Americans on patriotic occasions. Guthrie was a walking contradiction, a rambling folk singer who more or less abandoned his family while singing songs about the common man, and who decried the oppression of landlords and bankers while ignoring the genocide in the Soviet Union. Guthrie's legacy is incalculable and his songs served to both politicize numerous Americans and to evocatively capture the plight of the working poor, especially during the time of the Great Depression.

Guthrie's legacy also includes his most well-known son, singer Arlo Guthrie, author of the popular song "Alice's Restaurant" among many others, and Guthrie's music has been recorded by thousands of other artists in genres from punk to folk. Unpublished lyrics from Guthrie were later recorded in two volumes by folk/punk singer Billy Bragg with indie band Wilco in 1998 and 2000, called *Mermaid Avenue* and *Mermaid Avenue Volume II*.

H

HANNITY, SEAN. Sean Hannity (1961–) is a longtime conservative television and radio commentator and one of the key conservative commentators today, along with **Rush Limbaugh** and **Bill O'Reilly**. He currently hosts the hour-long *Hannity* show on the **Fox News** channel Monday through Friday evenings, as well as *The Sean Hannity Show* on radio WABC, which is syndicated to over 500 stations across the country. Hannity started in radio at the University of California Santa Barbara in 1989 and worked in Alabama and then Atlanta before Roger Ailes of Fox News noticed him and put him together with Alan Colmes, launching his television career.

Before his current television program, Hannity hosted the popular *Hannity and Colmes* show with liberal co-host Alan Colmes from 1996 to 2008 where their frequent fights with guests and themselves proved to be a powerful ratings draw, putting them at over 2.8 million viewers, the second highest in cable news talk shows. Hannity is also the author of two books, *Let Freedom Ring* and *Deliver Us from Evil*.

Hannity has been criticized by some, not only for his conservative views but about his tendency to shout at and sometimes drown out his guests. Critics believe that Hannity's style, where debates often turn personal and sometimes never get further than cursory dismissals of other people's opinions, is typical in today's television discourse. Hannity has also come under fire for using Colmes during their long tenure together as a straw man for various arguments. In his new show, Hannity, loved by many and questioned by many, is among the most popular and influential cable-television political hosts today.

HARVEST OF SHAME. Airing on Thanksgiving Day in 1960, *Harvest of Shame* brought to public attention the plight of migrant farm workers in the United States. Although it is widely cited as one of television's classic documentaries, *Harvest of Shame* was **Edward R. Murrow**'s swan song with *CBS Reports*. Murrow had earlier anchored *See It Now*, which, probably in large part due to the controversy it generated, was eventually replaced by *CBS Reports*. Murrow's role in the new show was diminished although he was allowed to anchor the *Harvest of Shame* segment. Following the broadcast, Murrow left *CBS Reports* and became director of the U.S. Information Agency under the **John F. Kennedy** administration.

HEARST, PATTY. Patricia Hearst (1954–) was a member of the powerful Hearst family (newspaper publishing) who caused a national media sensation when she was kidnapped by the Symbionese Liberation Army (SLA) on February 4, 1974, and even more shockingly when she reappeared several months later as a member of the SLA now calling herself "Tania" while robbing the Hibernia Bank in San Francisco. After many of the gang members had been killed in a police raid, Hearst went underground with two members, Emily and William Harris, before being captured in September 1975. The subsequent trial was a media circus, and Hearst's attorney, noted lawyer F. Lee Bailey, helped to spur on media coverage. Hearst gave a confusing and often rambling performance that helped the prosecution more than the defense, was convicted and sentenced to 35 years in prison, but her sentence was commuted by President **Jimmy Carter** in 1979, and she later gained a full pardon from President **Bill Clinton** in 2001. Today Hearst has appeared in several films and television shows, most notably in several films by schlock master John Waters.

The kidnapping was later parodied in the film *Network* where the Hearst character, Mary Anne Gifford, becomes part of a televised reality show about a revolutionary cell in America. At one point while arguing about the contracts for the program, Gifford shrieks, "You fucking fascist! Did you see the film we made of the San Marino jail breakout, demonstrating the rising up of the seminal prisoner class infrastructure?" to which the character Lorraine Hobbes (based on Angela Davis) shouts, "You can blow the seminal prisoner class infrastructure out your ass! I'm not knockin' down my goddamn distribution charges!"

For a while the Hearst case was a huge media draw in America and could be seen either as an example of the revolutionary impulse left over from the late 1960s or as an example of how human psychology could be affected by what could be called the "Stockholm Syndrome" (a hostage feeling sympathy for his/

Neverland: The Rise and Fall of the Symbionese Liberation Army (2005). Also known as *Guerrilla: The Taking of Patty Hearst*. Directed by Robert Stone. Shown: Patty Hearst (when she was known as Tania). (Magnolia Pictures/Photofest)

her captors). The Hearst case was one of the key events that helped transition American political movements from their fiery heyday in the 1960s to the transitional period of the 1970s. The Patty Hearst trial was also a media circus, akin to the O. J. Simpson trail in the 1990s, with attendant political issues of class and gender thrown in for good measure.

HILL, JOE (JOSEPH HILLSTOM, HJOE HAGGLUND). Joe Hill (1879–1915) was a Swedish immigrant, folksinger, member of the International Workers of the world (the **Wobblies**), and radical activist. Hill was executed by the state of Utah in 1915 for a murder after being convicted under circumstantial evidence and despite public outcry and an attempted intervention by President Woodrow Wilson. It is asserted by some that the execution was politically motivated and that Hill was not involved in the murder. Hill emigrated from Sweden in 1902 and became an activist after observing subpar living and working conditions on the Lower East Side of New York City. Hill joined the Wobblies in 1910 and wrote numerous folk songs about labor and working conditions, such as his most famous composition, "Casey Jones" (later parodied by the Grateful Dead). Hill's songs quickly grew popular with the labor movement and were collected in the Wobblies' *Little Red Songbook*. Jones was arrested for the murder of John Morrison, a store owner, although Hill's supporters blamed his conviction on a sinister plot by the "Copper Bosses" of Utah. Hill was influential on the left and greatly influenced the folk traditions from the 1940s onwards. The song "I Dreamed I Saw Joe Hill Last Night" has been covered by many artists including Paul Robeson, Pete Seeger, the Dubliners, and Joan Baez. **Bob Dylan** has particularly cited Hill as an influence on his work.

HIP-HOP SUMMIT ACTION NETWORK. Hip-Hop Summit Action Network is the hip-hop-oriented social activist group founded in 2001 and dedicated to promoting positive values, lobbying for voter rights, and agitating for reparations for slavery. According to the group's Web site, the members also "want advocacy of public policies that are in the interests of hip-hop before Congress, state legislatures, municipal governments, the media and the entertainment industry." Although the Web site is somewhat vague as to what kind of public politics are in the interest of hip-hop, the group does advocate for positive social change, as well as the repeals of "three strike laws" and the restoration of voting rights to convicted felons released from prison. The summit's board of directors includes hip-hop mogul Russell Simmons, founder of Def Jam records, as well as Dr. Benjamin Chavis, former head of the NAACP, and music industry heavyweights such as Sean P. Diddy Combs, Damon Dash, and Lyor Cohen. The Hip-Hop Summit Action Network demonstrates an increasing use of musical groups to lobby for social change and voter registration, as seen in other groups such as **Rock the Vote** and punkvoter.com. The Hip-Hop Summit Action Network goes beyond the goals of those organizations though, with more specific goals and issues of concern to the African American community being in the forefront of the group's advocacy positions.

HOPE, BOB. A popular comedian whose career spanned decades, Bob Hope (1903–2003) first attained celebrity status through the radio, eventually becoming the star of his own program.

In 1942, Hope took up a mission to entertain U.S. troops during times of military conflict. His live performances at army and naval bases sometimes served as episodes of his radio show. Later, when Hope made the successful transition to television, he continued his tradition of amusing U.S. military personnel. In particular, in the 1960s, he regularly gathered a group of other entertainers and traveled to Vietnam to stage shows. Some of his appearances were filmed and televised back home. These Bob Hope specials provided symbolic backing for the war effort, which, by the late 1960s, had become a contentious issue. As protests against the conflict became increasingly common, Hope's telecasts from Vietnam offered a different perspective that humanized and supported the troops.

Throughout his storied career, Bob Hope demonstrated sympathy toward government officials. For example, he played golf with presidents and presided as master of ceremonies at award ceremonies. In the late 1960s, when Vice President Spiro Agnew launched a protest against television because of its supposed liberal bias, Hope commissioned his writing team to devise jokes that Agnew could incorporate into his speeches. Although most of Hope's work centered on gags and light-hearted diversion, nonetheless, his entertaining broadcasts and other activities are notable for the political implications they sometimes conveyed.

HUFFINGTON POST. The *Huffington Post*, a left-leaning news **blog**, was started in 2005 by Arianna Huffington (1950–) and two other co-founders. In part, it was developed to serve as a counterpoint to the mostly conservative **Drudge Report**. A contradictory character herself, Huffington is a nationally syndicated columnist, book author, frequent guest on television talk and news shows, political activist, and renowned socialite. Formerly strongly aligned with the right wing (at one time, she was married to Republican millionaire Michael Huffington, who won a seat in the House of Representatives in 1992), she went through a conversion of sorts and today considers herself a political progressive. In 2003, she made a brief attempt to enter public office, running for governor of California. She was never a serious contender, however, and soon dropped out of the contest.

Doubted by many that it would ever survive when it was launched, the *Huffington Post* is now consistently rated as one of the most popular or powerful blogs in the nation—or even the world (it has held the top spot on some lists). The site features regular posts by Huffington, as well as a core group of routine contributors. Yet literally dozens of other personalities—comprising a wide range on the spectrum of fame—chime in from time to time. Writers hail from the worlds of politics, journalism, business, and entertainment, thus making the *Huffington Post* an exemplar in its blending of politics, media, and popular culture. Indeed, one of the aspects that separates it from other prominent political blogs is its emphasis on the power of celebrity. Huffington, herself, has the reputation of tirelessly recruiting would-be bloggers from her vast social network of well-known figures.

The *Huffington Post* provides many links to already existing news stories yet sometimes offers scoops of its own. Although, overall, the site advances liberal positions, because of the sheer quantity of its contributors—including members of the public who interact with the writers—it conveys an array of opinions. In 2006, and again in 2008, it received the "Webby Award" for Best Political Blog. Shortly after she introduced her Web site, Huffington was included in *Time* magazine's 2006 list of "100 most influential people." Still, the *Huffington Post* is not free of detractors, particularly from the conservative ranks of the punditry. (See Part I, Chapter 8, "Politics Online.")

I

IMUS, DON. Don Imus (1940–) began his radio career in 1968 in Palmdale, California. Eventually, he developed his persona as a "shock jock," a designation that refers to a talk radio host who emphasizes controversial and often crude humor that is sometimes perceived as racist or sexist. Quickly acquiring a reputation for being cantankerous, Imus later took on a more libertarian political bent beginning in the late 1980s on his show *Imus in the Morning*, which had been launched in New York in 1971.

Over the years, politicians and pundits have regularly appeared on his show. For example, during his run for office in 1992, **Bill Clinton** was interviewed on *Imus in the Morning* and temporarily endeared himself to the host, even though Imus had previously consistently derided the candidate. Yet Imus is also recognized for his tendency to make remarks about women and minority groups that many people find offensive. He has frequently been accused of rendering a juvenile persona, with a noticeable portion of his former show's standard fare consisting not only of serious political exchange, but scatological humor, and derogatory remarks toward homosexuals, women, and people of color as well. This pattern backfired in 2007, when Imus referred to the Rutgers University women's basketball team, the runner-up in the 2007 NCAA basketball tournament, as "nappy-headed hoes" (Steinberg, Jacques. "Imus Struggling to Retain Sway as a Franchise." *New York Times*, April 11, 2007), a comment that sparked countless news reports and debates about its appropriateness and soon contributed to his dismissal at both CBS radio and **MSNBC**, which had been simulcasting his program on television. Yet as of this writing, Imus is making a comeback. He returned to broadcasting, this time with ABC-Radio, on December 3, 2007.

AN INCONVENIENT TRUTH. Starring former vice president and 2000 presidential candidate **Al Gore**, *An Inconvenient Truth* (2006) explores the scientific evidence in support of human-generated global warming, its potential consequences, and what can be done to alleviate catastrophe.

Shortly before being elected as U.S. vice president in 1992, Al Gore established his keen interest in the environment with the release of his book, *Earth in the Balance: Ecology and the Human Spirit* (1992). Yet the two terms he served with President **Bill Clinton** in office were not particularly notable for any groundbreaking environmental policies. After failing in his bid for the presidency in 2000, however, Gore returned to the cause, becoming probably the world's most famous advocate for instituting wholesale measures to reduce the threat of climate change. He produced a slide show on the topic, which, over the years, he presented to hundreds of audiences around the world. Later, Davis Guggenheim, after seeing Gore's work, wanted to direct a film on the issue and decided to actually make the slide show presentation the central feature of the documentary. Yet the movie also follows Gore on his travels to educate the public about the urgency of the possible crisis, and includes biographical scenes of the politician that focus on the events and experiences that contributed to his evolving worldview and convictions about global warming.

A companion book, *An Inconvenient Truth: The Planetary Emergency of Global Warming and What We Can Do about It*, was also released about the time the film debuted in popular theaters and eventually topped the *New York Times* nonfiction best-seller list.

The movie is notable for the popularity it enjoyed, a rare achievement for a nonfiction film. It became the fourth largest grossing documentary in U.S. box office history, and won an array of awards, including an Academy Award for best documentary and another one for best original song. But perhaps more importantly, it brought the severity of the earth's changing climate to public attention. Though the movie was not without its critics and detractors who challenged some of Gore's facts and assumptions, nonetheless, probably to a greater extent than any other media vehicle, it at least stirred politicians and everyday citizens alike to debate how the earth's population should respond to the scientific community's dominant view on global warming.

Further making its mark on popular culture, *An Inconvenient Truth* and its main performer were parodied on an episode of *South Park* and in *The Simpsons Movie* (2007). Elsewhere, in an episode of the animated TV show *The Replacements*, a main character uttered a play on the title of the documentary in reaction to a villain who was planning to melt Antarctica. An installment of the TV program *Scrubs* also brought the film to mind through its title ("My Inconvenient Truth") and when a character known as The Janitor resolved to be more environmentally friendly after screening the documentary. Taking a different angle, in an edition of *The Colbert Report*, Steve Colbert poked fun at critics of the movie with an ironic presentation that illustrated the positive effects of global warming. These and other references to the film likely generated even more awareness of the dangers associated with a rise in temperature of the earth's climate.

"IN DER FURHER'S FACE." During World War II there were numerous patriotic songs designed to keep people enthusiastic and patriotic during the difficult rationing and unease during wartime. One of the most popular and silliest songs to advocate fighting against the Nazis was this song from 1942 by legendary comic bandleader Spike Jones (Lindley Armstrong Jones) and His City Slickers, entitled "In Der Furher's Face." The song, a pleasant novelty song in the vein of Jones's earlier hits became popular as public sentiment increasingly turned toward comedic patriotism.

Sample lyrics from the song include the lines "When der furher Says, 'Ve ist der master race!' We Heil (raspberry noise) Heil! (Raspberry noise) right in the Furher's face!" Jones, who had a long and prolific career writing novelty songs that often parodied popular songs of the day, created a truly inventive and humorous song that poked fun at the smug superiority of the Nazi war machine. Jones also created other "hits" such as "Cocktails for Two" and "My Old Flame" before the end of the big band movement signaled the end of his most prolific period, although Jones continued to write, drum, and arrange songs until his death from lung cancer in 1965.

IRAN HOSTAGE CRISIS. The central feature of this upheaval, an outgrowth of the Iranian Revolution of 1979, was the overthrow of the U.S.-backed Shah of Iran, Mohammad Reza Pahlavi, and the installation of the Ayatollah Khomeini, who wished to create a religious state rigorously faithful to the teachings of the Koran. Shortly after the coup, on November 4, 1979, a group of students loyal to Khomeini stormed the U.S. embassy in Tehran, Iran, and took over 50 Americans as hostages. Most of them were not released until 444 days later, just after the U.S. presidential election of 1980 had been decided. Network television provided daily coverage of the hostage crisis until it finally came to a close. Indeed, the news show *Nightline* was born just four days after the embassy was seized. Its original title was *The Iran Crisis—America Held Hostage: Day* ___ (the blank did not appear in the title but was filled in with how many days the country was into the crisis since the hostages were first taken). An announcer at the top of the program reinforced the words on the screen. (*Nightline* has continued until the present, although the program's future has been in jeopardy from time to time.) On CBS, **Walter Cronkite** ended each nightly newscast with the same day count as well.

Meanwhile, as the country waited with baited breath, the coverage of the hostage crisis was not merely confined to nightly news and newspaper accounts—it became a type of pop culture event as well. The cartoon strip *Doonesbury* regularly gave updates on the condition of "Uncle Duke," a Doonesbury character that had fictitiously been taken hostage. In one sequence, its creator, Garry Trudeau, depicted the Reverend Scott Sloan visiting Tehran in an attempt to talk to the hostages. The hostage crisis was also the source of numerous editorial cartoons urging action or decrying American inaction.

At one point, President **Jimmy Carter** initiated a rescue mission that failed. The hostage crisis, combined with the botched intervention, probably contributed to President Jimmy Carter's generally poor reputation with the populace and might have been a factor in his reelection defeat by **Ronald Reagan**.

When the hostages were released on the day of Ronald Reagan's inauguration, in January 1981, many suspected that some kind of hidden deal had been made. While this was denied at the time, it was later shown that indeed, such a transaction had been struck, with the United States unfreezing $8 billion in Iranian assets and indemnifying the country from lawsuits by former American hostages (also see **Political Scandals**). The importance of the Iranian hostage crisis on the 1980 presidential election, as well as the psyche of the American populace, was formidable. The continuous television coverage that reported on the hostage crisis kept Americans simultaneously engaged and frustrated throughout the duration of the situation.

IRAQ MOVIES (FICTION). Despite the fact that the United States has been engaged in a protracted conflict with Iraq since 2002, there have been relatively few movies made about Iraq and even fewer that have been successful. The most successful film made about Iraq was not even obliquely about the current war in Iraq: the film *Three Kings* (1999) predated the war by four years. The film's star George Clooney later did star in a film about the tensions created by the U.S. presence in the Middle East in the film *Syriana* in 2005. What is notable about many films about the conflict in Iraq is how spectacularly unsuccessful they have been at the box office. Films such as *In the Valley of Elah* (2007); *Home of the Brave* (2006); the Mariane Pearl memoir *A Mighty Heart* (2007); *Rendition* (2007); *The Kingdom* (2007; set in Saudi Arabia, but clearly meant to evoke Iraq); *Lions for Lambs* (2007); *The Kite Runner* (2007; set in Afghanistan, the less talked about war); *Redacted* (2007); and *Grace Is Gone* (2007) all attempted to seriously deal with various aspects of the conflict; however, the films' lack of success at the box office could indicate several different factors at play. It could be that the public is not yet ready for a film that analyzes the conflict seriously. In a time of a seemingly never-ending war, it could be that the public does not want to deal with cinematic representations of the war. Much like the Vietnam War, where representations of the war were only really shown after the end of the conflict (see **Vietnam War Movies [Fiction]**), it might well be that the time is simply not right. Other factors, such as a the fact that the War in Iraq is far more controversial than other wars such as World War II could be a major factor, as could the absence of direct government film-based propaganda as seen during World War I and World War II (see **World War Propaganda**). Either way, like films about Vietnam, the Iraq conflict may need to be distanced from the present before successful films can be made about the conflict.

I SPY. *I SPY* was a 1960s political spy television action series featuring Robert Culp as tennis player Kelly Robinson and comedian Bill Cosby as Alexander Scott, his tennis trainer, who travel the world fighting Soviet agents and others during the Cold War. Running from 1965 to 1968, the program was the first American program to have an African American actor playing one of the leads. While the show was fairly lighthearted, it was also one of the many spy programs popular during the 1960s that dramatized the espionage war between the Soviet Union and America during that time period. The program spawned numerous books and comic book tie-ins as well as a reunion movie in 1994.

J

JOHNSON, LYNDON BAINES (MEDIA PORTRAYALS). Lyndon Johnson (1908–1973) was the president of the United States from 1963 to 1969 following the assassination of President **John F. Kennedy**. Johnson was a polarizing figure, and many editorial cartoonists found him easy fodder for their caricatures. Herblock in particular found LBJ as a potentially polarizing figure, at one point even characterizing him as a Caesar figure, stunned by the duplicity of his aids. In addition, LBJ, as he was frequently called, was also referenced in the musical *Hair* in the song "L.B.J." that had the then president taking the IRT to 4th Street and seeing "the youth of America on LSD." LBJ was also caricatured in the satirical *Macbeth* revision *MacBird*.

K

KENNEDY, JOHN F. (MEDIA PORTRAYALS). Despite the good will engendered during the first years of the Kennedy administration, John F. Kennedy (1917–1963), America's thirty-fifth president, was not overly mocked as his womanizing was largely unknown to the American public at the time, and television did not at that point overtly satirize American presidents. Kennedy was satirized in a series of albums, *The First Family* records by comedian and impressionist Vaughn Meader, who essentially saw his career end after the Kennedy assassination. Later Kennedy was the subject of numerous television and movie portrayals, and his assassination film by Abraham Zapruder is probably one of the most viewed clips in American history. Kennedy also appeared in several superhero comic books including *Action Comics #285* and *Superman #170* (also see **Comic Books**). In the comics world, Kennedy was a friend of Superman and appeared in several issues of Action Comics. In one issue Kennedy is even called on to play Clark Kent so that Clark and Superman can appear in the same place at the same time, and he is later shown talking to Superman who thanks the president, asking, "if you can't trust the president of the United States, who can you trust?" Later treatments were not nearly as reverant in the Vertigo (a DC imprint) comic *Hellblazer*, where the former president walks across America holding in his head wound and speaking in political platitudes.

KENNEDY, JOHN F., JR. John F. Kennedy's son John F. Kennedy Jr. (1960–1999) had long been in the public eye from his birth in 1960 to the iconic photo of a three-year-old JFK Jr. saluting his father's coffin. Later in life, Kennedy became famous for his ubiquity in tabloids and gossip columns where he became a celebrity due to his stunning profile and his association with the mythology of the Kennedys. Much tabloid space was devoted to the mundanity of his life, his workout routine, his romantic dalliances, his attempts to become a lawyer (when he did not pass the bar after a second try, the *New York Post* reported the story with the headline "Hunk Flunks"). After settling down in his personal life after a marriage to Carolyn Bissette, Kennedy then started a magazine devoted to the intersection of politics and civic life in America called *George*. *George* was initially critically acclaimed, and it seemed as though Kennedy had finally found a niche for himself in the realm of public service so often associated with the Kennedys, but his life was cut short in a plane crash on July 16, 1999. John F. Kennedy Jr. was a rare American political figure not overtly involved in politics except as a social activist. Although Kennedy was part of one of the most prominent American political families, it is unclear if he would have entered politics, although what is clear is the role he played in the American popular imagination for his almost 40 years in the public eye.

KENNEDY-NIXON DEBATES. The presidential debates between then Republican Vice President **Richard Nixon** and Democratic contender **John F. Kennedy** in 1960 were a remarkable encounter that prefigured how television would become a dominant way of presenting information to American audiences. While there had been a long history of public debates in the United States, the Kennedy-Nixon contest was the initial one to be widely televised and, according to media scholar Marshall McLuhan (*Understanding Media: The Extensions of Man*. New York: Signet Books, 1964), represented the first time television had a major impact on the way citizens obtained and processed material on current affairs.

The Kennedy-Nixon debates are often pointed to as the most significant political communication event of the 1960 presidential campaign. The confrontations were staged, in part, to actually control advertising costs, since the networks were willing to donate time to the debates. But they could not have come about if the guideline in the Communications Act of 1934 that specified networks must provide equal time to all candidates had not been temporarily suspended, which allowed a two-person debate to occur, excluding smaller-party candidates.

The most heavily rated of the four debates was the first. In it, Nixon did not convey a visually appealing image—he looked exhausted, pasty, and not clean shaven. Kennedy, naturally handsome, projected a healthy energy. Interestingly, McLuhan (*Understanding Media: The Extensions of Man*. New York: Signet Books, 1964) suggested that television indirectly influenced not only the way in which audiences perceived the candidates visually but also how they received their messages. Although Nixon had carefully rebutted Kennedy's points and might have been the more skillful rhetorician, those who watched the debate on television, McLuhan explained, had thought that Kennedy had made the more compelling case and had won the debates. Conversely, those who listened to the debate on radio "received an overwhelming idea of Nixon's superiority" (261). This different perception by medium manifested the command that television could have over an election and how it could alter the rules by which campaigns would be fought. The power of the televised image suggested that a candidate's appearance could trump the content of his or her message in determining who takes office, a possibility that disturbed many scholars and other observers. Historian Daniel Boorstin argued in his book *The Image: A Guide to Pseudo-Events in America* (New York: Atheneum, 1975) that television had led to a new way of understanding both media and politics. The author noted that starting with the presidential debates of 1960, many supporters of Nixon came out "because they wanted to be seen on the television cameras" (28). Meanwhile, it was about this time that McLuhan coined the phrase, "the medium is the message," indicating that the medium through which a message is delivered shapes the meaning of the message more than the content itself. To Nixon, who had previously used television to his advantage in the famous **Checkers speech,** this would become a warning to keep in mind when he ran again in 1968 (for an example of how Nixon changed his tactics, see Joe McGinniss's classic, *The Selling of the President*). Ever since the Kennedy-Nixon debates, other politicians have also reasoned that visual presentation is more important than the content of a speech and have adjusted their campaigns accordingly. Yet the truth of McLuhan's contention continues to be widely argued over even today.

KENT STATE UNIVERSITY SHOOTINGS. At Kent State University on May 4, 1970, National Guard soldiers opened fire on student demonstrators after being unable to disperse a crowd of unruly students, killing four (including some who were not demonstrating) and wounding nine others. The event polarized America at the time, with many in the protest movement charging that the firing had been done deliberately and not simply out of panic by National Guardsmen with no experience in crowd control.

Shortly after the killings, Neil Young quickly wrote a song in response to the killing and recorded it with Crosby, Stills, Nash, and Young to get the song out while the killings were still topical. The resulting song is what many consider to be one of the best protest songs of the 1960s. "Ohio" was released in June 1970 and eventually climbed to No. 1 on the rock charts. The incident became a focal point for student protests against the war and the Nixon administration, helped mobilize a voter base, helped politicize a new generation of students, as well as continued the American tradition of protest songs written to commemorate tragic occurrences.

KISSING BABIES (AS SYMBOL). One of the great American campaign traditions is for candidates to kiss small babies given to them by members of the public. Although it has become increasingly more difficult for presidential candidates to engage in this ritual, it is still a staple of small-town campaigns and at best helps to humanize the candidate in front of an appreciative audience; at its worst it makes the inept or awkward candidate look unelectable.

KOS (MARKOS MOULITSAS ZÚNIGA). See Part I, Chapter 8, "Politics Online," and *Daily Kos*.

L

LEFT BEHIND. Popular series of novels by Tim LaHaye and Jerry Jenkins about a world after the rapture where half the living have been assumed bodily into heaven, and those who are left behind have to try and deal with the coming of the anti-Christ. The enormous popularity of the novels demonstrated the appeal of books to the Christian right since the first installment appeared in 1995 in the United States and also demonstrated the strong connection between politicized books that sell below the traditional radar of the mainstream media. The books to date have sold over 65 million copies so far and the franchise seems to expand almost on a daily basis.

LEHRER, TOM. Tom Lehrer (1928–) is a leftist satirical comic songwriter who was active primarily during the 1950s and 1960s. Lehrer wrote several records' worth of satirical songs that parodied the earnestness of the folk movement at the time. While numerous Lehrer songs were darkly comic, such as "Poisoning Pigeons in the Park," "In Old Mexico" (a typical line in that song states "we ate, we drank and we were merry/and we got typhoid and dysentery"), and "The Elements," which transposes the periodic table to the tune of "Major General's Song" by Gilbert and Sullivan, other songs were more biting, such as "The Vatican Rag," an attack on the Catholic Church, as well as the mildly anti-Army "It Makes a Fellow Proud to be a Soldier" and the attack on the nuclear arms race "We'll All Go Together When We Go" where Lehrer rhymes "We'll all burn together when we burn/they'll be no need to stand and wait your turn." Lehrer stopped performing in public in the early 1960s, but came back to write songs for the television series "That Was the Week That Was" (later also collected as an album). Later in life, Lehrer mostly retired after 1965 to concentrate full time on his career as a mathematics professor rather than continue as a musician, only writing the occasional satirical song, contributing to the *Electric Company*, later writing for Garrison Keillor, and supervising a revue of his music called

"Tomfoolery." Today Lehrer's work is regarded by many as some of the finest American satirical folk music of the time period, possessing a savage and keenly aware political wit. Although many folk musicians were political, none were as simultaneously witty and topical as Lehrer.

LENNON, JOHN. British rock star and ex-Beatle who lived in America from 1971 to his death in 1980, John Lennon (1940–1980) was a frequent critic of American foreign policy and was the subject of many deportation attempts by the U.S. government. Lennon is best known for his tenure in the Beatles, perhaps the most successful rock band of all time, but his later life was concerned more with raising a child as well as trying to raise political consciousness. His mid-1970s records were more controversial than most of his days with the Beatles and songs such as "Give Peace a Chance" and "Happy Christmas (War Is Over)." Lennon was also the subject of a longtime effort to deport him by the Nixon administration. The troubles dated back to a benefit concert that Lennon played in 1971 for jailed White Panther Party leader John Sinclair (also manager of the great 1960s proto-punk band MC5), which led to constant surveillance by the FBI and attempts to deport Lennon that went on from 1972 to 1975 when Lennon was finally granted his green card and allowed to stay permanently. His political battles with the U.S. government were later chronicled in the 2006 documentary *The U.S. vs. John Lennon*, which played to great acclaim in theaters across America. It may seem silly in retrospect that the government paid so much time and effort in trying to deport a musician whose most radical message was "Power to the People" but it may well demonstrate the perceived power that music has in protesting authority.

LIDDY, G. GORDON. G. Gordon Liddy (1930–) is a former Nixon administration official, general counsel, and campaign political intelligence director to the Republican reelection ticket in 1972 who was convicted of his role in the **Watergate** break-in, as well as conspiracy during the Daniel Ellsberg case and

G. Gordon Liddy, one of the seven convicted Watergate conspirators, arrives at the House Armed Services Subcomittee in Washington, D.C., on July 20, 1973, to testify. (AP Photo/Staff)

contempt of court, and he was sentenced to 20 years in prison before being pardoned by President **Jimmy Carter** in 1977. He later went on the lecture circuit, which included several notable debates with psychedelic pioneer Timothy Leary, and appeared on numerous television shows such as *MacGuyver* and, in 2006, the popular *Fear Factor* show. Liddy broadcasts a radio program carried on the Sirius and XM satellite networks and is a frequent guest on **Fox News** programs. Liddy's extraordinary celebrity is an interesting indication that political convictions are no longer an impediment to success and may even lead to a lucrative postpolitical career in show business. While Liddy has many detractors, his larger than life person and self-promotion have made him a political hero (or antihero, depending on one's politics) who successfully merged show business and politics to his advantage.

LIL' ABNER. *Lil' Abner* was a comic strip by noted cartoonist Al Capp involving a hillbilly family and their adventures in their rural community and in the big city. The strip, which ran from 1934 to 1977, featured the adventures of hillbillies Lil' Abner, Granny Yokum, Daisy Mae, and others who populated the small town of Dogpatch in the rural south. Capp, born Alfred Caplin, was outspoken politically and unafraid to offend all political affiliations. Some of the parody characters that Capp created included the ruthless and exploitative uber-capitalist General Bullmoose, whose slogan "What's good for General Bullmoose is good for the U.S.A." was based on a real life quote by Charles Wilson, the former head of General Motors who as secretary of Defense under Eisenhower in 1952 told a senate subcommittee that "what's good for the country is good for General Motors and what's good for General Motors is good for the country." Another political parody was the hapless senator Phogbound, a caricature of a slick and sleazy southern politician who seemed to spend most of his time campaigning in Dogpatch as opposed to attending votes in the senate. Phogbound's trademarks were his omnipresent rifle (in case some of his constituents wanted to do a little hunting) and his coonskin cap, solidifying his image as "just folks." Capp was sometimes uncomfortable with being seen as simply a satirist, as opposed to a storyteller. In a 1952 *Time* magazine article, an unnamed reporter noted that even Capp was worrying that too many serious themes were popping up in *Lil' Abner*, as the story noted, "A Wholesome Note: After 18 years, Capp has finally bowed to true love because he has become worried over the heavy load of satire his strip carries. Readers have begun to complain that it is 'un-American,' and he thinks a marriage, even a $1.35 (new inflation price) Dogpatch one, will introduce a wholesome note" (Time.com). Capp was also outspoken in real life as well as when he appeared on a variety of talk shows. He once insulted Yoko Ono in **John Lennon**'s presence, but he became more politically conservative as time went on, which critics charge reflected badly in the strip. Capp retired the strip in 1977, two years before his death, although its legacy lived on in two movie versions and a musical based on the comic strip. (For related discussion on politics and cartoons in general, see **Political Cartoons**.)

LIMBAUGH, RUSH. Rush Limbaugh (1951–) is a right-wing talk radio host who has gained fame for his brash commentary and possible influence on political opinions at large. Although he began his career in the early 1970s, Limbaugh did not receive large attention until he introduced his national radio show in New York in 1988. His popular appeal (by 1992, his show drew the genre's largest audience) has inspired numerous spin-offs that take a similar contentious approach to politics.

One of his key talents, according to a variety of researchers and critics who have analyzed his presentation, is his ability to articulate what everyday people might feel but are unable—or hesitant—to put into words. Yet Limbaugh, a self-declared proponent of conservatism, not only attempts to stir up passionate sentiments but to encourage listeners to act on them as well.

Limbaugh has received a large measure of criticism for his rabble-rousing tactics. Opponents have alleged that even as he has taken on the government and the corporate structure, Limbaugh repeatedly renounces the accomplishments of women, gays, lesbians, and nonwhite people. Somewhat paradoxically, though, Limbaugh has also constructed his primarily male audience through long-winded dialogues and highly emotional displays, two characteristics traditionally identified as feminine. Yet his sometimes hysterical tirades, including bashes against feminism, are commonly recognized by his fans as embodying a kind of authenticity. Ultimately, those who declare this format enacts a kind of gender politics conclude, women are marginalized not only by the content but also through their relative exclusion as hosts and members of the audience.

In addition, some critics contend that Limbaugh and others of his ilk are damaging to democracy because, they claim, there are few countervailing liberal voices on political talk radio, which undermines the standard of objectivity in journalism; thus the biased worldview of a select group is imposed on the public at large. Others would answer that such concerns are alarmist. Although it is true that the Fairness Doctrine, which demanded that political coverage be balanced, was disbanded in 1987 by the **Ronald Reagan** administration and that its dismissal subsequently created the conditions for heavily biased broadcasts to proliferate, they would counter, there are sufficient perspectives delivered throughout the media to ensure the free marketplace of ideas is preserved. Indeed, these proponents often state, the media in general contain a liberal bias.

Another attack against Limbaugh mounted by his adversaries centers on the disproportionate amount of political power he supposedly has for someone who merely serves as the host of a radio program. There might be some merit to this claim. In fact, at least for a while after the 2008 presidential election, a number of news pundits cited Limbaugh as the de facto leader of the Republican Party. In support of what perhaps seems to be a hyperbolic assertion, they pointed to the manner in which several Republican officials, including Michael Steele, the head of the Republican National Committee, expressed regret after making derogatory comments about the talk show celebrity. Yet even conservatives have debated whether or not Limbaugh's prominence is a positive development for the Republican Party.

LITTLE ORPHAN ANNIE. Popular comic strip *Little Orphan Annie* was originally started by prolific cartoonist Harold Gray in 1924 and continued under various writers until the present. Although the original *Little Orphan Annie* can be read as an escapist fantasy about a plucky and patriotic little girl who fought Nazis, Reds, and other saboteurs, the comic strip was unusual in its time period for its relatively conservative views, echoing the views of writer and artist Gray. Gray's views were mainly echoed in the words of the secondary character, Daddy Warbucks, the adopted father of Annie, and a self-made millionaire who railed against handouts and the New Deal. In an article in *The Public Opinion Quarterly* in 1954, Lyle Shannon noted that in the strip, the dynamic and self-reliant Warbucks is "a victim of the new deal, a martyr to success in the twilight of rugged individualism" ("The Opinions of Little Orphan Annie and Her Friends." *The Public Opinion Quarterly* 18, no. 5 [Summer]: 169). Warbucks, who would rather take things into his own hands with the aid of his two reliable (and magical) servants, The Asp and Punjab, frequently took on the world's problems by himself; just as he had made his millions by himself, there was no need to wait for government intervention. The strip today is written by Jay Maeder and artist Andrew Pepoy and is known for its patriotic, slightly conservative slant, which updated Annie to the modern world, in contrast to more liberal strips such as *Doonesbury*. In the new strip, *Daddy Warbucks*, The Asp and Punjab are frequently seen fighting (presumably) Middle Eastern terrorists in the country of Ratznestistan and traveling the world keeping America safe for democracy. (For discussion on political cartoons in general, see **Political Cartoons**.)

LIVE AID. Live Aid was an international series of concerts in England and the United States mounted by **Band Aid** co-founder Bob Geldof in 1985. The original Band Aid single had been inspired by Geldof's viewing of a BBC documentary on starvation in Ethiopia, and Geldof was moved to create the initial Band Aid single in a marathon 24 hour recording session. After Geldof (dubbed "St. Bob" by the press for his efforts) noted that massive response, he organized two concerts, one for Wembley Stadium in London and the other for Veterans Stadium in Philadelphia on June 13, 1985, featuring acts such as Queen, U2, Boomtown Rats and reunions from Black Sabbath and Led Zeppelin. The concerts ended up raising over $140 million for Ethiopia and reaching a global audience of over a billion people. However, famine continued in Ethiopia after Live Aid was over (due to the corruption of the then Ethiopian government) and famine continues to be a problem in Africa today. Movements such as Live Aid, which seem easy to support as a political action, raise the question of whether celebrity-based charity appeals create genuine political action and change, or whether they are simply a way for the audience to express a will to do something about a complex social and political problem without making too much effort. Later concerts, such as the Live 8 concert in June 2005 and the Live Earth concerts organized by former vice president **Al Gore** in July 2007, were also watched by billions of people, but it is also unclear how much awareness they raised for their respective causes.

LONG, HUEY. Elected in Louisiana in 1930 to serve as a U.S. senator, Huey Long (1893–1935) became well known for his incendiary radio broadcasts during the first part of the decade. Although he supported Franklin Delano Roosevelt's initial campaign for the presidency, Long soon turned against him. Vehemently opposed to FDR's New Deal policies, Long attracted a popular following with his demagoguery and propagandistic assertions. Adopting a "plain folks" style, Long entertained even as he spewed political venom. For a while, Roosevelt backers even feared that Long's influence could threaten FDR's reelection. Tragically, any threat he might have posed was cut short when the senator was assassinated on September 8, 1935, and died two days later.

Long stands as a forerunner of the likes of **Rush Limbaugh** and the political talk radio format that burst into the cultural environment in the 1980s and 1990s. Although he did not interact with listeners by phone as his successors do today, Long nonetheless conveyed the type of openly partisan and provocative tone that resonates with current fans of the genre.

LORENTZ, PARE. Working under the Franklin Delano Roosevelt administration, Pare Lorentz (1905–1992) directed or oversaw several significant government-sponsored documentaries designed to promote New Deal policies. During the Great Depression, a number of government agencies were created to help solve the problems sparked by economic hardship; these organizations some-times employed media vehicles to further their causes. Lorentz was hired by Rexford Guy Tugwell, who was the chief official of the Resettlement Administration. Although he had no previous filmmaking experience, Lorentz wrote and directed *The Plow that Broke the Plains* (1936), a picture that made the case that poor planning was responsible for the calamitous Dust Bowl. *The Plow* received positive reviews, yet it was poorly distributed and thus not seen by particularly large audiences. Lorentz followed up this effort with *The River* (1937), which argued that the Tennessee Valley Authority represented the means of turning devastated lands into the thriving resources they had once been. This time, Lorentz's film drew a huge audience. It was projected at over 5,000 theaters and, afterward, continued to be shown in schools and various community gather-ings; eventually, it even made its way to public television. Partly in response to *The River*'s monumental success, Lorentz helped set up the United States Film Ser-vice (USFS) in 1938. The USFS served as a propagandistic instrument of government, working to advance the goals of the Roosevelt administration. One of its products, *Power and the Land* (1940), was placed in over 5,000 theaters by Radio-Keith Orpheum (a company that spun out of RCA). Well received, the film enjoyed additional nontheatrical play throughout the decade. *Power and the Land* sought to persuade farmers to form cooperatives and secure electrical power through the government.

Eventually, however, partially due to resistance to the New Deal by Republi-cans and big business interests, as well as public opposition to government propaganda and flack from Hollywood, Congress stripped away funding for the USFS and rendered it defunct.

M

MACARTHUR, GENERAL DOUGLAS. American war hero and general during World War II, General Douglas MacArthur (1880–1964) was also considered a perennial presidential candidate due to his popularity with the American public. MacArthur is best known for his leadership during World War II and later in Korea, where he famously clashed with President Harry Truman who relieved him of command April 11, 1951. MacArthur returned home a controversial hero and the subject of much debate as to his political future. However, despite an electrifying address to Congress in 1952, his political aspirations soon faded away, as did the general himself who did not actively seek political office despite the success of Eisenhower in the 1950s. MacArthur is an example of how war heroes have always been automatically elevated to potential candidacy despite active political agendas.

MACINTOSH "1984" COMMERCIAL. One of the most famous commercials of all time, the Macintosh 1984 ad technically aired once during the Superbowl in 1984. (It actually had aired before the Superbowl, late at night in order to qualify for an award.) The ad featured a dystopian world, mirroring George Orwell's book *1984* (as well as movie versions of the book and the Fritz Lang film *Metropolis*) where people have been turned into mindless drones, working assembly lines and watching political speeches by an obvious "Big Brother" figure. In the ad, a woman, in color in contrast to the drab black and white outfits of the drones, comes in and throws a hammer into the screen, creating an explosion that dazzles the workers, as copy and a solemn voice-over announce that "On January 24th, Apple computer will introduce Macintosh, and you'll see why 1984 won't be like '1984.'" The advertisement was not only an attack on rival computer companies such as IBM, demonstrating symbolically how Macintosh users were rebellious against a conformist society, it also played into subliminal American fears of totalitarian regimes. The Cold War against the Soviet Union was still going on, and Americans were still worried about the outcome. In 2007, the ad was "mashed" or remixed by a member of the **Barack Obama** campaign, who replaced the image of Big Brother with an image of **Hillary Clinton** reciting one of her less exciting stump speeches. As the same colorful girl appears and throws her hammer, this time the picture of Clinton explodes and a voice proclaims that "On January 14th the democratic primary will begin, and you'll see why 2008 won't be like '1984.'" Although the Obama campaign did not officially release the video, it became extremely popular on the Web and was subsequently mass e-mailed, as well as put on **YouTube**, where by summer 2007, over 2 million people had watched or shared the video. While the overall effectiveness of the ad is questionable, the concepts of the mashup, where iconic images or videos are updated to the present seems like a trend that will continue, and certainly the viral spread of videos and commercials via services such as YouTube have provided a cheap and effective way for campaigns to release information without spending costly and precious advertising dollars on network advertising. Also, the idea that ordinary activists can now use relatively cheap technology to create their own political ads or responses on a viral basis seems much more likely. This certainly has the possibility to create new levels of participation unseen before the advent of file-sharing protocols and cheap editing and graphics programs.

"MADE IN AMERICA." Slogan and advertising symbol denoting that an article of clothing or a good or service was manufactured in the United States as opposed to in a factory in another country. The slogan has been used by companies for decades and is still a sign of populist responses to non-American imports and a sense of how Americans represent national pride in terms of consumer culture and national pride.

MAHER, BILL. Bill Maher (1956–) is an acerbic political comedian and television host, who is most well known for his programs *Politically Incorrect* and *Real Time with Bill Maher*. Maher started out as an actor in several forgettable films, such as *D.C. Cab*, but soon developed a topical stand-up routine that attacked what Maher saw as hypocrisy on the part of politicians, world leaders, and religious figures. Maher's persona of a flippant comedian disgusted with modern political machination and hypocrisy is reminiscent of early political comedians such as **Lenny Bruce**, but Maher takes edgy comedy to a new level, with vitriolic attacks on politicians of almost any stripes, although during the Bush administration he has notably attacked figures more on the right than the left. Maher was a popular host of the Comedy Central (and later ABC) show *Politically Incorrect*, where he allowed a wide range of guests from musicians to scientists to argue cogently about various political issues. This format was surprisingly unchanged when the show moved to ABC. But Maher learned the limits of the network's tolerance when he made an off-the-cuff remark that, "whatever they were, the 911 terrorists were not cowards." After an uproar from pundits, the show was cancelled by HBO in 2002. Since then Maher was picked up by HBO for his show *Real Time with Bill Maher* where his guests were allowed the sort of free-spirited debate not often seen on television. Maher is often a lightning rod for criticism, and he was heavily castigated by critics for calling Pope Benedict a "Nazi" upon his visit to America in April 2008, a position that Maher essentially did not apologize for. Maher remains today one of the most acerbic and politically involved comedians in American history. (For related discussion, see **Stand-Up Comedy and Politics.**)

MALLARD FILLMORE. A rare right-wing daily comic strip that runs in the *New York Post* and many other papers (at last count over 400) across the country. The strip, created by cartoonist Bruce Tinsley and originating in *The Daily Progress* in Charlottesville, Virginia, features the titular character making wry topical jokes about liberal foibles and government waste. The strip is a rare overtly conservative strip to appear on the comics' pages of major newspapers and demonstrates that not all comic strips are resolutely liberal. (For related discussion on politics and cartoons in general, see **Political Cartoons.**)

THE MANCHURIAN CANDIDATE. *The Manchurian Candidate* (original movie 1962; remake 2004) is a Cold War era political film about the fear of brainwashed undercover agents working against America secretly. The original film (it was later remade with Denzel Washington in the starring role in 2004) fed into the American fear of who to trust in an era when numerous high profile spy cases had dominated the headlines. The film was directed by John Frankenheimer and starred Frank Sinatra, Angela Lansbury, Janet Leigh, and Laurence Harvey, who was the brainwashed former army Officer Raymond Shaw. The plot of the film was that Harvey and his platoon (including Sinatra as Major Bennett Marco) had been captured in Korea, and he was brainwashed by the Chinese in an attempt to make him an assassin when his hypnotic trigger, a queen of hearts, was activated. Sinatra's character, Marco, is a former member of the platoon who suspects that something had happened in Korea and attempts to find out what is going on before it is too late. The film gleefully satirized both left and right, with James Gregory playing Senator Joseph Iselin, a McCarthy-esque figure who is planning to take over the government with the aid of his wife, played by Angela Lansbury, unaware that she is also attempting to take over the country for the communists. Shaw has been set up to kill the presidential candidate, who would die in Iselin's arms, after which Iselin would recite a dramatic speech (which, as Lansbury notes with glee, is "the most rousing speech I've ever read. It's been worked on, here and in Russia, on and off, for over eight years."). Although the convoluted plot is eventually foiled, the idea that no one could be trusted lends an ominous tone to the film's ending.

The title of the film became a pop culture phrase after the release of the film. As film critic Roger Ebert has noted "The title of *The Manchurian Candidate* has entered everyday speech as shorthand for a brainwashed sleeper, a subject who has been hypnotized and instructed to act when his controllers pull the psychological trigger" (Ebert, Roger. "The Manchurian Candidate," 2004. http://rogerebert.suntimes.com/apps/pbcs.dll/article?AID=/20040719/REVIEWS/40719005/1023 [accessed November 12, 2008]). The film also resonates as some American conspiracy theorists speculated if a similar job of brainwashing had been done on Kennedy assassin Lee Harvey Oswald. In an interesting note as to how conspiracies and suspensions have evolved since the film came out, the remake made the villains into a mysterious multinational corporation styled after Halliburton and other global corporations. As Ebert noted in his review of the new film, "It's a stretch to imagine a communist takeover of America, but the idea that corporations may be subverting the democratic process is plausible in the age of Enron" (Ebert 2004). In both versions *The Manchurian Candidate* demonstrates that many American films that dealt with the nexus of politics and popular culture were suspicious at best of the overall power of large corporations and foreign countries to influence the American electoral process.

THE MARCH OF TIME. Launched in 1935 by Henry Luce, the leader of Time-Life Fortune, Inc., *The March of Time* (MOT) was a series of documentary films that were screened in popular movie theaters throughout the 1930s and 1940s (a radio version, also created by Luce, established many of the conventions that the films would adopt). Covering current affairs by mixing actual news footage with dramatizations, the MOT sent a new film to theaters each month. Arguably, the MOT stands as one of the most popular documentary vehicles prior to the dawn of television. With its titles placed on movie marquees, the MOT films played before the feature selections. At its zenith, the MOT was viewed by over 20 million U.S. residents a month in over 9,000 theaters and was also distributed internationally. One of its most notorious offerings was the film *Inside Nazi Germany* (1938). At a time when many citizens embraced an isolationist position toward foreign affairs, the short documentary piece pictured a highly controlled German population and a governmental regime potentially gearing up for possible military aggression and economic expansion. Westbrook Van Voorhis became greatly recognized for his histrionic "Voice of God" narration in the MOT films. The MOT came to an end in 1951, just as television took the culture by storm and offered the capacity to render even more immediate news productions. Ultimately, the MOT established compilation editing techniques and other conventions that would influence public affairs programs to come.

MARX BROTHERS. A popular team of comedians (all of whom were brothers) active from the early part of the twentieth century until the 1960s (in various incarnations), the Marx Brothers included Groucho (Julius Marx, 1890–1977); Harpo (Adolph Marx, 1888–1964); Chico (Leonard Marx, 1887–1961); and occasionally Zeppo (Herbert Marx, 1901–1979), with Brother Gummo (Milton Marx, 1892–1977) moving to the business side of the equation before their movie career began. The brothers Marx (their real last name, not a nod to the father of communism) were known for their anarchic stage shows and movies and their sense of absurdist humor. Their most political film is the classic *Duck Soup* (directed by Leo McCarey, 1933) in which Groucho assumes the presidency of the small European nation of Freedonia and begins a futile and ridiculous conflict with the rival nation of Sylvania. The film, an uproarious comedy, is also one of the best political films to point out the absurdity of war. While the Marx Brothers were widely believed to be apolitical by most, Groucho was suspected of possible communist sympathies and the FBI had gathered a file of mostly useless information on him toward the end of his life.

M.A.S.H. *M.A.S.H.* is the title of both a 1970 satirical anti-Vietnam film (set during the Korean War) by director Robert Altman and a long-running television

A 1933 photo of the Marx Brothers. Left to right: Zeppo, Harpo, Chico, and Groucho. (AP Photo)

series starring Alan Alda that ran from 1972 to 1983. (It was briefly followed by a follow-up series called *AfterMASH* that ran for 30 episodes in 1983–1984.) *M.A.S.H.* was one of the most controversial and best-loved series of the 1970s and early 1980s and was uncompromising in its attacks on the hypocrisy and madness of war. *M.A.S.H.* was also one of the few political comedies during that time period that was allowed almost unparalleled freedom from network censorship due to its high ratings. The final episode was one of the most watched in American history, and ironically the series lasted much longer than the Korean War. The show continues on in reruns, and commentators frequently mention the parallels between *M.A.S.H.* and current American military ventures.

MATTHEWS, CHRIS. Chris Matthews (1945–) is a longtime journalist and ex-politician, best known for his nightly **MSNBC** show *Hardball with Chris Matthews*, as well as *The Chris Matthews Show* on NBC. Matthews started out as a Democratic Party staffer, working for many years for former Speaker of the House Tip O'Neill, before switching to journalism full time and working for the *San Francisco Chronicle* from 1987 to 2000. While Matthews is not nearly as vitriolic as some television show hosts, he has contributed to the era in which talking heads are each given a few minutes to comment on a political issue before risking getting cut off by the host. Matthew's often-eccentric persona is seen as endearing by many of his guests and fans, but he can also come across as highly opinionated. Although Matthews has been highly critical of the Bush administration toward the end of the second term of **George W. Bush**, many news articles also singled him out for being unfairly harsh toward Democratic primary candidate **Hillary Clinton**. Matthews's contract is up soon and it is unclear if he will continue as a television journalist or seek political office.

MAUDE. A politically oriented sitcom created by executive producer Norm Lear (also the creator of *All in the Family*, *Good Times*, and *The Jeffersons*), *Maude* was part of the wave of groundbreaking and controversial American sitcoms in the early 1970s. *Maude* was unique because the show concentrated more on feminism than other issues and was the first sitcom where a character (Maude) has an abortion, in an extremely divisive and controversial episode. The show lasted from 1972 to 1978 and was also the starting point for the popular sitcom spin-off *Good Times*. *Maude* was one of the key 1970s sitcoms to tackle serious and controversial political issues from a leftist slant in a way that was not meant to simply reassure the audience, but to engage them in a debate about controversial issues.

MCCAIN, JOHN. John McCain (1936–) is a long-serving senator from Arizona, decorated Vietnam War hero, and, most famously, Republican candidate for the presidency in 2008. McCain came from a military family (both his father and grandfather were admirals in the U.S. Navy), and McCain passed up a chance to serve as an admiral when he went into politics in 1981.

McCain, unlike most of his primary opponents in the Republican presidential primary in 2007 and 2008, served in the military during the Vietnam War. He joined the U.S. Naval Academy in 1958, was stationed in Vietnam, where he was shot down and captured in 1968, and was imprisoned in a prisoner-of-war camp for five and a half years. During McCain's time as a prisoner, he was repeatedly subjected to torture (as a result, today he cannot raise his arms above his head) and refused early release on more than one occasion. After returning to the United States, McCain resumed his military career, until in 1981 he ran successfully for congress in Arizona. In 1986 he became a U.S. senator and has held that position ever since.

In his years in congress and the Senate, McCain became known as a maverick, working with both sides of the aisle, and occasionally going against the Republican Party, as in the case of the Telecommunications Act of 1996 and the resolution of the tobacco company litigation. After being tarred by his involvement in the Keating Savings and Loan scandal in 1987, McCain made campaign finance reform one of his key issues, and the McCain-Feingold Act, which limited soft money to political campaigns, was passed in 2002.

In 2000 McCain ran in the Republican presidential primaries for president. During this particularly bitter campaign, rumors swirled in several battleground states, regarding untrue allegations that McCain had fathered an African American daughter out of wedlock. Although the Bush campaign denied being behind the whisper campaign, many attributed the smears to Bush advisor Karl Rove. McCain lost the primaries and ran again for president in 2008. After falling badly behind in early polls, McCain dusted off his "Straight Talk Express" bus and as an underdog cannily worked to regain his lead, eventually vanquishing Republican foes such as Rudy Giuliani, who had seemed to be the presumptive Republican nominee. During the 2008 election, he underwent more media scrutiny than ever before, with many questioning controversial positions McCain made during the campaign, to seemingly curry favor with the Republican Party base. McCain also took advantage of his age and his "Straight Talk Express" bus to reposition himself as a maverick, and even jokingly referred to his age and supposed infirmities to reassure voters that he was not too old to be president. On May 19, 2008, McCain even appeared on *Saturday Night Live* as himself, poking fun at his age and at the chaos in the Democratic primaries. Later on during the presidential race, McCain appeared to many to have stumbled, particularly with his choice of Alaska Governor Sarah Palin as his choice for running mate. The choice of Palin, with her numerous easy-to-mock mannerisms (especially well done by Tina Fey on *Saturday Night Live*), may have contributed much to McCain's defeat by Senator **Barack Obama** in the November election. McCain remains a senator and a strong voice for Republican and bipartisan issues to this day.

MCCARTHY, SENATOR JOSEPH. The controversial senator, best known for his relentless perusal of real and imaginary communists in the state department and other branches of government in the early 1950s, Senator Joseph McCarthy (1908–1957) was one of the most polarizing politicians of the twentieth century. Although he enjoyed great popularity for a time, his hubris and disregard for the truth eventually made him a laughingstock in much of America. McCarthy's famous televised battle with reporter **Edward R. Murrow** perhaps helped Murrow's career (although the newsman's treatment of contentious topics would eventually work against him) and helped lead to the demise of the senator's career. (See also Chapter 4, "Politics and Television Entertainment.")

MCGREEVEY, JIM. Jim McGreevey (1957–), former governor of the state of New Jersey, notoriously resigned from the governorship in August 2004, announcing on live television that he was a "Gay American" and resigning for personal reasons. However, McGreevey was not merely resigning because he was conflicted about his sexuality (at the time of his public disclosure McGreevey had been married twice and was the father of two daughters) but because he was involved with a legal dispute with an ex-aide, Israeli citizen Golan Cipel, over

McGreevey's alleged sexual harassment of Cipel. (McGreevey claimed that Cipel, a patronage appointment in New Jersey, had been a willing participant in a love affair, but Cipel never admitted to this.) Although McGreevey would later write an autobiography, *The Confession*, in 2006, detailing his struggles with his sexuality and his many sordid truck stop sexual encounters, he soon sought to leave the limelight behind. However, a year later his wife, Dina Matos McGreevey, responded with her own book, *Silent Partner: A Memoir of My Marriage*, renewing public interest in the scandal. Although the spotlight eventually faded from the McGreevey marriage, the salacious revelations proved that the public and the presses' appetite for gossip and scandal had not faded after the supposed new seriousness so many pundits predicted after 9/11/2001.

MEET JOHN DOE. *Meet John Doe* is a **Frank Capra** populist film from 1941 that involves the political movement led by a former homeless man, "John Doe" (played by Gary Cooper), who was created by journalist Anne Mitchell (Barbara Stanwyck). Long John Willoughby adopts the persona of the fictitious John Doe, who was supposed to have made a pledge to jump off the top of City Hall on Christmas Eve as a protest against hunger and social ills in a country that should be able to conquer all of its problems. He soon becomes a populist hero and inspires the formation of "John Doe" clubs across America, inspiring millions of Americans to pay attention to their neighbors. When he realizes that the clubs are actually being manipulated for political gain by the fascist D. B. Norton, Doe rejects his role and is exposed. After much soul searching, Doe decides to really commit suicide on Christmas Eve, but Norton is there determined to cover up any attempt to make a political statement. At the last minute, Anne and several "ordinary" people arrive and ask him to start again his mission of uniting the little people across America. The film is an example of Capra's populist streak in action; in films such as *Meet John Doe*, *Mr. Deeds Goes to Town*, and *Mr. Smith Goes to Washington*, Capra demonstrated a commitment to the power of ordinary citizens to affect real political change. The film was nominated for an Academy Award for best writing.

MEET THE PRESS. See **Sunday Morning Political Shows.**

MINUTEMEN (BAND). The Minutemen was a highly political American punk/indie band active during the 1980s. The band consisted of D. Boon on guitar and vocals, Mike Watt on bass and vocals, and George Hurley on drums. They played a politicized sometimes lyrically Marxist blend of free jazz and raucous punk rock. The band dissolved in December 1985 after Boon was killed in a highway accident, and bassist Mike Watt and drummer George Hurley later went on to form the less political Firehose.

MINUTEMEN (U.S. SOUTHERN BORDER GUARDS). Toward the end of the twentieth century, immigration became a much discussed political issue, and on the Mexican border, a group of vigilantes decided to form its own border patrol, taking its name from the legendary revolutionary war heroes. The Minutemen began in 2005 and immediately courted controversy with its strong support for border fences and strict restrictions on immigration. The group, who have taken to patrolling the border and reporting suspected immigrants to the border patrol, has gone through numerous schisms, and there are now several groups who are unaffiliated who use the name.

MOORE, MICHAEL. Acclaimed left-wing activist and documentary filmmaker, Michael Moore (1954–) is best known for *Bowling for Columbine* (2002), *Fahrenheit 9/11* (2004), and *Sicko* (2007). Initially gaining fame through his documentary work, Moore is also a writer and a comedian.

In 1988, with the release of *Roger & Me*, Moore established a personal film style that combines sensationalism, high on-camera involvement, ironic humor, satire, and social critique. Through the use of comedy and wit, Moore is often able to deliver scathing, sometimes even radical, invective and somehow make it seem palatable. The premise of *Roger & Me* revolves around the filmmaker trying to confront the inaccessible head of General Motors, Roger Smith, to ask him why he closed automotive plants in Moore's hometown of Flint, Michigan, which led to hardship for hundreds of workers and their families. Ultimately, the documentary challenges the benefits of globalization and the ethics of corporate leaders. The documentary performed well at the box office after its appearance at various film festivals.

Since the production of *Roger & Me*, Moore has continued to create controversial nonfiction films for theatrical distribution. In his documentaries, Moore, positioning himself as a populist, often portrays a kind of slovenly everyman, yet one

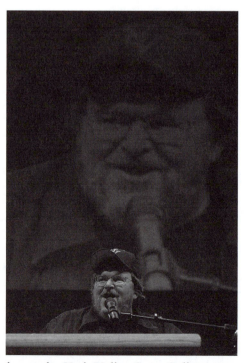

Michael Moore speaks on the Utah Valley State College campus, 2004, in Orem, Utah. The stop was Moore's 35th on his 61-city Slacker Uprising tour, a national trek aimed at mobilizing youth voters. (AP Photo/Douglas C. Pizac)

who is also a provocateur, taking on the powers that be, especially the corporate world and government officials. It appears as though he regards himself as being on a mission to let average Americans know what their political and corporate leaders are engaged in while they are not looking. At the same time, he seems to be pushing for greater political involvement from a generation that frequently opts out of political life. Moore is not interested in objective journalism. Instead, through heavy-handed juxtapositions and broad generalizations, he advances a strong point of view, producing his own brand of propaganda intended to counter the outlooks that he feels the popular media generally provide, which, he thinks, benefit big business and government more than common citizens. He is a muck-raker of sorts, exposing the underbelly of capitalist excess that traditional journalism typically shields from view. One of his distinctive traits, though, is his ability to accomplish his objectives in entertaining ways.

Moore has also translated his formula to television. In 1994, he created and starred in the series *TV Nation*, which aired in the summer on NBC. In each episode, Moore stages pranks with a satirical bite that are frequently designed to deliver social commentary on instances associated with the themes he generally covers—corporate abuse and the absurdities committed by government. When NBC dropped him, FOX contracted Moore in 1995 for another round of summer episodes. Afterward, FOX also decided to remove *TV Nation* from its lineup. Probably part of the motivation behind both cancellations was the networks' uneasiness with Moore's tendency to confront the very commercial forces they rely on for financial survival. The show took the type of risks that are usually anathema to broadcast television. Still, in 1999, the cable network Bravo offered Moore another chance to bring his style to the small screen. *The Awful Truth* was similar to its predecessor and ran for two seasons.

Moore's next theatrical feature to generate substantial debate is *Bowling for Columbine* (2002). Inspired by the late 1990s tragic massacre of students at Columbine High School, the film investigates the nation's violence and its fascination with guns. For his efforts, Moore collected an Oscar for Best Documentary Feature. Yet Moore was heavily criticized for his mocking confrontation with actor and then leader of the National Rifle Association Charlton Heston at the end of the movie. The scene, according to his detractors, is just one example of Moore's tendency to ridicule the people he engages in conversation, even sometimes the "little people" for whom he supposedly advocates.

Over the years, Moore has acquired an unprecedented level of celebrity for a documentarian, synchronizing his film activity with television shows, high-selling books (including *Stupid White Guys* [2004], *Dude, Where's My Country?* [2004], and *Will They Ever Trust Us Again?* [2005]), live events, and other communication avenues. He has been a frequent guest on the lecture tour and late night talk shows. In 2004, he toured across the country in a "slacker tour," promising free, clean underwear and ramen noodles as incentives to students for registering to vote in the 2004 presidential election (his 2008 film, *Slacker Uprising*, is a documentary of that tour).

Yet no other work has triggered more response and controversy than his anti–**George W. Bush** documentary, *Fahrenheit 9/11*, a vehement denunciation of the George W. Bush administration that was designed to indirectly persuade the population to vote for democratic challenger Senator John Kerry in the 2004 presidential election. The movie grossed more money than any documentary in history (far outstripping the previous leader, Moore's own *Bowling for Columbine*). With the film, Moore had established a financial pattern. When *Roger & Me*, his first notable feature, came out, it was the largest money-making documentary ever made at the time.

Moore's latest film to receive widespread attention, *Sicko* (2007), fervently rebukes the state of health care in the United States and indicates that it should be overhauled with a single-payer health care insurance system.

Without question, when measured by movie ticket sales, Michael Moore is the most successful nonfiction filmmaker the industry has ever known. But his popularity has gone hand-in-hand with an increasing level of scorn waged against him by his opponents. While a hero to many, he is frequently under attack from those on the right (and some on the left) who cannot stand what they view as his sense of self-importance. Some see an incongruity between his working-class film persona and the degree of wealth and fame he has achieved in his actual life. Another criticism focuses on the manner in which he tends to humiliate the people he interviews. His fans, however, praise him as a champion speaking truth to power.

Films as a director: *Sicko* (2007); *Fahrenheit 9/11* (2004); *Bowling for Columbine* (2002); *The Big One* (1997); *Canadian Bacon* (1995); *Pets or Meat: The Return to Flint* (1992; **PBS**); *Roger & Me* (1989).

MORAL MAJORITY. Christian political activist group founded in 1979 by the late Reverend Jerry Falwell and several other ministers including Drs. Tim and Beverly LaHaye. The group, which was dedicated to creating a base of Christian activists to push for political and social change, was heavily touted by the media in the 1980s and the early 1990s, but the overall direct influence is questionable. The group was also opposed by numerous left-wing and secular activists who believe that groups such as the Moral Majority were dangerous to the American political system. (A bumper sticker seen on some opponents' cars at the time read "The Moral Majority Is Neither.") Falwell officially dissolved the Moral Majority in 1989, but revived the group's name in 2004 as the Moral Majority Coalition, which he led up until his death in 2007. The influence of the evangelical vote on American elections, whether inspired by the Moral Majority, is unquestionable.

"MORNING IN AMERICA." "Morning in America" is a well-known 1984 political advertising campaign that sought to reinforce then President **Ronald Reagan**'s generally high standing with the public. Created by the renowned advertising man Hal Riney, who also provided a soothing voice-over, the spots featured emotionally moving images of everyday scenes involving ordinary Americans, many of which included American flags. The commercials are significant in that, probably more powerfully than in any previous presidential campaign season, they emphasized sentiment and good feelings over content. On Election Day, President Reagan easily won a second term in office.

MORRIS, ERROL. In 1988, Errol Morris (1948–) gained attention through his direction of the documentary *The Thin Blue Line*. Enjoying considerable distribution in movie theaters, the movie made the case that a man serving a life sentence for the murder of a police officer was actually innocent. *The Thin Blue Line* is widely credited with influencing the overturning of the man's conviction and his subsequent release from prison. Morris established a particular style in the film, mixing interviews, footage of actual events, and reenactments in a way that some critics found problematic. The director has admitted that people have told him his work has partly inspired certain "reality TV" conventions for shows such as *COPS*.

Years later, Morris won an Oscar for Best Documentary for *The Fog of War: Eleven Lessons from the Life of Robert S. McNamara* (2002), which, through extensive interview and other footage, probes the account of the Vietnam War of the man who served as secretary of defense for much of the conflict. Intercut with archival scenes from his younger days, an 85-year-old McNamara straightforwardly describes his former responsibilities, sometimes revealing gruesome events and disturbing thoughts. "LeMay [a general in Vietnam] said, 'If we'd lost the war, we'd all have been prosecuted as war criminals.' And I think he's right," McNamara states at one point in the film. Later, in 2008, Morris created another war documentary, this one centered on the Abu Ghraib scandal involving the torture of Iraqi prisoners by American soldiers. *Standard Operation Procedure* presents troubling interviews with some of the military personnel who participated in the acts of brutality.

Part of Morris's signature involves finding out-of-the-ordinary or eccentric people, and establishing a rapport and setting that allow them to talk openly about their lives, even as he promotes a vague feeling of detachment from his audience. Through his method, he attempts to connect individual oddity with larger social issues. For example, in *Mr. Death: The Rise and Fall of Fred A. Leuchter, Jr.* (1999), the protagonist discusses how he manufactures equipment meant to ease the pain of execution for prisoners sentenced to death, and discloses that he does not believe the Nazi Holocaust actually transpired. Applied to *Fog of War* and *Standard Operating Procedure*, Morris's techniques evoke matters of political consequence. The filmmaker is often recognized as one of the most important recent documentarians because of his distinctive approach.

"MOSH." "Mosh" is a politically charged rap song by noted Caucasian rapper Marshall Mathers (better known as Eminem) that urged voter turnout during the 2004 election. During the 2004 presidential season many previously apolitical rock stars and rappers became more politically engaged, and Eminem, who usually raps about controversial topics or how he is being persecuted, joined with many in the rap community to try and increase youth voter turnout. The lyrics, which at first are vague, soon address **George W. Bush** and what Eminem see as his failed war policy. As Eminem raps: "Stomp, push, shove, mush, Fuck Bush, until they bring our troops home (c'mon)."

The song itself was a straightforward call to action that infuriated many on the right and was applauded by many on the left, although some did not welcome the addition of the often controversial and profane rapper to the protest movement against Bush. The video was more explicit with hundreds (perhaps thousands) of animated youth in hoodies marching together, ultimately to the voting booths. Although none of the protest music during the election seemed to have a major effect on the outcome of the 2004 presidential election, it marked a turning point where popular artists were unafraid to make protest music in the wake of the controversy that the **Dixie Chicks** had previously caused several years earlier.

MOVEON.ORG. MoveOn.org is an influential liberal political advocacy group, with membership in the millions. (See Part I, Chapter 8, "Politics Online.")

MR. SMITH GOES TO WASHINGTON. *Mr. Smith Goes to Washington* (1939) is one of the most popular populist dramas made by director **Frank Capra**. The story involves idealistic Jefferson Smith, leader of the Boy Rangers, an organization analogous to the Boy Scouts, from (presumably) Mississippi who is appointed to fill out a Senate term. Although he is initially mentored by the state's senior senator, Joseph Paine (Frederic March), he soon realizes the extent of the corruption that infests Washington. When the state's political boss, Jim Taylor, tries unsuccessfully to corrupt him, he is later framed in a scandal and almost leaves the Senate in disgrace, before he learns the political ropes and holds a filibuster on the Senate floor while waiting for the American people to see the rightness of his cause. Eventually the people do respond, and Paine tearfully confesses his corruption, leaving Smith exhausted but triumphant. Although the film is critical of political corruption and bureaucracy, it was extraordinarily popular and was shown in other countries as an example of how the little guy can succeed against all odds in the American democratic system. To this day many politicians cite *Mr. Smith* as an example of why they went into politics in the first place. The film was eventually turned into a short-lived television show in the 1962–1963 season for six episodes. The show starred Davy Crockett popularizer Fess Parker as Mr. Smith, no doubt trading on his previous experience as an American icon. Notable guest stars included Edward Everett Horton and Buster Keaton. There was also a similarly titled documentary in 2001, "Mr. Smithereen Goes to Washington," about indie band the Smithereens' front man Pat Dinizio's unsuccessful run for the Senate in 2000 in New Jersey on the Reform Party ticket.

MSNBC. MSNBC was a joint venture between NBC and Microsoft, which first began to air on July 15, 1996. The network at first struggled to find its identity. The point was to make a splash as **Fox News** had done several years earlier, but with early low-rated programs filled with political analysis, such as the ill-fated Phil Donahue show, the network fell somewhere between **CNN** and Fox, without a discernible identity of its own. After almost a decade of struggling, Microsoft and NBC ended their partnership in 2005, with NBC assuming control of the network. The network consistently tried to boost ratings by luring celebrities over to the channel, but few lasted long. Even Tucker Carlson, who had been seen as an easy and natural success, did not make it past March 2008. However, the network has had success in political coverage or commentary with the shows *Hardball with Chris Matthews* and *Countdown with Keith Olbermann*, along with the new evening program *The Rachel Maddow Show*. Despite the best efforts of NBC to keep the network relevant, it consistently lags behind CNN and Fox in news coverage, though it had some success during the long presidential campaign of 2008.

MURROW, EDWARD R. Widely regarded as a true legend in the field of journalism, Edward R. Murrow (1908–1965) first rose to prominence during his radio coverage of World War II from London, England, for CBS. Standing in the midst of falling bombs, Murrow brought the harrowing sounds of warfare into people's homes. Throughout his career, though he generally adhered to the journalistic standard of objectivity, Murrow, nonetheless, was sometimes willing to take a side to uncover what he perceived as a larger truth. During his radio broadcasts, for example, he indicated that Great Britain was in need of assistance from the

CBS Newsman Edward R. Murrow (c. 1955). (Photofest)

United States. Later, when CBS ventured into television, Murrow followed. In 1951, *See It Now*, a descendant of the radio show *Hear It Now*, was launched, with Murrow serving as anchor. On the television documentary series, Murrow courageously explored a variety of controversial issues, including the anti-communism movement that became known as McCarthyism, named after its fiercest crusader, **Senator Joseph McCarthy**. Several *See It Now* episodes put McCarthy in a negative light and might have even contributed to his eventual fall from grace. In 2005, the chain of events involving Murrow and McCarthy was recaptured in the movie *Good Night and Good Luck* (the signature phrase Murrow used to end his newscasts) directed by George Clooney.

In 1958, *See It Now* was terminated, largely due to the nervousness among television and advertising executives who had tired of Murrow's treatment of contentious topics. He remained with CBS and worked on other fare, including occasional episodes of *CBS Reports*, which had been created shortly after the demise of *See It Now*. Perhaps his most famous appearance on *CBS Reports* was in a segment entitled ***Harvest of Shame***, an exposé of migrant workers in the United States. In 1961, Murrow left CBS and accepted the position of director of the U.S. Information Agency under the **John F. Kennedy** administration. A chain smoker even on camera, he succumbed to lung cancer in 1965.

MYSPACE. See Part I, Chapter 8, "Politics Online."

N

NASCAR. NASCAR stands for the National Association for Stock Car Auto Racing and is one of the most popular sports in the United States today. Many political candidates have tried to at least pretend an appreciation for NASCAR in order to demonstrate their "just folks" appeal to middle America. In 2004, Democratic presidential candidate Howard Dean used his connections with NASCAR racer Brian Weber to try and woo support within the racing community and with NASCAR fans. While Dean did not eventually win the democratic nomination, he did make inroads into the traditional Republican bastions of working-class southerners, although not to the extent that he had hoped. "NASCAR Dads" thus became a sought-after type of voter, especially in the 2008 campaign. Numerous other politicians, such as President **George W. Bush**, frequently used NASCAR winners as photo opportunities. As long as NASCAR remains popular, politicians will remain fans, whether they understand the sport or not as, like **kissing babies** and eating various rubber chicken dinners, has become a hallmark of the campaign season and an effective way of demonstrating that the candidate is "just folks." NASCAR, while not as popular in the northern "Blue States" is much more popular in the South and West and has become a touchstone of the modern political campaign.

NATIONAL LAMPOON. *National Lampoon* was a popular satirical monthly humor magazine founded by *Harvard Lampoon* alumni Douglas Kenney, Henry Beard, and Robert Hoffman in 1970. The magazine was a regular source of comedic gems during its prime and was a key source of American political satire for many years. Today the magazine is defunct (it officially ceased publication as of 1998), but the label is still used by a new company to market sophomoric teenage sex comedies and other branding opportunities, which lack any of the wit of subtlety that marked the lampoon at its best during the 1970s. The *Lampoon*, like the *Harvard Lampoon*, included both topical and political satire as a hallmark of its mission, and spared no one on the left or right as evidenced by the fact that conservative humorist P. J. O'Rourke was a writer and editor for the *National Lampoon* during its glory days. While several magazines have tried unsuccessfully to parody both politics and popular culture over the past few decades, few have been as imaginative or as clever as *National Lampoon* at its height.

NATIONAL PUBLIC RADIO. See Part I, Chapter 3, "Politics and Radio."

NATIONAL REVIEW. Influential conservative magazine founded by the late author and television commentator **William F. Buckley Jr.** (1925–2008) in November 1955, the magazine *National Review* has been credited, along with Buckley, with starting the modern-day conservative movement in America and was pivotal in making politics entertaining and engaging for a new generation of conservative intellectuals. Although Buckley left the day-to-day operations of the *National Review* in 1990 and later sold his shares into a trust, he still contributed columns until his death. The magazine has seen a new life with an influential Web site and the often-quoted writing of columnists Jonah Goldberg, David Frum, and Richard Lowry.

National Review was also a punch line in the 1977 Woody Allen movie *Annie Hall* when Allen's character Alvy Singer finds a copy of *National Review* in his ex-girlfriend Annie Hall's apartment while trying to kill a spider, and asks her "Why don't you ask William Buckley to kill your spider?"

NETWORK. *Network* was a 1976 satirical film that offers a look at American politics and our increasing obsession with popular culture. Written by classic television writer Paddy Chayefsky, directed by Sidney Lumet, and starring Faye Dunaway and William Holden, the film's plot revolves around the mad newscaster Howard Beale (Peter Finch) from fictional fourth network UBS who, after being fired, goes through a nervous breakdown and inadvertently creates a new kind of network news program, based on spectacle and entertainment as opposed to real news. While much of the film revolves around Beale and the way in which the news program morphs from serious coverage to entertainment, the film is also a biting satire of America's obsessions with popular culture. When Dianne Christiansen, the network's head of entertainment programming realizes the potential ratings of Beale, she quickly snatches him from news director Max Schumacher (William Holden), who represents the older more serious kind of journalism that seems ill suited for modern network television. *Network* parodies not only the inherent contradictions of the news industry but also corporate control of news, the way in which entertainment is valued more by the average American than civic discourse, and also the way in which current events can become fodder for an entertaining night's broadcast, despite their gravity. Despite the fact that the film was made in 1976 and based on the way in which news media and politics had become intertwined with entertainment, today the film resembles not so much prophecy as contemporary satire. The film was also hailed by critics and has been used as a touchstone of the way in which television news provides meaningless fluff as opposed to real news.

NEWS PARODIES. Since the 1960s there have been numerous parodies or satires of American news and the news industry. The most prominent examples include "Weekend Update" on *Saturday Night Live*, *The Daily Show*,

The Colbert Report, and the defunct *1/2 Hour News Hour* on television, as well as the weekly newspaper *The Onion* in print. A fascinating part of some of these parodies of traditional news programs is that many young people have reported actually using these programs to get their current news.

While these shows were directly copying the format of a news show in the name of satire, many sitcoms have also parodied the workings of news broadcasts or news stations over the past several decades. Many programs that were ostensibly about the news, actually had very little to do with news coverage. Although they may have parodied the excesses and idiocies of network television news, squandered the chance for any real satire, and instead concentrated on relationships and comedic plot lines such as in *The Mary Tyler Moore Show* (although from a political standpoint, *The Mary Tyler Moore Show* was political from its focus on a take-charge, unmarried woman in her thirties as a lead character).

9/11 CONSPIRACY DOCUMENTARIES. Conspiracy documentaries about 9/11 include short or full-length conspiracy films available via individual Web sites or video-sharing Web sites such as **YouTube**. After several years had passed and many Americans wondered if the details of the terrorist attacks on September 11, 2001, were improperly investigated or covered up, several hundred conspiracy buffs and legitimately concerned citizens conducted their own investigations using archival materials and several books published in the years following the attacks. A decade previously, the production and distribution channels were not available to provide the ability to make or publicize 9/11 conspiracy films, but new cheap video editing equipment and digital cameras have cut costs tremendously over the past decade. The proliferation of video-sharing Web sites, such as YouTube, have allowed greater distribution that would not have been possible outside of small independent film festivals. Some of the more popular videos include *9/11 and Conspiracy Crash Course* and *9/11 Conspiracy: The Legend of Flight 93*.

9/11 FILMS. After the attacks on America on September 11, 2001, few people were prepared to see dramatizations of the events of that tragic day. Although several documentaries were later shown that featured actual video images from inside the towers, including the documentary *911* by Gedeon and Jules Naudet, which won an Emmy in 2002, few expected movies dramatizing the events for several decades. The film was one of the most dramatic documentary features about the events of 9/11, in its own way as political as **Michael Moore**'s *Fahrenheit 9/11* documentary in 2004, which featured stunning footage of President **George W. Bush**'s initial reaction to being informed the country was under attack.

While these documentaries were somewhat successful, at first few filmmakers were willing to take a chance on releasing a dramatization of the events of 9/11. In 2006, the first true 9/11 film was released in America—*United 93*, a dramatization of the flight where passengers attacked the hijackers and the plane was forced to crash in a field in Pennsylvania. The film was critically hailed, and director Paul Greengrass was nominated for an Oscar for best direction. The same year saw noted political filmmaker **Oliver Stone**'s film, *World Trade Center*, which dramatized the rescue effort after the collapse of the towers and the real life stories of two Port Authority police officers, Will Jimeno and John McLoughlin, who were among the last survivors plucked from the rubble. *United 93* and *World Trade*

Center were hailed for their nonpolitical and nonexploitative looks at aspects of the tragic day. Another recent film was *Reign Over Me*, an Adam Sandler dramatic vehicle directed by Mike Binder where Sandler plays a fictional character who lost his family on 9/11, which opened to mostly tepid reviews.

Whether the public is ready for more works on 9/11 is unclear. Most national tragedies, such as Pearl Harbor, have been dramatized on film and television many times, but usually for propaganda purposes or after many years, and the existence of 9/11 films so soon after the actual events have caused much controversy amongst critics and the general public as many wondered if the country was ready to face the extremely emotional events of 9/11 dramatized on film. In addition, numerous 9/11 conspiracy theory documentaries of various qualities are available on YouTube and other Web sites.

9/11, SPORTS AFTER. After the tragic events of 9/11, numerous sports teams either stopped their seasons to honor the casualties or wore commemorative patches on their uniforms when playing commenced. Both the New York Mets and New York Yankees attempted "feel good" comebacks to try and win the 2001 season, but the Mets were unsuccessful in reaching the play-offs, while the Yankees were successful in reaching the World Series but fell to the Arizona Diamondbacks in seven games. In 2007, former Mayor Rudy Giuliani claimed to have spent "as much time, if not more" than the recovery and rescue workers at the pit in New York City. An exhaustive report from *Slate.com* on the time that Giuliani actually logged at Ground Zero, only 29 hours, were statistically far below the amount of time that Giuliani spent at Yankee games, a total of 58 hours. This demonstrates both the amount of passion New Yorkers had for a symbolic victory after 9/11 and the way in which politicians have a shaky grasp on their schedules.

9/11, TELEVISION ADVERTISING AFTER. After the tragic events of September 11, 2001, when Al Qaeda terrorists crashed planes into the World Trade Center, the Pentagon, and a field in Pennsylvania, the nation was shocked and politicians were united in their condemnation of the attacks. For several days the networks ran advertisement-free programming covering the attacks. In New York City, especially in the affected areas in downtown Manhattan, business had crawled nearly to a standstill due to the complexity of the search and recovery efforts that had commenced almost right away. After several days the major networks gradually began to add advertisements to their programming (and return to entertainment as well after a few weeks), although many of the more crass commercials for consumer goods were not shown again for several months. On the anniversary of 9/11 the next year many networks also gave commercial-free coverage of the commemorative services. By 2007 many of the networks were concerned that the continuous coverage of the 9/11 commemorative events were cutting into advertising time, and by 2008 it seemed clear that many networks would not run continuous coverage of the reading of the victims' names, which has been a hallmark of the ceremony since 2002.

1968 OLYMPICS AND BLACK POWER SALUTE. In the 1968 Olympic Games in Mexico City, American athletes Tommy Smith and John Carlos stunned

American audiences watching them from home when they chose to stand with their fists raised in the air in the Black Power salute and stand barefoot while the national anthem played. The International Olympic committee threatened to strip them of their medals and booted them from the Olympic camp. The furor caused at home (millions of Americans had been watching on television) and in magazines came alternately from pundits condemning and civil rights activists applauding the political stance of the two athletes. Australian runner Peter Norman wore an OPHR (Olympic Project for Human Rights) pin in solidarity. The controversy that erupted had as much to do with the state of civil rights in America as the supposedly sacrosanct nature of the Olympics themselves.

The Olympics games have often been used to make political points and political posturing. When Adolf Hitler presided over the Olympic games in Germany in 1936, he sought to turn the games into a demonstration of the superiority of Aryan might. In 1980, the United States boycotted the Olympic games because of the Russian invasion of Afghanistan. The 2008 Olympics to be held in China was the source of many protests throughout the world over the Chinese occupation of Tibet and China's record on human rights. The iconic image of the two athletes giving a Black Power salute (they shared one pair of gloves, so Smith wore his on his right hand and Carlos on his left so they could both share in the moment) was a powerful reminder of not only how far America had to go in race relations but once again of the power of the televised and photographic images to carry powerful political messages. The image proved to be iconic and is still available on posters, postcards, and computer wallpaper.

NIXON FAREWELL SPEECH. One of the most watched moments in American television history occurred on August 8, 1974, at 9 PM when President **Richard Nixon** publicly resigned in disgrace rather than be impeached for his role in the **Watergate scandal**. The live televised resignation occurred after over a year of televised hearings into the break-ins at the Watergate hotel and the Nixon administration's stonewalling and evasion regarding key pieces of evidence such as the audiotapes Nixon had secretly recorded. The resignation was the first by an American president and drew an audience of over 100 million viewers. This mass audience was an example of not only how Americans of all political stripes were fascinated by the public spectacle and disgrace of an American president resigning, but also of how television could be used as a source of mass ritual, or a "media event" as media analysts Katz and Dayan call "the high holy days of viewership" (Dayan, Daniel, and Katz, Elihu. *Media Events: The Live Broadcasting of History.* Cambridge, MA: Harvard University Press, 1992).

NIXON, RICHARD (MEDIA PORTRAYALS). Richard Milhouse Nixon (1913–1994), the thirty-seventh president of the United States, was one of the most controversial presidents in modern history, and also one of the most imitated and mocked presidents in history. While the caricatures of Nixon in editorial cartoons alone runs into the thousands, noted American political cartoonist Herblock (Herbert Block) started drawing satirical cartoons of Nixon as early as his entry into the House of Representatives in California in 1947. Along with his other frequent opponent, **Senator Joseph McCarthy**, Herblock drew both men "as sinister figures who were bent on destroying individuals and basic rights in their delusional attempts to rid the nation of Reds and fuels their own political careers" (Lordan, Edward. *Politics, Ink: How America's Cartoonists Skewer Politicians from King George III to George Dubya*. New York: Roman & Littlefield Publishers, 2006, p. 76). Herblock alone drew hundreds of cartoons of Nixon between 1947 and the cartoonist's death in 2001. (For related discussion, see **Political Cartoons**.)

The portraits of Nixon on television and movies also run to a considerable number. During Nixon's presidency various imitators were able to mock Nixon's awkward mannerisms, and celebrity imitator Rich Little did a particularly evocative Nixon. On *Saturday Night Live* Dan Aykroyd did a memorable Nixon impersonation where Aykroyd as Nixon forces a nervous Henry Kissinger (played by the late John Belushi) to pray with him on the eve of his resignation. Satirists regularly lampooned Nixon during this time period, and he remains a cultural icon, a sort of living caricature long after he had left office and long after his death. Nixon appeared as a regular character in the comic animated sitcom *Futurama*, where Nixon's head preserved in a fish bowl runs for president (he is equipped with a new robot body; hence he can circumvent the rule about no "body" being able to be elected to more than two terms as president). Naturally, as president, Nixon schemes, hunts his enemies, and frequently almost destroys the world, aided sometimes by the reanimated headless body of ex–vice president Spiro Agnew. While Nixon has not appeared on *The Simpsons*, his middle name, Milhouse, is the name of Bart's bumbling socially clueless best friend.

Nixon also appeared in numerous underground comics, as well as several mainstream ones, and in writer Alan Moore's acclaimed *Watchmen* comics series, Nixon is president of the United States during a time when the country is on the brink of nuclear war (for related discussion on politics and comic books in general, see **Comic Books**). In 1995 political activist director **Oliver Stone** made a film about the downfall of Nixon (called *Nixon*, of all things), which unsurprisingly cast Nixon in a decidedly unflattering light. In the film Nixon is a King Lear-esque character, in the words of critic Roger Ebert, a "Brooding, brilliant, tortured man, sinking into the gloom of a White House under siege, haunted by the ghosts of his past" (Ebert, Roger. "Nixon." 1995. http://rogerebert.suntimes .com/apps/pbcs.dll/article?AID=/20031207/REVIEWS08 [accessed September 4, 2007]). In the film, Nixon, played by British actor Anthony Hopkins, is tortured not only by his many political sins but also by a secret erased during the infamous missing 18-1/2 minute gap on the **Watergate** tapes that indicates that a secret anti-Cuban operation during the Eisenhower administration (when Nixon was vice president) somehow inadvertently led to the death of President **John F. Kennedy**. Although Stone indicates at the start of the movie that parts of the film are "based on hypothesis and speculation," he still finds new and unique ways to torment his old enemies. While Stone would certainly have had enough ammunition on Nixon without making it up, it seems that he could not resist revisiting his earlier film *JFK* while attacking Nixon.

Nixon also appeared as a character in the film *Dick* (1999) where he is portrayed as a bumbling schemer by Dan Hedaya, who becomes involved with the adventures of two young girls who inadvertently stumble into the Watergate cover-up. The movie mocks the image of Nixon as cold and calculating and instead shows him as a hapless idiot. Nixon also made himself the topic of many pop culture related discussions when his normal behavior sometimes bordered on the bizarre. One of the most unlikely photo opportunities in American political history occurred when iconic singer Elvis Presley and President Richard Nixon met at the White House in 1970. Presley, who was addicted to numerous prescription drugs, wanted to become an "agent at large" in the Bureau of Narcotics and Dangerous Drugs. The bizarre meeting and photo opportunity took place on December 21, 1970, after Presley had sent Nixon a letter requesting a meeting and Nixon had responded by inviting "The King" to the oval office. The meeting included an exchange of gifts (including a Colt 45 pistol brought by Presley along with family photos) and produced one of the most iconic images in popular culture of smiling Nixon shaking hands with a dazed looking Presley. For a brief instant it seemed as though Nixon could almost look hip; however, this lasted only a moment and was soon over. Elvis's motivations remain unclear, but it is likely that Elvis simply was concerned about hippies, or wanted a photo op with a president, and either explanation seems plausible in retrospect.

More recently actor Frank Langella won a Tony award for playing Nixon on Broadway in New York in the acclaimed play *Frost/Nixon* that had a limited engagement in 2007 and later in the Academy Award nominated film in 2008. It is unclear whether the constant use of Nixon as a comic foil is more because he was such a reviled man immediately after his presidency, or because of his partial rehabilitation later in his career, or simply because with his jowly face, suspicious eyes, five o'clock shadow, and distinctive voice, he was so readily imitable.

NORTH, OLIVER. Oliver North (1943–) is a former marine officer and Reagan administration official who riveted television viewers during his appearance in full uniform during the Iran Contragate hearings. He was convicted of several felony charges and later sentenced to a three-year suspended sentence and 1,200 hours of community service. After his conviction was reversed on appeal, he ran for a Senate seat from Virginia in 1994, and later worked as one of the new wave of right-wing radio political commentators. Today, North is a popular right-wing radio talk show host and also host of *War Stories with Oliver North* on **Fox News**. North is also a example of how television could be used for political purposes. Had North not chosen to wear his uniform during public hearings, it is less likely that he would have appeared as a hero to so many while admitting that he had broken U.S. laws and regulations. (For further discussion, see **Iran Hostage Crisis** and **Political Scandals**.)

O

OBAMA, BARACK (MEDIA PORTRAYALS). Barack Hussein Obama (1961–) is a political anomaly, a wildly charismatic Democratic presidential candidate who, despite his ethnic minority status, is one of the few political candidates in recent years to be treated more as a rock star or celebrity than a politician. Barack Obama is the son of a white mother and a Kenyan father and grew up originally in Hawaii, before moving to Indonesia for several years with his mother's new husband. (It was in Indonesia that Obama attended both Muslim and Christian schools, which during the presidential primaries came back to haunt him as an Internet rumor that he was secretly a Muslim pretending to be a Christian.) Obama later moved back to Hawaii and attended Columbia University, where he honed his debating skills, and then Harvard Law School where he headed the *Harvard Law Review*. After graduation, Obama worked for New York Public Interest Research Group and other organizations before returning to Illinois where he wrote his first book, *Dreams from My Father* (he would later write another best-selling book, *The Audacity of Hope*, in 2006). Soon he became a state senator, serving from 1998 to 2004, the same year in which he gave a riveting speech at the Democratic National Convention, making him instantly a rising star in the party as well as demonstrating his considerable oratorical skills.

As a first-term senator, few expected Obama to command attention immediately, but soon he was regarded by many in the party as a rising star. It was expected that he would run for president, the first black man to do so, in the near future of 2012 or 2016, after a successful **Hillary Clinton** White House bid in 2008. Obama surprised millions, including many in his own party, when he announced in February 2007 that he would be running for president. Although at the time few gave him much of a chance thanks to the formidable war chest and political organization of the Hillary Clinton campaign, after several early stumbles in the primary season Obama soon began to distinguish himself from the other second-tier candidates, such as Bill Richardson or Joe Biden. By the New Hampshire primary, the race had grown quickly to a three-way race with

Clinton and Edwards, and shortly afterward a two-way race when Edwards dropped out of the campaign. Obama, who raised considerable amounts of money from small donations, quickly amassed a considerable campaign treasury and could challenge Clinton directly in every state. Another key factor was the BlackBerry-addicted Obama's canny use of the Internet not only to keep in touch with his followers but also to mobilize them and get them to the polls. Obama may be the first astute user of the Internet to be elected president.

In March 2008, Obama was blindsided by media reports of incendiary and controversial speeches by his former pastor and spiritual mentor Jeremiah Wright. Previously videotaped speeches by Wright included allegations that the AIDS virus was a government plot against African Americans and that 9/11 was also just retribution for the evils perpetuated by the United States. Obama used the curve tossed at him by Wright to hit an inside-the-park home run with a powerful speech about race on March 18 entitled "A More Perfect Union," which calmed many voters confused as to how Obama could not previously have noticed Wright's comments. However, when Wright continued to be a political liability, Obama distanced himself from his longtime spiritual mentor and at the end of May 2008 severed ties with his longtime church. By the beginning of June 2008, it was clear that Obama had statistically clinched the Democratic nomination, and on June 4, Hillary Clinton conceded the nomination.

Obama had been the subject of much fawning treatment by the press during his career, and during the campaign, Senator Clinton and many of her aides made the case that Hillary Clinton was being asked hard questions and Obama merely being given softballs by an adoring press corps. *Saturday Night Live* parodied this in several episodes and Obama appeared in an episode as himself on November 3, 2007, attending a Halloween party at the Clinton's residence. Obama went on to successfully defeat Republican candidate **John McCain** in the November election, making him the first African American president in American history.

It is clear that Obama blurs the line between celebrities and politicians, becoming a figure of hope for many and a tabula rasa for others who project on him the legacy of the Kennedys and the idea that politics of inclusion from a progressive perspective can make a difference in ordinary citizens' lives.

"OBAMA GIRL." "Obama Girl" was a music video created by the Web site barelypolitical.com in 2007, which featured a scantily clad female singer/model who sang about how she had a "crush on Obama." The success of the viral clip led to answer songs such as "Hot for Hill," "I've got a crush on Giuliani," and finally "Obama girl vs. Giuliani girl" (which, of course, culminates in a pillow fight between the scantily clad supporters of Giuliani and Obama). While this most closely resembles the rap "answer" songs of the 1980s, such as "Roxanne Roxanne" by UTFO, "Roxanne's Revenge" by Roxanne Shante, and "The Real Roxanne" by UFTO with a model standing in for Shante who had sung the first answer song, it raises questions as to whether YouTube helps raise the bar for public participation in the democratic process as in the YouTube debates (see **YouTube**), or allows the crossover of politics and entertainment to become even more lurid than it had been in previous years.

OCHS, PHIL. Although lesser known today than many of his contemporaries in the 1960s folk scene, Phil Ochs (1940–1976) was one of the more politically astute folk singers who began to turn their attention to protest songs. Many of his classics, including "I Ain't Marching Anymore," "Outside of a Small Circle of Friends," and "Draft Dodger Rag" (which included the classic lines sung to the inducting sergeant at the draft board, "Sarge, I'm only eighteen, I've got a ruptured spleen and I always carry a purse") were fairly popular, yet Ochs became increasingly depressed as the 1960s wore on. Although he kept writing about political issues, he also became disillusioned with the folk scene. Ochs remained busy with various causes, including the May Day Demonstrations in 1971 where he famously proclaimed, "If the government can't stop the war, we'll stop the government" (West, Darrell M., and Orman, John. *Celebrity Politics: Real Politics in America*. Upper Saddle River: Prentice-Hall, 2003, p. 70). Ochs also played at a rally in tribute to Salvador Allende and at the rally celebrating the end of the Vietnam War in 1975. Depressed by a throat injury and plagued by substance abuse, Ochs committed suicide in 1976.

OFFICE OF WAR INFORMATION. The Office of War Information (OWI) was established by the Franklin Delano Roosevelt administration in 1942, soon after the United States entered World War II. The OWI was responsible for coordinating all of the government information distributed to the media, as well as creating its own media vehicles to influence U.S. citizens. Under the OWI's jurisdiction, the Motion Picture Bureau was assigned the duty of ensuring no Hollywood films undermined the war effort. At the same time, the bureau also produced original films. Although it largely failed to create and distribute movies that resonated with domestic viewers, the organization achieved a degree of success in reaching foreign audiences. Produced mostly by seasoned documentarians, these films sought to put the American military endeavors and way of life in a positive light.

The OWI, however, was more notable for its radio scripts than its newsreel films—the office is especially known for starting the long-lived *Voice of America* radio broadcasts. Although it was abolished in 1945, the kind of work it initiated would continue under other government programs.

OLBERMANN, KEITH. Former ESPN sports analyst turned political commentator on **MSNBC**'s *Countdown* program, Keith Olbermann (1959–) is a liberal counterpoint to **Rush Limbaugh** and **Bill O'Reilly**, although not as popular as either of them. Olbermann, who has hosted *Countdown with Keith Olbermann* since 2003, started out as a humorous analyst on ESPN's *SportsCenter* in 1992 with co-host Dan Patrick, where they reinvented the dull highlights reel as a source of catchphrases and cultural commentary. After leaving ESPN acrimoniously in 1997, Olbermann drifted from program to program, until eventually resurrecting his career on *Countdown* on MSNBC. In August 2006, Olbermann began to do "Howard Beale" type rants about politics on the air and cultivated feuds with O'Reilly and Limbaugh. Since then, Olbermann's popularity (and *Countdown*'s ratings) has increased dramatically; from 2006 to 2007, his audience more than doubled to over 730,000 viewers. Whether Olbermann can position himself as a left-wing populist answer to the prevailing right-wing television and radio hosts remains unclear at this writing.

ONE, TWO, THREE. *One, Two, Three* is the Billy Wilder film from 1961 featuring James Cagney as a Coca-Cola executive trying to open the cola market in the Soviet Union. The film satirizes not only the bumbling commissars and secret agents of the Soviet Union but also, to a much lesser extent, the provincialism of the American protagonists. Horst Buchholz also stars as a communist student who has married and impregnated the daughter of the CEO of Coca-Cola and whom Cagney must transform in the course of a day into a worthy and capitalist new husband. The film is an unusually cynical look at U.S.-Soviet relations; the Soviets are portrayed as jaded bureaucrats, well aware of how awful their system is (cars that fall apart, sullen musicians as the only entertainment in run-down hotels) and looking to make a buck as quickly as possible, while the Americans are shown as ardent capitalists, eager to demonstrate not only the superiority of American culture but of American products and consumerism as well. The film, despite its brilliance (it is now considered a classic by many, although it was inexplicably underrated during its release), was a failure at the time and precipitated Cagney's retirement until his comeback 20 years later in the film *Ragtime*. *One, Two, Three* is a rare film that can make comedic light of politics during what was an incredibly tense situation and also portray a nuanced, nonpropagandistic look at the conflict between capitalism and communism.

THE ONION. *The Onion* is the popular American satirical weekly that regularly parodies the American political system. *The Onion*, which was instantly successful, was founded in 1988 by Tim Keck and Christopher Johnson, two students at the University of Wisconsin–Madison, and later moved to New York City, where the weekly was relaunched in a slightly smaller format. *The Onion* also has a thriving Web site that it updates frequently with satirical news items as well as with serious interviews with musicians and actors. *The Onion*'s coverage has become so widespread that in a famous case of inaccurate journalism, a Chinese newspaper reported verbatim *The Onion* story about the U.S. Senate wanting to move out of the Capitol Building unless the rooftop was replaced with a retractable dome.

O'REILLY, BILL. Bill O'Reilly (1949–) is one of the most successful and widely followed conservative pundits currently active on television and in print. O'Reilly primarily broadcasts on the **Fox News** Network, where his regular program, *The O'Reilly Factor*, is viewed by over 2 million viewers on a regular basis and has increased its viewership every year since its debut in 1996. On every show O'Reilly proclaims that viewers are entering a "No Spin" zone where presumably only the plain facts will be presented. O'Reilly began his broadcast career in Scranton, Pennsylvania, before moving on to larger markets in Dallas, Denver, Boston, and Portland, Oregon, as a reporter and anchor on local news stations before joining WCBS in New York in 1980, later moving on to national news for CBS as well as ABC. O'Reilly later became host of *Inside Edition* before becoming a part of the embryonic Fox News Network in 1996. O'Reilly, despite his claims to be a centrist, has been an acknowledged cheerleader for numerous conservative causes, but his skills as a broadcaster are likely the main reason for his popularity. O'Reilly's popularity has led to a successful parody by comedian Stephen Colbert, first as a faux right-wing correspondent on **The Daily Show**

and later on his own program, *The Colbert Report*, where his winking version of O'Reilly's persona is a great success. Colbert, who affectionately refers to O'Reilly as "papa bear," appeared on *The O'Reilly Factor* as a guest, much to the confusion of O'Reilly. On the program, Colbert remarked that on his own program he spends so much time spinning that "being in the no spin zone gives him vertigo," and he argued that what he was doing was "emulation as opposed to imitation." O'Reilly mostly played along, allowing that his primary aim was to supply Colbert with more material. O'Reilly returned the favor by appearing on Colbert's program later that night. Although O'Reilly is best known for his television appearances, he is widely read in his syndicated column and listened to on his radio program, a two-hour call-in show named *The Radio Factor*, as well. O'Reilly, who has won two Emmy awards in his career, is the author of four books on politics and culture, *The O'Reilly Factor*, *The No Spin Zone*, *Who's Looking Out for You?* and *Culture Warrior*, as well as a children's book, *The O'Reilly Factor for Kids*. O'Reilly, based in Long Island, holds two master's degrees and, according to his official Fox News bio, enjoys "taking naps" in his spare time.

P

PAAR, JACK. Jack Paar (1918–2004) was a notable American comedian and television host best known for his stint hosting *The Tonight Show* from 1957 to 1962 where he pioneered the late night talk show interview and comedy segments that became staples of the genre. Paar was not an especially political comedian, and his barbs about political figures of the time would come across today as inconsequential jesting as opposed to the more acerbic attacks of today's late night hosts. Paar was also famous for interviewing both **Richard Nixon** and **John F. Kennedy** in 1960 as they ran for president, giving the public a rare televised look at both candidates in a more natural setting, and he also later aired a historic interview with Robert F. Kennedy following John F. Kennedy's assassination. Paar, as the man who largely created the form followed today by late night talk shows, albeit one far more intelligent and probing than current late night programming, is a key influence on late night political satire to this day.

PACIFICA AND COMMUNITY RADIO. "Community radio" refers to stations that are chiefly, if not completely, funded through the donations of listeners. Typically, community radio stations rely heavily on volunteer workers and eschew standardized programming. Ideally, each outlet is designed to serve the local community in which it is based and offer a heterogeneous mix of content that meets the needs of a diverse population. Because it does not depend on corporate sponsorship, community radio can avoid the pressure to provide an "advertising friendly" environment and, conversely, take far more risks than is generally the case with commercial radio.

The most well-known organization that is associated with this model is the Pacifica Foundation. In 1946, Lewis Hill, a critic of commercial radio at the time, created Pacifica and launched its first station in Berkeley, California (KPFA), as a dramatic alternative to the predictable fare listeners usually heard. Although he had hoped to integrate KPFA into the AM dial, Hill eventually settled for the largely neglected FM spectrum. KPFA presented an eclectic array of programming unlike any other station, regularly featuring politically radical commentary, music far from the mainstream, and challenging art criticism.

In time, Pacifica expanded its operation to five stations, including WBAI in New York. Over the years its guiding philosophies and programming have varied considerably, yet it has always stood apart from commercial radio.

Eventually, faced with economic hardship, Pacifica turned more and more to philanthropic institutions and federal subsidies to supplement the money it received from its audiences. No longer exclusively tied to its listeners, Pacifica modified its approach in ways that resulted in contentious debate among its fans. Its greatest controversy occurred in the late 1990s and early 2000s, when a power struggle developed between Pacifica's management, which desired a more autocratic and centralized structure, and numerous staff members, who sought to retain Pacifica's commitment to airing truly alternative perspectives. Many of these dissenters—as well as listeners—felt that Pacifica was softening its edges and would evolve into just another **National Public Radio** (NPR), which receives considerable funding through the government and, consequently, is less willing to advance any positions that might offend Washington. The conflict escalated into worker lockouts, firings, strikes, public demonstrations, and lawsuits. When the dust finally settled, Pacifica negotiated a new set of bylaws that kept the chain alive. Today, Pacifica is still a distinctive voice on the radio and continues to broadcast music and discussion that are seldom found on commercial radio—or even NPR. Programs such as *Democracy Now!*, a current affairs show hosted by Amy Goodwin that generally seriously challenges U.S. policies, remain a fixture; yet this flagship offering, too, did not escape the dispute of the late 1990s and early 2000s, spinning off into a more independent production that is also carried by other stations outside the Pacifica realm (as well as some cable outlets). Its liberal critics contend that Pacifica is no longer the radical vehicle it was when it joined the airwaves over 50 years ago.

PAULSEN, PAT. Comedian and perennial presidential candidate (1968–1996) who campaigned on the S.T.A.G. (Straight Talking American Government Ticket) for years without ever indicating if he was serious or not, Pat Paulsen (1927–1997) was a guest star on numerous programs from the 1960s onwards and extensively with the **Smothers Brothers**. Paulsen was also a serious actor and songwriter and did political commentary and editorials on the Smothers Brothers program long before news parody shows such as *The Daily Show* or ""**Weekend Update** (see **News Parodies**). Along with **Lenny Bruce** and Mort Sahl, Paulsen helped make controversial contemporary topics comedic fodder.

PBS (PUBLIC BROADCASTING SYSTEM). See Part I, Chapter 2, "Politics and Political Documentaries."

THE PEOPLE'S CHOICE. Regarded as one of the classic studies in the history of mass communication research, *The People's Choice* was directed by Paul Lazarsfeld in the 1940s and was summarized in print in 1948. Lazarsfeld's findings suggested that the media—and radio in particular—had little influence on people's

Comedian Pat Paulsen announces his candidacy for president in New York City in this August 1988 photo. (AP Photo/Marty Lederhandler, file)

voting behavior. Instead, he and his colleagues reported, political media campaigns most often either activate views, that is, bring to attention a person's stance on issues that has been lying dormant, or reinforce already consciously held positions. Only rarely do the media persuade citizens to actually change their minds in deciding for whom they will vote.

His investigation was a major influence on future communication researchers and a key impetus for a shift in the way scholars thought about media. Academics who had previously perceived the media as a very powerful or even irresistible source of persuasion now believed their impact was minimal within the context of the diverse array of other forces of socialization to which people were exposed, such as family and peer groups. Even to this day, many scholars accept Lazarsfeld's general conclusions in relationship to the short-term effects of media. There is considerable debate, however, regarding the media's long-term consequences, with many critics contending they are profound.

PINK RIBBONS (AS SYMBOL). In the 1990s it became popular for politicians to wear various colored ribbons to indicate their support for various causes. The pink ribbon, developed by Estée Lauder and Alexandra Penney in 1992, quickly became one of the most popular ribbons for politicians, particularly female politicians to wear on television to show their support for the fight against breast cancer. Many other charities and causes, such as AIDS awareness also use ribbons of different colors for supporters to show that they have donated money and/or are trying to raise awareness. As a first lady and later a senator and presidential candidate, **Hillary Clinton** in particular wore the pink ribbons publicly and at media appearances to indicate her support for breast cancer awareness.

PIRATE RADIO. See Part I, Chapter 3, section "Pirate Radio."

POGO. A popular and long-running (1948–1975) political comic strip by cartoonist Walt Kelly, *Pogo* featured a possum named Pogo and his friend who live in the Okefenokee Swamp where they discuss world affairs. *Pogo* was first syndicated in May 16, 1949, and continued to be seen in numerous papers until Kelly's death in 1973. *Pogo*'s creator, Kelly, originally worked for Walt Disney, where he perfected his cartoonist but realistic style, before moving to work on political cartoons for the short-lived newspaper *The New York Star*, where the character Pogo debuted during the last two months of the *Star*'s existence. In a biography written by Kelly in 1954, Kelly noted the great success of the comic and his inspirational aims, noting that:

> Pogo books have sold more than a million copies, and over 1,500,000 comic books were sold each year. Mail from enthusiastic readers is a major problem, albeit a flattering one. Two stenographers work at answering mail and clipping drawings and sending off books. Kelly, besides writing and drawing the strip, travels and speaks before fifty or more civic and college groups each year. His theme: The American Press is the last free voice of the world. It offers a rare opportunity to students despite its acknowledged frailties. (Kelly, Walt. "An Autobiography by the Creator of Pogo." http://www.pogopossum.com/walt.htm [accessed June 24, 2007])

When *Pogo* had risen to a level where it was being syndicated in over 400 papers, Kelly had the freedom to experiment and add more serious issues to the strip, including a series where Pogo runs for president as a noncandidate. Pogo is also well known for the phrase, "we have met the enemy, and he is us," which first appeared on a Kelly-drawn poster for Earth Day in 1970, and later appeared in a Pogo strip in 1971. Pogo also satirized current politicians, such as turning Vice President Spiro Agnew into a hyena and President Lyndon Johnson into a Longhorn steer. (For related discussion, see **Political Cartoons.**)

POLITICAL BLOGS. See Blogs.

POLITICAL CARTOONS. Since the founding of America, political cartoons on the editorial pages of newspapers and elsewhere have been used to satirize, ridicule, and lambaste public figures and politicians. In the book *Politics, Ink: How America's Cartoons Skewer Politicians from King George III to George Dubya* (2006), author Edward Lordan notes that political cartoons grew as the population did and as literacy increased: where "a talent for ridicule and a sense of injustice" existed, political satire via cartoons was never far behind (Lordan, Edward. *Politics, Ink: How America's Cartoonists Skewer Politicians from King George III to George Dubya*. New York: Roman & Littlefield Publishers, 2006, p. 6). Although early American cartoons had been used to attack King George III, to mobilize support for the American Revolutionary War, and to call for the ratification of the Constitution, most papers did not include many cartoons. While the partisan press existed, most attacks were in print as opposed to cartoon form. After the printing press became easier and more accessible in the seventeenth and eighteenth centuries, the importance and influence of cartoons again began to grow. Cartoons satirized presidents as early on as Andrew Jackson in 1828, and the editorial cartoon soon became an important part of newspapers and magazines. The Civil War and the Gilded Age led to an increase in cartoons as Americans tried to come to terms with an increasingly polarized America, where the industrialization of America caused many bewildering changes in city and country life that editorial cartoonists tried to contextualize. Some of the great editorial cartoonists of the latter half of the nineteenth century included the legendary Thomas Nast of *Harper's* and other publications, who not only gave us the modern depiction of Santa Claus but also was the first to use the symbol of the elephant to represent the Republican Party in 1874 (the donkey had been used prior to Nast's usage of it) as well as used his considerable talent to target New York City's corrupt Tammany Hall (which was the political organization that controlled the Democratic Party in New York City at the time, as well, sadly, also lampooning the Irish as a bestial and savage race of drunkards).

By the turn of the twentieth century, political cartoons had evolved further and pioneering cartoonists such as Frederick Burr Opper were tweaking President William McKinley in the *New York Evening Journal*. However, it was the presidency of Theodore Roosevelt after McKinley's assassination that led to a revolution in political cartooning. Roosevelt, a larger-than-life character who already looked like a walking cartoon caricature, was embraced by editorial cartoonists who saw him as easy to render and a source of constant material. Contributing new cartoons were artists such as John McCutcheon of the *Chicago Tribune* and Clifford Berryman of the *Washington Evening Star* who was also responsible for the creation of the iconic "Teddy Bear," which was consistently used by Berryman and later became the inspiration for the popular and enduring children's toy. The market for editorial cartoons had grown as well, and by the end of Roosevelt's term in office, almost every major American paper had at least one editorial cartoonist working on the editorial page. By the 1910s, new avenues for political cartooning grew with new socialist and leftist publications, and some American cartoonists became more politically aware as the war in Europe led to calls for both intervention and isolationism. Art Young, one of the most famous and stridently leftist editorial cartoonists of his time, soon began to do increasingly politicized cartoons for a new socialist publication in New York, *The Masses*. After American entry into the war, antiwar cartoons fell out of favor with the government; and in 1917 the Espionage Act was signed into law, which led to a mass roundup of editorial cartoonists, as Art Young, Boardman Robinson, and H. J. Glintenkamp were arrested for conspiracy to undermine the war, with some of their cartoons being entered into evidence. Although the case resulted in two hung juries, *The Masses* was forced to cease publication and a chilling precedent had been set for freedom of expression.

In the 1920s the increasing interest in women's rights and the start of prohibition had led to new material for editorial cartoonists such as Rollin Kirby, who developed a character "Mr. Dry," a mean and taciturn proponent of prohibition, much to the delight of the majority of the American populace who were against the ban on alcohol. Kirby also was notable for being the first American political cartoonist to win a Pulitzer Prize for editorial cartooning in 1922, the first of several others he would win that decade. The Wall Street Crash of 1929 and the advent of the Great Depression led to a target for editorial cartoonists and new cartoonists such as Herbert Johnson, Jacob Burck, and Blanche Mary Grambs attacking the wealthy and advocating for the rights of the oppressed. When Franklin Delano Roosevelt assumed the presidency, numerous cartoonists seized upon him as a larger-than-life figure, as easily caricaturable as his predecessor and distant cousin Teddy had been several decades earlier. The New Deal and the public works projects led to a more optimistic tone in many editorial cartoons, but a growing concern about the rise of the Nazi party in Germany led many cartoonists to presciently predict that America would soon be at war again, a prediction that was proven to be all too true.

The start of World War II led to an almost universal support for the war among editorial cartoonists, and many produced overly propagandistic cartoons supporting the war (for a discussion of the war and propaganda in general, see **World War Propaganda**). In the early 1940s artist Theodore Geisel, better known later as Dr. Seuss, drew numerous propagandistic cartoons for New York's *PM* magazine with caricatures of buck-toothed Japanese leaders and a grim Adolf Hitler personifying evil. (Geisel also did numerous cartoons for War bonds; see **Bond Drives.**) At the front, a new and more personalized view of the troops was provided by cartoonist Bill Mauldin, a private in the army's forty-fifth division who provided two notable characters, Willie and Joe, the sad-faced stubble-faced privates forced to suffer every kind of deprivation during the war, much to the chagrin of the military brass. Mauldin went on to a long and distinguished 50-year career as an editorial cartoonist and as the host of regular Veterans Day get-togethers with close friend Snoopy from the *Peanuts* comic strip, who regularly boasted of yearly gatherings where the men quaffed countless root beers and discussed old times.

After the war was over, cartoonists began to address issues in more complex terms, and two of the giants of the industry, Herbert Block (who often drew as "Herblock") and Pat Oliphant, pioneered a newly critical form of cartooning. While Block, who had started his career in the late 1920s, had consistently attacked authority, Oliphant was less ideologically consistent and preferred to attack targets on the left and right. Together they proved, along with Mauldin, who had moved into full-time editorial cartooning, to be the most prominent editorial cartoonists of their time.

The 1960s and the increased radicalization of many cartoonists led to a new group of cartoonists, many of whom started in college newspapers or in the underground press. Garry Trudeau started out writing and drawing a cartoon, **Doonesbury**, that, although it appeared in many newspaper comic pages, was also often featured on the editorial pages due to the strong political content of his work.

Although many political cartoonists had treated the Kennedy administration with kid gloves or a slightly reverent tone, the rise of Richard Nixon to the presidency in 1968 was an easy and consistent target for many cartoonists who both loathed the president and saw his jowls and slouching stance as easy to caricature and mock. Some may have been almost sorry to see him leave office, as his successor Gerald Ford was less easy to mock. Jimmy Carter's rise to the presidency led to a new range of caricatures, some featuring the former peanut farmer in simple farmer's garb, and others as a "Mr. Peanut" type character. When Ronald Reagan became president, his hair, large, thick, and dark for a man his age, led to numerous caricatures of Reagan as a cowboy-type/ex-actor, overly concerned with appearances and initially shown as a warmonger, but later during the Iran-Contra hearings as a senile old man.

If Reagan was polarizing and good fodder for leftist cartoons, his successor, George H. Bush, was consistently displayed as a man who was too wishy-washy to make a serious decision and was mired in self-doubt. It did not help George H.'s image that his successor, William Clinton, was enormously charismatic. Clinton's larger-than-life style led to numerous caricatures of him as Elvis or a walking southern stereotype with an outlandish appetite for food and women. Clinton's philandering and the Monica Lewinsky scandal (see **Political Scandals**) reinforced this image of Clinton as a relentless womanizer, perhaps abetted by the coldness with which many cartoonists used to display his wife, who was vilified by many conservatives for her seemingly icy and calculating demeanor.

After the Clinton years, many cartoonists did not know how to label the compassionate, conservative George W. Bush, although the caricature of a bumbling frat boy over his head was an early choice. After 9/11 and especially after the U.S. invasion of Iraq in 2002, new images started to appear, that of an imperial presidency, and Bush as a warmonger with little interest in the facts. In *Doonesbury* Trudeau depicted Bush as a large empty war helmet, floating in mid-air and making speeches that had little or no connection to the facts on the ground. Other cartoonists were less kind and modern-day underground cartoonists such as Ted Rall and Tom Tomorrow were particularly vicious in using Bush's statements against him. One cover of the *Village Voice* drawn by comic art painter Alex Ross depicted Bush as a vampire draining the blood from the Statue of Liberty.

Bush got off easy (in comparison) to Vice President Dick Cheney. The relentlessly dour, seemingly never smiling Cheney was not only the subject of numerous television and stand-up comic routines but was also the subject of increasingly harsher media portrayals, including in comic strips where many parodied him as a Darth Vader character. *Doonesbury* in 2007 redrew Cheney as "Lord Cheney," a dark-hooded and mysterious robed character who barked orders at terrified underlings to commence the propaganda buildup for the looming war against Iran. But despite the viciousness of Cheney or Bush's depiction, it is clear that there are a long line of cartoonists who drew potentially libelous cartoons in an effort to protest against various policies or government actions. The modern-day viciousness may be a return to the old-fashioned gloves-off style of political cartooning that used to dominate the industry. Unlike the past though, and despite some rumblings from talk radio, no cartoonists have been arrested for nonobscene cartoons in America during the war in Iraq, and it seems that the actions taken during World War I were an aberration. Either way, political cartoons, whether in newspapers or on the Web, will continue to serve the same function as the court jester of the Middle Ages, to caricature and satirize the foibles of those in power. (For related discussion, see entries on presidents, beginning with **John F. Kennedy**.)

POLITICAL CONVENTIONS. While political party conventions have existed since the 1830s as a way to rally the party stalwarts and showcase the leading contenders for office, it has only been since the 1950s that political conventions have been the source of network coverage and debates on the way in which presidential tickets are chosen. In the past several decades, however, the two main political conventions have received less and less airtime.

At the same time as networks started concentrating less on the conventions themselves, as the presidential choices were inevitable by that point, the Republican and Democratic parties began to use them more to showcase rising stars within the party. Also, networks have responded to what they see as viewer disinterest. In 1976 political conventions received an average of a 28 share of the ratings with the average American viewer watching up to 11 hours, whereas by 2000 the average viewership was down to 15 percent and the average viewer watched only two hours (Kennedy Center. "Kennedy School Poll: Interest Lagging in Political Party Conventions." 2004. http://www.ksg.harvard.edu/press/press%20releases/2004/vanishing_voter_poll_072204.htm [accessed December 12, 2007]). It may be the pomp and spectacle of the convention are no longer needed in an age when fewer Americans follow political stories closer, or that conventions are now most useful in providing an expected "bounce" in the polls prior to election time.

POLITICAL MEMORABILIA AND MERCHANDISE. Political campaigns have long included promotional items—such as T-shirts, hats, and buttons—in order to remind citizens to vote, as well as for supporters to demonstrate in public that they support a specific candidate. The twentieth century has also seen an increase in availability of cheap campaign merchandise, and buttons, stickers, and caps are now within the price range of even those candidates who are running for a local office.

Hillary Clinton Nutcracker. In September 2007, a pair of Minneapolis businessmen developed a new piece of political memorabilia, the Hillary Nutcracker. The tool, which retailed for $19.95, featured a nutcracker built into the figure that resembled **Hillary Clinton** designed to "pulverize even the toughest shells," according to a story in the *New York Post*. The nutcracker came complete with fake testimonials attributed to **Barack Obama, John McCain**, and even former president **Bill Clinton**, who seemingly replied, "No Comment." The makers of the nutcracker defended their invention as being a bipartisan joke that would appeal to both parties —according to one, it would make everyone laugh, "regardless of their politics" (Venezia, Todd. "Nut Buster: Wacky Hillary Gizmo Is a Real Easy Shell." *New York Post*, September 7, 2007, p. 3). While the joke of the nutcracker is aimed at Clinton's steely demeanor and reputed toughness, it is unclear if a male candidate would have been targeted with such obvious sexual connotations. During the years of the Clinton campaigns one of the frequent attacks on Hillary Clinton was her supposed coldness and presumed toughness, and this satirical campaign novelty item clearly reflects what some members of the populace thought about the senator during her presidential campaign.

Sunflower Buttons. Sunflower buttons were campaign buttons worn by supporters of Republican presidential candidate Alf Landon during his unsuccessful campaign against Franklin Delano Roosevelt during the 1936 election. The sunflower on the button symbolized the "sunflower state" of Kansas. These buttons were frequently used by Landon and his running mate, Frank Knox, to communicate a rural and folksy appeal that did not help Landon from being crushed during the general election. The buttons are an early example of how politicians tried to associate themselves with a specific image or slogan (see **Political Slogans**) in order to be both more memorable and evocative to voters.

POLITICAL NOVELS. There have been numerous political novels published over the past 100 years. From many early political books such as Upton Sinclair's *The Jungle* (1906), to the books of John Steinbeck, or even to the feminist works of Joyce Carol Oates, such as *Where Are You Going, Where Have You Been?* (1974), clearly many novels have tackled serious political themes. In more recent years there has been a plethora of political books written more exclusively for a pop culture audience. From the widest possible classification, the military novels of Tom Clancy, the Blackford Oaks spy novels by **William F. Buckley**, the White House mysteries by Margaret Truman (*Murder at the White House*, for example), and even the *Left Behind* novels by Tim LaHaye and Jerry Jenkins have all been seen as politically motivated. The genre of politically themed novels has also inspired numerous politically themed films.

POLITICAL SCANDALS. Political scandals have been occurring as long as there has been politics, but in the twentieth century these scandals have become particularly conspicuous with the advent of tabloid journalism, radio, newsreels, and later television. Because of the close relationship between political participation and personal involvement and investment in political life, the private lives of politicians have become more and more transparent as the twentieth century progressed (although there have certainly been political scandals in American history from the founding of the country). Since the founding of the nation there has been a tactic agreement between the press and the government that certain things would not be reported, even if obvious to some in the press (such as the fact that then President Franklin Delano Roosevelt was confined to a wheelchair during his presidency, or that the press was reluctant to expose the womanizing of President **John F. Kennedy**). In the 1960s, the press became more aggressive, especially after the Vietnam exposures of the Pentagon Papers and the **Watergate** incident, when the investigative reporting of Carl Bernstein and Robert Woodward of the *Washington Post* led to more public and press scrutiny of the lives of politicians.

Although many scandals have dealt with political corruption or the bribery or financial proclivities of many politicians, many others have dealt with the personal lives of politicians (such as the Wilbur Mills and Fanne Fox scandal, the Mark Foley page boy scandal, the numerous scandals surrounding President Warren G. Harding, the Teapot Dome scandal, and Larry Craig's allegedly "wide stance" in airport men's bathrooms) or have become more publicized as sex scandals (such as those involving President **Bill Clinton** and White House intern Monica Lewinsky [1998] or presidential aspirant Gary Hart and Donna Rice [1987–1988]). The Kennedy family has also long been embroiled in political scandals, such as the Chappaquiddick incident where Senator Ted Kennedy was driving home late in the evening and drove off the Chappaquiddick Bridge, killing his passenger, Mary Jo Kopechne (1969) (Kennedy was charged with leaving the scene of an accident and was sentenced to a suspended sentence of two months), the William Kennedy Smith rape trial in 1991, as well as the problems with drugs and alcohol by several sons of the Kennedy family. Republicans, of course, have not been immune from sex scandals as well, with Senator David Vitter admitting his involvement in a prostitution ring on capital hill in the summer of 2007 (his official statement acknowledged that he had committed a "serious sin"). The outspoken conservative senator from Louisiana had been a steadfast proponent of marriage and family values, a stark contrast to the allegedly corrupt tradition of Louisiana politics, but was embarrassed when his name was found in the "black book" of Deborah Jeane Palfrey, referred to by the press as the "D.C. Madam."

Political scandals take on new dimensions when mediated, particularly when televised. Scandals such as Nixon's involvement in the slush fund scandal that led to his famous "**Checkers Speech**" in 1952 would not have been as highly publicized were it not for the popularity of television as a medium, nor would Nixon have been as capable of using the medium and the visual image of a cute dog to deflect criticism. Likewise, the Watergate scandal became much more of a political liability for the Nixon administration, as millions of Americans watched enraptured as the scandal unfolded and subsequent hearings were televised, often preempting popular programs on network television. The Iran-Contra hearings of the Reagan administration in the 1980s and the Clinton impeachment hearings during the 1990s were also more highly publicized because of television.

More recent scandals included Republican Senator Larry Craig from Idaho being arrested for soliciting sex in a public bathroom at the airport. (The senator pleaded guilty, although he later claimed that he had responded to the charges too quickly and without being told exactly what he was acknowledging.) Craig had also been previously targeted by bloggers who claimed that he had for years been carrying on affairs with men while opposing gay marriage in the Senate.

Marilyn Monroe Scandal. Iconic American actress born Norma Jean Mortensen (1926–1962), Marilyn Monroe was best known for her many acting turns, usually as a ditzy blonde, and was the most popular comedic actresses in America during the height of her popularity. While best known for her film career, she married two American popular culture icons, baseball player Joe DiMaggio and playwright Arthur Miller, but may also have had affairs with both President John F. Kennedy and Attorney General Robert F. Kennedy. Monroe was also well known for her sultry version of "Happy Birthday" she sang to President Kennedy on May 29, 1962, at Madison Square Garden at the president's forty-fifth birthday party. Some conspiracy theorists have speculated that her death of a drug overdose in 1962 was a staged suicide, masterminded by Bobby Kennedy as a result of her liaisons with the president and his brother, although most serious scholars dispute this as a conspiracy theory. Through her connection to the Kennedys as well as two opposing pillars of popular culture in DiMaggio (baseball) and Miller (theater), she is a key icon and one of the most reproduced images of the twentieth century. Monroe was also the subject of a famous silk-screened painting by Andy Warhol.

Iran Contragate Scandal. The Iran Contragate political scandal involved the selling of weapons to Iran (possibly done in exchange for the release of Western hostages by militant group Hezbollah, funneling the resulting profits to arm the Contra rebels in Nicaragua during the early 1980s; also see **Iran Hostage Crisis**). The resulting televised hearings helped make a media darling of Colonel **Oliver North** who appeared on camera at the hearings in full military uniform and captivated the nation during his testimony. North was later convicted of several felony charges (later overturned on appeal) and today is a popular right-wing radio talk show host as well as host of *War Stories with Oliver North* on **Fox News**. North's secretary, Fawn Hall, also became a minor celebrity during the hearings and later married Jim Morrison biographer Danny Sugerman. Both were frequently parodied in print and on late night talk shows during this time period. The hearings demonstrated the way in which scandals become much more evocative to the general public when presented live on television, and continued the tradition of applying the suffix "gate" to any scandal post-Watergate.

Gary Hart Scandal. In 1987 during the presidential primaries, Gary Hart, a leading contender for the Democratic nomination, was dogged with rumors of infidelity. Hart initially denied the allegations of impropriety and dared reporters to make the charges stick. Unfortunately for Hart, the *Miami Herald* staked out an apartment and found Hart leaving the building the next morning with a young woman named Donna Rice. After several more embarrassing pictures of Hart and Rice together were released, including one of Rice sitting on Hart's lap on a boat called *Monkey Business*, Hart's campaign was finished and the nomination went to Michael Dukakis, who lost to George H. Bush in the general election. While sex scandals are nothing new to politics, the Hart scandal illustrated that the press had taken on a more engaged role in covering political figures and that political coverage had become both more thorough and more sensational at the same time.

The Clinton-Flowers Scandal. Gennifer Flowers was one of several women who accused presidential candidate Bill Clinton of sexual improprieties prior to his election in 1992. Flowers alleged that she and Clinton had engaged in a prolonged affair while Clinton was governor of Arkansas. Flowers, unlike other women with similar accusations, also had incriminating taped phone conversations, which proved embarrassing for the Clinton campaign at that time. Clinton denied that any affair had taken place and in a shrewd political move, appeared on the CBS show *60 Minutes* along with his wife, **Hillary Clinton,** to announce that, although there had been problems in his marriage, the accusations were categorically untrue. The appearance, including affectionate gestures between the two Clintons, was seen as a superb piece of political damage control and also indicated how well the Clintons were able to tap into the power of television to showcase their natural charisma. Flowers later posed for *Penthouse* magazine at the height of her popularity before moving to New Orleans and opening a nightclub with her husband. Gennifer Flowers is an example of the blurred line that exists now between the press and politicians about how much of their private lives are subject to press scrutiny. Also, it could be argued that Clinton's relentless womanizing and his wife's refusal to disavow him were a boon to his presidential campaign as opposed to an impediment.

The Clinton-Lewinsky Scandal. Monica Lewinsky was an intern of President Bill Clinton who famously embroiled him in a sex scandal in 1996 that led to a move to impeach the president. The outcome of the affair was highly publicized by the media and became the butt of numerous jokes and parodies on television. Lewinsky (1973–) joined the Clinton White House as an intern in 1995, eventually working near the president. When the affair initially broke, Lewinsky initially denied any involvement as did Clinton; however, she later was forced to testify, leading to a televised denial by Clinton. Eventually a prolonged and torturous mediated affair began where the media closely followed the scandal as it broke, leading to relentless media coverage that exhausted most Americans' patience. Lewinsky later went on to parody her affair with Clinton in a *Saturday Night Live* spoof, design her own line of handbags, and attend graduate school for a master's degree in social psychology. Lewinsky's legacy unfortunately was apparent in an episode of the popular crime television program *Law & Order* where the name "Lewinsky" was used as a term for oral sex.

POLITICAL SLOGANS. Since the nineteenth century, many presidential candidates (and many who were running for state or federal positions) have often used slogans to sum up their campaign themes. Although many of these early slogans may have primarily been used by the candidate (or by members of the campaign, or even were attributed to the candidate erroneously) to sum up their campaign in a neat little package, others may have been trying to appeal to a less literate public who could understand and remember campaign slogans. This is also true of campaign songs (see Part I, Chapter 6) and other forms of **political memorabilia and merchandise,** designed to show support as well as sometimes to summarize more difficult messages into something easily memorable, such as William Henry Harrison's 1840 campaign slogan "Tippecanoe and Tyler Too" (which referred to Harrison's purported heroism at the battle of Tippecanoe and his vice presidential running mate John Tyler). In the twentieth century many memorable campaign slogans were used to address either some aspect of the candidate's personality or part of his/her platform. Memorable slogans from the first half of the twentieth century included William McKinley's "A Full Dinner Pail" in 1900 (referring to the improved economic conditions under his leadership), Woodrow Wilson's extremely premature "He Kept Us Out of War" in 1916, and the seldom spoken Calvin Coolidge's "Keep Cool with Coolidge" in 1924. Although Eisenhower is most associated with the somewhat simplistic "I Like Ike" in 1952, the phrase "peace and prosperity" was also associated with his 1956 campaign. Somewhat reminiscent of this was the phrase associated with the 1968 **Richard Nixon** campaign, "Nixon Is the One." **Ronald Reagan** famously used "It's Morning Again in America" to represent the end of the recession-prone 1970s, as well as presumably the resumption of American foreign policy success under the more hawkish Reagan administration (also see "**Morning in America**"). While the past two decades have seen numerous unofficial campaign slogans associated with aspects of the presidential candidates' campaigns, such as Clinton's theme based on the Fleetwood Mac song "Don't Stop Thinking about Tomorrow," the **George W. Bush** campaign relied on a variety of unofficial phrases such as "Compassionate Conservatism" and "A Reformer with Results," there have been relatively few memorable campaign slogans in recent years, possibly because, due to modern micromarketing campaigns, one slogan would not be resonant with a majority of possible voters. Another explanation could be that buttons, once a key way of expressing support for a candidate via slogan, are no longer as vital to a presidential campaign as they had been in previous elections.

POLITICAL THEATER. Over the past 100 years there have been numerous political plays, performances, and acts of political theater produced. While there had been some mockery of politicians in vaudeville and in Yiddish theater, one of the first mainstream political musicals was *I'd Rather Be Right*, a Rodgers and Hart musical from 1937, which starred George Cohan as a character based on Franklin Delano Roosevelt who meets a young man named Phil, who cannot get married till he gets a raise and cannot get a raise till FDR balances the budget.

Cohan, one of the grand old men of Broadway, sings several songs, including the extremely prescient "Off the Record," where Roosevelt sings:

> My speeches on the radio have made me quite a hero—
> I only have to say "My friends" and stocks go down to zero
> (Lorenzhart.org. "I'd Rather Be Right." http://www.lorenzhart.org/rather2.htm)

While the political satire of "I'd Rather Be Right" seems almost quaint today, it does indicate not only how well received Roosevelt's **"Fireside Chats"** were but also a growing sense that Americans could lampoon politicians and be accepted, within reason. Although during the war in the 1940s political satire in theater more or less ended, by the late 1950s and early 1960s numerous small and underground theater groups had formed with much less stake in the status quo than in previous generations.

In the 1960s the satirical *MacBird* by underground playwright Barbara Garson parodied both Shakespeare's *Macbeth* and the Johnson administration. The original play included Stacy Keach as MacBird and Rue McClanahan as Lady MacBird and was produced in 1966. The 1960s had numerous political theater groups such as the Living Theater and Bread and Puppets, who consistently satirized American politics and middle-class norms. While the 1970s did not see as many overtly political plays, numerous small underground theater companies were still working, and new innovators such as gay playwrights Harvey Feirstein and Tony Kushner were adding new political themes to American theater. In the early part of the twenty-first century, playwrights also satirized the Bush administration, most notoriously in the extremely controversial *I'm Going to Kill the President, A Federal Offense* by the Imagination Liberation Front, which brought Guerilla Theater to a new and shocking dimension.

POWELL, COLIN. Colin Powell (1937–) is an African American four-star general, former Secretary of State, and Chairman of the Joint Chiefs of Staff during the **George H. Bush** and **George W. Bush** administrations. Powell was one of the most popular African American politicians and former military officials after the Gulf War and was widely seen as the first serious African American to be considered as a strong candidate for president from either party. Powell was born in Harlem and quickly rose in the ranks in a 35-year military career to become the twelfth chairman of the Joint Chiefs of Staff. After his retirement from the military at the end of the Gulf War, Powell published a successful 1995 autobiography, *My American Journey*, which also led to Powell's success as a sought-after speaker on the lecture circuit.

Powell's star was tarnished in the second half of the Bush administration when it was revealed that Powell, either under his own knowledge or inadvertently, had misled the United Nations in presenting a rationale for the invasion of Iraq in 2003, leading to the scandal involving the leaked identity of CIA agent Valerie Plame, an affair later labeled Plamegate by the press when Plame was outed by columnist Robert Novak. Many saw Plamegate as retaliation for an editorial her husband, Joseph Wilson, had written doubting the evidence of Iraqi agents buying enriched uranium from Niger. (Powell's political career is in doubt at this point, and it may well be that the once incredibly popular general will take on the role

General Colin Powell, when he was Chairman of Joint Chiefs of Staff, 1993. Powell is the first African American to hold the highest office in the U.S. Department of Defense. (AP Photo)

of an elder statesman in American politics rather than accept a future cabinet job or advisory work to the next few presidents.)

PRESS CONFERENCES. Press conferences are the key way in which the president of the United States or the press secretary communicates with reporters to announce major events or simply give updates on policy. The first electronic press conference held by an American president was held in January 1955 by President Dwight Eisenhower and quickly established the precedent that major press conferences should be televised, a practice that continues to this day. While for many years the live press conference had been an opportunity for presidents to demonstrate their command of the issues, in the modern form the press conference is a carefully staged tool in which presidents rarely stray off message and usually field only softball questions (or in the absence of the president at the more frequent White House briefings, the press secretary answers questions for the president and attempts to clarify presidential public statements). While it is very difficult to be issued a press pass for the White House, nonetheless the process can be corrupted from time to time, such as in 2005 when former male prostitute Jeff Gannon (James Guckert) was given a press pass for his journalistic work on Talon, what was essentially a Web site set up by the Republican party. When Gannon, who had asked a softball question involving the Democrats now that they have "seem to have divorced themselves from reality," was revealed to have had more experience in porn than in journalism, his press pass was revoked. (Gannon now has a Web site at http://www.jeffgannon.com/ [accessed March 19, 2007] where he covers news with a right-wing slant.) The modern press conference continues to be a source of information for the general public, although major networks often complain that most press conferences are poorly watched and, unless during a time of grave national crisis, are better off on C-SPAN or other government-run channels.

PRIMARY. One of the first major documentaries that became associated with the practices of direct cinema is *Primary* (1960), produced by Drew Associates. The company head, Robert Drew, would come to be regarded as a central force in the direct cinema movement (Richard Leacock is widely held to be another). He and the rest of the Drew Associates team had initiated the approach in the ABC TV series *Close Up!* In *Primary*, the director follows the campaigns of Democrats Hubert Humphrey and **John F. Kennedy** as they compete against each other in the 1960 primary season. Part of the film's distinction is that not only does it display the politicians in action at rallies and other public settings, but it also portrays private moments with the candidates in their hotel rooms and other locations away from the crowds. This type of intimate coverage was unprecedented. With television still in its relative infancy, and with little experience in documentary production, the candidates often appear more candid and honest than the later politicians who had become especially media savvy and had learned to cultivate visual personas that worked to their advantage. Other notable documentaries that follow the campaign trail and were perhaps inspired by the trailblazing work of *Primary* include *The War Room* (1993), *A Perfect Candidate* (1996), and *The Road to the Presidency* (2004).

PRIMARY COLORS. *Primary Colors* was a book and later a film that satirized the contradictions between a thinly disguised womanizing Bill Clinton figure called Jack Stanton, his domineering wife, and their idealistic campaign rocked by sexual scandals. The book was originally released in 1996 and attributed to "Anonymous." After much press speculation, it was later revealed that the book was written by Joe Klein of *Newsweek*. (Klein had previously worked at *New York* magazine and later worked at the *New Yorker*.) The book was made into a film in 1998 starring John Travolta as the Bill Clinton character and Emma Thompson as a thinly disguised **Hillary Clinton**. The idea of publishing the book anonymously did as much as any marketing campaign to sell copies, and Klein was vilified by some and praised by others for using his campaign access to publish a satirical look at the Bill Clinton campaign. After the success of the book, the movie paled in comparison, although it featured dead-on performances by Travolta and Thompson. The success of *Primary Colors* raises questions about journalistic objectivity and access to politicians, as well as questions about how much of a politician's private life is off limits for public consumption. (For additional discussion of depictions of Bill Clinton and the media, see **Bill Clinton [Media Portrayals]**.)

PRIVATE SNAFU. *Private Snafu* was an army cartoon and comic book character created by Theodore Geisel, who would later go on to find fame and fortune as the far better known Dr. Seuss, and Phil Eastman, who was an example for soldiers about what not to do. ("Snafu" is a military term that stands for situation normal, all "fouled" up, or another word in some cases.) The series of risqué shorts were done by some of the most popular names in animation such as Chuck Jones, Fritz Freling, and Bob Clampett. *Private Snafu* was another example of trying to use comic animation for propaganda and training purposes (for a full discussion of propaganda techniques in general that were used in the World Wars, see **World War Propaganda**; for a full discussion of politics and cartoons in general, see **Political Cartoons**).

R

RAGE AGAINST THE MACHINE. Rage Against the Machine was a popular group of activist musicians who wrote explicitly political songs that attacked the American system and capitalism. Active during the 1990s and again in 2007, the band consisted of Zack de la Rocha on lead vocals, Tom Morella on guitar, Brad Wilk on drums, and Tim Commerford (Tim C.) on bass. The band played a strident mix of politically minded hard rock/punk with rap influences that made them one of the most popular politically active left-wing bands in the United States, supporting causes such as the freeing of convicted murderer Mumia Abu Jamal as well as protesting against capitalism and the American system in songs such as "Killing in the Name" and "Bulls on Parade." While the band's politics were informed by the outspoken and politically active Morella, and to a slightly lesser extent by de la Rocha, the band's precedents were not only in older protest songs in the tradition of **Woody Guthrie** and **Bob Dylan** but drew influence equally from politicized music across the globe, earlier American punk bands such as MDC, and early rap such as EMPD. A question that dogged the band throughout its early years was what machine they were raging against, particularly once they were signed to Epic Records, a subsidiary of global recording giant Sony. While this may have cost the band some initial street credibility, they were, in their initial short-lived first period, one of the few bands to discuss political issues (albeit from a particular political slant) on a consistent basis and not see a resultant loss in sales and popularity, as the **Dixie Chicks** did in 2004. The band repeatedly restated its commitment to political activism, and their protest concert outside the Democratic National Convention in 2000 was a rallying cry for many left-wing intellectuals. The band broke up in 2000 after the departure of de la Rocha and the remaining members formed the less politicized Audioslave with Chris Cornell, formerly of Seattle band Soundgarden. When Cornell left in late 2006, de la Rocha rejoined the band and played a politically charged set at Coachella in California. Currently, the band is touring again and considering recording new music. (Also see Part I, Chapter 6, for a full discussion of politics and music in general.)

REAGAN, RONALD (MEDIA PORTRAYALS). The American president from 1980 to 1988 and acknowledged as one of the most telegenic and persuasive presidents of the twentieth century, Ronald Reagan (1911–2004) was nicknamed the "Teflon President" (as well as his preferred nickname, "The Great Communicator") for his ability to remain untarnished by some of the scandals including the Iran Contragate scandal (see **Political Scandals**) that rocked his presidency, but usually left his personal popularity unscathed. Reagan was one of the most well-liked presidents in American history, and that was partly a result not only of his personal charisma and magnetism but also of his years of training as an actor and politician.

Reagan worked as a sportscaster in Des Moines before becoming an actor in the late 1930s. Reagan ended up making over 50 movies and numerous television appearances. Although he is best known for mediocre B films such as *Bedtime for Bonzo* (1951), Reagan could also be an effective actor when given the right material such as in *Kings Row* (1942) (which also provided one of his most effective lines as an actor when the disabled Drake McHugh wakes up in bed to discover that both of his legs have been amputated and exclaims in horror, "Where's the rest of me?" which later became the title of Reagan's autobiography published in 1981) and *Knute Rockne, All American* (1940) (which also led to one of his many nicknames, the "Gipper," for the character of George Gipp, the doomed college football player Reagan played in the film) where he was allowed to display more dramatic range than in previous years. From 1947 to 1952 and 1959 to 1960 Reagan was also the president of the Screen Actors Guild where he became involved in anti-communist causes and urged actors to cooperate with the HUAC. Reagan continued to work less on his acting, became prominent in Republican circles, and in 1966 was elected governor of California where he served two terms. Based on his popularity (despite numerous controversies and his unpopularity on the left), Reagan parlayed his governorship of California into

President Ronald Reagan, "The Great Communicator," at a presidential conference. (Photofest)

a race for president, first in the 1968 election, later in the 1976 primaries, and then successfully in 1980, with a landslide reelection in 1984.

During his career as president, Reagan was a master of the televisual image, and his training as an actor served him well in presenting information to the American people on screen. Just as Franklin Delano Roosevelt had been a master of radio's power to feel intimacy and connection (see **Fireside Chats**), Reagan used television to project an image of "just folks" and intimacy where it felt as though he was speaking to the average American and had his/her best interests in mind, despite the nuances of whatever proposal he was presenting at the time. Reagan was also a powerful voice for Western notions of freedom, and his image as a powerful "cowboy" type might also have been a catalyst for both much loathing from communist leaders and admiration from the citizens of Eastern European countries. Reagan's image as someone not afraid to fight also contributed to numerous protests against him. Punk bands in particular, alarmed by Reagan's saber rattling, wrote numerous songs against him, and one New York band even named themselves "Reagan Youth" after the president. In a famous media hoax, the English radical anarchist band Crass doctored a tape of Thatcher and Reagan talking to make it seem that Thatcher had let a British war ship be sunk by the Argentinean navy with Reagan's blessing in order to facilitate the Falklands War. Although the U.S. government originally thought it was a KGB plot, eventually the band was caught by a British newspaper and admitted its involvement (also see "**Thatchergate Tapes**"). Other parodies of Reagan included the "**Rapping Ronnie**" rap single where a Reagan impersonator rapped about trying to get at least 2 percent of the black vote, while Nancy Reagan played bass in the background and Edwin Meese manned the wheels of steel (turntables, for those of you not as hip as Rapping Ronnie).

Despite the many parodies of Reagan, in particular in editorial **political cartoons** Reagan's popularity continued to soar. A major factor in Reagan's continuing popularity as president was his image consultant, Michael Deaver. Deaver, a former aide to Reagan as governor, was well known for creating popular images of Reagan, such as Reagan posing at the Great Wall of China and famously atop the cliffs at Normandy on the 40th anniversary of the Allied invasion of Europe. Although in 1985 Deaver caused controversy for allowing Reagan to lay a wreath at the Bitburg cemetery where former SS officers were buried, he quickly recovered by adding a stop at the Bergen-Belsen concentration camp. Deaver famously accepted no credit for the numerous photo ops created for Reagan, but instead simply insisted that "the only thing I did was light him well" and that "I didn't make Ronald Reagan, Ronald Reagan made me." Deaver, who died in 2007, also choreographed Reagan's funeral in 2004, concluding the funeral as the sun set over the Pacific Ocean for a dramatic end to the services.

Reagan was also an eloquent and powerful speaker, although some critics claimed that toward the end of his presidency he was already suffering from early symptoms of Alzheimer's, and other critics felt that he fudged stories and confused facts with fiction. However, Reagan and his speechwriters were responsible for numerous iconic quotes. A particularly evocative image was of Reagan at the Berlin Wall in 1987 challenging Soviet Premier Mikhail Gorbachev to "tear down this wall." Reagan was always quick with a quip, whether scripted or otherwise, including tweaking Walter Mondale during the presidential debates in 1984 about his age, saying, "I will not make age an issue of this campaign. I am not going to exploit, for political purposes, my opponent's youth and inexperience." After an assassination attempt on his life, he first joked with doctors that he "hoped they were all Republicans" and later joked to his wife, Nancy Reagan, in the hospital, "Honey, I forgot to duck!" Reagan had the uncanny ability to diffuse a situation while simultaneously disarming an opponent, as when he famously told President **Jimmy Carter** during the one and only televised presidential debate in 1980, "There you go again" as a dismissal of Carter's opinions (PBS.org. www.pbs.org /wgbh/amex/carter/peopleevents/e_1980.htm).

When Reagan died in 2004 during the presidential election campaign, many critics noted that the national outpouring of grief and mourning that surrounded the funeral might have inadvertently boosted the Bush campaign. The Reagan funeral was the first state funeral held since the death of Lyndon Johnson in 1973, and Reagan was buried at his Presidential Library in Simi Valley, California. Whatever critics from the left or right thought about Reagan's particular policies, Reagan was the most telegenic president since **John F. Kennedy** and the first president to master the art of the presidency as performance in an age of electronic media. Reagan's natural charm, combined with years of training in the fields of acting and politics, made him an enormously effective communicator and, unlike his successor, **George H. Bush**, a man who clearly was at home in front of the camera; one could argue that Reagan was the preeminent pop culture president of the twentieth century.

"REVOLVING DOOR." See Part I, Chapter 7, "Political Campaign Advertising," and **Furlough Commercial**.

ROCK, CHRIS. Chris Rock (1965–) first came to public attention as a cast member on *Saturday Night Live* from 1990 to 1993, and although he had not used his full potential, Rock was soon spotted as a major talent and began a series of popular movies including the rap parody *CB4*. However, it was stand-up where Rock found his true calling once again, and for the past 15 years he has been one of the most astute political comedians of his time. Starting with the *Bring the Pain* special on HBO in 1996, Rock has made a career of wry political and social commentary. From hilarious but logical comments on gun control (simply raise the price of bullets enough to make them unaffordable) to lambasting those in the African American community who claim that simply taking care of their children is enough to make them good men ("you're supposed to take care of your children!"), Rock's sketches drew praise from many in the African American community who saw his work on social responsibility as upholding traditional values. Recently Rock created a mostly nonpolitical show about the travails of his younger self, the popular CW show, *Everybody Hates Chris*. (See also **African American Stand-Up Comedians** and **Stand-Up Comedy and Politics**.)

ROCK THE VOTE. A youth-centered, ostensibly nonpartisan political institution, Rock the Vote (RTV) was founded in 1990 by several members of the music recording industry who wished to challenge what they perceived as a surge of assaults on freedom of speech and artistic expression. Its first campaign, "Censorship is UnAmerican," presented a series of public service announcements

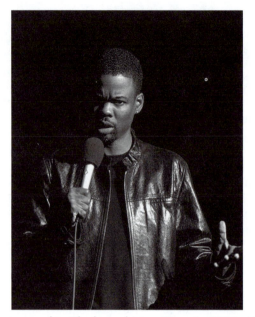

Chris Rock performing on his Black Ambition Tour in 2004. (AP Photo/Douglas Healey)

(commercials for nonprofit causes) that featured appearances by Iggy Pop, Red Hot Chili Peppers, Woody Harrelson, and other celebrities. The following year, however, RTV extended its program to promote youth voter registration. Since then, its mission has mostly been dedicated to motivating this base of younger voters that, until the presidential election of 2004, had been steadily decreasing for the past several decades. (Eventually, a spin-off coined "Rap the Vote" supplemented the effort, turning to artists and spokespeople specifically associated with the rap genre.) The group supported the National Voter Registration Reform Act, which was intended to help voters register by allowing them to do so at government motor vehicle facilities. The bill was passed by Congress, vetoed by President **George H. Bush**, and then later enacted by President **Bill Clinton** in 1993.

RTV secured still greater attention in 1992 when it partnered with several network television sponsors, including MTV, a cable channel that was originally almost entirely music oriented and has been targeted toward young people since its birth in 1982. With the use of MTV celebrities spreading the message through public service announcements, this alliance was meant to help RTV get in touch with a younger audience. Through its efforts, according to its own reporting, RTV helped register 350,000 young people and prompt over 2 million new youth voters to head to the polls. The increase in voting by this demographic halted a 20-year skid in youth turnout. Following this success, RTV has continued to mount "get out the vote" campaigns during subsequent presidential elections. Though the organization has also been involved in other goals, such as health care education and antidiscrimination advocacy, it has received most of its recognition through its voting drives. To further its objectives, RTV has consistently applied and enhanced several tactics, which include:

- **Reliance on celebrities.** RTV has sought to maintain a high profile and resonate with young audiences by incorporating the collaboration of prominent celebrities. Some of the notable figures who have functioned as spokespeople or served in other ways are Drew Barrymore, LL Cool J, Chuck D, the Beastie Boys, Alicia Keys, Lenny Kravitz, Madonna, Justin Timberlake, Ricky Martin, Snoop Dogg, Black Eyed Peas, Samuel L. Jackson, and a host of others. RTV has staged a number of television events and specials featuring popular actors, musicians, comedians, and athletes.

- **Making voting registration easier.** In 1996, RTV introduced a program to register voters by phone, as well as a Web site offering online registration. It has also organized bus tours (for example, MTV's "Choose or Lose" bus traveled around the country) and "Street Teams" of volunteers to facilitate registration.

- **Strategic partnerships.** In addition to its celebrity involvement, RTV has fueled its endeavors by building relationships with many valuable sources, such as corporations, radio stations, schools, and concert tours.

- **Comprehensive use of media.** RTV has tried to maximize its reach and effectiveness with well-synchronized media plans. Its public service announcements and other promotions have been placed in magazines and on television, radio, and the Internet.

RTV continued its mission during the 2004 presidential election between incumbent **George W. Bush** and Senator John Kerry. Over 1.2 million people completed voter registration forms on RTV's or its partners' Web sites. On-the-ground efforts, such as the RTV Bus Tour and the organizational tactics of its Community Street Teams, resulted in an additional 200,000 potential voters signing up. RTV also used two Internet social network portals—**MySpace** and Meetup—to reach young Americans. Through Meetup, people could identify others with like-minded political interests and plan face-to-face meetings. In another instance of mining the latest technologies, RTV disseminated political information via cell phone text messaging. Again, RTV formed alliances with an array of corporations, media companies, and nonprofit outfits. Still, celebrity endorsements stood at the heart of RTV's strategy. Artists buttressed the cause in several ways, including attending RTV gatherings staged as Hollywood-style parties, performing at bus tour events, and serving as RTV spokespeople in public service announcements or at other settings. Some prominent figures were at the very core of a few specific programs. The **Dixie Chicks**, for example, sponsored "Chicks Rock, Chicks Vote," an initiative designed to resonate specifically with young women.

Eventually, RTV's alliance with MTV strained the organization's nonpartisanship stance, as most of the celebrities used by RTV in conjunction with MTV were unabashedly partisan and working to remove Republican candidates from office. After the 2004 election, RTV fell on hard times. The institution came to be regarded by many as a tainted organization. Furthermore, the group's failure to become either an advocacy group for the left or a truly nonpartisan group complicated its mission. By 2006, it was reported through the news that RTV was $700,000 in debt, had lost much of its donor support, and had cut its staff to just two employees. As of the writing of this book, RTV is essentially a skeleton operation. While its overall success is still up in the air, it does seem as though RTV and other similar organizations make inroads into getting younger voters interested in politics, as well as help to increase voter registration and possibly turnout on Election Day.

RONNIE'S RAP/RAPPING RONNIE. Ronnie's Rap/Rapping Ronnie refers to novelty rap singles from the 1980s that involved a Ronald Reagan imitator spouting folksy Ronald Reagan-esque quips about helping African Americans over a primitive rap beat. The record was produced by Ron and the D.C. Crew in the mid-1980s and remains one of the few early novelty rap songs that satirized American politics.

ROWAN AND MARTIN'S LAUGH-IN. *Rowan and Martin's Laugh-In* (1968–1973), an American comedy and variety show, was one of the most popular programs of the late 1960s, mixing politics and pop culture jokes along with vaudeville era jokes and blackouts as well as cameos by film stars and politicians. One episode featured John Wayne reading a poem that went "Roses are red/Violets are green/Get off your butts/And join the marines." **Richard Nixon** also appeared, looking somewhat confused and asking in a confused tone of voice, "sock it to me?" While the program may look relatively mild in comparison to many of today's programs, it was still one of the most popular programs that satirized American culture and politics during the 1960s.

S

SALON. *Salon* is a popular left-leaning online magazine, founded in 1995 by David Talbot, with some support by Apple Computer. (See Part I, Chapter 8, "Politics Online.")

SATURDAY NIGHT LIVE. *Saturday Night Live (SNL)* is an irreverent late night comedy series started by producer Lorne Michaels in 1975. The show immediately gained attention for the antics of the show's stars, the "Not Ready for Prime Time Players," as well as for a satiric take on politics and political humor. From the very first season, the show was not afraid to take on politics. A memorable sketch had Dan Aykroyd as **Richard Nixon** forcing a bewildered John Belushi as Henry Kissinger to pray with him for guidance about his resignation. Aykroyd, a gifted mimic, was also adept at skewering **Jimmy Carter**, whom he portrayed as a good old boy and born-again Christian, but one with "lust in his heart." Nixon's successor, **Gerald Ford**, was treated no less irreverently, with a masterful impression by Chevy Chase giving many Americans the impression that the president, as portrayed by Chase, was constantly taking pratfalls and was terminally clumsy.

During the Reagan years a variety of actors played him, including Phil Hartman, and for the most part he was portrayed as a senile and bumbling old fool, except when in some sketches the façade went down and **Ronald Reagan** was revealed as the mastermind behind the Iran-Contra scandal (see **Political Scandals**) and in command of every detail, even speaking in Farsi to a contact on the telephone. When **George H. Bush** took over as commander in chief, Dana Carvey took over as the president, and his nasally whining and trademark "not gonna do it" were actually less harsh than the portrayal of Reagan had been a few years previously. When **Bill Clinton** was elected, Darrell Hammond played him first as a good old boy with a knack of explaining complex economic problems while glomming free fries from fast-food customers, to a lascivious and lecherous president, faking remorse at his near impeachment. As **George W. Bush** took over,

Hammond switched to a Gore impersonation and Will Ferrell took over as the frat-boy-esque hard-drinking persona of George W. Bush.

Although Jan Hooks had played **Hillary Clinton** in the early 1990s, Amy Poehler was extremely adept at portraying the former first lady and current senator as a smug and slightly cold first lady. In a memorable event Clinton herself showed up as a guest on *SNL* on March 1, 2008, during the presidential primary campaign in an episode that indicated that *SNL* was parodying the fact that **Barack Obama** seemed to get preferential treatment by the press. The show, which had been struggling with ratings, became more popular during the primary and election season of 2008, with hilarious depictions of debates and of the major players, including Obama, Republican presidential running mates Senator **John McCain** and Governor Sarah Palin, and Democrat running mate to Obama, Senator Joe Biden. Since the 2008 election Fred Armisen, a white performer, has been playing President Obama in moderate blackface. (For additional examples of satirical depictions of presidents, see names of presidents, beginning with **John F. Kennedy.**)

SCHLESSINGER, LAURA (DR. LAURA). Best known as the host of a talk radio show named after her, Dr. Laura (full name, Laura Catherine Schlessinger; 1947–) has also written popular books and appeared often on television, even once serving as the star of her own short-lived television talk show. She has a Ph.D. in physiology and certification as a counselor.

Her radio career began in the 1970s as a featured guest on a program hosted by Bill Balance in California. After a successful rise in the field, she finally landed her own daytime show, which became nationally syndicated in 1994. The program centers on Dr. Laura giving advice to listeners who call in and seek her counsel on various concerns, especially regarding marriage, romantic relationships, parenting, sexuality, and other interpersonal matters. Widely recognized for her politically conservative stance on social issues, Dr. Laura is generally openly critical of what she considers immoral practices, such as premarital sex, "permissive" parenting, and placing children in day care rather than foregoing work to take care of them at home. Her style is straightforward, even blunt—she frequently cuts off long-winded callers to quickly get to what she perceives as the core of a problem and offer a prompt solution. Because of her strong political views and sometimes abrasive manner, she has generated controversy even as she has attracted a loyal base of fans (her program has consistently been among the highest rated talk radio shows for years).

Her positions on homosexuality, in particular, have sparked public outcry. Adamantly opposed to same-sex marriage, Dr. Laura has described homosexuality as a "biological error." In response to her increasingly strident expression toward nonheterosexual behavior, members of the GLBT (Gay-Lesbian-Bisexual-Transgendered) community staged a string of protests in various cities around the country. Other controversies have entailed her apparent lack of credentials to practice any form of psychiatry and the discovery that, earlier in her life, Schlessinger had allegedly engaged in some of the very activities that she condemns on her program.

In spite of the flak she has generated, however, Dr. Laura continues to command a sizable audience today.

SCHWARZENEGGER, ARNOLD. Austrian-born former film star best known for a series of action films in the 1980s and 1990s, Arnold Schwarzenegger (1947–) improbably became the governor of California in 2003, after announcing his candidacy on *The Tonight Show with Jay Leno* on August 6, 2003, in a recall election on October 7 of that year. Schwarzenegger had long been active in Republican causes and fund-raising before his run for governor (ironically he is married to Maria Shriver, a niece of President **John F. Kennedy**). Although his terms as governor of California were sometime contentious, he won reelection easily in November 2006 with over 57 percent of the vote. Schwarzenegger was not the first actor to become governor of California, as future president **Ronald Reagan** had held that distinction before him for two terms in the 1960s and 1970s. Schwarzenegger's future political ambitions are uncertain, but some members of Congress have in the past suggested amending the constitution to allow foreign-born Americans to run for president, an outcome that seems unlikely as of this writing, but then again so did Schwarzenegger becoming governor of California. Schwarzenegger has also long been parodied as the German actor Rainier Wolfcastle in the popular animated television show *The Simpsons*, and a character called President Schwarzenegger appeared in the 2007 *The Simpsons Movie* (for more information about the television show, see *The Simpsons*). Schwarzenegger is often the butt of jokes on late night talk shows regarding his accent and persona. He has also been given various comic nicknames such as "Conan the Republican" and "The Governator."

He had co-starred with another budding politician, professional wrestler and future governor of Minnesota **Jesse Ventura**, in the 1987 film *Predator*.

SCHWARZKOPF, GENERAL NORMAN. Popular and telegenic four-star general who appeared regularly on television during the Gulf War in the early 1990s providing updates for viewers, General Norman Schwarzkopf (1934–) became an iconic spokesman for the Bush administration's war plans and was considered a viable presidential candidate for some time. He retired from the military in August 1991 and now primarily works as a television analyst on military affairs. Although Schwarzkopf wrote a popular book after retirement, *It Doesn't Take a Hero*, he never actively sought political office and largely retired from public life after the Gulf War.

SEE IT NOW. Regarded as the first regular television documentary series, *See It Now* took up many contentious subjects, including school segregation and, most notably, the actions of anti-communist crusader **Senator Joseph McCarthy**. An offshoot of the radio show *Hear It Now*, it catapulted the newsman **Edward R. Murrow** to even greater prominence. In 1954, one show combined clips from McCarthy speeches with brief commentary by Murrow that debunked the senator's points. Another installment featured a cafeteria worker who had been accused of being a communist; yet its portrayal made the idea of her being a threat to the nation seem ridiculous. McCarthy was offered an episode to reply. The following week, Murrow delivered a rebuttal. Some media scholars reason that Murrow's bold coverage had an impact on events. Within months after the telecasts, the Senate had voted to censure McCarthy and his popularity dramatically declined.

Largely due to the tendency of *See It Now* to cover controversial topics, advertising sponsorship for the show began to wane. Some CBS executives also tired of the stress evoked by the risky programming. *See It Now* consequently shifted from a weekly feature to a show that appeared only occasionally. In 1958, it was cancelled altogether and eventually replaced by **CBS Reports**.

THE SELLING OF THE PRESIDENT. A book written in 1969 by Joe McGinniss that documents the 1968 political campaign of Republican **Richard Nixon**, *The Selling of the President* helped intensify the debate about the appropriate place of marketing in politics and whether candidates should be sold like cigarettes and soap. Readers were exposed to the inner mechanisms of transforming a politician into a likeable TV commodity. To accomplish the feat, according to McGinniss, Nixon's media advisors attempted to carefully control every televised appearance. Some political historians, however, do not fully accept McGinniss's central points, suggesting the author handpicked the evidence he needed to support the case he had already decided to make. Other criticisms include the contention that marketing alone can rarely—if ever—dupe an audience into embracing a candidate image that is entirely incongruent with the real person, and the assertion that Nixon's consultants by no means inaugurated the processes of image and media management by outside professionals—such procedures were in operation well before the Republican's run in 1968. Several of the key figures who worked on Nixon's behalf claim they were not creating an image from scratch as much as merely calling attention to several of the candidate's actual and most desirable qualities.

THE 700 CLUB. A popular television program that examines political, social, and moral issues, broadcast by televangelist Pat Robertson on CBN (the Christian Broadcasting Network), *The 700 Club* was founded in 1966 and grew to be televised on 95 percent of the television marketplace during its peak. The program is now syndicated on CBN and carried on the ABC Family Channel, as well as Trinity Broadcasting, and now is hosted by Pat Robertson, Terry Meeuwsen, and Gordon Robertson, with news anchor Lee Webb.

The current program features not only emphasis on prayer and spiritual issues but also reporting on global religious and Christian issues. The show was hosted for some time by James and the late Tammy Faye Bakker before they left to host the PTL (Praise the Lord) Network in the early 1970s. The program is now available in Asian and Spanish language markets and a version of the show debuted in England in 2004. Although *The 700 Club* claims to be apolitical, Robertson has used the show as a soapbox for his sometimes-controversial statements, such as in 2005 suggesting that Venezuelan president Hugo Chávez should be assassinated. Christian broadcasting is one of the most prominent ways in which the Christian right has used television and the Internet to try and engage their voter base into contemporary politics.

THE SIMPSONS. *The Simpsons*, an extremely popular American animated program that has aired since 1989, is known for its humorous skewering not only of popular culture but also of various politicians. Several episodes have included

The Simpsons (FOX Television). The show frequently takes on political issues, such as this episode featuring Bob Dole, Homer Simpson, and Bill Clinton. (Fox/Photofest)

cameos from major political figures (British Prime Minister Tony Blair made an appearance while in office) and many major American figures have been parodied. In one episode Homer Simpson was engaged in a running battle with new neighbor former President **George H. Bush**, who was later replaced in the neighborhood by former President **Gerald Ford**. During the 1996 presidential election, the *Treehouse of Horror* Halloween episode featured candidates **Bob Dole** and President **Bill Clinton** kidnapped and replaced by alien invaders, Kang and Kodos. (The two candidates are later accidentally sent out in an air lock by Homer.) Although no American politicians have lent their voices to the Simpsons, the show parodies theme and American social and political life on a regular basis. When the two presidential candidates are revealed as aliens, the American people vote for them anyway, as opposed to voting for a third party candidate and "throwing your vote away" in the words of one of the aliens. In a later episode, Kang and Kodos invade earth in a parody of the *War of the Worlds* remake and lament the fact that "we were supposed to have been greeted as liberators" (satirizing the presumed Iraqi response to American occupying troops. In addition, the show has also made strong statements against commercialism, and has attacked the Fox network (who air *The Simpsons*) as being right wing (in one episode after the 2004 election, a **Fox News** truck is seen going by with a Bush/Cheney banner, playing the Queen song "We Are the Champions") and against consumer culture. Of course in other episodes, Homer is portrayed as the quintessential American voter, fat, lazy, and uninformed, muttering about "liberal bias" and "slick Willie" under his breath, but this is not meant to suggest apathy as a political choice, just to demonstrate the futility of being uninformed. The Simpsons have also been mentioned by political figures, according to the Web site www.snpp.com, "In a speech to the National Religious Broadcasters convention (1/27/92), then President George Bush said 'The nation needs to be closer to the Waltons than the Simpsons.' " This time, Matt Groening replied "Hey, the Simpsons are just like the Waltons. Both families are praying for the end of the Depression." The clip later played at the opening of an episode, and Bart used the same line as Groening. (For discussion on political cartoons in general, see **Political Cartoons**.)

60 MINUTES. Started in 1968 by CBS, *60 Minutes* is probably television's most well-known news magazine—or even one of its most successful shows in general. A descendant of former CBS news programs such as *See It Now* and *CBS Reports*, the investigative journalism program was one of the ten highest rated shows for years and is still running strong today. Likely due to its achievements, other network executives later followed suit and created spin-offs of their own, including ABC's *20/20* and *Dateline NBC*. Together, these and similar shows that string together several short segments have almost completely shoved the traditional, long-format documentary off of commercial television. The resulting emphasis has been much more on personalities, "human interest" stories, current affairs, and individual cases of corporate malfeasance than on the kind of broader social issues treated in documentaries before the dawn of television (see Part I, Chapter 2). Still, from time to time, *60 Minutes* has featured and continues to address political figures and issues.

SLATE. An influential online magazine of progressive, moderately liberal slant, *Slate* was started in 1996 by Michael Kinsley, with corporate backing from Microsoft. (See Part I, Chapter 8, "Politics Online.")

SMOTHERS BROTHERS. The Smothers Brothers were a popular team of comedians and musical brothers who fought numerous censorship battles over political content during the course of their popular program *The Smothers Brothers Comedy Hour* (CBS 1967–1969). The real life brothers, Tommy and Dick Smothers, consistently pushed the envelope during the Vietnam War with their topics, jokes about Vietnam, racism, and other topics that were considered taboo by the network's censors during that time period. The show also showcased the career of comedian and perennial presidential candidate **Pat Paulsen** who started running for president in 1968 under the S.T.A.G. (Straight Talking American Government) ticket. Scenes that were cut from the program before it aired included a performance by folk singer Pete Seeger singing "Waist Deep in the Big Muddy" and even a skit where Tommy Smothers and Elaine May played network censors. The brothers later revived the show various times for reunion specials.

SPIN CITY. Long-running television show about the mayor of New York City and his misfit staff, *Spin City* starred Michael J. Fox and Barry Bostwick. The show ran on ABC from 1996 to 2002 (although Fox left due to health reasons and was replaced during the last season by Charlie Sheen). The show demonstrated a healthy dose of cynicism about local politics, featuring a mayor (Barry Bostwick) who had to be constantly guarded and massaged by his political staff to keep him from making a misstep or verbal gaffe. The show was one of the few American sitcoms (numerous British sitcoms such as *Yes, Minister* and *Yes, Prime Minister* had already broken this ground on British television) to attack the absurdity of American politics and the behind-the-scenes steps that are often taken so that voters do not find out the true capabilities of those they have elected to office. Fox was later notable for appearing in campaign commercials for Senate candidate Claire McCaskill, a Missouri Democrat, and for Wisconsin Governor Jim Doyle (D), as well as Democratic challenger Benjamin Cardin in Maryland. The actor's haggard appearance, general shakiness, and slurred words led talk show host **Rush Limbaugh** to attack him for intentionally not taking his medication that day, a charge Fox vigorously denied.

SPITZER, ELIOT. Eliot Spitzer (1959–) was the governor of New York State from January 2007 until his resignation in March 2008, who is now best known for resigning his office in disgrace after it was disclosed that Spitzer was a client of a high-priced prostitution ring. Spitzer, who was state attorney general from 1998 to 2006, was elected governor with an overwhelming majority in 2006 and with his credential as a crusader against crime, it appeared that Spitzer would govern from a bully pulpit. However, Spitzer soon courted controversy-involving feuds with the Republican state senate majority leader Joe Bruno and other petty squabbles. Still, Spitzer had an enormous amount of political capital to spend, when suddenly and surprisingly he was named the subject of a probe into a prostitution ring on March 10, 2008. Spitzer, after a weekend's indecision, resigned the governorship and was succeeded by Lieutenant Governor David Patterson. Spitzer's meteoric and improbable fall will doubtlessly make him fodder for comedians for generations to come, and the man who dreamed of once being the first Jewish president instead set a new standard for political scandals. (For a discussion of other noteworthy political scandals, see **Political Scandals**.)

SPURLOCK, MORGAN. A documentarian who has also translated his work into a popular book, Morgan Spurlock (1970–) rose to unlikely fame through his 2004 documentary, *Super Size Me*. An unexpected success in theaters, the film traces Spurlock's commitment to eating nothing but fast food for a month. Along the way, he gains considerable weight and develops health concerns. The nonfiction work serves as an indictment of the fast-food industry.

Probably largely due to his success with *Super Size Me*, Spurlock secured the credibility to produce his own television show. In each episode of *30 Days*, created for the cable network FX, an everyday person (or sometimes Spurlock himself) is placed into a situation far different from his or her normal circumstances for 30 days. The scenarios are designed to challenge the status quo thinking on a topic, which gives the series political significance. For instance, in one installment, a conservative, heterosexual, Christian man agreed to live for a month with a gay man in San Francisco's Castro District. By the end of the program, he has acquired a more tolerant attitude toward homosexuals. In another episode, to shed light on the U.S. prison system, Spurlock spends 30 days in incarceration, including three days in solitary confinement.

Spurlock later produced another full-length documentary, *Where in the World Is Osama Bin Laden?*, which depicted the filmmaker hunting for Osama bin Laden, the notorious mastermind behind the terrorist attacks of September 11, 2001.

STAND-UP COMEDY AND POLITICS. Ever since the founding of America, there has been a long tradition of political satire. While many of the early attacks were particularly vicious and largely confined to newspapers and pamphlets, songs and sheet music, and political cartoons, by the turn of the twentieth century, there had developed new forms of political satire. Early vaudeville had political overtones, reminiscent of the plays and musicals that had dominated New York theater since the time of Lincoln.

By the mid-twentieth century, a new type of comedian had emerged, one who could be categorized under the title of "stand-up" comedian, or one who did a solo comic set for five minutes to an hour on topical situations. In the 1960s a new group of politically active stand-up comedians challenged the status quo of using risqué jokes, the borscht belt style of poking fun at relationships; instead comedians such as **Lenny Bruce**, Woody Allen, Shelly Berman, Mort Sahl, and Mike Nichols and Elaine May pioneered a new kind of stand-up that brought in both contemporary topics and overtly sexual topics and also challenged the political institutions of the United States. The first overtly political comedian was Mort Sahl, who changed the nature of stand-up by offering stream of consciousness intellectual observations instead of standard jokes. Sahl once remarked, "I'm not so much interested in politics as I am in overthrowing the government." Although a risky statement to make in the mid-1950s, Sahl persisted, also asking the rhetorical question, "Is there anyone I haven't offended?" During a time when many comedians were afraid of being called before the HUAC, Sahl instead deliberately made jokes poking fun at Dwight Eisenhower, **Richard Nixon**, and even **Senator Joseph McCarthy**, an approach that made Sahl nationally famous and landed him on the cover of *Time* magazine. In the mid-1960s Sahl lost popularity as he focused relentlessly on the Warren Commission and various conspiracy theories about the **John F. Kennedy** assassination. While audience members booed and Sahl often got into heated exchanges, he remained a cult favorite, becoming even more popular as his vocal attacks on the Vietnam War and frequent appearances with the **Smothers Brothers**, Steve Allen, and others exposed his witty acerbic style to a new generation of fans unaware of his earlier infamy. Although Sahl maintained a low profile in the 1970s and 1980s, he also took jobs as a script doctor, and with the advent of his records being reissued on compact discs a new generation became Sahl fans.

Lenny Bruce is perhaps the best-known political comedian in American history, and his long-running battles with his many obscenity cases and arrests for violating public standards of decency make him more well known for his legal troubles than for the content of his act. Bruce also pioneered a free-form string of associated topics, sometimes not caring if the audience was following him or not. While many of Bruce's earlier routines were attacks on contemporary morality, he later became even more provocative, talking about oral sex and using the words "to" and "come." As Bruce's legal troubles mounted, his drug habit escalated and Bruce was found dead of an apparent morphine overdose on August 3, 1966. Other comedians in the mold of Bruce and Sahl, including an early Woody Allen during his stand-up years, were also known for their insightful political observations.

The 1970s saw many of the earlier comedians moving on to filmmaking, semi-retirement, or an inability to change with the times. A new breed of younger, angrier comedians took over the limelight, such as Richard Pryor and George Carlin.

George Carlin was a notorious stand-up comedian active since the 1960s who attacked right-wing hypocrisy and censorship. One of his most famous routines, the seven words you can never say on television, was the source of a Supreme Court case when the Pacifica radio network was fined for playing the routine on the radio; in their decision the Supreme Court ruled against Pacifica 5–4 (for additional discussion of Pacifica in general, see **Pacifica and Community Radio**). Carlin, who had performed stand-up since the late 1950s, had always been politically outspoken, and in more recent years in his stand-up routines, HBO specials, and appearances on programs such as *Real Time with Bill Maher* he had been particularly critical of the United States and the political system, labeling both parties as beholden to corporate interests and providing no real choice for the voter. According to Carlin,

> There is a certain amount of righteous indignation I hold for this culture, because to get back to the real root of it, to get broader about it, my opinion that is my species—and my culture in America specifically—have let me down and betrayed me. I think this species had great, great promise, with this great upper brain that we have, and I think we squandered it on God and Mammon. And I think this culture of ours has such promise, with the promise of real, true freedom, and then everyone has been shackled by ownership and possessions and acquisition and status and power. (Murray, Noel. "Interviews: George Carlin." http://www.avclub.com/content/node/42195/1 [accessed on August 26, 2008])

Carlin was, until his death in June 2008, one of the few active comedians left from the original group of antiestablishment comedians from the late 1950s to still remain in the public eye, and with his performances in the *Bill and Ted* movies and *Thomas the Tank Engine* Carlin had also expanded his audience base to a new generation not yet born when he was first doing the "seven words" monologue.

Pryor, with his profanity-laced monologues about race and his prominent use of the term "nigger" in routines, specialized in not only making people laugh but also making them uncomfortable while they laughed. On live albums documenting his routines, such as *Is It Something I Said?* (1975), *Bicentennial Nigger* (1976), and *Wanted: Richard Pryor Live* (1979), Pryor's frank musings about race were considered outrageous by critics even by today's standards. When Pryor was booked to appear on **Saturday Night Live** in 1975, the show for the first time instituted a five-second tape delay in case Pryor cursed on air, a technique they did not use for similarly edgy comedian George Carlin who was also a frequent host. After a trip to Africa in 1979, Pryor repudiated his frequent use of the word "nigger" and concentrated more on his film career, appearing in over 50 films, mostly forgettable roles that hardly showcased his comedic style. Ironically, the one film that best showcased his style during his prime was the Pryor and Mel Brooks scripted *Blazing Saddles*, a Western parody that Pryor was unable to star in due to his problems with cocaine. Pryor's drug use and complicated life began to eclipse his genius, and in 1986 he was diagnosed with multiple sclerosis (MS), an affliction that gradually robbed him of his ability to walk. Pryor died of MS in 2003, although his original records and DVD and CD reissues attract new fans and inspire new comedians to do edgier material to this day.

A contemporary of Pryor's who died young was Bill Hicks, an acid-tongued underground comedian who ranted about American culture and was considerably more popular in Britain. Hicks, a former drug user, used many of his monologues to attack U.S. policy on drugs and drug legalization. Although Hicks appeared many times on David Letterman, his last routine there was cut by network censors, which showed that up until his untimely death from cancer in 1994, Hicks was still considered too edgy and extreme for network television.

The legacy of comedians such as Carlin, Hicks, and Pryor lived on and numerous comedians such as **Chris Rock** and **Dave Chappelle** carried on this legacy (see **African American Stand-Up Comedians**). Rock, a former ensemble member of *Saturday Night Live*, came into his own when he hosted a series of comedy specials on HBO that included several edgy pieces about race relations. Chappelle, a stand-up comedian best known for his routines about smoking pot, became a star on the edgy and unpredictable *Chappelle's Show*, which included sketches about a blind (and black) white supremacist, scenarios about what would have happened if President **George W. Bush** had been black, as well as less political but equally hilarious send-ups of Rick James and Prince. Chappelle famously walked away from the show during production for a third season and has kept a low profile since then, appearing occasionally to do stand-up unannounced at various clubs. Some other notable modern comedians who include political material in their acts include the absurdist David Cross and Patton Oswalt, who although completely different in style and temperament, also work in the vein of the best political comedy of the past 50 years. Others in a more traditionalist vein include ranter par supreme Lewis Black, Kate Clinton, Will Durst, and Barry Crimmins.

Other stand-up comedians who used politically charged material included many who did so outside of the constraints of stand-up, such as former stand-up comedian Jon Stewart, who in 1999 took over as host on **The Daily Show** (see **News Parodies**) and quickly turned it from a pop culture–obsessed show to one of the most politically insightful entertainment and news programs in the

United States. *The Daily Show* also led to a spin-off show almost as popular, *The Colbert Report* (see **News Parodies**), where former *Daily Show* correspondent Stephen Colbert mocks right-wing talk show hosts in the character of the same name, Stephen Colbert, an often contradictory right-wing talk show host.

Another stand-up comedian who became a political force is **Bill Maher**. Maher, a former bit-part actor and stand-up comedian, first began tackling serious political comments on his first program, *Politically Incorrect*, which ran late night from 1994 to 2002 when it was unceremoniously cancelled for a remark Maher made on air stating that the terrorists who attacked America on September 11, 2001, were reprehensible, but not "cowards," as a suicide mission takes courage. Maher's comments spurred outrage from critics, and although ABC did not cite that as the cause, it certainly precipitated the cancellation. Maher returned with another comedy show about politics, *Real Time with Bill Maher*, on HBO from 2003 to the present, where he continues to attack the powers that be in his usually acerbic style. Maher's guests have included presidential candidates, senators, and politically active actors such as Sean Penn and Ben Affleck, as well as Maher's longtime friend **Ann Coulter**. *Real Time* is one of the most freewheeling and open debate shows that resembles nothing so much as a foul-mouthed version of **William F. Buckley**'s old *Firing Line* program during its heyday. (Also see **News Parodies**.)

Al Franken is one of the most politically active comedians working from the left. Al Franken started his career as a writer and performer on *Saturday Night Live* during the mid-1970s along with then partner Tom Davis before branching out on his own as a performer and writer. Franken worked on and off for *Saturday Night Live* for several decades before leaving in 2004 to host a radio program on the fledgling left-wing talk radio network **Air America**. He hosted this program until 2007 when he left to run for the senate seat in Minnesota formerly held by Franken's hero, the late Paul Wellstone, and next held by Republican Norm Coleman. Franken is one of the first stand-up comedians outside of **Pat Paulsen** to run for office, although his chances are taken more seriously than Paulsen's were. Air America was also known for a program by stand-up comedian Janeane Garofalo, who became more political later in her career. Others with a long-standing career include musical comic Mark Russell, the more benign comedic stylings of Garrison Keillor, and the late night monologues of David Letterman, Jay Leno, and Conan O'Brien. Comedy is one of the key ways in which the American public encounters politics, and sometimes political scandals or issues only become important to the American public though humor. As Jeffrey Jones argued in his book *Entertaining Politics: New Political Television and Civic Culture*, comedy, particularly televised comedy, had the potential to "offer voices, positions and perspectives not found in traditional television presentations of politics" (Jones, Jeffrey P. *Entertaining Politics: New Political Television and Civic Culture*. Lanham, MD: Rowman & Littlefield, 2005, p. 9). If the country is too large and diverse to have any sense of what Jürgen Habermas referred to as a "Public Sphere," or a sense of a national conversation, then political comedy must be an important source not only of political entertainment but of some level of participation as well for many Americans who might otherwise feel disenfranchised or powerless before the seeming inaccessibility of contemporary politics.

STERN, HOWARD. One of the most famous personalities in talk radio, Howard Stern (1954–) is widely regarded as one of the genre's premier "shock jocks," a label often used to indicate the provocative nature of the form. He began his career as a more traditional disc jockey, landing his first morning show, which featured a rock and roll format, in 1978. After radio stints in Detroit and Washington, D.C., in 1982 Stern moved to New York City, where he further perfected the inflammatory persona he had already set in motion. He eventually enjoyed a meteoric rise in the 1990s, even starring in a movie about his life. In addition, his radio show was translated into a television program. Through the years, Stern has consistently challenged authority and taboos of many flavors. Often contradictorily displaying both conservative and liberal positions, Stern, critics charge, nonetheless has also persistently presented women as sexual objects and privileged the voice of the boorish, arrogant male. He has repeatedly come into conflict with the Federal Communications Commission because of his emphasis on vulgarity and relatively explicit sexual themes.

Largely because of these run-ins, Stern departed "terrestrial" radio in 2006 for the less regulated realm of satellite radio.

STONE, OLIVER. Prolific leftist film director, best known for films such as *Born on the Fourth of July* (1989), *JFK* (1991), *Wall Street* (1987), *Natural Born Killers* (1994), and *Platoon* (1986), Oliver Stone (1946–) was very much influenced by his own experiences as a soldier in Vietnam, which radicalized him and inculcated a desire to expose what he considers the basic hypocrisy of the American system. While not all of Stone's films approach political issues as directly as films *JFK*, *Nixon*, or *Born on the Fourth of July*, even films such as *Wall Street* deal with not only the motivations of the main characters but also the inherent limitations of capitalism and democracy, as in the scene in *Wall Street* where Gordon Gekko (played by Mike Douglas and clearly modeled on ex-Wall Street tycoon Ivan Boesky) justifies the pillaging of small business to help fatten the purses of stockholders by declaring, "Greed, for lack of a better word, is good." Gekko's character is as much a victim as captain of industry, trapped, in Stone's world, in a system that demands that the individual is sacrificed to the system. Stone has also worked extensively as a script writer/doctor on many supposedly apolitical films such as *Conan the Barbarian* (1982), *Midnight Express* (1978), and *Scarface* (1983; which can easily be seen as another indictment of the American dream), but overall he can be seen as a leftist version of **Frank Capra**, a filmmaker who approaches film as a struggle between corrupt political systems where the only hope is the redemption of the individual. His latest film as of this writing, *World Trade Center* (2006), surprised many critics on the right, who expected Stone to make a polemic piece instead of a nuanced human drama about two trapped Port Authority officers and the rescue efforts that united their families (also see **9/11 Films**). Stone's career as one of the most politically active filmmakers ever to engage the public is remarkable for its longevity and success in a marketplace where overtly political films no longer sell as well as they have in the past.

Films as director: *W.* (2008); *World Trade Center* (2006); *Alexander* (2004); *"America Undercover": Looking for Fidel* (2004, TV); *"America Undercover": Persona Non Grata* (2003, TV); *Comandante* (2003); *Any Given Sunday* (1999); *U Turn* (1997); *Nixon* (1995); *Natural Born Killers* (1994); *Heaven & Earth* (1993); *JFK* (1991); *The Doors* (1991); *Born on the Fourth of July* (1989); *Talk Radio* (1988); *Wall Street* (1987); *Platoon* (1986); *Salvador* (1986); *The Hand* (1981); *Mad Man of Martinique* (1979); *Seizure* (1974); *Last Year in Viet Nam* (1971).

"SUN CITY" (SONG). "Sun City" is an all-star protest song against the racist policies of the South African government and its "Sun City" resort. The single was released in 1985 and was organized by E-Street guitarist (and future *Sopranos* star) Steve Van Zandt under the name "Artists Against Apartheid." The single featured vocal contributions from many luminaries in the rock and rap worlds, including Joey Ramone, **Bob Dylan**, Lou Reed, Jackson Browne, Run DMC, Ron Carter, Miles Davis, Pete Townsend, Jimmy Cliff, and Darlene Love. The single opposed Western bands, such as Queen and Ray Charles, and criticized the Reagan administration's policy of constructive engagement. "Sun City" was released during a particularly fertile time for musicians to take political stands and attempt to influence public opinion about political issues. While many punk bands had been doing this for quite some time during the 1970s and 1980s, efforts such as "**Live Aid**," "**Band Aid**," and "Sun City" saw the dawning of a new brand of mainstream political music, which would abate somewhat in the 1990s but come back with a vengeance during the Bush administration under such organizations as **Rock the Vote**, PunkVoter.Com, and "**Vote or Die.**" It is still unclear how successful such musical efforts at political change are, or whether they lead to more voter involvement or participation. (For a full discussion of politics and music in general, see Part I, Chapter 6.)

SUNDAY MORNING POLITICAL SHOWS. Sunday morning political talk shows are public affairs programs telecast on Sunday morning that feature national leaders in politics and other civic concerns such as U.S. presidents, senators, members of the House of Representatives, state governors, White House officials, military leaders, ambassadors, and high-profile journalists and political pundits. Because of their focus on politics, economics, foreign policy, and current affairs, they help television networks fulfill their legal obligation to serve the public interest. The most prominent shows within this genre include *Meet the Press*, *Face the Nation*, and *This Week (with George Stephanopoulos)*. The format originated in the United States, but has spread to other countries around the world. Through the use of satellite technology, on occasion, a politician wishing to strongly promote a certain policy or point of view will seek to appear on more than one of the Sunday shows on the same day. Another common tactic entails being interviewed on at least two of the programs on successive weeks.

Meet the Press is recognized as television's longest running show and, for years, has generally received the highest ratings of any Sunday morning political talk show. Every U.S. president since **John F. Kennedy** has been on the program, although not always while in office. Its origins can be traced to 1945, before its television debut, with the introduction of the radio program *American Mercury Presents: Meet the Press*. Part of the motivation behind the creation of the radio forerunner was to advertise the magazine *The American Mercury*. The NBC television version made its entrance in November 1947 and its name was changed to simply *Meet the Press*. During its early seasons, it sometimes aired in prime time, although it has remained a Sunday morning staple since 1965.

The show originally ran in 30-minute installments, with each episode centering on a single guest being interviewed by a panel of questioners. Martha Roundtree served as the program's first moderator—the only woman to have ever held the position. Over the years, ten other journalists have occupied the moderator's seat.

Perhaps the most famous of all was Tim Russert, who, beginning his reign near the end of 1991 and maintaining it until his untimely death in 2008, also become the show's longest performing host. With Russert at the helm, the program expanded to 60 minutes in length. Moreover, the format shifted from a type of televised press conference (indeed, the show had long billed itself as "America's Press Conference of the Air") to a venue that placed far greater emphasis on Russert's questions and remarks. Although the journalist continued to lead round-table discussions with a panel of experts, he also conducted often lengthy one-on-one interviews with public officials. After his sudden death in June, Tom Brokaw, who had recently retired from anchoring NBC's nightly national news broadcast, became interim moderator. In December 2008, David Gregory was named the program's new host, a role he continues to retain today.

Face the Nation debuted on CBS in 1954 and has remained on the network ever since. Like *Meet the Press*, the show also aired in prime time for short periods in the early 1960s, but then became a Sunday morning fixture. Unlike its NBC counterpart, however, it has always kept its length to 30 minutes. Ted Koop served as its first moderator for roughly one year. Seven other journalists have held the position after Koop left the post, including Bob Schieffer, the program's current host, who began his run in 1991. In its initial seasons, *Face the Nation* usually included a panel of newspeople posing questions to key public figures. Presently, each episode features at least one interview; a round-table discussion involving correspondents, guests, and other contributors on events of the day; and a brief commentary at the end of the telecast.

Issues and Answers, premiering in 1960, represented ABC's entry into the field. In 1981, the show was renamed *This Week with David Brinkley*, with the reputable Brinkley performing as its original moderator. Since Brinkley's retirement in 1996, the talk show has continued to feature the name(s) of its anchor(s) in the title. Cokie Roberts and Sam Donaldson co-hosted the show from 1996 to 2002. Since then, George Stephanopoulos, a chief consultant during **Bill Clinton**'s run for the presidency in 1992, has assumed the position. Like its competitors, *This Week* also presents a panel discussion on pressing issues of the day, although it formally labels this part of the show, the "Roundtable." Through the years, a number of journalists and pundits have appeared as regular panelists, especially George Will, the only person to contribute in this capacity since the program began. Before hosting *This Week*, Roberts, Donaldson, and Stephanopoulos also worked as recurring panelists. Roberts and Donaldson returned to the panel after Stephanopoulos took over as moderator. Another distinctive element of the show, one that directly pulls from the realm of popular culture and entertainment, is the "Sunday Funnies," which replays excerpts of jokes from late-night television programs that ran the previous week.

Although *Meet the Press*, *Face the Nation*, and *This Week* are the most enduring and highly rated Sunday morning political talk shows, other commercial and public broadcasting programs are sometimes associated with the category, such as NBC's *The Chris Matthews Show* (2002–), *The Journal Editorial Report* (2004–), which spent its first season on **PBS** before joining FOX, and *Inside Washington* (1998–), which is currently distributed to PBS.

SWIFT BOAT VETERANS FOR TRUTH. During the 2004 presidential election campaign, "527" groups, a designation that referred to independent political organizations that had been made possible through a recent revision to the U.S. tax code pertaining to political funding, proliferated. The 527 that came to stand out among all the others, though, was the one labeled "Swift Boat Veterans for Truth." It produced a series of advertisements, paid for by Republican operatives, featuring ex-Vietnam service men claiming that Democratic candidate Senator John Kerry had not really deserved the Silver Star, Bronze Star, and the three Purple Heart medals he had received in Vietnam. Less than a week after the Democratic convention, a gathering that made heavy reference to Kerry's purported Vietnam heroism, the group launched its first spot. In it, veterans who supposedly had served with Kerry accused him of lying about his war record and betraying the soldiers with whom he fought. Although the media buy for the commercial was relatively small, once it caught enough people's attention, it took on a life of its own, receiving substantial play and discussion on news shows. Even though several of the claims uttered in the advertisement were debunked by investigators, Kerry hesitated to offer a refutation, an act that, according to many observers, badly damaged his campaign. Not until two weeks after the Swift Boat spot's initial run did Kerry challenge its facts. Yet he did so not through advertising but in a single speech. The next day, the Swift Boat organization placed another commercial in the media and continued to sponsor additional spots. In the midst of the assault, polls showed that about 30 percent of those surveyed believed that Kerry "did not earn" all his wartime medals.

The results of the Swift Boat attacks were to distract the Kerry election team, forcing the candidate to spend time and resources fighting accusations not made by a rival politician, but by an advocacy group. Ultimately, the Swift Boat campaign sparked heated postelection commentary because of it dubious assertions. Moreover, a variety of analysts postulated that it had played a deciding role in Republican **George W. Bush**'s reelection, despite misleading its audience.

SYRIANA. *Syriana* (2005) is a left-wing political film, starring George Clooney as CIA agent Bob Barnes, that was essentially an attack on the U.S. roles in Middle Eastern affairs. It was written and directed by Stephen Gaghan based on the book *See No Evil* by Robert Baer. The film is an extremely cynical look at the political and moral corruption surrounding the oil industry and the role of the CIA and American corporate interests in destabilizing the region. The term "Syriana" refers to a supposed idea from Washington, D.C.–based think tanks that refers to a possible realignment of borders in the Middle East in a way that would stabilize the region and make it more friendly to U.S. interests.

T

TEAM AMERICA. *Team America* (2004) is a film by *South Park* creators Trey Parker and Matt Stone that featured a team of puppets involved in counterterrorism activities. The film itself is a parody of the simplistic jingoistic action films of producer Jerry Bruckheimer, only done with blatantly obvious marionettes. (Stone and Parker had originally wanted to do a puppet version of the film *Pearl Harbor*, but realized that movie was already practically a satire.) It is interesting not only for its entertainment value and inherent absurdism but also because it reflects a largely libertarian view of politics, the points of view of Stone and Parker. Although there is gratuitous action and violence (including a terrorist attack on the Eiffel Tower led by a puppet version of Osama bin Laden) and idiocy by the American counterterrorism agents, there is also an underlying message that American culture is superior to other cultures, and that left-wing actors such as Sean Penn, Janeane Garofalo, and director **Michael Moore** are more dangerous than American military might. The film was condemned by actors such as Sean Penn, who were presumably not amused by their caricatures or the film's politics. However, it still ended up grossing over $30 million in the United States and over $50 million overseas, although it is unclear whether this is in response to the film's implicit politics, or despite them.

TELEVISED WARS. The first use of television to bring dramatic images of war into the American living room has been traced primarily to the Vietnam War, but the first real televised war was the first Iraq conflict where satellite images brought the war into American households in real time as opposed to the time taken during the Vietnam War where film had to be transported, developed, and edited before it could be shown on network television. During the 1970s and 1980s as satellite transmission and videotape technology changed the way conflicts were covered in other countries, war became more immediate because images could be seen almost as soon as they were shot and edited into a news package. Whereas in the past war seemed somewhat impersonal, war was not immediate and appeared only on the nightly news. However, during the First Gulf War, hostilities were over so quickly, and reports so complimentary to the American war effort, that it almost seemed as though the war itself was a recreation, leading French philosopher Jean Baudrillard to write, in a series of essays and eventually in a short book, *The Gulf War Did Not Take Place* published in 1995, that the Gulf War itself had been a simulacrum, although this was a difficult argument to make to the thousands killed on both sides during the war or the many civilians displaced. (Also see **CNN**.)

"THATCHERGATE TAPES." In 1983 the anarchist British punk band Crass was responsible for a notorious hoax that caused alarm in both England and America over a possible KGB attempt to spread anti-American propaganda. Crass doctored several Reagan and Thatcher speeches to create the so-called "Thatchergate Tapes" to mimic a phone call between then British Prime Minister Margaret Thatcher and U.S. President **Ronald Reagan** where Thatcher indicated her responsibility for the sinking of a British warship during the Falklands War. The band's prank led to a statement from the U.S. State Department denouncing the tape as a KGB forgery and considerable media outcry in both countries until the hoax was discovered by British paper *The Observer* and discredited. The prank was not merely a political controversy, but also demonstrated the ease, starting in the 1980s, with which tape doctoring could be used to create political statements. This method was used increasingly during the 1980s by punk bands, and later by those in the techno movements, leading to not only dance records with politicians such as **George W. Bush** but also remixes of the famous "Dean Scream" and novelty records such as **"Rapping Ronnie."** The technique is also analogous to the video mashups featuring **Hillary Clinton** and **Barack Obama** that were prevalent on **YouTube** during the 2007 and 2008 democratic presidential primaries. (For related discussion on the role of mashups in the 2008 primary election season, see **Macintosh "1984" Commercial**.)

THAT'S MY BUSH. *That's My Bush* was a briefly aired television show created by *South Park* creators Trey Parker and Matt Stone. The show parodied the Bush administration in a classic sitcom style and portrayed Bush as a hopeless bumbler who inadvertently steals cable television and accidentally ingests the drug ecstasy. Although Parker and Stone claimed that they would have created a similar show about candidate **Al Gore** had he won the election (the *South Park* creators are notorious for their nonpartisan skewering of both the left and right), the show lasted less than one season and was cancelled in 2001. It is unclear if the show was really cancelled because of excessive production costs as the network claimed or because overt political satire was not seen as feasible after a divisive election. (For related discussion, see **George W. Bush [Media Portrayals]**.)

THAT WAS THE WEEK THAT WAS. A satirical spoof of the happenings of the week, *That Was the Week That Was* became an early precursor to *Saturday Night Live*'s "Weekend Update" and *The Daily Show* (see **News Parodies**), although with more emphasis on topical stand-up routines and songs. Based on an earlier British version that contained future members of Monty Python Graham Chapman and John Cleese as writers, the program ran in America for only one season. The show retained David Frost from the British version, as well as guest appearances from Tom Poston, Woody Allen, Steve Allen, Bill Cosby, and Alan Alda, among others. While the show did not last long in America, it was an indication that political humor could be successfully aired on American television. Even *Rowan and Martin's Laugh-In* was clearly influenced by *That Was the Week That Was*.

THIS WEEK WITH GEORGE STEPHANOPOLOUS. See Sunday Morning Political Shows.

THOMPSON, FRED. One of the few American politicians to also maintain an acting career, Fred Thompson (1942–) first worked in the Nixon administration but was also always eager to act. He has appeared in numerous movies such as *No Way Out* (1987), *The Hunt for Red October* (1990), and *Days of Thunder* (1990) but is best known in terms of television for his recurring role (from 2002 to 2007) as District Attorney Arthur Branch on the long-running television program *Law & Order*. When Thompson announced his intent to run for the Republican nomination for the presidency in 2007 (ironically, on *The Tonight Show*), cable channels stopped showing reruns of Thompson episodes of *Law & Order*.

On September 5, 2007, the former Republican senator and actor from *Law & Order* announced his bid for the Republican nomination for president in 2008 on *The Tonight Show* hosted by comedian Jay Leno. Thompson followed in the footsteps of Republican Governor **Arnold Schwarzenegger** who had announced his candidacy on *The Tonight Show* in October 2003. Thompson, who had been building a campaign team for months before his announcement, used the wider access of *The Tonight Show* in order to reach more voters than his Republican opponents who had been engaged in a debate on the Fox Network that afternoon. The strategy worked, at least in terms of number, as the Republican debate reached 3.1 million viewers on Fox, while Thompson was able to reach 6 million voters. The show was watched by curious Americans (Leno's usual ratings were up 15 percent that night) who saw Thompson, a seasoned actor, talk about his town-to-town tours in a pickup truck as he tried to cast himself as a populist outsider alternative to the other candidates.

24. "My name is Jack Bauer, and this is the longest day of my life."

24 is a very popular American television program (2001–) featuring Keifer Sutherland as an agent of the C.T.U. (Counter Terrorism Unit, a secret government agency) who each season has 24 hours to solve a mystery and thwart a terrorist threat. *24* was created by Joel Surnow and Robert Cochran, and Surnow, unlike most Hollywood producers, unabashedly wears his conservative beliefs on his sleeve. The program's unique concept is that each episode takes place in "real time" where an hour of programming equals one hour of the day. The program has been extremely popular, but also controversial for its seeming approval of torture as a legitimate way of gathering information. *24* has been acknowledged as a favorite show by various government officials, including Vice President Dick Cheney and Supreme Court justices Anton Scalia and Clarence Thomas.

The show is not clearly right wing on many issues, but Surnow has made it clear that the motivation behind much of the show is the U.S. war on global terror. As Jane Mayer pointed out in her article in *The New Yorker*:

> [24 is] ripped out of the Zeitgeist of what people's fears are—their paranoia that we're going to be "attacked," and it "makes people look at what we're dealing with" in terms of threats to national security. "There are not a lot of measures short of extreme measures that will get it done," he said, adding, "America wants the war on terror fought by Jack Bauer. He's a patriot."
>
> For all its fictional liberties, "24" depicts the fight against Islamist extremism much as the Bush Administration has defined it: as an all-consuming struggle for America's survival that demands the toughest of tactics. Not long after September 11th, Vice-President Dick Cheney alluded vaguely to the fact that America must begin working through the "dark side" in countering terrorism. On "24," the dark side is on full view. (http://www.newyorker.com/reporting/2007/02/19/070219fa_fact_mayer)

The show's frequent use of torture as a method of interrogation even became part of the U.S. debate on the usefulness of using torture to extract information from America's enemies. In November 2006, U.S. Army Brigadier General Patrick Finnegan, dean of the U.S. Military Academy at West Point, went to Los Angeles to meet with the producers in charge of *24*. According to Mayer, "Finnegan arrived on the set as the crew was filming. At first, Finnegan—wearing an immaculate Army uniform, his chest covered in ribbons and medals—aroused confusion: he was taken for an actor and was asked by someone what time his 'call' was" (http://www.newyorker.com/reporting/2007/02/19/070219fa_fact _mayer).

Finnegan was concerned that his students at West Point had watched *24* and concluded outside of the classroom that the arguments presented in favor of torture in the case of necessity were sound. Other military sources had indicated that DVDs of *24* were popular in the battlefield and wondered if there was a connection between interrogation techniques on the small screen and in real life. It was not simply that the chain of command had gone awry that had led to American abuses of prisoners in the war against Iraq, but somehow television was so influential that it had reframed the debate on how to deal with prisoners and had led to torture becoming an acceptable interrogation technique for the military and, presumably, for the American people (or at least those who watch *24*). Other fans include the White House, which had Surnow in as a guest for a private event, where fans such as Karl Rove and the Cheneys congratulated him on the success of the show. The conservative Heritage Foundation organized a panel on *24* featuring Homeland Security Secretary Michael Chertoff and others to discuss how *24* reflected the real-life war on terror. John Yoo, the professor and former Justice Department lawyer who helped draft the 2002 "torture memo" that helped the Bush administration's rationale for using extreme forms of interrogation, mentioned *24* as mirroring a situation in real life in which torture would be permissible in his book *War by Other Means*.

The enduring popularity of *24* later led to an even bigger honor than the meeting at the White House: a *Simpsons* parody where Bart and Lisa attempt to stop a group of bullies from setting off a potent stink bomb in the school, with special guest star Keifer Sutherland as his character Jack Bauer (for further discussion of politics and *The Simpsons* in general, see **The Simpsons**).

Surnow also tried his hand at writing *The 1/2 Hour News Hour*, which debuted in January 2007 as a satirical treatment of the week's news with a conservative slant, which would presumably offer a counterpoint to the liberal slant of **The Daily Show with Jon Stewart** and **The Colbert Report** (also see **News Parodies**). The program featured anchors Kent McNally (Kurt Long) and Jennifer Lange (Jennifer Robinson), celebrities such as Lorenzo Lamas in fake celebrity public service announcements, as well as conservative comic Dennis Miller who provided commentary. The program was cancelled in August 2007, but may return in a different format in the future.

TWITTER. See Part I, Chapter 8, under "Related New Media and Politics."

V

VENTURA, JESSE. Former professional wrestler and actor Jesse "the Body" Ventura (1951–; his birth name was James Janos, he took "Ventura" from the town in California), who became governor of Minnesota in 1998 as a member of the Reform Party, is an example of how actors and celebrities were increasingly becoming bankable political figures in the twentieth century. At the time of the election it was widely assumed that Ventura had won because of voter disenchantment with the political establishment during the 1990s. Although Ventura served only one term, he was a colorful often-quoted figure, who, along with California Governor **Arnold Schwarzenegger** (who co-starred with Ventura in the 1987 film *Predator*), demonstrated that pop culture figures such as actors and wrestlers with a natural fan base and a seeming lack of connection to conventional politics and political organizations could become viable political figures. Ventura had previous political experience, having served one term as mayor of the small town Brooklyn Park in Minnesota.

VIETNAM WAR MOVIES (FICTION). Normally during war time in America, propaganda films are a staple of the public's cinematic diet, as demonstrated during World War I and World War II where numerous propaganda films were made to boost morale and keep the war effort going (for related discussion, see **World War Propaganda**). However, during the war in Vietnam, the film industry largely kept quiet for most of the war, and the conflict was not examined to any serious degree until after American involvement in the war was over.

Despite the fact that the controversy over the war in Vietnam was causing upheavals across the nation, Hollywood largely avoided it, with only John Wayne managing to get funding for his film *The Green Berets* (1968), which shows the righteous American forces fighting the good fight against the cowardly and despicable North Vietnamese. Despite the fact that public opinion was turning against the war, the Wayne vehicle was the last major film to be made about Vietnam until the 1970s. In particular, the late 1970s saw a surge in Vietnam films, with films such as *Go Tell the Spartans* (1978), *Rolling Thunder* (1977), *Heroes* (1977), *The Boys in Company C* (1978), *Who'll Stop the Rain?* (1978), *The Deer Hunter* (1978), *Coming Home* (1978), *More American Graffiti* (1979), and *Apocalypse Now* (1979). These films offered a sober and largely pessimistic look at the conflict in Vietnam, as well as the toll it took on the American psyche and on the returning veterans that often suffered from post-traumatic stress disorder.

This is not to suggest that Vietnam was ignored by Hollywood during its time period. There were several, more explicitly political comedies that while not overtly mentioning Vietnam, could not be read outside of the time period, such as *M.A.S.H.* (1970) and the film adaptation of the classic antiwar novel *Catch-22* (1970), both of which highlighted the absurdity of war and its often surrealistic consequences. Although these films were not always the most popular films, they did demonstrate that in the 1960s, the studio system and independent filmmakers were trying to make films that resonated more with audiences who increasingly wanted more realistic fare rather than just entertainment. When the time was judged more appropriate for showing the war on screen, the result was uniformly films that at first looked at the conflict as a horrible and draining war of attrition, fought nonsensically by brass who were miles from the action (and any sense of reality). In *The Boys in Company C* (1978) the war is depicted as brutal and senseless, and absurdity, as in *M.A.S.H.* (1970), is the only appropriate way of dealing with the war. A similar film, *Go Tell the Spartans* (1978), also cast the film as rife with irony and moral ambiguity, with characters forced to make moral choices that would not have made sense on any other battlefield, inevitably leading to death or madness. Two other films made that year also looked at the cost of the war on servicemen when they returned to civilian life. In *Coming Home* (1978) Jon Voight as a wheelchair-bound soldier and **Jane Fonda** try and make sense of a war that has changed the notion of America as a land of infinite promise. In the more pessimistic *The Deerhunter* (1978), which won a best picture Oscar, the horror of war is made evident by characters who, if they make it off the battlefield at all, are so scarred by their experience that only the twisted game of Russian roulette can come close to making them feel anything real again.

The most famous Vietnam film of that era, *Apocalypse Now* (1979), expands on that theme of madness, featuring the charismatic, mad Colonel Kurtz leading an unsanctioned fiefdom where the law of the jungle leads straight down a path to a heart filled with darkness. In the period of 1977–1979, Hollywood tackled Vietnam and found only horror and death. However, in the 1980s, a more diverse group of films would not only analyze the scars of Vietnam, but also ask the question, this time, do we get to win?

The character of Rambo, created by Sylvester Stallone in the hugely successful Rambo films, is usually portrayed by critics as a jingoistic American gladiator, fighting for patriotic values. However, the first Rambo film in the trilogy, *Rambo: First Blood* (1982), is less a feel good "let's kill them all" movie than a sad indictment of the consequences of Vietnam and the neglect of deeply traumatized Vietnam veterans. When Rambo is first introduced, he is not a glorious warrior but instead is a paranoid drifter, scared and traumatized from experiences he initially will not reveal, and he simply wants to be left alone to drift wherever the road takes him. When a small-town sheriff first bullies him and then arrests him, Rambo's natural instincts kick in with disastrous consequences for local law enforcement officials who clearly do not know how to handle a threat of the magnitude of Rambo and his superior survival skills.

The second film, *First Blood II* (1985), takes a turn toward wish fulfillment as Rambo is allowed to go back to Vietnam to find and rescue POWs who were abandoned by an uncaring government. Although the film is similar to the first movie in its treatment of the scarred psyche of John Rambo, it also walks an uneasy line between action and political commentary, made plain early on in the film when Rambo, after being assigned his mission, asks his handler Colonel Troutman (Richard Crenna), "this time, do we get to win?" By the time the third film, *Rambo III* (1988), was made, Rambo had gone to fight against the Russians with the Mujaheed, and the silliness implicit in the material had caused the once nuanced character to be turned into caricature, albeit with sufficiently violent carnage to satisfy its younger audience. In retrospect, the fact that Rambo was fighting on the side of Osama bin Laden is also a bit unsettling in the light of September 11, which may have been more due to the spectacular special effects of the series and the action quota, rather than the overt political messages of the time. Other films, such as the Chuck Norris Missing in Action series, also took a more patriotic look at Vietnam from an action adventure perspective.

Other films at that time took a particularly un-Rambo-like view of the conflict. In particular, the films of **Oliver Stone**, such as the Vietnam epics *Platoon* (1986) and *Born on the Fourth of July* (1989), also take critical looks at American foreign policy during the height of when the country was supposed to have gone resolutely to the right. Other movies such as *Hamburger Hill* (1987) and *Full Metal Jacket* (1987) also took a particularly dark view of the war in Vietnam. An interesting aspect of many of these films was that they were successful at the box office despite their dark and often chiding tone. It seemed as though for a decade from the late 1970s to the late 1980s the audience had an appetite for films that analyzed the moral lessons of

Vietnam. This is particularly fascinating analyzed next to the relative lack of success of films that analyzed the conflict in Iraq.

"VOTE OR DIE." "Vote or Die" was a motivational voter slogan used during the 2004 election by the group **Citizen Change** (founded by hip-hop mogul Sean "P. Diddy" Combs). For some time during the 2004 election the slogan was a popular one on T-shirts among celebrities as well as youth activists, whether they were actually registered to vote or not. The saying was later parodied on a *South Park* episode where P. Diddy attacks *South Park* character Stan because he had not voted and also had not died. As P. Diddy sings when he confronts Stan:

Get out there and vote or I will ***' kill you.

Although it was clearly a send up of P. Diddy/Puff Daddy, and not actually lyrics by the rapper, it did demonstrate the absurdity behind a slogan with as blatant a message as "vote or die." Vote or Die was one of the many ways in which celebrities tried to make their presence felt in the political arena at the dawn of the new century.

W

WALLACE, GEORGE. George Wallace (1919–1998) was one of the most polarizing figures in American politics from the 1950s until his death in 1998. Although Wallace later recanted his segregationist ways and tried to make amends for his past, his legacy will be forever overshadowed by his earlier televised actions as a staunch segregationist. Wallace was first elected governor of Alabama in 1962, but had previously run in 1958 as a fairly progressive candidate who refused the endorsement of the Ku Klux Klan, which his opponent, John Paterson, willingly accepted. Wallace, who received the endorsement of the NAACP during the 1958 election, drastically changed his campaign strategy in 1962, this time running as a staunch segregationist. His first terms were marked with controversy and much playing on racial fears by Wallace, including a notorious incident on June 11, 1963, where Wallace, in response to a campaign pledge, stood in the doorway of the University of Alabama to block two African American students, Vivian Malone and James Hood, from entering. Wallace did not relent until President **John F. Kennedy** mobilized the Alabama National Guard to the campus, which led to Wallace retreating, his point having presumably been made to the segregationists of Alabama. This incident and its attendant news coverage caused Wallace to become a nationally known figure, and the pictures of Wallace blocking the doors and the attendant interviews made Wallace a de facto spokesman for the segregationist movement in America. Wallace parlayed his notoriety to enter national politics and ran in the presidential primaries in 1964, in 1968, and most famously in 1972. During the 1972 primary, Wallace took several states in the Democratic primary, until his career was derailed by an attempted assassination by Arthur Bremer, which led to Wallace's confinement in a wheelchair for the rest of his life.

Wallace resumed the governorship of Alabama, and by the time of his last campaign in 1982, Wallace had changed his politics so dramatically that he captured the State House with the majority of the black vote. While Wallace did eventually change his views, he will still go down in history thanks to his high profile on television, on radio, and in newspapers as the most vocal proponent of segregationist politics in the United States during the 1960s and 1970s. **David Duke** aside, it is inconceivable that a proponent of racism could receive such a high profile today, but Wallace, always controversial and an aggressive speaker, made good news copy. Wallace also illustrated that television does not always favor the most eloquent candidate, but can often be as effective a platform for demagogues as saints. In 2007, it was announced that Arthur Bremer would be paroled after 35 years in prison for attempting to assassinate Wallace.

WALTERS, BARBARA. A pioneering woman in television news and entertainment programs, Barbara Walters (1929–) worked her way up the ladder, starting in local television stations in New York and then moving on to the *Today Show*, where she eventually became a co-anchor. When she resigned in 1976 to become co-anchor of the *ABC Evening News* with Harry Reasoner, many complained about the way in which news was becoming increasingly oriented toward both celebrity news and the increasing rise of news anchors as celebrities themselves. She eventually went on to fame as a skillful interviewer of celebrities and political figures, including world leaders, and was a host of ABC-TV's newsmagazine show *20/20*. Since 1997, Walters has been co-executive producer and host of *The View*, a morning talk show focusing primarily on issues of interest to women. ABC continues to carry her periodic interview "specials," featuring people in the news, from celebrities of dubious talent to significant political and religious figures.

WAR OF THE WORLDS RADIO BROADCAST. On October 30, 1938, an adaptation of H. G. Wells's novel *War of the Worlds* was broadcast on the CBS radio network. Directed by Orson Welles, who also starred in the drama, *War of the Worlds* evoked a reaction that places it among the most famous episodes in radio history. The show was presented in the form of news coverage about a hostile Martian invasion. Although an announcer stated more than once that the piece was fictional, some people either did not hear the disclaimer or did not allow it to register with them and they panicked. Consequently, the broadcast sparked an outcry from those who felt Welles and his associates had acted irresponsibly.

The incident motivated a team of media researchers headed by Hadley Cantril to conduct a study to determine why some people had been so scared by the drama. Cantril revealed that the vast majority of listeners did not panic, as some critics had believed (even to this day the legend persists that *War of the Worlds* incited widespread terror). Moreover, he explained, those who did give in to fear were more likely to have certain personality characteristics and backgrounds than others.

The research was significant in that it led to a modified outlook on media. Previously, some scholars had held that the power of the media was nearly irresistible and affected everyone in the same way. Cantril showed that the media's impact varied depending on a person's makeup and predispositions (for discussion on another important study that further challenged the belief in media as an overwhelming cultural force, see *The People's Choice*). The radio broadcast itself is politically relevant because it provides a classic example of how audiences often interpret products of the media within the political atmosphere of the day. Many scholars have argued that the looming threat of Hitler and World War II put people in an anxious state of mind that inclined them to overreact to particular symbolic scenarios. Their suggestion is that if the political climate had been more serene, citizens would have been less likely to have perceived the drama as real. In this manner, the *War of the Worlds* radio event provides a cautionary lesson on why audiences should attempt to maintain a neutral stance toward the media even in the face of an emotionally charged political environment.

THE WAR ROOM. Reminiscent of the 1960 documentary *Primary*, *The War Room* (1993), in cinéma vérité style, follows the 1992 presidential campaign of **Bill Clinton**, particularly emphasizing the work of campaign managers **James Carville** and George Stephanopoulos, both of whom, probably due in part to the recognition they received in the feature, went on to become political TV news pundits. Released in 2004, *The Road to the Presidency* also retraces the 1992 campaign, this time with Clinton the center of focus; yet the film did not generate the same notice as its predecessor. *The War Room* was nominated for an Academy Award for best documentary.

WATERGATE SCANDAL. Watergate was one of the key political scandals of the twentieth century and led to the first ever resignation of a U.S. president, as well as a popular movie and many subsequent **political scandals** being labeled with the term "gate." The main impact of Watergate was that it led to impeachment proceedings against President **Richard Nixon** and Nixon's eventual resignation in disgrace from the office of the presidency in 1974. Watergate (a term that referred to the name of the hotel where agents of President Nixon broke into the Democratic National Committee's offices) began with news reports on June 17, 1972, that five burglars had been caught breaking into the Democratic Party headquarters, armed with burglars' tools, suspicious amounts of money, as well as an address book that listed the name of Howard Hunt at the "WH" (presumably the White House). Although most major networks either played down the story at first or treated it as one of the risks inherent in dealing with politics, the scandal was not contained so easily. Conservative commentator **William F. Buckley** speculated on his program, *Firing Line*, that some of the burglars, anti-Castro Cuban nationals, were trying to find evidence of links between the Democratic Party and Fidel Castro. By the time of the election, where Nixon won over George McGovern in a legendary landslide of 49–1 states (McGovern also won the District of Columbia) and 520–17 electoral votes, Nixon's return to power with clear mandate seemed to spell the end of any traces of scandal from Watergate, but in reality the scandal was just beginning. Although the original conspirators had simply been paid off and had accepted their sentences meekly, the congressional investigation in the summer of 1973 was far harder for Nixon to avoid. Even though Nixon skillfully used television to combat his critics, according to television historian Erik Barnouw, there was one factor he could not fight against, "congressional television" (Barnouw, Erik. *Tube of Plenty: The Evolution of American Television*. 2nd rev. ed. New York: Oxford University Press, 1990, p. 454). While public television covered the hearings gavel-to-gavel, network television, afraid of audience bleed, decided on a strategy of alternating coverage between the big three networks. Much to the surprise of the networks, the Watergate hearings often got better ratings than long-running game shows such as *Let's*

Make a Deal and *The Newlywed Game*, as well as popular soap operas such as *All My Children* and *Days of Our Lives* (although many soap opera viewers did call in to complain when their favorite programs were preempted). Senator Sam Ervin, chair of the committee, gathered damaging testimony live on national television, none so damaging as when former White House aide Alexander Butterfield noted the presence of numerous voice-activated tape recorders in the president's offices. After originally refusing to release the tapes, Nixon eventually did release several, but not all tapes, including one with a curious 18-1/2 minutes gap. Nixon's refusal to release more was based on the concept of "national security" (an excuse that would also be used by future President **George W. Bush**). Nixon then released another 1,308 pages of White House transcripts of tapes that Nixon, in a televised address, called potentially "damaging and confusing" but suggested that overall, they exonerated the White House in any criminal behavior. In an example of how much the scandal had engaged the American public, numerous public broadcasting radio stations broadcast live dramatic readings of the transcripts to increasing ratings.

Reporters Carl Bernstein and Robert Woodward of the *Washington Post* began to dig deeply into the scandal and were tipped off by a White House mole nicknamed "Deep Throat" (after a popular porno movie) who gave them information about where the money ("follow the money" was a particularly telling clue) was coming from and told them to explore the inconsistencies in the testimony of key figures.

In 2005 Deep Throat revealed his identity as W. Mark Felt, the former number two man at the FBI during the time of Watergate, now in his nineties and in frail health. (Felt later published a book assembled by John O'Connor about his identity.) The fact that this was kept secret to most of the American public for over 30 years is impressive considering the amount of time and research done by reporters in trying to figure out who Woodward and Bernstein's source had been.

As it became increasingly obvious to Nixon that he was going to be publicly impeached for his role in Watergate, he was dealt another blow when the Supreme Court voted 8–0 to force the president to release the material subpoenaed by Congress. After the release of the remaining tapes, the magnitude of Nixon's crimes became clear and the congressional committee voted unanimously to recommend impeachment. Full votes in Congress and the Senate seemed inevitable. After Republican Brahmins met with the president privately, Nixon finally announced his resignation live on national television on August 8, 1974, at 9 PM. Nixon, who had used television to his advantage during the "**Checkers Speech**" and during the 1968 campaign, found himself at a loss as to how to act on television on his final day as a president. Cameras followed Nixon as he rambled to staff and friends, before he was whisked away by Air Force One. He was finally seen briefly waving at supporters at the airport in California as he finished his journey home in disgrace. Nixon's successor, **Gerald Ford**, appeared on television, in contrast to Nixon, looking relaxed and amiable as he picked up his morning delivery of milk before proceeding to be sworn in later that day.

Watergate not only was a key political scandal and immeasurably important in terms of questions about presidential power but also was one of the most compelling mixtures of politics and popular culture ever seen. The hearings were broadcast live on national television (much to the chagrin of many Americans, who had programs preempted for the hearings) and were watched by millions of people at various times. Just as the famous "Checkers Speech" had humanized then Vice President Nixon, the Watergate hearings served as a further televised example of politics in action. The fact that America (and much of the world) could watch an American president struggling for his political career live on television proved that not only were politics increasingly becoming adapted to the needs of television (as would later be demonstrated by the advent of self-aware senators and representatives using makeup and hair spray for appearances on the barely watched C-SPAN channel) but that television served as a way to involve Americans with the political system in ways unimagined previously. The televised Watergate hearings demonstrated how television could ritualize important events and turn them into what media theorists Elihu Katz and Daniel Dayan called "Media Events" or the high holy days of television, where people are united in a common conversation by watching television. Although politics is a major part of the fabric of American life, very rarely outside of election years do people converse almost exclusively about the same political subjects. The Watergate scandal was an example of a true media event where literally millions of Americans were held spellbound by a compelling political drama involving real people with genuine consequences for America.

By its ubiquity, its hold on the national conversation, and the fact that it brought a sitting president down, Watergate ranks as the most important political scandal that was televised and covered by national media. Watergate is notable as one of the first political scandals of the 1960s to be presented as a popular film within a few years of the actual scandal. The film, *All the President's Men* (1976, directed by Alan Pakula), starred Dustin Hoffman as Carl Bernstein and Robert Redford as Robert Woodward. The film won three Academy Awards (including one for Jason Robards for best supporting actor) and was part of a wave of 1970s films that analyzed America through a lens of cynicism and alarm. The Watergate scandal's ramifications can be felt to this day and, although many previous scandals had been forgotten, Watergate still contains an enormous amount of emotional resonance, particularly as many of the major players are still alive as of this writing. Today, Bob Woodward, one the two reporters who helped uncover Watergate, still writes about politics, although his access to the George W. Bush presidency has led to many claiming that Woodward now values access more than a hard scoop. Nixon was later to make more television news with a notable series of interviews with reporter David Frost in 11 dramatic interviews in 1977. (For related discussion, see **Richard Nixon [Media Portrayals]**.)

"WE ARE THE WORLD." "We Are the World" was an American charity single (and album) designed to follow in the footsteps of **Band Aid** to aid in African famine relief. The single featured Michael Jackson, Cyndi Lauper, Bruce Springsteen, Stevie Wonder, **Bob Dylan**, and other luminaries of the pop world. In the 1980s, celebrities and musicians increasingly became concerned with global issues and began banding together in groups to raise funds and awareness for projects such as USA for Africa. Although money was raised for famine relief, it is unclear how much actually reached Ethiopia, and how much political awareness among fans was caused by the We Are the World project.

WEATHER UNDERGROUND. Weather Underground was an American radical terrorist group active in the 1960s that agitated for social change and was responsible for a series of bombings and terrorist actions during its career. The group broke away from the less activist SDS (Students for a Democratic Society) and took their name from the **Bob Dylan** song "Subterranean Homesick Blues" from the line, "You don't need a weatherman to know which way the wind blows." Many of the group were killed in an explosion in a New York City townhouse weapons-making factory in March 1970. The others were splintered into underground cells, but few remained active by the end of the decade. The Weathermen represented the extreme radical fringe of the American student revolutionary movement of the 1960s and demonstrated the degree to which many Americans believed that revolution was imminent toward the end of that decade.

THE WEAVERS. The left-wing folk group The Weavers, led by renowned singer Pete Seeger, originally started in the late 1940s. The group consisted of Seeger, Lee Hays, Ronnie Gilbert, and Fred Hellerman. Seeger and Hays, dedicated communists both, had been in an earlier group, the Almanac Singers, who had to embarrassingly change their stance on U.S. involvement in World War II after the Soviet Union was invaded. The four singers who later became The Weavers had met at a series of musical salons called "people's songs," a group of musicians who met regularly at Seeger's house in Greenwich village starting in 1948 and who took their name from a play by Gerhart Hauptmann. The group, known for folk songs such as "Good Night Irene," "Wimoweh," "Kisses Sweeter Than Wine," as well as many other million-selling discs, were involved with a contentious

The Weavers, organized in 1948, perform in a 25th Anniversary Reunion concert at Carnegie Hall in New York City in 1980. From left are Pete Seeger, Lee Hays, Ronnie Gilbert, and Fred Hellerman. (AP Photo/Richard Drew)

confrontation with the American government over their socialist leanings and their past as political activists. Although most of the Weavers' songs were not political at all, scrutiny by booking agents left the Weavers without any potential gigs or recordings and the group broke up for the first time in 1952. They re-formed in 1955, but Seeger left the band in 1958. Ironically, it was not the government but a business dispute that broke up the group—infighting over money when Seeger left the group in protest of using the Weavers' music in a cigarette commercial. The Weavers carried on without Seeger for several years, before calling it quits again in 1961. In 1980, the band reunited for a series of concerts and an acclaimed documentary, "Wasn't That a Time," directed by Jim Brown. Hays died the following year, essentially ending the Weavers. The Weavers, along with **Woody Guthrie**, Leadbelly, and **Joe Hill** are examples of how the origins of American folk music were concerned with political issues, and they were a major influence on the folk boom of the late 1950s and early 1960s, and in particular on **Bob Dylan**, who Seeger had mentored early in his career. Seeger made headlines again in 2007 when he finally admitted that he had been wrong about Stalin and should have asked to see the Gulags when he was in Russia. According to a *New York Times* article, Seeger had recently written a song about Stalin, entitled "Big Joe Blues."

"WEEKEND UPDATE." "Weekend Update" is an ongoing weekly network news parody on NBC's long-running *Saturday Night Live* sketch show. The "Weekend Update" segment parodies recent news events and skewers political figures and celebrities, many of whom either appear on camera in brief cameos or are played by cast members of the repertory company.

The sketch has appeared since the first episode of *Saturday Night Live* on October 11, 1975, where the first host was comedian Chevy Chase, who playfully mocked the solemnity of network news by intoning just before a commercial break, "Still to come, earthquake claims San Diego, Four million die in Turkey, and Arlene visits an art museum" in the manner of a typical anchor supplying a tease before a commercial. Chase, who supplied the slightly surreal opening line "I'm Chevy Chase and you're not" (based on the opening line of longtime real news anchor Roger Grimsby, who opened each broadcast with the line "I'm Roger Grimsby, and here's the news"), was also a writer for *Saturday Night Live* who contributed much to the early version's best bits of satire, including the Garrett Morris segment of "News for the Hard of Hearing," which featured Morris repeating the previous headlines by shouting them with cupped hands. While many early "Weekend Update" sketches and characters were resolutely apolitical such as the semantically confused Emily Littela, as played by Gilda Radner (who, nonetheless, read an editorial confusing "presidential erections" with "presidential elections," while **Gerald Ford**'s press secretary Ron Nessen was a guest host), as the sketch developed it gradually became more political. Soon Washington senators were remarking that they watched the program weekly to see which of their colleagues were parodied that weekend.

After Chase left the program at the end of the first season, he was replaced by new hosts Jane Curtin and later Dan Aykroyd and Bill Murray (followed by a variety of others, including Christopher Guest, Mary Gross, Brian Doyle-Murray, Brad Hall, Christine Ebersole, Charles Rocket, and more notably Dennis

Miller and Norm MacDonald). After the original cast left, the humor level varied, with guest hosts poking fun at the president du jour, but also toning down some sketches that were considered to be too offensive. By the time Norm MacDonald was a host in 1994–1997, pressure had come down on the program and MacDonald's caustic style and wry jokes were not a good match for a program that many argued had become increasingly safe and predictable. (MacDonald was fired in 1997, allegedly at the request of NBC executive Don Ohlmeyer, reportedly because of Ohlmeyer's friendship with O. J. Simpson, a frequent target of MacDonald's cutting humor.) When Jimmy Fallon took over with Tina Fey in 2000, the segment mostly took on easy celebrity targets such as Paris Hilton and Lindsey Lohan, with occasional sharp and cutting jabs at various politicians (especially during the 2004–2006 Amy Poehler and Tina Fey seasons), demonstrating the considerable power that the "Weekend Update" bully pulpit has when it works well. During the 2007–2008 season with co-hosts Seth Meyers and Amy Poehler, more political issues were broached, especially with references during the 2008 presidential primary and election season. However, in contrast to programs such as *The Daily Show with Jon Stewart* and *The Colbert Report*, "Weekend Update" is mainly a pale imitation of what it once was, a legitimately biting satirical look at the clichés of network news, as well as a sometimes scathing look at Washington. Nonetheless, during the months of 2007 and 2008 that saw presidential candidate debates and a seemingly endless stream of primaries, many opening skits on *Saturday Night Live* were about **Hillary Clinton, Bill Clinton, Barack Obama**, Mike Huckabee, other candidates, and the television news media. Further, Hillary Clinton, Barack Obama, Sarah Palin, and **John McCain** all appeared on the program as themselves. The show, in fact, was credited with possibly giving a favorable bump to the Hillary Clinton primary campaign one week when a skit showed her being consistently challenged by male TV news moderators of the debate, while Obama received fawning attention and easy questions (Itzkoff, Dave. "SNL Writer Narrows the Gap between Politics and Farce." *New York Times*, March 3, 2008). While "Weekend Update" had to walk a fine line between what was permissible in terms of edgy material (particularly during the Bill Clinton/Monica Lewinsky scandal), they also shifted focus gradually away from potentially controversial political subjects and more to strictly pop culture jokes, including digs at the celebrity crisis du jour. It remains to be seen if, inspired by competition from *The Daily Show with Jon Stewart*, "Weekend Update" can regain its edge. (See also **News Parodies**.)

THE WEST WING. *The West Wing* (1999–2006) was a politically oriented show about an American left-leaning president who presumably continued the moderate liberal legacy of Clinton. The show's center-left politics appealed to numerous liberal and centrist Americans who no doubt had wished for a Gore victory in the 2000 election. The program featured Martin Sheen as president Josiah Jed Bartlet, a very human president with his own set of problems. The program lasted as long as two regular presidential terms and ended with Bartlet being replaced by Democratic Congressman Matt Santos, played by Jimmy Smits, in the 2006 election. Many critics regard *The West Wing* as one of the most astute and accurate shows about insider relations and back-room dealing in modern American politics.

A scene from *The West Wing*, Episode "20 Hours in America," Season 4. 2002. Martin Sheen as President Josiah Bartlet. (NBC/Photofest)

WHY WE FIGHT. Although it represented his first foray into documentary filmmaking, a series of seven inspirational army training films entitled *Why We Fight* were spearheaded by the legendary Hollywood director **Frank Capra**, a lieutenant during World War II. Adding to the films' high production values, Walt Disney Studios provided some of the graphics. Made over the course of two years, the collection of *Why We Fight* films attempted to explain the events leading up to U.S. participation and the reasons why involvement was crucial. At the same time, the series hoped to persuade military personnel to replace any isolationist sentiments they might be harboring with complete dedication to furthering the cause. U.S. enemies were portrayed as cruel or even inhuman. (Many modern viewers who have screened the films claim they display racist tendencies and are overly jingoistic.) Those people scheduled for military duty overseas were required to view all seven films before departure. Though the movies were originally intended for only a military audience, some of them were later distributed to theaters for screening by members of the general population as well.

Despite the high expectations for the *Why We Fight* films and their subsequent attention, however, they were not necessarily successful in achieving their purpose. Ultimately, the films were found to be too simple and propagandistic to be effective indoctrination films for soldiers (for a discussion on the war and propaganda in general, see **World War Propaganda**). In a seminal group of studies, now often cited in media studies textbooks, the researchers presented mixed evidence as to whether the movies functioned as effective tools of persuasion. Their findings significantly contributed to an evolving understanding of the power of media. Critics had formerly held that the media's influence is nearly irresistible.

The *Why We Fight* studies and others demonstrated that additional variables—including the characteristics and dispositions of the audience—are equal, if not more important, factors in predicting and analyzing audience responses to the images and sounds of the media.

WOBBLIES. Wobblies were members of the socialist organization better known as the International Workers of the World (IWW), primarily active toward the first part of the twentieth century. The IWW is still active, but less powerful and less a presence in the political life of America than it was during its heyday. The origin of the term itself is unclear, even to the IWW, but may refer to the idea of "wobbling the works" (industrial sabotage) or to an insult from the bosses that was adapted by the Wobblies as a proud term, as the word "queer" was by many in the gay and lesbian community. (Another story also details how a Chinese restaurant worker may have mispronounced the name as "Eye Wobble Wobble," but this may also be apocryphal.)

WORLD WAR PROPAGANDA. The term "propaganda" was originally taken from the Latin word for sowing or propagating ideas and derives from the Vatican office for the propagation of the faith, the *Sacra Congregatio de Propaganda Fide*, originally founded in 1622. Although, at first, the word was perceived as fairly neutral, it gradually became associated less with simple persuasion and more with messages intended to confuse or obfuscate the truth.

World War I Propaganda. While there had always been campaigns designed to change the opinions of a populace in regard to war, social issues, or political support, the rise of modern propaganda in the United States can be traced back to the years immediately preceding World War I and during the actual war itself. Many propaganda techniques that could be used as templates for advertising and political campaigns were developed to great success. Notable progressives, advertising men, and theorists, such as Walter Lippmann, **Edward Bernays** (considered one of the "founding fathers" of American public relations), and George Creel, who was put in charge of the Committee on Public Information (dubbed the "Creel Commission"), sought to develop educational counterpoints to German propaganda and educate the American public about the reasons for U.S. involvement in the war. The nation's comprehensive propaganda campaign proved so adept at achieving its goals that soon after the war, when it was discovered that the populace had sometimes been deceived through misrepresentations, the field of media effects research was born. These initial studies into the impact of media by outside observers were motivated by the fear that propaganda was a powerful force that could be used to ignoble ends.

World War II Propaganda. As in World War I, the United States made a concentrated push to counter anti-American propaganda, as well as produce its own propaganda to rally support for the war effort. The campaign included posters, movies, training films, slogans, and other tools that were meant to influence Americans to embrace the necessary sacrifices the war entailed.

In his classic book *Propaganda*, originally issued in 1928, Edward Bernays (the nephew of Sigmund Freud) argued that propaganda was useful and beneficial for the construction of a well-ordered society. Bernays, Walter Lippmann (author of numerous books, including the enormously influential 1922 publication, *Public*

Opinion), and Bruce Barton (a prominent advertising man and the author of *The Man Nobody Knows*, a book that positions Jesus Christ as a founder of modern business) were members of the progressive movement and were concerned that ordinary citizens could not think clearly in a complex and newly industrialized "mass society"—therefore, these prominent men believed, a class of "invisible governors" was needed to help shape public opinion. Bernays and other propagandists laid the foundations of modern political propaganda that the allies (as well as the Germans) later used during World War II.

One of the major propaganda initiatives put in motion during the war involved the production of various training films. The government believed it was necessary to quickly instruct new soldiers about exactly who they were fighting and indoctrinate them into its positions on what had caused the war and the reasons the nation needed to join the fray. Given that many Americans had been opposed to entry into another "European" war so soon after the last one, fresh recruits, the government felt, often required a lesson not only in patriotism, but in history as well. The most important training film series made for the war was the ***Why We Fight*** films, which were headed up by noted film director **Frank Capra**.

Other famous figures—such as the director John Ford and the actor Jimmy Stewart—also took part in training films that were created for the war effort. A number of mainstream Hollywood movies served as vehicles for American propaganda as well, although some were more subtle in achieving this end. A classic film like *Casablanca*, for example, can be looked at as equal parts love story and anti-German sentiment. Numerous combat films, which at least indirectly endorsed a pro-war point of view, were also made during the conflict, including topical films such as the John Wayne vehicle *Sands of Iwo Jima*. Even comedies set within the context of war could buttress the mission—Abbott and Costello's *Buck Privates* is a case in point.

World War II Radio Entertainment Propaganda during World War II. In the run-up to the nation's engagement in World War II and during actual U.S. involvement, the Franklin Delano Roosevelt administration turned to the relatively new and hugely popular medium of radio in particular as a means of spreading propaganda. The government produced a number of its own shows, in both news and entertainment formats, in an attempt to persuade listeners to accept its stance on the war. At the same time, however, FDR and his officials also tried to convey propaganda with more covert tactics by infiltrating commercial entertainment to its advantage (for a complete discussion of these tactics, see Part I, Chapter 3).

Y

YOUTUBE. The YouTube Web site is one of the great success stories of the twenty-first century and has revolutionized how political messages (as well as old episodes of *Sesame Street* and clips from current cable shows and homemade movies) can be disseminated quickly. During the 2006 and 2008 elections, You-Tube was increasingly used by candidates of all stripes to get their message out, and the Democrats in particular used YouTube not only for disseminating information (such as the widespread sharing of the **Hillary Clinton** Sopranos campaign commercial) but also for spoofs such as "**Obama Girl.**" On July 23, 2007, the Democratic candidates also took part in a live debate where the questions were submitted previously online on YouTube—the questioners included a snowman. Later in November 2007, the Republicans also took part in a combination **CNN**/YouTube debate. While many questioned the process (CNN co-sponsored the debate and promised to not use embarrassing or "gotcha" questions, leading some to think that the debate had been co-opted before it had begun), it was a sign that YouTube had spawned a new way of sharing that could not be overlooked by the major candidates. (See **Macintosh "1984" Commercial.**)

Selected Bibliography

"About Us; The Christian Coalition." http://www.cc.org/about.cfm (accessed April 3, 2007).

"A Brief Biography of Joe Hill." http://www.newyouth.com/archives/music/joehillbio.asp (accessed June 14, 2007).

Ackerman, Seth. "The Most Biased Name in News." http://www.fair.org/index.php?page=1067 (accessed March 18, 2008).

"Alf Landon 1936 Presidential Race Campaign Posters & Ephemera." http://www.the-forum.com/ephemera/LANDON.HTM (accessed July 12, 2006).

Andrejevic, Mark. "Faking Democracy: Reality Television Politics on American Candidate." *Politicotainment: Television's Take on the Real*, ed. Kristina Riegert. New York: Peter Lang, 2007.

Arthur, Paul. "Jargons of Authenticity (Three American Moments)." *Theorizing Documentary*, ed. Michael Renov. New York: Routledge, 1993.

Aucoin, Don. "Hollywood Votes the Rascals Out." *Boston Globe*, November 4, 1990, B.6.

Barkin, Steve. *American Television News: The Media Marketplace and the Public Interest*. Armonk, NY: M. E. Sharpe, 2003.

Barnouw, Erik. *The Sponsor: Notes on a Modern Potentate*. Oxford, U.K.: Oxford University Press, 1978.

Barnouw, Erik. *Tube of Plenty: The Evolution of American Television*. 2nd rev. ed. New York: Oxford University Press, 1990.

Barnouw, Erik. *Documentary: A History of the Non-Fiction Film*. 2nd rev. ed. New York: Oxford University Press, 1993.

Barnouw, Erik, et al. *Conglomerates and the Media*. New York: The New Press, 1997.

Battone, Richard. "Person to Person." http://www.museum.tv/archives/etv/P/htmlP/persontoper/persontoper.htm (accessed May 12, 2007).

Baudrillard, Jean. *The Gulf War Did Not Take Place*. Bloomington: Indiana University Press, 1995.

Bennett, Tony, and Janet Wollacott. *Bond and Beyond: The Political Career of a Popular Hero*. New York: Methuen Books, 1987.

Benoit, William L., et al. *Campaign 2000: A Functional Analysis of Presidential Campaign Discourse*. Lanham, MD: Rowman & Littlefield, 2003.

Bernays, Edward. *Propaganda*. Brooklyn, NY: IG Publishing, 2005.

"Bill O'Reilly." Biography on. http://www.billoreilly.com/g/Bill-O'Reilly's-Bio/515.html (accessed June 1, 2007).

"Billy Brew Ha Ha." http://www.cbsnews.com/stories/1999/05/26/earlyshow/saturday/main48690.shtml (accessed September 23, 2006).

Binelli, Mark. "The Most Honest Man in News: Keith Olbermann Is Mad as Hell—and Unlike Rush Limbaugh, He's Not Faking It." *Rolling Stone*, issue 1021, March 8, 2007.

"Bio: William F. Buckley Jr." http://author.nationalreview.com/bio/?q=MjE0Ng (accessed August 10, 2007).

"Biography: Jim Bunning." bunning.senate.gov (accessed July 25, 2006).

Bloom, Harold. "Heroes and Icons: Billy Graham." http://www.time.com/time/time100/heroes/profile/graham01 (accessed October 4, 2006).

"The Bombing Halt: Johnson's Gamble for Peace." http://www.time.com/time/magazine/article/0,9171,902482-1,00.html (accessed July 25, 2007).

Boorstin, Daniel. *The Image: A Guide to Pseudo-Events in America*. New York: Atheneum, 1975.

Boroff, Philip. "Marketplace: News Archives." http://marketplace.publicradio.org/shows/1996/10/07_mpp.html (accessed March 12, 2007).

Brooks, Tim, and Earle Marsh. *The Complete Directory to Prime Time Network and Cable TV Shows 1946–Present*. 8th ed. New York: Ballantine, 2003.

Brynen, Rex. "Mirror, Mirror? The Politics of Television Science Fiction." *It's Show Time! Media, Politics, and Popular Culture*, ed. David A. Schultz. New York: Peter Lang, 2000.

Bullert, B. J. *Public Television: Politics and the Battle Over Documentary Film*. New Brunswick, NJ: Rutgers University Press, 1997.

Butsch, Richard. "Ralph, Fred, Archie, and Homer: Why Television Keeps Re-creating the White Male Working-Class Buffoon." *Gender, Race, and Class in Media: A Text-Reader*. 2nd ed., ed. Gail Dines and Jean M. Humez. Thousand Oaks, CA: Sage, 2003.

Canby, Vincent. "Bob Roberts." http://movies2.nytimes.com/movie/review?_r=1&res=9E0CE7D91E31F937A3575AC0A964958260&oref=slogin&pagewanted=print (accessed March 19, 2008).

Castleman, Harry, and Walter J. Podrazik. *Watching TV: Six Decades of American Television*. 2nd ed. Syracuse, NY: Syracuse University Press, 2003.

Christensen, Terry, and Peter Hass. *Projecting Politics: Political Messages in American Films*. Armonk, New York: M. E. Sharpe Press, 2005.

"The Claiming of Patty Hearst." http://www.crimelibrary.com/terrorists_spies/terrorists/hearst/1.html (accessed June 23, 2007).

Clymer, Adam. "Obituary: Michael Deaver, Shaper of Reagan's Image, Dies at 69." *New York Times*, August 19, 2007, Metro Section, 29.

"CNN/YouTube Debate Questions, Which Ones Will Make the Cut?" http://www.cnn.com/2007/POLITICS/07/20/debate.preps/index.html (accessed July 22, 2007).

Cohen, Jeff. *Cable New Confidential: My Misadventures in Corporate Media*. Sausalito, CA: PoliPoint Press, 2006.

Cohen, Norman. *Folk Music: A Regional Exploration*. Westport, CT: Greenwood Press, 2005.

Collins, Sue. "Traversing Authenticities: *The West Wing* President and the Activist Sheen." *Politicotainment: Television's Take on the Real*, ed. Kristina Riegert. New York: Peter Lang, 2007.

Corner, John, and Dick Pels. "Introduction: The Re-Styling of Politics." *Media and the Restyling of Politics: Consumerism, Celebrity and Cynicism*, ed. John Corner and Dick Pels. London: Sage, 2003.

Cornfield, Michael. "Going Broadband, Getting Netwise: The Cyber-Education of John Kerry and Other Political Actors." *Divided States of America: The Slash and Burn Politics of the 2004 Presidential Election*. New York: Pearson-Longman, 2006.

Craig, Douglas B. *Fireside Politics: Radio and Political Culture in the United States, 1920–1940*. Baltimore: John Hopkins University Press, 2000.

Crew, Danny. *American Political Music: Volume 1: Introduction, Alabama–New York*. Jefferson, NC: McFarland and Company, 2006.

Croteau, David, and William Hoynes. *Media/Society: Industries, Images, and Audiences*. 3rd ed. Thousand Oaks, CA: Pine Forge, 2003.

Davis, Richard. *Politics Online: Blogs, Chatrooms, and Discussion Groups in American Democracy*. New York: Routledge, 2005.

Dayan, Daniel, and Katz, Elihu. *Media Events: The Live Broadcasting of History*. Cambridge, MA: Harvard University Press, 1992.

DeBauche, Leslie Midkiff. *Reel Patriotism: The Movies and World War I*. Madison: University of Wisconsin Press, 1997.

DeFrank, Thomas, and Michael McAuliff. "YouTube Yackfest Does Dems Some Good." *New York Daily News*, July 24, 2007, p. 8.

Devine, Jeremy. *Vietnam at 24 Frames Per Second*. Austin: University of Texas Press, 1995.

Diamond, Edwin, and Stephen Bates. *The Spot: The Rise of Political Advertising on Television*. 3rd ed. Cambridge, MA: MIT University Press, 1992.

Diamond, Edwin, and Robert Silverman. *From the White House to Your House: Media and Politics in Virtual America*. Cambridge, MA: MIT University Press, 1995.

Dickerson, Ben. *Hollywood's New Radicalism: War, Globalization and the Movies from Reagan to George W. Bush*. London: I. B. Taurus and Compnay, 2006.

Dirks, Tim. "Review: Meet John Doe." http://www.filmsite.org/meet3.html (accessed July 25, 2007).

Dirks, Tim. "Review: Manchurian Candidate." *American Culture and World War II*. New York: Columbia University Press, 1993.

Doherty, Thomas. *Cold War, Cool Medium: Television, McCarthyism, and American Culture*. New York: Columbia University Press, 2003.

"Doonesbury at 35: What a Long Strange Trip It's Been." Doonesbury.com (accessed July 20, 2008).

"Doonesbury, Drawing and Quartering for Fun and Profit." http://www.time.com/time/magazine/article/0,9171,917981-3,00.html (accessed June 22, 2007).

Douglas, Susan J. "Letting the Boys Be Boys: Talk Radio, Male Hysteria, and Political Discourse in the 1980s." *Radio Reader: Essays in the Cultural History of Radio*, ed. Michele Hilmes and Jason Loviglio. New York: Routledge, 2002.

Douglas, Susan J. *Listening In: Radio and the American Imagination*. Minneapolis: University Press of Minnesota, 2004.

Dowd, Maureen. "America's Anchors: Jon Stewart and Stephen Colbert Faked It until They Made It. Now They Are the Most Trusted Names in News." *Rolling Stone*, issue 1013, November 16, 2006.

Dylan, Bob. *Chronicles, Volume One*. New York: Simon and Schuster, 2004.

Easton, Jake. "Dixie Chicks and Alex Baldwin: Fighting for 'Centre Square' on *The Hollywood Squares*?" *Radok News; Tabloid Column*. http://www.tabloidcolumn.com/dixie-chicks.html (accessed March 12, 2007).

Ebert, Roger. "The Manchurian Candidate." http://rogerebert.suntimes.com/apps/pbcs.dll/article?AID=/20031207/REVIEWS08/40802006/1023&template=printart (accessed September 3, 2007).

Ebert, Roger. "The Manchurian Candidate." 2004. http://rogerebert.suntimes.com/apps/pbcs.dll/article?AID=/20040719/REVIEWS/40719005/1023 (accessed November 12, 2008).

Ebert, Roger. "Nixon." http://rogerebert.suntimes.com/apps/pbcs.dll/article?AID=/20031207/REVIEWS08 (accessed September 4, 2007).

Elasmar, Michael, Kazumi Hasegawa, and Mary Brain. "The Portrayal of Women in U.S. Prime Time Television." *Journal of Broadcasting and Electronic Media* 44, no. 1 (1999): 20–34.

Ellis, Jack C., and Betsy A. McLane. *A New History of Documentary Film*. New York: Continuum, 2005.

Ellul, Jacques. *Propaganda: The Formation of Men's Attitudes*. New York: Vintage Books, 1965.

Eyerman, Ron, and Andrew Jamison. *Music and Social Movements: Mobilizing Traditions in the Twentieth Century*. Cambridge, U.K.: Cambridge University Press, 1998.

Farhi, Paul. "Calling on Hollywood's Terrorism 'Experts': Homeland Security Chief Compares Reality and '24.'" *Washington Post*, June 24, 2006, C01.

Fergusen, Andrew. "All Quiet on the Firing Line: William F. Buckley Jr. Flicks His Tongue and Skewers His Guests One Last Time." http://www.cnn.com/ALLPOLITICS/time/1999/12/20/firing.line.html (accessed April 23, 2007).

Fiske, John. "Technostruggles: Black Liberation Radio." *Radio Reader: Essays in the Cultural History of Radio*, ed. Michele Hilmes and Jason Loviglio. New York: Routledge, 2002.

Flynt, Larry. "Larry Flynt Exposes GOP Senator David Vitter." http://www.larryflynt.com/mycms/ (accessed August 10, 2007).

Foote, Timothy. "Fish in the Brandy Sifter." http://www.time.com/time/magazine/article/0,9171,904627,00.html? (accessed August 1, 2007).

Franklin, Daniel. *Politics and Film: The Political Culture of Film in the United States*. Lanham, MD: Rowman & Littlefield, 2006.

Frantzich, Stephen E. "C-SPAN: A Window on the Political Process." *It's Show Time! Media, Politics, and Popular Culture*, ed. David A. Schultz. New York: Peter Lang, 2000.

Freedman, Paul. "Swift Boats and Tax Hikes: Campaign Advertising in the 2004 Election." *Divided States of America: The Slash and Burn Politics of the 2004 Presidential Election*. New York: Pearson-Longman, 2006.

Fyne, Robert. *The Hollywood Propaganda of World War II*. Lanham, MD: Scarecrow Press, Inc., 1997.

Gauntlett, David. *Media, Gender and Identity: An Introduction*. London: Routledge, 2002.

"George Corley Wallace." http://www.archives.state.al.us/govs_list/g_wallac.html (accessed May 24, 2007).

"George Magazine to Fold in March." http://cnnstudentnews.cnn.com/2001/ALLPOLITICS/stories/01/04/george.magazine/index.html (accessed June 20, 2007).

Giglio, Ernest. *Here's Looking at You: Hollywood, Film & Politics*. New York: Peter Lang Publishing, 2007.

Gitlin, Todd. *The Whole World Is Watching: Mass Media and the Making & Unmaking of The New Left*. Berkeley: University of California Press, 1980.

"The Goldwater Who Came in from the Cold: The Exclusive CONELRAD Interview." Conelrad.com: Cold War Music from the Golden Age of Homeland Security. http://www.conelrad.com/media/atomicmusic/sh_boom.php?platter=25 (accessed July 25, 2007).

Graham, Polly. "Oprah Makes U2's Bono Sick." *Sunday Mirror*. http://findarticles.com/p/articles/mi_qn4161/is_20020922/ai_n12845552 (accessed December 15, 2007).

Grimes, William. "The Endlessly Unimproved American Pie." *New York Times*, October 20, 2004, p. F4.

Gunning, Tom. *D. W. Griffith and the Origins of American Narrative Film: The Early Years at Biograph*. Urbana and Chicago: University of Illinois Press, 1991.

Gunter, Barrie. *Television and Gender Representation*. London: John Libbey, 1995.

Hall, John. "Update from Congress—August 16, 2007." http://www.johnhallforcongress.com/ (accessed August 23, 2008).

Hill, Doug, and Jeff Weingard. *Saturday Night: A Backstage History of Saturday Night Live*. New York: Vintage Books, 1986.

Hilmes, Michele. "Rethinking Radio." *Radio Reader: Essays in the Cultural History of Radio*, ed. Michele Hilmes and Jason Loviglio. New York: Routledge, 2002.

Hinckley, David. "They Elude Questioners' Net." *New York Daily News*, July 24, 2007, p. 8.

Hollihan, Thomas A. *Uncivil Wars: Political Campaigns in a Media Age*. Boston: Bedford/ St. Martin's, 2001.

Horten, Gerd. *Radio Goes to War: The Cultural Politics of Propaganda during World War II*. Berkeley: University Press of California, 2002.

Huff, Richard. "Thompson Is Ahead—At Least in the Ratings." *New York Daily News*, September 7, 2007, p. 12.

"I'd Rather Be Right 1937." http://www.lorenzhart.org/rather.htm (accessed November 12, 2006).

Indiana, Gary. *Schwarzenegger Syndrome: Politics and Celebrity in the Age of Contempt*. New York: New Press, 2005.

Iyengar, Shanto, and Donald Kinder. *News that Matters: Television and American Opinion*. Chicago: University of Chicago Press, 1987.

Jamieson, Kathleen Hall. *Dirty Politics: Deception, Distraction and Democracy*. Oxford, U.K.: Oxford University Press, 1992.

Jamieson, Kathleen Hall. *Packaging the Presidency: A History and Criticism of Presidential Campaign Advertising*. 3rd ed. New York: Oxford University Press, 1996.

Johnson, Lyndon. *Public Papers of the Presidents of the United States: Lyndon B. Johnson, 1968–69*. Volume I, entry 170, pp. 469–476. Washington, DC: Government Printing Office, 1970.

Johnson, Thomas J., and Barbara K. Kaye. "Democracy's Rebirth or Demise? The Influence of the Internet on Political Attitudes." *It's Show Time! Media, Politics, and Popular Culture*, ed. David A. Schultz. New York: Peter Lang, 2000.

Jones, Jeffrey P. *Entertaining Politics: New Political Television and Civic Culture*. Lanham, MD: Rowman & Littlefield, 2005.

Jowett, Garth, and Victoria O'Donnell. *Propaganda and Persuasion*. Thousand Oaks, CA, and London: Sage Publications, 2006.

Kaid, Lynda Lee (ed.). *Handbook of Political Communication Research*. Mahwah, NJ: Lawrence Erlbaum Associates, 2004.

Kaid, Lynda Lee. "Political Web Wars: The Use of the Internet for Political Advertising." *The Internet Election: Perspectives on the Web in Campaign 2004*, ed. Andrew Paul Williams and John C. Tedesco. Lanham, MD: Rowman & Littlefield, 2006.

Keith, Michael C. "Turn On . . . Tune In: The Rise and Demise of Commercial Underground Radio." *Radio Reader: Essays in the Cultural History of Radio*, ed. Michele Hilmes and Jason Loviglio. New York: Routledge, 2002.

Kellner, Douglas. *Television and the Crisis of Democracy*. Boulder, CO: Westview, 1990.

Kelly, Walt. "An Autobiography by the Creator of Pogo." http://www.pogopossum.com/ walt.htm (accessed June 24, 2007).

Kennedy, Helen. "Singer Rockin' Vote, GOP Boat." *New York Daily News*, September 17, 2006, p. 26.

"Kennedy School Poll: Interest Lagging in Political Party Conventions." http:// www.ksg.harvard.edu/press/press%20releases/2004/vanishing_voter_poll_072204. htm (accessed December 12, 2007).

Keren, Michael. *Blogosphere: The New Political Arena*. Lanham, MD: Lexington Books, 2006).

Koppelman, Alex. "After 9/11 Rudy Wasn't a Rescue Worker—He Was a Yankee." http:// www.salon.com/news/feature/2007/08/18/rudy_yankees/ (accessed August 20, 2007).

Koppes, Clayton, and Gregory Black. *Hollywood Goes to War; How Politics, Profits and Propaganda Shaped World War II Movies*. Berkeley: University of California Press, 1987

Krasner, Paul. "The Trial of Abbie Hoffman's Shirt." http://www.huffingtonpost.com/ paul-krassner/the-trial-of-abbie-hoffma_b_2334.html (accessed August 23, 2007).

Lacey, Kate. "Radio in the Great Depression: Promotional Culture, Public Service, and Propaganda." *Radio Reader: Essays in the Cultural History of Radio*, ed. Michele Hilmes and Jason Loviglio. New York: Routledge, 2002.

Lankford, Ronald. *Folk Music USA: The Changing Voice of Protest*. New York: Schirmer Trade Books, 2005.

La Salle, Mick. "Sundance Kid Looks Back: 'Bagger' Director Redford Reflects on 40-year Career." *San Francisco Chronicle*, October 29, 2000, p. 51.

Lenthall, Bruce. "Critical Reception: Public Intellectuals Decry Depression-Era Radio, Mass Culture, and Modern America." *Radio Reader: Essays in the Cultural History of Radio*, ed. Michele Hilmes and Jason Loviglio. New York: Routledge, 2002.

Lloyd, Mark. *Prologue to a Farce: Communication and Democracy in America*. Urbana: University of Illinois Press, 2006.

Lordan, Edward. *Politics, Ink: How America's Cartoonists Skewer Politicians from King George III to George Dubya*. New York: Roman & Littlefield Publishers, 2006.

Louw, Eric. *The Media and Political Process*. London: Sage, 2005.

Lowery, Shearon, and Melvin DeFleur. *Milestones in Mass Communication Research: Media Effects*. New York: Longman Publishers, 1995.

"MacArthur." http://www.empereur.com/G._Douglas_MacArthur.html (accessed August 5, 2007).

"MacBird: A Play by Barbara Garson." http://www.brumm.com/MacBird/ (accessed August 27, 2007).

"Mallard Fillmore: About the Character." King Features Syndicate.com, http://www.kingfeatures.com/features/comics/mallard/aboutMaina.php (accessed June 1, 2007).

Manoff, Robert, and Michael Schudson (eds.). *Reading the News*. New York: Pantheon Books, 1987.

Marchand, Roland. *Advertising the American Dream: Making Way for Modernity 1920–1940*. Berkeley: University of California Press, 1985.

Mark, David. *Going Dirty: The Art of Negative Campaigning*. Lanham, MD: Rowman & Littlefield, 2007.

Mayer, Jane. "Whatever It Takes: The Politics of the Man Behind 24." http://www.newyorker.com/reporting/2007/02/19/070219fa_fact_mayer (accessed March 12, 2007).

McCauley, Michael P. "Radio's Digital Future: Preserving the Public Interest in the Age of New Media." *Radio Reader: Essays in the Cultural History of Radio*, ed. Michele Hilmes and Jason Loviglio. New York: Routledge, 2002.

McEnteer, James. *Shooting the Truth: The Rise of American Political Documentaries*. Westport, CT: Praeger, 2006.

McGinniss, Joe. *The $elling of the President*. New York: Penguin Books, 1968.

McLuhan, Marshall. *Understanding Media: The Extensions of Man*. New York: Signet Books, 1964.

McNair, Brian. *An Introduction to Political Communication*. 4th ed. London: Routledge, 2007.

McNeil, Alex. *Total Television: The Comprehensive Guide to Programming from 1948 to the Present*. 4th ed. New York: Penguin, 1996.

"Media Awareness." http://www.family.org/entertainment/A000002511.cfm (accessed June 1, 2007).

Miller, Mark Crispin. "Introduction." *Propaganda*, ed. Edward Bernays. Brooklyn, NY: IG Publishing, 2005.

Minh-ha, Trinh T. "The Totalizing Quest for Meaning." *Theorizing Documentary*, ed. Michael Renov. New York: Routledge, 1993.

Mitchell, Jack. "Lead Us Not into Temptation: American Public Radio in a World of Infinite Possibilities." *Radio Reader: Essays in the Cultural History of Radio*, ed. Michele Hilmes and Jason Loviglio. New York: Routledge, 2002.

Moraes, Lisa. "Colbert Still Digesting His Correspondents' Dinner Reception." http://www.washingtonpost.com/wp-dyn/content/article/2006/05/01/AR2006050101558.html (accessed September 1, 2007).

"Moral Majority Timeline." http://www.moralmajority.us/index.php?option=com_content&task=view&id=5&itemid=29 (accessed July 21, 2008).

"Mort Walker: About the Cartoonist." http://www.kingfeatures.com/features/comics/bbailey/about.htm (accessed November 25, 2006).

Mosk, Matthew. "Michael J. Fox Records TV Ad for Cardin; Actor Questions Steele's Stance on Funding for Stem Cell Research." *Washington Post*, October 24, 2006, B01.

Murray, Noel. "Interviews: George Carlin." http://www.avclub.com/content/node/42195/1 (accessed August 26, 2008).

Newman, Kathy M. "Poisons, Potions, and Profits: Radio Rebels and the Origins of the Consumer Movement." *Radio Reader: Essays in the Cultural History of Radio*, ed. Michele Hilmes and Jason Loviglio. New York: Routledge, 2002.

Nichols, Bill. *Introduction to Documentary*. Bloomington: Indiana University Press, 2001.

"The Nixon-Presley Meeting: December 21st 1970." http://www.gwu.edu/~nsarchiv/nsa/elvis/elnix.html (accessed December 20, 2006).

Nossiter, Adam. "A Senator's Moral High Ground Gets a Little Shaky." *New York Times*, July 11, 2007.

Novak, Viveca, and Michael Weiskopf. "New Questions about Roger Clinton's Slippery Schemes." http://www.time.com/time/nation/article/0,8599,165992,00.html (accessed July 7, 2007).

O'Connor, John E., and Peter C. Rollins. "Introduction." *The West Wing: The American Presidency as Television Drama*, ed. Peter C. Rollins and John E. O'Connor. Syracuse, NY: Syracuse University Press, 2003.

O'Connor, William F. "Expatriate American Radio Propagandists in the Employ of the Axis Powers." *Radio Reader: Essays in the Cultural History of Radio*, ed. Michele Hilmes and Jason Loviglio. New York: Routledge, 2002.

Olver, Lynne. "American Apple Pie." http://www.foodtimeline.org/foodpies.html#applepie (accessed September 6, 2007).

Patterson, Troy. "Dinner Theater: Why Stephen Colbert Didn't Bomb in D.C." http://www.slate.com/id/2140921/nav/tap2 (accessed September 1, 2007).

Peddie, Ian (ed.). *The Resisting Muse: Popular Music and Social Protest*. Hampshire, England: Ashgate, 2006.

"People & Events: Billy Carter (1937–1988)." http://www.pbs.org/wgbh/amex/carter/peopleevents/p_bcarter.html (accessed September 23, 2006).

"People and Events: The Election of 1980." www.pbs.org/wgbh/amex/carter/peopleevents/e_1980.htm (accessed September 24, 2006).

Pfau, Michael, J. Brian-Houston, and Shane M. Semmler. *Mediating the Vote: The Changing Media Landscape in U.S. Presidential Campaigns*. Lanham, MD: Rowman & Littlefield, 2007.

Postman, Neil. *Amusing Ourselves to Death: Public Discourse in an Age of Show Business*. New York: Penguin, 1985.

Postman, Neil, and Steve Powers. *How to Watch TV News*. New York: Penguin Books, 1992.

"Presidential Campaign Slogans." http://www.presidentsusa.net/campaignslogans.html (accessed July 21, 2007).

"President Lyndon B. Johnson's Biography." http://www.lbjlib.utexas.edu/johnson/archives.hom/biographys.hom/lbj_bio.asp (accessed July 22, 2007).

"Private Snafu." http://www.toonopedia.com/snafu.htm (accessed August 3, 2007).

"Reagan's Image Maestro Dead at 69." *New York Daily News*, August 19, 2007, p. 26.

"Remarks by the President at New England Presidential Dinner, Park Plaza Hotel, Boston, Massachusetts, January 31st, 1995." www.bostonyouthzone.com/myc/PDFs/Jan_95_WJC_at_Pres_Dinner.pdf (accessed August 10, 2007).

Renov, Michael. "Introduction: The Truth about Non-Fiction." *Theorizing Documentary*, ed. Michael Renov. New York: Routledge, 1993.

Renov, Michael. "Toward a Poetics of Documentary." *Theorizing Documentary*, ed. Michael Renov. New York: Routledge, 1993.

Richards, Jeffrey. "Frank Capra and the Cinema of Populism." *Movies and Methods: An Anthology*, ed. Bill Nichols. Berkeley: University of California Press, 1976, pp. 65–77.

Richardson, Glenn W., Jr. *Pulp Politics: How Political Advertising Tells the Stories of American Politics*. Lanham, MD: Rowman & Littlefield, 2003.

Riegert, Kristina. "The Ideology of *The West Wing*: The Television Show that Wants to Be Real." *Politicotainment: Television's Take on the Real*, ed. Kristina Riegert. New York: Peter Lang, 2007.

Riegert, Kristina. "Introduction." *Politicotainment: Television's Take on the Real*, ed. Kristina Riegert. New York: Peter Lang, 2007.

"Right Wing Organizations: Focus on the Family." http://www.pfaw.org/pfaw/general/default.aspx?oid=4257 (accessed June 1, 2007).

Riismandel, Paul. "Radio by and for the Public: The Death and Resurrection of Low-Power Radio." *Radio Reader: Essays in the Cultural History of Radio*, ed. Michele Hilmes and Jason Loviglio. New York: Routledge, 2002.

Robb, David. *Operation Hollywood: How the Pentagon Shapes and Censors the Movies*. Amherst, NY: Prometheus Books, 2004.

Rollins, Peter, and John O'Connor. *Hollywood's White House: The American Presidency in Film and History*. Lexington: University Press of Kentucky, 2003.

Rosenbaum, Jonathan. *Movies as Politics*. Berkeley: University of California Press, 1997.

Rosenberg, Shawn W., and Patrick McCafferty. "The Image and the Vote: Manipulating Voters' Preferences," *Public Opinion Quarterly* 51, no. 1 (1987): 31–47.

Ross, Steven (ed.). *Movies and American Society*. Malden, MA: Blackwell Publishing, 2002.

Roston, Allen. "Carter and Capra." *Journal of Popular Film & Television* 25, no. 2 (Summer 1997): 57–68.

Rothenbuhler, Eric, and Tom McCourt. "Radio Redefines Itself, 1947–1962." *Radio Reader: Essays in the Cultural History of Radio*, ed. Michele Hilmes and Jason Loviglio. New York: Routledge, 2002.

Ruhlman, William. "Woody Guthrie: Biography." http://www.allmusic.com/cg/amg.dll?p=amg&sql=11:jifoxql5ldte~T1 (accessed March 13, 2007).

Sabato, Larry J. "The Election That Broke the Rules." *Divided States of America: The Slash and Burn Politics of the 2004 Presidential Election*. New York: Pearson-Longman, 2006.

Sabato, Larry J. "Introduction." *Divided States of America: The Slash and Burn Politics of the 2004 Presidential Election*. New York: Pearson-Longman, 2006.

Sanders, Arthur. *Losing Control: Presidential Elections and the Decline of Democracy*. New York: Peter Lang, 2007.

Saulny, Susan. "Thompson Enters Race from 'Tonight Show' Couch." http://www.nytimes.com/2007/09/06/us/politics/06Thompson/.html (accessed September 6, 2007).

Savage, Barbara. "Radio and the Political Discourse of Racial Equality." *Radio Reader: Essays in the Cultural History of Radio*, ed. Michele Hilmes and Jason Loviglio. New York: Routledge, 2002.

Scagg, Austin. "Pearl Jam: Censored." *Rolling Stone*, issue 1034, September 6, 2007, p. 30.

Schimmler, Stuart. "Singing to the Oval Office: A Written History of the Political Campaign Song." http://www.presidentelect.org/art_schimler_singing.html (accessed June 1, 2007).

Schudson, Michael. *Discovering the News: A Social History of American Newspapers*. New York: Basic Books, 1978.

Schudson, Michael. *Advertising, the Uneasy Persuasion: Its Dubious Impact on American Society*. New York: Basic, 1986.

Schultz, David A. "Kenny Meets George Washington or, 'Come on Down, Your 15 Minutes of Fame Are Now!' " *It's Show Time! Media, Politics, and Popular Culture*, ed. David A. Schultz. New York: Peter Lang, 2000.

Schwartz, Tony. *The Responsive Chord*. Garden City, NY: Anchor Books, 1973.

Scott, Ian. *American Politics in Hollywood Film*. Edinburgh: Edinburgh University Press, 2000.

"Secretary of State Colin Powell" http://www.whitehouse.gov/government/powell-bio.html (accessed March 23, 2007).

Seelye, Katharine. "Former First Couple Mimics TV's Former First Couple." *New York Times*, June 20, 2007. http://www.nytimes.com/2007/06/20/us/politics/20netwatch.html? scp=1&sq=%20"Former%20First%20Couple%20Mimics%20TV's%20Former%20First%20Couple."%20New%20York%20&st=cse (accessed June 21, 2007).

Shales, Tom. "Fox News Channel's '1/2 Hour News Hour': Right Funny, in Spots." http:// www.washingtonpost.com/wp-dyn/content/article/2007/02/16/AR2007021602098. html (accessed February 27, 2007).

Shane, Peter M. "Introduction: The Prospects for Electronic Democracy." *Democracy Culture: The Prospects for Political Renewal through the Internet*, ed. Peter M. Shane. New York: Routledge, 2004.

Shannon, Lyle. "The Opinions of Little Orphan Annie and her Friends." *The Public Opinion Quarterly* 18, no. 5 (Summer 1954): 169–179.

Sheppard, Noel. "Bill O'Reilly Meets Stephen Colbert." http://www.newsbusters.org/node/ 10248 (accessed April 23, 2007).

Simons, Jon. "Popular Culture and Mediated Politics: Intellectuals, Elites and Democracy." *Media and the Restyling of Politics: Consumerism, Celebrity and Cynicism*, ed. John Corner and Dick Pels. London: Sage, 2003.

Sloan, Kay. Excerpt from "The Loud Silents: Origins of the Social Protest Movie." *Movies and American Society*, ed. Steven Ross. Malden, MA: Blackwell Publishing, 2002.

Smith, Judith E. "Radio's 'Cultural Front,' 1938–1948." *Radio Reader: Essays in the Cultural History of Radio*, ed. Michele Hilmes and Jason Loviglio. New York: Routledge, 2002.

Standora, Leo. "Dan Would Rather Not See Katie's Changes." *New York Daily News*, June 12, 2007, p. 66.

Steinberg, Jacques. "Imus Struggling to Retain Sway as a Franchise." *New York Times*, April 11, 2007, http://www.nytimes.com/2007/04/11/business/media/11imus.html (accessed March 24, 2008).

Steinberg, Jacques. "Talking Politics, Drawing Viewers." *New York Times*, December 23, 2007, p. 34.

Stephens, Mitchell. *A History of News*. Fort Worth, TX: Harcourt Brace, 1997.

Stewart, John Craig. *The Governors of Alabama*. Gretna, LA: Pelican Publishing, 1975.

Street, John. *Politics & Popular Culture*. Philadelphia: Temple University Press, 1997.

Street, John. "The Celebrity Politician: Political Style and Popular Culture." *Media and the Restyling of Politics: Consumerism, Celebrity and Cynicism*, ed. John Corner and Dick Pels. London: Sage, 2003.

Sun, Chyng Feng. "Ling Woo in Historical Context: The New Face of Asian American Stereotypes on Television." *Gender, Race, and Class in Media: A Text Reader*. 2nd ed., ed. Gail Dines and Jean M. Humez. Thousand Oaks, CA: Sage, 2003.

"Superman and John F. Kennedy." http://www.geocities.com/utherworld/comixpix/ zsuperjfk.html (accessed August 30, 2008).

Tedesco, John C. "Web Interactivity and Young Adult Political Efficacy." *The Internet Election: Perspectives on the Web in Campaign 2004*, ed. Andrew Paul Williams and John C. Tedesco. Lanham, MD: Rowman & Littlefield, 2006.

"This Land Is Your Land." http://www.arlo.net/resources/lyrics/this-land.shtml (accessed June 15, 2007).

Toner, Michael. "The Impact of the New Campaign Finance Law on the 2004 Presidential Election." *Divided States of America: The Slash and Burn Politics of the 2004 Presidential Election.* New York: Pearson-Longman, 2006.

Trent, Judith S., and Robert V. Friedenberg. *Political Campaign Communication: Principles & Practices.* 5th ed. Lanham, MD: Rowman & Littlefield, 2004.

Tuchman, Gaye. "Introduction: The Symbolic Annihilation of Women by the Mass Media." *Hearth and Home: Images of Women in the Mass Media*, ed. Arlene Kaplan Daniels and James Benét. New York: Oxford University Press, 1978.

"The Unthinkable." http://www.time.com/time/magazine/article/0,9171,935599,00.html (accessed May 15, 2007).

Van Zoonen, Liesbet. " 'After Dallas and Dynasty We Have ... Democracy': Articulating Soap, Politics and Gender." *Media and the Restyling of Politics: Consumerism, Celebrity and Cynicism*, ed. John Corner and Dick Pels. London: Sage, 2003.

Van Zoonen, Liesbet. *Entertaining the Citizen: When Politics and Popular Culture Converge.* Lanham, MD: Rowman & Littlefield, 2005.

Venezia, Todd. "Nut Buster: Wacky Hillary Gizmo Is a Real Easy Shell." *New York Post*, September 7, 2007, p. 3.

"Vote or Die Lyrics." http://www.sing365.com/music/lyric.nsf/Vote-or-Die-lyrics-South-Park/18A9D53C122E19D248256F5700099A4B (accessed May 22, 2007).

Wakin, Daniel. "This Just In: Pete Seeger Denounced Stalin Over a Decade Ago." http://www.nytimes.com/2007/09/01/arts/music/01seeg.html?_r=1&adxnnl=1&oref=slogin&adxnnlx=1188666708-dsoTJRr3WipfY9JV5ZKmjQ (accessed September 1, 2007).

Walker, Jesse. *Rebels on the Air: An Alternative History of Radio in America.* New York: New York University Press, 2001.

"Walter Cronkite: U.S. Broadcast Journalist." http://www.museum.tv/archives/etv/C/htmlC/cronkitewal/cronkitewal.htm (accessed July 17, 2006).

Wang, Jennifer Hyland. " 'The Case of the Radio-Active Housewife': Relocating Radio in the Age of Television." *Radio Reader: Essays in the Cultural History of Radio*, ed. Michele Hilmes and Jason Loviglio. New York: Routledge, 2002.

Weiss, Philip. " 'Watching Matt Drudge': He Hides, but Craves attention. He is Prurient and prudish, powerful and paranoid, an icon of the right who seems obsessed with making Hillary Clinton our next president. And he has America caught in the grip of his contradictions." *New York Magazine*, September 3–10, 2007.

West, Darrell M., and John Orman. *Celebrity Politics: Real Politics in America.* Upper Saddle River, NJ: Prentice-Hall, 2003.

"What We Want." http://www.hsan.org/Content/main.aspx?pageid=27 (accessed August 25, 2006).

"What Would Jesus Drive?" http://www.whatwouldjesusdrive.org/ (accessed March 23, 2007).

Williams, Andrew Paul, and John C. Tedesco. "Introduction." *The Internet Election: Perspectives on the Web in Campaign 2004*, ed. Andrew Paul Williams and John C. Tedesco. Lanham, MD: Rowman & Littlefield, 2006.

Wilson, Clint C., II, Félix Gutiérrez, and Lena M. Chao. *Racism, Sexism, and the Media: The Rise of Class Communication in Multicultural America.* 3rd ed. Thousand Oaks, CA: Sage, 2003.

Witt, Louise. "Scud Stud Lobs a Missile at Bush." *Salon.com.* http://dir.salon.com/story/news/feature/2003/03/17/scud_stud/index.html

Wright, Bradford. *Comic Book Nation: The Transformation of Youth Culture in America.* Baltimore and London: The John Hopkins University Press, 2001.

Zook, Kristal Brent. *Color by Fox: The Fox Network and the Revolution in Black Television.* Oxford, U.K.: Oxford University Press, 1999.

Index

About the Authors

BRIAN COGAN is an associate professor in the Communication Arts Department of Molloy College, Rockville Centre, New York. He has written for numerous journals and newspapers on subjects ranging from Irish immigration and cultural assimilation to popular culture, politics, media, and music. He is a member of the New York Irish History Roundtable and has presented there, and at the American Conference for Irish Studies, the first Galway conference of Irish Studies, as well as many other national and international conferences. Dr. Cogan is the author, coauthor, or coeditor of six books on music, politics, and popular culture, including the popular *The Encyclopedia of Punk Music and Culture* and *The Encyclopedia of Heavy Metal*. He is a member of the editorial board of the *Journal of Popular Culture* and reviews books and journal articles for numerous other publishers. He is coeditor of the book *Mosh the Polls: Youth Voters, Popular Culture and Democratic Engagement* (2008).

TONY KELSO is associate professor in the Department of Mass Communication at Iona College, New Rochelle, New York. His research interests include mediated political communication, as well as the intersection of advertising and religion. He is coeditor of the book *Mosh the Polls: Youth Voters, Popular Culture, and Democratic Engagement* (2008). Some of his other recent work has appeared in *It's Not TV: Watching HBO in the Post-Television Era* (2008), the *Encyclopedia of Religion, Communication, and Media* (2006), and the journal *Implicit Religion*.

DATE DUE